SUFFOL
MILDREL ☞ W9-BKU-012
8 ASHBURTON PLACE
BOSTON, MASS. 02108

Texts in Theoretical Computer Science
An EATCS Series

Editors: W. Brauer G. Rozenberg A. Salomaa
On behalf of the European Association
for Theoretical Computer Science (EATCS)

Advisory Board: G. Ausiello M. Broy C.S. Calude
A. Condon D. Harel J. Hartmanis T. Henzinger
J. Hromkovič N. Jones T. Leighton M. Nivat
C. Papadimitriou D. Scott

D. Bjørner

Software Engineering 1

Abstraction and Modelling

With 38 Figures

 Springer

Author

Prof. Dr. Dines Bjørner
Computer Science and Engineering
Informatics and Mathematical Modelling
Richard Petersens Plads
2800 Kgs. Lyngby, Denmark
bjorner@gmail.com

Series Editors

Prof. Dr. Wilfried Brauer
Institut für Informatik der TUM
Boltzmannstr. 3
85748 Garching, Germany
Brauer@informatik.tu-muenchen.de

Prof. Dr. Grzegorz Rozenberg
Leiden Institute of Advanced
Computer Science
University of Leiden
Niels Bohrweg 1
2333 CA Leiden, The Netherlands
rozenber@liacs.nl

Prof. Dr. Arto Salomaa
Turku Centre of
Computer Science
Lemminkäisenkatu 14 A
20520 Turku, Finland
asalomaa@utu.fi

Library of Congress Control Number: 2005936099

ACM Computing Classification (1998): D.1, D.2, D.3, F.3, F.4, G.2.0, K.6.3, H.1, J.1

ISBN-10 3-540-21149-7 Springer Berlin Heidelberg New York
ISBN-13 9-783-540-21149-5 Springer Berlin Heidelberg New York

This work is subject to copyright. All rights are reserved, whether the whole or part of the material is concerned, specifically the rights of translation, reprinting, reuse of illustrations, recitation, broadcasting, reproduction on microfilm or in any other way, and storage in data banks. Duplication of this publication or parts thereof is permitted only under the provisions of the German Copyright Law of September 9, 1965, in its current version, and permission for use must always be obtained from Springer. Violations are liable for prosecution under the German Copyright Law.

Springer is a part of Springer Science+Business Media
springer.com

© Springer-Verlag Berlin Heidelberg 2006
Printed in Germany

The use of general descriptive names, registered names, trademarks, etc. in this publication does not imply, even in the absence of a specific statement, that such names are exempt from the relevant protective laws and regulations and therefore free for general use.

Cover design: KünkelLopka, Heidelberg
Typesetting: Camera ready by the author
Production: LE-TeX Jelonek, Schmidt & Vöckler GbR, Leipzig
Printed on acid-free paper   45/3142/YL - 5 4 3 2 1 0

Kari Skallerud Bjørner

the best thing that ever happened to me

Caminante, son tus huellas
el camino, y nada más;
caminante, no hay camino,
se hace camino al andar.
Al andar se hace el camino,
y al volver la vista atrás
se ve la senda que nunca
se ha de volver a pisar.
Caminante, no hay camino,
sino estelas en la mar.

Walker, your footseps
are the road, and nothing more.
Walker, there is no road,
the road is made by walking.
Walking you make the road,
and turning to look behind
you see the path you never
again will step upon.
Walker, there is no road,
only foam trails on the sea.

Proverbios y cantares, 29
Campos de Castilla
Antonio Machado
Page 280 [31]

Proverbs and Songs, 29
Fields of Castilla
Page 281 [31], Translated by Willis Barnstone
Border of a Dream:
Selected Poems of Antonio Machado

Preface — to Vols. 1–3

This preface covers the three volumes of *Software Engineering,* of which this volume is the first.

- **Software engineering — art/discipline/craft/science/logic:** Software engineering is the art [326–328], discipline [194], craft [441], science [245], logic [275] and practice [276] of
  - ⋆ **synthesizing** (i.e., building, constructing) software, i.e., technology, *based on scientific insight,* and
  - ⋆ **analysing** (i.e., studying, investigating) existing software technology *in order to ascertain and discover its possible scientific content.*

To succeed in this,

- **Software engineering — abstraction and specification:** Software engineering makes use of abstraction and specification.
  - ⋆ **Abstraction** is used to segment development into manageable parts, from high-level abstractions in phases, stages and steps to low-level abstractions, i.e., concretisations.
  - ⋆ **Specification** records and relates all levels of abstraction.

Volumes 1 and 2 of the three-volume book cover abstraction and specification in detail.

- **Software engineering — the triptych:** Software engineering composes analysis of *application domains* with synthesis and analysis of *requirements* (to new software) into *design* (i.e., synthesis and analysis) of that *software.* Hence software engineering consists of
  - ⋆ **domain engineering,** which, as these volumes will show you, is a rich field of many disciplines, etc.,
  - ⋆ **requirements engineering,** which, as we shall again see, in these volumes, has many aspects and facets not usually covered in textbooks, and

    ⋆ **software design,** with concerns of software *architecture, component* composition and design, and so on.

Volume 3 of the book covers this triptych in detail.

- **Software engineering — practical concerns:** Software engineering, besides, consists of many *practical concerns:* Project and product management; principles, techniques and tools for making sure that groups of possibly geographically widely located people work effectively together, for choosing, adapting, monitoring and controlling work according to one of a variety of development process models; planning, scheduling and allocating development resources (people, materials, monies and time); and related matters, including cost estimation, legacy systems, legalities, etc.

We shall not be covering these management-oriented facets of software engineering in this book.

● ● ●

Each chapter of this volume and its companion volumes starts with a synopsis. An example — relevant for this preface — follows:

- **Assumptions:** You have taken this book into your hands since you are interested in knowing about, and possibly learning a new approach to software engineering.
- **Aims:** The main aim of these volumes is to introduce you to a new way of looking at software: One that emphasises (I) that software engineering is part of informatics, and that *informatics* is a discipline otherwise based on (i) mathematics, (ii) the computer & computing sciences, (iii) linguistics, (iv) the availability of the hard information technologies (computers and communication, sensors and actuators) and, last but not least, (v) applications. Furthermore (II) that informatics "hinges" on a number of philosophical issues commonly known under the subtitles — epistemology, ontology, mereology, etc.
- **Objectives:** To help you become a truly professional software development engineer in the widest sense of that term, such as promulgated by these volumes.
- **Treatment:** Nontechnical, discursive.

To develop large-scale software systems is hard. To construct them such that they (i) solve real problems, (ii) are correct and pleasing and (iii) will serve well in the acquiring organisation is very hard.

    This series of volumes offers techniques that have proven (i) to make the development of large-scale software systems much less hard than most current software engineers find it, (ii) to result in higher-quality systems than normally experienced and (iii) to enable delivery on time.

    Thus we emphasise the software engineering attributes aimed at in this series: Trustworthy and believable methods, higher-quality software products, higher-quality software development projects, and the personal satisfaction of developers and acquirers, that is, the software engineers and their management, respectively the users and their management. We aim at much less, if any, frustration, and much more fascination and joy!

Reasons for Writing These Volumes

A number of reasons[1] can be given for why these volumes had to be written:

- *Formal techniques apply in all phases, stages and steps of software engineering, and in the development of all kinds of software.* But there was no published textbook available that covered software engineering, such as we shall later characterise that term, from a basis also in formal techniques (besides other, "non-formal" bases).
- Formal development (that is, specification, refinement and verification) books were more like monographs than they were textbooks, and they covered their topic from a rather narrow viewpoint: usually just specification of software, that is, of abstract software designs and their concretisation. *Formal specification, in these volumes, applies not just to software, but also to their requirements prescription, and, as a new contribution (in any book or set of lecture notes), also to domain descriptions.*
- The author of these volumes has long been less than happy with the way in which current textbooks purport to cover the subject of software engineering.
  - ★ "All" current textbooks on software engineering fail[2] with respect to very basic issues of programming methodology, in particular with respect to (wrt) formal techniques. If they do, as some indeed do, bring material on so-called "Formal Methods", then that material is typically "tucked away" in a separate chapter (so named). In our mind, the interplay between informal and formal techniques, that is, between informal descriptions and formal specifications, informal reasoning and formal verification, and so on, permeates all of software engineering. The potential of (using) formal techniques shapes all phases, stages and steps of development. Classical software engineering topics, such as software processes, project management, requirements, prototyping, validation (not to speak of verification), testing, quality assurance & control, legacy systems, and version control & configuration management, these auxiliary, but crucial, concerns of software engineering, can be handled better, we show, through a judicious blend of informal and formal techniques. Needless to say, these volumes will redress this "complaint".

---

[1]Usually, when more than one "excuse" is given for some "mistake", none apply. This series of volumes, however, is no mistake.

[2]With the notable exception of [240].

* All current textbooks, in our mind, fail in not properly taking into account the issue of the software developer not having a thorough understanding of the domain in which the software is to be inserted, that is, the domain from which sprang the desire to have "that new software"! As mentioned above, a major new "feature" of our books is the separation of concerns illustrated in the software development process — when the developer initially spends much time and effort to understand and document an understanding of the application domain.

* All current textbooks, in our mind, fail in not systematically, i.e., methodically, presenting principles, techniques and tools that "carry through" and "scale up". By carry through I mean principles, techniques and tools that are shown, by extensive examples, to cover all the major phases, stages and steps of development. By scaling up I mean principles, techniques and tools that can be applied to the largest-scale software development projects.

* Some current textbooks, in our mind, fail the programming, that is, the design issues completely. There is no assumption on any methodological approach to the development of software from the point of view of programming methodology.[3]

* Other current textbooks, in our mind, fail the stepwise refinement, that is, the implementation relation development point of view.[4]

* And yet other current textbooks fail the design point of view.[5]

* Finally all current textbooks fail, we believe, in not properly integrating the above, albeit more theoretical, points of view, with the points of view of mundane, engineering issues such as (i) development process models ("waterfall", "spiral", "iterative", "evolutionary", "extreme programming", etc.), (ii) quality management, (ii) testing & validation, (iv) legacy systems, (v) software re-engineering, and so on.

Shortcomings of These Volumes

The major shortcoming of the current set of three volumes is our all too brief coverage of correctness issues, that is, of the verification (theorem proving, model checking) of properties of single and pairs of (development-step-related) specifications.

---

[3]By the `programming` methodology point of view we mean a view that concerns itself with such issues as establishing invariants when specifying loops, as securing proper programming abstractions in terms of routines (procedures, functions), etc.

[4]By the stepwise refinement point of view we mean the concern that abstractions, even when informally expressed, are rendered into correct concretisations — when expressed as code.

[5]By the design point of view we mean the programming concern for choosing appropriate algorithms and data structures, for their justification and validation.

Elsewhere, and where appropriate in these volumes, we explain why we have not introduced substantial material on verification.

The reader, seeking this knowledge, is referred to an abundance of texts (books, and articles in journals and in proceedings), or may have to wait till we feel competent to write a textbook of sufficient generality on this topic. Current texts are very much linked to a specific notational system (i.e., specification language).

• • •

Obviously we do not know all there is to know about how to develop all possible kinds of software, and not all that we know is in these volumes. To develop software, in general, takes a diverse range of techniques and tools.

Whatever special techniques and tools we cover, we cover them to some non-trivial depth, but not to the depth that is sufficient for a professional engineer in the relevant field. For example:

- **Development of compilers:** We cover quite a lot, but not all that is necessary for the really professional compiler developer. We cover what we believe all software engineers ought know. And we cover it in a way that we find is sorely missing from all compiler textbooks. We refer to Chaps. 16–20 of Vol. 2.
- **Development of operating and distributed systems:** We cover only general principles and techniques of specifying concurrent systems.
- **Development of embedded, safety-critical and real-time systems:** Basically the same coverage as for operating and distributed systems development: We emphasise that Vol. 2 covers techniques for specifying embedded, safety-critical and real-time systems. These techniques and their underlying notations are those of Petri nets [313, 421, 435–437], message [302–304] and live sequence charts [171, 270, 325], statecharts [265, 266, 268, 269, 271], temporal logics [205, 360, 361, 400, 429] and the duration calculi [537, 538].

Chapter 28 in Vol. 3, Domain-Specific Architectures, will, however, go into some depth, showing which principles, techniques and tools apply in the development of translation systems (interpreters and compilers), information systems (database management systems), reactive systems (i.e., embedded, real-time and safety-critical systems), workpiece systems (worksheet systems), client/server systems, workflow systems, etcetera. Our treatment in that chapter is novel, and is inspired, strongly, by Michael Jackson's concept of Problem Frames [310].

Thus we cover what we believe all software engineers, whatever their specialty is, should know. And we believe they should know far more than most textbooks in software engineering offer.

As explained elsewhere, these volumes suggest that education and training in the specialised fields mentioned above can follow after having studied Vol. 3.

And much of the textbooks of those specialised fields really, then, ought be rewritten: be adapted to formal specification, and so on.

Methods of Approach

Our didactics seeks to go to the "roots of the matter". We see these roots to be formed from basic understandings of such issues as (i) the linguistics of "how to describe", (ii) the near-philosophical issues of "what to describe", (iii) the linguistic, i.e., *semiotic* issues of *pragmatics, semantics and syntax*, and (iv) the issues of constructing concise, objective formulations in terms of mathematics, i.e., of using formal specification languages (and, in turn, understanding their pragmatics, semantics and syntax — independent of the pragmatics, semantics and syntax of the application phenomena).

Thus this book begins by exploring the above four issues. In Vol. 2 we then take up this theme of semiotics (pragmatics, semantics and syntax) in four separate chapters (Chaps. 6–9 incl.).

Also this is new: Existing textbooks on software engineering completely avoid any mention of these issues. For a modern, professional software engineer to graduate from any reputable academic institution without a proper grasp on these four didactic bases (i–iv) is, to this author, unthinkable! Alas! It is today the rule rather than the exception: That they do not even see these issues at all!

A New Look at Software

These volumes will provide the reader with a new way of looking at software and at the process of developing software. They will provide the reader with an altogether dramatically different approach to understand and to develop software. That "new look" can perhaps best be characterised as follows: Software is seen as intellectual artifacts, as the product of a rather intellectual process of thinking (analysing), of describing (of synthesising) and of contemplating (of reasoning). Software, as a product, has less material, quantitative measures by which to be grasped (no cheaper, faster, smaller, etc., catchwords) than it has intellectual, qualitative measures — such as affinity to application domain (it is, or is not, the right product), fitness for human use (computer–user interaction), correctness (the product is, or is not, right), etc.

Grasping abstraction — a major issue of these volumes — affords any developer a far better chance of getting the right product and the product right than not grasping abstraction — even when these same people do not use many of the formal techniques of these volumes. Most practicing software engineers do not grasp abstraction. Yet software, by its very nature is and must be abstract: When supporting the automation of what used to be human work processes, the automating software is not "those human processes", it is only a model, an approximation, an abstraction of them.

We wish to perpetrate a view of software development as something that proceeds in phases, stages and steps of development and for which there are now available clear techniques of relating these phases, these stages, these steps to one another. Yet such development is hardly covered in standard textbooks on software engineering. We wish to perpetrate a view of software development where the specification of the phases, stages and steps can be done formally, and where the relations can be formalised and, in cases where warranted, can even be formally verified. This view has been possible, at least in the small to medium, for at least 20 years. Yet such development is hardly covered in standard textbooks on software engineering. We wish to further a view of software development where the developers create, nurture and deploy abstractions. Where the programmers at all levels take pride and have fun in "isolating", as it were, beautiful abstractions and let them find their way into programs. In the end these programmers let those abstractions determine major structures of systems, and beauty: Simplicity and elegance, as felt by users, arises! Such development is scalable to large systems. It is now possible, manageable and affordable. It can be taught and it can be learned by most academically trainable students.

Formal Techniques "Light"

Many practicing programmers abstain from and some academics express reservations about formal reasoning[6] or just formal specification.[7]

Our approach is a pragmatic one. We allow for a spectrum from systematic via rigorous to formal development. By a systematic development we mean one which specifies some of the steps of development formally. By a rigorous development we mean one which expresses and formally proves some of the proof obligations of a systematic development. By a formal development we mean one which formally proves a significant majority of proof obligations as well as other lemmas and theorems of a rigorous development.

> In order to follow the principles and techniques of these volumes, we advise going "light": Start by being systematic. Specify crucial facets — of your application domain, your requirements and your software designs — formally. Then program (i.e., code) from there!

It seems, from practice [155], that by far the most significant improvements in correctness of software development accrues from being systematic. And these

---

[6]Example: Proving, in some mathematical logic, some lemma about program properties.

[7]Example: Describing, in addition to informally, but concisely, some domain, or prescribing some requirements, or specifying some software design formally, in some formal specification language.

volumes are primarily, possibly almost exclusively, focused on being systematic. Certain kinds of applications warrant higher trust, and it then seems that being rigorous achieves the next higher step of believability. Finally, a few customers are willing to accept today's rather high cost of formal development: heart pacemakers, hearing-aid implants, hybrid controllers for nuclear power plants, driverless metro trains, and the like.

Volume 3, Chap. 32, Sect. 32.2 discusses a rather large number of dogmas, misconceptions and myths about so-called "formal methods". Section 1.5.3 of this volume and Vol. 3, Chap. 3, Sect. 3.1 discuss why methods cannot be formal, but that some techniques can.

The "Super Programmer"

Many practicing programmers and some academics believe strongly in the unchecked individualism of the programmer: They are worried that having to adhere to a number of method principles and formal techniques may squash the creativity and productivity of "super programmers". We are not worried. We have generated well over a 100 MSc thesis candidates. Most work in fewer than eight software houses in Denmark. All follow, more-or-less, many of the principles and techniques of these volumes. Most of them are super programmers.

The following has been expressed by other academics and most of my former students and likewise those of my colleagues around the world who similarly teach and propagate principles and techniques like those of these volumes. I emphasise it here:

> The principles and techniques of these volumes, even when adhered to only "lightly", even when hardly followed explicitly, are such that if you have grasped them, while studying these volumes, they will have changed your attitude to software engineering. It will never be the same.

We are sure that you will, from then on, enjoy far more doing "super programming", being a super programmer, and *being clever in many small ways, devising smart tricks to do things better and faster.* We shall not deny a central role[8] for being low level clever, for being smart. We will augment whatever skills you may have in this direction with a number of teachable engineering principles and techniques. *The successful programmer is both beast and angel.*

We claim that we can also point to several medium-scale software development projects where knowing or being aware of the principles of these volumes seems to have helped significantly in devising elegant, beautiful products. And *'Beauty is our Business'* [224].

---

[8]The two *slanted* "quotes" of this paragraph are from an e-mail, Sunday, January 20, 2002, from Prof. Bertrand Meyer [5,375,376], ETH Zürich, Switzerland, and ISE, Santa Barbara, California, USA.

What Is Software Engineering?

We continue the characterisation of software engineering that we began on the very first page of this preface.

- **Software engineering:** To us, in a most general sense, 'software engineering', as are all kinds of engineering, is a set of professions which based on scientific insight construct technologies, or which analyses technologies to ascertain their scientific content (including value), or, usually, do both.
- **"Software Engineer":** Thus the software engineer (but see the following for a critique of this term) *"walks the bridge"* between computer and computing science, on one side, and software artifacts (software technologies), on the other side, and constructs — or studies — the latter based on insight gained from the body of knowledge established in the many disciplines of computer and computing sciences.

In a more mundane way, software engineering embodies general and specific principles, techniques and tools (i) for analysing problems amenable to solution or support through computing; (ii) for synthesising such (program, such as software) solutions; (iii) for doing this analysis and synthesis in large projects, that is, projects involving more than one developer, and/or projects for which the resulting software is to be used by other (people) than the developer(s); and (iv) for managing such projects and products (including planning, budgeting, monitoring and controlling the projects and the products).

But because we can term a subject software engineering does not necessarily mean that we can speak of "software engineers". As formulated above, and this must be understood clearly by all readers of these volumes, software engineering is a body of principles, techniques and tools available to such people as we may otherwise have wished to label "software engineers". But for any one person to be labeled a software engineer without further, more "narrowing" qualifications seems problematic. It would give the "recipient" of the message *that person is a software engineer* the belief that the person in question is able to professionally tackle the development of well nigh any software. With Jackson [307] we claim that there are no software engineers! There are compiler engineers, there are embedded systems (software) engineers, there are information (cum database) systems (software) engineers, there are banking software engineers, and so on, just as we speak of automotive engineers and of electrical power engineers rather than mechanical or electrical engineers.

Thus the principles, techniques and tools of these volumes apply, we claim, across a broad spectrum of specialty software engineers. These volumes bring examples of applications of the principles, techniques and tools across the broadest possible spectrum. The fact that principles, techniques and tools are generally useful and can be deployed across a broad field of occupations and applications only means that the student must also, additionally, study special texts on the chosen profession, compiler development, development of safety-critical real-time software, database systems, etc., to become a proper specialty software engineer.

The Author's Aspirations

So these then were and are my aspirations: To provide you with a different kind of textbook; to bring more than 30 years of exciting programming methodological studies and controlled experimental practice into the larger arena of software engineering; to show you what a beautiful world software development can be when following the didactic cornerstones of linguistics, philosophy, semiotics and mathematics; and to unload more than 25 years of evolving lecture notes into a set of three coherent, consistent and relatively complete volumes.

> I have written these volumes because I wanted to understand how to develop large-scale software systems. When I started, some 25 years ago, writing lecture notes on this subject, I knew less than I do now. Meanwhile I have had the great pleasure of having many clever and eager students follow the practice. I have initiated the large-scale commercial developments of compilers for such unwieldy programming languages as CHILL [254, 255] and Ada [128, 129, 155], and I have thus honed and corrected my thinking. Writing about software engineering while testing out the ideas has been a sobering experience. There are still many corners of software engineering that I have to write about, think and experience. Meanwhile, this is what you get!

These volumes thus represent my chef d'œuvre.

Role of These Volumes in an SE Education Programme

Who are the target readers of these volumes? That question is indirectly answered in the following.

What roles do we see these volumes serve in the larger context of an academic software engineering education, one that leads to a Master's degree in the subject? Figure 1 shall assist us in answering that question.[9]

---

[9]The labelled boxes of Fig. 1 designate topics that enter into the software engineer's daily practice, and which are therefore useful topics of learning. In Fig. 1 two-way arrows between boxes indicate that the designated topics can be studied simultaneously. Directed (one-way) arrows between boxes designate a suitable, proposed precedence relation between the learning of these topics. A "fan in" (multiple source) arrow shows that a topic may need (i.e., have as prerequisites) the knowledge of one or more (predecessor) topics. A "fan out" (possibly multiple target) arrow shows that the arrow source topic is a "must" for one or more successor topics.

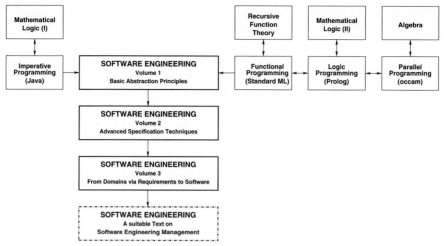

Fig. 1. Courses based on these volumes: a first setting

We emphasise that we here place these volumes in the context of an academic Software Engineering MSc education programme — not to be confused with an academic Computer Science MSc education. The former aims at the production of industry programmers: developers of commercial software. The latter aims at theoreticians, useful in an academic institution of study. Another explanation, wrt. another diagram, would thus have to be given for an equally likely setting in the context of an academic programme for an MSc degree in (theoretical) computer science, and yet another one for an undergraduate course of an academic software engineering BSc education programme.

- **Prerequisite or "concurrent" courses:** We assume that the reader of these volumes is — or while following a course based on Vol. 1 of these volumes becomes — familiar with the general topics of imperative, functional, logic, parallel and machine programming. Teaching in these topics must cover both skill-learning and training wrt. specific languages such as, for example, SML (Standard ML) [261, 389] for functional programming, Prolog [295,351] for logic programming, Modula-3 [262,401], Oberon [527] and Java [10,20,243,348,470,511] for modular (i.e., object-oriented) programming, and occam [364] and a machine language for some well-chosen, "current-technology" hardware (e.g., Intel-like) chip. Their teaching must also cover — to a basic extent — the knowledge acquisition wrt. the theoretical background for these programming styles and languages: recursive function theory [136, 444], logic for logic programming [295, 351], Hoare Logic for imperative programming [15,16] and process algebras for concurrency (CSP [288, 289, 448, 456] and Petri nets [313, 421, 435–437]). The machine programming topic [379, 501, 511] is the only real hardware-oriented, but not hardware-design-oriented [279, 418], course. Codesign [482], that is, design of combined hardware/software systems (typical, for example, for embedded systems, see below) is not covered. But one could "add other boxes"! Included in the above kinds of course, or additional to these, we expect the reader to have some working knowledge of algorithms and data structures, i.e., to be familiar with the classical as well as modern such algorithms and data structures and measures of concrete complexity [7, 357, 371, 495, 524].

- **Auxiliaries:** The reader is assumed to be — or to become, in conjunction with the software engineering study of which these volumes are part — comfortable with mathematics — to a Bachelor's degree level in the subjects listed. We suggest [534], a delightful "smallish" introduction, and the substantial introduction to discrete mathematics [213]. We find [213] to be an excellent textbook for an entirely separate, and major, course on that topic. One that every software engineer is assumed to take.

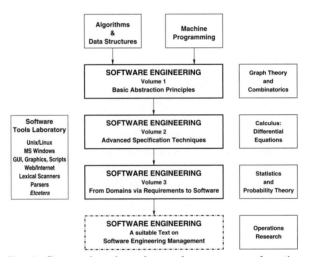

Fig. 2. Courses based on these volumes: a second setting

Similarly, but more thought of as part of term projects and other forms of laboratory (including self-study) work, we expect the reader to be reasonably comfortable with practical, existing platform technologies (the Software Tools Laboratory box).

- **Main course:** These volumes are then to serve in a main set of three courses on software engineering — and before the breadth and depth of the follow-on courses are attempted. We additionally would advise acquisition of the two books [236, 238], the first as supplementary, the second to fill out especially the verification (i.e., the design calculi) parts which are not developed in these volumes.

- **Follow-on courses:** Classical software engineering has focused rather much on the "navel-gazing", i.e., introspective parts of computing systems: compilers, database systems, distributed systems, operating systems, real-time (fault-tolerant and) embedded systems, etc. Ideally such topics should now be covered on the basis of, and from the point of view of, formal specification and design calculi. The embedded systems topic (given 1–3 units of work load) could go as far as including hardware/software codesign [482] and otherwise rely strongly on other systems engineering issues.

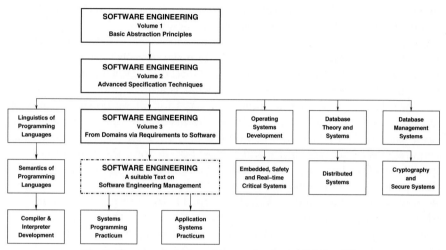

Fig. 3. Courses based on these volumes: a third setting

Additionally we plead that each software engineering student take two "practica": A large, project and colloquium/seminar-oriented "systems programming" and a similar "applications systems" course which experimentally and exploratively researches and develops a non-trivial hardware/software control system, respectively a commercial, industrial, or other application such as amply hinted at in these volumes!

- A final software engineering course is hinted at: "Software Engineering Management". We have quite some material for lectures on this topic. For the time being we refer to the excellent book by Hans van Vliet [512].

The linguistics of formal languages, including theories of formal semantics, is crucial knowledge to be possessed by the professional engineer. Two courses relate to this: the leftmost boxes in rows three and four of Fig. 3. The linguistics course could be based, for example, on David A. Schmidt's or John Reynolds' works. References are [455], respectively [442]. The semantics course could be based, for example, on any of [183, 252, 443, 454, 497, 521].

Why So Much Material?

These volumes are more-or-less self-contained. We expect these volumes to be used in university and college courses, and to be studied by readers on their own. Some universities and some colleges cover material in courses that lie early in the course curriculum that we also bring here. So it could be assumed, and left out? No, not quite, since other universities and colleges do not cover such prerequisite material. Hence these volumes, again and again, must make these excursions. Since these volumes significantly rely on mathematics — not anything advanced, not something for which any deep theorems need be known or used — we need to recapitulate some of this material in Chaps. 3–9. There we also explain and illustrate the λ-calculus.

Since actual life phenomena have to be perceived, whether manifest or not, that is, have to be conceptualised, we make deep excursions, in Vol. 3's Chaps. 3, 5, 6 and 7, into what constitutes a methodology, what are definitions, what are phenomena and concepts, and what is a description.

Since language is such an important basis for all we do in software engineering, and since we cannot rely on the necessary topics having already been learned, i.e., being known, we need also to make deep excursions into the pragmatics, the semantics and the syntax, in toto, the semiotics of languages, whether formal or informal. Since automata and finite state machines likewise form an indispensable component of our science and engineering we need also cover that topic in Vol. 2's Chap. 11. In covering all these adjunct ideas we supply their treatment with a twist: We present them from unconventional angles. We expect, thereby, that the reader achieves a different view on these matters, one that is more relevant to engineering than perhaps science, more relevant to practice than to theory. In any actual course the lecturer can therefore, based on local course curricula, leave out some of the "excursion" material.

How to Use These Volumes in a Course

Together with these volumes it is planned to make available over the Internet:

- `http://www.imm.dtu.dk/~db/The-SE-Books`

a comprehensive set of electronic documents:

- a large variety of suggested course structures (with references to volume chapters and slides)
- group project descriptions — some with solutions
- large-scale development examples
- URLs to formal methods pages
- URLs to formal methods tools

Via the publisher there will, from the day the book is published, be available, for bona fide lecturers,

- several thousand postscript/pdf lecture slides
- selected exercise solutions
- representative (student) project reports

The slides will cover a large subset of the text of these volumes. By means of viewing facilities on most computers the lecturer will be able to personally select those slides that cover suitable lectures.

Brief Guide to the Book

The book is divided into three volumes. Each volume is divided into several parts. Most parts are composed from several chapters or appendixes.

Most chapters offer exercises. A special set of exercises has been formulated. Their presentation spans almost the entire Vol. 1. These exercises are introduced in Appendix A.

All volumes have extensive cross-referencing indexes and bibliographic references. There is, in Vol. 1, a Glossary, Appendix B. It is intended to cover all three volumes. The glossary can be read independently of the rest of these volumes.

Appendix A of Vol. 2 brings our conventions for naming identifications of types, values, functions, variables, channels, objects and schemes, as well as parameters over most of these.

Brief Guide to This Volume

This volume has several chapters. The chapters are grouped into parts. Figure 4 abstracts a precedence relation between chapters. It is one that approximates suggested sequences of studying this volume.

- Chapter 1 is considered a prerequisite for the study of any chapter.
- Chapters 2–4 may be skipped by readers with some schooling in discrete mathematics.
- Chapters 5–6 may be skipped by readers with a bit more schooling in discrete mathematics.
- Chapters 7–9 can only be skipped by readers who have a reasonably firm grip on the topics mentioned.
- Chapters 10–16 form the core of Vol. 1.
- If, after Chap. 1, you continue with Chap. 2, then you should study all of Chaps. 2–9.
- If, after Chap. 1, you continue with Chap. 5, then you should study all of Chaps. 5–9.

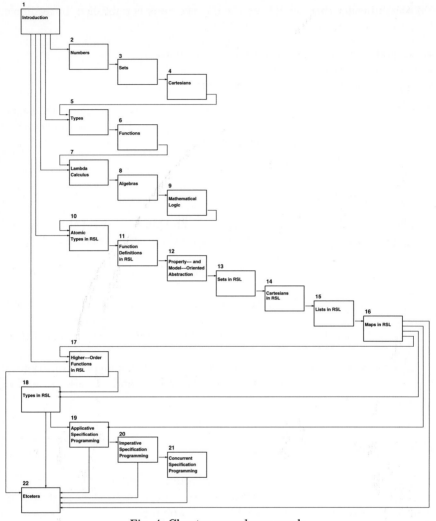

Fig. 4. Chapter precedence graph

- If, after Chap. 1, you continue with Chap. 7, then you should study all of Chaps. 7–9.
- You can skip Chaps. 17 and/or 18 before continuing with Chaps. 19–21.
- You can exit your study of this volume after any of Chaps. 16–21.
- It is no harm to study Chap. 22.

Within most chapters many sections can be skipped. Typically those with larger examples or towards the end of the chapters.

In this way a teacher or a reader can compose a number of suitable courses and studies.

Acknowledgments

The author explicitly acknowledges the following colleagues, most of whom I have worked with, and who over the years have greatly influenced my thoughts and actions: Cai Kindberg, Jean Paul Jacob, Gerald M. Weinberg, Peter Lucas, Gene Amdahl, John W. Backus, Lotfi Zadeh, (the late) E.F. (Ted) Codd, Cliff B. Jones, (the late) Hans Bekič, Heinz Zemanek, Dana Scott, (the late) Andrei Petrovich Ershov, Hans Langmaack, Andrzej Blikle, Neil D. Jones, Jørgen Fischer Nilsson, David Harel, Bo Stig Hansen, Søren Prehn, Sir Tony Hoare, Mícheál Mac an Airchinnigh, Michael Jackson, Zhou ChaoChen, Chris George, Jim Woodcock, Kokichi Futatsugi, Joseph A. Goguen, Larry Druffel and Wolfgang Reisig — listed more-or-less chronologically. I wish in particular to acknowledge my deepest thanks and gratitude to Søren Prehn and Chris George — for more than a quarter century of inspiration.

I also express my gratitude to the members of IFIP Working Groups WG 2.2 and WG 2.3 (not already mentioned above). The meetings of these working groups, with their "free for all" *topics for discussion sessions and debates*, have helped me sharpen and focus on what these volumes are about: Jean-Raymond Abrial, Jaco W. de Bakker, Manfred Broy, (the late) Ole-Johan Dahl, (the late) Edsger W. Dijkstra, Leslie Lamport, Zohar Manna, John McCarthy, Bertrand Meyer, Peter D. Mosses, Ernst-Rüdiger Olderog, Amir Pnueli, John Reynolds, Willem-Paul de Roever and Wlad Turski — listed alphabetically.

From the writing (and copy-editing) phase of these volumes invaluable thanks goes to my former students, Christian Krog Madsen (who wrote Chaps. 12–14 of Vol. 2), Steffen Holmslykke (who wrote Sect. 10.3 of Vol. 2), Martin Pěnička (who basically wrote Sects. 12.3.4, 14.4.1 and 14.4.2 of Vol. 2), and to Hugh Anderson. Final, dearest and warmest thanks goes to my editors at Springer. First Ingeborg Mayer, then Ronan Nugent. I also thank the Copy Editor, Tracey Wilbourn — whose thorough work is deeply appreciated.

Dines Bjørner
National University of Singapore, 2004–2005

Contents

Part II DISCRETE MATHEMATICS

Part III SIMPLE RSL

Part IV SPECIFICATION TYPES

Part V SPECIFICATION PROGRAMMING

Part XI AND SO ON

Part XII APPENDICES

Part I

OPENING

1

Introduction

- The **prerequisites** for studying this chapter are that you have academic training in programming, that is, in algorithms and data structures, say using two or more of the `Standard ML`, `Java` and `Prolog` programming languages.
- The **aims** are to set the stage for the entire set of volumes, to introduce the "triptych" concept of domain engineering, requirements engineering and software design, to emphasize the importance of documentation and of descriptions, to preview the concepts of formal techniques, methods and methodology, and to introduce the concepts of syntax, semantics and pragmatics.
- The **objective** is to guide you in the direction of what we think are to be the important aspects of software engineering; that is, to set, with respect to the aims and objectives of this book, your "spinal chord" to as close as possible a "state" as that of their author.
- The **treatment** is informal and discursive.

This chapter has been written so as to be read, if not in excruciating detail, then at least such that the reader is hopefully "tuned" to somewhere near the "wavelength" of the author of this chapter. The present chapter may thus be read in between the study of most subsequent chapters.

1.1 Setting the Stage

Characterisation. *Engineering* is the mathematics, the profession, the discipline, the craft and the art of turning scientific insight and human needs into technological products. ∎

The sciences of software engineering are those of computers and computing.

Characterisation. *Computer science* is the study and knowledge of what kind of "things" may (or can) exist "inside" computers, that is, *data* (i.e., *values* and their *types*) and *processes*, and hence their *functions, events* and *communication.*   ∎

Characterisation. *Computing science* is the study and knowledge of how to construct those "things".   ∎

These volumes will provide material for teaching you some of the core aspects of the mathematics, the profession, the discipline, the craft and the art of software engineering. The engineer walks the bridge between science and technology, creating technology from scientific results, and analysing technology to ascertain whether it possesses scientific values. These volumes will teach you some of the science of computing, exemplify current software technologies, and help you to become a professional engineer "walking that bridge"!

Students of these volumes are not expected to have any acquaintance with the disciplines in the following list of computer science topics: automata, formal languages and computability [296,319], programming language semantics [183,252,443,454,497,521], type theory [1,241,407], complexity theory [319], cryptography [363], and others as covered in, for example, [344]. The topics of the above list, other than the first, will either be introduced in these volumes or can be studied after having studied the present text.

Students of these volumes are expected to possess some fluency in the following computing science topics: functional programming [261], logic programming [295,351], imperative programming [20,243,290], parallel programming [449], and algorithms and data structures [7,161,326–328].

The keywords *art* [326–328], *discipline* [194], *craft* [441], *science* [245], *logic* [275], and *practice* [276], are also prefix terms of the titles of seminal textbooks on programming, as referenced. In a sense these references also serve to indicate our basic approach to programming. But software engineering goes beyond what has been implied by the above listings of computer and computing science topics. Software engineering goes beyond the algorithm and data structure, cum programming language skills. These computer and computing science skills can and must first be reasonably mastered by the individual, by the professional, academically educated and trained programmer. Software engineering is as much about making groups of two or more programmers work productively together.[1] And software engineering is about producing software which can be further deployed in the development of larger computing systems by other developers.

To fulfill these latter aspirations, software engineering must augment the knowledge of computer and computing sciences with such disciplines as project and product management. By *project management* we colloquially mean: How do project leaders plan (schedule and allocate) development resources, how

---

[1]However, the principles, techniques and tools covered by these volumes are also required to be used even by the "lone" programmer developing her "own" software.

do they monitor and control "progress", and so on? By *product management* we colloquially mean: How does a software house determine a, or its, product strategy and tactics, that is, which projects to undertake, which products to market, how to price, service and extend them, and so on?

We detail a number of project management issues: (1) choice and planning of development process, (2) scheduling and allocation of resources, (3) monitoring and control of work progress, (4) monitoring and control of quality: assurance and assessment, (5) version control and configuration management, (6) legacy systems, (7) cost estimation, (8) legal issues, etc. There are other issues, but listing just these shows, up here, early in these volumes, the large variety of development concerns.

(1) *Process (choice and) modelling* is a project management issue. How do the engineers proceed, what does one do first, then after that, etc.? There is not just one right way of doing things, of proceeding in phases, stages and steps, rather there are many eligible process models. First, the development process is determined by the problem frame; second, by the novelty of the problem; third, by the experience of the programmers and of management; and so forth.

(2) *Planning, scheduling and allocation of resources* is another project management issue. In planning we decide on which things to do. In scheduling we decide on when to do these things, and in allocation we decide on which resources (monies, people, machines, etc.) to deploy.

(3) *Monitoring and control of work progress* extends the list of project management concerns. Once the project proper starts, after planning, one needs to regularly and continuously check what has been achieved. And, if what has been achieved is according to plan, then just continue. But if plans are not being followed, then control must be asserted by possibly changing the plan, rescheduling and/or reallocating development resources.

(4) *Monitoring and control of quality assurance and assessment* further extends our project management concern list. The web of application domain knowledge that goes into a software product, the maze of hundreds of mostly unrelated requirements that are expected fulfilled from the software product and the "Babylonic towers" of software design techniques and tools (languages, etc.) all necessitate careful formulations of what is meant by product quality, as well as close scrutiny of the development process, in order to ascertain whether quality objectives are at risk or are being met.

(5) *Version control & configuration management:* In the development of software the programmers usually construct several versions, or "generations", of code. One must monitor and control these generations and versions. This is called *version control*. It can be a sizable undertaking when, as is often the case, there exist hundreds, if not up towards thousands, of such alternative and complementary versions. Some of these versions may enter into one release of a product, while other subsets of versions enter into other releases of related products. Combining such versions into software products is called *configuration management*.

(6) *Legacy systems:* At any time customers (users, acquirers, buyers) of software operate computing systems composed from often "age-old" parts, and these have to be maintained: *adapted* to new hardware and to new software, *perfected* to offer relevant performance, and *corrected* (by removing "bugs"). All three maintenance aspects become increasingly problematic as the original software is either programmed in languages for which there are no longer adequate, let alone "recent" compilers and related support tools, or is documented in a style basically unfamiliar to new generations of programmers, or not documented at all. This kind of software and these kinds of problems constitute the concept of *legacy software.*

(7) *Cost estimation:* Two issues of cost estimation may be relevant: estimating the cost of developing new (or maintaining old) software, and estimating competitive, profitable prices for software. The problem of *cost estimation* is intertwined with the problems of software development process models, project and product management, quality assurance, version control and configuration management, legacy systems, etc.

(8) *Legal issues related to software:* There are many legal issues related to software. There are software patents, which establish intellectual, and property rights. There is *software curriculum accreditation,* that is, the approval of a university or college curriculum in software engineering. And there is *software house accreditation:* the approval (usually, typically by, or through some ISO-related agency), generally, of a software house as a trustworthy developer of software. There is *software engineer certification:* the approval (usually by some national engineering society) of a person being a bona fide professional. Finally there is *software product certification:* the approval (usually by some international agency, such as Lloyd's Register of Shipping, Bureaux Veritas, Norwegian Veritas, TÜV, or others) of a specific software product to meet certain standards of quality.

• • •

Software engineering is anchored in programming: (1) in the design of software, (2) before that in constructing the software requirements, (3) and before that in understanding the application domain.

These volumes spend most of their pages on the development aspects of software engineering: on principles and techniques for developing proper application *domain* understandings, on principles and techniques for developing proper software *requirements* and on principles and techniques for developing proper *software designs.* These volumes unfold these principles and techniques based on the tools of both informal and formal languages for *describing domains, prescribing requirements* and *specifying (designing) software.*

1.2 A Software Engineering Triptych

It is a definite new contribution of Vol. 3 that it focuses, in a "special way", on the triptych[2] of *domain engineering, requirements engineering* and *software design*. That way emphasises that domain engineering, *"ideally and logically speaking"*, precedes requirements engineering, which (and there is nothing new in this), *ideally and logically speaking,* precedes software design. The new contribution is the central role given to domain engineering.

1.2.1 Software Versus Systems Development

Although these volumes are primarily about the engineering of software, we cannot avoid getting involved, to a nontrivial degree, in the more general engineering of computing systems.

Characterisation. By a *computing system* we mean a combination of hardware and software that together implement some requirements.   ∎

Typically a computing system is distributed, over local areas as well as globally, and thus very typically requires extensive data communication hardware and software. When, in the following, we say 'software' or 'system' we can usually substitute the more general term 'computing system'.

1.2.2 Motivating the Triptych

We motivate the roles of the three triptych constituents as follows: *Before we can (3) design software we must understand the (2) requirements put to this software. And before we can prescribe the (2) requirements we must understand the application (1) domain.* What is discussed, again and again in these volumes, is how we interpret the *"ideal and logical"* precedences mentioned above. But first we will take a look at the three triptych components, or, as we shall also refer to them in these volumes, *the three phases of software development.*

1.2.3 Domain Engineering

Characterisation. By *domain engineering* we mean the engineering of domain descriptions.   ∎

---

[2] *Triptych:* (i) From Greek 'triptychos', having three folds, (ii) an ancient Roman writing tablet with three waxed leaves hinged together, (iii) a picture (as an altarpiece) or carving in three panels side by side, (iv) something composed or presented in three parts or sections. Same as trilogy.

Characterisation. By a *domain* we mean (i) an area of human activity, (ii) and/or an area of semi- or fully mechanised activity, (iii) and/or an area of nature that can be described, and parts or all of which that can potentially be subject to partial or total computerisation. ∎

Example 1.1 *Three Domains:* Examples of (respective) domains, related to the above enumeration (i–iii), are: (i) book-keeping; (ii) the sending of freight from a harbour of origin, on ships via other harbours, to a destination harbour; and (iii) the planetary movements, i.e., celestial mechanics [494]. ∎

We understand a domain when we can describe it in an objective way.

Characterisation. By a *domain description* we mean an indicatively expressed description of the properties of the following domain facets: the *intrinsics* (the basic, invariant, and core), the *enterprise* (business, institution) *processes*, the *technology supports*, the *management and organisation*, the *rules and regulation*, the *human behaviour*, and possibly of other facets of the domain. ∎

Domain descriptions explain the domain *as it is*. No reference can be made to any requirements to desired software — that comes later! Furthermore, no reference can be made to the desired software — that also comes later! So, a domain description really has nothing to do with information technology (IT) or software — other than what is already installed and deployed in the domain, and then only if reference to such existing IT and software is deemed relevant.

Example 1.2 *A Logistics Domain:* We are not describing the example domain, only informing about it, but in almost descriptional terms: A logistics domain consists (a) of senders and receivers of freight; (b) of logistics firms which arrange for senders and receivers to send or, respectively, receive freight; (c) of hubs (like harbours, railway stations, truck terminals and airport air cargo centres) where freight may be loaded onto or, respectively, unloaded from conveyors; (d) of conveyors (such as ships, freight trains, trucks, respectively air planes) that are owned and/or operated by transport companies; (e) of transport companies (like cargo liners, railway operators, trucking companies, airlines); and (f) of the networks of transport routes (shipping lanes, railway lines, highways or, respectively, air corridors).

Some further descriptions can be hinted at: A conveyor path[3] is a connection between two hubs. A conveyor route is a sequence of one or more connected paths. Some hubs are of two or more kinds, viz., harbours and railway stations, air cargo centres and truck terminals, etc. Conveyors travel their routes according to fixed time tables. A conveyor fee table prescribes costs of transporting freight, per cubic meter, between hubs. This example is continued in Example 1.3. Notice that there were no references to either requirements or to possibly desired software (i.e., computing system), let alone to such a system. ∎

A domain description, to repeat, describes the domain as it is. Chapter 5 of Vol. 3 covers principles, techniques and tools for describing any *universe of discourse*, whether domain, requirements or software. Part IV (Chaps. 8–16) of Vol. 3 covers principles, techniques and tools for proper domain description. Domain knowledge need be acquired, that is, elicited from those who work in and are affected by the domain.

1.2.4 Requirements Engineering

Characterisation. By *requirements engineering* we mean the engineering of *requirements prescriptions.* ∎

Requirements arise as a natural consequence of a *contractual relation* between a *client* who procures (who is to acquire) some desired software (i.e., software to be delivered), and the *deliverer* or the *developer* of that software. By *requirements* we mean a list of one or more putatively expressed statements as to which *properties* are expected from the software to be developed. Requirements must be acquired, that is, elicited from those who may be affected by the eventually acquired software.

Example 1.3 *Some Logistics Requirements:* This example continues Example 1.2. We do not exemplify a proper requirements prescription, we just hint at what it might deal with. A logistics system needs software support for (at least) the following kinds of activities:

First we exemplify some *domain requirements*. These are requirements that solely pertain to the domain, and whose professional terms are domain terms. Examples are: Software support for handling inquiries, from potential senders, with logistics firms, as to possible routing of freight, schedules and costs; software support for handling requests, from actual senders, to logistics firms, for the dispatch of freight, and hence the issuance of bills of lading (waybills) and the handling (passing on) of freight to be sent; software support for logistics firms tracing the whereabouts of freight at hubs or with the owner transport companies of scheduled conveyors; software support for the hub management of conveyors in and out of hubs, the unloading and loading of conveyors, and the receipt of freight from, and delivery of freight to logistics firms.

Then we exemplify some *machine requirements*. These are requirements that primarily pertain to the machine to be built, that is: the software+hardware of the desired computing system, in other words, whose professional terms additionally include information technology terms in general.

---

[3]Examples of paths: Sea lanes, rail lines, roads, and air corridors.

Examples are: The computing system shall have a mean time between failures of two years; when the system is "down" it must at most be so for two hours, and so on.

Finally, we exemplify some *interface requirements*. These are requirements that pertain both to the domain and to the machine to be built, to the interface between the machine and the domain, human users of the domain as well as (other) natural phenomena and man-made equipment of the domain. Interface requirements are about the phenomena that are shared between the domain and the machine. Examples are: senders and receivers shall be able to ascertain the transport status of their own freight from their own, home PCs based on standard Internet browsers; the computing system shall display, for logistics firms, the route networks in some "zoom-able" manners, and so on.

This example is continued in Example 1.4.   ∎

Notice how Example 1.3 introduced three notions of requirements: domain requirements, interface requirements and machine requirements.

This decomposition represents a pragmatic separation of concerns. Domain requirements, to repeat, are requirements that pertain solely to domain phenomena, i.e., they are requirements whose professional terms are domain terms. Interface requirements, to repeat, are requirements that pertain both to the domain and to the machine to be built, to the interface between the machine and the domain, human users of the domain as well as (other) natural phenomena and man-made equipment of the domain. That is, to phenomena shared between the environment and the machine. Machine requirements, to repeat, are requirements that primarily pertain to the machine to be built, that is, the software + hardware of the desired computing system. In other words, the professional terms of machine requirements additionally include information technology terms in general.

Notice how we, in rough sketching some requirements, relied on domain terms having been previously described. We did, however, not precisely describe those terms. But we hinted at how it is the purpose of a domain description to explicate all such domain specific terms. We likewise relied on machine (hardware + software technology, that is: IT) terms also having been precisely specified, elsewhere!

Notice also how we "sneaked" the crucial concepts of *domain, interface* and *machine requirements* into the example! Part V (Chaps. 17–24) of Vol. 3 covers principles, techniques and tools for the proper prescription of requirements.

A popular view of requirements makes the following distinctions: user requirements, system requirements, and non-functional requirements. How are we to take these? User requirements form one entire set of requirements: domain, interface and machine requirements. So do system requirements. Non-functional requirements are what we refer to as some interface and most, if not all machine requirements. How does this work? User requirements do not need to be complete, they can be, as we shall call them, rough-sketches, although they are typically well-structured and carefully cross-referenced, and they form input for the development of system requirements. System requirements must be consistent and relatively complete: they "improve" upon the user requirements, and they form input to software design.

1.2.5 Software Design

Software: Code and Documents

Characterisation. By *software* we mean not only the *code* based on which computers can act, but also all the *documentation* that is necessary for the proper deployment of the code. This includes the *business process reengineering manuals* that are necessary for the enterprise (the institution) acquiring the computing system to function most optimally when using this system, the *installation manuals* that are necessary when initially installing the computing system, the *user training and daily use manuals* that are needed in preparatory training of future system users as well as in their daily use of the system as installed, the *maintenance manuals* that are needed during the daily facilities management of the installed system (for (adaptive) up- or downgrades, for performance (perfective) enhancements, and for error corrections), and the *disposal manuals* that are needed when dismantling the system. Ideally software also includes a precise record of the software validation and verification history: stakeholder responses, verification and tests, including test suites and the results expected from, and actually recorded during, actual tests using these test suites. By a *test suite* we mean a collection of data serving as input to a test.   ∎

Software Design, I

Characterisation. By *software design* we mean the implementation of (required) software, not just coding, but its stage and stepwise development and documentation.   ∎

Phases, Stages and Steps of Development

Characterisation. By *software development* we mean the combined development of domain descriptions, requirements prescriptions, and software designs.   ∎

Software, as well as domain descriptions and requirements prescriptions, is usually rather complex. Hence these need be developed according to the principle of *separation of concerns*, i.e., of *divide and conquer*. Therefore we divide the development phases of domain descriptions, requirements prescriptions and software design into stages and steps. A first development, one that is reasonably illustrative of a multistep development, is given in Examples 16.10 to 16.21. Part VI (Chaps. 25–30) of Vol. 3 covers software design.

Software Design, II

Conventionally we think of establishing, in *stages of software design,* first the *software architecture,*[4] which in a sense explained, in Chap. 26 of Vol. 3, implements a "high-level design" of the domain requirements, the interface requirements and the machine requirements. In the second stage we establish the *program components* which in a sense, explained in Chaps. 27 and 28 of Vol. 3, designs the gross and detailed modular structure of the software. The final or *implementation stage,* which usually consists of many steps, includes *platform reuse design* in which available *software components* are examined for their possible reuse in the implementation, *modularisation* or *objectivisation,* in which a fine grained decomposition of the program organisation into modules takes place, and finally the *coding* itself in which final lines of code are specified. That is, the instructions to the computer as expressed in some programming languages and in calls to run-time system facilities and (other platform) components.

In Example 1.4 we give an informally expressed software architecture design.

Example 1.4 *A Logistics System Software Design:* This example continues Examples 1.2 and 1.3. We do not exemplify a proper software design specification. We just hint at what it might deal with. A logistics computing and communication system is implemented as follows: Each sender or receiver, each logistics firm, each transport firm, each hub and each conveyor (of a transport firm) is implemented as a separate, concurrently operating process with its own state. None of the processes share global state components, but instead operate based on synchronised and communicated messages. Freights are not implemented as objects, i.e., as independent processes. Shared data is implemented as a separate process whose state represents the shared data (i.e., a database). ∎

1.2.6 Discussion

General Issues

This ends our exposition of core concepts of the software development triptych. In summary we emphasise two sets of relations between the three software development phases. The three kinds (cum phases) of engineering development can be summarised as follows: In domain engineering we describe the domain *as it is.* In requirements engineering we prescribe the requirements to software (i.e., a computing system) for the support of activities in the domain *as we*

---

[4]Wherever we say software architecture we could say computing systems architecture.

would like to have them. In (the early stages of) software design we specify the software such *as we have decided it shall be.*

The relations between the three kinds of documents arise from respective development phases. Domain descriptions are *indicative* [308], as we seriously believe the domain essentially is. We must make sure to describe all possible behaviours of the domain, including as we normally expect well-functioning actors to perform, but to also include erroneous, faulty, less diligent, sloppy, or even outright criminal behaviours. Requirements prescriptions are *putative* [308], as we would mandate the software to behave. A requirements prescription would naturally focus on well-functioning behaviour and try to ensure correct behaviour of all actors, whether men or machines. Software specifications are *imperative* [308], that is, mandatory.

When a domain description is formalised, the hedge 'may' is lost. And when a requirements prescription is formalised, the hedge 'must' is likewise lost. Formal domain descriptions, requirements prescriptions and software (design) specifications have in common a certain "authoritative air" which the domain description can never have. A domain description is only an abstraction, or a model of some reality, but it is not that reality, whereas a requirements prescription is intended to be a precise exact model of the software to be implemented.

The triptych approach to software engineering is central to these volumes. We shall endeavour to enunciate clear principles, techniques and tools for the development of domain descriptions, requirements prescriptions and software specifications. Within domain descriptions we find such concepts as domain attributes, stakeholders and their perspectives, and domain facets. Within requirements prescriptions we find such concepts as domain requirements, interface requirements, and machine requirements. Independently of these we find such requirements techniques as domain projection, instantiation, extension and initialisation. Within software design we find such concepts as software architecture, program organisation and structure, and modularisation.

1.3 Documentation

This section is a precursor for a later chapter, Chap. 2 of Vol. 3, which includes many examples and enunciates many documentation principles, techniques and tools. Since documentation is all pervasive and is all important in software engineering, we shall this early in these volumes "lift the curtain" on documents enough that we can refer broadly and generally to the document types in the text that follows between this section and Chap. 2 of Vol. 3 in which we finally dispose of the subject.

We saw, in the previous section, that software development entails three major phases, possibly several stages within phases and possibly several steps within stages. Carrying out each of the steps results in documents. These are documents on domains descriptions, requirements prescriptions and software specifications.

There is nothing else[5] emanating from steps, stages and phases than documents, on paper or electronically. So the question is: What kind of documents? In this section we will briefly overview three kinds of documents that result from the engineering of the steps, stages and phases. It is important that the reader keeps the *universe of discourse* in mind, either the domain, the requirements, the software, the two first (domain and requirements), the two last (requirements and software) or all three (an entire development). That is, the various documents, even the informative ones, all have a specific *universe of discourse* in mind. It must first be clearly stated, lest one of the "parties" to a development contract gets confused from the very start!

1.3.1 Document Kinds

There are basically three kinds of documents that emerge from the development process, and which the developer hence should be aiming at. These are: (1) *informative documents,* or document parts, such as partners and current situation, needs and ideas, product concepts and facilities, scope and span delineations, assumptions and dependencies, implicit/derivative goals, synopsis, design briefs, contracts, logbook; (2) the *description documents,* or document parts, such as rough sketches (records of "brainstorming"), terminologies, narratives, and formal models; and finally (3) the *analytic documents,* or document parts, such as description property verifications, verification of correctness of development transition (i.e., development step), and validation of formal and informal descriptions.

We will briefly review these kinds of documents, both as concerns their pragmatics: why they are necessary, and as concerns their multitude: why there are so many seemingly different kinds of documents.

1.3.2 Phase, Stage and Step Documents

A development phase results in a comprehensive, definitive set of informative, descriptive and analytic documents. A development stage results, similarly, in a comprehensive set of informative, descriptive and analytic documents, or in a set of relatively complete domain, interface or machine requirements prescriptions.

The boundaries between a subphase and a stage, and the comprehensiveness of either, are not sharp. It serves no purpose here, or for the approaches advocated in these volumes, to try sharpen such distinctions. The stage and

---

[5]Strictly speaking: Understanding also emerges, and so do closer relations between client (acquirer, customer) and developer (deliverer, provider), etcetera. But, contractwise, unless, for example, education and training is also part of a project, documents are the only tangible goods delivered!

step concepts are simply pragmatic. One could go on defining sub-steps, etc., but we refrain. Let the actual project determine a need for finer granularities!

If a distinction need be made between a phase and a stage, then the comprehensive set of stage documents represents one of more than one "stage" of development within the phase.

A step of development produces only a part of a comprehensive set of documents, for example: a comprehensive set of informative, descriptive or analytic documents or document parts, or just, as a substep, one of these documents, or document parts. More will emerge as we progress deeper into these volumes.

1.3.3 Informative Documents

Characterisation. By an *informative document* we mean a document, or a document part, which informs, it does not necessarily describe a designatable, manifest phenomena or concept.   ∎

As the name implies, informative documents give information which takes many forms. Informative documents include those of perceived or already enunciated needs, product concepts and facilities, scope and span delineations, assumptions and dependencies, implicit/derivative goals, synopsis, contracts, design briefs, and so on.

Current Situation Documentation

Need for software development, or for requirements prescription, or for domain description usually arise out of a *current situation*. A current situation may be that the domain is not well-understood, or that software is required. Professional software development projects therefore produce an informative document — two–three pages — which inform of the current situation that leads to needs.

Needs Documentation

Needs refer to perceived or actual needs for the product being desired, whether a domain description, a requirements prescription, a software design (i.e., specification), or just plainly, as is most often the case, the software itself. Needs can be expressed in many ways: We must understand the domain; we must establish requirements; *"So ein Ding muss Ich auch haben"*[6]; software to automate humanly menial, boring processes; software to speed up slow processes; and so on. Needs must be quantified, if possible.

---

[6] "I must also have such a 'thing'" (i.e., software).

Product Concepts and Facilities

Product concepts and facilities refer to "brainstorming" or ideas ("dreams"). That is, what the universe of discourse "contains", or is to contain, what aims and objectives the proposers have for the "product", what roles, in a larger socioeconomic context, the product is to serve (or fulfill). That is, what are the strategic or tactical objectives of the developer and/or customers, how it might complement earlier products, and/or how it might open the way for, or be, a next-generation product.

Design Briefs

Design briefs refer to documents which state what kind of project is to take place: for which universe of discourse, specifically (aiming at a very specific client), or generally (aiming at a largest class of such clients), or something in-between. Whether the project is an ordinary development, or a research, or some advanced project encompassing both R&D. Finally it also encompasses what general deliveries are expected, the time frame, costs, institutions involved, and so on.

Usually a scope and span delineation is part of or strictly adjoins the design brief. To this we turn next.

Scope and Span Delineations

Scope and span delineations refer to the more specific subjects of the universe of discourse to be dealt with in the project, that is, the target and modal scope, for example: *railways,* or *health care,* or *financial services;* respectively new development (incl. R&D), or maintenance, or other. The target and modal span, for example, *rolling stock monitoring and control,* or *electronic patient journals,* or *stock trading;* respectively off-the-shelf commercial, one-of-a-kind, or other product.

Synopsis

Synopsis refer to a "capsule" (i.e., short overview) characterisation of the product being desired, whether a domain description, a requirements prescription or a software design. A synopsis is like a movie "trailer". It tells, in a few words, what the whole thing (domain, requirements or software) is all about. A synopsis is not a description (a prescription, a specification), "but almost". It mentions all the most important phenomena of the universe of discourse, their entities, types, values, actions, events and behaviours. It mentions their semantics and syntax, but it does so incompletely. And a synopsis "links" these phenomena components to their pragmatics, that is what role they serve, and so on.

Synopses often form an important introductory part of contracts.

Contracts

A contract describes *parties to the contract, the subject matter* and *considerations.*

   Contracts refer to the legal documents that name contractors (the parties: clients and developers); and that define what is to be developed: If software, then the contract would normally refer to an already existing requirements prescription; if requirements, then the contract would normally refer to an already existing domain description; or if a domain description then the scope and span delineation would be an important document part. In addition (the considerations) contracts prescribe the development costs (estimates): If software is to be developed, then the estimate should be rather binding. If requirements are to be developed, then costs could be based on fixed hourly rates and some usually negotiable rough time estimates. Precise numbers cannot be given since much, unforeseeable interaction needs to take place between the contracting parties. Or if a domain description is to be developed—in which case the project is basically a joint research effort—then the costs are usually negotiable, and billed on a, say, monthly basis. A contract would (further considerations) refer to legal conditions. Many other considerations may be part of a contract document.

Discussion

We have outlined essential informative documents. We emphasise that the developer (and/or client) may, in the extreme, have to "repeat" such documents for each phase, stage and, in a few cases, step of development and their transitions. That is, informative documents may be needed for each and all of the triptych phases: domains, requirements and software design.

   We have chosen the wording *documents* (and documentation) so as to indicate that one may view each of the listed informative document types as designating instantiation of individual, separately "bound" documents. For the next category of documents, the descriptive ones, we choose a wording that allow their various types to designate document parts that can be "mingled" (woven together) into larger documents.

1.3.4 Descriptive Documents

Characterisation. By a *descriptive document* we mean a document, or a document part, which describes a manifest phenomenon or a concept.   ∎

The term describe, and hence the terms description, and descriptive, are here used in a rather specific, narrow sense. A description designates (i.e., is some text that sets forth, in words) either some physically existing part of nature (one that centres around physical behaviours usually governed by laws of physics) or some man-made part of the world (one that centres around human activities, including their interaction with artifacts) or some combination of these two classes of worlds.

Thus a description, such as we shall deploy the term, tends to focus on what might eventually "fit within a computer". It may well be that what we describe concerning a domain is not computable and cannot be "mimicked" by a computer. A requirements prescription, however, "cuts down" on its underlying domain description and makes sure that what is required is also computable. Hence opinions, emotions, metaphysical, political or such other similar subjective texts are not here considered descriptions.

It can be seen from the above, and it will reappear, again and again later, that it is not a simple, straightforward matter to delineate precisely when something is a description (a prescription, a specification), and what can be described, that is, what can exist. Chapters 5, 6 and 7 of Vol. 3 focus on principles and techniques for forming proper descriptions (specifications) and touch on the philosophical issues of being.

We (thus) consider three kinds of descriptions: domain descriptions, requirements prescriptions, and software designs. We point out that we use three different terms synonymously: descriptions, prescriptions and designs (specifications). Domain descriptions are about what already exists, "the world as it is".[7] Michael Jackson [308] refers to domain descriptions as indicative. Requirements prescriptions are about what we expect from software, "the world as we would like it to be". Michael Jackson [308] refers to requirements prescriptions as putative. Software (design) specifications then outline the design structure of software, that is, specifications of specific types, values, functions, events and behaviours. Michael Jackson [308] refers to domain descriptions as imperative.

Descriptive Document Kinds and Types

We see basically two kinds of description documents: informal and formal. And we see basically four types of description documents: rough sketches (documents which record results of "brainstorming"), terminologi.e., narratives and formal models. One could consider the latter two types (narratives and formal models) to stand for one type, the type of 'proper description documents', both informal and formal. We shall stick with the above compartmentalisation.

Rough Sketches

Characterisation. By a *rough sketch document* we mean a descriptive document which is a draft and whose description is incomplete, and/or is not well structured.   ∎

---

[7]From an epistemological point of view we may have to say: a world as we subjectively observe it.

When we first, as an initial act of proper development, attempt to develop something, we then "brainstorm". Recording the ideas that arose during "brainstorming" results in a rough sketch. We are told either to develop a domain description or a requirements prescription or a software design. And we are not quite sure where to begin in the chosen universe of discourse. So we "doodle", or we rough sketch. A rough sketch is basically an unstructured nonsystematic effort at describing whatever has to be described (prescribed, specified).

A rough sketch serves the purpose — in the style of explorative, experimental work — of coming to grips with the concepts that are central to the universe of discourse, and from there with the derivative concepts. A rough sketch shall then serve, as it is being developed, i.e., as a means to identify the core concepts, and their relations. This identification process is of utmost importance. It is of analytic nature, and is further discussed in Section 1.3.5. Section 2.5.1 of Vol. 3 presents examples, principles and techniques of rough sketching.

Terminology

Characterisation. By a *terminology document* we mean a description document which, in a systematic, but not necessarily a complete or exhaustive manner, lists and briefly explains a number of terms.   ▪

The rough sketch descriptive step together with the concept formation analytic step serves to identify and consolidate the important concepts (i.e., abstractions of phenomena, whether in domains, requirements or software). This identification contains an element of naming these concepts. A list of all these concept names and their characterisation (description, explanation, definition) is what call a *terminology*. We could also call the list a *glossary* or a *dictionary* or even an *ontology*. We refer to Sect. B.1 for discussions of these four and the related terms of encyclopedia and thesaurus.

> We consider it to be a very important and indispensable part of every phase of software development to perform the following four terminology-related actions: (1) to *establish* a (phase-oriented) terminology; (2) to *use* and hence *adhere* to such a terminology; (3) to *update*, i.e., *maintain* such terminologies and let changes be reflected back in all the documents where referenced terms are used; (4) and to *make available* such terminologies.

Failure to do as advised above usually has dire consequences.

Section 2.5.2 of Vol. 3 will present examples, principles and techniques for creating a terminology.

Narrative

Characterisation. By a *narrative document* we mean a description document which systematically and reasonably comprehensively, in natural, yet most likely (application domain-specific) professional language, explains the entities, functions and behaviours (including events) of a designated universe of discourse.

■

To narrate is to "tell a story". The story (the narration) to be told here is that of the chosen universe of discourse, be it a domain, or part of a domain, a requirement, or a software design. The narrative must be such that the listener (i.e., the reader) as well as, of course, the narrator, can formalise the story: That is, we put down as a constraint upon the narratives that they can be given mathematical, i.e., computing science, models or otherwise be characterised mathematically. It is not a constraint on domain descriptions that what is described is computable: that it can be "mimicked" (mechanised, simulated) by a computer. It is indeed a constraint on domain requirements prescriptions as well as on software design specifications that they constitute computational models.

This insistence on formalisation can be justified as follows: The domain requirements must imply something computable. After all, they are about a computing system. The software design certainly must also imply something computable.

But why insist on the domain description being formalisable? First, we must accept that domain requirements, as mentioned in Example 1.3, are derived from domain descriptions, and we would like the derivation operations to be formally well understood. Second, we must accept that the original role, as well as the successful pursuit of this role over the last two and a half millennia, has been to formalise phenomena of the actual world, first the physical ones, and now the human-made ones. So why not also attempt this for domains — essential parts of which cannot be said to be understood unless we indeed have a formal model. Third, it must be understood that we shall only attempt to formalise the semantic and the syntactic aspects of domains, not their pragmatic imports.[8] Finally, we must accept that we today, November 2, 2005, do not quite know how to formalise all aspects of domains and requirements! That last caveat applies in particular to domain descriptions and to interface and machine requirements prescriptions.

Thus the task is clear: describe, principally, what can or what ought be formalised. The style of the informal narrative follows from this dogma: Present first text on the classes of entities (i.e., types: abstract type (sorts) and concrete types). Then postulate any fixed, i.e., constant, instantiations (i.e., values), if and when needed. Then postulate all the functions that apply to entities (i.e., observers, generators, predicates, auxiliaries), and characterise these functions: Start by stating to which types of entities they apply (the input) and the type of the resulting, the yielded (the output) entity; then characterise the functional relationship between inputs and outputs. Similarly identify the

---

[8]For a discourse on pragmatics, semantics and syntax we refer to later material in Sect. 1.6.2 and in Part IV (Chaps. 6–9 inclusive) of Vol. 2.

behaviours (i.e., processes); and their interaction (i.e., their shared events, such as synchronisation and communication).

We are guided in the task of informally describing something when we follow the above "recipe", the above "narration" dogma — which leads on to the formalisation itself.

Chapter 2 of Vol. 3 (Sect. 2.5.3) presents examples, principles and techniques for the construction of proper narratives. These principles and techniques emerge from most chapters in Vols. 1 and 2. Specific domain, requirements, and software design narration principles and techniques are then covered in Parts IV–VI, respectively, of Vol. 3.

Formal Model

Characterisation. By a *formal document* we mean a document which expresses a model (of some universe of discourse) in a formal language.   ∎

A formal model is a model expressed in some mathematical notation or in some formal language. A mathematical expression permits conventional, albeit precise reasoning, such as is normally done in textbooks on mathematics. A formal language is one with a precise syntax, a precise semantics and a mathematical logic proof system, that is, a set of proof rules that allow formal reasoning, such as is done in textbooks on mathematical logic but here with a twist! The informal narrative and a formal model may be intertwined, textually, such as we often see in mathematics and physics textbooks. The relation between the informal narrative and its formal model is necessarily informal. That is, is one that can never be proven correct, it must be validated.

Volumes 1 and 2 contain many chapters which present examples, principles and techniques for the construction of proper formal models. Specific domain, requirements and software design formalisation principles and techniques are then covered in Parts IV–VI, respectively, of Vol. 3.

Discussion

The informal rough sketch, the more structured, but still informal narration, and the formal model, may be manifested in separate documents or may be combined and intertwined with the analytic documents. Usually the rough sketch is not documented in a manner suitable for release other than to the directly involved client and developer staff, and then usually only to the development staff. We say that the informal narratives, the terminologies and the formal models may constitute deliverables. And we normally assume that the rough sketches remain proprietary documents of the development enterprise.

1.3.5 Analytic Documents

Characterisation. By an *analytic document* we mean a document whose subject is a descriptive document. The text of an analytic document analyses a descriptive document.   ∎

As the term indicates, analytic documents are documents whose content represents analyses of other documents, here the descriptive documents. We consider four kinds of analytic documents: those that represent (i) formation of concepts from rough sketches (during brainstorming), (ii) validation of formal and informal description documents, (iii) description property verifications, and (iv) verification of the correctness of development transitions (i.e., development steps).

There may be other analytic documents. Examples: documents whose content analyses behavioural aspects of the intended computing system, such as expected interface response times based on queueing theoretic studies; expected machine computation times based on complexity theoretic studies; details of dictionary or database hashing algorithms based on statistical studies of reference patterns; and so on. Also included may be documents whose contents analyse pragmatic issues such as, production line flow (congestion), based on statistical studies, for a project and production planning, monitoring and control computing system; company cash flow, based on similar studies, for a financial services or an electronic trading computing system; and so on. Further kinds of analytic documents can be imagined. We shall, in these volumes, only cover those just mentioned.

Rough Sketch Analysis and Concept Formation

The most important task in describing a domain, prescribing some requirements or specifying some software design is to identify the core concepts around which the universe of discourse evolves. On one hand are the phenomena in the domain, the facilities that are desired from the software or the software program constructs (data structures, procedures, etc.). On the other hand these phenomena, in the actual world, these facilities (to be made manifest in the required software), or these program code constructs are to be conceptualised (as for the domain) or are indeed concepts, that is, abstract ideas, once captured as requirements or in software code.

Thus we see a transition from a concrete, manifest, actual world of usually tangible phenomena to an abstract, intellectually perceivable, but usually intangible world of concepts. It is this transition, from what is perceivable, via what is conceivable, to that which is "made into" software, that we need to record.

We do so for the domain by first brainstorming, that is by sketching rough domain descriptions and, from those, through analysis, identifying domain concepts. Then for the requirements by conceiving. In that case by sketching rough requirements "prescriptions" and, from those, through analysis, identifying requirements concepts. And finally we do this for the software by "casting", that is, by sketching rough software "designs" and, from those, through analysis, identifying proper software constructs.

Analysis with the aim of forming concepts is an art. Perhaps the hardest thing to learn is to do it right, or at least to do it in such a way that pleasing, elegant and "economic" concepts emerge. But reading lots of analysis examples might help. Chapters 13 and 21 of Vol. 3 therefore present analysis and concept formation examples, principles and techniques that are found useful in conducting the analyses hinted at above.

Validation of Descriptions, Prescriptions and Specifications

Characterisation. By a *validation document* we mean an analytic document which validates the text of a description document (*&c.*) with respect to the stakeholders of the described universe of discourse.   ∎

By *&c.* we mean: prescription and specification document.

Domain descriptions must be validated, they are, most likely, written by a small group of primarily developers, aided by a likewise small group of client staff. But larger, more definitively representative groups of client staff need review domain descriptions in order to concur. The same holds for requirements prescriptions.

Domain description and requirements prescription validation is necessarily a process of interaction between client staff and developers, and is necessarily a process based on informal narrative and terminology descriptions. This kind of validation is a crucial one: It is necessarily an informal, human process, and it serves the role of getting the right product. Chapters 14 and 22 of Vol. 3 present validation examples, principles and techniques that are found useful in conducting the analyses hinted at above.

Verification of Properties of Specifications

Characterisation. By a *verification document* we mean an analytic document which proves, model checks, or tests statements made about the properties of a description or a prescription or a specification.   ∎

A domain description denotes a theory. The description is only a model of the domain, not the real domain. Expressed in precise English, and especially expressed in some formal language, the model designated by a domain description possesses some properties. The sum total of all these properties is a theory for the domain. The same is true for requirements prescriptions and software design specifications.

We can informally reason about such properties when given a consistent and relatively complete description (or prescription or specification). And we may record this reasoning formally when we also have a formal description (formal prescription, formal [design] specification). The usefulness of formal models is that such theorems may be proven. Proof of such theorems affords a higher trust in the descriptions.

Example 1.5 *Towards a Domain Theory:* Assume that we have described a railway system, its network of lines and stations, its train timetables and the actual train traffic according to timetables. Let us further assume that the train timetables, and hence the traffic is modulo 24 hours: repeats itself daily and is always on time. Now a property that transpires only very indirectly from the train timetables (and hence the train traffic) could be the following variant of Kirchhoff's Law: For any station in the network, the number of trains arriving, over any 24 hour period, at that station, minus the number of trains ending their journies at that station, plus the number of trains starting their journey at that station, equals the number of trains departing from that station, all over the same 24 hour period. ∎

Informatics models of domains can be made into theories, just as were models of physical phenomena such as Newton's Theory of Mechanics, Thermodynamics, etc. Chapter 15 of Vol. 3 presents domain theory examples, principles and techniques that are useful in establishing domain theories as above.

Correctness of Development Phase, Stage or Step Transition

When we make the transition from the phase of describing a domain to the phase of prescribing requirements to software for support of activities in that domain we correctness-relate that transition, from the latter to the former. When we make the transition from the phase of prescribing requirements to software to the phase of specifying the required software we correctness-relate from the latter to the former. These correctness relations, when stated properly (and so they must be if we are to have trust in the development), can be informally reasoned about. And, if the descriptions, prescriptions and (design) specifications are formally expressed and the relations likewise, then the reasoning may be formally supported: Formal proofs of correctness may be made.

Phases can be decomposed into stages of development, and transitions between stages may be correctness-related and argued about. Stages can similarly be decomposed into steps, and transitions between steps may be correctness-related and argued about.

Note that we sometimes used the term 'can', and sometimes 'may'. We can always try reason informally, as do mathematicians. But it is not always possible today to formally prove properties and transition correctness. Reasons for this may be of the following: We may have constructed some unwieldy models that make the proofs too cumbersome. Or computing science, cum specification language designers, may not yet have researched and developed appropriate specification language constructs and proof systems. Or we, the developers, are simply not good enough at stating and proving auxiliary lemmas and theorems. Or we are trying to prove a non-theorem, something that is false.

Discussion

We have surveyed the analytic documents that may arise during software development. There are at least four kinds of analytic document parts: concept formation, description (prescription and design specification) validation, property verification and correctness verification. Some analytic work is "inspiration-guided", such as concept formation seems to be. Other analytic work is guided by human interaction, such as validation is. And yet other analytic work is formalisable, such as property and correctness verification can be.

To give a proper, comprehensive presentation of these three kinds of analytic work is, however, not a goal of these volumes. Instead we refer to specialised texts and monographs on software verification.

1.4 Formal Techniques and Formal Tools

Reading of this section can be skipped till the reader has read Chaps. 2–9 of the present volume. The section may to some lay readers appear a bit esoteric.

The aim of this early section is to make the reader aware of the fact that the languages in which one expresses domain descriptions and requirements prescriptions are not programming languages, but are specification languages. These specification languages need allow the expression of abstractions, so as to make easy the expression of essential properties, while allowing freedom of software design implementations.

1.4.1 On Formal Techniques and Languages

Characterisation. By a *formal technique* we mean both of the following: a technique that has a mathematical foundation, and thus can be explained mathematically, and a technique by which its user expresses descriptions, prescriptions and (design) specifications formally and is able to reason formally about what is expressed.   ∎

Thus a formal technique implies: Formal specification using subsidiary techniques and the possibility of formal verifications, with their subsidiary techniques. Therefore a formal technique requires a formal specification language.

Characterisation. By a *formal specification language* we mean all of the following: a language which has: a formal, mathematical syntax; a formal, mathematical semantics; and a formal, mathematical logic proof system.   ∎

In Chap. 9 of this volume we explain what is meant by a proof system. In Vol. 2, Part IV we will explain what is meant by formal syntax and formal semantics.

Normally, in conventional software engineering, only the last step of development uses an almost[9] formal language, namely the coding (i.e., the computer programming) language. We shall advocate the use of formal languages from the very beginning, for all phases, stages and steps of development. In conventional software engineering many different kinds of informal description, prescription and (design) specification languages are deployed, some with one form of diagrammatic constructs, others with other constructs, but all without a proper syntax, let alone any discernible semantics.

1.4.2 Formal Techniques in SE Textbooks

The aims and objectives of these volumes hinge crucially on the ideas of formal techniques and formal tools. The purpose of this section is to motivate this central role of formality. Most, if not all, existing textbooks on software engineering shy away from propagating these ideas of formalism. If other textbooks on software engineering bring any material on what they call 'formal methods', it is usually in the form of a separate chapter appearing somewhere in the book. In these volumes formal techniques permeate all technical chapters. Formal techniques are deployable, and are hence to be taught in connection with all technical aspects of software engineering.

1.4.3 Some Programming Languages

A language, when seen as the means for expressing an engineering objective, can be considered a tool. As such, formal languages represent one class of software engineering tools. As for all crafts, many tools are needed, different size hammers, different size saws, different size screwdrivers, different size planners, etc., are needed for carpentry. That is, the artifact to be constructed, that is, its "nature" or its attributes (properties), determines exactly which of many different tools are to be deployed.

We have very many different kinds of programming languages, "past" and "current"[10]: functional programming languages such as LISP [370], • Standard ML [261,389], • Miranda [502], and • Haskell [498], to mention a few; logic programming languages, including • Prolog [295,351], and CLPR

---

[9]Usually most programming languages still do not possess a proof system.

[10]'Current' programming languages are marked with a bullet: •.

[312]; the imperative[11] programming languages of Fortran [14], Cobol [12], Algol 60 [24], Algol 68 [510], Pascal [522],• C [321]; object-oriented programming languages, such as Simula 67 [54], • C++ [489], Modula 2 and Modula 3 [262,401,525], • Eiffel [377,378], Oberon [434,526,528–530], and • Java [10,20,243,348,470,511]; and finally the parallel programming languages of PL/I [13,37], CHILL [145], Ada [128], and • occam [301,364,449].

1.4.4 Some Formal Specification Languages

We can also expect to have many different kinds of formal specification languages that are model-oriented or property-oriented.

On Model-Oriented Specification Languages

Some specification languages are model-oriented:[12] • VDM-SL [120, 121, 226, 317], • Z [281, 476, 477, 533], and • B [3].

Characterisation. By a *model-oriented specification language* we mean one which expresses whatever it specifies in terms of mathematical constructions (i.e., models) such as sets, Cartesians, lists, functions, etc.   ∎

On Property-Oriented Specification Languages

Other specification languages are property-oriented (algebraic semantics) specification languages:[13] OBJ3 [233], • CafeOBJ [190, 232], and • CASL [49,397,399].

Characterisation. By a *property-oriented specification language* we understand one which expresses whatever it specifies in terms of logical properties of what is specified.   ∎

---

[11] An imperative programming language is one which primarily focuses on assignable variables, hence assignments, and hence has statements, and usually therefore statement labels and GOTOs. Statements, in a sense, prescribe: *Do this, then do that* — "imperially".

[12] A model-oriented specification language allows for the expression of models in terms of mathematical entities such as sets, Cartesians, lists, maps, functions, etc. Chaps. 12–16 (of the present volume) will make the first presentations of model-orientedness.

[13] A property-oriented specification language allows for the expression of models in terms of logically expressed algebras. Chapters 9 and 12 will make the first presentations of algebras and property-orientedness.

On Property-Oriented + Model-Oriented Specification Languages

Other specification languages are "mixed" property- and model-oriented specification languages: • RSL [236, 238, 239].

In these volumes we mostly use the RAISE Specification Language, RSL. But, really, nothing prevents a lecturer from using, for example, VDM-SL or Z instead.

More on Programming Languages

One selects a programming language according to what one wishes to express, that is, the values one wishes to speak of. Different programming language categories, as listed above, favour different value spaces.

In *functional programming* we handle functions, their definition, application and composition, because functions (including ordinary operator/operand expressions) are thought to best capture the problem at hand.

In *logic programming* we express propositions and predicates, i.e., handle logical values, because it is thought that one can best express certain computing problems by characterising their properties.

In *imperative programming* we establish, initialise, update and read states, i.e., assignable variables, because states and state changes are thought to best capture the problem to be solved.

In *object-oriented programming* we establish, initialise, update and read special clusters of state components called objects, because dividing the problem up into a set of such objects and solving the problem by expressing the interaction between objects is thought to best capture the problem at hand.

In *parallel programming* we establish, initialise and compose processes, and select among processes in various deterministic or nondeterministic ways. In addition we express cooperation among processes through their synchronisation and communication because it is thought that one can best express certain computing problems by their decomposition into cooperating and concurrently operating processes.

Specification Languages Resumed

The situation is not that simple with formal specification languages. Indeed, there is the distinction between model-oriented and property-oriented formal specification languages mentioned above. So one can choose one from either category depending on what it is one wishes to express, and how.

Purists might choose either the Z (since 1980) or the B (since around 1990) specification language paradigm. Both are based on simple set theoretic notions, are utterly elegant and can traditionally handle what one would consider simple state-oriented sequential problems. Z has been extended in various ways: to express concurrency, or to express objects beyond its own basic, elegant modularity concept.

VDM [120,121,226] represents possibly the first full-fledged formal specification language concept (since early 1970s), and is still flourishing in the form of the ISO standardised VDM-SL. The RAISE [236,238] Specification Language (RSL) was conceived, in the mid-1980s, as a successor to the VDM specification language, then colloquially known as Meta-IV.

RSL, which we primarily use in these volumes, features both property-oriented and model-oriented means of expression, has a somewhat sophisticated object-oriented means of compositionality, and borrows from CSP [288, 289, 448, 456] to offer a means of expressing concurrency. Extensions to RSL have also been proposed, for example with timing [535], and with Duration Calculus, that is, temporal logic ideas [274].

1.4.5 Insufficiency of Current, Formal Languages

The story as told above may give you the impression that the formal (programming as well as specification) languages offer sufficient expressibility to handle all situations, but this is not so. Few, if any, professionally supported programming languages offer means for expressing temporal notions such as absolute times, relative time (intervals), delays, etc. The same is true for specification languages. Accordingly we see a bevy of very fascinating programming languages focusing on expressing synchrony: Esterel [47,48], Lustre [256] and Signal [248]. We also see specification languages involving temporal notions: Timed Automata [9], TLA (Temporal Logic of Actions) [331] and Duration Calculus [537,538]. We also find some which provide for the expression of state transitions: Petri Nets [313,421,435–437], MSCs (Message Sequence Charts) [302–304] and LSCs (Live Sequence Charts) [171,270,325], and Statecharts [265,266,268,269,271]. We shall have more to say about Petri nets, sequence charts, statecharts and the duration calculi [537,538] in Vol. 2's Chaps. 12–15.

What does this plethora of programming and specification languages signify? First, it tells us that we are still in the early days of computing science, and hence software engineering. Proposals for new and better languages, or for altogether different language paradigms, are being put forward continually. It also probably tells us that we should not seek "universal" languages, that could handle all the "things" that one wishes to express. We shall probably have to settle for using combinations of different languages when specifying and when implementing problems.

More generally, it tells us that we shall, in these volumes, be content with the formal specification languages that are available today, while recognising their (and our) shortcomings. That is, there are situations in these volumes where we would like to show a formal specification of a problem, but where that would entail a longer introduction of a "new" notation, or where we simply have to give up because no pleasing or adequate or even known such language can be found!

1.4.6 Other Formal Tools

The most well-known formal tool for software development is a compiler: It accepts programs in a formal language, the source programming language, it checks that input programs satisfy a wide variety of static properties, and if so, it generates an output program in a target coding language, such that the meaning of the input program is preserved in the meaning of the output program. To do this properly a compiler embodies a number of instantiations of *theoretical artifacts*. These include a *finite state machine* which processes (ASCII) character strings into either keyword or identifier tokens, and other symbols into appropriate delimiter or operator tokens; a *push-down stack machine* which processes strings of tokens and creates, while checking, suitable internal representations of the input program (dictionaries, a parse tree, etc.); a *rewrite system* that transforms these internal representations into other, sometimes claimed optimised representations; and another *rewrite system* that finally transforms possibly resulting internal representations into output code.

Other formal tools are possible and exist: type checkers for abstract specifications; general data or control flow analysers, proof checkers, proof assistants; model checkers, theorem provers, and program interpreters. These, together with compilers, are all examples of what we in general call *abstract interpreters*, or *partial evaluators*. The current understanding of the role and possibilities of *abstract interpretation* is far from complete [163, 164, 215, 231, 320].

1.4.7 Why Formal Techniques and Formal Tools?

Some Rationale

Engineering, in its classical forms, civil, mechanical, electrical, all deploy calculations in one form or another. They do so in order to determine structural properties and design parameters, for example, for reinforced concrete or steel constructions, aircraft wing design, electrical transformer design, and so on. When we drive over a bridge, fly in an aircraft, or use some electrical appliance, we do so with some confidence that the classical design engineers have been properly trained in how to, and, when required, can, and indeed do, perform such calculations.

When we use an ordinary text processing system, yes, even when we send otherwise "innocent" (read: unimportant) e-mails, then we do not bother much about the "error-freeness" of that software. But when we fly an aircraft, or live next to a nuclear power plant, or receive our monthly paycheck (calculated from a myriad of interdependent tax regulations), or follow instructions from a medical doctor, and when we are told that any of these, the aircraft, the power plant, the paycheck processing and the medical advice, are monitored and partly or fully controlled by a computer, we may wonder about the correctness of the relevant software! But are the software engineers comparatively well trained in the many calculi that do indeed exist today for securing trust in the software, and, if so, are they actually deploying such calculi? The answer is, wrt. current practice, sadly, no! These volumes will teach you some, but certainly far from enough, such calculi, i.e., formal techniques.

The answer to the rhetorical question of this section, *Why formal techniques and formal tools?* is therefore: *Because we need the highest possible degree of trust, given today's knowledge, in our software!* Since it can be done, namely, *ensuring highest possible degree of trust*, it must be done. Not ensuring so would be tantamount to cheating the customer — also known as criminal neglect!

Anecdotal cum Analogical Evidence

Until the mid-1700s most ships' captains (and their ships' mates) did not know how to reckon the longitude[14]. The chronometer was first fully available and known by the last quarter of the 1700s. Samuel Pepys[15] commented on the pathetic state of navigation:

> It is most plain, from the confusion all these people are in, how to make good their reckonings, even each man's with itself, and the nonsensical arguments they would make use of to do it, and the disorder they are in about it, that it is by God's Almighty Providence and great chance, and the wideness of the sea, that there are not a great many more misfortunes, and ill chances in navigation than there are.

We bring that story here for analogical purposes.

We claim that developing software without using formal techniques is like sailing the high seas without knowing how to compute the current longitude. We claim that nobody can become a ship's mate, much less a captain, if they do not know how to compute the longitude.

It is as simple as that, but the problem itself is not simple. It was, perhaps, more obvious, that the chronometer had indeed solved the longitude problem. To some it is still not obvious that formal specification and related techniques (verification, etc.) have brought us a long way towards having solved the software development problem.

1.5 Method and Methodology

We refer to Vol. 3's Chap. 3 for a more thorough treatment of the concepts of method, methodology, principles, techniques and tools. Suffice it here to give a brief account of these terms.

---

[14]Those "funny" lines (on a map of the world, or, as here, more appropriately, of the seas) which stretch between the arctic poles.

[15]From a trip as a high official of the British Royal Navy, 1683, from England to Tangier.

1.5.1 Method

Characterisation. By a *method* we understand a set of *principles* for *selecting* and *applying* a number of *analysis* and *synthesis* (*construction*) *techniques* and *tools* in order *efficiently* to *construct* an *efficient* artifact, here software (i.e., a computing system).   ∎

The above will be our guiding characterisation of the concept method. It will flavour these volumes. We will endeavour to enunciate such principles, techniques and tools that will guide the software engineer in where to start, how to proceed and where to end.

In the above characterisation we have also *emphasized* the things about or to which the principles, techniques and tools are concerned or apply, *selecting, applying, analysis, synthesis (construction)* and *efficiency*. Humans select the principles, techniques and tools. Hence choices of selection form a crucial aspect of a method. We, humans, or machines, i.e., *tools, apply techniques.* Hence *modes* of *application* form a crucial aspect of a method, likewise for *analysis* and *construction*. *Efficiency*, as a concept, applies both to the development process and to the developed artifact. We have added *efficiency* as an attribute of the concept of a method.

1.5.2 Methodology

Characterisation. By *methodology* we understand the study of, and the knowledge about one or more *methods*.   ∎

These volumes also cover *methodology:* We will contrast several *methods*, including several alternative *principles, techniques* and *tools*. No one *method* suffices for all software. There are a number of *principles, techniques* and *tools* that can help us. But for any one *method* there are still *principles, techniques* and *tools* to be identified, studied and tried out.

1.5.3 Discussion

The *principles* are to be interpreted by humans. The *selection* and *analysis* is to be mostly performed by humans. Some *techniques* and some *tools* can be used by machine, i.e., are formalised. But far from all. Hence it is a misnomer to refer to a concept of *formal methods*. It seems appropriate to refer to some techniques and some tools as being *formal*. So we conclude: Methods cannot be formal.

1.5.4 Meta-methodology

In this book, that is, in these volumes we shall highlight certain pieces of texts. These highlighted texts are concerned with

- *characterisations,*
- *definitions,*
- *principles,*
- *techniques,*
- *tools,* and
- *examples*

as follows. In the text the following kinds of highlighted texts will stand out. Please take appropriate note of these texts.

Characterisation. Characterisations are descriptive texts. They are not precise definitions.   ∎

Definition. Definitions are descriptive texts at the level of mathematical precision. We present definitions either as shown in the present definition, as numbered and highlighted paragraphs, or as mathematical texts or as RSL specifications.   ∎

Principles. Principles are here seen as comprehensive and fundamental laws, doctrines, assumptions or rules (codes) of conduct underlying the pursuit of software engineering. It is our principle to enunciate characterisations, definitions, principles, techniques and tools, and to bring many examples.   ∎

Techniques. Techniques are here concerned with the manner in which technical details are treated by the software engineer. The techniques of presenting highlighted characterisations, definitions, principles, techniques and tools are basically those used for descriptive texts.   ∎

Tools. Tools are here seen as intellectual (or even software) devices that aid in accomplishing a task, that is, are used in performing an operation or necessary in the practice of the profession of software engineering. The tool for presenting highlighted characterisations, definitions, principles, techniques and tools is that of English.   ∎

Example 1.6 The previous five **boldface** highlighted paragraphs together exemplified the ideas enunciated in this section. They all ended with the "∎" symbol; and so does does this example.   ∎

1.6 The Very Bases of Software

> This section previews the core issues of software engineering. The treatment here is, perhaps, a bit taxing, that is, it requires careful reading. You may wish to skip this section and return to read it after having studied, for example, the first half of this volume!

Before introducing types, functions and relations, algebras, and logic, we must, however, first cover some even more basic material: What is meant by didactics and paradigms, and what is meant by semiotics, that is, pragmatics, semantics and syntax. In other words, this section collects and presents a number of basic concepts, and as such it is a prelude to Part II of this volume.

1.6.1 Didactics and Paradigms

> Life is rather a subject of wonder, than of didactics
>
> *Ralph Waldo Emerson 1803–1882*

We are guided by *paradigms*, see Sect. 1.6.3. Good paradigms, we claim, reflect reasonably clarified *didactics*.

The Shorter Oxford English Dictionary [350] (*OED*) defines: didactics *having the character or manner of a teacher; characterised by giving instructions; instructive; preceptive;* and *systematic instruction.*

We shall, in these volumes, take the word *didactics* to mean *the basic ideas of practical or theoretical nature upon which the practice of a field of human activity is (best, or reasonably) pursued.* We claim that our rendition is commensurate with the OED explanation. There are other didactic and practical bases for software engineering than just types, functions, algebras and mathematical logic such as mentioned earlier. Although we shall in later volumes devote separate chapters to covering these other didactic bases in detail, we shall, in order that we may be able to refer to the very essence of these bases (before we reach those chapters), cover the concepts briefly. They are semiotics and descriptions.

1.6.2 Pragmatics, Semantics and Syntax

Semiotics can, for our purposes, fruitfully be understood as the study and knowledge of pragmatics, semantics and syntax of language. That is, respectively the use, meaning, and analysis and synthesis of language texts.

Pragmatics

Characterisation. By the *pragmatics* of a language we mean its use in social context: Why a particular expression used? What "ultimate" motive lies (seems to lie) behind an utterance, an expression.   ∎

We have some ulterior motives when specifying: What is it? What are they? Pragmatics, characterised somewhat convolutely, is that *which cannot be formalised!* Pragmatics is the "real thing". Syntax and semantics enable us to convey and, it is hoped, to understand, those "real things"!

Software specification languages and, more generally, computing systems specification languages serve to describe domains, prescribe requirements and specify software designs. Thus their pragmatics, as well as the pragmatics of the individual domain, requirements and software design specifications, are that they are able to cover that spectrum, and that they, individually, allow for certain kinds of for example trustworthy and manageable development. Thus the design of any specification language, such as B, Cafe-OBJ, CASL, RSL, VDM-SL and Z, has taken into account which target applications that language best caters to. The main specification language of these volumes is RSL. As we shall see, RSL covers a rather broad spectrum. Two, amongst several more, important aspects of RSL are that it allows modular, reusable development and provably correct development.

Semantics

Characterisation. *Semantic* is about the meaning of what we express syntactically. ∎

We shall later sharpen this characterisation, but first we express some deeply felt dogmas. Semantics, in some sense, *is what it is all about abstractly!* Pragmatics, in that sense, is what it is about concretely, in a specific social, human context. If we cannot express the essence abstractly, then we have not understood it. Then we can only have little trust in any software derived from such an incomplete understanding. Software is, by nature, abstract and is necessarily conceptual. Therefore it is more important to capture, mentally, the semantics before we search for a way to express it syntactically. Our best abstractions are those of mathematics. Mathematics is the science of abstraction.

So what is the semantics of RSL specifications? To appreciate and understand the choice made for the semantics of RSL, let us consider some very basic RSL specifications. Usually a specification names "things".

Example 1.7 *Semantics of Class Specifications:* Our example is just that: It does not model anything "practical", but illustrates, at a minimum cost of symbols, what we wish to say about semantics.

```
[0]  scheme EXAMPLE =
[1]    class
[2]      type
[3]        A = Int, B = Nat
[4]      value
[5]        f: A → B
[6]      axiom
[7]        [ bijection ]
[8]          ∀ a:A,a′:A • a≠a′ ⇒ f(a)≠f(a′)
[9]    end
```

Five things are named: (i) A class expression (**EXAMPLE**, lines [1–8]), (ii–iii) two types of values, A and B (lines [2–3]), (iv) a function, a value, f (lines [4–5]) that maps As (integers) into Bs (natural numbers), and (v) an **axiom** bijection (lines [6–7]) that expresses that f for distinct arguments yields distinct results.

Of the five things named only four designate specific mathematical entities. The **axiom** name, always enclosed in brackets, [...], may be put before the **axiom** keyword, and is there for a pragmatic reason so that we can refer to that **axiom**. Thus **axiom** names are optional and can be omitted.

Now what semantics does RSL ascribe to the identifiers **EXAMPLE**, A, B and f? We start "inside out": A and B stand for the sets of integer, respectively sets of natural number values, and f for any function that satisfies the axiom. The class definition, **EXAMPLE**, etc. (lines [0–8]) now stands for a set of models, where a model provides a mapping from identifiers, such as A, B and f, into their meanings. All members of the set of models have A and B stand for the same universes of integers, respectively natural numbers, but each member of the set has f map into a distinct function from A into B, such that this set of models exhibits all such functions f in fact infinitely many! Hence **EXAMPLE** stands for an infinite set of models.

We summarise: Each **type** and **value** thing named by the specifier, e.g., you, in a specification, has a meaning. And that meaning may deterministically be a value, or a specific set of (typed) values, as for type names, or nondeterministically be one or another from amongst a possible infinity of values, as for the illustrated function name. So, functions can be values. The set of all values contains the set of all functions. Combining two or more such meaningful identifiers as here in a class expression, or just as a juxtaposition of definitions without the **class** keyword and class name results in a named, respectively unnamed set of (one or more) models. Axioms may be so constraining that there may be no model that satisfies the axioms. Or there may be a finite number of models, including just one!

Let us "display" the set of models for the class expression (lines [0–8]):

{

    [A $\mapsto$ { ...,−2,−1,0,1,2,... },
    B $\mapsto$ { 0,1,2,... },
    f $\mapsto$ λa • **if** a<0 **then**
          3∗(2∗(−a)) **else if** a=0 **then** 0 **else** 3∗(1+2∗a) **end end**,
    ...],
    [A $\mapsto$ { ...,−2,−1,0,1,2,... },
    B $\mapsto$ { 0,1,2,... },
    f $\mapsto$ λa • **if** a<0 **then**
          5∗(2∗(−a)) **else if** a=0 **then** 0 **else** 5∗(1+2∗a) **end end**,
    ...],
    [A $\mapsto$ { ...,−2,−1,0,1,2,... },
    B $\mapsto$ { 0,1,2,... },
    f $\mapsto$ λa • **if** a<0 **then**

$7*(2*(-a))$ **else if** a=0 **then** 0 **else** $7*(1+2*a)$ **end end**,

...], ...

}

By $\lambda a{:}A{\bullet}E(a)$ we mean the function which when applied to an argument x in A yields a value as prescribed by the function body $E(x)$, i.e., where all free a in $E(a)$ have been replaced by x. By the ellipses, that is, ..., we intend to show that the model may contain parts which map other identifiers into other mathematical values.   ∎

In the rest of these volumes we shall return, again and again, to semantic models of the above kind.

Syntax

Characterisation. *Syntax* is about how we can, in our case, write down specifications: rules of form, basic forms and their proper compositions. These rules for formal languages are to be of such a nature that the forms, that is, the language expressions, can be analysed, and such that, from the analysis, one can 'construct' (construe) the meaning.   ∎

Syntax is, of course, important, but its importance is secondary to semantics! We should strive for semantic clarity, then syntactic elegance. If the idea to be expressed is "muddled", then no matter how beautiful the syntactic forms may be, humans will not easily understand them!

You have already seen some RSL syntax, for example, the scheme definition of Example 1.7. Since RSL is aimed at a rather wide spectrum of applications and at a full spectrum of development, from descriptions of actual domains, via requirements prescriptions to abstract software designs, the RSL syntax is rather "rich". That is: has many entities. We shall try unravel these, gently, as we go along in these volumes, and only introduce the syntax that we need up to any given point in these volumes.

The syntax of class expressions, as exemplified above, thus appears to be covered by:

```
<class_expression> ::=
    class
        type
            <type_definitions>
        value
            <value_definitions>
        axiom
            <axiom_definitions>
    end
```

But since there are many more aspects to class expressions than illustrated so far, the syntax is more complicated than hinted at above.

When explaining a specification language construct we ought systematically cover its general forms and its static semantics, that is: which constraints limit the use of for example identifiers, operator symbols, keywords, delimiters, etc. and its meaning. We will, however, only give cursory explanations, leaving details to the RSL Reference Handbook [236].

1.6.3 On Specification and Programming Paradigms

We are guided by *paradigms:*

> (1) **Paradigm:** thing copied.
> (2) **Model:** pattern, standard, rule, original, mirror;
> (3) **Prototype:** archetype, antetype;
> (4) **Precedent:** lead, representative, epitome
>
> *Roget's International Thesaurus* [445].

Using paradigms we construct artifacts:

> The universe ... was made exactly conformable
> to its Paradigme, or universal Examplar.
>
> *(The Shorter Oxford English Dictionary* [350].)

These volumes are structured according to a set of specification paradigms. And these again rest on what we believe are the didactic bases of the practice and theory of software engineering.

So which are the "most basic" paradigms? Generally, we can say this: Abstraction is a specification paradigm; so is "favouring, encouraging" nondeterminism in specification. Respective programming styles — functional (also referred to as applicative), logic, imperative, and parallel programming — represent a programming paradigm. Favouring a specification style that allows formally verifiable transformations of (more) abstract specifications into (more) concrete ones, and these finally into 'executable programs — is a software development paradigm. There are then paradigms within paradigms: Practicing the functional specification (or the functional programming) paradigm may then be according to, for example, the *continuation* [59, 63, 315, 392, 404, 440, 471, 487, 513, 514] programming paradigm. Likewise practicing the parallel specification (or the parallel programming) paradigm may then be according to, for example, the CSP, i.e., the *communicating sequential processes,* [287, 288, 448] paradigm, and so on.

1.6.4 Descriptions, Prescriptions and Specifications

We shall, in these volumes, try strictly to use the following terms consistently and according to the following overlapping classification:

- Description: As a general term encompassing the below, and as a special term in connection with textual characterisations of domains.
- Prescription: As a specific term used primarily in connection with requirements.
- Specification: As a general term encompassing the above, and as a special term in connection with textual characterisations of software designs.
- Definition: As a general term encompassing formalisations, also of the above; and as a special term in connection with certain textual characterisations, namely and specifically, those parts that constitute proper definitions as distinguished from designations and refutable assertions.

Software Specifications, Requirements Prescriptions and Domain Descriptions

To direct a computer to perform any computation it must be so instructed. These instructions form a program. A program is a finite specification of possibly infinite sets of possibly infinite computations. So, descriptions, prescriptions and specifications form the most essential object of our endeavour: to develop software. We first explain the idea of specification, then the idea of prescription, and finally we explain the idea of description.

We *specify* computations; thus: to *design software* we *specify* how the computations should proceed: *the how* is an end goal. We *prescribe the what*, that is, the *requirements* that we expect the subsequently designed software to fulfill. And, before all that we *describe* the actual world in which these computations are to occur, that is, the *(application) domain*.

1.6.5 Metalanguages

We use language, say $\mathcal{M}$, to describe or "to talk about" other languages, say $\mathcal{L}$. One cannot use $\mathcal{L}$ to describe $\mathcal{L}$. It leads to nonsense. $\mathcal{M}$ is said to be a metalanguage for $\mathcal{L}$. To describe $\mathcal{M}$ we need another metalanguage, or, as we could call it, a meta-metalanguage $\mathcal{M}'$.

The language, say $\mathcal{M}$, in which we explain mathematics, i.e., the notation of mathematics and its meaning, $\mathcal{N}$, is thus necessarily different from $\mathcal{N}$. We do not describe $\mathcal{M}$.

1.6.6 Summary

We have briefly introduced the notions of didactics and paradigms; and of semiotics: pragmatics, semantics and syntax. We have also introduced documents: informative, descriptive and analytic, as well as (domain) descriptions, (requirements) prescriptions and (software) specifications. We have finally introduced the notions of metalanguages, and object languages.

We shall later cover these in quite some detail. Suffice it, for now, to say that the reader now knows that these are basic concepts whose reasonable understanding is indispensable when pursuing professional software engineering.

1.7 Aims and Objectives

By the 'aims of these volumes' we mean the topics that we will be covering or dealing with. By the 'objectives of these volumes' we understand that which we wish to achieve through covering certain material.

1.7.1 Aims

The Main Aims

The main aims are to teach you general software engineering principles, techniques and tools. That is (in Vol. 3): those of domain engineering, of requirements engineering and of software design. Among these we additionally single out and teach principles, techniques and tools of abstraction and modelling in (Vols. 1–2); of description (in Vol. 3); and of documentation (in Vol. 3).

Some Other Aims

Additional aims are those of providing appropriate mathematical foundations, (Vol. 1, Part II), of ensuring appropriate understanding of semiotics issues: pragmatics, semantics and syntax (Vol. 2, Part IV), and of doing all of this within an appropriate framework of models and definitions (Vol. 3, Chaps. 4 and 6).

An aim, altogether "orthogonal" to the other aims above, is to illustrate development components of software for the support of large, distributed and concurrent infrastructure subsystems and systems.

1.7.2 Objectives

The Main Objectives

The main objectives are to help ensure that you become a professional engineer within software, to thus help ensure that the software (cum computing) systems, in whose development you are involved, become trustworthy systems of highest attainable quality, and through our emphasis on exemplifying the development of software (cum computing) systems for infrastructure components to help ensure that you, with colleagues, believably can develop highly sophisticated systems.

Some Other Objectives

Other objectives are to put the broader concerns of software engineering, such as treated in these volumes, in the context of other, indispensable and more specialised computing science disciplines such as artificial intelligence and knowledge-based systems, compiler systems, concurrent, safety-critical and real-time application systems, database management systems, distributed systems, operating systems, secure, en- and decryptable systems, and so on. Another objective is to show that formal techniques are applicable, in all phases, stages and steps of development, and to all kinds of computing systems.

1.7.3 Discussion

The usual *aims and objectives* section has been dispensed with, but with a change: usually the two concepts, aims and objectives, are "lumped" into one treatment. Here we have separated them, properly.

There is a conceptual triangle: there is the author of these volumes; there is you, the reader, who studies its contents; and there is the most important thing: the subject itself: software engineering. Aims are about which software engineering topics the author wishes to cover, i.e., to teach you. Objectives are about which effects, with respect to the discipline of software engineering, the learning of these topics is to have on you. In other words aims are about 'what'; objectives are about 'why'.

1.8 Bibliographical Notes

This book, all three volumes of it, is different from most other textbooks on software engineering. We shall single out the following major ways in which this book differs from the following textbooks: [423, 430, 475, 512]. First they really are short on real development examples: there are hardly any real examples of specification and design. The present book, all three volumes of it, hinges crucially on real examples of specification and design. Second, when they bring a chapter on formal methods, do so in a separate chapter "tucked away" somewhere, ad hoc. The present book emphasises the use of formal techniques in all phases, stages and steps of development. Third, they, also including [240], do not bring any material on domain engineering. It is perhaps the last thing, domain engineering, in which this book is really new.

One very nice book, [240], does show a lot of formal techniques. Ours show almost all, if not all, of these techniques, and many, many more, and puts these techniques in the context of an overall methodology. The book by Watts Humphrey [298] is a wise book on management. "Hard to beat". The book by Hans van Vliet [512] is, in our mind, the best overall of the above-referenced books when it comes to these practical and management issues.

1.9 Exercises

Exercise 1.1. *The Sciences:* Can you define what we, in these volumes, mean by computer science, and what we mean by computing science.

Exercise 1.2. *Project Management Issues:* Can you list some of the more practical, i.e., project management issues of software engineering.

Exercise 1.3. *The Triptych of Software Engineering:* Please list the three main phases of software engineering as put forward in this volume.

Exercise 1.4. *Documentation:* Can you list the three major classes of documents (as put forward in this volume) and, within each of the classes, can you list some of the major document parts.

Exercise 1.5. *Formal Techniques and Formal Languages:* Please define what these volumes mean by formal techniques and by formal languages.

Exercise 1.6. *Method and Methodology:* What does these volumes mean by (an efficient) method, and by methodology?

Exercise 1.7. *The Very Bases:* What does this chapter hint at as the meaning of a specification?

Part II

DISCRETE MATHEMATICS

We cover basic notions of mathematics in a somewhat circuitous way: in-between treatments of numbers (Chap. 2), sets (Chap. 3), Cartesians (Chap. 4), functions (Chap. 6), λ-calculus (Chap. 7), algebras (Chap. 8) and logics (Chap. 9), we put a treatment of types (Chap. 5). There is a reason for this. A reasonable sequence of topics would be numbers, sets, Cartesians, functions, λ-calculus, algebras and logics. Each of these mathematical domains entails sets of values. We group characterisable subsets of these into types, where types, naïvely, are sets of values: types whose values are sets, and types whose values are Cartesians. The members of sets and the elements of Cartesian values are just postulated to be of some type.

From types (of values) we can then construct new types: types whose values are functions, typically from values of Cartesian types to values, etc. And then we can present algebras as typed sets of entities and operations over these. Finally, we can introduce mathematical logic — allowing quantifications to range over specified types. Types thus permeate our treatment of the mathematical universes of numbers, sets, Cartesians, functions, λ-calculus, algebras and logics. Some textbooks on discrete mathematics are [260, 420, 425, 481].

2

Numbers

- The **prerequisite** for studying this chapter is that you possess at least a simple level of mathematical maturity.
- The **aim** is to introduce the simple concepts of numbers.
- The **objective** is to help ensure that the reader, in the future, handles the various types of numbers: natural numbers, integers, rationals, reals, transcendentals, with ease, naturally and correctly.
- The **treatment** is informal, but systematic.

> "God created the integers, all else is the work of man," so said Kronecker, or so it is believed he said.

2.1 Introduction

Our interest, in these volumes, and hence in modelling some universe of discourse phenomenon by means of numbers, is not in the deeper number-theoretic properties,[1] but in the simpler, rather more shallow properties: Numbers are strictly ordered and reals are densely packed.

There are many kinds of numbers, to wit: natural numbers: $0, 1, 2, \ldots$; integers: $\ldots, -2, -1, 0, 1, 2, \ldots$; rationals: consisting of both integer (viz., i, j) and fractions, $\frac{i}{j}$, for all integers i, j where $j \neq 0$; irrational numbers; real, imaginary and complex numbers; and transcendental numbers. Although we shall have occasion, even for a very large variety of typically man-made "systems", to use only natural numbers, integers and reals, it may be a good idea to become familiar with all these other number concepts as well. The aim is to make sure that you are well aware of those means we have chosen to make available for our modelling endeavours, and those we have not!

---

[1]Properties such as prime numbers, factorisation, irrationality or transcendental numbers: Euler's Theorem and Fermat's Little Theorem, Euler's phi-function, de Polignac's formula, Mersenne primes, Möbius's function, Euclid's algorithm, Pell's equation, and so on [263].

2.2 Numerals and Numbers

A *numeral* is a *name* for a *number*. No-one (in a state of sober mind) has ever seen a number. Numbers are abstract mathematical quantities. They are characterised by their properties. For every number that exists in the universe of mathematics, there is exactly one copy: the original. For many numbers there are simple names, and often there is more than one distinct simple name for the same number:

> *7, seven, sieben, sept, syv, ...*

For most numbers there are simple or composite names:

> *14/2, 6+1, 2∗4−1, ... ; vii, III, IIIIII, ...*

By a *digit* we understand a simple numeral for a special number: If in radix (i.e., base) ten, then the digits are the *decimal digits,* usually written 0, 1, 2, 3, 4, 5, 6, 7, 8 and 9. If in radix two, then the "digits"[2] are the binary digits, usually written O and I. If in radix one (!), the "digit" is a marker, or its absence: ı. If we can speak of Roman "digits" they would be: I, V, X, L, C, D and M.

2.3 Subsets of Numbers

We shall briefly survey such facts about numbers that will turn out useful in specifications, natural numbers and integers, rational numbers and reals. We also take a brief look at other kinds of numbers: irrational and transcendental numbers.

2.3.1 Natural Numbers: Nat

By the natural numbers we understand those that are basically characterised by Peano's Axioms (Example 9.21 on page 190). By **Nat** we designate the set of all natural numbers. We write the natural numbers based on the following BNF[3] grammar:

```
<NatNum> ::= <DecDig> | <DecDig> <NatNum>
<DecDig> ::= 0 | 1 | 2 | 3 | 4 | 5 | 6 | 7 | 8 | 9
```

<DecDig> stand for decimal digits.

---

[2]We really should reserve the name digit only for the base numerals in base-10 systems, since 'digitus', in Latin, stands for finger.

[3]By BNF we mean 'Backus Normal (or Naur) Form'. We assume that the reader is familiar with the notion of such BNF grammars, including is familiar with the notion of context-free grammars.

Example 2.1 *Semantics of Decimal Digit Natural Numerals:* Let us perform the following thought experiment: Let **0, 1, 2, 3, 4, 5, 6, 7, 8, 9** "somehow be" the natural numbers corresponding, left to right, to the decimal digits 0, 1, 2, 3, 4, 5, 6, 7, 8, 9; then

> M: <NatNum> → Num
> M(d,n) ≡ 10∗M(d) + M(n)
> M(d) ≡ **case** d **of** 0→**0**,1→**1**,...,9→**9 end**

informally explicates the meaning of a natural number numeral.   ∎

Notice that M is a morphism (see Sect. 8.4.4 for the concept of morphism).

We explain the notation used in the above example. We owe you an explanation as to how M is able to distinguish between the natural number, <NatNum> which is just a decimal digit, <DecDig> and one which is the composite form, <DecDig><NatNum>. Later, when we have introduced the appropriate "machinery", we can also present the syntax and type definition forms by means of which RSL, and other specification languages, solve the distinguishability problem.

But we can explain the rest: If the number is of the composite form then M(d,n) is *the sum of ten times the value of the first digit and the value of the rest of the numeral.* If the number is just a digit then there are 10 cases to distinguish. If the digit is the digit 0 then the value is the mathematical number **0**, etc. Had we chosen to write the digits by the character strings zero, one, two, . . . , nine then the case distinction would have been on these character strings, but resulting, to the right of the →'s, in the same boldfaced number designators.

Example 2.2 *Semantics of "Quadruplet" Binary Digit Natural Numerals:* By "quadruplet" binary numerals we mean those strings of one or more special quadruplets of Os and Is, namely: OOOO, OOOI, OOIO, OOII, . . . , IOOO, IOOI. Then we again have the same right-hand sides:

type
> ⟨QuaNum⟩ ::= ⟨QuaNum⟩ ⟨QuaDig⟩ | ⟨QuaDig⟩

value
> M: ⟨NatNum⟩ → Num
> M(d,n) ≡ 10∗M(d) + M(n)
> M(d) ≡ **case** d **of** OOOO→**0**, OOOI→**1**, ..., IOOO→**8**, IOOI→**9 end**

∎

Explanation of Some RSL Constructs

In other words, the "**case** e **of** $p_1 \rightarrow e'_1$, $p_2 \rightarrow e'_2$, . . . ,$p_n \rightarrow e'_n$ **end**" construct has a first argument which is an expression e of any value and of any type, and a second argument which is a sequence of "triples" separated by commas: $p_i \to e'_i$, for i being 1 for the first triple, right after the **of** keyword, 2 for the next, etc. If the value of e can be expressed as the *pattern*, inclusive, as here, of having the value of that pattern, then the value of the whole **case** construct is that of the value of e'_i, else we try the next triple. If no triple yields a comparison that equals, that is, that 'matches', then the value of (the whole **case** construct) expression is **chaos.** We shall have more to say about patterns later.

2.3.2 Integers: Int

Integers derive from natural numbers by including those numbers that are negations of natural numbers. That is, if i is an integer, and $-i = j$ is its negation, then $i + j = 0$.

Properties

Let a, b and c stand for integers. Some important properties of integers are:

[Associativity and Commutativity of + and ∗:]
   a+(b+c) = (a+b)+c, a+b = b+a
   a∗(b∗a) = (a∗b)∗c, a∗b = b∗a
[Distributivity **of** ∗ over +:]
   a∗(b+c) = a∗b + a∗c
[Properties of 0 and 1:]
   0+a = a, 1∗a = a, 0∗a = 0
[Properties of −:]
   (−a)+a = 0, (−a)∗b = −(a∗b), (−a)∗(−b) = a∗b
[Cancellation Laws:]
   a+b = a+c ⇒ b=c, a≠0 → (a∗b=a∗c ⇒ b=c)
[Properties of Order:]
   a>0 ∧ b>0 ⇒ a∗b > 0
   ∀ a:**Int** • a<0 ∨ a=0 ∨ a>0 [Trichotomy]
[Definition of Addition and Multiplication:]
   s:**Int**→**Int**, s(i) ≡ i+1 ≡ i′
   a+0 = a, a+s(b) = s(a+b) = a+b+1
   a∗0 = 0, a∗s(b) = (a∗b)+a
[Integer Division:]
   a / b **as** (q,r) where a = b∗q+r ∧ 0≤r<b

The RSL Integer Algebra

The RSL integers can be indefinitely large, positive or negative. The usual operators are defined, as well as some not so usual operators \ and /.

value

$+,-,/,*,\backslash$: **Int** $\times$ **Int** $\overset{\sim}{\rightarrow}$ **Int**

$<,\leq,=,\neq,\geq,>$: **Int** $\times$ **Int** $\rightarrow$ **Bool**

$-,\uparrow$: **Int** $\rightarrow$ **Int**

abs: Int $\rightarrow$ $\{|$ i:**Int** $\bullet$ i$\geq$0 $|\}$

axiom

$\forall$ n:**Nat** $\bullet$ **abs** $-$n $=$ n $=$ **abs** n

The slash, /, and the backslash, \, operators designate the integer division and remainder functions:

$\forall$ i,j:**Int** $\bullet$ j$\neq$0 $\Rightarrow$ i $=$ (i / j)$*$j $+$ (a \ b)

The $\uparrow$ designates the integer exponentiation function. The second argument must be a natural number. If both arguments are zero then the result is **chaos.**

2.3.3 Real Numbers: Real

Real numbers, besides the integers, are additionally those that can be written (i.e., can be represented) as a pair of possibly infinite sequences of digits separated by, for example, a period. We indicate two extremes, the finitely writable reals:

$$d_n d_{n-1} \ldots d_1 . d_1' d_2' \ldots d_{m-1}' d_m'$$

and the doubly infinitely writable reals:

$$\ldots d_i'' d_{i-1}'' \ldots d_1'' . d_1''' d_2''' \ldots d_{j-1}''' d_j''' \ldots$$

for all combinations of digits $d_k, d_{k'}', d_{k''}'', d_{k'''}'''$ ranging over $0, 1, 2, 3, 4, 5, 6, 7, 8$ and 9, for k, k' finite, and for $-\infty \leq k'', k''' \leq \infty$, whatever that means!

Obviously, in RSL we can only write the finitely representable reals.

Rational Numbers

A rational number is a real which can be expressed as the division of two integers where the denominator is non-zero.:

Rat $=$ $\{|$ i/j $\bullet$ i,j:**Int** $\wedge$ j$\neq$0 $|\}$

Every integer is a rational number.

Operations on Reals

RSL defines the following operations on real numbers:

value
    $+,-,/,*$: **Real** $\times$ **Real** $\overset{\sim}{\to}$ **Real**
    $<,\leq,=,\neq,\geq,>$: **Real** $\times$ **Real** $\to$ **Bool**
    $-$: **Real** $\to$ **Real**
    abs: **Real** $\to$ {| r:**Real** • r$\geq$0 |}
    int: **Real** $\to$ **Int**
    real: **Int** $\to$ **Real**
axiom
    $\forall$ n:**Nat** • **abs** $-$n = n = **abs** n

The **int** and **real** functions convert a real to the integer nearest 0, respectively an integer to a real:

    int 2.71 = 2, **int** $-$2.71 = $-$2, **real** 5 = 5.0, and so on

Thus **int**r is the greatest integer that is smaller than or equal to the absolute value of the real (r), with the sign being that of the real.

2.3.4 Irrational Numbers

The irrational numbers are all those reals which are not rational.

2.3.5 Algebraic Numbers

The algebraic numbers are all those real or imaginary numbers which are roots, r, of polynomial equations of the form:

$$a * x^n + b * x^{n-1} + \cdots + c * x + d = 0$$

where n is any integer and where coefficients $a, b, \ldots, c, d$ are integers. $\sqrt{2}$ is an algebraic number. A root is any number, r, which makes the value of the polynomial expression:

$$a * x^r + b * x^{r-1} + \cdots + c * x + d$$

equal 0. We shall not have any basic need to deal with algebraic numbers. If, however, we were to develop a software system for calculations over polynomials, then we would abstractly define polynomials as syntactic structures, and we would define functions that, for example, solve polynomial equations.

2.3.6 Transcendental Numbers

A real number which is not algebraic is called transcendental. Existence of transcendental numbers was first shown by the French mathematician Joseph Liouville[4] in 1844. Examples of transcendental numbers are e and π. Again, in these volumes, we shall have no occasion to wish to express transcendental numbers, but we will provide means for modelling them.

---

[4]See, e.g., `http://www.stetson.edu/~efriedma/periodictable/html/Lu.html`.

2.3.7 Complex and Imaginary Numbers

Complex numbers arise as the solution to certain kinds of polynomial equations. Such numbers (c) are, in ordinary mathematics, normally written as a pair of a real (a) and an imaginary $(i\,b)$ number (where a and b are themselves reals):

$$c : a + ib$$

There is no explicit means for writing complex numbers in RSL, as RAISE was not intended for such applications where expressing or denoting complex numbers arise. If, however, we need to deal with complex number "representation" and operations, then we model them as pairs:

type
   Complex = **Real** × **Real**
value
   add, sub, mpy, div: Complex × Complex → Complex

   add((a1,ib1),(a2,ib2)) ≡ (a1+a2,ib1+ib2)
   sub((a1,ib1),(a2,ib2)) ≡ (a1−a2,ib1−ib2)
   mpy((a1,ib1),(a2,ib2)) ≡ (a1∗a2−ib1∗ib2,a1∗ib2+a2∗ib1)
   div((a1,ib1),(a2,ib2)) ≡ ... /∗ left as exercise ∗/ ...

2.4 Type Definitions: Numbers

So when and where are numbers used when modelling domains, requirements and software? We model certain (concrete) phenomena and certain (abstract) concepts by means of numbers when operations on the phenomena and concepts necessarily entail those of for example addition, subtraction, multiplication, and, more rarely, division.

   A (concrete) type definition is something which to a type name associates a type expression. The type expressions introduce in this chapter were:

type
   Nat, Int, Real

Let N, I and R be (arbitrarily selected) type names, then:

type
   N = **Nat**
   I = **Int**
   R = **Real**

are examples of type definitions. N stands for the type, i.e., the class, of natural number values. I and R for integers and reals.

With a person one can associate a height and a weight. With a country one can associate a population (i.e., number of citizens) and its decomposition into females and males. With that same population one can associate the annual increment or the decrement in population, i.e., deviation. Suggested types are therefore:

type
  Height, Weight = **Real**
  Population, Female, Male = **Nat**
  Deviation = **Int**

The above just constitutes a very first beginning in which we model 'kinds' of phenomena and concepts

2.5 Summary

We have introduced the natural number **Nat**, the integer **Int** and the real **Real** number types. In addition, we have shown how to express their values, and covered the usual operations on each of these kinds of values. The other number types mentioned are not directly designatable in RSL.

Integers are usually deployed to model indices into arbitrary arrays of mathematics and hence in such programming languages which are used for mathematical calculations over arrays (vectors, matrices, tensors, etc.). Similarly natural numbers larger than 0 are usually deployed to model indices into list data values, including, for example, sequences of sentence structures. Sometimes, in ordinary programs of ordinary programming languages, integers and natural numbers are occasionally used as programmer-chosen encodings of other phenomena than numbers themselves.

Example 2.3 *Undesirable Encodings:* Typical encodings in "old" programming styles were: 1 for truth and 0 for falsity; the numbers $1, 2, 3, 4$ for designating the suit, s, of a card, in a deck of cards: $1 \simeq \clubsuit, 2 \simeq \diamondsuit, 3 \simeq \heartsuit$ and $4 \simeq \spadesuit$; and the numbers $1, \ldots, 13$ for representing, within each suit, the face value, v, of the card: $1 \simeq$ ace, $i = $ i, $1 \le i \le 10$, $11 \simeq$ knight, $12 \simeq$ queen, and $13 \simeq$ king. As a result any ordinary (i.e., non-joker) card is encoded as a number pair (s, v), and such that the joker (card) may be represented as, for example, $(5, 14)$! ∎

We leave it to the reader to imagine for which purposes we use reals in abstract model specifications.

2.6 Bibliographical Notes

The classical textbook cum monograph on number theory is that of Hardy [263].

2.7 Exercises

Exercise 2.1. *A Radix 0 Numeral Number System.* Let natural numerals be represented by sequences of diamonds, $\diamond$, such that $\diamond$ designates 0, $\diamond\diamond$ designates 1, $\diamond\diamond\diamond$ designates 2, etc.

(1) Define a BNF[5] grammar for these radix 0 numerals.

(2) Define a function R0R10, and another function R10R0, such that R0R10 converts a radix 0 numeral to a radix 10 numeral, and such that R10R0 converts a radix 10 numeral to a radix 0 numeral. Assume a modulo function which when applied to numbers m and n, i.e., modulo(m,n), yields a pair, (m',d), of numbers such that $0 \leq d \leq n$, and $m = n \times m' + d$.

(3) Define suitable arithmetic operators, addition, multiplication and integer division, that take radix 0 numerals and return radix 0 numerals.

Exercise 2.2. *A Radix 8 Numeral Number System (I).* Based on the idea of the informal Example 2.1, devise a grammar for a radix 8 natural number system, and an informal meaning function that converts radix 8 numerals into radix 10 numbers.

Exercise 2.3. *A Radix 8 Numeral Number System (II).* Given a radix 10 number, convert it to a radix 8 numeral. That is: Define, informally, a function which takes a natural number and yields a radix 8 numeral. Assume a function modulo which takes two arguments, m, n, both natural numbers, both larger than 0, and yields a pair w, r such that $w \times n + r = m$.

Exercise 2.4. *Real Numerals.* Suggest a BNF grammar for real numerals, that is, a pair of sequences of digits separated by a period. Then suggest an informal function definition which converts a real numeral to a real number.

Exercise 2.5. *Imaginary Numbers.* We refer to Sect. 2.3.4. Please define the division of complex numbers (i.e., complex reals).

Throughout this volume we shall use the triplets of ♣s to set off exercises that pertain to the "running" exercises of transportation nets, container logistics and financial service industries. The single ♣ after the initial **Exercise** literal and exercise number shall signal that the exercise in question belongs to these running exercises.

---

[5]We refer to Page 46 for an example BNF grammar.

Exercise 2.6. ♣ *Numbers in the Transportation Net Domain.*

We refer to Appendix A, Sect. A.1, *Transportation Net.*

Reading, carefully, the rough sketch description given in Sect. A.1, try to identify as many entitites which can be, in a reasonable way, modelled as numbers. State their type definitions as outlined in Sect. 2.4 on page 51.

Exercise 2.7. ♣ *Numbers in the Container Logistics Domain.*

We refer to Appendix A, Sect. A.2, *Container Logistics.*

Reading, carefully, the rough sketch description given in Sect. A.2, try to identify as many entitites which can be, in a reasonable way, modelled as numbers. State their type definitions as outlined in Sect. 2.4 on page 51.

Exercise 2.8. ♣ *Numbers in the Financial Service Industry Domain.*

We refer to Appendix A, Sect. A.3, *Financial Service Industry.*

Reading, carefully, the rough sketch description given in Sect. A.2, try to identify as many entitites which can be, in a reasonable way, modelled as numbers. State their type definitions as outlined in Sect. 2.4 on page 51.

3

Sets

- The **prerequisite** for studying this chapter is that you are willing to learn about simple mathematical concepts.
- The **aim** is to introduce the basic mathematical concepts of simple sets.
- The **objective** is to help ensure that the reader gets a head start on the most important of all model-oriented abstractions: sets.
- The **treatment** is rigorous to formal.

Characterisation. By a *set* we shall, loosely, understand an unordered collection of distinct elements (i.e., entities), something for which it is meaningful to speak about (i) an entity *being a member* of a set (or not) $\in$, (ii) the *union* (merging) of two or more sets into a set (of all the elements of the argument sets) $\cup$, (iii) the *intersection* of two or more sets into a set (of those elements which are in all argument sets) $\cap$, (iv) the *complement* of one set with respect to another set $\setminus$, (v) whether one set is a subset of another set $\subset$ and $\subseteq$ and (vi) the cardinality of a (finite) set (i.e., how many members it contains), **card** and a few more. ∎

The concepts of *sets* and *set elements* are left undefined. Above we have hinted at some set forming and other operations over sets and their elements. What sets "really are" is usually defined in mathematics by establishing what is called an axiom system[1]. Axiomatically speaking, sets and their operations are what a number of axioms of a set theory define them to be! There are several axiom systems for set theory. They each define a set theory. The different set theories may therefore not be exactly the same. The perhaps best-known axiom system for set theory is that put forward by Zermelo/Fraenkel (ZF) [211, 230][2].

---

[1] We shall later, in Chap. 9, define what we mean by axiom system.

[2] See, for example:

http://plato.stanford.edu/entries/set-theory/ZF.html

http://mathworld.wolfram.com/Zermelo-FraenkelAxioms.html

3.1 Background

Set theory is a major branch of mathematics. One can start by explaining mathematics from a basis of set theory, or from a basis of mathematical logic. We refer to seminal texts in set theory for a discussion of sets as a foundation for mathematics [46, 211, 230, 258, 273, 394, 491, 500, 505]. These texts also put set theory into a historical context.

3.2 Mathematical Sets

Let $e_1, e_2, \ldots, e_n$ be arbitrary elements (i.e., mathematical entities). Let us assume, without loss of generality (of what we shall have to say next), that they are all distinct and elementary, i.e., atomic. That is, no e_i involve functions, or other sets, etc. Then when writing $\{e_1, e_2, \ldots, e_n\}$ we mean the set, which we may name s, of n distinct elements e_i for $i = 1 \ldots n$. $\{\}$ designates the empty set[3] (of no elements). $\{$ and $\}$ are the set-forming braces.

We take membership, $\in$, of a set, $e \in s$, to be a further unexplained primitive function. $e \in s$ holds, i.e., is **true**, if e is one of the e_i for $i = 1 \ldots n$. Otherwise the expression $e \in s$ is **false.**

Based on the membership function we can now define[4] the standard collection of operations over sets. Let e, s, s' designate any element and any two sets:

$$s \cup s' = \{e \mid e \in s \vee e \in s'\} \tag{3.1}$$

$$s \cap s' = \{e \mid e \in s \wedge e \in s'\} \tag{3.2}$$

$$s \setminus s' = \{e \mid e \in s \wedge e \notin s'\} \tag{3.3}$$

$$s \ / \ s' = \{e \mid e \in s' \wedge e \notin s\} \tag{3.4}$$

$$s \subset s' = \forall e \bullet e \in s \Rightarrow e \in s' \wedge \exists e \bullet e \in s' \wedge e \notin s \tag{3.5}$$

$$s \subseteq s' = \forall e \bullet e \in s \Rightarrow e \in s' \tag{3.6}$$

$$s \ = \ s' = s \subseteq s' \wedge s' \subseteq s \tag{3.7}$$

$$s \ \neq \ s' = \neg(s = s') \tag{3.8}$$

Since this an early exposition of logical formulas, let us "read" these:

- Equation (3.1): The union of two sets, s and s', is the set of elements e such that e is a member of either the set s or the set s', or both.
- Equation (3.2): The intersection of two sets, s and s', is the set of elements e such that e is a member of both the set s and the set s'.

---

http://planetmath.org/encyclopedia/ZermeloFraenkelAxioms.html
http://www.britannica.com/eb/article?tocId=24035, etc.

[3]Sometimes the empty set is designated ∅.

[4]Definitions 3.1–3.8 are all in the classical style of mathematics.

- Equation (3.3): The difference of set s wrt. set s' is the set of elements e such that e is a member of s but not of the set s'.
- Equation (3.4): The complement of set s wrt. set s' is the set of elements e such that e is a member of s' but not of the set s.
- Equation (3.5): s is a proper subset of set s' if all ($\forall$) members of s are also members of s', and such that there exists ($\exists$) members of s' which are not members of s.
- Equation (3.6): s is a subset of set s' if all members of s are also members of s'.
- Equation (3.7): Two sets are equal if one is a subset of the other, and vice versa.
- Equation (3.8): Two sets are unequal if they are not equal.

Definitions (3.1)–(3.4) exemplify *set comprehension:*[5]

$$\{e \mid \mathcal{P}(e)\}$$

Figure 3.1 illustrates six of the above operations. The black circle to the left of the upper-leftmost subfigure stands for a set A; the other black circle to the right stands for another set B. The same is true for the subfigures of the first two rows.

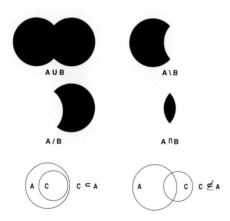

Fig. 3.1. Informal illustration of six set operations

Thus the operator symbols of Eqs. (3.1)–(3.8) read as follows: $\vee$: or, $\wedge$: and, $\notin$: not member of, $\forall e\bullet$: for all elements it is the case that, $\exists e\bullet$: there exists an element such that, $\neg$: not. The first four definitions are by *set comprehension*. The last four definitions use universal and existential quantification.

---

[5]When expressing set comprehension in the RSL notation we shall "add" a type binding: $\{e \mid e : T \bullet \mathcal{P}(e)\}$.

The symbol | reads: such that. The logic of these equations (i.e., definitions) is covered in Chap. 9.

In summary: There are two ways of expressing sets: by enumeration: $\{\}$, $\{a\}$, $\{a,b\}$, etc., and by comprehension: $\{e \mid e : T \bullet P(e)\}$. We did not show the typing, T, of elements e in Eqs. (3.1)–(3.8). Take, for example, Eq. 3.1:

$$s \cup s' = \{e \mid e : T \bullet e \in s \vee e \in s'\}$$

That is, we shall later bind elements of sets to specific types, and hence express that sets are typed sets. But we did show the use of the predicate (P over e). Later we will explain typing (Chap. 5) and predicates (Chap. 9).

3.3 Special Sets

3.3.1 Axiom of Extension

The *axiom of extension* states that a set is completely determined by its elements.

3.3.2 Partitions

Let s be a set, say $\{a_1, a_2, a_3, a_4, a_5, a_6\}$. A partition of s is a set of disjoint, i.e., nonoverlapping, sets, for example, $\{s_1, s_2, s_3\} = \{\{a_1\}, \{a_2, a_3\}, \{a_4, a_5, a_6\}\}$, such that the union of these: $\{a_1\} \cup \{a_2, a_3\} \cup \{a_4, a_5, a_6\}$, forms the set s.

3.3.3 Power Sets

Given a set, s, the power set of s, $\mathcal{P}(s)$, is the set of all its subsets. Thus, for $a = \{a_1, a_2, a_3\}$, $\mathcal{P}(s)$ is $\{\{\}, \{a_1\}, \{a_2\}, \{a_3\}, \{a_1, a_2\}, \{a_1, a_3\}, \{a_2, a_3\}, \{a_1, a_2, a_3\}\}$.

3.4 Sorts and Type Definitions: Sets

3.4.1 Set Abstractions

So when and where are sets used when modelling domains, requirements and software? We model certain concrete phenomena and certain abstract concepts by means of sets when operations on these phenomena and these concepts necessarily entail those of for example a phenomenon (or a concept) being a member of a class of such, or a set union of such, or a set intersection of such, or one phenomenon (or concept) being set included in another, etc.

3.4.2 Set Type Expressions and Type Definitions

A (concrete) type definition is something which to a type name associates a type expression. The set type expression introduced in this chapter was:

B-set

where B is any type (expression). Let B be an already defined type name, then:

type
   A = B-**set**

is an example of a type definition. A then stands for the type, i.e., the class, of sets of B elements.

Example 3.1 *Sociology:* If a neighbourhood, N, of people consists of a set of people, if a clan (i.e., a family), C, similarly, and if a society (of people), S, consists of a set of neighbourhoods, then:

type
   P
   N = P-**set**
   C = P-**set**
   S = N-**set**

models neighbourhoods, clans, and societies, in terms of the undefined sort of people, P. ∎

The above just constitutes a very first beginning in which we model kinds of phenomena and concepts.

3.4.3 Sorts

By a sort we shall understand a type about whose elements we make no further statements, that is, we do not, at present, say what they are. In other words, we leave them further undefined.

3.5 Sets in RSL

In Chap. 13 we shall cover, in excruciating detail, the concept of sets in RSL: how they are typed, enumerated, comprehended, operated upon, and used in various abstractions.

3.6 Bibliographical Notes

Set theory and logic are classical mathematical disciplines, and are strongly related. Seminal textbooks in set theory are: [46, 211, 230, 258, 273, 394, 491, 500, 505].

3.7 Exercises

Exercise 3.1. *Simple Set Enumerations and Operations.* (1) List, as set expressions, i.e., with curly braces and separated by commas, i.e., $\{\_, \_, ..., \_\}$ the following finite sets: (a) The set of the first 10 Fibonacci numbers, (b) the set of the first 6 factorial numbers, and (c) the set of the first 6 square numbers. (2) Then list the set of elements resulting from the intersection set of a and b, the complement of a wrt. b (i.e., a\b), and the complement of b wrt. to a (i.e., a/b).

Exercise 3.2. *Set Statements.* Fill in the texts implied by $\boxed{1}$ and $\boxed{2}$ below:

- If *an element e is in* $A \cap (B \cup C)$ *then it is the same as saying that e is in* $\boxed{1}$ *and in* $\boxed{2}$.
- If *an element e is in* $(A \cap B) \cup C$ *then it is the same as saying that e is in* $\boxed{1}$ *or in* $\boxed{2}$.
- If *an element e is in* $A \setminus (B \cap C)$ *then it is the same as saying that e is in* $\boxed{1}$ *but not in* $\boxed{2}$.

Notes for the next exercises: Let A be the main type of some domain (i.e., the *Transportation Net*, the *Container Logistics*, or the *Financial Service Industry* — such as outlined in Appendix Chap. A). If some major, i.e., an immediate subentity of entities of type A can be modelled as sets of entities of type B, then we can also say that we can **observe** these sets of (type B) entities:

type
    A, B
value
    obs_Bs: A → B-**set**

Here **obs_Bs** is said to be an observer function that applies to entities of type A and yields sets of entities of type B. We say that we can observe these latter sets from elements of type A.

Exercise 3.3. ♣ *Sets in the Transportation Net Domain:*
    We refer to Appendix A, Sect. A.1, *Transportation Net*.
    Reading, carefully, the rough sketch description given in Sect. A.1, try identify as many entities which can be, in a reasonable way, modelled as sets. State their type definitions as outlined in Sect. 3.4 on page 58. Suggest related observer functions.

Exercise 3.4. ♣ *Sets in the Container Logistics Domain.*
    We refer to Appendix A, Sect. A.2, *Container Logistics*.
    Reading, carefully, the rough sketch description given in Sect. A.2, try identify as many entities which can be, in a reasonable way, modelled as sets. State their type definitions as outlined in Sect. 3.4 on page 58. Suggest related observer functions.

Exercise 3.5. ♣ *Sets in the Financial Service Industry Domain.*
    We refer to Appendix A, Sect. A.3, *Financial Service Industry*.
    Reading, carefully, the rough sketch description given in Sect. A.3, try identify as many entities which can be, in a reasonable way, modelled as sets. State their type definitions as outlined in Sect. 3.4 on page 58. Suggest related observer functions.

4

Cartesians

- The **prerequisite** for studying this chapter is that you possess at least a simple level of mathematical maturity.
- The **aim** is to cover the classical mathematical concept of Cartesians.
- The **objective** is to make sure that the reader, in the future, will handle the issues of certain kinds of aggregations, compounds, products, records, structures, etc., as possible examples of Cartesians.
- The **treatment** is informal, yet precise.

We have chosen the name Cartesians, for the kind of mathematical structures unveiled in this chapter, after the French philosopher and mathematician René Descartes. Other, more common, terms are: structures, records, groupings or aggregations. At the end of the chapter we provide a "borrowed" biography of René Descartes.

Characterisation. By a *Cartesian* we understand, loosely, a fixed grouping (i.e., aggregation) of a number of not necessarily distinct entities such that it is meaningful to speak of (i) the composition of these entities, e_i, into a Cartesian, $(e_1, e_2, \ldots, e_n)$, and of (ii) the decomposition of a Cartesian, c, into its components: **let** $(id_1, id_2, \ldots, id_n) = c$ **in** ... **end**, etc. ∎

4.1 The Issues

Between elements (i.e., members) of a set there is no other relation than their being distinct members of that set. If one wishes to express a mathematical entity which has a fixed number of possibly distinct entities such that their position is fixed, but not ordinal, then it is suggested to model such an entity as a Cartesian.

4.2 Cartesian-Valued Expressions

By a Cartesian we understand a finite grouping of two or more values.[1] By a grouping we understand a composite value which can be uniquely decomposed:[2]

type
    X, Y, Z
value
    x:X, y:Y, z:Z
    (x,y,z) /∗ expresses a Cartesian ∗/
    /∗ assume k to be a three−component Cartesian: ∗/
    let (x,y,z) = k **in** ...x...y...z... **end**
axiom
    ∀ x:X,y:Y,z:Z •
        let k=(x,y,z) **in let** (x′,y′,z′)=k **in** x ≡ x′∧y ≡ y′∧z ≡ z′ **end end**

Thus left and right parentheses are used to delineate a comma-separated list of two or more elements and to form, i.e., to construct, a Cartesian.

The **axiom** (see Chap. 9) expresses that for any Cartesian structure (i.e., grouping, composition) of individual values we uniquely get exactly these values back when decomposing the structure.

While emphasising the semantic idea of compositions, parts and wholes, we incidentally also illustrated extensions to the syntax of **let ... in ... end** clauses.

4.3 Cartesian Types

To express the type of Cartesian values, say over respective sorts[3] X, Y, and Z, we write the type expression:

    X × Y × Z

That is: × is the infix Cartesian type constructor. Giving names, for example K, to Cartesian types is exemplified below:

---

[1]It does not make sense, we think, to speak of Cartesians of zero elements, or of just one element. (), as an expression, in RSL, stands for the value of type **Unit,** that is: A type of just one value: (). Let v be of type A, then the type of the value of the expression (v) is A.

[2]In the formulas below (i.e., above!) we introduce some first bits of the RSL notation: By **type** X we roughly mean a set of entities of the same type, here named X. By **value** x:X, y:Y, z:Z we mean the naming of, as here, arbitrary values, x, y, z of respective types. By **axiom** ∀ x:X,y:Y,z:Z • $\mathcal{P}$(x,y,z) we mean to express a property $\mathcal{P}$(x,y,z) that always holds for all the values x, y, z.

[3]The term sort is used in lieu of the term type when the type is not further defined.

type
   X, Y, Z
   K = X × Y × Z

The meaning of X × Y × Z is the (unnamed) type whose values are uniquely decomposable into exactly three components of respective types X, Y and Z.
   Any type expression can be grouped:

   X×Y×Z, (X×Y×Z), (X×Y)×Z, X×(Y×Z), etc.

The first two of the parenthesised expressions are not different, X×Y×Z and (X×Y×Z) denote the same type spaces. But the last two, repeated below, are different. That is, the three spaces, K1, K2 and K3 are distinct:

type
   K1 = X×(Y×Z)
   K2 = X×Y×Z
   K3 = (X×Y)×Z
axiom
   [informally:]
      K1 ∩ K2 = {} ∧ K1 ∩ K3 = {} ∧ K2 ∩ K3 = {}
   [formally:]
      ∀ x:X,y:Y,z:Z • (x,(y,z))≠(x,y,z)∧(x,y,z)≠((x,y),z)∧((x,y),z)≠(x,(y,z))

Although we have yet to introduce the concept of **axiom**s, we can read the informal and the formal bits: The three type spaces share no values. For no combinations of x, y, and z values in respective types (i.e., type spaces) are the specific combinations, which correspond to the three type spaces K1, K2 and K3, equal.

4.4 Cartesian Arity

In general, let $D_1, \ldots, D_n$, (also written as D_1, etc.) stand for type names (or type expressions), then

   D_1 × D_2 × ... × D_n
type
   C = D_1 × D_2 × ... × D_n

stand for the n-ary Cartesians over respective D_is. The *arity* of a Cartesian is thus its number of components.

4.5 Cartesian Equality

We define only one operator on Cartesians. The equality expression:

$$(a_1, a_2, \ldots, a_m) = (b_1, b_2, \ldots, b_n)$$

holds if and only if $m = n$ and, for all i in the interval $[1..m]^4$ we have that $a_i = b_i$.

4.6 Some Construed Examples

The examples of this section are construed, or made up, to serve as illustrations, however artificial, of uses of Cartesians. They furthermore violate our edict, our language design decision, that Cartesians have at least arity 2, in that we also, in the below examples, claim to deal with Cartesians of arity 0 and 1.[5]

Example 4.1 *A Simple Language of Cartesian Numerals:* Consider the following encoding of natural numbers in terms of Cartesians. Let token be any atomic value.

> 0: token,
> 1: (token),
> 2: (token,token),
> 3: (token,token,token),
>
> ...
>
> n: (token,token,...,token) n times token
>
> ...

Now consider the following "operations" on these Cartesian numerals:

> +: (token,token,...,token)+(token,token,...,token) = (token,token,...,token)
>   n times token   m times token   m+n times token

The question is: How do we express this operation? Here is a proposal:

> cn1 + cn2 ≡
>   **case** (cn1,cn2) **of**
>   (token,("lst2")) → cn2,
>   (("lst1"),token) → cn1,

---

[4]In RSL, the specification language mostly used in these volumes, an interval of integers from j to k is designated by the two period range expression: $[j..k]$.

[5]Of course, we could just change our design decision wrt. the arity of Cartesians and allow arities 0 and 1. We would then have to provide a way in which to express Cartesians of those arities, and could perhaps choose: () and (A), where A is any type.

$(("lst1"),("lst2")) \rightarrow (lst1,lst2)$
        end

where "lsti" stands for any list of tokens, for example, t1,t2,...,tn.

The proposal works only if you believe it works! That is, you have to agree with the writer of the above formulas that "lst1" and "lst2" stand for lists of "token,token,...,token". This form of "text and ellipss" expressions may work, intuitively, but rarely works in formal practice. That is, one can easily, or maybe not so easily, come up with examples where the above-suggested metalinguistic variables (i.e., "lst1" and "lst2") lead to ambiguities.

Along that line: How is one to represent the subtraction, the multiplication and the integer division operations?

We have brought this example so as to motivate the need for a metalanguage, here RSL, in which to model constructions like those of the present example. We say metalanguage, since it is being used in order to express properties about another language — here that of Cartesian numerals.   ∎

Example 4.2 *A Simple Language of Cartesian Lists:* Consider $\langle$ and $\rangle$ to be delimiters of list expressions, that is, $\langle$a,b,c$\rangle$ designates the list of elements a, b and c, and in that order: a being the first list element, b being the second, and c being the third element. Now consider using just pairs of Cartesians to designate lists:

(token,token) $\equiv$ $\langle\rangle$
((a),token) $\equiv$ $\langle$a$\rangle$
((a),((b),token)) $\equiv$ $\langle$a,b$\rangle$
((a),((b),((c),token))) $\equiv$ $\langle$a,b,c$\rangle$
...

That is, (token,token) designates the empty list, and $((a),\ell)$ designates the list whose first element is a and whose tail is the Cartesian list ℓ.

Does this work? Well, only if the pairs obey, for example, this restricted syntax:

<CL> ::= (token,token) | (<A> , <CL>)
<A> ::= a | b | c | ...

A is any set (i.e., type) of, for example, atomic (non-Cartesian) values.

With this language of Cartesian lists, how do we express concatenation, ⌢, of two lists:

$\langle$a,b,c$\rangle$ ⌢ $\langle$d,e$\rangle$ = $\langle$a,b,c,d,e$\rangle$?

Well, let us try:

⌢: (token,token)⌢((a),ℓ) $\equiv$ ((a),ℓ)
⌢: ((a),ℓ)⌢(token,token) $\equiv$ ((a),ℓ)
⌢: ((a),ℓ)⌢((a'),ℓ') $\equiv$ ((a),ℓ⌢((a'),ℓ')).

Let us define **hd** (head) and **tl** (tail) of lists:

> **hd** $\langle\rangle \equiv$ **chaos**
> **hd** $\langle$a$\rangle\widehat{\ }$tail $\equiv$ a
> **tl** $\langle\rangle \equiv$ **chaos**
> **tl** $\langle$a$\rangle\widehat{\ }$tail $\equiv$ tail

i.e.:

> **hd** (token,token) $\equiv$ **chaos**
> **hd** ((a),ℓ) $\equiv$ a
> **tl** (token,token) $\equiv$ **chaos**
> **tl** ((a),ℓ) $\equiv \ell$.

chaos denotes the undefined value.   ∎

We leave it as an exercise to define the following operations on Cartesian lists: length of a list, **index** set (**inds**) of a list, **element** set (**elems**) of a list and the list indexing operation $\ell(i)$.

4.7 Sorts and Type Definitions: Cartesians

4.7.1 Cartesian Abstractions

So when and where are Cartesians used when modelling domains, requirements and software? We model certain concrete phenomena and certain abstract concepts by means of Cartesians when these are seen as consisting of a fixed combination of an a priori known number of distinct entities.

4.7.2 Cartesian Type Expressions and Type Definitions

A concrete type definition is something which to a type name associates a type expression. The Cartesian type expressions introduced in this chapter were of the form:

> $B \times C \times ... \times D$

where B, C, ..., D are any types (i.e., any type expressions). Let B, C, D be already defined type names, then:

type
> $A = B \times C \times D$

is an example of a type definition. A then stands for the type, i.e., the class, of Cartesians of (b,c,d) elements, that is: Where b is in B, c is in C and d is in D, also written b:B, c:C, d:D.

Example 4.3 *Complex Numbers:* Let R be real numbers, and I likewise, then

type
    R, I = **Real**
    C = R $\times$ I

models complex numbers.   ∎

The above just constitutes a very first beginning in which we model kinds of phenomena and concepts.

4.8 Cartesians in RSL

In Chap. 14 we shall cover, in excruciating detail, the concept of Cartesians in RSL: how they are typed, enumerated, operated upon, and used in various abstractions.

4.9 Bibliographical Notes

We refer to an Internet-based biography about René Descartes:

`www-gap.dcs.st-and.ac.uk/~history/Mathematicians/Descartes.html`

It is authored by J. J. O'Connor and E. F. Robertson, of the Univ. of St Andrews, Centre for Interdisciplinary Research in Computational Algebra. The book of historical interest to us is *Discours de la méthode pour bien conduire sa raison et chercher la vérité dans les sciences,* with three appendices: *La Dioptrique, Les Météores,* and *La Géométrie* [185, 189].

4.10 Exercises

Exercise 4.1. *Simple Cartesians.* Is $(1, 2) = (2, 1)$? And is $(\sqrt{16}, (-2)^3, \frac{1}{4}) = (4, \sqrt{64}, 6/24)$?

Exercise 4.2. *Cartesian Sets.* Let the sets A, X be $\{a, b, c\}$, respectively $\{p, q\}$. List the elements of the sets $A \times A, A \times B, B \times B$, and $B \times A$.

Exercise 4.3. *Further Operations on Cartesian Lists.* We refer to Example 4.2 on page 67.
    Define the following operations on Cartesian lists:
    (1) **length** of a list: The number of (zero, one or more) elements that it contains.

(2) **index set** (**inds**) of a list: The set of indices, from 1 to and including the length of the list. If the list is empty then the index set is the empty set.

(3) **element set** (**elems**) of a list: The set of distinct elements of the list. If the list is empty then the element set is the empty set.

(4) The list indexing operation $\ell(i)$. where, if the list is empty then the operations is undefined, i.e., ends in the result **chaos.**

Exercise 4.4. ♣ *Cartesians in the Transportation Net Domain*
We refer to Appendix A, Sect. A.1, *Transportation Net*.

Reading, carefully, the rough sketch description given in Sect. A.1, try to identify as many entities which can be, in a reasonable way, modelled as Cartesians. State their type definitions as outlined in Sect. 4.7 on page 68.

Hint: The directions of traffic along a segment may be modelled in terms of a set of zero (the segment is closed to traffic), one (it is a one way segment), or two pairs of distinct segment identifiers.

Find more examples yourself.

Exercise 4.5. ♣ *Cartesians in the Container Logistics Domain.*
We refer to Appendix A, Sect. A.2, *Container Logistics*.

Reading, carefully, the rough sketch description given in Sect. A.2, try to identify as many entities which can be, in a reasonable way, modelled as Cartesians. State their type definitions as outlined in Sect. 4.7 on page 68.

Hint: A container terminal consists of a quay (or a set of quays), and a container storage area. [You may wish to also include the harbour basin in "what a container terminal consists of".]

Find more examples yourself.

Exercise 4.6. ♣ *Cartesians in the Financial Service Industry Domain.*
We refer to Appendix A, Sect. A.3, *Financial Service Industry*.

Reading, carefully, the rough sketch description given in Sect. A.3, try to identify as many entities which can be, in a reasonable way, modelled as Cartesians. State their type definitions as outlined in Sect. 4.7 on page 68.

Hint: (i) A bank consists of a catalog of customers and (all their) accounts. (ii) A buy [sell] order consists of a customer identification, a securities instrument identification, a quantity indication (of number of to be bought [sold]), a time period during which the ordered transaction is expected to be fulfilled, and a price interval ("lo"–"hi") within which the 'buy' ['sell'] price is expected to fall.

Find more examples yourself.

5

Types

- The **prerequisites** for studying this chapter are that you possess knowledge of the type concept of ordinary programming languages as well as of the mathematical concepts of sets and Cartesians as covered in earlier chapters.
- The **aim** is to give a first overview of the type concept that we shall further develop in subsequent chapters.
- The **objective** is to help ensure that the reader eventually becomes fluent in the selection, expression and use of types.
- The **treatment** is from systematic to semiformal.

> The type concept is, perhaps, the greatest contribution computer science has made to mathematics. The type concept is all pervasive, but it is not quite the same as the dimension and unit concepts of, for example, physics.

Characterisation. By a *type* we shall, loosely speaking, understand a named (i.e., an identified) set of values. ∎

Types are, simplifying, taken to be sets of values. The values of type sets, i.e., their elements, are such as Booleans, numbers, sets, Cartesians, functions, relations, lists and maps where the composite types (sets, Cartesians, functions, relations, lists and maps) themselves consists of values.

In this section we will briefly introduce the reader to the fundamental concept of types. The professional software engineer repeatedly thinks in terms of types. That is, the concept of type and its abstract and concrete mastery is crucial to professional software engineering.

This section is cursory. The type concept will be identified. Chaps. 2–4 have introduced types, and Chaps. 6–9, as well as Chaps. 10 and 13–16 will introduce type concepts. The RSL type concept will then be summarized in Chap. 18. Thereafter it will be used in the rest of these volumes. So, with the present introductory section we will start a long journey into possibly that most important concept of software engineering, type theory and practice!

• • •

The world is full of manifest things (i.e., of phenomena): entities that one can point to. Some share properties and are "of the same kind", others do not, and are "of different kinds". The type concept was introduced first, in some abstract sense, by philosophers, then by mathematicians and, much later, in programming languages to cope with "sameness", respectively "distinctness".

We assume some basic familiarity with rudimentary aspects of the type concept of some programming languages. From examples of such a programming language type concept and its analysis, we unfold, below, some very basic ideas of more abstract type concepts. In this way we can, little by little, introduce a concept of specification language type concept.

In this section we shall introduce the very basics of the type concept upon which we shall later be basing further ideas of type. These basics are: *sorts* (i.e., *abstract types*), *concrete types*, *atomic types*, *type names*, *type expressions*, *type constructors*, and the fact that *values* and *types* form complementary notions.

5.1 Values and Types

How do we motivate the concept of types? We do so as follows: Around us we see phenomena such as a person being 1 meter, 79 centimeters tall, 67 years old, and weighing, oh well, too much! We shall, in these volumes, refer to the 'person' phenomenon as an *entity*. The person is an *entity* describable, i.e., characterisable, through, in this example, the three *entity attributes* just mentioned. On first reflection, the attributes represent, i.e., characterise *values*, and on second thought, these attributes are *types*: *height*, *age*, and *weight*. So an *entity* has an *attribute value* which is of an *atomic* or *composite type*.

The person **attribute value** was of, or had composite type, and the composite type components included the height, age and weight types, which were atomic types, that is, could not be further decomposed. Some entities have *constant values*, others have *variable values*. A person's birth date is definitely fixed. A person's gender is (usually) fixed. A person's age changes all the time!

Entities rarely change type. A rather construed example of an entity that may be considered to change type is the following: Some thing, an entity, which, "to begin with" may be considered or registered as a wooden chair. That is, of utility. Then the chair "changes" type to become an antique, exhibited, but not sat in. It is no longer of utility depending on one's viewpoint, of course. Or it is wrecked and becomes a "heap of wood", and is thence possibly considered burning material for a stove. That is, again of utility, but of a different one! Modelling types — including type changes — is often referred to as *data modelling*. In other words: *types* and *values* go hand-in-hand.

In these volumes we shall have much more to say on the concepts of types, attributes (a kind of types) and values, as well as on the use of these concepts in (domain) modelling the actual world, in (requirements) modelling expectations to software and in expressing software implementation models.

5.2 Phenomena and Concept Types

5.2.1 Phenomena and Concepts

Characterisation. By a *phenomenon* we mean some physically manifest thing, something that one can point to or measure by means of some physical instrument. ▪

Any specific person is such a phenomenon.

Characterisation. By a *concept* we mean an abstraction, something of our mind. ▪

Concepts usually abstract classes of related phenomena.

We bundle, following what was expressed in earlier sections, classes of like phenomena or like concepts into types. In this section we shall examine relations between phenomena, concepts and types.

5.2.2 Entities: Atomic and Composite

Characterisation. By an *entity* we mean a representation of a phenomena or a concept. ▪

Characterisation. By a *representation* (of something) we loosely mean "a way of talking" about that "something", a way of "writing it down". ▪

A representation of a phenomenon *is not that phenomenon,* but it is *only our way of referring to it.*

As an aside: A representation of a phenomenon, however represented, as long as it is not represented "inside" a computing (and communications) system, is spoken of *as information.* Once represented inside a computing (and communications) system we *speak* of it as *data.* Data is formalised representation of information.

Characterisation. By an *atomic entity* we mean an entity which does not itself consist of proper sub-entities. ▪

A person could be considered an atomic entity in that that person's head, arms, legs, etc., should not from some point of view be considered entities in their own right. Perhaps they are considered so by a surgeon, but certainly not desirably so by any one person: one does not compose, as in mechanical engineering, a person from one head, one left leg, etc.!

Please note that it is you who decides whether to consider a phenomenon (or a concept) to be atomic, that is, indivisible or not.

Characterisation. By a *composite entity* we mean an entity which can be said to be independently composed from other proper subentities.   ∎

A motor car can be said to be a composite entity in that it can be said to be composed from an engine, a transmission system, a left front door, etc., where each of these subentities are being considered entities in their own right, as entities, by those who manufacture, that is, assemble them.

5.2.3 Attributes and Values

Characterisation. By an *attribute* we mean a named property which has an associated type that for the same named attribute of different entities may have different or the same values.   ∎

Atomic Entity Attributes and Values

An atomic entity may possess one or more attributes.

A person, which we here consider an atomic entity, has, we decide, amongst many other attributes, the following ones: *name* (with some fixed value, say *Dines Bjørner*), (current) *height* (with some varying value, say *179 centimeters*), gender (with fixed value, *male*), etc.

So, the "full value" of an atomic entity may be a composite value!

Composite Entity Attributes and Values

The way in which a composite entity is composed can be said to be an attribute of the composite entity which is different from the composition of the attributes of the proper subentities.

Example 5.1 *Roadnet: Entities and Attributes:* A roadnet *is composed* from a *set* of segments and a *set* of connectors. Segments do not contain connectors, but *ends in, or has* exactly two such. A segment is an entity. Connectors do not contain segments, but *connect one or more* segments (one if a road is a cul-de-sac). A connector is an entity. Each segment, we decide, has attributes: unique segment identity, road name, segment length, segment curvature, segment cover (tarmac, or other), etc., none of which are separable entities. Each connector, we decide, has attributes: connector identity, possibly a connector name, set of identifiers of segments incident (and/or emanating from) the connector, etc., none of which are (separable) entities. The roadnet has as attribute that of the compositions of its entities (consists of, ends in, connects). ∎

Characterisation. *Composite Entity Attributes:* We make the distinction between the attributes of component entities of a composite entity and the attribute of the composite entity: Let composite entity $\rfloor$ *consist of* entities $c_1\ c_2,\ \ldots,\ c_m$. Each of the individual c_i, for $i = 1 \ldots m$, have attributes $\mathcal{C}_{i_1}$, $\mathcal{C}_{i_2}, \ldots, \mathcal{C}_{i_n}$. In addition, the composite entity c has attributes $\mathcal{C}$. The latter attribute outlines how the *consist of* relation is manifested, i.e., how we decide it is so. For example: $\mathcal{C}$ is: c consists of a *sequence of* components c_j, or $\mathcal{C}$ is: c consists of a *set of* components c_k, or $\mathcal{C}$ is: c consists of a component c_{ℓ_p} *next to* a component c_{ℓ_q} *next to* $\ldots$ *next to* a component c_{ℓ_r}. ■

It is this ontology of *sequence of, set of, next to,* etcetera, which we shall later capture by means of type operators, that is, operators on types that define how component types make up overall types

Characterisation. *Composite Entity Values:* To each attribute we associate a current value. Let composite entity c *consist of* entities $c_1, c_2, \ldots, c_m$. Each of the individual c_i, for $i = 1 \ldots m$, have overall current values $v_{v_{i_1}}$, $v_{c_{i_2}}, \ldots,$ $v_{c_{i_n}}$. In addition, the composite entity c has value v_c for attribute $\mathcal{C}$. The overall current value of c is thus v_v, combined, as prescribed by $\mathcal{C}$, with the overall current subentity values: $v_{c_{i_1}}, v_{c_{i_2}}, \ldots, v_{c_{i_n}}$. ■

Example 5.2 *Roadnet Values:* We continue Example 5.1 on the preceding page. A particular roadnet is composed from three segments, as shown in Fig. 5.1 subfigures [A]–[C]. The composition that two connected segments meet in a connector is adhered to. Subfigures [A] and [B] show two, respectively three cul-de-sacs.

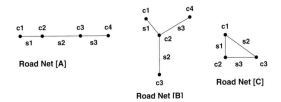

Fig. 5.1. Representation of three different roadnet values

The overall roadnet values are different by virtue, primarily of their specific topologies. The three segments could all have the same values, that is, same length, the same identifications, the same names, etc., as also indicated. But what you first notice, we claim, when observing Fig. 5.1, is the difference in the three attribute roadnet values. ■

• • •

We have tried, somewhat informally, to outline some ideas of atomic and composite entities, and of their attributes and values. These ideas need to be sharpened, i.e., made more precise. That is a main rationale of the present volume!

Discussion

In ordinary mathematics, some would abstract roadnets in terms of graphs:

$$G : (S, C, K)^1$$

S stands for a set of segments. For example, $\{s_1, s_2, s_3\}$. C stands for a set of connectors. For example, $\{c_1, c_2, c_3, c_4\}$, as in either of subfigures [A] and [B] of Fig. 5.1 on the preceding page, or $\{c_1, c_2, c_3\}$ as in subfigure [C] of Fig. 5.1 on the page before. K stands for the specific connections of segments to connectors. For example, $[s_1 \mapsto \{c_1, c_2\}]$ as in subfigure [A] of Fig. 5.1 on the preceding page. The gist of Chaps. 12–18 is that we offer several ways in which roadnets (i.e., graphs) can be abstractly modelled:

The property-oriented algebraic sort and analytic function presentation:

type
    G0, S, C
value
    obs_Ss: G0 → S-**set**
      obs_Cs: G0 → C-**set**
      obs_K: G0 → (C $\overrightarrow{m}$ (S $\overrightarrow{m}$ C))

would for g0 being the roadnet of subfigure [A] of Fig. 5.1 on the page before yield:

    obs_Ss(g0) = {s1,s2,s3}
    obs_Cs(g0) = {c1,c2,c3,c4}
    obs_K(g0) = [c1↦{s1},c2↦{s1,s2},c3↦{s2,s3},c4↦{s3}]

The model-oriented set-, Cartesian- and map-oriented specifications:

type
    G1 = (C × S × C)-**set**
    G2 = C $\overrightarrow{m}$ (S $\overrightarrow{m}$ C)

yield the following values of g1 and g2 for the same roadnet (subfigure [A] of Fig. 5.1):

    g1: {(c1,s1,c2),(c2,s1,c1),(c2,s2,c3),(c3,s2,c2),(c3,s3,c4),(c4,s3,c3)}
    g2: [c1↦[s1↦c2],c2↦[s1↦c1,s2↦c3],c3↦[s2↦c2,s3↦c4],c4↦[s3↦c3]]

---

[1]The expression G: (S,C,K) is not in the style we shall be using in these volumes.

That is, the type definition facility promulgated by this volume replaces the ordinary way in which mathematicians define mathematical structures. Our type definition facility ties in with the function definition facility and permits the definition of very rich and novel mathematical structures with entities and functions.

5.3 Programming Language Type Concepts

We review some standard concepts of programming languages.

Some Examples

From classical programming languages, such as Algol 60, Pascal, C, C++ and Java, we know of a type concept similar to the one now summarised.

Example 5.3 *Simple Types:* The three syntactic constructs after the keyword var:

```
[1]    var i integer,
[2]        b Boolean,
[3]        c character;
```

prescribe that storage for three variables be allocated, one ([1]), i, to have enough storage space to contain integer values ranging, for example, between -2^n and $+2^n - 1$ (for some such n as, for example, 16 or 32 or 64) where n is the size, in bits, of a storage cell (also called a half-word, a word, or a double word). Another ([2]), b, to have enough storage space, say one bit, to contain a Boolean value — either **true** or **false.** And a final ([3]), c, to have enough storage space, say a byte or two bytes, to contain character values such as the characters "a", "b", ..., "z", and possibly others (such as digits, symbols and operators: "0", "1", ..., "9", ",", ";", ".", ..., "-", "+", "*", "/", ...).

We observe a number of things that seem relevant for the understanding of the above examples: (i) the use of the keyword var (or *declared variable* or some such variant) to indicate that a *variable* is *declared;* (ii) that there seem to be three *declarations;* (iii) that each of these *declarations* has two parts: a *variable name* (i, b, respectively c), and a *constant ("built-in") type name* (integer, Boolean, respectively character); (iv) that to each *variable* a *concrete storage representation* is (implicitly) prescribed; and (v) that *variable names* (most likely uniquely) identify *storage space* that may *contain values* of the *prescribed type.*   ∎

Example 5.4 *Composite Types:*

```
[4]    type r =
[5]       record (i integer,
[6]               b Boolean,
[7]               a array[1..m,1..n] of char);
[8]    var p r;
```

As before we observe a *variable declaration* (line [8]), but now the *variable name*, p, is associated with a *defined type*, of name r (rather than, as previously, a *constant*, *built-in type*). The *defined type name* is shorthand for, i.e., is defined by, the right-hand side of the '=' in line [4] of the example, i.e., by lines [5–7]. There we observe that the *defined type* is of type record, i.e., certain compositions of values of other types, and that it is to have three *named fields* whose corresponding *storage location parts* are to *contain values* of types integer, Boolean and a matrix of m rows and n columns of character elements. Included in our examples above is the illustration of the variable bounds ([1..m,1..n]) array type (actually a matrix such as defined). Incidentally, just to provoke some possible confusion (see Example 5.5) we have chosen *field selector names* "similar" (with respect to identifiers), to the previously (correspondingly) introduced *variable names*.

Concerning p ([8]): It is an entity (a variable) of type r, and p (besides having the overall attribute of being a variable) also has part attributes integer, Boolean and character.   ∎

Example 5.5 *Type Checking Expressions and Assignments:*

```
[9]    i := i + 1;
[10]   b := (if i > p.i then true else false end);
[11]   p.i := p.i + i;
[12]   c := p.a[i,p.i];
```

This last example is really extraneous to our main purpose of bringing and discussing these examples. That purpose was to introduce the type concept as it is found in classical programming languages. Instead the current example illustrates such imperative programming language concepts as assignment, expressions, and record field value selection. The above illustrates four assignment statements. In line [9] we show a simple assignment: The integer variable i has its value incremented by one. In line [10] we show another assignment, a conditional expression, and a record field value selection: The Boolean variable b has its value set to **true** if the value of variable i is larger than the value contained in record p field i, otherwise it is set to **false**. And, finally, in line [12] we show an assignment involving a seemingly "tricky" array element indexing: The value of character variable c is prescribed set to the value of the character element of the record array field that is indexed along one dimension by the value of the simple integer variable i and along the other dimension by the value of the record i field.   ∎

Discussion

We observed that two kinds of keywords are used in connection with types: *type names* and *type constructors*. Type names are those, like integer, Boolean and character that denote types of specific kinds of values, viz.: integers, Booleans and characters. These keywords stand for built-in or given types. Type constructore are those, like record and array which, together with other *linguistic markers* (delimiters), identifiers and type names, help *construct* or form new, *defined types*. These keywords stand for higher-order functions. That is, we speak of *type names*, which are identifiers, either built-in (as integer, Boolean, character) or defined (such as) r, and of composite *type expressions* such as record(id1 te1, id2 te2, ..., idn ten) where idj and tej stand for *record field selector identifiers* and *type expressions*, respectively. *Type names* are *simple type expressions*. We also observe, in the above examples, that we pair *type definitions*, a *type name*, such as r, with a *type expression*, such as record(id1 te1, id2 te2, ..., idn ten).

We say that the *type name* r is being defined *concretely:* It is given a *model*. The *model* given for r is that of records as laid out in storage: selector-named consecutive fields of proper storage location (and cell) parts. We shall soon see that not all *type names* need be given *concrete models*.

The *record type* forming type constructor looks something like:

```
record(* *,* *,...,* *)
```

where the first * of the replicated pairs of * * are thought of as places into which one can insert distinct *record field selector identifiers*, and where the second * (of the replicated pairs) are similarly thought of as places into which one can insert not necessarily distinct type names or, more generally, type expressions.

The *array type* forming type constructor looks something like:

```
array[*..*,*..*,...,*..*]  of  *
```

where the first, respectively second * of the replicated pairs of * * are places where one can insert integer-valued expressions designating lower, respectively upper, bounds for respective dimensions of the array, and where the last *, after the keyword of, is a placeholder for a type expression.

Apart from the storage space allocation, with its possible constraints on layout,[2] the above type and value concepts are to be found in well-nigh any

---

[2]Such constraints could, for example, be: vector arrays are consecutively laid out in storage from "higher addresses down"; matrix arrays have first dimension elements referred to as columns, and second-dimension elements as rows; and are

abstract specification language, and hence in RSL. We consider the examples given to be those of concrete data structures, whereas what we shall initially be modelling (in domain specifications and in requirements prescriptions) are information structures. We consider data to be computerised representations of information. That is, in domain specification and requirements prescription we abstract from any storage representation. But otherwise we shall have great use for types, and for typed variable names (even though we shall mostly be using nonassignable, that is applicative or functional programming, variables).

5.4 Sorts or Abstract Types

We now turn to type issues, not of programming languages, but of specification languages. Most specification languages offer built-in types such as integers, Booleans and characters. Such built-in type names usually stand for *atomic types,* that is, for types of values which are atomic, in other words, those for which it is not meaningful to decompose the value into proper part values. Some specification languages, typically the primarily model-oriented ones, say RSL, VDM-SL and Z, offer type constructors not unlike the `record` and `array` constructs, to build composite types from other, already existing or defined types. We shall in this section only introduce the Cartesian type constructor.

A number of specification languages, archetypically the algebraic ones, Cafe-OBJ [192, 234] and CASL [398], allow the introduction of *abstract types* or *sorts. Sorts* are types for which no model (say, in terms of sets, Cartesians, functions, etc.) has been explicitly suggested:

type
    A, B, C

The *sorts* A, B and C are named, but no further definition is given.

We have introduced a bit of RSL syntax: The keyword **type** signals to the reader that what follows — before other such keywords — are type declarations. The above-illustrated type declarations introduced the names A, B and C, as names of types. To help you think of the *sorts* A, B and C, we suggest that you imagine them as spaces (i.e., sets) of values of type A, B or C.

It may turn out, now or later, in your considerations, that a sort is either atomic, or it is composite. In the latter case, its values can be analysed into proper constituent parts (i.e., values) of specific component types.

---

to be laid out row-orderwise, that is, they are laid out consecutively, first row first, etc., and again from "higher addresses down".

5.5 Built-in and Concrete Types

The RSL type concept will be introduced in stages. We have already introduced some parts of the concept above. We will introduce some more now, and then, throughout the next many chapters, we will introduce even more. For now, we ask you to simply think of a type as a set, possibly an infinite set, of values, i.e., of entities of some kind.

We need some syntax to name and to define types:

[0] **type**
[1]   I = **Int**, B = **Bool**, C = **Char**
[2]   P, Q, R
[3]   K = P × Q × R

Int, Bool and **Char** are *literals*. They are built-in names; they come with RSL. They name, respectively, disjoint sets of integers, Booleans and characters. P, Q and R are user-defined *type names*. They denote *sorts*, i.e., *abstract types*. K is a user-defined *type name*. It denotes a set of Cartesians, i.e., of products, or "three-groupings", of *values* of respective *sorts*. The RSL form:

[4] **value**
[5]   p,p′,...,p″:P, q,q′,...,q″:Q, r,r′,...,r″:R

designates a set of bindings. The identifiers p,p′,... and p″ are all distinct and designate arbitrary (nondeterministically chosen) values of *type* P. Similarly, the identifiers q,q′,... and q″ are all distinct and designate arbitrary (nondeterministically chosen) values of *type* Q, and the identifiers r,r′,... and r″ are all distinct and designate arbitrary (nondeterministically chosen) values of *type* R.

The value bindings (in line [10]):

[6] **type**
[7]   A, B
[8]   L = A × B × ... × C
[9] **value**
[10]   (a,b,...,c),(a′,b′,...,c′),(a″,b″,...,c″), ..., (a‴,b‴,...,c‴):L

bind the free and distinct names a, a′, ..., a″, b, b′, ..., b″, c, c′, ... and c″ to arbitrary values of respective types. The *types* K and L stand for Cartesian values.[3]

Let us comment on the bits and pieces of syntax that have been introduced in lines [0..10]. In this case it is RSL syntax. The keyword **type** [0,6] expresses that what follows are type names or type definitions. In [1], the first line after the keyword **type**, we show three *concrete type definitions*; in [2], the

---

[3]The use of ellipses, . . . , is metalinguistic: RSL expressions do not allow for the use of ellipses such as in ordinary mathematics.

second line, we show three *abstract type definitions*, that is, *sort definitions;* and in [3], the last line, we again show a *concrete type definition*. The first three *concrete type definitions*, [1], merely give other names (namely I, B, C) to **Int**eger, **Bool**ean, respectively **Char**acter types. The *concrete type definition*, [3], K=P×Q×R, gives the name K to the Cartesian types P×Q×R. The *infix* × symbol is similar to the *distributed-fix* record (, ,...,) type constructor. That is, × is a Cartesian type constructor, and similarly for line [8].

The keyword **value**, [4,6], expresses that what follows, first [5], are usually *typed names of values:* p,p′,...,p″, and thus are distinct names which stand for not necessarily distinct values, all of type P, etc.

The composite bindings, [10], (a, b, ..., c), (a′, b′, ..., c′), (a″, b″, ..., c″), ... and (a‴, b‴, ..., c‴) express that the individual values of (unprimed, single or multiply primed) a, b, c's are grouped into Cartesian (or product, or grouping, or record, or structure) values. That is, to repeat: We shall use the terms: *Cartesians, products, groupings, records,* and *structures* synonymously.

5.6 Type Checking

The idea of associating types with identifiers is twofold: to inform the reader as to the intentional use of the identifiers, while at the same time to allow a specification language processor, a type checker, to analyse whether incorrect uses are made of the typed identifiers. We shall briefly examine the last proposition.

5.6.1 Typed Variables and Expressions

Let us consider the following program fragment, from Sect. 5.3:

```
[0]     var i integer    := 7,
[1]         b Boolean    := true,
[2]         c character := 'd';
        . . .
[3]     type r =
[4]       record (i integer,
[5]               b Boolean,
[6]               a array[1..4,1..2] of char)
        . . .
[7]     var p r;
        . . .
[8]     i := i + 1;
[9]     b := (if i > p.i then true else false end);
[10]    p.i := p.i + i;
```

The above expressions and statements seem pretty innocent!

5.6.2 Type Errors

If in line [9] we had written b*7, or if in line [10] we had written if b > p.a, or if in line [11] we had written p.i := c, then, somehow, we could argue that something was wrong.

What is wrong?

In line [9] (now with b*7) b is known as a Boolean, and one cannot multiply with Boolean-valued operands. In line [10] (now with if b > p.a) b is (still) known as a Boolean, and p.a is known as a character, and one cannot compare Booleans and characters. In line [11] (now with p.i := c) p.i is known as an integer-valued variable, and c is known as a character-valued variable, and one cannot assign characters to integer variables.

Example 5.6 *Well-formed Roadnets:* We continue the roadnet Example 5.1 on page 74 and 5.2 on page 75.

We exemplify two kinds of type constraints for which an appropriate roadnet must be checked.

(1) If, by a roadnet we meant one in which no roads were isolated then the characterisation of Example 5.1 on page 74 must be sharpened: (1') The roadnet must be such that from any connector one can reach any other connector (of the same roadnet). (1'') Another way of formulating this is: The roadnet graph must not deteriorate into two or more isolated subgraphs. Isolation in the above sense hinges on all roads being two way roads.

(2) If, by a roadnet we meant one in which non-cul-de-sac segments were either one-way or two-way segments, then the characterisation of Example 5.1 on page 74 must be extended to ensure nonisolation: (2') cul-de-sacs are all two-way segments, and (2'') any other segment is either a one-way segment or a two-way segment. (2''') From any connector one can reach any other connector (of the same roadnet), only by following the direction of the connected segments. (That is: A one way segment has a single direction.) ∎

5.6.3 Detection of Type Errors

Having "annotated" various variables with types we can deduce which operators, indexing and assignments seem correct, and which do not. This is called type checking. We shall later, much later in these volumes, define, more properly what is meant by *is known to be of type*, and how to assess such knowledge. That is, we shall show how to formalise and possibly automate certain type checks.

Many computer scientists and software engineers consider the concept of type to only be related to, i.e., motivated, by type checking. We shall take a broader view: Type checking is important to catch specification mistakes early. But abstracting in terms of sorts and concrete types is also considered important, because it focuses the mind.

5.7 Types as Sets, Types as Lattices

In this chapter we have treated types as sets of values. This is often a reasonable way of modelling types, but not always. When a type, D, is expected to include the space of functions from D into D, then a set-theoretic treatment does not suffice. It would simply not be able to explain the meaning of the type equation:

$$D = D \rightarrow D$$

To solve such equations as $D = D \rightarrow D$ one may need to impose, for example, an ordering amongst the "type set" elements, called the "type domain". We shall just hint at this type theory here. It is a type theory in the sense of being able to solve arbitrary type equations. That is, to give proper meaning to reflexive function types is a hallmark of computer science. Dana Scott founded type theory in the sense hinted at above [251, 458–462, 464, 466–468]. We refer to [241, 282, 424, 532] for introductions to type theory.

5.8 Summary

This completes our first coverage of the RSL type concept. It is the naming of *basic, primitive*, that is, *built-in types* (**Int, Bool, Char**), which all stand for *concrete*, in this case *atomic types*. We also covered the definition of *abstract types*, that is, *sorts*, and the definition of *concrete, composite types*, in this case Cartesians (record, products, groupings, structures), by means of the *infix type constructor* ×.

We shall, throughout these volumes, introduce further aspects of the RSL type concept. Section 6.5.2 enlarges upon the type concept.

5.9 Exercises

♣ **Note:** The next three exercises, 5.1, 5.2 on the next page and 5.3 on the facing page share the same three 'Common Exercise Topics'. Hence they are marked ♣. See Appendix Sect. A.1, *Transportation Net*, Sect. A.2, *Container Logistics*, and Sect. A.3, *Financial Service Industry*. We also refer to Sect. 5.2 and to Examples 5.1 on page 74 and 5.2 on page 75. The exercises of this chapter are in line with the referenced section and examples.

Exercise 5.1. ♣ *Atomic Entities of the Transportation Net, Container Logistics, or Financial Service Industry Domain.*

1. Identify (i.e., name) a number of possible atomic entities.
2. For each entity identify (i.e., name) a number of attributes.
3. For each named attribute identify its possible values.

Exercise 5.2. ♣ *Composite Entities of the Transportation Net, Container Logistics, or Financial Service Industry Domain.* We refer to Exercise 5.1 on the preceding page (above). The questions below refer to the same physical phenomenon, either in the *Transportation Net, Container Logistics,* or *Financial Service Industry* domain.

1. Identify (i.e., name) some possible composite entities.
2. For some such (distinct kind of) entity list its component (i.e., sub-)entities.
3. For some composite component (i.e., sub-)entity list its component (i.e., subsub-)entities, etcetera.
4. For some composite component entity identify (i.e., name) a number of composite component attributes.
5. For some such named composite component entity attribute identify its possible composite component values.

Exercise 5.3. ♣ *Type Checking Entity Descriptions of the Transportation Net, Container Logistics, or Financial Service Industry Domain.* We refer to Exercises 5.1 on the facing page and 5.2. The questions below refer to the same physical phenomenon, either in the *Transportation Net, Container Logistics,* or *Financial Service Industry* domain.

1. *Atomic Entity Attribute Value Constraints.* Recall Question 3 on the facing page of Exercise 5.1. Can you think of some type check that has to be performed when presented with some possible atomic entity attribute values? Please list some such. Hint: The constraint on the value of an atomic entity attribute may to be formulated relative to the values of some other (atomic or composite) attributes.
2. *Composite Entity Attribute Value Constraints.* Recall Question 2 of Exercise 5.2. Can you think of some type check that has to be performed when presented with some possible composite entity attribute values? Please list some such. Hint: The constraint on the value of a composite entity attribute may to be formulated relative to the values of some other (atomic or composite) attributes.

6

Functions

- The **prerequisite** for studying this chapter is that you understand the notions of sets and Cartesians as covered in earlier chapters.
- The **aim** is to introduce you to the mathematical concept of functions such as we understand it in computing science and software engineering.
- The **objective** is to enable the reader to use and handle that concept of functions, with ease, in order to achieve one of the most important aspects of software development, namely abstraction. We shall endeavour to ensure that the reader learns to think in terms of mathematical functions.
- The **treatment** is from systematic to semiformal.

> The function concept, such as we shall introduce and use it, is a mathematical concept. It is, next to types, of paramount importance. Nobody has ever seen a function. Mathematical functions can be "observed" through their being *applied* to *argument values* and *yielding result values*.

Characterisation. By a *function* we understand a mathematical entity that can be *applied* to an *argument* (i.e., an entity) and then *yields*, i.e., *results*, in a *value* "of the function of that argument". ∎

To speak of spaces (or classes, or types) of functions and relations we need the type concept, first illustrated in Chap. 5. In Chap. 8 we shall cover the concept of algebras, but to do so we need the concept of functions. That explains our sequence: first types, then functions and relations, and then algebras.

  Some presentations of the concepts of functions and relations start with relations, and then bring in functions later. We shall start with functions because we find introducing functions first, in a software engineering setting,[1] more natural, and relations could, in this context, be considered a "mechanical" means of explaining functions. If this reasoning puzzles you, then read on and return, after having read the present chapter, to reread this paragraph.

---

[1] We will be dealing more, throughout these volumes, with functions than with relations.

Example 6.1 *Example of Everyday Functions:* We refer to Example 5.1 on page 74 and 5.2 on page 75 of Sect. 5.2.

Let S, C and V name the types of segments, connectors and vehicles. Let, accordingly, suitably decorated lower case versions of these type names stand for segment, connector and vehicle values. Let N name the type of roadnets. Thus n stands for specific nets. From, or in, a roadnet one can observe its segments and connectors. Now let any segment, as a composite entity include the values of zero, one or more vehicles (on that segment). Similarly for connectors. That is, from a segment and from a connector one can observe the set of vehicles on that road (respectively in that intersection). To "observe" is to apply a function to an argument value and obtain a result value.

type
  N, S, C, V, Si, Ci, Vi
value
  obs_Ss: N $\rightarrow$ S-set
  obs_Cs: N $\rightarrow$ C-set
  obs_Vs: (S|C) $\rightarrow$ V-set
  obs_Cis: S $\rightarrow$ Ci-set
  obs_Sis: C $\rightarrow$ Si-set

From a segment one can observe the identity of the two connectors it is connected to. From a connector one can observe the set of identities of segments leading to (and from) that connector.

When driving a vehicle on a segment, to enter that vehicle into a connector is to perform a function. Likewise when leaving a connector and entering a segment.

value
  enter: S $\times$ V $\times$ C $\xrightarrow{\sim}$ S $\times$ C
  enter(s,v,c) **as** (s',c')
  pre: v $\in$ obs_Vs(s) $\wedge$ v $\notin$ obs_Vs(c)
  post: v $\notin$ obs_Cs(s') $\wedge$ v $\in$ obs_Vs(c') $\wedge$
          obs_Cs(s') = obs_Cs(s)\{v} $\wedge$ obs_Vs(c') = obs_Vs(c) $\cup$ {v}

  leave: C $\times$ V $\times$ S $\xrightarrow{\sim}$ C $\times$ S
  leave(c,v,s) **as** (c',s') ...

Entering a vehicle, v, from a segment, s, into a connector, c, results in changing the segment and connector values into s', c'. The vehicle value is unchanged, hence not mentioned as a result value. The only difference in the before, s, and after value, s', of the segment is that the segment no longer "contains" vehicle v, with the reverse being true for the connector. ∎

The gist of Chaps. 12–18 is to explain the kind of abstractions exemplified above, while the gist of the present chapter is to introduce you to the basic notion of functions, f, that is, those things whose value was expressed above as **type** f: A → B.

6.1 General Overview

We shall first place the concept of a function in context and present some intuitive notions of functions: function definitions, maps (i.e., function graphs), types and attributes. Then we shall "restart" by presenting an attempt at informally motivating *"how functions come about"*.

Structure of This Chapter

Three indispensable topics occupy this chapter: (1) the function algebra: what functions "really" are, function space type constructors, function attributes (nondeterministic, constant, and strictness) and operations (abstraction, application, composition, definition, respectively range set); (2) Currying[2]; and (3) relations as models of functions.

6.1.1 Special Remarks

Different ways of looking at functions will be introduced:

(a) functions which can be defined syntactically,
(b) functions whose meanings are mathematical functions, and
(c) functions whose syntax and meaning are "one and the same thing".

These three facets (a–c) should emerge from items below. There are (i) functions which (i.a) can be defined syntactically, as textual entities (see function definitions, Sect. 6.2.2) and (i.b) where these syntactical forms have a semantics, or a meaning, which resembles the functions known from mathematics (see function maps (graphs), Sect. 6.2.2 on the following page). Furthermore (ii) there are functions which (ii.a) can, again, be defined syntactically, but (ii.c) which can be given a "syntactic" meaning by a set of *rewriting rules* that "massage" (edit, translate) these syntactic expressions into syntactic expressions of the same form (Chap. 7).

To repeat: There are two different syntactic function expression forms, and two different notions of functions: one syntactic, the other mathematical. We also introduce the mathematical concept of *relations*. Relations are then used to explain the abstract concept of functions.

---

[2]The term Currying derives from the name of the American mathematician Haskell B. Curry.

6.2 The Issues

We start by placing the notion of functions in both a mathematical context and a programming language context. We proceed to informally present some easy-to-understand notions of function definitions, function "maps" (graphs), function types and attributes of functions, that is, special classes of functions.

6.2.1 Background

In mathematics we use and define functions. The sine and cosine functions of trigonometry were used and were (as we shall see, axiomatically) defined by their properties before we, in numerical mathematics, learned to approximate their computation through suitably defined functions. And in programming we define and use functions only we may call them by some other names: procedures, routines, methods, etc. In this section we shall take a first look at the kind of functions that we shall be dealing with in these volumes the functions that we wish to be abstract counterparts of the procedures or methods of programming languages; and the functions that we wish to represent the meaning (the denotations) of described phenomena of some actual world, or of requirements-prescribed phenomena.

Functions are obviously fundamental to any understanding of computing, and, we shall argue, to any understanding of the actual world around us! Functions, in mathematics, are not just abstract notions. They sometimes need be computed, whether, as in the old days, by hand, through *reckoning*, or, as now, by computers, through *computation*. The function concept that we focus mostly on in this section ties the above together: The definable as well as the denoting functions, that is, the mathematical functions. We do not necessarily focus on those for which we can devise an algorithm for their computation, but on functions in general.

6.2.2 Some Concepts of Functions

We shall, in turn, treat ideas of function definitions, function "maps" (i.e., function graphs), function types and classes of functions.

Function Definitions

Characterisation. By a *function definition* we shall understand a text, say, $f(a) \equiv \mathcal{E}(a)$, which states the name, f, of the function, the name of an archetypical argument (or argument list), a, a definition symbol, $\equiv$, and a *body*, $\mathcal{E}(a)$, which is usually some clause (expression or statement) in which the argument, a, is free. ∎

First some example formal function definitions and some intuition.

Example 6.2 *Two Function Definitions:* You are familiar with the factorial and the Fibonacci functions. These two functions are chosen only as examples. In RSL we might express these functions as follows:

type	**value**
Nat1 = {| n:**Nat** • n$\geq$1 |}	fib: Nat1 $\to$ Nat1
value	fib(n) $\equiv$
fact: Nat1 $\to$ Nat1	**case** n **of:**
fact(n) $\equiv$	1 $\to$ 1,
if n=1	2 $\to$ 1,
then 1	_ $\to$ fib(n$-$2)+fib(n$-$1)
else n∗fact(n$-$1)	**end**
end	

The "underline" (wildcard) symbol stands for the "otherwise" alternative. ∎

Since the above formulas represent another early occurrence of some formal RSL text, let us "read" these definitions "aloud":

Nat1 is the set of natural numbers larger than or equal to 1, i.e., **Nat**, but excluding 0. (We say that Nat1 is a proper subtype of **Nat**.) Both factorial and Fibonacci, as identifiers, denote functions (as indicated by the right arrow: $\to$), and they both take natural numbers as arguments and yield non-zero natural numbers as results (as indicated by the left and right Nat1s). The factorial function definition body expresses that if the argument is one then the result is one, otherwise the result is the value of the product of the argument and the factorial of an argument which is one smaller than the original argument. The situation is similar for the Fibonacci function definition. Its body expresses that if the argument is one, then the result is one, otherwise, if the argument is two, then the result is (also) one, otherwise,[3] i.e., for all other larger values of the argument, the result is the sum of the "two previous Fibonacci numbers"! Thus the first and the second Fibonacci numbers are both 1.

Now to some RSL syntax: The keyword **value** signals, to the reader, that RSL bindings of identifiers to values now follow.[4] The names being bound are here fact and Fib. These names are bound in this case to function values. Thus we here have two *function definitions* each consisting of a pair of clauses: the *function signature* and the *function definition* proper. The former consists of the function name and a function space type expression, usually a type expression that contains (at least) one infix function space type constructor, either $\to$ or $\overset{\sim}{\to}$. The latter consists, in the above example, of a triple: (i) a *function*

---

[3]The "otherwise" is designated by the "wildcard" symbol _.

[4]An abstract **type** clause: **type** A, or a concrete **type** clause: **type** A = ... designates a binding of type identifiers to sorts, respectively concrete types (i.e., value spaces).

name and a possibly empty list of arguments enclosed in parentheses,[5] (ii) the identity symbol ≡, which separates the *function definition header* from (iii) the *function definition body*, which is always an RSL expression — here both are simple conditional expressions.

The reason for presenting the above two function definition examples is now to relate them, still as examples, to an informal concept of function "maps".

Function "Maps" (Graphs)

Characterisation. By a *function* "*map*" we understand, loosely, the set of pairs, (a, r), of all those function arguments, a, for which the function is defined and then yields a result value r.   ∎

We use the terms function "map" and function graph interchangeably. We deliberately use quotation marks around the term map here. Unquoted map references shall, later, designate a special kind of functions. That is, functions for which the *definition set* can be computed. A *function definition set* is the set of argument values for which the function is defined.

Figure 6.1 on the next page illustrates two function "maps".[6] They purport to illustrate how *arguments* of the *definition sets*, "under" the *functions*, *map into*, i.e., *yield results* of the *range (range set)*, or *image (image set)* of the *functions*.

The idea of the function "map" (graph) is to visualise that specific elements of the definition set "map" into specific elements of the range set. Please refer to the definition of the **factorial** and the **Fibonacci** functions (Example 6.2) in order to see that the function "maps" of Fig. 6.1 "correspond to", i.e., visualise fragments of these functions.

Later we shall see examples where there are elements of what is claimed to be the definition set for which the function "map" prescribes no corresponding range element (Fig. 6.3). We refer to the question symbol **?** of the injective, partial function and the surjective, likewise partial function.

Types of Function Spaces and Function Signatures

This is the first of two sections on function types. The presentation is informal, and short. The subsequent (Sect. 6.5.2) is a bit more systematic. Here we

---

[5]The parentheses (...) surrounding two or more arguments effectively compose these into a Cartesian. RSL does not provide for one element Cartesians. Hence a function invocation expression $f(a)$ could as well be written $f\ a$. The parentheses in $f(a)$ are merely there for disambiguation should one happen to write fa but mean $f\ a$ (i.e., $f(a)$).

[6]The figure title of Fig. 6.1 lists names of functions in double quotes. As is common practice, we use double quotes to signal that we do not quite mean what the quote says! In the case of Fig. 6.1 the pictures only purport to show something: They *are not the functions* named, only "pictures" of fragments of them!

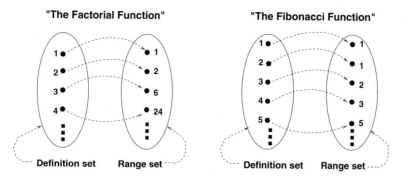

Fig. 6.1. Concrete function "maps" (i.e., graphs)

outline our form of writing down type expressions for functions spaces. Later we will assume this intuition.

The two function "maps" of Fig. 6.1 both contain three elements: the function definition sets, the function range sets and the function "map arrows" (the graph arrows, i.e., the "map" set of the function). These three are summarised in Fig. 6.2.

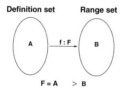

Fig. 6.2. Function Types

The notation B^A is sometimes used to designate the function space $A{\to}B$. If $|X|$ expresses the "cardinality" of the set X then $|B|^{|A|}$ expresses the "cardinality" of the set B^A.[7]

These three elements naturally form the basis for our linguistic way of expressing function spaces:

$$A \to B, \quad \textbf{type } F = A \to B$$

The *type expression* A → B denotes the *space* of all *total functions* from *definition set* A into (or onto) *range set* B. The *type definition* F = A → B "assigns" the *identifier* F as the *type name* for that space of functions. The form: F = A → B is also called the *signature* of a function, or its *function signature*.

---

[7]Of course, if either of the cardinalities are infinite, then it really does not make sense to talk of a cardinality, hence the double quotes.

Classes of Functions

Functions whose results are *truth values* are called *predicate functions* and the others just *functions* (optionally, of *nontruth value result types*).

Without detailing what the specific functionalities could be, we can "picture" some other functions (Fig. 6.3). By the *definition set* of a function we mean the set, $A' \subseteq A$, of exactly all the arguments for which a function is defined. By the *image* (or *range*) of a function we mean the set, $B' \subseteq B$, of exactly all the result values for defined arguments. A function which is not defined for all values of its postulated definition set is a *partial function*. We syntactically express the space of all total and partial functions from definition set A into (or onto) range set B by $A \tilde{\rightarrow} B$.

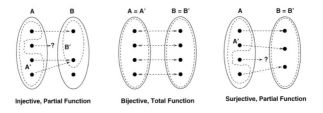

Injective, Partial Function   Bijective, Total Function   Surjective, Partial Function

Fig. 6.3. Conceptual function "maps" (i.e., graphs)

A function which maps values of its postulated definition set into some, but not all elements of its range is an *injective function*. A function which maps values of its postulated definition set into all elements of its range is a *surjective function*. A function which is *surjective* and which maps all definition set elements (i.e., a function which is a *total function*) into distinct range elements is a *bijective function*.

6.3 How Do Functions Come About?

In a few steps of reasoning we shall try motivate how functions come about! In the next paragraphs we first cover the concepts of (1) names and (2) values, including constant and variable names; (3) then the concepts of expressions, of expression evaluation and of free variables. And from that we (4) introduce the concepts of functions and abstracted functions. From this we, very cursorily, (5) mention the notions of function application, function result and the substitution of values for free variables. This sequence, from names, via expressions with free variables, to functions, thus motivates the concept of λ functions — to be more formally introduced in Chap. 7. So here we go!

(1–2) There are *names*, and names *designate values*, either *constant* or *variable*: 7, true, and "a", respectively i, b and c are examples of *constant*, respectively *variable, names.* [8] Some such constant or variable values are values like numbers, Booleans, characters, records or arrays of these etc. Thus, 7, true, "a", r(i:7,b:true,c:"a"), and <1,2,3,5,8,13> are example constant value expressions. Other such constant or variable values are function values like addition (of numbers) +, subtraction -, etc., or conjunction (of Booleans) ∧, disjunction ∨, list concatenation ˆ, etc. Thus: +, -, ∧, ∨, and ˆ, respectively, are example function names. When written as shown, as noncharacter symbols, we call them operator names or operator symbols or just operators, or, if Boolean, we call them connectives.

(3) There are *expressions,* and expressions are built up from constant or variable names and delimiters (such as, for example, (,), >, < and ,), and such expressions designate values: i+7, <"a">ˆ<1,2,3,5,8,13>, and a∧true. If all expression names designate constant values, then the expression designates, i.e., *evaluates*[9] to, a constant value. If one or more names of an expression designate variable values, such as i in i+7, or a in a ∧ true, or p and q in <1,p,3,q,8,13>, then we say that they are *free variables* in those expressions.

(4) Expressions, typically with free variables — generally written: $\mathcal{E}(x, y, \ldots, z)$, where x, y and z are the free variables of expression $\mathcal{E}(x, y, \ldots, z)$ — *denote*[10] a function. That is, a function from values (eg. α, β and γ) that can be associated with x, y, respectively z, to the value of the (constant) expression where α, β and γ have been substituted for x, y, respectively z. We say that the expression has been *(function) abstracted* and that the expression constitutes the *body* in the *abstracted function.* An example is: If α and β are the values 7 and 9, respectively, and are associated with p and q in <1,p,3,q,8,13>, then the value of <1,p,3,q,8,13> becomes $\langle 1, 7, 3, 9, 8, 13 \rangle$.[11]

(5) We express by: $\lambda x \bullet \lambda y \bullet \ldots \lambda x \bullet \mathcal{E}(x, y, \ldots, z)$ *"the function of $x, y, \ldots, z$ which when applied to arguments $\alpha, \beta, \ldots, \gamma$, yields the value of $\mathcal{E}(x, y, \ldots, z)$ where $\alpha, \beta, \ldots, \gamma$ have (first) been substituted for $x, y, \ldots, z$ in $\mathcal{E}(x, y, \ldots, z)$."* $\mathcal{E}(x, y, \ldots, z)$ is the *body* of the function expression $\lambda x \bullet \lambda y \bullet \ldots \lambda x \bullet \mathcal{E}(x, y, \ldots, z)$

---

[8]We have written in *italic* those terms which stand for computing science concepts. We have written in `teletype font` those terms which stand for examples. Having done this in the introductory lines we shall only, in this section, use these type fonts when introducing new concepts.

[9]See Sect. 6.4 for an informal explanation of the term *evaluate.*

[10]We have used the two terms *designate* and *denote* almost interchangeably: We use *designate* when an *evaluation* should lead to what one would normally consider the value (of the expression). And we use *denote* when an *evaluation* should lead, not to such a value, but to a function from contexts into such values — where the contexts associate variables to values.

[11]Observe our two uses of digits: The syntactic use expressed in the `teletype` `font`: 0, 1, 2, ..., 9, and the semantic use which is expressed in the mathematical font: $0, 1, 2, \ldots, 9$, and the two uses of 'angles': The < and > in expressions, and the $\langle \ldots \rangle$ in value forms as if we could "write" values! We cannot, of course, but use numerals to speak of numbers, etc.

Thus functions arise from free variable names of expressions. To summarise the above: From (1) constant names we abstracted to (2) variables, from there to (3) expressions over constants and variables, and from there to (4) functions. The latter were seen as abstractions of expressions with free variables. It is on this basis that, in Chap. 7, we introduce the "pure" λ-calculus. Notice that the λx in $\lambda x \cdot \mathcal{E}(x)$ makes us say: *"the function of x that when applied to an argument a yields a value as denoted by $\mathcal{E}(a)$".*

6.4 An Aside: On the Concept of Evaluation

We cover, briefly, concepts of evaluation, interpretation and elaboration; examples of function evaluation (etc.); and the concept of function application (i.e., invocation).

6.4.1 [E]Valuation, Interpretation and Elaboration

In the previous section we mentioned the term *evaluate*. The concept of *evaluation* applies to *syntactic* quantities and can be thought of as a *procedure*, or as a *metafunction*, which is applied to a *syntactic construct*, and usually something we call its *semantic context*, and which then *yields* a *value*. That is, if we wish to find the value of an expression, then we evaluate the expression. If the expression contains variables, then we need look up, somewhere, namely in the *semantic context*, to find the value of these variables. Usually we shall use the term *environment*[12] in lieu of the term *semantic context*.

Other words for *evaluate* (*evaluation*) are *valuate* (*valuation*), *interpret* (*interpretation*), and *elaborate* (*elaboration*). Much later in these volumes we shall distinguish between these three terms. Meanwhile, we refer the reader to the present volume index.

6.4.2 Two Evaluation Examples

Examples help.

Example 6.3 *Function Evaluations:* The Fibonacci function as given in Example 6.2 can be represented as a set of argument/result value pairs, i.e., as a relation, as implied by Fig. 6.1:

$$\{(1,1), (2,1), (3,2), (4,3), (5,5), (6,8), \ldots\}$$

---

[12]Note that we now use the term environment in two senses in these volumes: (i) as above, for a semantic context in which free variables are associated with values, and (ii) as the context, in some domain, in which some machine, i.e., some computing system (hardware + software) is placed and with which that machine interacts.

Correspondingly, we can talk of two bases of evaluating the Fibonacci function. Based on the relational representation above we can very informally sketch one form of evaluation by:

fib = {(1,1),(2,1),(3,2),(4,3),(5,5),(6,8),...}

evaluate(fib,4) =

evaluate({(1,1),(2,1),(3,2),(4,3),(5,5),(6,8),...},4) =

select the pair (i,j)
whose first element ≡ 4
and yield its second element, here 3

We shall later return to this form of function representation (Sect. 6.7). We shall call the above form of evaluation a *relation search*. Based on the function definition in Sect. 6.2 we can likewise, without much explanation and thus very informally sketch another form of evaluation. In the present form we replace invocation text, viz., fib(i), for some (constant) i, with the function definition body text where the function argument, n, has been replaced by the constant i:

fib(4) =
  case 4 **of:** 1 → 1, 2 → 1, _ → fib(2) + fib(3) **end**
  =
  fib(2) + fib(3) =
  case 2 **of:** 1 → 1, 2 → 1, _ → fib(0) + fib(1) **end** +
  case 3 **of:** 1 → 1, 2 → 1, _ → fib(1) + fib(2) **end**
  =
  1 + fib(1) + fib(2)
  =
  1 +
  case 1 **of:** 1 → 1, 2 → 1, _ → fib(−1) + fib(0) **end** +
  case 2 **of:** 1 → 1, 2 → 1, _ → fib(0) + fib(1) **end**
  =
  1 + 1 + 1
  =
  3

We shall later have more to say about this form of combined syntactic rewriting and simple arithmetic and Boolean test expression calculation. We shall call this form of evaluation *symbolic interpretation*.

6.4.3 Function Invocation/"Function Call"

We have used the term function application. Above, in the informal function evaluation examples, we saw what application might imply: some form of evaluation. The examples show several examples of function applications, or, as we shall also call them, function invocations, or function calls:

> evaluate(relation,argument), or
> fib(4),fib(3),fib(2),fib(1),fib(0),fib(−1),fib(−2),...

In Example 6.3, *evaluation by relation search* is a metainvocation: In other words, the metalinguistic evaluator function **evaluate** "simulates" the application of the function representation **relation** to the function argument **argument**:

> `relation`(`argument`)

By *function application* we understand the mathematical phenomenon of applying a function, as a mathematical quantity, to an argument of its definition set, also mathematical quantities. By *function invocation*, or *function call*, we understand the same: namely the first step in simulating or evaluating the "application of a function". By *symbolic function evaluation*, we understand the "sequence of things" that goes on, as shown in the syntactic rewriting and simple arithmetic and Boolean test expression calculations shown above for the Fibonacci example (Example 6.3).

6.5 Function Algebras

We can summarise a number of things said earlier in this section on functions. That is, basically no new material is now presented, but a review of what we shall need in the future is given. We do so by presenting the notion of functions as an algebra. As we shall see in Chap. 8, an algebra consists of a set of values and a set of operations. To this we add a name for the algebra. In this section we shall treat these three issues in a permuted order: Values, names of algebras and operations.

6.5.1 Functions

The values of a function algebra is the space of all functions of that algebra. A *function* is that "mysterious thing" *which when applied to an argument of its definition set yields a result of its range set*. Nobody has ever seen a function — just as nobody has ever seen a number. Rather, these are mathematical entities that are characterised by their properties.

6.5.2 Function Types

First, we treat how we write down type expressions that denote function spaces, then how we express higher-order function types. We syntactically distinguish between total, $\rightarrow$, and partial, $\overset{\sim}{\rightarrow}$, functions:

Type expression: Type definition:

$\quad$ A → B   **type**
$\quad$ A $\overset{\sim}{\to}$ B $\quad$ TF = A → B
$\qquad\qquad\qquad\qquad\qquad\qquad\qquad$ PF = A $\overset{\sim}{\to}$ B

These are understood as follows: The type expressions A→B and A$\overset{\sim}{\to}$B are the composite names (i.e., signatures) of function algebras. The type names TF and PF are the simple names of function algebras. The fact that we write f = A $\overset{\sim}{\to}$ B amounts to typing the function f.

$\quad$ Thus → is an infix type constructor function: It takes two argument types (i.e., sets of values), A and B, and yields the space of all total functions from all of the definition set (i.e., type) A to within[13] the range set (i.e., within the type) B. And $\overset{\sim}{\to}$ is an infix type constructor function: It takes two argument types (i.e., sets of values), A and B, and yields the space of all partial functions from within the type A to within the range set (i.e., type) B. That is, there are (possibly different) values in A for which each function in A$\overset{\sim}{\to}$B is not defined.

$\quad$ Above we explained the → and $\overset{\sim}{\to}$ symbols semantically. Now we explain them syntactically: → is an infix operator. Its two operands are to be type expressions. Likewise for $\overset{\sim}{\to}$.

6.5.3 Higher-Order Function Types

Types A and/or B may themselves be function types:

type
$\quad$ A = P → Q
$\quad$ B = U → V
$\quad$ F = (P → Q) → (U → V) ≡ A → B

More generally, the type expressions:

$\quad$ A → B → C ≡ A → (B → C) ≠ (A → B) → C

That is, the infix function space type constructor associates to the right. Above we have used the ≡ and the ≠ operators in a metalinguistic sense: They look like RSL operators, but they are not. They are here to be understood as mathematical operators (since in RSL one cannot compare types).

6.5.4 Nondeterministic Functions

Let f and g be functions defined by:

---

[13]By within A we mean either all of A or a proper subset of A.

value
   m,n:**Nat**

   f: **Nat** $\overset{\sim}{\to}$ **Nat**, f(i) ≡ **let** j:**Nat** • j>i **in** i+j **end**
   ... f(7) ... f(9) ... f(13) ...

   g: **Real** → **Nat**, g(j) ≡ m
   ... g(1/**if** n=0 **then** 100000000000000 **else** n **end**) ... g(1/(1+n)) ...

where **Real** and **Nat** stand for the types of reals, respectively natural numbers, then we say that function f is *nondeterministic*. That is, it delivers an arbitrary, but some natural number, not necessarily the same for every invocation of f, but "skewed upward". Nondeterministic functions, from type A to type B are given the partial function signature: A $\overset{\sim}{\to}$ B.

6.5.5 Constant Functions

Function g (defined above) is a *constant function*. In the above definition of g, the definition relies on the nondeterministic definition of m; m may take on any natural number value. But m is defined only once. Thereafter it is a constant, hence g is a constant function. Constant functions, when invoked, each yield the same result value irrespective of their argument value(s), if any. Specifically:

type
   A
value
   a:A
   f: **Unit** → A, f() ≡ a

hints at the view that values of arbitrary type can be seen as constant functions:[14]

value
   zero, one, two, ..., nine: **Unit** → **Nat**
   zero() ≡ 0, one() ≡ 1, two() ≡ 2, ..., nine() ≡ 9
   tt, ff: **Unit** → **Bool**
   tt() ≡ **true**, ff() ≡ **false**

---

[14]The literal **Unit** designates the value (). It is used wherever we wish to define functions of no arguments. Invocation of such argumentless functions, f, is written f().

6.5.6 Strict Functions

Function g (defined above) is a *strict function:* It depends on whether the argument is defined, i.e., **chaos** — value m above could be 0 — or not. Note that g(**chaos**) = **chaos**. **chaos** is not a real number, hence the function signature is that of a total function.

RSL functions are all strict. The RSL **if .. then .. else .. end** operator is the only RSL operator (i.e., function) which is not strict:

type
    A, B, C
value
    h: A × B × C → D, p: A → **Bool**
    h(a,b,c) ≡ **if** p(a) **then** b **else** c **end**

If the language in which h is expressed is nonstrict, in other words is not RSL, then the result of a function h invocation depends on whether chaotic arguments are being evaluated in the body of the function. Argument c may thus be the totally undefined value (**chaos**). If the predicate function (p) invocation (p(a)) prevents, i.e., "circumvents" evaluation of argument c, then a function invocation f(a′,b′,c′) may still yield a defined result value. The above example generalises to any function of one or more arguments, i.e., of nonzero arity.

6.5.7 Strict Functions and Strict Function Invocation

A strict function is one which, no matter what its function definition body may prescribe, but when given any **chaos** valued argument, always yields the totally undefined value **chaos.** Programming languages with *Call-by-Value* have *function* (including procedure) *invocations* that are strict. Strict function invocation should not be confused with strict functions: Strict function invocation is a property, typically of programming languages, usually having the *Call-by-Value* property, whereas strict functions, typically in specification languages, usually have the *Call-by-Name* property. RSL has a *Call-by-Value* semantics.

6.5.8 Operations on Functions

So far we can speak of five operations which apply to or result in functions, three ([1–2–3]) that are "computable", and two ([4–5]) that are not. The computable functions are: ([1]) function abstraction, $\lambda x : X \cdot \mathcal{E}(x)$;[15] ([2]) function

---

[15]By the expression $\lambda x : X \cdot \mathcal{E}(x)$ we denote the function of x which when applied to arguments of type X yields values of the kind found by evauation of the body $\mathcal{E}(x)$. In Chap. 7 we introduce the λ-calculus.

application, •(•); and ([3]) function composition, •°•. (The symbol • indicates an argument placeholder.)

They (i.e., [1–3]) are "computable" in the sense that we can define and evaluate them. This computability still allows for evaluations that do not terminate. But whereas we can ([4]) speak of the definition set, $\mathcal{D}(•)$, and ([5]) speak of the range set, $\mathcal{R}(•)$, of functions, we can, in general, given a function, not compute these sets.

([6]) As we shall see later, we can add a sixth operation on functions: The fix point taking operation, **Y** (Sect. 7.8).

We can illustrate the above:

type
    $F = A \rightarrow B, G = B \rightarrow C, H = A \rightarrow C$
value
[1] λa:A•e
[2] (λa:A•e)(e′)

[3] f°g ≡ λa:A•g(f(a))
      pre $\mathcal{R}$f ⊆ $\mathcal{D}$g

[4] $\mathcal{D}$: F → A-**set**, G → B-**set**
[5] $\mathcal{R}$: F → B-**set**, G → C-**set**

A, B and C are arbitrary types, and F, G and H are function spaces.

[1] expresses the abstraction of expression e into an (unnamed) function; a may, or may not, be *free* in e. Given that evaluation of e for arguments replacing all free occurrences of a in e by any applied value yields a value of type B, the function is of type F. [2] expresses the application of such a function to an argument, expressed by expression e′. Given that evaluation of e for arguments replacing all free occurrences of a in e by the value of e′ yields a value of type B, the function result is of type B. [3] f°g expresses the composition of two functions. Provided the range of the first function, f, is a subset of the definition set of the second function, g, the result of the composition is defined, and is of type H. [4] $\mathcal{D}$ postulates a function that applies to (any type of) function and yields its definition set, while [5] $\mathcal{R}$ postulates a function that applies to (any type of) function and yields its range set.

The problem with [4–5] is that these functions are not "definable", that is, cannot be computed. It is not possible to decide, i.e., it is not decidable, given an arbitrary function, say in the form of its definition, which are exactly all the elements of its definition and range sets. But we can, in mathematics, speak of the definition set and the range set of a function.

6.6 Currying and λ-Notation

6.6.1 Currying

Sometimes we think of functions as being functions of more than one argument. We therefore, in function definitions, group these arguments into Cartesian structures.

Instead of writing:

type
  X, Y, Z, R, K = X×Y×Z
value
  f: X → Y → Z → R

we may write:

  f: X × Y × Z → R, or: f: K → R

And, instead of expression function application as:

  f(a)(b)(c),

for suitable a, b, and c, we may write:

  f(a,b,c),

or, if k is some Cartesian structure — like (a,b,c) — we may write:

  f(k).

6.6.2 λ-Notation

This subsection is a precursor for Chap. 7.

The following are equivalent ways of expressing function definitions in RSL:

type
  A, B, C
value
  f: A × B → C
  f(a,b) ≡ $\mathcal{E}$(a,b)

  f: A → B → C
  f(a)(b) ≡ $\mathcal{E}$(a,b)
  f(a) ≡ λb:B.$\mathcal{E}$(a,b)
  f ≡ λa:A.λb:B.$\mathcal{E}$(a,b)

That is: Moving a rightmost argument, y, "across" the definition symbol ≡, from a function header g(x)(...)(y), causes it to appear on the righthand side as a prefix, λy:Y., to the function definition body $\mathcal{E}$(x,...,y).[16]

---

[16]Recall an arithmetic (calculus) "analogue": $p \times q = r$ is the same as $p = r/q$ for $q \neq 0$.

6.6.3 Example of Currying and λ-Notation

Example 6.4 *Curryed and Uncurryed Function Definitions:* Let:

type
   X, Y, Z
   $K = X \times Y \times Z$

Next we look at various examples of expressing simple, explicit function definitions:

[1] **let** $f = \lambda x{:}X{\cdot}\lambda y{:}Y{\cdot}\lambda z{:}Z{\cdot}\mathcal{E}(x,y,z)$ **in** f(a)(b)(c) **end**
[2] **let** $f'(x)(y)(z) = \mathcal{E}(x,y,z)$ **in** f'(a)(b)(c) **end**
[3] **let** $g = \lambda(x,y,z){:}(X{\times}Y{\times}Z){\cdot}\mathcal{E}(x,y,z)$ **in** g(a,b,c) **end**
[4] **let** $g'(x,y,z) = \mathcal{E}(x,y,z)$ **in** g'(a,b,c) **end**
[5] **let** $g'' = \lambda(x,y,z){:}K{\cdot}\mathcal{E}(x,y,z)$ **in** g''(a,b,c) **end**
[6] **let** $g''' = \lambda k{:}K{\cdot}\mathcal{E}(k)$ **in** g'''(abc) **end**
[7] **let** $g''''(k) = \mathcal{E}(k)$ **in** g''''(abc) **end**
[8] **let** $h = \lambda(x,y){:}(X{\times}Y){\cdot}\lambda z{:}Z{\cdot}\mathcal{E}(x,y,z)$ **in** h(a,b)(c) **end**
[9] **let** $h'(x,y)(z) = \mathcal{E}(x,y,z)$ **in** h'(a,b)(c) **end**

The nine functions f, f', g, g', g'', g''', g'''', h and h', are meant to be identical due to the common function type and common body expression $\mathcal{E}(x,y,z)$. But $[\alpha - \beta]$ below, although the same function, is not a function of the same kind (i.e., type) as [8–9] above:

[α] **let** $h'' = \lambda x{:}X{\cdot}\lambda(y,z){:}(Y{\times}Z){\cdot}E(x,y,z)$ **in** h''(a)(b,c) **end**
[β] **let** $h'''(x)(y,z) = E(x,y,z)$ **in** h'''(a)(b,c) **end**.

This is so since the two types:

$$(X \times Y) \to Z, \quad \text{and} \quad X \to (Y \times Z)$$

are different. ∎

6.7 Relations and Functions

Characterisation. By a *relation* we shall understand a set of groupings of the same arity and component types. ∎

Example 6.5 *An Abstract Relation:* Let e_{i_j} for $1 \leq i \leq n$, then:

$$\left\{ \begin{array}{l} (e_{1_{1_1}}, e_{2_{1_2}}, \ldots, e_{n_{1_n}}), \\ (e_{1_{2_1}}, e_{2_{2_2}}, \ldots, e_{n_{2_n}}), \\ \cdots \quad \cdots \quad \cdots \quad \cdots \\ (e_{1_{m_1}}, e_{2_{m_2}}, \ldots, e_{n_{m_n}}) \end{array} \right\}$$

where each row designates a grouping, and the collection of rows designating a set could be generically a representation of a relation.   ∎

Typically we may define:

type
    D_1, ..., D_n
    T = D_1 × ... × D_n
    R = T-**set**

Any subset of R is now said to be a *relation*.

6.7.1 Predicates

We can now explain predicate functions, for example, of signature:

value
    p: D_1 × ... × D_n → **Bool**

as a finite or a possibly infinite subset, a relation, p_rel, of R:

    p_rel:R, e.g., p_rel = {(d_1,...,d_n),...,(d'_1,...,d'_n),...}
    p(r) ≡ **if** r ∈ p_rel **then true else false end** ≡ r ∈ p_rel

The type expressions **R-set** and **R-inset** denote the set of finite, respectively possibly infinite, subsets of R, also known as the *power set* of R.

6.7.2 Function Evaluation by Relation Search

We can thus explain a function (from, for example, D_1 × ... × D_n into D) as a relation, f_rel, over D_1 × ... × D_n × D:

type
    F = D_1 × ... × D_n × D
value
    f_rel:F-**inset**, e.g.: $\{(d_1, ..., d_n, d), ..., (d'_1, ..., d'_n, d')\}$

    f: D_1 × ... × D_n $\overset{\sim}{\to}$ D
    f(r) ≡
        if ∃ (d_1,...,d_n,d):F•(d_1,...,d_n,d) ∈ f_rel∧r=(d_1,...,d_n)
           then
               let (d_1,...,d_n,d):F•(d_1,...,d_n,d) ∈ f_rel∧r=(d_1,...,d_n)
               in d **end**
           else chaos end

6.7.3 Nondeterministic Functions

An n-ary nondeterministic function, f, is now a function for which several groupings in f_rel have the same first n-grouping:

value
    is_nondeterministic: **F-infset** $\rightarrow$ **Bool**
    is_nondeterministic(f_rel) $\equiv$
        $\exists$ (d_1,...,d_n,d),(d'_1,...,d'_n,d'):F •
            {(d_1,...,d_n,d),(d'_1,...,d'_n,d')} $\subseteq$ f_rel $\wedge$
            (d_1,...,d_n) = (d'_1,...,d'_n) $\wedge$ d$\neq$d'

Note that we use the type constructor $\overset{\sim}{\rightarrow}$ to express either that the function space is one of partial functions, or one of nondeterministic functions, or, for that matter, both! Please also note that the above definitions of predicate function p, of function f, and of is_nondeterministic are all metalinguistic: they are not expressed in RSL, but in the informal, yet precise language of ordinary mathematics.

6.8 Type Definitions

Although covered in detail in Chap. 11 we shall briefly summarise how, in RSL, one defines function spaces, i.e. function types:

type
    A, B
    $F = A \rightarrow B$
    $G = A \overset{\sim}{\rightarrow} B$

A and B are any types, mentioned here as sorts. F denotes the space of all total functions, defined over all of A, into B. G denotes the space of all partial functions, defined over all or some of A, into B.

6.9 Conclusion

We have introduced the essence of functions: that they map arguments of their definition set into (i.e., yield) results of their range, and that they can be expressed (i.e., defined), named, applied and abstracted. We have also introduced the notion that functions have type — from (type of) definition set into (type of) range set. Together with the name of the function, this is called the signature of the function. We have seen that functions are either total or partial, and that functions can be further attributed as either being surjective, injective or bijective.

6.10 Bibliographical Notes

A classic introduction to recursive function theory, a theory "lurking" behind our presentation in this chapter, is that of Hartley Rogers [444].

6.11 Exercises

Exercise 6.1. *Simple Arithmetic Operations, I.* Let there be given just the simple RSL expression constructs:

value
    f: A → B
    f(a) ≡ **if** $\mathcal{P}_{\text{test}}$(a) **then** $\mathcal{E}_{\text{con}}$ **else** $\mathcal{E}_{\text{alt}}$ **end**
    pre: $\mathcal{P}_{\text{pre}}$;

where $\mathcal{P}_{\text{test}}$ is a simple Boolean value expression which tests whether invocation of f should terminate; where $\mathcal{E}_{\text{con}}$ is the *consequence* expression, a simple expression which does not contain a (recursive) reference to f; where $\mathcal{E}_{\text{alt}}$ is the *alternative* expression, also an expression which does contain a (hence recursive) reference to f; and where $\mathcal{P}_{\text{pre}}$ is a simple Boolean value expression which tests whether f should be applied, a *pre*-condition.
    Define

1. arithmetic (natural number) multiplication ($i \times j$), and
2. arithmetic (natural number) exponentiation (i^j)

using just addition and subtraction, or already defined functions. That is: A is the Cartesian of the Natural Number type, and B is that type.

Exercise 6.2. *Simple Arithmetic Operations, II.* We refer to Exercise 6.1.
    Define

1. integer division (with remainder) ($i/j = (d,r)$)

Where $d \times i + r = i$.

Exercise 6.3. *Function Application Evaluation by Relation Search.* We refer to Exercise 6.1 and to the first part of Example 6.3 on page 96.
    Compute the sets of argument/result value pairs, i.e., as a relation (as implied by Fig. 6.1 on page 93) for the two functions:

1. mult for arguments between 0 and 4, and
2. exp for arguments between 0 and 3.

Exercise 6.4. *Function Evaluation by Recursive Function Invocation.* We refer to Exercise 6.1 and to the last part of Example 6.3 on page 96.
    Evaluate mult(3,4) and exp(2,3) in the manner of that part.

Exercise 6.5. *Higher-order Arithmetic Functions.* Define a function, thrice, which when applied to a 2-argument (i.e., a binary) arithmetic function, f, results in a 3 argument (etc.) function, τ, which, when applied to three arguments yields the result of applying f to the result of appying f to the first two arguments and the third argument !

Test your function, thrice, on the mult and exp function of Exercise 6.1. Show that $(\tau(\text{mult}))(4, 3, 2) = 24$, and that $(\tau(\text{exp}))(4, 3, 2) = 4096$.

7

A λ-Calculus

- The **prerequisite** for studying this chapter is that you understand the concept of functions as covered in Chap. 6.
- The **aims** are to introduce the concept of λ-calculus, to introduce the concept of fix points of recursively defined functions and to relate the λ-calculus expressions to the notation of RSL, the RAISE Specification Language.
- The **objective** is to ensure that the reader can use and handle the RSL λ-notation at ease and for proper abstraction purposes.
- The **treatment** is formal and systematic.

> There is a family of calculi called the λ-calculi. A calculus is a set of rules for calculating "something".[1] We shall present two λ-calculi: A "pure" λ-calculus, and a λ-notation, i.e., an embedding of the (new, less than) "pure" λ-calculus into the RSL notation. That λ-calculus, and variants thereof, have become a de facto standard for modelling computation.

The λ-calculus was first proposed by Alonzo Church [152], in the mid-1930s, as a model for computation.

Characterisation. By a *λ-calculus* we understand a specific language (1) of syntactic entities called λ-expressions, e: Namely (1.i) λ-variables x, (1.ii) λ-functions $\lambda x : T \cdot e$, and (1.iii) λ-applications $e_f(e_a)$ (or $(e_f e_a)$, $(e_f)e_a$, $(e_f)(e_a)$, or $e_f e_a$); and (2) of related "semantic" λ-conversion (i.e., calculus) rules: (2.i) α-renaming, (2.ii) β-reduction, and possibly other rules. ∎

In this chapter we shall briefly outline some essentials of the λ-calculi.

---

[1] You are well familiar, from first grade, with the calculus of ordinary arithmetic: Adding and subtracting, multiplying and dividing numbers. You are also assumed to be familiar with the calculi of differentiation and integrals. Later, in Chap. 8, you will encounter the calculi of the Boolean algebra, propositions and predicates.

Using the background of the previous chapter we systematically, yet very cursorily present a version of what we shall refer to as the "pure" λ-calculus: its syntax, its semantics and its various forms of (terminating or possibly nonterminating) conversions. We then enlarge the scope by incorporating the λ-calculus, as a notation, in the main specification language of these volumes, RSL. As part of that, we introduce the indispensable language construct **let ... in ... end**, explained in terms of λ-function application.[2] We end with an introduction of the notion of recursively defined functions, fix points, a fix point operator and fix point evaluation of function application.

7.1 Informal Introduction

In the λ-calculus everything is functions. To express such λ-calculus function values we write λ-expressions. The following are the only forms of λ-expressions:

$$x, \quad \lambda y{\cdot}e, \quad f(a)$$

where λ is a keyword, x and y are referred to as *variables* (or *λ-variables*), and e, f and a are arbitrary λ-expressions. λ-variables are simple identifiers. The form $\lambda y{\cdot}e$ is referred to as a λ-function: It *abstracts* the λ-expression e. Note that y may or may not occur in e, the *function expression body*. We "read" the expression $\lambda y{\cdot}e$ as follows: *The function of x that the expression e designates*, or, in more detail: *The λ-function expression which when "applied" to an argument λ-expression a yields a resulting λ-expression that arises from λ-converting expression e substituting all free occurrences of the variable x with λ-expression a*. The form $f(a)$, which we also allow to be written as $(fa), (f)a$, and $(f)(a)$, is referred to as a λ-application (or a λ-combination, or just a function application).

7.2 A "Pure" λ-Calculus Syntax

We briefly introduce the "pure" λ-calculus. The pure λ-calculus does not contain general expressions. The λ-notation, see later, will. We define the set of all λ-expressions in an informal, yet precise style, one that we shall often be using.

Definition. λ-expression syntax.

- Basis clause: If x is a variable, then x is a λ-expression.
- Inductive clause: If x is a variable and e, f, a are λ-expressions, then so are $\lambda x{\cdot}e$ and $f(a)$.

---

[2]This construct has been used in very many functional programming and computer science notations since it was first introduced, it is believed, by Peter Landin in the early 1960s [333, 334, 337–339].

- **Extremal clause:** Only forms that are constructed using a finite number of applications of the above clauses (rules) are λ-expressions.

The above is an example of an inductive definition.   ∎

Since this is the the first time, in these volumes, that we properly introduce a language, and since we have yet to cover the material that shall later enable us to present such a language definition formally, we use the above informal, yet very precise style of presentation. This presentation represents a classical, mathematical way of presenting inductive[3] structures, that is, usually infinite sets of entities (here they are syntactic entities) which have a structure. Here the structure is that of expressions either being atomic (no structure, really), as for the basis clause, or pairs of entities, a variable and an expression, or two expressions (i.e., the structuring is that of those two forms of composition).

The basis clause usually lists a finite or infinite number of terms (instances), here a family of variables. The inductive clause is of recursive nature: It assumes the existence of some terms and expresses the construction — the existence — of further terms. The basis clause secures the existence of initial terms. The inductive clause adds further terms to the language of terms. The extremal clause ensures that unwanted terms do not accidentally creep into the language. The adjective extremal expresses exclusion.

We can give a BNF grammar[4] for pure λ-expressions:

type /∗ A BNF Syntax: ∗/
$\langle L \rangle ::= \langle V \rangle \mid \langle F \rangle \mid \langle A \rangle$
$\langle V \rangle ::=$ /∗ variables ∗/
$\langle F \rangle ::= \lambda \langle V \rangle \bullet \langle L \rangle$
$\langle A \rangle ::= (\langle L \rangle \langle L \rangle)$

value /∗ Examples ∗/
$\langle V \rangle$: x, y, z, f, a,
$\langle F \rangle$: λ x • λ y • z
$\langle A \rangle$: (f a)
/∗ Application ∗/
$\langle A \rangle$: (f a), f(a), (f)(a), etc.

There are thus three basic kinds of "pure" λ-expressions: variables (V), function definitions (F) and function applications (A).

We relax the BNF syntax to allow for the variant forms of expressing function application. Which form (f a, (f a), f(a), (f)a, (f)(a) and ((f)(a))) is chosen depends on the "size" of the respective f and a expressions, i.e., is chosen for reasons of readability. The syntax relaxation can be justified by extending the initial BNF syntax rule:

$\langle L \rangle ::= \langle V \rangle \mid \langle F \rangle \mid \langle A \rangle \mid (\langle L \rangle)$

---

[3] By inductive we mean: inferring (inducing) general conclusions from particular instances.

[4] By BNF we mean "Backus–Naur Form". We assume that the reader is familiar with the notion of such BNF grammars, including is familiar with the notion of context-free grammars.

Elements of ⟨V⟩ are called *variables*. Elements of ⟨F⟩ are called λ-*functions*. We say that the expression ⟨L⟩ in λ⟨V⟩•⟨L⟩ has been *abstracted*, that is, "lifted" to a function, also called λ-*abstraction*. Expressions ⟨A⟩ are called *function applications*.

7.3 A λ-Calculus Pragmatics

We shall not really examine, in detail, the statement that in the λ-calculus "all things are functions". We do, however, emphasize that even variables denote functions. Arguments to and results of function application are also functions.

   Thus, to model ordinary mathematics or calculi, like arithmetic or logic, we ought to indicate that Boolean truth values and Boolean operations, that integers and the arithmetic operations, and that conditional expressions, can indeed be modelled by λ-expressions.[5] We do so in Exercises 7.1–7.2. We do this so that you may better accept why we put such an emphasis on the λ-calculus. From working with these exercises the reader may then become "relatively convinced". For more formal treatments, and "full convictions" we refer to the literature [26, 28, 152, 284, 334, 338, 465, 517].

7.4 A "Pure" λ-Calculus Semantics

The idea of the λ-calculus is that a function expression, λx•e, designates *that function which when applied to an argument expression, a, substitutes a for all free occurrences of x in e.*

Example 7.1 λ-*Expression Evaluation:* Let us try, informally, to see some examples of a substitution process: Wherever we have a function application of the form $(\lambda p \cdot e)(q)$ we substitute q for all occurrences of p in the body e:

1. $(\lambda x \cdot x)(a) \Rightarrow a$
2. $(\lambda x \cdot y)(a) \Rightarrow y$
3. $(\lambda x \cdot (xy))(a) \Rightarrow (ay)$
4. $(\lambda x \cdot \lambda y \cdot (xy))(\lambda z \cdot z) \Rightarrow \lambda y \cdot ((\lambda z \cdot z)y) \Rightarrow \lambda y \cdot y$
5. $(\lambda x \cdot \lambda y \cdot (yx))(\lambda z \cdot (zy)) \Rightarrow \lambda y \cdot (y(\lambda z \cdot (zy)))$

The first four examples are straightforward, and are okay. The last example, line 5, is not okay! The problem is that the *free* y in the argument $\lambda z \cdot (zy)$, when substituted for x, becomes *bound* by the y in $\lambda y \cdot (yx)$.   ∎

The two λ-functions, $\lambda u \cdot u$ and $\lambda v \cdot v$, or, more generally, the two λ-functions, $\lambda u \cdot \mathcal{E}(u)$ and $\lambda v \cdot \mathcal{E}(v)$, are conditionally considered the same. By changing

---

[5]Showing integers, Booleans and conditionals indicates some of the computational power we need in order to informally convince most readers that the λ-calculus indeed can handle "what is computable".

$\lambda y{\bullet}(yx)$ above to $\lambda r{\bullet}(rx)$, the *free* y in the argument $\lambda z{\bullet}(zy)$ now does not become bound.

The function application expression (a y) pragmatically assumes that a is a function, or can at least be made into something of the form λv•e.

7.4.1 Free and Bound Variables

To explain, more systematically, this and the problem of turning a free variable into a bound one, we introduce the notions of (i) *free* and *bound variables*, of (ii) *substitution*, of (iii) *α-renaming* and of (iv) *β-reduction* — the latter covering the notion of *function application*.

Definition. Free and bound variables. Let x, y be variable names and e, f be λ-expressions.

- $\langle V \rangle$: Variable x is free in x.
- $\langle F \rangle$: x is free in $\lambda y \bullet e$ if $x \neq y$ and x is free in e.
- $\langle A \rangle$: x is free in $f(e)$ if it is free in either f or e (i.e., also in both).

A variable is bound in an expression, if it occurs in the expression, but is not free.   ∎

7.4.2 Binding and Scope

We also say that free occurrences of a variable x in some expression e become *bound* in λx•e. Thus the formal parameter variable, x in λx•e, serves as the *binding variable*, and the free occurrences of x in e become bound in λx•e.

The *scope* of a binding variable is the *body* of its function expression exclusive of any inner, i.e., properly embedded, function expressions in which that same binding variable is reintroduced by some ("other") function expression. Thus the scope of the first x in

$$\lambda x{\bullet}\lambda y{\bullet}(x \ \lambda x{\bullet}(x \ y))$$

extends to the second (left to right), but not the third nor the fourth occurrence of x in the λ-function expression just above.

7.4.3 Collision and Confusion of Variables

The first occurrence, left to right, of variable x in the expression below is said to *collide* with the second (left-to-right) occurrence:

$$\lambda x{\bullet}\lambda y{\bullet}\lambda x{\bullet}x.$$

The first occurrence, left to right, of variable y in the expression below is the binding occurrence. It binds only the second (left to right) occurrence:

$$\underbrace{(\lambda x \cdot \lambda y \cdot (xy))}_{f}(y) \quad \text{apply } f \text{ to } y \text{ yields } \lambda y \cdot (yy)$$

However, the third (left to right) occurrence. But when performing the intended substitution of the argument, i.e., the third y for the free x in λy·(xy), it becomes *confused* with the second y in λy·(xy). We thus speak of *confusion* of variables.

Collisions, as it turns out, create no problems, but may seem "confusing". Confusion can be avoided by simple *renaming*:

$$\lambda x \cdot \lambda y \cdot \lambda x \cdot x \quad \text{renaming last bound variable yields} \quad \lambda x \cdot \lambda y \cdot \lambda z \cdot z$$

7.4.4 Substitution

To deal with the *confusion* of *free* and *bound* variables, as illustrated above, we introduce a proper substitution function. Substitution is a very important and nontrivial notion. It is needed here in order to understand function application in the λ-calculus, i.e., the meaning of writing f(e). Somehow, intuitively the idea is that the e replaces all occurrences of the formal parameter of the function expression f. And if f is the λ-expression λx·e', then e replaces all free occurrences of the variable x in e'. Problems with collision and confusion of free and bound variables, however, dictate some caution as to "what replaces what".

Substitution of an expression N for all free occurrences of x in M will be expressed by: **subst**([N/x]M). Depending on the form of the expressions N and M we get either of the cases shown below:

Definition. Substitution.

- **subst**([N/x]x) ≡ N
- **subst**([N/x]a) ≡ a for all variables a≠x.
- **subst**([N/x](P Q)) ≡ (**subst**([N/x]P) **subst**([N/x]Q)).
- **subst**([N/x](λx·P)) ≡ λy·P.
- **subst**([N/x](λy·P)) ≡ λy·**subst**([N/x]P) if x ≠ y and y is not free in N or x is not free in P.
- **subst**([N/x](λy·P)) ≡λz·**subst**([N/z]**subst**([z/y]P)) if y ≠ x and y is free in N and x is free in P (where z is not free in (N P)).

Substitution is a very important concept of computer science and, as you can see from the above, not quite a simple one.   ∎

7.4.5 α-Conversion and β-Conversion Rules

The substitution function mandates prior renaming (see last rule above) if a substitution might collide a free variable with a bound scope. We single this renaming out, referring to it in the future as α-renaming (or α-conversion). Furthermore we isolate the real purpose of substitution, namely function application, in the β-reduction (or β-conversion) rule.

Definition. α-renaming: $(\lambda x \cdot M) \equiv \lambda y \cdot \textbf{subst}([y/x]M)$.

If x, y are distinct variables then replacing x by y in $\lambda x \cdot M$ results in $\lambda y \cdot \textbf{subst}([y/x]M)$. Renaming the formal parameter of a λ-function expression is allowed if no free variables of its body M thereby become bound. ∎

Definition. β-reduction: $(\lambda x \cdot M)(N) \equiv \textbf{subst}([N/x]M)$.

All free occurrences of x in M are replaced by the expression N provided that no free variables of N thereby become bound in the result. ∎

7.4.6 λ-Conversion

As illustrated in the informal "substitution" examples (Example 7.1), one can re-apply the conversion rules multiple times. The question, naturally, is: *"Will it, the conversion, end?"* To see that there might be a *termination* problem, let us look at the following four examples:

Example 7.2 *Four λ-Conversions:*

(a) $(\lambda x \cdot (xy)(z)) \rightarrow_\beta (zy)$
(b) $(\lambda x \cdot (xx))(\lambda y \cdot (yy)) \rightarrow_\beta (\lambda y \cdot (yy))(\lambda y \cdot (yy)) \rightarrow_\alpha$
  $(\lambda z \cdot (zz))(\lambda y \cdot (yy)) \rightarrow_\beta (\lambda y \cdot (yy))(\lambda y \cdot (yy)) \rightarrow_\alpha$ ... ad infinitum!
(c) $(\lambda x \cdot y)(\lambda u \cdot (uu) \lambda v \cdot (vv))$
  either: $\rightarrow_\beta y$, or $\rightarrow_\beta (\lambda x \cdot y)(\lambda v \cdot (vv) \lambda v \cdot (vv))$
  either: $\rightarrow_\beta y$, or $\rightarrow_\beta (\lambda x \cdot y)(\lambda v \cdot (vv) \lambda v \cdot (vv))$
  etcetera!

We show example (c) again, graphically laid out for visual grasp!

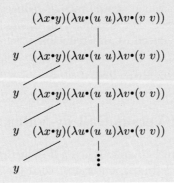

(d) The last example shows all the (always) terminating conversions of a λ-expression. First the visual picture:

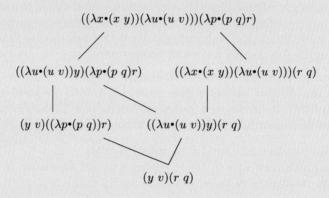

Then a more textual, linear layout:

[1] $((\lambda x\bullet(x\ y))(\lambda u\bullet(u\ v)))(\lambda p\bullet((p\ q)r))$
[2] $\Rightarrow ((((\lambda u\bullet(u\ v))\ y)))(\lambda p\bullet((p\ q)r))$

[1] $((\lambda x\bullet(x\ y))(\lambda u\bullet(u\ v)))(\lambda p\bullet((p\ q)r))$
[3] $\Rightarrow ((\lambda x\bullet(x\ y))(\lambda u\bullet(u\ v)))(((r\ q)))$

[2] $((((\lambda u\bullet(u\ v))\ y)))(\lambda p\bullet((p\ q)r))$
[4] $\Rightarrow (((((y\ v)))))(\lambda p\bullet((p\ q)r))$

[2] $((((\lambda u\bullet(u\ v))\ y)))(\lambda p\bullet((p\ q)r))$

[5] $\Rightarrow (((\lambda u\bullet(u\ v))\ y))(((r\ q)))$

[3] $((\lambda x\bullet(x\ y))(\lambda u\bullet(u\ v)))(((r\ q)))$
[5] $\Rightarrow (((\lambda u\bullet(u\ v))\ y))(((r\ q)))$

[4] $(((((y\ v))))) (\lambda p\bullet((p\ q)r))$
[6] $\Rightarrow ((((y\ v))))(((r\ q)))$

[5] $(((\lambda u\bullet(u\ v))\ y))(((r\ q)))$
[6] $\Rightarrow ((((y\ v))))(((r\ q)))$

We observe that some λ-expressions always (Example 7.2(a) and Example 7.2(d)[1–6]) reduce to a form that no longer contains any syntactic occurrence of a λ-function which can be further reduced. Such a form is called an *irreducible λ-expression*. We also observe, Example 7.2(b), that some λ-expressions cannot be reduced to an irreducible form. Others have their conversion either terminate, or not terminate, depending on which reducible λ-functions are chosen — as in Example 7.2(c).

7.5 Call-by-Name Versus Call-by-Value

Characterisation. *Call-by-name:* When a β-reduction is possible, and when one always chooses the leftmost, outermost such (i.e., the leftmost with the fewest parentheses surrounding it), then we call that sequence of reductions, that is, the conversion, a *call-by-name*, or *leftmost outermost conversion*.   ∎

Characterisation. *Call-by-value:* When a β-reduction is possible, and when one always chooses the rightmost, innermost such (i.e., the rightmost with the largest number of parentheses surrounding it), then we call that sequence of reductions, that is, the conversion, a *call-by-value*, or *rightmost innermost conversion*.   ∎

Example 7.2(a) and (b) are examples of both leftmost outermost and a rightmost innermost conversion. One leads to an irreducible form, the other never! In Example 7.2(c) the leftmost outermost conversion leads to an irreducible form, whereas the rightmost innermost conversion never leads to an irreducible form.

7.6 The Church–Rosser Theorems — Informal Version

The Church–Rosser Theorems state:

- If a λ-expression has an irreducible form, then a *leftmost outermost conversion* will find it.
- If two different λ-conversions lead to irreducible forms, then they are, modulo α-renaming, the same.

So: call-by-name reduction is the "safest"! Usually programming languages provide call-by-value.

7.7 The RSL λ-Notation

We like the ability to designate functions without always having to name them. We also like the ability, also through λ-function abstraction, to express functions, concisely without too much syntactic "machinery", i.e., "syntactic sugar". The simple rules for free and bound variables, for substitution, for α-renaming and for β-reduction also apply in the larger context of all programming, and hence also all specification languages. Therefore, as is common practice in the computer and computing science literature, we introduce an extended version of λ-expressions, here into RSL.

7.7.1 Extending λ-Expressions

We now embed λ-expressions in our specification language, RSL, by allowing any RSL **value**-designating clause (statement or expression) to occur wherever a λ-expression may occur. We type (i.e., we give a type to) the bound variable argument of λ-functions: $\lambda x{:}X{\bullet}\mathcal{E}(x)$. The type X is not necessarily coincident with (equal to) the definition set of the function. It is just a conveniently expressible type expression, usually a type name. The function definition set, however, falls within the type. Below we show a slight revision of the BNF Grammar for the "pure" λ-syntax.

type /∗ An Extended BNF Syntax ∗/
    ⟨Tn⟩ ::= /∗ Type names ∗/
    ⟨L⟩   ::= ⟨V⟩ | ⟨F⟩ | ⟨A⟩
    ⟨V⟩   ::= /∗ variables, i.e., identifiers ∗/
    ⟨F⟩   ::= λ⟨V⟩ : ⟨Tn⟩ • ⟨E⟩
    ⟨A⟩   ::= (⟨E⟩⟨E⟩)
    ⟨E⟩   ::= ⟨L⟩ | (⟨E⟩) | etcetera
                          /∗ Any ordinary RSL (or other) ∗/
                          /∗ expression, statement or clause ∗/
value /∗ Examples ∗/
    ⟨E⟩: 0, 1, **if** n=0 **then** 1 **else** n ∗ f(n−1) **end**, 4
    ⟨V⟩: n, f
    ⟨F⟩: λ n:**Nat** • **if** n=0 **then** 1 **else** n ∗ f(n−1) **end**
    ⟨A⟩: (λ n:**Nat** • **if** n=0 **then** 1 **else** n ∗ f(n−1) **end**)(4)

We have embedded into RSL the λ-notation as a syntactic way of expressing functions without naming them. For cases of use where evaluation of RSL text does not imply side-effects (i.e., hidden state changes or communication over channels, etc.) we can resort to the λ-calculus in order to grasp the meaning of an embedded λ-expression. Otherwise we cannot! We shall later have occasion to clarify the above, seemingly cryptic statements.

7.7.2 The "let ... in ... end" Construct

A very useful expression construct of RSL is the **"let ... in ... end"** clause. It can be basically explained in terms of the λ-Calculus. To do so we say that the three expressions:

    (λ a:A • E(a))(b)
    let a:A = b **in** E(a) **end**
    let a = b **in** E(a) **end**

are, for nonfunctional, or for functional expressions b that are nonrecursive (in a) — the same.

    The case where a occurs free in b amounts to a recursive mentioning of a in b. We shall deal with these cases in Sect. 7.8.

7.8 Fix Points

Recursive definitions can be intriguing, whether of types, of functions, or of other values. Here we shall, from a practical point of view, briefly investigate the λ-calculus meaning of recursive function definitions.

Recursive function theory is predominantly focused on fix points. So fix points are very important in computer and computing science; and if we get these wrong, as software engineers, then we can get "things" terribly wrong.

7.8.1 The Issue

An important notion of mathematics and of both specification and programming languages is that of *recursion*. In mathematics the notion of recursion "belongs" to what is sometimes called *meta-mathematics*, or sometimes *recursive function theory*.

In this section we first outline the problem. Then we "massage" a λ-expression in a few stages. We perform both conversion and short-hand substitution, the latter of an expression for a name (the F below). That conversion and substitution leads us to a concept of fix points and of a fix point-yielding operator (the **Y** below). Finally, we show an example of a fix point evaluation using the fix point identity: $\mathbf{Y}F = F(\mathbf{Y}F)$. The identity applies to any functional, i.e., for any higher-order function, but it does not necessarily lead to what is called a minimal fix point.

7.8.2 Informal Outline

We will now deal with the case in which a occurs free in b in the expression E(a) below:

> **let** a = b **in** E(a) **end**

Assume:

type
> F

value
> **let** f = λx:X•B(f,x) **in** E(f) **end**.

If by a free f inside B(f,x) we mean the same as the lefthand side f, then the two expressions ([1–2]):

> [1] **let** f:F = λx:X•B(f,x) **in** E(f) **end**,
> [2] (λf:F•E(f))(λx:X•B(f,x))

are not the same. The f inside B(f,x), of the second (λf•E(f))(λx:X•B(f,x)), is not bound by the λf in λf•E(f) as was probably the intention. Let us assume:

value

    fact: **Nat** → **Nat**

    fact(n) ≡ **if** n=0 **then** 1 **else** n∗fact(n−1) **end**.

This example illustrates the issue of recursive function definitions.

7.8.3 The Fix Point Operator Y

We now treat the general example systematically: We omit typing the λ-function arguments.

    let f(x) = B(... f ... x ...) **in** E(f) **end**

The next, numbered items refer to the formal, line-by-line derivation which follows. (1) Let the f inside the righthand side B(... f ... x ...) mean the same as the lefthand side f (i.e., in f(x)). (2) move x from the lefthand to the beginning of the righthand side — this is done by *abstracting* in x, i.e., by prefixing the moved x with a λ and suffixing the moved x with a •. (3) Now rename the f inside the righthand side (... f ... x ...) into g by lifting the expression (... f ... x ...) to a function λg•(... g ... x ...) which is then applied to f — whereby we get the original expression (... f ... x ...).

1 **let** f(x) = (... f ... x ...) **in** f(a) **end**
2 **let** f = λx•(... f ... x ...) **in** f(a) **end**
3 **let** f = λg•λx•(... g ... x ...)(f) **in** f(a) **end**
4 **let** f = F(f) **in** f(a) **end** −−− **where** F = λg•λx•(... g ... x ...)
5 **let** f = **YF in** f(a) **end**
6 **The fix point Identity Law: YF = F(YF)**

    From 1 to 2: λ-abstraction.
    From 2 to 3: λ-abstraction + λ-application.
    From 3 to 4: Abbreviation.
    From 4 to 5: If f satisfies $f = Ff$ then f is a fix point of F.
    (4) Now observe the expression f = F(f), where F = λg•λx•(... g ... x ...). Any function f which satisfies the equation f=F(f) is said to be a fix point of F.

    (5) The operator **Y** is an example of a fix point-taking operator.

    Thus one can eliminate named references to a recursively defined function by replacing the function name by its fix point. **Y** produces one such fix point. There are many such fix points but we refer to more foundational language semantics texts for a proper treatment of this. Any one of [28, 183, 250–252, 280, 284, 319, 396, 443, 454, 497, 521] will do. We remind the reader that we have omitted typing the formal variable of the above λ-function expressions. We will continue, in this section, to omit such typing.

7.8.4 Fix Point Evaluation

Example 7.3 *Fix Point Evaluation:* We show an example of evaluation using the **Y** fix point operator and the fix point identity **YF = F(Y(F))**.

We leave it to the reader to decipher which of the conversion rules have been applied in each step below: α-renaming, β-reduction (or its inverse, function abstraction, as for the introduction of g), or fix point identity **YF = F(Y(F))**.

let f(n) = if n=0 then 1 else n∗f(n−1) end in f(3) end
let f = λn•if n=0 then 1 else n∗f(n−1) end in f(3) end
let f = (λg•λn•if n=0 then 1 else n∗g(n−1) end)(f) in f(3) end
let f = F(f) in f(3) end
   where F = (λg•λn•if n=0 then 1 else n∗g(n−1) end)
let f = YF in f(3) end
(YF)(3)
(F(YF))(3)
((λg•λn•if n=0 then 1 else n∗g(n−1) end)(YF))(3)
(λn•if n=0 then 1 else n∗((YF))(n−1) end)(3)
(if 3=0 then 1 else 3∗(YF)(3−1) end)
(3∗(YF)(2))
(3∗(F(YF))(2))
(3∗((λg•λn•if n=0 then 1 else n∗g(n−1) end)(YF))(2))
(3∗(λn•if n=0 then 1 else n∗(YF)(n−1) end)(2))
(3∗(if 2=0 then 1 else 2∗(YF)(2−1) end))
(3∗(2∗(YF)(1)))
(3∗(2∗(F(YF))(1)))
(3∗(2∗((λg•λn•if n=0 then 1 else n∗g(n−1) end)(YF))(1)))
(3∗(2∗((λn•if n=0 then 1 else n∗(YF)(n−1) end))(1)))
(3∗(2∗((if 1=0 then 1 else 1∗(YF)(1−1) end))))
(3∗(2∗((1∗(YF)(0)))))
(3∗(2∗((1∗(F(YF))(0)))))
(3∗(2∗((1∗((λg•λn•if n=0 then 1 else n∗g(n−1) end)(YF))(0)))))
(3∗(2∗((1∗((λn•if n=0 then 1 else n∗(YF)(n−1) end))(0)))))
(3∗(2∗((1∗((if 0=0 then 1 else 0∗(YF)(0−1) end))))))
(3∗(2∗((1∗((1)))))) = 3∗2∗1∗1 = 6

We have shown yet another example of symbolic function evaluation. This time, in contrast to the second example of Example 6.3, we used a mixture of α-conversion, β-reduction and fix point conversion using the fix point identity. The fix point operation is an operation of the function algebra.

7.9 Discussion

It is time to conclude this brief overview of the λ-calculus.

7.9.1 General

We have introduced the essence of the λ-calculus. First, λ-function expressions have a bound variable which binds all free occurrences of that variable within its scope (i.e., the body). Second, functions can be modelled by the λ-calculus with its concepts of free and bound variables, substitution, α-renaming and β-reduction. Finally, that one can define notions of fix points, of a fix point-taking operator, of a fix point identity and of fix point evaluation.

7.9.2 On Minimal, Maximal and All Fix Points

The fix point operator shown above does not necessarily lead to what is called a minimal fix point. A minimal fix point of a recursively defined function is the smallest set of argument and result pairs such that there are no other argument and result values for which the recursive function definition is satisfied. We refer to readily available papers and textbooks on semantics or on recursive function theory for the story on fix points and why it is important to deal with *minimal, maximal* and all fix points [28, 183, 250–252, 280, 284, 319, 396, 443, 454, 497, 521]. RSL's recursive definitions yield a set of models corresponding to *all fix points*.

7.9.3 Emphasis

As mentioned in Sect. 6.1.1 two different concepts of functions were introduced in the last two chapters: a syntactic notion, in the form of λ-expressions (in this chapter), and a semantic notion, in the form of mathematical functions, depictable as function "maps" (in the previous chapter).

The two are worlds apart: With the former view, the λ-calculus view, we remain within a set of syntactic forms that are said to model the latter view. With the latter view we are postulating entities that no-one has ever seen! But entities whose properties can be fully satisfactorily described — so that we know that they exist, mathematically!

7.9.4 Principles, Techniques and Tools

Principles. *λ-Abstraction:* Every expression can be raised, i.e., abstracted into a function of the free variables of the expression such that the function for values of these free variables yields the same value as would the expression with those values substituted for the free variables.   ∎

The same is true for clauses like statements, etc.

Techniques. *λ-Conversion:* The techniques of λ-conversion include those of α-renaming, β-reduction, and fix-point expansion.   ∎

Tools. *The λ-calculus* is a tool needed to express functions, their definition and their application.   ∎

7.10 Bibliographical Notes

7.10.1 References

The λ-calculus was introduced in the 1930s by Alonzo Church and his students [152,322], in their rather successful attempt to explain the notion of computability: *What can be computed?* The λ-calculus has turned out to be the simplest device for explaining programming concepts [222, 334, 338, 391, 426] and is at the basis of functional programming [51, 175, 225, 261, 278, 380, 433, 520]. The mathematical foundations of λ-calculi were first given by Dana Scott, inspired by Christopher Strachey [251, 458–462, 464, 466–468]. Barendregt has covered the λ-theory from a scholarly viewpoint [25]- [28]. A good textbook is [284].

7.10.2 Alonzo Church, 1903–1995

We refer to an Internet-based biography of Alonzo Church:

> http://www-gap.dcs.st-and.ac.uk/~history/Mathematicians/Church.html

It is due to J. J. O'Connor and E. F. Robertson, University of St Andrews, Scotland: Centre for Interdisciplinary Research in Computational Algebra.

7.11 Exercises

We shall pose some applied λ-expression exercises. They are put forward to help you see that one can model the Boolean truth values and their operations, integers and their arithmetic operations as well as lists within the λ-calculus.

We refer to standard references for exercises in general λ-conversion using the substitution, α-renaming, β-reduction and the fix point identity conversion rules [26, 29, 284].

Exercise 7.1. *λ-Expressions for Boolean Truth Values and Connectives.* Consider:

if b **then** c **else** a **end.**

Think of c and a in **if** b **then** c **else** a **end** as a pair, or more generally, as a list and b as a selector into that list. If b is **true** then c is selected. If b is **false** then a is selected. This determines our representation of **true** and **false** in the λ-calculus:

T,**true**: λx.λy.x
F,**false**: λx.λy.y

λ-calculus representation of the Boolean connectives are now suggested:

~: λx((xF)T)
∧: λx.λy.((xy)F)
∨: λx.λy.((xT)y)

1. Writing out T and F in full (i.e., as λ-expressions), show apply ~ to F to get T, and apply ~ to T to get F.
2. Writing out T and F in full apply ∧ to all four combinations of T and F and get what you expect.
3. Similarly for ∨.

Notice that these representations of the Boolean connectives expect operands that reduce to T or F. For operands (i.e., arguments) that do not reduce to Booleans these λ-calculus connectives define "other" functions!

Exercise 7.2. *λ-Expressions for Lists and List Element Selection.* Consider the list:

$$\langle \phi_0, \phi_1, ..., \phi_{n-1} \rangle$$

being represented in the λ-calculus as follows:

$\langle \phi_0 \rangle$: λx.((xϕ_0)ψ)
$\langle \phi_0, \phi_1 \rangle$: λx.((x$\phi_0$)$\langle \phi_1 \rangle$)
$\langle \phi_0, \phi_1, \phi_2 \rangle$: λx.((x$\phi_0$)$\langle \phi_1, \phi_2 \rangle$)
...
$\langle \phi_0, \phi_1, ..., \phi_{n-1} \rangle$: λx.((x$\phi_0$)$\langle \phi_1, \phi_2, ..., \phi_{n-1} \rangle$)

ψ is a "dummy" 'end of list' delimiter. It can be any λ-expression.

The idea, in Exercise 7.1 on the page before, to let T and F select into a list of length 2 and yield the 1st, respectively the second element, is now iterated:

T: λx.λy.x
FT: λx.λy.(y λx.λy.x) ≡ λx.λy.(y T)
F^2T: λx.λy.(y λx.λy.(y λx.λy.x)) ≡ λx.λy.(y FT)
...
F^{i+1}T: λx.λy.(y F^iT)

Now show that:

1. $\langle\phi_0,\phi_1,...,\phi_{n-1}\rangle T \;=\; \phi_0$
2. $\langle\phi_0,\phi_1,...,\phi_{n-1}\rangle FT \;=\; \phi_1$
3. $\langle\phi_0,\phi_1,...,\phi_{n-1}\rangle F^n T \;=\; \phi_{n-1}$

Exercise 7.3. λ-*Expressions for Integers and Arithmetic Operators.* Church illustrated the following representation of natural numbers:

$0 \;\equiv\; \lambda a.\lambda b.b$
$1 \;\equiv\; \lambda a.\lambda b.(ab)$
$2 \;\equiv\; \lambda a.\lambda b.(a(ab))$

...

$n \;\equiv\; \lambda a.\lambda b.(a(a(\;...\;(ab))))$

where the natural number n is represented by the n-fold application of the first argument (a) to the second argument (b).

With the following representation of the arithmetic operators:

$m + n$: $\lambda x.\lambda y((m\ x)((n\ x)y))$,
$m \times n$: $\lambda x.(m(n\ x))$, and
m^n: $(n\ m)$,

calculate the following:

1. $2+3$
2. 2×3
3. 2^3

8

Algebras

- The **prerequisite** for studying this chapter is that you understand the mathematical concepts of sets and of functions as covered in earlier chapters.
- The **aims** are to cover the mathematical concepts of algebras such as they are used in computing science and software engineering and to cover, even in this early chapter, the algebraic specification of what is known, in computing science and software engineering, as abstract data types (ADTs).
- The **objective** is to ensure that the reader from as early as possible can use and handle this concept of specification algebras, at ease and with determination.
- The **treatment** is systematic to semiformal.

It is a main purpose of this chapter to basically just introduce the jargon — the language, as it were — of algebras. We do so for the sake of convenience: The mathematical concept of algebras equip us with suitable terms. When using those terms they help us delineate what we are presenting.

Characterisation. By an *algebra* we, loosely, mean a possibly infinite set of entities and a usually finite set of operations over these entities. ∎

In software engineering algebras play two central mathematical roles. The way we structure specifications and programmes (in schemes, classes, modules, objects) can perhaps best be understood with reference to algebra. Steps of development, from abstract specifications to concrete ones, can likewise best be understood as some algebra morphisms.

8.1 Introduction

Algebras are defined in terms of functions, hence this section follows the previous section on functions. Algebras capture the very essence of grouping entities together with actions upon, events and behaviours over, and communications between these entities. In ordinary programming parlance, "algebras are objects". We refer to [53, 349] as appropriate introductions to modern algebra.

The concept of *algebra* is a mathematical concept that allows us to abstract observations that may have their background in topics other than mathematics. The concept of function can be seen as one such concept, which we, in Chap. 6, "related back" to phenomena in some actual world. Our concept of functions, as well as the basis of the concept of mathematical logic (Chap. 9) can both have their presentation improved by presenting some of their structure algebraically. The *function algebra* thus consists of the space of all functions and a few operations such as function abstraction, function application, function composition, taking the definition set of a function, taking the range set of a function and, last, taking the fix point of a function.

8.2 Formal Definition of the Algebra Concept

We shall primarily take an algebraic approach when determining, i.e., when deciding upon, the form of, and developing software development descriptions. An *algebraic system* is a set,[1] A (finite or infinite), and a set[2], Ω, (usually finite), of operations:

$$(A, \Omega)$$

$$A = \{a_1, a_2, ..., a_m, ...\}, \Omega = \{\omega_1, \omega_2, ..., \omega_o\}$$

Set A is the *carrier* of the algebraic system, and Ω is a collection of operations defined on A. Each operation $\omega_i : \Omega$ (ω_i in Ω, i.e., ω_i of type Ω) is a function of some *arity*, say n, taking operands, i.e., argument values in A, and yielding a result value in A:

$$\omega(a_{i_1}, a_{i_2}, \ldots, a_{i_n}) = a$$

That is, ω_i is of type $A^n \to A$.[3] Different functions (in Ω) may have different arities. Think of arity as a functional, a function that applies to functions and yields their arity:

type arity: $\Omega \to$ **Nat**,   arity(ω_i) $= n$

---

[1]We usually do not say what the elements of this set are, it is just a set!

[2]Similarly: Just a set!

[3]The expression $A^n \to A$ is not an expression of RSL. First, we are explaining basic mathematical concepts not in RSL but in an informal notation of mathematics already assumed understood. Second, if we wish to express in RSL what may seem to be a Cartesian of arity n, for a known, fixed n, then we write it out in full: $A_1 \times A_1 \times \cdots \times A_n$. If n varies, then it is probably not to be modelled, i.e., thought of, as a Cartesian, but rather as a list, A^*, where A is then the union type of all the A_i's.

8.3 How Do Algebras Come About?

Popular *software devices*, also known as *abstract data types*, such as *stacks, queues, tables, graphs*, etc., can all be seen as algebras.

Example 8.1 *"Everyday" Algebras:*

1. *A Stack Algebra:* The *stack algebra* has, as *carrier*, the union of the set of all stack element values with the set of all stack values, and create empty stack, top of stack, push onto stack, pop from stack and is_empty stack as *operations*.
2. *A Queue Algebra:* The *queue algebra* has, as *carrier*, the union of the set of all queue element values with the set of all queue values and, for example, create empty queue, enqueue, dequeue, first ("oldest"), last ("youngest"), and is_empty queue as *operations*.
3. *A Directory Algebra:* The *directory algebra* has, as *carrier*, the union of the set of all directory entry values (i.e., of value triples of entry name, date and information values) with the set of all directory values and, for example, create empty directory, insert entry in directory, directory look-up, edit directory entry and remove directory entry as *operations*.
4. *A Directed, Acyclic Graph Algebra:* The *directed acyclic graph algebra* has, as *carrier*, the union of the set of all node labels, the set of all edges, and the set of all acyclic graphs of (these) labeled nodes and unlabeled edges, and, for example, create empty graph, insert_node in graph, insert_edge in graph, trace edges in graph from node to node, depth_first_search in graph and breadth_first_ search in graph, as *operations*.
5. *Patient Medical Record Algebra:* The *patient medical record algebra* has, as *carrier*, all conceivable patient medical records, each consisting of one dossier. Each dossier consists of one or more sheets (i.e., records) that are of the following kinds: prior medical history, interview records, analysis records, diagnostics determination, treatment plans (including prescriptions), observations of effects of treatment, etc. In addition the *carrier* also includes these different kinds of sheets. That is, the *carrier* is quite complex. The *patient medical record algebra* has, for example, the following *operations:* creation of a new medical record, inserting new information, editing previous (i.e., old) information, copying a sheet or a dossier and shredding a dossier.

■

Algebras may have finite or infinite carriers, i.e., carriers with finite or infinite numbers of elements of possibly different types.

8.4 Kinds of Algebras

> There are various kinds of algebras. It is important to understand which kinds of algebras are of interest to software engineering and which are not. For that purpose we explicate the variety of algebras that you may come across.

8.4.1 Concrete Algebras

The examples above were all examples of *concrete algebras*.

Characterisation. A *concrete algebra* has sets of known, specific values as carrier, and a set of specifically given operations.   ∎

That is, one knows that one has a concrete algebra when one knows the elements of the carrier and when one knows the operators and how to evaluate operation invocations. The Boolean algebra of Chap. 9 is an example of a concrete, mathematical algebra. Other concrete, mathematical algebras are found in Example 8.2.

Example 8.2 *Number Algebras:*

- *An Integer Algebra:* (Integer,$\{+, -, *\}$), an infinite carrier algebra whose operations yield all the integers.
- *A Natural Numbers Algebra:* (NatNumber,$\{$gcd,lcm$\}$) an infinite carrier algebra where gcd, lcm are the greatest common divisor, respectively the largest common multiple (viz.: gcd(4,6)=2, lcm(4,6)=12) operations, which yield all the natural numbers.
- *A Modulo Natural Number Algebra:* ($\Im_m = \{0, 1, 2, \ldots, m - 1\}, \Omega = \{\oplus, \otimes\}$) is a finite carrier algebra: $\oplus$ and $\otimes$ are the addition and multiplication operations modulo m.

Several other algebras over numbers are possible.   ∎

As software engineers we shall mostly be developing concrete algebras. As computing scientists we shall often have occasion to explain things in terms of abstract or universal algebras, to which we now turn.

8.4.2 Abstract Algebras

Whereas concrete algebras are known, i.e., effectively constructed, abstract algebras are postulated, That is, they are what we shall call (and define as) 'axiomatised' in Chap. 9.

Characterisation. An *abstract algebra* has a sort, i.e., a presently further undefined set of entities as carrier, a set of operations, and a set of axioms that relate (i.e., constrain) properties of carrier elements and operations.   ∎

The algebraic system of an abstract algebra is thus defined by a system of postulates, to be known henceforth as axioms — and to be treated in depth later. See Sect. 9.6.

We shall often be using axioms to describe manifest phenomena in an actual world; and we shall likewise often be using axioms to prescribe software devices — which will later be made "concrete", as concrete as such "phenomena" which can exist inside computers can "be". The axiom systems should not be seen as actually "being" this or that concrete world, but "only" models of it.

A "concrete" example of an informally postulated abstract algebra may be in place:

Example 8.3 *Another Stack Algebra:* We present another version of the stack algebra of Example 8.1(1). There is a distinguished, unique carrier element called the empty stack: empty(). Let s stand for any carrier stack value, i.e., stack, and let $E = \{e, e', \ldots, e'', \ldots\}$ stand for carrier stack element values. The members of E will become the elements of stacks. is_empty(empty()) always holds (is always true), whereas is_empty(push(e, s)), for any e and s, always fails to hold (is always false). Inquiring as to the top of a stack, s — which can be thought of as one onto which one has just pushed the element e — yields that e for any stack s: pop(push(e, s')) = e, while popping an element from the stack s' (i.e. pop(push(e, s))) yields s. Popping an element from, respectively inquiring as to, the top element of an empty() stack always yields the **chaotic** value, of no type, and representing the universally undefined element.   ∎

We shall more explicitly use the concept of abstract algebras whenever we "lift" an example like the above by not being concrete about exactly what the elements of the stack are. That is, we use it when we define a *parameterised algebra*, that is, abstract, like for function abstraction, in one or more of the *sub-carriers* of the abstract algebra being defined. Thus we introduce the concept of *heterogeneous algebras*.

8.4.3 Heterogeneous Algebras

Characterisation. A *heterogeneous algebra:*

$$(\{A_1, A_2, \ldots, A_m\}, \Omega\})$$

has its carrier set A be expressible as the union of a set of disjoint sub-carriers A_i, and associates with every operation ω in Ω a signature:

$$\mathsf{signature}(\omega) = A_{i_1} \times A_{i_2} \times \cdots \times A_{i_n} \to A_{i_{n+1}}$$

Thus the kth operand of ω is of type A_{i_k}, and the result value is of type $A_{i_{n+1}}$.

Example 8.4 *Stack Algebra:* We expand on the stack algebra example, Example 8.3. Viewing that stack algebra as a heterogeneous algebra, the stack operations are (now) of the following signatures: S is the stack type, and E is the type of stack elements: empty: **Unit** $\rightarrow S$, is_empty: $S \rightarrow$ **Bool**, push: $S \times E \rightarrow S$, top: $S \overset{\sim}{\rightarrow} E$, and pop: $S \overset{\sim}{\rightarrow} S$.   ∎

Unit is a literal. It denotes a type of one element. That element is designated by the empty parameter grouping: (). We shall later return to a more thorough treatment of **Unit**.

8.4.4 Universal Algebras

Characterisation. A *universal algebra* is a carrier and a set of operations with no postulates, i.e., the operations are not further constrained.   ∎

The Morphism Concept

When, in software development we transform abstract specifications to more concrete ones, then, usually, an *algebra morphism* is taking place.

Let there be two algebras:

$$(A, \Omega), (A', \Omega')$$

A function $\phi : A \rightarrow A'$ is said to be a *morphism* (also called a *homomorphism*) from (A, Ω) to (A', Ω') if for any $\omega \in \Omega$ and for any $a_1, a_2, \ldots, a_n$ in A there is a corresponding $\omega' \in \Omega'$, such that:

$$M : \phi(\omega(a_1, a_2, \ldots, a_n)) = \omega'(\phi(a_1), \phi(a_2), \ldots, \phi(a_n))$$

We say that the homomorphism relation M *respects* or *preserves* corresponding operations in Ω and Ω' (Fig. 8.1).

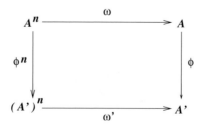

Fig. 8.1. Morphism mapping diagram

ϕ^n is the n-fold Cartesian power of $\phi : A \to A'$, that is, the map $A^n \to (A')^n$, and is defined by:

$$\phi^n : (a_1, a_2, \ldots, a_n) \mapsto (\phi(a_1), \phi(a_2), \ldots, \phi(a_n))$$

If $\phi : A \to A'$ is a homomorphism of Ω-algebras, then, by definition ϕ preserves all the operations of Ω.

A special rendition, i.e., manifestation and version, of the morphism concept will be expressed when we cover the model-oriented set, list and map data types (of RSL), in terms of their set, list and map comprehension forms. We refer to Sects. 13.2.2, 15.2.2 and 16.2.2, respectively.

Special Kinds of Morphisms

We classify morphisms according to their properties as functions. If $\phi : A \to A'$ is a morphism, then we call ϕ an *isomorphism* if ϕ is *bijective*; an *epimorphism* if ϕ is *surjective*, and a *monomorphism* if ϕ is *injective*.

Some further characterisations: The *abstract properties* of an *algebraic system* are exactly those which are *invariant* (i.e., which do not change) under *isomorphism*. For *epimorphisms*, A' is called the *homomorphic image* of A, and we regard (A', Ω') as an *abstraction* or a *model* of (A, Ω). A monomorphism $A \to A'$ is sometimes called an *embedding* of A into A'.

We single out morphisms that map algebras onto themselves. We call a morphism $\phi : A \to A'$ that maps (A, Ω) into itself an *endomorphism*. If ϕ is also bijective, hence an isomorphism, $\phi : A \to A$, then we call it an *automorphism*.

8.5 Specification Algebras

The mathematical concept of algebras has had a great influence on our way of presenting software designs, prescriptions for software, and, in general, any kind of documentation related also to software development. The whole concept of *object-orientedness* is basically an algebraic concept. Giving meaning, i.e., semantics, to syntactic constructs by means of presenting morphisms from syntactic algebras to semantics algebras is obviously another algebraic concept.

Thus it is that in programming as well as in specification languages we find syntactic means for presenting what amounts to heterogeneous algebras. In RSL the syntactic construct for presenting a heterogeneous algebra is called a **class** expression. In an RSL **class** expression one therefore expects to find syntactic means for defining the carriers and the operations of a heterogeneous algebra. We now turn to this subject. But we first remind the reader of Sect. 1.6.2 in which we first introduced the class concept. We shall not formally introduce the pragmatics, semantics and syntax of the RSL **class** and **scheme** concepts till Vol. 2, Chap. 10.

8.5.1 Syntactic Means of Expressing Algebras

To define the various carriers we define their **types**, and to define the various operations over these carriers we define these as function **values**. Schematically:

class
  type
    A, B, C, D, ...
  value
    f: A → B
    f(a) ≡ ...
    g: C → D
    g(c) ≡ ...
    ...
end

The above class expression defines carriers A, B, C and D (etcetera), and operations f and g (etcetera).

8.5.2 An Example Stack Algebra

Example 8.5 *Stack Algebra:* We bring a third version of the stack algebra of Examples 8.1(1) and 8.3.

Let us define an algebra of simple stacks. E and S are the stack element type, respectively the stack types, i.e., are the *types of interest.* They are two disjoint carrier sets. The operations empty and is_empty generate empty stacks, i.e., stacks of no elements, respectively tests whether an arbitrary stack is empty; push, top and pop are the *operations of interest.* An empty stack is empty. One cannot pop from an empty stack (i.e., *generate* a remaining stack), nor can one *observe* the top of an empty stack. *Observing* the top of a stack which is the ["most recent"] result of having pushed the element e "onto" a ["previous"] stack s yields that element e. *Generating* the stack after a pop of a stack which is the ["most recent"] result of having pushed any element e "onto" the ["previous"] stack s yields that stack s.

class
  type
    E, S
  value
    empty: **Unit** → S
    is_empty: S → **Bool**
    push: E → S → S
    top: S $\overset{\sim}{\to}$ E
    pop: S $\overset{\sim}{\to}$ S

axiom
  is_empty(empty()),
  top(empty()) ≡ **chaos**,
  pop(empty()) ≡ **chaos**,
  ∀ e,e':E, s:S •
    top(push(e)(s)) ≡ e ∧
    pop(push(e)(s)) ≡ s
end

The above formalisation should, by now, look rather conventional!   ∎

Informal Explanation of Some RSL Constructs

Since this is one of the earlier examples of a full-scale use of several hitherto unexplained, but nevertheless rather simple RSL constructs, let us explain them in anticipation of material of Chap. 9 on Mathematical Logic. The RSL *keywords* **class** and **end** delineate the class expression. The class expression, in this case, contains three kinds of definitions: **type**, function **value** and **axiom.** The **type** definitions you should be familiar with. The **value** definitions name a number of values. Here, all these values are functions: one 0-ary (nullary), one 2-ary (binary, dyadic), and three 1-ary (unary, monadic). These function values are given just their type, called their signature (no function definition [body]).

The **axiom** definitions, that is, the axioms, constrain the function values to lie within a smaller function space than defined by their signatures. We leave deciphering the specific functionality of these axioms to the reader, but close by explaining the use of the ∀ "binder". The clause: ∀ e,e':E, s:S • $\mathcal{A}_1, \mathcal{A}_2, \ldots, \mathcal{A}_n$, (where the individual $\mathcal{A}_i$ are the axioms — expressions that may or may not contain the quantifier variables e, e', and s) expresses that these axioms' variables take values that *range* over the types E, E, and S, respectively.

8.5.3 An Example Queue Algebra

Example 8.6 *Queue Algebra:* We give a formal example of the queue algebra of Example 8.1(2). Let us define an algebra of simple queues: E and Q are the queue element type, respectively the queue type, i.e., are the *types of interest.* The operations **empty** and **is_empty** generate empty queues, i.e., queues of no elements, respectively tests whether an arbitrary queue is empty, and **enq** and **deq** are the *operations of interest.* The interesting functions are here defined in terms of the *hidden functions* dq and rq.

hide
  dq,rq **in**

```
class
  type
    E, Q
  value
    empty: Unit → Q, is_empty: Q → Bool
    enq: E → Q → Q, deq: Q ∼→ (Q × E)
    dq: Q ∼→ E, rq: Q ∼→ Q
  axiom
    is_empty(empty()), deq(empty()) ≡ chaos,
    dq(empty()) ≡ chaos, rq(empty()) ≡ chaos,
    forall e,e':E, q:Q •
      ~is_empty(enq(e)(q)),
      dq(enq(e)(empty())) ≡ e,
      rq(enq(e)(empty())) ≡ empty(),
      dq(enq(e)(enq(e')(q))) ≡ dq(enq(e')(q)),
      rq(enq(e)(enq(e')(q))) ≡ enq(e)(rq(enq(e')(q))),
      deq(enq(e)(q)) ≡ (rq(enq(e)(q)),dq(enq(e)(q)))
end
```

Operation dq is called an *auxiliary operation*. It finds the first element en-
queued, i.e., the, "oldest", or the most distantly, in time, inserted element.
Auxiliary operation rq reconstructs the queue less its currently dequeued element.   ∎

Some Notation: hide

The functions dq and rq are defined as *hidden functions*. They are not intended to be used outside the class expression inside which they only serve
as *auxiliary functions*, that is, *auxiliary operations*. The marker **hide** effects
that it can be syntactically checked that they are not used outside the scope
of the class definition. Hiding values (or types) enable us to reasonably simply
characterise, as here, the *functions of interest* deq and enq.

8.5.4 Towards Semantic Models of "class" Expressions

So, a **class** expression, even the little we have so far introduced about class
expressions, can be seen to "cluster" the introduction of a number of identifiers, to wit: A, B, C, D, f, g, or E, S, empty, is_empty, push, pop, top, or E, Q,
empty, is_empty, deq, enq, dq, and rq. *But what does it all mean?* We return
now to a thread first begun in Sect. 1.6.2. Namely to informally explain the
semantics of RSL constructs. The "story" applies, inter alia, here.

As already outlined, in Sect. 1.6.2, the meaning of a class expression is a
set of *models*. Each model in the set maps all identifiers defined in the class
expression, whether hidden or not, into their meaning.

The meanings of the above-mentioned identifiers, for example, E, S, empty, is_empty, push, pop, and top, are as follows: Any type identifier is mapped into the set of values as constrained by the axioms over these values, and a function identifier is mapped into a function value, as constrained by the axioms over these function values. Since the axioms do not normally constrain the function values to one specific function, but to a (possibly infinite) space of functions over suitable input argument value and result value relations, we have that the meaning of a class expression is a possibly infinite set of models: one for each combination of defined function values, etc. We shall later see a need for allowing these models to further map identifiers not (at all) mentioned in the class expression into arbitrary values (including set values).

The meaning of the stack class expression is thus a set of models, with each model mapping at least the seven identifiers mentioned in the stack class expression into respective meanings: the value type of all elements, of all stacks, and specific values for empty, is-empty, push, pop and top functions.

8.6 RSL Syntax for Algebra Specifications

8.6.1 "class" Expressions

We have several times illustrated the RSL syntax for presenting an algebra in the form of a class of models:

class
   type
      ... [sorts and type definitions] ...
   value
      ... [value, incl. function definitions] ...
   axiom
      ... [properties of types and values (functions) ...]
end

The meaning of a class expression is a set, possibly empty, possibly singleton, possibly infinite, of models in the form of bindings, i.e., associations between the type and value identifiers introduced in the class expression and mathematical entities such a numbers, sets, Cartesians and functions.

We shall only occasionally wrap our type and value definitions and our axioms into a class expression, but in a sense we really ought to so so! The intended meaning is of course the same.

8.6.2 "scheme" Declarations

The scheme construct of RSL allows us to name classes:

scheme A =
  class
  type
    ... [sorts and type definitions] ...
  value
    ... [value, incl. function definitions] ...
  axiom
    ... [properties **of** types and values (functions) ...]
end

Identifier A now names the class of all the models denoted by the class expression.

8.7 Discussion

8.7.1 General

We have made a *tour de force* of covering, ever so cursorily, some concepts of mathematical algebra. The purpose has been twofold. First, to put names to a number of algebra concepts, names that have been properly defined, and which can be used for later characterising a number of specification (cum programming) concepts, principles and techniques. Second, we showed notation and elegance of the definitions, something that we, as software engineers, can learn from and ought to copy. That is, there are so many ideas of specification and of development that can be characterised using these algebraic concepts, and knowing this may induce us to further study (especially the universal) algebraic notions. Although such a study is outside the aims of these volumes it would reveal the usefulness of the lemmas and theorems of universal algebra. We shall endeavour, however, to communicate, wherever relevant, the spirit of the underlying algebraic concepts.

We have finally, in this section on algebra, shown how the software community has taken the *prescribed medicine:* The concept of algebra, as a mathematical structure of carriers and operations, has found its way into programming and into specification languages. We have shown the initial concepts of the RSL class specification construct, syntactically as well as semantically. In programming languages this algebra concept is usually manifested in so-called *object-orientedness*. In specification languages this algebra concept is usually manifested in so-called *module, class* or *abstract data type* constructs.

8.7.2 Principles, Techniques and Tools

Principles. *Algebraic Semantics:* is that of capturing core notions of a domain, or of requirements, or of software designs, by expressing these as algebras. ∎

Techniques. *Algebra construction* consists in expressing (i) the sorts (i.e., abstract types) of the carrier by naming them, (ii) the signature of the operations (functions), and (iii) in providing an appropriate (small) set of axioms that relate elements of the carrier and the operations. ∎

Tools. *Algebra* tools include the **class** and **scheme** constructs of RSL (and of similar, basically model-oriented languages (for example: B [3], event-B [4], VDM++ [201–204], and Object-Z [144,199,200])), CASL, the Common Algebraic Specification Language [49,395,399], and CafeOBJ [193,232]. ∎

8.8 Bibliographical Notes

A classical textbook on algebra is Birkhoff and MacLane's [53]. We owe our debt to that book and, for the treatment of this chapter, to Lipson's delightful [349]. Universal algebras are covered by Cohn in [157]. Another good algebra book is also by Cohn: [158].

8.9 Exercises

♣ **Note:** The next three assignments are, in a sense, premature. They ask that you express something in RSL, of which you have yet to learn the essentials. But try anyway! In the present and in the previous chapters there is indeed enough material on RSL to build upon. But that material will be reintroduced, and then very much more systematically, from Part III on.

Exercise 8.1. ♣ *Suggest a Transportation Net Algebra,*
    We refer to Appendix A, Sect. A.1, *Transportation Net.*
    Suggest short sort (or type) names for *Transportation Net* entities (nets, segments, connections), and signatures for (four) functions that insert [delete] a new [an "old"] segment, and that insert [delete] a new [an "old"] connection (intersection). Write out axioms, in English, stating properties that must hold of any input argument or result value segment, intersection and transportation net. "Wrap" the whole thing into a **scheme** declaration.

Exercise 8.2. ♣ *Suggest a Container Logistics Algebra.*

We refer to Appendix A, Sect. A.2, *Container Logistics*.

Suggest short sort (or type) names for the following *Container Logistics* entities: Container Ship, Container, Quay, Container Storage Area, Bay, Row, and Stack, as well as Bay, Row, and Stack Identifiers (Names, Indexes). Suggest signatures for (four) functions that load [unload] Containers onto [from] Container Ship Stacks from [to] a Quay, respectively that load [unload] Containers onto [from] Container Storage Area Stacks from [to] a Quay. (Remember to identify Bays, Rows and Stacks of both Container Ships and the Container Storage Area.) Write out axioms, in English, stating properties that must hold of any input argument or result value amongst the many container terminal entities. "Wrap" the whole thing into a **scheme** declaration.

Exercise 8.3. ♣ *Suggest a Financial Service Industry Algebra.*

We refer to Appendix A, Sect. A.3, *Financial Service Industry*.

Suggest short sort (or type) names for the *Financial Service Industry*, in particular Bank entities (Customer, Bank Account, etc.), and signatures for (four) functions that open and close accounts, that establish shared accounts, that deposit and withdraw funds, and that transfer funds between accounts. (Remember to also identify the types of such internal bank "books" that keep track of customers account numbers, and of the sharing of accounts.) Write out axioms, in English, stating properties that must hold of any input argument or result value amongst the many financial service industry entities. "Wrap" the whole thing into a **scheme** declaration.

9

Mathematical Logic

- The **prerequisite** for studying this chapter is that you understand the mathematical concepts of sets, functions and algebras as covered in earlier chapters.
- The **aims** are to cover the concepts of Boolean algebra, propositional and predicate logic, to cover the concepts of proof theory and model theory and to cover the concept of axiom systems and exemplify its application in abstract specifications.
- The **objective** is to help ensure that the reader becomes reasonably fluent in the use of logic as a specification tool and to begin the long road in ensuring that the reader will eventually become reasonably versatile in logic reasoning.
- The **treatment** is semiformal to fully formal.

Mathematical logic is, without any doubt, the most important mathematical subdiscipline of software engineering.

Characterisation. By a *mathematical logic* we mean a formal language: A *syntax* defining an infinite set of formulas, and a *"semantics"* — here in the form of a set of *axioms* concerning these formulas and a set of *rules of inference* over these formulas. ∎

Logic is the study of reasoning. Logic was, for a long time, part of philosophy. Mathematical logic is the study of the kind of reasoning done by mathematicians, and mathematical logic was, for some time, a stepchild of mathematics.[1]

---

[1]It seems, without exaggerating, that many mathematics university departments still have a somewhat problematic relationship to mathematical logic.

> We shall basically be using mathematical logic as undoubtedly the most important part of our specification notation. That is, we shall be using all the sublanguages of mathematical logic: the sublanguage of Boolean ground terms, the sublanguage of propositions and the sublanguage of predicates. Therefore it is important that the reader — from the very beginning, that is, now! — is at ease with many of the concepts of mathematical logic. This, then, is the purpose of this chapter: to teach you those concepts, and to teach you how to express yourself, formally, in those sublanguages.

Correctness of software, and proving properties of their specifications and implementations, are concerns of core importance. So is proving properties of domain descriptions, of requirements prescriptions, and of relations between them and software designs. The languages (i.e., tools) and techniques of mathematical logic are used in securing fulfillment of desired properties.

We shall be covering, also, some of the proof aspects of mathematical logic. But our presentation in this section is from the point of view of mathematical logic as an abstract specification language. We will not cover theories of mathematical logic, but refer to many good textbooks, for example, [235, 259, 372, 457].

9.1 The Issues

We shall first treat basically nine issues of logics, including three sublanguages: (i) a language of Boolean-valued ground terms, (ii) a language of Boolean-valued propositional expressions, and (iii) a language of Boolean-valued predicate expressions. And we shall also cover some diverse issues: (iv) Boolean-valued expressions, (v) **chaos** — undefined expressions, (vi) axiom and inference systems, (vii) proof systems, (viii) the axioms of the logic languages, and the axiom definition facility of RSL, and (ix) the meaning of the **if ... then ... else ... end** clause.

We first survey these nine issues, then we treat the three languages in more detail in Sects. 9.3–9.5. But, before that, we survey the distinction between *proof-theoretic* and *model-theoretic* logic (Sect. 9.2). That distinction will bring out the distinctions between syntax and semantics, between provable and true, and between completeness and soundness.

9.1.1 Language of Boolean Ground Terms

First, there is the *Boolean ground term*[2] *algebra*, or simply the *Boolean calculus*, its syntax, semantics and pragmatics.

---

[2] By a ground term we mean an operator/operand expression with no variables, just, as here, the Boolean literals and connectives.

We refer to the Boolean ground term algebra by the type name **Bool**.[3]

Syntactically the *Boolean algebra* is a *language of ground terms*, having a syntax including: Boolean (constant) literals (**true** and **false**), a set of connectives: $\{\sim, \wedge, \vee, \Rightarrow, =, \neq, \equiv\}$, a set of (syntax) rules for forming ground terms, and a set of axioms relating ground terms and connectives, a calculus.

true, false, ∼true, ∼false, true ∧ false, ∼true ∧ false, ...

Semantically we have truth tables for these connectives: the truth values and the three-valued logic.[4] We explain this semantics by presenting a procedure for evaluating (i.e., interpreting) ground terms.

Speaking on the pragmatics of the Boolean ground term algebra, with this (ground term) algebra there is little we can express. But it forms a smallest basis, even with just the first two connectives listed above!

9.1.2 Language of Propositional Expressions

Next, we present the *propositional calculus*, its syntax, semantics and pragmatics. The propositional calculus builds on the language of Boolean ground terms.

There is the syntax of propositional (operator/operand) expressions built from Boolean literals, connectives, and variable identifiers, axioms and inference rules. The axioms and inference rules define the calculus part of the propositional calculus. Variables are intended, in the semantics, to denote truth values.

true, false, ∼true, ∼false, true ∧ false, ∼true ∧ false, ...
a, b, ..., a ∧ true, a ∧ b, ...

There are the semantics rules (an evaluation procedure) for interpreting propositional expressions.

And there is the pragmatics: With the propositional calculus we can express a few more things than with just Boolean ground terms.

9.1.3 Language of Predicate Expressions

Finally, we have the *predicate calculus*, with its syntax, semantics and pragmatics. The predicate calculus includes the propositional calculus.

Thus there is the syntax of predicate (operator/operand) expressions, including propositional expressions, extended with constant values of any type,

---

[3]The type name **Bool** will also refer to the propositional and the predicate calculi.

[4]As noted later we must, in general, be aware of undefined, e.g., nonterminating, expression evaluations. A three-valued logic is to deal with nonterminating expression evaluation.

variables denoting such values, and hence operator/operand expressions also over these, as well as quantified expressions (∀, ∃), and axioms and inference rules.

The axioms and inference rules define the calculus part of the predicate calculus.

true, false, ~true, ~false, true ∧ false, ~true ∧ false, ...
a, b, ..., a ∧ **true**, a ∧ b, ...
∀ x:X • **true**, ∀ x:X • x ∧ ..., ∃ x:X • x ∧ ...

There are the semantics rules for interpreting (evaluating) predicate expressions — leading to truth values (or **chaos!**).

And there is the pragmatics: With the predicate calculus we can express quite a lot. It is sufficient for a long while!

9.1.4 Boolean-Valued Expressions

Syntactically we can thus speak of four categories of expressions: Boolean ground terms, propositional expressions, predicate expressions and quantified expressions. Figure 9.1 informally indicates that *Boolean ground term expressions* syntactically are a proper subcategory of *propositional expressions;* that *propositional expressions* syntactically are a proper subcategory of *predicate expressions;* that *quantified expressions* syntactically are a proper subcategory of *predicate expressions;* but that *quantified expressions* syntactically are not a proper subcategory of *propositional expressions.* It also expresses that all are *Boolean-valued expressions.*

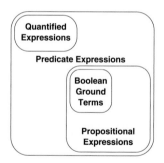

Fig. 9.1. Languages of Boolean-valued expressions

9.1.5 "chaos" — Undefined Expression Evaluations

We reintroduce, at this point, the literal **chaos**, first introduced in Sect. 6.5.6 (in the subsection named Strict Functions (Page 101)). It pertains to possible evaluations (i.e., of finding the values) of arbitrary expressions — yet to be introduced — throughout these volumes. If an expression cannot be evaluated ($e/0$ never evaluates!), then its value is said to be **chaos**. That is, we can speak of never terminating, or undefined evaluations, and we give the name **chaos** to the "value", i.e., the result of such evaluations.

9.1.6 Axiom Systems and Inference Rules

Just as we have the calculus of integers, that is, rules for adding, subtracting, multiplying and integer-dividing integers, and rules for eliminating certain additions, subtractions, multiplications and divisions:

$$0 + a = a, \ 1 \times a = a, \ 0 \times a = 0, \ a/1 = a, \ 0/a = 0 \text{ (where } a \neq 0), \text{etc.}$$

so we have rules, in general called inference rules, for "reducing" or "rewriting" syntactic logic expressions into other (usually simpler) such expressions.

Axioms and inference rules (of some logic) together make up the calculus for that logic. A logic is defined by its axioms and inference rules. We shall, in subsequent sections introduce, various axiom systems.

Axioms and Axiom Systems

An *axiom* is a predicate expression with free variables. These variables designate arbitrary predicate expressions. An axiom thus designate an infinity of predicates without variables, where all (former free) variables have been replaced by propositions.

A "classical" logic axiom is:

$$\phi \vee \neg \phi$$

ϕ is the free variable. It reads: Either ϕ holds, or ϕ does not hold. The axiom is called the axiom of the *excluded middle*, also colloquially referred to as the axiom of the *excluded miracle*!

The pragmatics of an axiom, of a logic, is that it represents, in some or all semantics of that logic, a self-evident truth. An *axiom system* is a collections of one or more axioms.

Inference Rules

An *inference rule* is a pair: a set of predicates with free variables (the premise), and an inferred predicate with some of the same free variables (the conclusion).

The most famous logic inference rule is that of *modus ponens*:

$$\frac{P, P \supset Q}{Q}$$

P and Q are the free variables. It reads: If we know that P holds and that $P \supset Q$ holds, then we can infer (conclude) that Q holds.

The pragmatics of an inference rule, of a logic, is that it represents, in some or all semantics of that logic, a self-evident way of reasoning, from one set of logic expressions to the next, or to another logic expression.

9.1.7 Proof Systems

By a proof system for a logic language we mean: a set of axiom schemes, a set of rules of inference, and a set of theorems provable from the axiom schemes and rules of inference. The latter can be considered as being axioms. Some theorems may be reformulated as "additional" rules of inference:[5]

$$\frac{\Gamma, \phi \vdash \psi}{\xi}$$

The verifier, a person or a mechanised system, has "more to choose from"!

In our presentation of proof systems, in particular that of RSL, we present not only *not* the entire proof systems, but also *not* the full details of how to carry out full proofs, and certainly *not* how to do even small proofs using available theorem prover or proof assistant software systems. To learn how to do real proofs for real developments is a deep study by itself, and we refer to specialised text books on this subject: $[181, 242, 359–361, 419, 472, 533]$.

Summarising we can say: Proof systems are specially tailored versions of axiom schemes and rules of inferences — augmented by theorems and special syntactic conventions on how to present proofs.

9.1.8 A Note on Two Axiom Systems

Axioms are self-evident truths, i.e., can be considered laws. But we have to keep track of two kinds of notions of axioms and axiom systems: The axioms that define proof systems of logic languages, including RSL, and the axioms that a user of RSL defines when specifying properties of sorts and functions.

The two relate as follows:

The axioms of the proof systems of logic languages, like RSL, are given, a priori[6], and are not expressed in those same languages. However, the reader may get the impression that RSL's proof system is defined in RSL, since the axioms look very much like the axiom definition facility of RSL. The axioms that are expressed in RSL, using RSL Boolean valued and other expressions,

---

[5] $\frac{\Gamma, \phi \vdash \psi}{\xi}$ reads: If, assuming the set of axioms (etc.) Γ, ψ can be proved from ϕ, then ξ holds (i.e., has [thus] been proved).

[6] a priori, relating to or derived by reasoning from self-evident propositions, presupposed by experience, being without examination or analysis, formed or conceived beforehand (Merriam–Webster Dictionary [373]).

and which rely on RSL's proof system when proving properties of what these user-defined axioms express.

In the next sections (Sects. 9.3–9.5) on the logic languages of Boolean ground terms, propositions and predicates, respectively, we shall be speaking about the axioms of RSL's proof system. In Sect. 9.6 we shall, in contrast, illustrate the use of RSL' axiom definition facility in defining data types like *Euclid's plane geometry, natural number (Peano's axiom system), simple sets,* and *simple lists* (Examples 9.20, 9.21, 9.23 and 9.24, respectively).

9.1.9 The "if ... then ... else ... end" Connective

The **if...then...else...end** construct "anchors" around a basic understanding of logic. We therefore explain this construct. Let e be:

if b then e′ else e″ end

e is a syntactic construct of, for example, RSL. It allows b to evaluate to a value of any type and to **chaos** (which has no type). The expression e only makes sense if b evaluates to **false** or **true**:

if false then e′ else e″ end ≡ e″
if true then e′ else e″ end ≡ e′
if chaos then e′ else e″ end ≡ chaos

If b evaluates to any other value **chaos** is still the result.[7] **chaos** stands for *chaotic behaviour* of the result of evaluating an expression, including nontermination.

Nonstrictness of a functional, like the *distributed fix,* **if...then...else-...end**, means that applying the functional to arguments that may evaluate to **chaos** does not necessarily lead to **chaos**:

if true then e′ else chaos end ≡ e′
if false then chaos else e″ end ≡ e″

We refer to **if...then...else...end** as a *distributed-* or *mix-fix connective.*

9.1.10 Discussion

We are building up our treatment of logics in small, easy steps. In this section we have basically identified three languages of logic, a language of Boolean ground terms, a language of propositions and a language of predicates. Each of these languages will be dealt with in more detail in Sects. 9.3–9.5. But first, in Sect. 9.2, we treat a number of issues common to the three languages.

---

[7]But RSL is so designed as to out-rule such, so-called type errors, and therefore such expressions, b, will not even be considered correct RSL expressions.

9.2 Proof Theory Versus Model Theory

Above we have made the distinction between the syntax and the semantics of a language. In this section we will elucidate this distinction. In this section we shall assume a classical two-valued logic.

9.2.1 Syntax

What we write is syntax. When we manipulate written text, in some language, using certain (for example inference) rules and axioms, and thereby obtain other text in the same language, then these rules are basically of syntactic nature.

Example 9.1 *Differentiation of Analytic Expressions, I:* We take, as an example, that of the formal language of analytic expressions where some expressions are shown in the left column below. And we take as rules those which define differentiation, shown in the right column below. We observe that the rules are recursively defined.

Analytic Expression		Rule of Differentiation
$y:$	a	$\frac{\partial y}{\partial x} = \frac{\partial a}{\partial x} \rightsquigarrow 0$
$y:$	x	$\frac{\partial y}{\partial x} = \frac{\partial x}{\partial x} \rightsquigarrow 1$
$y:$	x^n	$\frac{\partial y}{\partial x} = \frac{\partial (x^n)}{\partial x} \rightsquigarrow n \times x^{n-1}$
$y:$	$f(x) + g(x)$	$\frac{\partial y}{\partial x} = \frac{\partial (f(x)+g(x))}{\partial x} \rightsquigarrow \frac{\partial (f(x))}{\partial x} + \frac{\partial (g(x))}{\partial x}$
$y:$	$f(x) \times g(x)$	$\frac{\partial y}{\partial x} = \frac{\partial (f(x) \times g(x))}{\partial x} \rightsquigarrow \frac{\partial (f(x))}{\partial x} \times g(x) + \frac{\partial (g(x))}{\partial x} \times f(x)$
etc.		*etc.*

We observe that the rules of differentiation when applied to any analytic expression terminate with the result being an analytic expression. In other words, the language plus the rules remain syntactic. We are just "fiddling" with symbols. ∎

The notions of proofs and theorems (in logic) are syntactic notions. There is a large body of theory that deals only with the syntax of any, or some, logic language(s). Similarly, there is a large body of theory that deals only with the differentiability of analytic expressions, also a syntactic theory.

Mathematical logic can be pursued, at length and in depth, while remaining at the syntactic level.

9.2.2 Semantics

What we mean by the written text, in contrast, is semantics.

Example 9.2 *Differentiation of Analytic Expressions, II:* Why we perform differentiation is of no concern to the rules of differentiation as they are being applied. The semantics of an analytic expression may express distance covered over time. Differentiation wrt. time may therefore be done in order to express the velocity. Differentiation wrt. time performed twice may therefore be done in order to express the acceleration.   ∎

Semantics is about truth, about the 'holding' or 'not holding' of a logical sentence. Thus the Boolean ground terms **false** and **true** denote the semantic values *falsity* and *truth,* respectively.

Example 9.3 *Meaning of Logical Expressions:* A logical expression, ϕ, may mean that it designates the properties of a requirements prescription. Another logical expression, ψ, may mean that it designates the properties of a software specification. The logical expression, $\psi \supset \phi$, may then mean that the software specification implements the requirements.   ∎

9.2.3 Syntax Versus Semantics

To sum up: When speaking in the syntactic realm of a logic language the logic expressions are mere symbols — we are not interested in their meaning. We manipulate strings of symbols using the axioms and rules of inference. When speaking in the semantic realm of a logic language the logic expressions denote values, and these values are obtained through interpretation. There is a *context* which, among others, maps expression symbols (including variable identifiers) to their truth values. Different contexts (we say different 'worlds') may map the same variable identifier to different truth values.

9.2.4 Formal Logics: Syntax and Semantics

This and the next sections (Sect. 9.2.4–9.2.6) are inspired by John Rushby's 1993 report *Rapid Introduction to Mathematical Logic* [451].

The various logic languages, their syntax and semantics, all manifest formal systems. A formal logic system, syntactically, consists of several parts. First, it contains (i) a logic language given by some concrete grammar which elucidates constant and function (i.e., operation) literals, for example, **false, true, chaos,** ¬ (or ∼), ∧, ∨, and ⊃, variable, function and predicate identifiers, delimiters (like commas: ",", parentheses: "(", ")", etc.), and their combination (say in terms of a set of BNF rules). Second, a formal logic system, syntactically, also consists of (ii) an axiom system: a set of axioms, viz.:

$$\phi \lor \neg\phi.$$

In other words, the axiom system is a subset of sentences of the language, in which variable identifiers (ϕ) are metalinguistic: they designate proper sentences (viz.: $(P \vee Q) \wedge R$) of the language. Finally, a formal logic system, syntactically, also consists of (iii) a set of rules of inference: a set of pairs of antecedents and consequents, viz.:

$$\frac{\phi, \phi \supset \psi}{\psi}$$

The former is a set of sentences, and the latter is a sentence, such that all variable identifiers of these sentences are metalinguistic. They designate proper sentences of the language.

More on the Semantics of Formal Logic Systems

Semantically, a formal system extends its syntax along two lines. Along one line, a context is provided, something which to every symbol of the language associates appropriate semantic notions. To literals (**false, true, chaos**) one associates the semantic truth values (**ff**, **tt** or *falsity, truth*), respectively the semantic undefined value ($\perp$). $\perp$ "propagates" by making any expression evaluation in which it occurs denote that value. To variable identifiers one associates some proper truth or other value, etcetera. What the "etcetera" stands for will be revealed later, suffice it here to hint at operator, function and predicate symbols.

Along the other line, a semantics prescribes an evaluation (an interpretation) procedure which when applied to a sentence in a context results in a value: *falsity, truth* or $\perp$.

More on the Syntax of Formal Logic Systems

There are usually two parts to a formal system: One part, the *logical part* that is shared by all logic languages, and another, the *non-logical part*.

The symbols that belong to the *logical part* are called the *logical symbols* of the system. The *connectives* are logical symbols:

$$\neg, \quad \vee, \quad \wedge, \quad \supset, \equiv$$

In the predicate calculi we additionally introduce:

$$f_1, \quad f_2, \quad \ldots, f_n, \quad \forall, \quad \exists$$

where f_i are function symbols, and $\forall$ and $\exists$ are the universal, respectively the existential quantifiers.

The non-logical symbols are given special interpretations:

$$+, \quad -, \quad \times, \quad /, \quad <, \quad \leq, \quad =, \quad >, \quad \geq, \quad \ldots$$

The connectives are chosen to "mimic" every language use, with some more precision, of the terms: 'and' ($\wedge$), 'or' ($\vee$), 'not' ($\neg$), 'equal' ($\equiv$), and 'imply' ($\supset$). In $P \supset Q$ P is called the *antecedent*. Q is called the *consequent*.

On the Meaning of Material Implication, $\supset$

Let us dwell, for a moment, on the issue of the intended (semantic) meaning of implication $\supset$:

$$P \supset Q$$

When we say that a logical expression holds we mean that it evaluates to **true**.

$P \supset Q$ reads: If P holds, then Q holds; if P then Q.

Example 9.4 *Informal Uses of Implication, I:* Let us illustrate some examples of uses of implication. The examples are taken from [451]:

> The deduction "the *jaberwocky* is a *tove*; all *toves* are *slithy*; therefore that *jaberwocky* is *slithy*", seems OK even though we have do not know what *jaberwocky, tove* and *slithy* means.
>
> What about "The air plane is a Boeing 737; therefore it has two engines"? That does not seem OK, even though its conclusion is true. It jumps to a conclusion that is not supported by the facts that are explicitly mentioned.
>
> What about: "the car is a Chrysler; therefore it has two engines"? We see this as palpable nonsense. We can repair the above "The air plane is a Boeing 737; all Boeing planes, except the 747, have two engines; therefore that plane has two engines." Now the reasoning is sound. And soundness does not depend on whether we understand the terms 'Boeing', 'engine', '737', or '747'.

∎

Following John Rushby[8] we show an example, and then analyse possible semantics of the implication connective.

Example 9.5 *Informal Uses of Implication, II:*

> Consider the four implications: (1) $2+2 = 4 \supset$ Paris is the Capital of France; (2) $2 + 2 = 4 \supset$ London is the Capital of France; (3) $2 + 2 = 5 \supset$ Paris is the Capital of France; and (4) $2 + 2 = 5 \supset$ London is the Capital of France.
>
> What truth values can we ascribe to (1–4)? (1) is true because both the antecedent and the consequent are true. (2) is false because the consequent is false. (3) is what? (4) is what? To answer (3) and (4) we turn to the next analysis.

∎

---

[8] *Rapid Introduction to Mathematical Logic*, 1993 Appendix to [451]

We continue quoting from [451]:

> Thus if, in $P \supset Q$, P does not hold, then we do not (based on what we have presented up till now) know whether Q holds, and hence we do not know whether $P \supset Q$ holds. If P holds, but Q does not hold, then our intuition dictates that $P \supset Q$ does not hold.
>
> So what are we to say about the holdings of $P \supset Q$ when P does not hold? If we say that $P \supset Q$ does not hold, when P and Q do not hold, then $P \supset Q$ is the same as $P \wedge Q$. If we say that $P \supset Q$ holds exactly when Q holds, then $P \supset Q$ is the same as Q. If we say that $P \supset Q$ holds exactly when Q does not hold, then $P \supset Q$ is the same as $P \equiv Q$. Thus we conclude that $P \supset Q$ holds when P and Q hold, and when P does not hold (irrespective of holding of Q).

Metalinguistic Variables

In axioms, such as:

$$\phi \vee \neg\phi$$

and in rules of inference, such as:

$$\frac{\phi, \phi \supset \psi}{\psi}$$

the identifiers ϕ and ψ stand for arbitrary logic sentences. They are metalinguistic variables. In any particular use of logic in some specification we may have some propositions or some predicates P and Q.

They can now be substituted in lieu of ϕ and ψ

$$P \vee \neg P$$

respectively

$$\frac{P, P \supset Q}{Q}$$

Since any Ps and Qs are acceptable we see that axiom and rules of inference really are schemes of axioms, respectively schemes of inference. That is, they stand for infinities of axioms and infinities of rules of inference.

Given a metalinguistic variable, say ϕ, and given some instance of a propositional or predicate sentence, say P, we may express that P is to take the place of ϕ in some (designated) axiom scheme or in some (designated) rule of inference scheme as follows:

$$[\phi \mapsto P]$$

The form $[\phi \mapsto P]$ is called a substitution specification clause. Substitution specifications may contain several clauses:

$$[\phi_1 \mapsto P_1, \phi_2 \mapsto P_2, \ldots, \phi_n \mapsto P_n]$$

9.2.5 Issues Related to Proofs

Proofs

Given a sentence ϕ. A *proof* of ϕ, from a set, Γ, of sentences is a finite sequence of sentences, $\phi_1, \phi_2, \ldots, \phi_n$, where $\phi = \phi_1$, where $\phi_n = $ **true**, and in which each ϕ_i is either an axiom, or a member of Γ, or follows from earlier ϕ_js by one of the rules of inference.

We say that ϕ is *provable* from *assumptions* Γ, or simply Γ proves ϕ:
$\Gamma \vdash \phi$

Proofs and provability are syntactic notions, i.e., are notions of proof theory.

Theorems and Formal System Theories

A *theorem* is a sentence that is provable without assumptions, that is purely from axioms and rules of inferences. We say that a *theory* of a given formal system is the set of all its theorems.

Theorems and theories are syntactic notions, i.e., are notions of proof theory.

Consistency

A formal system is *consistent* if it contains no sentence ϕ such that both ϕ and its negation $\neg\phi$ are theorems.

It is a meta-theorem of all the two-valued logics that all sentences are provable in an inconsistent formal, two-valued logic system.

Consistency is a syntactic notion, i.e., is a notion of proof theory.

Decidability

A formal logic system is *decidable* if there is an algorithm which prescribes computations that can determine whether or not any given sentence in the system is a theorem (or not).

9.2.6 Relating Proof Theory to Model Theory

In modelling domains, requirements and software using logic, we are modelling some "worlds". So far we have emphasised the syntactic aspects of logic. To establish a relationship between the syntactic aspects of the sentences of a formal language and some world we must turn to semantics.

The goal, then, of mathematical logic is to make sure that theorems are true in the chosen world, or worlds. We wish to make sure that the theorems we can prove will correspond to true statements about a chosen world, or all worlds.

Interpretation

The connection between syntax and semantics is, as always, established through an interpretation, $\mathcal{I}$. So we start with a formal logic system, $\mathcal{L}$. An interpretation $\mathcal{I}$ identifies some chosen world, Ω, and associates a true or a false statements with each sentence of the formal system. Statements are of the kind: *"the logic expression ϕ (about such-and-such) is true in Ω"*, or *"the logic expression ϕ (about such-and-such) is false in Ω"*.

The interpretation, $\mathcal{I}$, has two parts: A context, an environment, ρ, which to every symbol in $\mathcal{L}$, associates some value in Ω, and a procedure for evaluating any sentence ϕ in $\mathcal{L}$.

Example 9.6 *The Factorial and The List Reversal Functions:* This example is inspired by [359]. Let ϕ be the sentence:

$$\exists F \bullet ((F(a) = b) \land \forall x \bullet (p(x) \supset (F(x) = g(x, F(f(x))))))$$

which, model-theoretically, reads: there exists a mathematical function F such that ($\bullet$) the following holds, namely: $F(a) = b$ (where a and b are not known, model-theoretically), and $\land$ for every (i.e., all) x it is the case ($\bullet$) that if $p(x)$ is true, then $F(x) = g(x, F(f(x)))$ is true (where x, g and f are not known, model-theoretically).

Now there are (at least) two possible interpretations of ϕ. In the first interpretation we establish first the world Ω of natural numbers and operations on these, and then the specific context ρ:

[F $\mapsto$ fact,
  a $\mapsto$ 1,
  b $\mapsto$ 1,
  f $\mapsto$ λ n.n$-$1,
  g $\mapsto$ λ m.λ n.m+n
  p $\mapsto$ λ m.m>0]

And we find that ϕ is true for the factorial function, fact. In other words, ϕ characterises properties of that function.

In the second interpretation we establish first the world Ω of lists and operations on these: and then the specific context ρ:

[F $\mapsto$ rev,
  a $\mapsto$ $\langle\rangle$,
  b $\mapsto$ $\langle\rangle$,
  f $\mapsto$ **tl**,
  g $\mapsto$ $\lambda\ell_1.\lambda\ell_2.\ell_1\,\hat{}\,\langle$**hd** $\ell_1\rangle$
  p $\mapsto$ $\lambda\ell.\ell\neq\langle\rangle$]

And we find that ϕ is true for the list reversal function, rev. In other words, ϕ characterises properties of that function.

We leave it to the reader to find worlds and/or context associations for which ϕ does not hold.   ∎

Models

An interpretation $\mathcal{I}$ is a *model* for a formal system $\mathcal{L}$ if it evaluates all its axioms to true.

An interpretation $\mathcal{I}$ is a *model* for a set of sentences Γ if it (the set) additionally evaluates all the sentences in Γ to true.

The concept of model is a semantics notion.

Satisfiability, Entailment: $\models$ and Validity

A set of sentences Γ is *satisfiable* if it (the set) has a model.

A set of sentences Γ *entails* a sentence ψ

$$\Gamma \models \psi$$

if every model of Γ is also a model of ψ, that is: ψ evaluates to true in every model of Γ.

A sentence ψ is (universally) *valid*, and we write $\models \psi$, if it valuates to true in all models of its formal system.

Soundness and Completeness, $\vdash$ Versus $\models$

A formal system is *sound* if $\Gamma \models \psi$ whenever $\gamma \vdash \psi$. Soundness helps ensure that every provable fact is true. A formal system is *complete* if $\Gamma \vdash \psi$ whenever $\gamma \models \psi$. Completeness helps ensure that every true fact is provable. Inconsistent systems cannot be sound. The formal systems used in the formal techniques for specification and verifying properties of specifications must be consistent, but are usually incomplete and not decidable.

9.2.7 Discussion

So the syntax (sentences, axioms and rules of inference) determines a proof theory. Issues like proofs, theorems, consistency and decidability are proof theoretic concepts. And an interpretation determines a model theory. Interpretations tie proof and model theories together. And so do issues like models, satisfiability, entailment, validity, soundness and completeness. We remind the reader that all of this section (Sect. 9.2) has assumed a classical two-valued logic.

9.3 A Language of Boolean Ground Terms

On one hand, we have the semantic notion of an algebra. And on the other hand, we have the syntactic notion of Boolean ground terms. The two together with appropriate syntactic and semantic extensions define a language of Boolean ground terms. In this section we will present these notions and extensions.

9.3.1 Syntax and Semantics

The Boolean algebra to be put forward in these volumes can be presented as if it was an RSL **class**:[9]

class Boolean
    type
      Bool
    value
      true, false, chaos
      $\sim$: **Bool** $\to$ **Bool**
      $\wedge, \vee, \Rightarrow, =, \neq, \equiv$: **Bool** $\times$ **Bool** $\to$ **Bool**
    axiom
      $\forall$ b,b':**Bool** •
        $\sim$b $\equiv$ **if** b **then false else true end**
        b $\wedge$ b' $\equiv$ **if** b **then** b' **else false end**
        b $\vee$ b' $\equiv$ **if** b **then true else** b' **end**
        b $\Rightarrow$ b' $\equiv$ **if** b **then** b' **else true end**
        b $=$ b' $\equiv$ **if** (b$\wedge$b')$\vee$($\sim$b$\wedge\sim$b') **then true else false end**
        (b $\neq$ b') $\equiv$ $\sim$(b $=$ b')
        (b $\equiv$ b') $\equiv$ (b $=$ b')
    end

We refer to Sect, 9.1.9 for the axioms that govern the use of the **if ... then ... else ... end** clause. Notice that we henceforth, for proper RSL, use the implication symbol $\Rightarrow$ instead of the usual mathematical logic symbol used earlier $\supset$. However, they designate the same thing

We emphasize that the above presents only an algebra: its values (by their designators **true, false, chaos**, that is a semantic presentation) and its operations (by their signatures, and by axioms defining the meaning of the operations). And we emphasize that we have, in a sense, "misused" RSL. We can, of course, not use RSL to explain RSL. We are, above, informally using mathematics, but couch it in the style of some RSL-like text.

---

[9]We remind the reader that we cannot define the axioms of the logic sublanguage of RSL in RSL. That would lead to a meaningless circularity. Thus the **class** clause shown above (after where this footnote was first referenced), is not to be read as RSL, but as an ordinary mathematics text.

In the next section we shall informally explain these operations. Later we shall introduce a language of Boolean ground terms by presenting the syntactic notions of grammar, axioms and rules of inference.

9.3.2 The Connectives: $\sim$, $\wedge$, $\vee$, $\Rightarrow$, $=$, $\neq$, $\equiv$

We explain the connectives, semantically, and as if we already allowed their operands to attain the undefined value **chaos**. For the algebra of Boolean ground terms we do not need the concept of 'undefined value'. Later we shall extend our logic to the language of predicate expressions, which have the same connectives as for Boolean ground terms. Below we therefore explain the connectives as if they occurred in propositional expressions, i.e., in truth-valued expressions whose variables were truth-valued.

Negation, $\sim$

The logical connective $\sim$ is called 'negation'. We may read $\sim$P as 'not P'. The *law of the excluded middle* implies that we cannot have both 'not P' and 'P'; exactly one of the propositional expressions is true. Some three-valued logics (cf. Cheng and Jones's *Logic for Partial Functions* (LPF) [150, 151, 318]) do not enjoy the "excluded middle" property.

Conjunction, $\wedge$

The logical connective $\wedge$ is called 'and' and 'conjunction'. The $\wedge$ connective is applied not only to express the simultaneous truth of both operands, but also to express that if the left operand has truth value falsity, then one need not consider (evaluation of) the right operand! This non-commutativity of the $\wedge$ connective cuts down on the size of expressions that one may need to write down:

$$a \wedge b \equiv \textbf{if } a=\textbf{false then false else } b \textbf{ end}$$

The expression to the left of $\equiv$ above is shorter than the expression to the right of $\equiv$.

Disjunction, $\vee$

The logical connective $\vee$ is called 'or', 'logical or', 'inclusive or' and 'disjunction'. Normally in the English language using 'or' means 'exclusive or' — for which latter exactly one of its two arguments are true, the other is false. But for P$\vee$Q we accept if both are true. So beware! But if the left-hand operand is **true** then we may skip evaluating, i.e., even considering the right-hand operand.

Equality, $=$

Equality, $=$, is to be seen in contrast to identity, $\equiv$. In $E = E'$ the propositional expressions E and E' may contain arbitrary identifiers, i.e., variables, whose (in the present situation: truth) values may vary. Evaluation of $E = E'$ thus takes place in a context[10] where these variables are bound to some values. And evaluation of $E = E'$ considers only the "current" context. That is, $E = E'$ may be evaluated several times, say because that expression occurs in a function definition body which is evaluated each time the function is invoked. The value of $E = E'$ is determined only by the context relevant for the specific invocation. For two different invocations the value of the same expression, $E = E'$, may thus differ!

Implication, $\Rightarrow$

The logical connective $\Rightarrow$ is called 'implication'. In P$\Rightarrow$Q the propositional expression P is called the *hypothesis*, the *antecedent* or the *premise*, while the propositional expression Q (of P$\Rightarrow$Q) is called the *consequence* or *conclusion*.

The proposition P$\Rightarrow$Q is **false** only when P is **true** and ($\wedge$) Q is **false**. One can 'read' P$\Rightarrow$Q in a number of ways: *If P then Q, P only if Q, P is a sufficient condition for Q, Q is a necessary condition for P, Q if P, Q follows from P, Q provided P, Q is a logical consequence of P*, or *Q whenever P*.

Identity, $\equiv$

To explain the identity connective, $\equiv$, is a bit more complicated than to explain the equality connective, $=$. As expressed above, when testing for equality of values one evaluates both operand expressions, once, in some current binding of their free identifiers to values, then tests them for equality.

For $\equiv$(e′,e″) (also written, more naturally, e′ $\equiv$ e″), one has to evaluate the two operand expressions in all possible bindings of their free identifiers to values, and for all bindings the same result must be yielded: Either always **true** or always **false** for the identity to hold, i.e., be **true**. If some evaluate to **chaos**, then **chaos** is the value. If none evaluate to **chaos** and not all to the same (**true** or **false**) truth value, then **false** is the value.

9.3.3 Three-Valued Logic

The present section presents a proof-theoretic, i.e., a syntactic view of a three-valued logic of the emerging language of Boolean ground terms. Syntactically

---

[10]We shall later in this section explain, in more detail, what we mean by the term 'context', and we shall then contrast this context concept with the concept of 'model' introduced already in Sect. 1.7 and discussed more extensively in Sect. 8.5.4.

we should now present a set of axioms and, possibly, a set of rules of inference. We shall do so, but instead of presenting the rules of inference in the form of "something above a bar and something below that bar", we exemplify below a *tabular representation* of these rules of inference.

The **axioms** are **true** and ~**false**. But note that the above do not explain RSL in terms of RSL, but in terms of informal mathematics.

∨, ∧, and ⇒ Syntactic Truth Tables

∨	true	false	chaos
true	true	true	true
false	true	false	chaos
chaos	chaos	chaos	chaos

∧	true	false	chaos
true	true	false	chaos
false	false	false	false
chaos	chaos	chaos	chaos

⇒	true	false	chaos
true	true	false	chaos
false	true	true	true
chaos	chaos	chaos	chaos

≡ Versus =

Assume e_1 and e_2 are defined expressions, both with deterministic (i.e., definite) values, without effects, that is, side effects (changes to assignable variables), and without communication, that is, as we shall first see in Chap. 21 (this volume), CSP-like input/output communication. Assume further that e_1 and e_2 evaluates to v_1, and v_2, respectively. Then the two three-valued logic truth tables are:

≡ and = Syntactic Truth Tables

≡	e1	e2	chaos
e1	true	false	false
e2	false	true	chaos
chaos	false	false	true

=	e1	e2	chaos
e1	true	false	chaos
e2	false	true	chaos
chaos	chaos	chaos	chaos

Form of Inference Rule

From the tabular form we arrive at the standard way of presenting a rule of inference

$$\frac{\text{antecedent}(s)}{\text{consequent}}$$

as follows: There is one rule of inference for each entry in each table. The antecedent of such a rule of inference is formed by composing three symbols: the row index ground term, the "upper left corner" operator, and the column index ground term, and in that order. The consequent of the rule of inference is now the entry term:

$$\frac{\textbf{false} \Rightarrow \textbf{chaos}}{\textbf{true}}$$

Above we have shown an example from the third table above, second row, third column!

Truth and Falsity (Syntactic) Designators and Semantic Values

As the truth tables are presented we may get the syntactic understanding that the truth designators are **true** and **false**. That is how we syntactically express them. Pragmatically we need a way to write down truth values — so we use the literals **true** and **false**. We distinguish between the syntactic literals — which are the ones we write down in our specifications — and the names of their meaning (i.e., semantics or interpretation). Some authors, when making this distinction, for example use the metalinguistic literals tt, ff and ⊥. That is, the interpretation context (ρ) associates **true** with tt, etc. We could then use these latter as entries in three tables defining the interpretation context meaning of the connectives:

Interpretation Context: Semantic Truth Tables

∨	tt	ff	⊥
tt	tt	tt	⊥
ff	tt	ff	⊥
⊥	⊥	⊥	⊥

∧	tt	ff	⊥
tt	tt	ff	⊥
ff	ff	ff	ff
⊥	⊥	⊥	⊥

⇒	tt	ff	⊥
tt	tt	ff	⊥
ff	tt	tt	tt
⊥	⊥	⊥	⊥

But we cannot use the interpretation designators in any of the identities expressed earlier. That is, we cannot use them in the **if ... then ... else ... end** axioms. They are metalinguistic: They are the means of explaining something.

Non-commutativity of Boolean Connective

We refer to a logic of three values, as above, as a three-valued logic. The first such, for computing science, was introduced by John McCarthy [367]. For VDM, RSL's predecessor, Cliff B. Jones proposed a *logic for partial functions* [150, 316, 317]. Several forms of three-valued logic exists [131–133, 329].

Let an expression be:

(E1 ∧ E2) ∨ E3

where evaluation of E2 for E1=**false** might not terminate. If E1∧E2 yields **true**, evaluation of the expression E3 need not take place. If E1∧E2 yields **false**, evaluation of the expression E3 must take place.

To express the above for commutative, two-valued logics of ∧ and ∨, we need, for example, write:

if E1 then (if E2 then true else E3 end) else E3 end

9.3.4 Ground Terms and Their Evaluation

Let us first give some examples:

Example 9.7 *Ground Terms:* Examples of ground terms are:

true, false, ∼true, ∼false,
true∧true, true∨true, true⇒true, true=true, true≠true, true ≡ true
true∧false, true∨false, true⇒false, true=false, true≠false, true ≡ false
  ...
(true∧((∼true)∨false)⇒true)=false, ...

∎

Syntax of Boolean Ground Terms, BGT

The *Boolean language of ground terms*, BGT, is now defined:

- The Basis Clause: **true, false** and **chaos** are Boolean ground terms.
- The Inductive Clause: If b and b′ are Boolean ground terms, then so are:
  ∼b, b∧b′, b∨b′, b⇒b′, b=b′, b≠b′, b≡b′ and (b).
- The Extremal Clause: Only those terms that can be formed from a finite number of uses of the above two clauses are Boolean ground terms.

Since this is only the second time in these volumes that we properly introduce a language, and since we have yet to cover the material that shall later enable us to present such a language definition formally, we use the above informal, yet very precise style of presentation.[11]

We can present the above inductive definition in the form of a BNF Grammar:

---

[11] Our first such structured, yet informal presentation was that of λ-expressions (Sect. 7.2).

The basis, inductive and extremal clause presentation represents a classical, mathematical way of presenting inductive structures. These are typically infinite sets of entities (here they are syntactic entities), which have a structure. The three-clause presentation aims at presenting this structure. The structure contains atomic entities, as for the basis clause, or composite, as here, pairs or triples of entities: operands and prefix or infix operators as well as parenthesised structures. The basis clause usually lists a finite, or refers to an infinite, number of terms. The logic clause lists

⟨BGT⟩ ::= **true** | **false** | **chaos**
      | ∼ ⟨BGT⟩
      | ⟨BGT⟩ ∧ ⟨BGT⟩
      | ⟨BGT⟩ ∨ ⟨BGT⟩
      | ⟨BGT⟩ ⇒ ⟨BGT⟩
      | ⟨BGT⟩ = ⟨BGT⟩
      | ⟨BGT⟩ ≠ ⟨BGT⟩
      | ⟨BGT⟩ ≡ ⟨BGT⟩
      | (⟨BGT⟩)

The trouble with the above grammar is that it is ambiguous. Is the term:

true ∧ **false** ∨ **true**,

the same as

true ∧ (**false** ∨ **true**),

or

(**true** ∧ **false**) ∨ **true**?

The inductive definition gave no hint as to the binding priority of the connectives.

To do so, through a BNF grammar, we introduce an alternative grammar:

⟨BGT⟩ ::= ⟨aBGT⟩ | ⟨pBGT⟩
⟨aBGT⟩ ::= **true** | **false** | **chaos**
⟨pBGT⟩ ::= (⟨BGT⟩)
      | (∼ ⟨BGT⟩)
      | (⟨BGT⟩ ∨ ⟨BGT⟩)
      | (⟨BGT⟩ ∧ ⟨BGT⟩)
      | (⟨BGT⟩ ⇒ ⟨BGT⟩)
      | (⟨BGT⟩ = ⟨BGT⟩)
      | (⟨BGT⟩ ≠ ⟨BGT⟩)
      | (⟨BGT⟩ ≡ ⟨BGT⟩)

Now it would not be possible to write:

true ∧ **false** ∨ **true**.

The above would have to be written either as

---

just two. The inductive clause is usually of recursive nature: It assumes the existence of some terms and expresses the construction, the existence, of further terms. The basis clause secures the existence of initial terms. And the inductive clause adds further terms to the language of terms. The extremal clause ensures that unwanted terms do not accidentally creep into the language. The adjective 'extremal' expresses exclusion!

true ∧ (**false** ∨ **true**),

or as

(**true** ∧ **false**) ∨ **true**.

By suitably designing a BNF grammar that directly "embodies" operator (binding) precedence rules, one can achieve an expression form that avoids excessive parenthesisation.

Boolean Ground Term Evaluation, Eval_BGT

Given any Boolean ground term, we can provide an interpretation. That is, we can evaluate it.

The evaluation rules are: If the ground term is **true**, its value is tt. If the ground term is **false**, its value is ff. If the ground term is ∼b and the value of b is tt, then the value of ∼b is ff. b value ff leads to ∼b result value tt. If the ground term is b∧b' and the values of b and b' are τ and τ' — where τ and τ', individually are one of tt or ff — then the value of b∧b' is found by looking up under the corresponding entry in the ∧ table. The same holds for b⊙b' where ⊙ is any of ∨, ⇒, =, ≠, or ≡, for which appropriate tables are selected.

We "pseudo-formalise" this interpretation function. It is a pseudo-formalisation since it is not expressed in a proper formal notation. Why not, i.e., why not use RSL? The answer is: Because we have yet to introduce all the RSL machinery that is needed in a proper formalisation. The pseudo-formalisation shall serve to acquaint the reader with the form and possible content of formal function definitions.

The tables are presented as maps (finite size, enumerable functions) from truth values to truth values. They are straightforward "mathematical" forms of the tables given above. One table was missing: that of negation. We leave it to the reader to provide that table. Thus the type of the Boolean ground term evaluation procedure, Eval_BGT, is:

value
    Eval_BGT: BGT → TBLS → **Bool**
type
    TBLS = uTBL×bTBL×bTBL×bTBL×bTBL×bTBL×bTBL
    uTBL = **Bool** $\overrightarrow{m}$ **Bool**
    bTBL = **Bool** × **Bool** $\overrightarrow{m}$ **Bool**

The six tables above are to be those of negation, conjunction, disjunction, implication, equality, none-quality, respectively identity (equivalence).

value
    Eval_BGT(bgt)(tbls) ≡

     let (n,a,o,i,eq,neq,id) = tbls **in**
    case bgt **of**
       true → tt,
       false → ff,
       chaos → ⊥,
       ∼t → **let** b = Eval_BGT(t)(tbls) **in** n(b) **end**,
       t′∧t″ →
          let b′=Eval_BGT(t′)(tbls), b″=Eval_BGT(t″)(tbls)
          in a(b′,b″) **end**,
       ... /∗ similar for p′∨p″, p′⇒p″, p′=p″, p′≠p″, and ∗/ p′is p″
    end end

Later we shall see how to express the above pseudo-formalisation of Eval_BGT.

9.3.5 "Syntactic" Versus "Semantic Semantics"

Thus there are two ways of looking at most of the languages that we will present in these volumes (for the various subsets of RSL, as well as for languages (or language fragments) separate from RSL).

One way of looking at a language is *semantically* — as we have just done. Here we explained the meaning of (in this case Boolean ground) terms by exhibiting an evaluation procedure which "translated" the syntactic literals **true** and **false** into tt, respectively ff. And where we did not otherwise bother much about telling you what these "new" markers, tt and ff, stood for!

Another way of looking at a language is *syntactically* — which we did earlier, for example on Page 159. Then we basically "rewrote" an operand term in the Boolean literals **true** and **false** and connectives (∼, ∧, ∨, ⇒, =, ≡) into one of these literals.

In the former semantics the meaning of a term was a mathematical value, one that "nobody has ever seen"! In the latter "semantics" the value of a term was a term, i.e., a syntactic "thing" that "everybody has seen"!

The former style of semantics definition will be repeated, again and again in these volumes, and will be referred to, especially as we go on to the next examples, as the denotational style of semantics definitions. The latter style, the syntactic one, will be referred to as a 'rewrite rule' semantics. The λ-calculus, as given earlier (Sect. 7.2) was thus given a syntactical, that is, a rewrite rule semantics.

"Syntactic semantics" is the basis for proofs of properties of formal specifications, and for proofs of certain relations (including correctness) between pairs of formal specifications. We shall return to this subject in due course.

9.3.6 Discussion

We have introduced the "barest" of a language, the language of Boolean ground terms, BGT. We have separated our presentation into one of presenting the syntactics of BGT and one of presenting the semantics of BGT. And we have just, immediately above, briefly discussed a recurrent theme: a proper semantics view of syntax as well as a "syntactic semantics" as are most calculi. Finally, wrt. the pragmatics of BGT we said earlier: Using just the language of Boolean ground terms, there is not much of interest we can express.

With the next logic language, that of propositions, there also is not much of interest we can express. We shall have to wait till we master the syntax (and semantics) of some language of predicates, then we can start expressing something.

The reason for this seemingly slow, pedantic unfolding of two, we claim, not so "powerful" languages before we present the "real thing" is one of pedagogics and didactics: For some readers the concepts of logics, and in particular its three "sublanguages", such as we have presented them, is not familiar. Additionally, the distinction between the syntactics of calculi (including proof systems) is so different from what they may be familiar with, that a direct, an immediate presentation of just a language of predicate calculus is an unnecessary intellectual challenge as compared to a stepwise unfolding such as we have attempted it.

9.4 Languages of Propositional Logic

By *propositional logic* we syntactically understand (i) a set of truth values, (ii) an infinite set of *propositional expressions*, with connectives, and *truth-valued propositional variables*, (iii) a set of axioms and (iv) a set of rules of inference. The above determines a syntax, i.e., a proof theory of a propositional calculus.

Semantically we equip the (syntax of the language of) propositional logic with (v) a suitable context for determining the value of *propositional literals* and *symbols*, and (vi) an *interpretation function* that allows one to *calculate* the *truth value* of *propositional expressions*. By a propositional expression we thus mean an expression like a Boolean ground term, but where some Boolean literals (**true, false** or **chaos**) are replaced by *propositional variables*. A *propositional variable* is an identifier which, semantically, is intended to stand for a Boolean truth value (which could be **chaos**). We shall only cover propositional logic from the viewpoint of its practical use in formal specifications: (i–iv) Making precise the syntax of the expressions, and (v–vi) presenting an interpretation procedure for evaluating their values.

9.4.1 Propositional Expressions, PRO

Examples of Propositional Expressions

Let V be an alphabet of variable identifiers (i.e., variables), and let v, v', ..., v'' be examples of such variables.

value $v,v',...,v''$:**Bool**
... **true**, v, $v \wedge$**true**, ..., $(\sim(v \wedge v') \Rightarrow (v' \Rightarrow v'')) =$ **false**, ...

The last line above exemplifies some propositional expressions.

Syntax of Propositional Expressions, PRO

- Basis Clause I: Any Boolean ground term is a *propositional expression*.
- Basis Clause II: There is given an *alphabet* V of (further un-analysed) *variable identifiers*. If v, v', ..., v'' are in that alphabet, then v, v', ..., v'' are propositional expressions.
- Inductive Clause: If p and p' are propositional expressions, then so are $\sim p$, $p \wedge p'$, $p \vee p'$, $p \Rightarrow p'$, $p = p'$, $p \neq p'$, $p \equiv p'$ and (p).
- The Extremal Clause: Only such terms which can be formed from a finite number of uses of the above two clauses are propositional expressions.

An example BNF grammar could be:

$$\langle\text{PRO}\rangle ::= \textbf{true} \mid \textbf{false} \mid \textbf{chaos}$$
$$\mid \sim \langle\text{PRO}\rangle$$
$$\mid \langle\text{PRO}\rangle \wedge \langle\text{PRO}\rangle$$
$$\mid \langle\text{PRO}\rangle \vee \langle\text{PRO}\rangle$$
$$\mid \langle\text{PRO}\rangle \Rightarrow \langle\text{PRO}\rangle$$
$$\mid \langle\text{PRO}\rangle = \langle\text{PRO}\rangle$$
$$\mid \langle\text{PRO}\rangle \neq \langle\text{PRO}\rangle$$
$$\mid \langle\text{PRO}\rangle \equiv \langle\text{PRO}\rangle$$
$$\mid (\langle\text{PRO}\rangle)$$
$$\mid \langle \text{Identifier}\rangle$$
$$\langle \text{Identifier}\rangle ::= ...$$

We leave it to the reader to complete the BNF definition of $\langle$ Identifier$\rangle$s, say as strings of alphanumeric characters commencing with lower case alphabetic characters, possibly having properly embedded, separating underscores (_). The above BNF grammar is ambiguous, as was the BNF grammar for Boolean ground terms, cf. Sect. 9.3.4.

Above we saw an example of an inductive definition. Next we shall see an example of a semantics which is presented in the style of a morphism, i.e., a homomorphism, such as earlier explained in Sect. 8.4.4.

The two concepts go hand-in-hand: The inductive definition describes composite structures in terms of postulated structures and operator symbols. A morphism is explained in terms of a function ϕ being applied to postulated (semantic) structures, i.e., values. The induction definition was here used to explain syntax. And homomorphisms will be used to explain the semantics of inductively, i.e., recursively, defined syntactic structures.

9.4.2 Examples

The below examples relate to corresponding *Common Exercise Topics* outlined in Appendix Chap. A.

Example 9.8 ♣ *Propositions: Transportation Net:*
We refer to Appendix A, Sect. A.1, *Transportation Net.*
   Let the following propositions be expressible:

- *a: Segment 17 of Broadway has connectors 34th Street and 35th Street.*
- *b: Segment 18 of Broadway has connectors 35th Street and 36th Street.*
- *c: Segment 17 of Broadway is connected to Segment 18 of Broadway.*

Given the above abbreviations we can express:

- $a \wedge b$, and $a \wedge b \Rightarrow c$,

If a and b holds then these propositions hold, i.e., c holds.   ∎

Example 9.9 ♣ *Propositions: Container Logistics:*
We refer to Appendix A, Sect. A.2, *Container Logistics.*
   Let the following propositions be expressible:

- *a: "Quay locations 7–12 are free at container terminal PTP."*
- *b: "The Harald Maersk ship is 6 terminal PTP quay locations long."*
- *c: "Harald Maersk can enter container terminal PTP."*

Given the above abbreviations we can express:

- $a \wedge b$, and $a \wedge b \Rightarrow c$,

If a and b holds then these propositions hold, i.e., c holds.   ∎

Example 9.10 ♣ *Propositions: Financial Service Industry:*
We refer to Appendix A, Sect. A.3, *Financial Service Industry.*
   Let the following propositions be expressible:

- *a: Anderson has account α with a balance of US $ 1,000.*
- *b: Peterson has account π.*
- *c: Anderson can transfer US $ 200 from account α to Peterson account π.*

Given the above abbreviations we can express:

- $a \wedge b$, and $a \wedge b \Rightarrow c$,

If a and b holds then these propositions hold, i.e., c holds.   ∎

The above examples are, in a sense, continued in Sect. 9.5.3.

9.4.3 Proposition Evaluation, Eval_PRO

To evaluate a propositional expression we must postulate a context function $\mathcal{C}$:

type
$\mathcal{C} = \text{V} \underset{m}{\rightarrow} \textbf{Bool}$
value
  $c{:}\mathcal{C}$

where $\mathcal{C}$ maps some, but not necessarily all, variables of any given propositional expression into a truth value.

    The meaning of a propositional expression p, in the type of all propositional expressions PRO, is now a (function of type) partial function from contexts (i.e., $\mathcal{C}$) to Booleans! To see this, we show how to evaluate, how to find not the meaning, but the value of a propositional expression. And then we "lift" that value, that is, we abstract that propositional expression with respect to contexts, to obtain its meaning!

    So, let some $c : \mathcal{C}$ be given, and postulate any propositional expression p. The value of any properly embedded Boolean ground term is found by the procedure outlined previously. If p is a variable v then the value of p is found by applying c to v, i.e., $c(\textsf{v})$. If p, i.e., v, is not in the definition set of c, the result is the undefined value **chaos**. If p is a prefix expression $\sim\!\textsf{p}'$, then first find the value, τ, of $\textsf{p}'$, then negate it. If p is an infix expression $\textsf{p}'\!\odot\!\textsf{p}''$, then first find the values, τ', τ'' of $\textsf{p}'$, respectively $\textsf{p}''$. Then proceed as for ground term evaluation. If p is a parenthesised expression $(\textsf{p}')$, then its value is that of the value of $\textsf{p}'$.

    This evaluation procedure will terminate since inductively (i.e., recursively) applied sub-evaluations apply to "smaller" and "smaller" subexpressions, and finally to ground terms and variables.

    The type of the propositional expression evaluation procedure is:

value
  Eval_PRO: PRO $\rightarrow$ TBLS $\rightarrow \mathcal{C} \xrightarrow{\sim}$ **Bool**

The meaning of propositional expressions are therefore semantic functions $\mathcal{C}\xrightarrow{\sim}$**Bool**, while the value of a propositional expression is a **Bool**ean.

value
  Eval_PRO(pro)(tbls)(c) $\equiv$
    case pro **of**
        true $\rightarrow$ tt,
        false $\rightarrow$ ff,
        chaos $\rightarrow \perp$,

$\sim$p $\to$ **let** b = Eval_PRO(p)(tbl) **in** Eval_BGT(b)(tbls) **end**,
p$'$ o p$''$ $\to$
    let b$'$ = Eval_PRO(p$'$)(tbls)(c), b$''$ = Eval_PRO(p$''$)(tbls)(c)
    in Eval_BGT(b$'$ o b$''$)(tbls) **end**,
(p) $\to$ Eval_PRO(p)(tbls)(c),
v $\to$ c(v)
end

9.4.4 Two-Valued Propositional Calculi

Preliminaries

A propositional expression may evaluate to true for some (combinations of) values of its propositional variables, and to false for other (combinations of) values.

A *tautology* is a propositional expression whose truth value is true for all possible values of its propositional variables. A *contradiction*, or *absurdity*, is a propositional expression which is always false. A propositional expression which is neither a tautology nor a contradiction is a *contingency*.

Some Proof Concepts

The material of this section is based on [481].

An *assertion* is a statement. A *proposition* is an assertion which is claimed *true*.

An *axiom* is a true assertion — typically about some mathematical structure. That is: axioms are *a priori* true; are not to be proven; cannot be proven; are not theorems.

A *theorem* is a mathematical assertion which can be shown to be true. A *proof* is an argument which establishes the truth of the theorem.

A proof of an assertion is a sequence of statements. The sequence of statements (re)presents an argument that the theorem is true. Some proof assertions may be *a priori* true: Are either axioms or previously proven theorems. Other assertions may be *hypotheses* of the theorem — assumed to be true in the argument. Finally, some assertions may be *inferred* from other assertions which occurred earlier in the proof.

Thus, to construct proofs, we need a means of drawing conclusions, or deriving new assertions from old ones. This is done by *rules of inference*. Rules of inference specify conclusions which can be drawn from assertions which are known, or can be assumed to be true.

Axioms and a Rule of Inference, I

The material of this section is based on [451].[12]

There are many ways of defining a propositional logic. First there is the issue of whether it is to be a two- or a three-valued logic, then there is the issue of which axioms and rules of inference to choose. Here we select a two-valued logic. Then we select a simple set of axioms and one rule of inference. Let ϕ, ψ and ρ designate metalinguistic variables. Any propositional expression may be put in their place.

The following three axiom schemes are axioms of the chosen propositional calculus:

$$\phi \supset (\psi \supset \phi)$$
$$\phi \supset (\psi \supset \rho) \supset ((\phi \supset \psi) \supset (\phi \supset \rho))$$
$$(\sim (\sim (\phi))) \supset \phi$$

There is a single rule of inference, *modus ponens:*

$$\frac{\phi, \phi \supset \psi}{\psi}$$

Here we chose $\supset$ to designate implication. In the next example of a two-valued propositional logic we choose $\Rightarrow$ to designate implication.

We can introduce additional connectives — other than $\neg$ (or $\sim$) and $\supset$ (or $\Rightarrow$) — through rules of inference. For example, disjunction ($\vee$): can be presented as:

$$\frac{\phi \vee \psi}{(\neg \phi) \supset \psi}, \quad \frac{(\neg \phi) \supset \psi}{\phi \vee \psi}$$

Axioms and Inference Rules, II

The material of this section is based on [481].

We shall now present another *formal proof system* allows proofs of propositional expressions to be fully done by machine. We can do this because there is only a finite number of propositional variables in any propositional expression, and each such variable's value ranges only over true or false, or is not defined at all, i.e., results in **chaos.**

Here is a set of rules of inference for the propositional expressions of a two-valued logic. This set and those expressions, form a propositional calculus. Let ϕ, ψ, ρ, and ξ designate metalinguistic variables.

---

[12]We remind the reader that the axioms given in this and the next subsection are axiom schemes of the proof system of the logic language of propositions. They are not expressed in RSL.

- Substitution of equals for equals: Wherever a propositional expression of any interpreted value may occur, any other propositional expression of the same value may occur.

- $\frac{\phi}{\phi\lor\psi}$ Addition

The form $\frac{\Phi}{\Psi}$ reads: From Φ conclude Ψ.

- $\frac{\phi\land\psi}{\phi}$ Simplification

- $\frac{\phi,\phi\Rightarrow\psi}{\psi}$, $\frac{\sim\psi,\phi\Rightarrow\psi}{\sim\phi}$ Modus Ponens versus Modus Tollens

The form $\frac{\Phi,\Psi}{\Omega}$ reads: From Φ and Ψ conclude Ω.

- $\frac{\sim\phi,\phi\lor\psi}{\psi}$, $\frac{\phi\Rightarrow\psi,\psi\Rightarrow\rho}{\phi\Rightarrow\rho}$ Disjunctive versus Hypothetical Syllogism

- $\frac{\phi,\psi}{\phi\land\psi}$ Conjunction

- $\frac{(\phi\Rightarrow\psi)\land(\rho\Rightarrow\xi),\phi\lor\rho}{\psi\lor\xi}$, $\frac{(\phi\Rightarrow\psi)\land(\rho\Rightarrow\xi),\sim\psi\lor\sim\xi}{\sim\phi\lor\sim\rho}$ Constructive vs. Destructive Dilemma

The RSL proof system is different from the above since the RSL logic is a three-valued logic. We refer to the authoritative [238] for not only a listing of the full RSL proof system, but also for a treatise on provably correct stepwise RSL developments using that proof system.

9.4.5 Discussion

We have completed the second step of our unfolding of "the real thing": a language of predicates, calculus and interpretation. The structures of our presentation followed that of our previous presentation of the language of Boolean ground terms. The introduction of Boolean-valued identifiers, i.e., of propositional variables, is what distinguishes, syntactically, the language of Boolean ground terms from the language of propositions. Semantically these variables lead to a context which is expected to bind these variables to Booleans. We kindly ask the reader to compare, line-by-line, the two informally stated evaluation definitions: Eval_BGT and Eval_PRO. But in order to make a logic language useful in dealing with actual world phenomena, there is also a need for allowing variables to designate other than Boolean values. To this we turn next.

9.5 Languages of Predicate Logic

> We now come to the "high point" of applied mathematical logic as far as this volume is concerned. With predicate logic expressions of the kind that, for example, RSL allows us, we can express quite a lot. That is, predicate logic will be be a "work horse" for us.

9.5.1 Motivation

In the propositional logics we cannot[13] express the idea that *"if x is even then x + 1 is odd"*. To see this, following [451], let us carefully examine this statement. There are two independent propositions expressed here: is_even(x) and is_odd(succ(x)), where succ(x) yields the successor of x. The statement is_even(x)$\Rightarrow$is_odd(succ(x)) is not a proposition. Its two terms are, but x is not a propositional variable, that is, one having a truth value. It "obviously" has a number value.

The *predicate calculus*[14] extends propositional logic with *individual variables*, which model-theoretically may range over other than Boolean values, thus giving us the expressive power (in terms of quantifications) which allows us to express the above statement. For example:

$$\forall x : \mathbf{Int} \bullet \mathcal{O}(x) \Rightarrow \mathcal{E}(x + 1)$$

where $\mathcal{O}$ and $\mathcal{E}$ designate the is_odd, respectively the is_even, predicates.

9.5.2 Informal Presentation

By a *predicate logic* we syntactically, i.e., proof-theoretically, understand (i) a set of truth and other non-truth values; (ii) a usually infinite set of *predicate expressions* with (ii.1) connectives, (ii.2) *truth-valued propositional variables,* (ii.3) *usually other non-truth-valued quantified or free variables,* (ii.4) *quantified expressions;* (iii) a set of axiom schemes; and (iv) a set of rules of inference.

Semantically, i.e., model-theoretically, we understand a predicate calculus to extend the above with: (v) for every predicate expression, a context, $c : \mathcal{C}$, which maps individual variables to values, and (vi) an interpretation procedure for determining, given any context and any predicate expression, the value of that expression.

Predicate expressions are thus extensions of propositional expressions: Where a propositional expression may occur, it now becomes possible to express a property by expressing some truth-valued relations between other than truth values.

Example 9.11 *Predicate Expressions:* Informally, an example is:

$$((e-1 \leq 3) \Rightarrow e') \Rightarrow (\exists\ i:\mathbf{Int} \bullet i > e * (e'' + 3))$$

which we can read: if $e-1$ less than or equal to 2 *implies* e' then that *implies* that there *exists* an *integer* which is *larger* than the *value* of the non-truth

---

[13]This example, which intuitively motivates the concept of predicate logics, is taken from Ruth E. Davis's [181] via John Rushby's [451].

[14]Other names for predicate calculus are: *first-order logic (FOL), elementary logic* and *quantification theory*.

valued expression e ∗ (e″ + 3). The example illustrates a number of new constructs that — from now on — may occur in logical, i.e., *predicate* expressions. In the above the new constructs were:

$$\le, >, \exists, -, *, +$$

More generally, and in this case schematically. we can list the constructs of a predicate calculus:

[1] p(e,e′,...,e″)
[2] f(t,t′,...,t″)
[3] ∀ x:X•E(x)
[4] ∃ x:X•E(x)
[5] ∃ ! x:X•E(x)

which we can read semantically: [1] The formula p(e,e′,...,e″) expresses the holding, or non-holding of some relation, p, between the values of subexpressions e, e′, ..., e″. Examples of p above are ≤ and >, as well as many user-defined *n*-ary (n > 1) predicates. [2] The value of expression f(t,t′,...,t″) is the result of applying the non-truth result valued function, f, to the values of subexpressions t, t′, ..., t″. Examples of f above are −, ∗ and +, as well as many user-defined unary (n = 1) predicates. [3] For all values x of type X it is the case that E(x) holds. [4] There exists at least one value x of type X for which it is the case that E(x) holds. [5] There exists a single, unique value x of type X such that E(x) holds.

Whether these predicate expressions ([1-5]) hold, i.e., are **true** or not (**false** or **chaos**) is not guaranteed just by writing them!

Forms [3-4-5] illustrated the concepts of binding and typing, $x : X$: A typing is, generally, a clause of either of the forms:

identifier : type_expression
identifier_1,identifier_2,...,identifier_n : type_expression

Typings bind their identifier[_i]s to (arbitrary) values of the type designated by the type_expression.

9.5.3 Examples

The below examples relate to corresponding *Common Exercise Topics* outlined in Appendix A. They also continue, in a sense, the examples of Sect. 9.4.2.

Example 9.12 ♣ *Predicates: Transportation Net:*
We refer to Appendix A, Sect. A.1, *Transportation Net*.

Assume that from nets, $n : N$, we can observe segments, $s : S$, and connections, $c : C$, and that from segments [respectively connections] we can observe connection identifiers [respectively segment identifiers], then we must assume that the latter observations fit with the former: That all segments [respectively connections] of the net have unique identifiers, and that any segment [respectively connection] identifier observed from a connection [respectively segment] is the identifier of a segment [respectively connection] observed in the net.

type
    N, S, C, Si, Ci
value
    obs_Ss: N $\to$ S-**set**
    obs_Cs: N $\to$ C-**set**
    obs_Sis: (N|C) $\to$ Si-**set**
    obs_Cis: (N|S) $\to$ Ci-**set**
axiom
    $\forall$ n:N •
      card obs_Ss(n) = **card** obs_Sis(n) $\land$
      card obs_Cs(n) = **card** obs_Cis(n) $\land$
      $\forall$ s:S • s $\in$ obs_Ss(n)
        $\Rightarrow$ obs_Cis(s) $\subseteq$ obs_Cis(n) $\land$
      $\forall$ c:C • c $\in$ obs_Cs(n)
        $\Rightarrow$ obs_Sis(c) $\subseteq$ obs_Sis(n)

The first axiom clause expresses uniqueness of identifiers: the cardinality of segments [respectively connections] and segment [respectively connection] identifiers are the same. If you do not like that form, then try this instead:

type
    N, S, C, Si, Ci
value
    obs_Ss: N $\to$ S-**set**
    obs_Cs: N $\to$ C-**set**
    obs_Si: S $\to$ Si
    obs_Ci: C $\to$ Ci
axiom
    $\forall$ n:N •
      $\forall$ s,s':S • {s,s'} $\subseteq$ $\in$ obs_Ss(n) $\land$ s$\neq$s'
        $\Rightarrow$ obs_Si(s) $\neq$ obs_Si(s') $\land$
      $\forall$ c,c':C • {c,c'} $\subseteq$ $\in$ obs_Cs(n) $\land$ c$\neq$c'
        $\Rightarrow$ obs_Ci(c) $\neq$ obs_Ci(c')

Example 9.13 ♣ *Predicates: Container Logistics:*
We refer to Appendix A, Sect. A.2, *Container Logistics*.

Assume that from container terminals, ct:CT, we can observe (i) the container storage area, csa:CSA and (ii) containers, c:C (in the container storage area). That from the former we can observe (iii) bays, bay:Bay, (iv) rows, row:Row, and (v) stacks, stk:Stk, and that from any of these (bays, rows and stacks) one can observe containers. Finally assume that from the latter we can observe (vi) containers, c:C:

type
    CT, C, CSA, BAY, ROW, STK
value
    obs_Cs: (CT|CSA|BAY|ROW|STK) → C-set
    obs_CSA: CT → CSA
    obs_BAYs: (CT|CSA) → BAY-set
    obs_ROWs: (CT|CSA|BAY) → ROW-set
    obs_STKs: (CT|CSA|BAY|ROW) → STK-set

Now containers observed in the container terminal must be containers of some unique stack, of some unique row and of some unique bay of the container storage area:

axiom
    ∀ ct:CT •
        ∀ c:C • c ∈ obs_Cs(ct) ⇒
        let csa = obs_CSA(ct) in
        ∃!bay:BAY •
            bay ∈ obs_BAYs(csa) ∧ c ∈ obs_Cs(bay)
            ⇒ ∃!row:ROW •
                row ∈ obs_ROWs(bay) ∧ c ∈ obs_Cs(row)
                ⇒ ∃!stk:STK •
                    stk ∈ obs_STKs(row) ∧ c ∈ obs_Cs(stk)
        end

∎

Example 9.14 ♣ *Predicates: Financial Service Industry:*
We refer to Appendix A, Sect. A.3, *Financial Service Industry*.

Assume that from a bank, bank:Bank, one can observe (i) the unique identities, cid:Cid, of all its customers, (ii) the unique identities, aid:Aid, of all their accounts, (iii) the collection, accs:Accs, of all these accounts, (iv) the identities of all the accounts, acc:Acc, in the collection, accs:Accs, of all accounts, (v) the account numbers owned by any one identified customer and (vi) the identities of customers possibly sharing any one (identified) account.

type
　Bank, Cid, Aid, Accs, Acc
value
　obs_Cids: Bank → Cid-**set**
　obs_Aids: (Bank|Accs|(Bank×Cid)) → Aid-**set**
　obs_Accs: Bank → Accs
　obs_Cids: Bank × Aid → Cid-**set**

(vii) If a customer is registered in a bank then we assume that customer to have one or more accounts. (viii) If an account is known by the bank then it is an account in the collection of accounts. (ix) And if that account is shared by one (!) or more customers then they are all known to the bank and as having that account.

axiom
　∀ bank:Bank •
　　∀ cid:Cid • cid ∈ obs_Cids(bank) ⇒
　　　obs_Aids(bank,cid) ≠ {} ∧
　　∀ aid:Aid • aid ∈ obs_Aids(bank) ⇒
　　　aid ∈ obs_Aids(obs_Accs(bank)) ∧
　　　∀ cid′,cid″:Cid •
　　　　cid′ ∈ obs_Cids(bank,aid) ⇒
　　　　　cid′ ∈ obs_Cids(bank) ∧ aid ∈ obs_Aids(bank,cid′)

9.5.4 Quantifiers and Quantified Expressions

Syntax

Quantified expressions, like ∀x:X•E(x), ∃x:X•E(x) and ∃!x:X•E(x), are *predicate expressions*. In general, *quantified expressions* are of the *inductive* form: Let x be any identifier, let X be any type expression, and let E(x) be any *propositional* or *predicate* expression in which x may (or may not) *occur*, and if it *occurs*, may *occur free* or *bound*. Now ∀x:X•E(x), ∃x:X•E(x) and ∃!x:X•E(x), are *quantified predicate expressions*. The *extremal* clause follows.

　　We refer to the above ∀, ∃ and ∃! as *quantifiers*, to x's as *binding* variables, E(x) as the *body* of the *quantified expression*, and to X as the *range set* (designated by a type expression) of the *quantification*.

　　More generally, *quantified expressions* have the syntactic form:

　　quantifier typing_1,typing_2,...,typing_2 • bool_expr

where simple forms of *typings* have the syntactic form:

　　id_1,id_2,...,id_m: type_expr

Free and Bound Variables

In the λ-calculus we define a concept of *free* and *bound* variables. Let E(x) be an expression which is not of the form Qx:X•E(x), where Q is either of ∀, ∃ or ∃!, and in which there are no further embedded, i.e., proper subexpressions of those forms, then any occurrence of x in E(x) is *free*. Let E(x) be an expression which is of the form Qx:X•E(x), where Q is either of ∀, ∃ or ∃!, then any occurrence of x in E(x) is *bound*. Let E(x) be an expression which is not of the form Qx:X•E(x), where Q is either of ∀, ∃, or ∃!, but in which there are some further embedded, i.e., proper sub-expressions of those (x binding) forms, then any occurrence of x in E(x), which is not within those latter forms, is *free*, whereas, of course, the others are *bound*.

Compound Quantified Expressions

Since in Qx:X•E(x) the expression *body* may itself be of the form Qy:Y•E'(y), we may get multiple *bindings*:

$$... \ \forall \ x{:}X \ \bullet \ \forall \ x'{:}X \ \bullet \ \exists \ y{:}Y \ \bullet \ \forall \ z{:}Z \ \bullet \ E(x,x',y,z)$$

for which we provide a shorthand:

$$... \ \forall \ x,x'{:}X, \ z{:}Z, \ \exists \ y{:}Y \ \bullet \ E(x,x',y,z)$$

Example 9.15 *Compound Predicate Expression:* For all natural numbers i larger than 2 there exist two distinct natural numbers j, k larger than 0 (but not necessarily distinct from i) such that i is the product of j and k:

$$\forall \ i{:}\textbf{Nat} \ \bullet \ i{>}2 \Rightarrow \exists \ j,k{:}\textbf{Nat} \ \bullet \ j{\neq}k \wedge i = j{*}k$$

∎

Example 9.16 *Compound Predicate Expression:* For all sets s of integers such that if i is in the set then also $-i$ is in the set; it is the case that the sum of all integers equals 0.

type
   S = **Int-set**
value
   sum: S → **Int**
   sum(s) ≡
      if s={} **then** 0 **else let** i:**Int** • i ∈ s **in** i + sum(s\{i}) **end end**
axiom
   ∀ s:S • ∀ i:**Int** • i ∈ s ⇒ −i ∈ s ⇒ sum(s) = 0

Here **Int-set** designate the type all of whose values are sets of integers. ∎

9.5.5 Syntax of Predicate Expressions, PRE

We present the syntactic quantities of predicate expressions: the symbols, the terms, the atomic formulas, the well-formed formulas (wffs), and a BNF grammar. That is, we divide the presentation of the language of predicate expressions into the presentation of language of terms, upon which we build a language of atomic formulas, and from those we build the well-formed formulas, i.e., the predicate expressions.

The Symbols of a Predicate Calculus

The symbols of a predicate calculus include a number of elements. There are the variables b, b', ..., b'' and x, x', ..., x'', where we think of the b's being truth valued propositional variables, and the x's being otherwise typed variables (integers, etc.). There are the Boolean connectives $\sim$, $\vee$, $\wedge$, etc. There are the existential quantifiers $\exists$, $\exists!$ and $\forall$. For every suitable arity n there are sets of predicate function symbols $\{p_{n_1}, p_{n_2}, \ldots, p_{n_{p_n}}\}$. For every suitable arity m there are sets of otherwise typed function symbols $\{f_{m_1}, f_{m_2}, \ldots, f_{m_{f_m}}\}$.

The idea is that:

$$p_{i_j}(t_1, t_2, \ldots, t_i), j : 1, 2, \ldots, i_p;$$

and

$$f_{k_\ell}(t'_1, t'_2, \ldots, t'_k), \ell : 1, 2, \ldots, i_f;$$

are two expression forms. The first is a *formula* and ostensibly has a truth value; that the second is a *term* and ostensibly has a value of any kind (i.e., of any type). Finally the arguments $t_j, t'_{j'}$ are also *terms* of any kind (i.e., of any type) of value. Note that we now distinguish between *terms* as the basic building blocks of expressions, and *formulas* as the expressions that have truth values.

The Term Language of a Predicate Calculus

The term language is defined inductively:

- **Basis Clause:** A variable, b, etc., or x, etc., that is, whether truth valued or not, is a *term*.
- **Inductive Clause:** If $t_1, t_2, \ldots, t_n$ are terms and f_n is an n-ary function symbol, and if p_n is an n-ary predicate symbol then, $f_n(t_1, t_2, \ldots, t_n)$ and $p_n(t_1, t_2, \ldots, t_n)$ are terms.
- **Extremal Clause:** Only those expressions that can be formed from a finite number of applications of the above clauses are terms.

The idea is that Boolean literals are nullary predicate function symbols: true() $\equiv$ **true**, false() $\equiv$ **false** and chaos() $\equiv$ **chaos**; and that, for example, numerals are nullary function symbols: one() $\equiv$ 1, etc. More complex examples are: and(b, b') ($\equiv b \wedge b'$), etc.; and ift(equalzero(i), one(), mult(i, fact(sub(i, 1)))) ($\equiv$ **if** i=0 **then** 1 **else** i×fact(i-1) **end**), etc.

The Atomic Formula Language of a Predicate Calculus

The atomic formula language is defined inductively:

- Basis Clause: Any propositional expression is an atomic formula (and is a term).
- Inductive Clause: If $t_1, t_2, \ldots, t_n$ are terms and p_n is an n-ary predicate function symbol, then $p_n(t_1, t_2, \ldots, t_n)$ is an *atomic formula*. [15]
- Extremal Clause: Only such terms which can be formed from a finite number of uses of the above two clauses are atomic formulas.

The Well-formed Formulas of a Predicate Calculus

The wff language is defined inductively:

- Basis Clause: *Atomic formulas are formulas, i.e., predicate expressions.*
- Inductive Clause: If x is a variable ranging over type X, and u, v and $\mathcal{E}(x)$ are formulas (i.e., predicate expressions), then: $\sim u$ is a formula; $u \wedge v$, $u \vee v$, $u \Rightarrow v$, $u = v$, $u \neq v$, and $u \equiv v$, are formulas; $\forall x{:}X{\cdot}\mathcal{E}(x), \exists x{:}X{\cdot}\mathcal{E}(x)$, and $\exists! x{:}X{\cdot}\mathcal{E}(x)$ are formulas.
- Extremal Clause: Only those terms that can be formed from a finite number of uses of the above two clauses are formulas, i.e., predicate expressions.

An Informal BNF Grammar for Predicate Expressions

We refer to previous BNF grammar examples for Boolean ground terms (Sect. 9.3.4) and propositional expressions (Sect. 9.4.1). Instead of building on these, we present a new BNF grammar:

```
⟨Fn⟩ ::= ⟨Identifier⟩        /* Fn: non−truth valued functions */
⟨Pn⟩ ::= ⟨Identifier⟩        /* Pn: truth valued predicates */
⟨Term⟩ ::= ⟨Identifier⟩
     | ⟨Fn⟩ ( ⟨Term−seq⟩ )
     | ⟨Pn⟩ ( ⟨Term−seq⟩ )  /* true, false, chaos: nullary terms */
⟨Term−seq⟩ ::=               /* empty sequence */
     | ⟨Term⟩
     | ⟨Term⟩ ⟨Comma−Term−seq⟩
⟨Comma−Term−seq⟩ ::= ⟨Comma−Term⟩ ⟨Term−seq⟩
⟨Comma−Term⟩ ::= , ⟨Term⟩
⟨Atom⟩ ::= ⟨Identifier⟩      /* Boolean valued */
     | ⟨Pn⟩ ( ⟨Term−seq⟩ )
⟨Wff⟩ ::= ⟨Atom⟩
```

---

[15]The truth and the non-truth-value relational operators (to wit: $=$, $\neq$, $\equiv$, respectively $=$, $\neq$, $\equiv$, $<$, $\leq$, $>$, $\geq$, etc.) are examples of p_{2_i}'s, and hence of atomic formulas, as would be any user-defined predicate applied to terms.

$$| \sim \langle \text{Wff} \rangle$$
$$| \langle \text{Wff} \rangle \wedge \langle \text{Wff} \rangle \mid \langle \text{Wff} \rangle \vee \langle \text{Wff} \rangle \mid \langle \text{Wff} \rangle \Rightarrow \langle \text{Wff} \rangle$$
$$| \langle \text{Wff} \rangle = \langle \text{Wff} \rangle \mid \langle \text{Wff} \rangle \neq \langle \text{Wff} \rangle \mid \langle \text{Wff} \rangle \equiv \langle \text{Wff} \rangle$$
$$| \langle \text{Quant} \rangle \langle \text{Identifier} \rangle : \langle \text{Tn} \rangle \bullet \langle \text{Wff} \rangle$$
$$\langle \text{Quant} \rangle ::= \exists \mid \exists ! \mid \forall$$

9.5.6 A Predicate Calculus

In Sect. 9.4.4 we presented a system of axioms and rules of inference for a propositional calculus. We now wish to present such a system for a predicate calculus.

Axiom Schemes

The material of this and the next section is based on [451]. Quoted parts are expressed in *slanted text font*.

Let $\phi[x \mapsto t]$ designate the expression ϕ' which is like ϕ except that some or all of the free x in ϕ have been replaced by the term t — where x does not occur free in t.

One such system for the predicate calculus extends one, or the other of the sets of axiom schemes given (earlier) for a propositional calculus with the following:

- *Provided that no free occurrence of x in ϕ lie in the scope of any quantifier for a free variable appearing in the term t, we have:*

$$\forall x : X \bullet \phi(x) \;\Rightarrow\; \phi[x \mapsto t]$$

  Expressed semantically: *If some formula ϕ is true for all x, then it is certain true when some particular term t is substituted for x in ϕ.*
- And, *provided that t is free for x in ϕ, we have:*

$$\phi[x \mapsto t] \;\Rightarrow\; (\exists x : X \bullet \phi(x))$$

  Expressed semantically: *We can conclude that there exists some x satisfying the formula ϕ if some substitution instance of ϕ is true.*

Rules of Inference

The above leads to the following rules of inferences:

- First:

$$\frac{\psi \supset \phi(v)}{\psi \supset (\forall x : X \bullet \phi(x))},$$

- *and:*

$$\frac{\phi(v) \supset \psi}{(\exists x : X \bullet \phi(x)) \supset \psi},$$

where the variable v is not free in ψ.
- *The rule of universal quantification can best be understood semantically by considering the simpler case when ψ is true. Then the rule becomes:*

$$\frac{\phi(v)}{\forall x : X \bullet \phi(x))}$$

which, semantically says, that if ϕ is true for some arbitrary v, then it must be true for all x.
- *Universal and existential quantification are related:*

$$\exists x : X \bullet \phi(x) \ \equiv\ \sim (\forall x : X \bullet \sim \phi(x)))$$

This definition, as an axiom, can be done if we have already defined equivalence.

9.5.7 Predicate Expression Evaluation

As we did for Boolean ground terms (Eval_BGT), and for propositional expressions (Eval_PRO), so we shall now do for predicate expressions: namely provide an informal, yet precise description of an evaluation procedure (Eval_PRE).

Evaluation Contexts

Semantically we may understand the predicate calculus by constructing models. There are two parts to any such model: a context, $\rho : \mathcal{R}$, which maps all user-defined symbols in the language of predicate expressions to their meaning in some world Ω, and an interpretation function. Thus, in order to find the value of a given predicate expression, one must provide a context which maps some, all or more of the *free variables*, v:V (of that predicate expression), into values, VAL, of appropriate types; some, all or more of the *type names*, Tn (of the range type [name] expressions of that predicate expression), into their respective — finite or even infinite value spaces; some, all or more of the predicate function symbols, p (of that predicate expression), into appropriate arity predicate functions; and some, all or more of the non-truth result value function symbols, f (of that predicate expression), into appropriate arity non-truth result value functions:

type
    Vn, Tn, Pn, Fn, VAL
    $\mathcal{R} = (\text{Vn} \rightarrow \text{VAL})$
        $\cup\ (\text{Tn} \rightarrow \text{VAL-set})$
        $\cup\ (\text{Pn} \rightarrow (\text{VAL}^* \rightarrow \textbf{Bool}))$
        $\cup\ (\text{Fn} \rightarrow (\text{VAL}^* \rightarrow \text{VAL}))$

Recall that $A{\to}B$ stands for the type whose values are functions from A into B, that A-**set** stands for the type whose values are sets of element values of type A and that A^* stands for the type whose values are lists of element values of type A. The unusual, non-RSL construct $(A{\to}B)\cup(C{\to}D)$ stands for the type whose values are functions from A into B and functions from C into D.

Example 9.17 *Predicate Expression Evaluation Context:* Let us review an example. See the first formula line below. To evaluate the next expression we seem to need a context, $c : \mathcal{C}$, like the one shown further below:

value
$$(a \wedge (v \geq 7)) \Rightarrow \forall\ k{:}K \bullet fact(j) \leq k$$

ρ: $\lambda x{:}(Vn|Tn|Pn|Fn) \bullet$
       if $x \in Vn$ **then**
          case x **of**
             a$\to$t,v$\to$i,j$\to$m, ...
          end
       else if $x \in Tn$ **then**
          case x **of** K$\to$\{$-2,-1,0,1,2$\}, ... **end**
       else if $x \in Pn$ **then**
          case x **of**
             "larger-than-or-equal" $\to$ $\lambda(x,y){:}(\mathbf{Int}{\times}\mathbf{Int}){\bullet}x{\geq}y,$
             "smaller-than-or-equal" $\to$ $\lambda(x,y){:}(\mathbf{Int}{\times}\mathbf{Int}){\bullet}x{\leq}y,$
             ...
          end
       else /$*$ assert: $*$/ $x \in Fn$:
          case x **of**
             "factorial" $\to$ $\lambda n{:}\mathbf{Int}{\bullet}\mathbf{if}\ n{=}0\ \mathbf{then}\ 1\ \mathbf{else}\ n{*}fact(n{-}1)\ \mathbf{end},$
             ...
          end
          end end end

As an example, let $(a{\wedge}(v{\geq}7)){\Rightarrow}\forall k{:}K{\bullet}fact(j){\leq}k$ be the predicate expression to be evaluated. Variables a, v and j are free and so is type name K — the latter is assumed to be some (finite or infinite) set of integers. For that expression we need a context preferably like $\rho : \mathcal{R}$ above — where t is some Boolean truth value, and i and m are some integers. If the values of t, i, m are **true**, $9, -2$ then we see that the predicate evaluates to **true**.   ∎

Meaning Versus Values of Predicate Expressions

The meaning of a predicate expression p, in the type of all predicate expressions PRE, is now a function from context, that is, $\rho : \mathcal{R}$ to Booleans!

value

   Eval_PRE: PRE $\rightarrow \mathcal{R} \xrightarrow{\sim}$ **Bool**

To see this, we show how to evaluate — how to find — not the meaning, but the value of a predicate expression. And then we "lift" that value, we abstract that predicate expression with respect to contexts!

Evaluation Procedure, Eval_PRE

Term Evaluation

Let $\rho : \mathcal{R}$ be some context, and let t be the term subject to evaluation in context ρ.

   If t is variable v then c is applied to v to find its value. If v is not in the definition set of ρ then the undefined value **chaos** is yielded.

   If, instead, t is of the form f(t,t',...,t''), then the values v, v', ..., v'' of the terms t, t', ..., t'', respectively, are evaluated; the function f is "looked up" in ρ (i.e., c(f)), and the resulting function ψ applied to v, v', ..., v'': ψ(v,v'...,v''). If f is not in the definition set of ρ, then the undefined value **chaos** is yielded.

Formula Evaluation

Let e be a formula.

   If e is a propositional expression, that is, if e is of any of the forms: $\sim$e, e$\wedge$e', e$\vee$e', e=e', e$\neq$e', or e$\equiv$e', then evaluate as prescribed earlier (Eval_pro).

   If e is of the form p(t,t',...,t'') then the values v, v', ..., v'' of the terms t, t', ..., t'', respectively, are evaluated, the predicate function p is "looked up" in c (i.e., ρ(p)), and the resulting function ϕ applied to v, v', ..., v'': ϕ(v,v'...,v''). If p is not in the definition set of c, then the undefined value **chaos** is yielded.

   If, instead, e is of either of the forms $\forall$x:X$\bullet$E(x), $\exists$x:X$\bullet$E(x) or $\exists$!x:X$\bullet$E(x), i.e., if it is of the general form $\mathcal{Q}$ x:X$\bullet$E(x), then the value, Ξ, of the range set X is found from ρ. If X is not in the definition set of ρ, then the undefined value **chaos** is yielded, and becomes the value of $\mathcal{Q}$ x:X$\bullet$E(x).

   Otherwise three case distinctions must be made:

- If $\mathcal{Q}$ is $\forall$ then the possibly infinite conjunction: $E(\xi_1) \wedge E(\xi_2) \wedge ... \wedge E(\xi_i) \wedge ...$ is evaluated. Here the ξ's range over all, possibly infinite values of Ξ.
  Note: *The $\wedge$ is here constrained to be commutative.*
  All $E(\xi_i)$ must yield **true** for $\forall$ x:X$\bullet$E(x) to yield **true**. Any **chaos** results in **chaos**. Any **false** with no **chaos** yields **false** for $\forall$ x:X$\bullet$E(x).
  We can rephrase the above: The value of $\forall$x:X$\bullet$E(x) is **true** if E(x) holds for all models as implied by x:X. That is, x:X defines a set of models, that is, a set of contexts, at least one for each element x in X. Each of these models further defines bindings of all other free identifiers in E(x).

- If Q is $\exists$ then there must exist a disjunction:

$$E(\xi_1)\vee E(\xi_2)\vee...\vee E(\xi_i)\vee...$$

This disjunction is evaluated. For it to yield **true** $E(\xi_1)$ must yield **true** with all other $E(\xi_j)$ for all j>1 yielding **true, false** or **chaos.**
Or rephrased: $\exists x:X\bullet E(x)$ is true if $E(x)$ holds for at least one model in the set of models induced by X.

- If Q is $\exists!$ then there must exist exactly one i in some arbitrary disjunction:

$$E(\xi_1)\vee E(\xi_2)\vee...\vee E(\xi_i)\vee...$$

such that $E(\xi_1)$ yields **true** and all other $E(\xi_i)$, for all i>1, yield **false** or **chaos!**
Rephrased: $\exists!x:X\bullet E(x)$ holds if and only if $E(x)$ holds for exactly one of the induced models.

We shall later present a formal definition of Eval_PRE.

9.5.8 First-Order and Higher-Order Logics

If the *range set* of quantifications permit values that are, or contain, functions, then we say that the *predicate logic* is a *higher-order logic*. Otherwise it is a *first-order logic*.

An example may be in order to illustrate the need for higher-order logics:

type
    P = A → **Bool**
value

axiom
    $\forall$ p:P • ...

RSL's logic is higher-order.

9.5.9 Validity, Satisfiability and Models

We briefly introduce such concepts as validity, satisfiability and models. But first we take yet another look at interpretations and their contexts, i.e., their possible worlds.

Contexts and Interpretations

We have seen that predicate expressions only have values if a suitable context is given. In mathematical logic such a context is called an interpretation. Generally a context, that is, an interpretation, is a mapping of identifiers to mathematical values. Predicate symbols p_n of arity n can be thought of as being mapped $(p_n \mapsto \pi)$ into possibly infinite sets π of n groupings: $(v_1, v_2, \ldots, v_n)$, with the meaning that $p_n(v_1, v_2, \ldots, v_n)$ represents truth for all $(v_1, v_2, \ldots, v_n)$ in π, and falsity otherwise. Function symbols f_n of arity n can likewise be thought of as being mapped $(f_n \mapsto \phi)$ into possibly infinite sets, ϕ of $n + 1$ groupings: $(v_1, v_2, \ldots, v_n, v)$ — with the meaning that $f_n(v_1, v_2, \ldots, v_n)$ has value v for respective $(v_1, v_2, \ldots, v_n, v)$ in ϕ, and is otherwise undefined. Non-function symbols, i.e., variable identifiers, i are mapped $(i \mapsto v)$ into values v in some type.

Example 9.18 *Predicate Expression Interpretation:* An example may be in order. We interpret the predicate ... $\forall$ i:Integer, $\exists$ n:Natural • square(i) = n ... in two models:

type
    Integer, Natural
value
    square: Integer $\rightarrow$ Natural
    ... $\forall$ i:Integer, $\exists$ n:Natural • square(i) = n ...

    /* interpretation_1: */
      [Integer$\mapsto$\{ ...,-2,-1,0,1,2,... \},
       Natural$\mapsto$\{ 0,1,2,... \},
       square$\mapsto$\{ ...,(-2,4),(-1,1),(0,0),(1,1),(2,4),... \}]

    /* interpretation_2: */
      [Integer$\mapsto$\{ ...,-2,-1,0,1,2,... \},
       Natural$\mapsto$\{ 0,3,5,7,9,... \},
       square$\mapsto$\{ ...,(-2,4),(-1,1),(0,0),(1,1),(2,4),... \}]

The above predicate is true in interpretation_1 and false in interpretation_2. ∎

Validity and Satisfiability

Let there be given a possibly infinite set of interpretations. A predicate expression is said to be *valid* if it is true for all interpretations. A predicate expression is said to be *satisfied* if it is true for at least one interpretation. There is no mechanical procedure by which one can determine the validity or satisfiability of predicate expressions. That is, one cannot write a computer program which determines validity or satisfiability. A predicate expression is said to be *contradicted* if it is false for all interpretations.

Models

Let there be given a set, α, of predicate expressions, and an interpretation ι. If every w in α holds in the interpretation ι, then ι is said to be a *model* of α.

Contexts, Interpretations and Models

We now take up the line on models begun in Sect. 1.6.2 and continued in Sect. 8.5.4. We have earlier introduced the following related terms: context and interpretation. It is time to sort out any possible differences in our use of the terms: model, context and interpretation.

At the start of this section we equated, within the subject of mathematical logic, the two concepts: context and interpretation. We shall henceforth use the term context (or later the term environment) — in connection with the actual development and presentation of language interpreters — as standing for the above use of both the terms context and interpretation.

And we shall, likewise, use the term interpretation to stand for the function of doing what is prescribed by such language interpreters. For matters of mathematical logic we shall not use the term context any more. For the term model, until we reach Vol. 3, Chap. 4, technical uses of this term will be in connection with the meaning of RSL definitions being sets of models: bindings between identifiers, in a space of all such, to type values (which themselves are set of values), or function values or, as we shall see, later, many other kinds of values including variables, channels. In Vol. 3, Chap. 4 we shall then discuss the looser, not necessarily technical, but usually more pragmatic use of the term model — in the senses of modelling, of creating models.

9.5.10 Discussion

We have introduced languages of predicate calculi. We now have several languages since we can either choose a two-valued or a three-valued logic, and since we can choose one or another set of rules of inferences. RSL basically has a three-valued logic. We say basically, as we can safely restrict particular uses of RSL to a two-valued logic — one that is consistent with a three-valued logical interpretation. That is, the **chaos** will never occur in expressions for which the two-valued logic is claimed to be sufficient. Whenever necessary, we are thus encouraged to state which logic we require. We remind the reader of the distinction between proof-theoretical (i.e., syntactical) presentations of a logic, and model-theoretical (i.e., semantical) presentations of the same logic.

This and the previous two sections have thus provided a basis for our use of the RSL predicate calculus as a specification language. Since these volumes basically emphasises specification development rather than verification of such developments, we refer the reader to specialised textbooks and monographs for more comprehensive treatments of verification. Such references are: [181, 242, 359–361, 419, 472, 533].

9.6 Axiom Systems

Axioms are self-evident truths. That is, they are laws or postulates that we accept without proof.

> When mathematics students study mathematical logic they learn about proof and model-theoretic properties of families of predicate logics, and about what axiom systems are, in general, possible.
>
> With this section you shall, in contrast, learn the first steps towards constructing pleasing and elegant axiom systems for actual-world phenomena and — later — for computing.

In this section we shall illustrate uses of RSL's linguistic facilities for specifying properties of sorts and functions over these sorts in terms of axioms. That is, in contrast to the previous three sections' treatment of proof systems for logic languages, including that embedded in RSL. We shall now be using RSL itself to express axioms.

Some of the examples given now may be said to be presented prematurely or to be redundant: Either they rely on arithmetics for which no semantics, including no axioms, have been given, or they have already been presented before or will be presented more fully later. Be that as it may; our aim is to familiarise you with RSL specifications of axioms. We refer to the Sect. 9.1 for remarks on the two kinds of axiom systems. Some of the text in this section summarises earlier material.

9.6.1 General

An axiom system is usually a set of type definitions, a set of function signatures (of observer and generator functions, including predicates), and a set of predicate expressions (the axioms themselves).

Example 9.19 *Euclid's Plane Geometry:* The following illustrates an axiom system. It is informally expressed: [0] Every *line* is a collection of *points*. [1] There exist at least two *points*. [2] If p and q are distinct *points*, then there exists one and only one *line* containing p and q. [3] If ℓ is a line then there exists a *point* not on ℓ. [4] If ℓ is a line and p is a point not on ℓ, then there exists one and only one *line* containing p and *parallel* to ℓ. ∎

In these expressions we can identify, for example, three kinds of plane geometry terms. They are: line, point and parallel. We can also identify the *ontologically* determined terms: collection, containing and on; as well as other natural language terms. The axioms assume that you understand the ontologic and natural terms, but define, as a set of axioms, the plane geometry terms.

9.6.2 Axioms

An axiom, for us, is a predicate expression that always holds, that is, which is *valid*. In other words, whatever quantification set is implied by some quantification range identifiers (viz. X above) they are constrained to make the axiom true.

If we, for example write:

type
    X, Y
axiom
    $\forall$ x:X • $\forall$ y:Y • x $\neq$ y

then the sorts X and Y have at least been constrained to not contain similar elements. If instead

type
    X
axiom
    $\forall$ x:X • $\exists$ i:**Int** • x = i$*$i

then the sort X is the type of all square numbers. We could instead define X by a subtype definition:[16]

type
    X = {| n:**Nat** • $\exists$ i:**Int** • n = i$*$i |}

To repeat: Axioms are predicate expressions. Predicate expressions are only valid for certain interpretations. These interpretations are exactly what the axioms are (pragmatically) intended to model. Thus axioms are used to model the properties of structures, either abstract, as above, or seemingly manifest, such as the Euclidean system of plane geometry.

9.6.3 Axiom System

An *axiom system*, that is, a set of predicate predicate expressions, also contains some type type (including sort) definitions and function signatures. One of the quantification range set identifiers — which may be mentioned in one or more of the axioms — are sorts, and a purpose of the axioms are to characterise those sorts. Usually at least one of identifiers — which may be mentioned in one or more of the axioms — is a function name, and a purpose of the axioms is to characterise that function.

Example 9.20 *Euclid's Plane Geometry:* The Euclidean geometry informally described in Example 9.19 can be formally axiomatised by first introducing the sorts P and L:

type
    P, L
value

---

[16]We shall use subtypes extensively between here and the formal introduction of the concept of subtypes, in Sect. 18.8.

[0] obs_Ps: L → P-**infset**
    parallel: L × L → **Bool**

Observe how the informal axiom in Example 9.19 has been modelled by the *observer function* obs_Ps. It applies to lines and yields possibly infinite sets of points.

Now we can introduce the axioms proper:

axiom
  [1] ∃ p,q:P • p ≠ q,
  [2] ∀ p,q:P • p ≠ q ⇒
        ∃! l:L • p ∈ obs_Ps(l) ∧ q ∈ obs_Ps(l),
  [3] ∀ l:L • ∃ p:P • p ∉ obs_Ps(l),
  [4] ∀ l:L • ∃ p:P • p ∉ obs_Ps(l) ⇒
        ∃ l':L • l≠l' ∧ p ∈ obs_Ps(l') ∧ parallel(l,l')

The concept of being parallel is modelled by the predicate symbol of the same name, by its signature and by axiom [4].   ∎

Thus (also in RSL) an axiom system is usually represented by (i) a set of sort definitions, (ii) a set of observer and generator functions, and (iii) a set of quantified expressions, the axioms proper.

9.6.4 Consistency and Completeness

A *theory* is, formally speaking, a set of axioms and a set of theorems derived, through proofs,[17] from these axioms using the inference rules of the logic in which the axioms were stated. Whether the set of inference rules and the set of axioms together is sufficient for proving all valid assertions, i.e., whether the axiom system is *complete* with respect to all valid predicates, is undecidable: One cannot devise a mechanical procedure which can test an axiom system and its inference rules for completeness. Furthermore, whether the set of inference rules and the set of axioms together is such that one can prove validity of an assertion and its negation, that is, whether the axiom system is *inconsistent*, is undecidable: One cannot devise a mechanical procedure which can test an axiom systems and its inference rules for consistency.

9.6.5 Property-Oriented Specifications

We give a number of examples of axiom systems. They each characterise one or more model(s). We say that they specify this (or these) model(s) in a *property-oriented* manner. This is as opposed to presenting the model directly in terms of for example such discrete mathematical concepts as sets, Cartesians, lists, maps, functions, etc.

---

[17]We refer to the paragraphs on 'Some Proof Concepts' in Sect. 9.4.4.

Example 9.21 *Peano's Axioms:* The purpose is to define the algebra of *natural numbers* and *successor* (+1) and *equal to zero functions* (=0).

[1] Zero (0) is a natural number. [2] For each natural number n there exists exactly one other natural number $n + 1$. [3] For no natural number n, is $n + 1$ equal to zero. [4] For any natural numbers m and n, if $m + 1 = n + 1$ then $m = n$. [5] For any set N of natural numbers containing zero, if $n \in A$ implies $n + 1 \in A$, then A contains every natural number.

type N
axiom
  [1] $0 \in N$
  [2] $\forall$ n:N • $\exists!n':N$ • $n' = n+1 \wedge n' \in N$
  [3] $\sim\!\exists$ n:N • $n+1 = 0$
  [4] $\forall$ m,n:N • $m+1 = n+1 \Rightarrow m = n$
  [5] $\forall$ A:N-**infset** • $(0 \in A \wedge n \in A \Rightarrow n+1 \in A) \Rightarrow A \equiv N$

[5] is a specialisation of the *principle of induction*: If p is a property, i.e., p is expressible as a predicate function which may hold of (applies to) natural numbers n; if $p(0)$ holds; and if, whenever $p(n)$ holds for some natural number n, then $p(n + 1)$ also holds, then that implies that all natural numbers satisfy p. Formulated, in general, we have:

axiom
  [6] $\forall$ p:(N $\rightarrow$ **Bool**) • $(\forall$ n:N • $p(n) \Rightarrow p(n+1)) \Rightarrow \forall$ n:N • $p(n)$

∎

Another example:

Example 9.22 *Sine & Cosine:*
  There is given a sort of angles, A, and a sort of rational numbers, R^{18}, between -1 and 1. There is also given a pair of functions sin and cos (for sine, resp. cosine). Finally there are given the axioms:

type
  A = **Real**
  R = {| r:**Real** • $-1 \leq r \leq 1$ |}
value
  sin,cos: A $\rightarrow$ R
axiom
  forall a:A •
    $-1 \leq \sin(a), \cos(a) \leq 1,$
    $\sin^2(a) + \cos^2(a) = 1$

---

[18]In Example 9.22 R is defined as a subtype of reals. We refer to Sect. 18.8 for a proper introduction of the concept of subtypes.

Here we have introduced a variant of the ∀ quantification: The keyword
forall lets the quantifier bindings which follow it, distribute across the axioms
now separated by commas.

Under the assumption of appropriate axioms for the rational numbers,
their squaring and sum, and the ≤ relation, Figure 9.2 exemplifies one model
of this axiom.   ∎

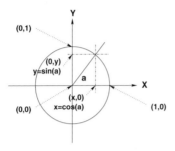

Fig. 9.2. Definition of the trigonometric sin and cos functions

Further examples.

Their formal parts are presented, as were those of the above examples, in
RSL. It is not RSL, however, in that it has the simple semantics of the predicate
calculus. To repeat: One cannot explain, i.e., give semantics, to a language by
using that language itself. One must use a language already defined.

Example 9.23 *Simple Sets:* By a simple set we understand an unordered
finite collection of simple, say in the present example, distinct atomic elements.
Let the latter belong to sort A. Let the sort of simple sets be designated by
S. Now simple sets are characterised, as already hinted at above, by being
collections, by being finite, by having distinct elements, by being unordered
such collections, and by the following operations: ∈ is taken as a primitive
and stands for *"is the left-hand operand (an atomic element) a member of
the right-hand operand (the set)."* {} is an *overloaded function symbol:* {}
either stands for the nullary constant function that yields the empty set (of
no elements), or {} stands for the unary function that yields the singleton
set of its operand. ={} stands for the unary *isempty-set* predicate function
which tests whether its operand set is empty. ∪ stands for the *union* operator
which, when applied to two operand sets, yields the set of all elements of
these operands. ∩ stands for the *intersection* operator which, when applied
to two operand sets, yields the set of elements common to both operands. \
stands for the *set complement* operator which, when applied to two operand
sets, yields the set of elements of the first operand not in second operand.
= stands for the *equality* operator which, when applied to two operand sets,

yields truth if they are the same set, otherwise falsity. $\subset$ stands for the *proper subset* operator which, when applied to two operand sets, yields truth if all the elements of the left-hand operand set are in the elements of the right-hand operand set and there are elements of the right-hand operand set which are not elements of the left-hand operand set. $\subseteq$ stands for the *subset* operator which, when applied to two operand sets, yields the truth if all the elements of the left-hand operand set are in the elements of the right-hand operand set. **card** stands for the *cardinality* operator which, when applied to a finite operand set, yields its number of elements. The axiom system provides the characterisation.

The membership operation, $\in$, is, to repeat, taken as a primitive. That is, is not explained!

A Sketch Formal Axiom System Defining S = A-set

Types and Signatures:

type
 A, S
value
 $\in$, $\notin$: A $\times$ S $\rightarrow$ **Bool**
 {}: **Unit** $\rightarrow$ S
 {}: A $\rightarrow$ S
 $\cup$, $\cap$, \: S $\times$ S $\rightarrow$ S
 =, $\neq$, $\subset$, $\subseteq$: S $\times$ S $\rightarrow$ **Bool**
 card: S $\xrightarrow{\sim}$ **Nat**

Axioms:

axiom
 forall a:A, s,s':S •
  {a} $\in$ S,
  ((a $\in$ s $\cup$ s') $\equiv$ (a $\in$ s $\vee$ a $\in$ s')),
  ((a $\in$ s $\cap$ s') $\equiv$ (a $\in$ s $\wedge$ a $\in$ s')),
  ((a $\in$ s \ s') $\equiv$ (a $\in$ s $\wedge$ a $\notin$ s')),
  s = s' $\equiv$ (a $\in$ s $\equiv$ a $\in$ s'),
  s $\subseteq$ s' $\equiv$ (a $\in$ s $\Rightarrow$ a $\in$ s'),
  s $\subset$ s' $\equiv$ (s $\subseteq$ s' $\wedge$ s $\neq$ s'),
  card({}) $\equiv$ 0,
  a $\notin$ s $\Rightarrow$ **card**({a} $\cup$ s) = 1+**card**(s)

Chapter 13 continues our presentation of sets. It focuses on the way in which RSL, the main specification language of these volumes, provides for sets, as well as on the choice and use of sets in abstract specifications.

Example 9.24 *Simple Lists:* By a simple list we understand an ordered finite collection of, say in the present example, atomic, but not necessarily distinct elements. Let the latter belong to sort A. Let the sort of simple lists be designated by L. Now simple lists are characterised, as already hinted at above, by being collections, by being finite, by allowing multiple occurrence of some elements, by being ordered such collections and by the following operations: $\langle\rangle$, $=\langle\rangle$, **hd, tl,** $\hat{\ }$, **elems, inds, len** and $[\cdot]$. $\langle\rangle$ is an *overloaded function symbol:* $\langle\rangle$ either stands for the nullary constant function that yields the empty list (of no elements), or $\langle\rangle$ stands for the unary function that yields the singleton list of its (only) operand. $=\langle\rangle$ stands for the unary *test for empty list predicate operator.* It applies to a list and yields truth if that list is empty, otherwise falsity. **hd** stands for the *head* operator which, when applied to an operand list, yields the first element of that list. **tl** stands for the *tail* operator which, when applied to an operand list, yields the list of all but the first element of that list, and in the same order as in the operand. $\hat{\ }$ stands for the *concatenation* of two operand lists of which the first must be finite. The result is the list whose first list elements are exactly those of the first operand list in the order and multiplicity of that list, and whose remaining list elements are exactly those of the last operand list in the order and multiplicity of that list. **elems** stands for the *elements* operator which, as a function, when applied to an operand list, yields the set of all the distinct elements of that list. **inds** stands for the *indices* operator which, as a function, when applied to an operand list, yields the set of all the indices into the list. If the list is of length *ell* then **inds** of that list is the set of all natural numbers from and inclusive 1 to and inclusive *ell*. If the list is empty, the yielded index set is empty. **len** stands for the *length* of list operator operator which, when applied to a finite operand list, yields the length of that list, i.e., the number of not necessarily distinct elements of the list, otherwise **chaos.** $\cdot(\cdot)$ stands for *list element selection,* i.e., for the (distributed fix) list operator which when applied to a "left" operand list and a "right" operand index, i.e., a natural number within the index set of the list, yields the list element having the index position in the list. The above explication was "loose" wrt. the "border" cases of when certain argument lists were either infinite or empty, or not of sufficient length — for which cases the results amount to **chaos.**

The axiom system provides a fuller characterisation.

A Sketch Formal Axiom System Defining L = A*

Types and Signatures:

type
    A, L
value
    $\langle\rangle$: L
    $\langle\,\bullet\,\rangle$: A $\rightarrow$ L

$\bullet = \langle\rangle$: $L \to$ **Bool**
hd $\bullet$: $L \overset{\sim}{\to} A$
tl $\bullet$: $L \overset{\sim}{\to} L$
$\bullet \,\hat{}\, \bullet$: $L \times L \to L$
elems $\bullet$: $L \to A$-**set**
inds $\bullet$: $L \to$ **Nat-set**
le n$\bullet$: $L \overset{\sim}{\to}$ **Nat**
$\bullet\,[\,\bullet\,]$: $L \times$ **Nat** $\overset{\sim}{\to} A$

Axioms:

axiom
$\forall$ a:A,ℓ:L $\bullet$
$\quad \langle\rangle \in L,$
$\quad \langle\rangle = \langle\rangle,$
$\quad \mathbf{hd}\langle\rangle = \mathbf{chaos}$
$\quad \mathbf{hd}\langle a\rangle\hat{}\,\ell \equiv a \equiv (\langle a\rangle\hat{}\,\ell)[1],$
$\quad \ell\hat{}\langle\rangle \equiv \ell \equiv \langle\rangle\hat{}\,\ell$
$\quad \mathbf{tl}\langle\rangle = \mathbf{chaos},$
$\quad \mathbf{tl}\langle a\rangle\hat{}\,\ell \equiv \ell,$
$\quad \mathbf{chaos}\,[\,i\,] \equiv \mathbf{chaos},$

$\quad \forall$ i:**Nat** $\bullet$ i>0 $\Rightarrow$ l[i+1] $\equiv$ (**tl** l)[i]
$\quad \mathbf{elems}\langle\rangle \equiv \{\},\ \mathbf{elems}\langle a\rangle\hat{}\,l \equiv \{a\} \cup \mathbf{elems}\ l$
$\quad \mathbf{inds}\langle\rangle \equiv \{\},\ \mathbf{inds}\ l \equiv \{i | i{:}\mathbf{Nat} \bullet 1 \leq i \leq \mathbf{len}\ l\},$ i.e.,
$\quad \mathbf{inds}\langle a\rangle\hat{}\,l \equiv \{1\} \cup \{i{+}1 | i{:}\mathbf{Nat}\bullet i \in \mathbf{inds}\ l\}$
$\quad \mathbf{len}\langle\rangle \equiv 0,\ \mathbf{len}(\langle a\rangle\hat{}\,l) \equiv 1{+}\mathbf{len}\ l,$ i.e.,
$\quad \mathbf{len}(l\hat{}l') \equiv \mathbf{len}\ l + \mathbf{len}\ l',$
$\quad \forall$ i:**Nat** $\bullet$ i>**len** l $\Rightarrow$ (l$\hat{}$l')[i] $\equiv$ l'[i$-$**len** l]

In general, lists will be allowed to contain any kinds of elements: Functions, integers, Booleans, sets, etc. So, when we say 'simple list' we only mean it as an example; as a simple example which does, i.e., should not complicate matters.

Chapter 15 continues our presentation of lists. It focuses on the way in which RSL, the main specification language of these volumes, provides for lists, as well as on the choice and use of lists in abstract specifications.

Example 9.25 *Syntax of Simple Arithmetic Expressions:* The first abstract syntax proposal was put forward by John McCarthy in [366]. An *analytic abstract syntax* was given for arithmetic expressions. In an analytic abstract syntax we postulate — as sorts — a class of terms. You may consider terms as a subset of all the things that can be analysed. We associate a number of observer functions with these.

These examples are drawn from McCarthy [366].

Analytic Syntax

We define abstractly a small language of arithmetic expressions. We focus on constants, variables and infix sum and product terms.

type
    A, Term
value
    is_term: A → **Bool**
    is_const, is_var, is_sum, is_prod: Term → **Bool**
    s_addend, s_augend, s_mplier, s_mpcand: Term → Term
axiom
    ∀ t:Term •
        (is_const(t)∧∼(is_var(t)∨is_sum(t)∨is_prod(t))) ∧
        (is_var(t)∧∼(is_const(t)∨is_sum(t)∨is_prod(t))) ∧
        (is_sum(t)∧∼(is_const(t)∨is_var(t)∨is_prod(t))) ∧
        (is_prod(t)∧∼ (isc_onst(t)∨is_var(t)∨is_sum(t))) ∧
    ∀ t:A • is_term(t) ⇒
        (is_var(t)∨is_const(t)∨is_sum(t)∨is_prod(t)) ∧
        (is_sum(t) ≡ is_term(s_addend(t))∧is_term(s_augend(t))) ∧
        (is_prod(t) ≡ is_term(s_mplier(t))∧is_term(s_mpcand(t)))

A is a universe of things. Some are terms, some not! The terms are restricted, in this example, to constants, variables, two argument sums and two argument products. How a constant, a variable, a sum or a product is represented is immaterial to the above.

One could think of the following alternative, external, written representations of arithmetic expressions:

$$a + b, +ab, (\text{PLUS } A \ B), 7^a \times 11^b.$$

The last $(7^a \times 11^b)$ is some form of Gödel number representation [180,319,444] of arithmetic expressions.

Synthetic Syntax

A synthetic abstract syntax further introduces generators of sort values, i.e., of terms:

value
    mk_sum: Term × Term → Term
    mk_prod: Term × Term → Term
axiom
    ∀ u,v:Term •
        is_sum(mk_sum(u,v)) ∧ is_prod(mk_prod(u,v)) ∧
        s_addend(mk_sum(u,v)) ≡ u ∧ s_augend(mk_sum(u,v)) ≡ v ∧
        s_mplier(mk_prod(u,v)) ≡ u ∧ s_mpcand(mk_prod(u,v)) ≡ v ∧
        is_sum(t)⇒mk_sum(s_addend(t),s_augend(t)) ≡ t ∧
        is_prod(t)⇒mk_prod(s_mplier(t),s_mpcand(t)) ≡ t

Analytic and synthetic syntaxes are truly abstract.   ∎

McCarthy's notion of abstract syntax, both the analytic and the synthetic aspects, are to be found in most abstraction languages, thus also in RSL.

9.6.6 Discussion

We have shown one of the most powerful means of abstraction: namely property-oriented abstraction by means of sorts, observer functions (predicates and other value "selection" functions) and generator functions.

Specific principles of when to choose and of how to express, axiomatic property-oriented abstractions are given primarily in Chap. 12.

9.7 Summary

We have presented an overview of mathematical logic as a specification, rather than as a verification language. There were many parts to our exposition. In three stages of development we unravelled first the basis, a Boolean algebra; then a propositional logic, and finally a predicate calculus. We write an "algebra", a "logic", a "calculus", since there are many possible Boolean algebras — ours was one of a specific three-valued logic — and hence many propositional logics and predicate calculi. We also distinguished between algebra, logic and calculus: The algebra is just a simple one, the logic is more extensive — and hints at a theory (with axioms, rules of inference, and theorems) which we did not elaborate on — and the calculus is indeed to become a calculus: a set of rules, the inference rules, for calculation, just as the λ-calculus had rules (α-renaming and β-reduction). It is the predicate calculus, for very many chapters to come, that will serve us in abstraction and in specification.

In Chap. 8 we explained the notion of an algebra morphism (Sect. 8.4.4) Two algebras, one of syntax and one of semantics. In this chapter on logic we applied this concept repeatedly: in structuring our presentation of Boolean ground terms and their evaluation (Sect. 9.3.4), in structuring our presentation of propositional expressions and their evaluation (Sect. 9.4.3), and in structuring our presentation of predicate expressions and their evaluation (Sect. 9.5.7). It was perhaps not until the last of the above that we saw the full benefits of adhering to an inductive style of presenting the syntax and a homomorphic style of presenting the semantics. We claim that deploying the morphism idea helps structure our understanding of induction with its demand for three clauses: the basis, the inductive, and the (often implicitly understood) extremal clauses. In particular the inductive clause makes it easier for the specifier to decide on what — and how much — to develop, to define and present. Morphisms "tell" us how to develop the semantics: first the semantics corresponding to the basis clauses, then to the inductively defined syntax.

The choice of a three-valued logic is necessitated by our dealing, not with executable programs, but with specifications: from those of abstract models of the application domain, as it is, via requirements, to abstract software designs. That choice, however, complicates the semantics and hence the proof rules. So far we have only presented inference rules for a two-valued logic.

Finally, taking up a line that was begun in the chapter on algebras, in Sect. 9.6 we presented a thorough coverage of the predicate calculus with its quantified expressions — the practical idea of an axiom system. We applied this idea immediately, without going into logic theories of for example *undecidability* issues of axiom systems, *consistency* or *completeness*. We did so in order to present actual examples of abstract specifications. With a reasonable, albeit specification-oriented, view of logic, we can now proceed to apply the concepts of logic discussed in this chapter.

9.8 Bibliographical Notes

Classical textbooks on mathematical logic are:

- Willard van Orman Quine: *Mathematical Logic* (1951) [509]
- Alonzo Church: *Introduction to Mathematical Logic* (1956) [153]
- Elliott Mendelsohn: *Introduction to Mathematical Logic* (1964) [372]
- Patrick Suppes: *A First Course in Mathematical Logic* (1964) [492]
- Stephen Kleene: *Mathematical Logic* (1967) [324]
- Joseph R. Schoenfield: *Mathematical Logic* (1967) [457]
- Herbert B. Enderton: *A Mathematical Introduction to Logic* (1972) [210]

There are many others, including: [136, 235, 259, 294, 402]. The reader should, however, be duly warned.

On one hand is the mathematical subject of mathematical logic. On the other hand is the computing science subject of the same name, but their foci are different. To logicians mathematical logic is a study of which kinds of logics there are, their expressive power, which issues are decidable, i.e., what can be proved. To the software engineer mathematical logic is a tool to be used for the expression of abstractions and for the oftentimes long-winded and cumbersome proofs of stated, desirable properties. In Sect. 9.2 we discussed several of the interface issues between these two viewpoints, and we did so on the basis of John Rushby's delightful report [451].

9.9 Exercises

Exercise 9.1. ♣ *Predicates over the Transportation Net Domain.* We refer to Appendix A, Sect. A.1, *Transportation Net*.

We also refer to Example 9.12 in which we suggested some types, some observer functions, and an axiom covering two constraints.

But those constraints were not enough to satisfy suitably well-formed transportation nets.

(i) If from any segment one can observe some connections, then from each of these connections one should be able to observe (at least) that segment. And: (ii) If from any connection one can observe some segments, then from each of these segments one should be able to observe (at least) that connection.

1. Formulate suitable axioms (i.e., a predicate expressions) expressing these two constraints.
2. Can you think of other constraints?
3. We wish to insert in a given transportation net a new segment, and assume that it is to be connected to existing connections. State the signature of a suitable insert_segment function, and state the pre- and post-conditions for this function.
4. We wish to insert in a given transportation net a new connection, and assume that it is to be inserted in an existing segment. State the signature of a suitable insert_connection function, and state the pre- and post-conditions for this function.

Exercise 9.2. ♣ *A Predicate over the Container Logistics Domain.* We refer to Appendix A, Sect. A.2, *Container Logistics*.

We also refer to Example 9.13 in which we suggested some types, some observer functions, and an axiom covering one constraint.

Assume that associated with every bay of a ship or a container storage area there is associated a maximum height for any of the stacks of any of its rows of such. Thus assume that the maximum height is an attribute that can be observed from any bay, and that the current height of a stack can be observed from any stack.

Express a predicate which applies to any bay:Bay and yields truth if none of its stacks are higher than the stated maximum height.

Exercise 9.3. ♣ *A Predicate over the Financial Service Industry Domain.* We refer to Appendix A, Sect. A.3, *Financial Service Industry*.

We also refer to Example 9.14 in which we suggested some types, some observer functions, and an axiom covering three constraints (vii, viii, and ix).

For a transaction concerning a named securities instrument to take place at a securities (e.g., a stock) exchange, at a given time, t, its name, i, must be given and there must be buy and sell orders, buy_orders$_i$, sell_orders$_i$ for that securities instrument such that their time interval of consideration embraces the given time, t, such that the sum totals of quantities of buy_orders$_i$, i.e., q_{b_i}, and of sell_orders$_i$, i.e., q_{s_i}, equal, and such that their ("lo–hi") price interval of consideration all embraces some transaction price, p_i.

Express the above constraints as a pre-condition for a transact function whose arguments include the name, i, of the securities instrument, the current time, t, and the securities exchange, sec_exchg.

Thus assume suitable observer functions such as: (i) observe buy [sell] orders for a given, i.e., a named, securities instrument, (ii) observe from a buy or a sell order its requested buy, respectively sell quantity, its transaction period (time interval), and its "lo–hi" (buy, respectibely sell) price interval.

Part III

SIMPLE RSL

General

We have covered very basic, and very simple aspects of discrete mathematics and functions. We are now ready to "embed" such notions in the main tool of these volumes: The RAISE Specification Language, RSL.

Our first systematic presentation of RSL will basically follow the "pattern" set in Part II, except that we will now cover functions, as they can be defined in RSL early in the present part, and then again, later!

For other introductions to the RSL and the RAISE Method we refer to [236, 238].

RSL Versus VDM-SL, Z and B

There are other specification languages. We shall settle for RSL. We could have chosen, instead, VDM-SL, the current author being one of the instigators and first researchers into and developers of VDM-SL [120, 121, 226] (as he is also an instigator *&c.* of RAISE hence RSL).

Or we could have chosen Z [476, 477, 533], or B [3, 4]. We chose RSL for a number of reasons:

- of the specification languages just mentioned, RSL is closest in some sense, to discrete mathematics;
- like VDM-SL, RSL also expresses the imperative specification style, i.e., with assignable variables and statements;
- RSL, in addition, can handle the expression of concurrency (see Chap. 21) — none of VDM-SL, Z, B can do that;

- RSL, like algebraic specification languages (CASL [399] and CafeOBJ [191]), allows for introduction of sorts, postulation of observer function, and then having axioms determine the "shape" of the sorts and the signature defined functions; finally
- RSL, like Z, B, CafeOBJ and CASL, can structure its specifications in a modular fashion (see Vol. 2, Chap. 10).

> It is the "extension" of VDM-SL with sorts and axioms and with CSP-like process concepts, which to this author makes RSL preferable to VDM-SL. If you have learned and use VDM-SL before you can rather easily "move" on to RSL.

B, with its follow-on event-B, has yet to settle, so it would be premature to base a text book whose primary aim is not to teach a specific language (but to teach abstraction) on B/event-B.[19]

The modular structuring facilities of Z seems very elegant. The emerging such facilities of event-B likewise. Both Z and B seem to emphasize formal proofs as mandatory in every step of development — where VDM-SL and RSL emphasises specification. All in all it seems to this author that RSL is a best choice: Most versatile.

But we should claim that it is more important to express (model-oriented) abstraction, than to pick (on) a specific language. So we suggest lecturers to use these volumes, but work out themselves supplementary notes in either of the model-oriented specification languages VDM-SL, Z or B.

What, Syntactically, Constitutes a Specification?

We shall, in the present volume, take a specification to consist of:

- one or more **type** definitions,
- one or more function **value** definitions,
- zero, one or more **axioms**,
- zero, one or more **variable** declarations, and
- zero, one or more **channel** declarations.

For now we shall be content with the first three kinds of specifications.

Chapter 20 will introduce **variable**s, and Chap. 21 will introduce **channels**.

Volume 2, Sect. 10.2 will slightly change the above view of the syntax of a specification, to allow for **schemes** and **classes** to contain the **type, value** and **axiom** parts, while extending RSL with **objects**.

---

[19]The current author finds that the principles of event-B represents a fascinating specification paradigm.

Towards an RSL "Standard"

RSL[20] is currently maintained, as a language, by Chris George[21]. The main reference to RSL is [236]:

The RAISE Specification Language.
Chris George, Peter Haff, Klaus Havelund, Anne Haxthausen, Robert Milne, Claus Bendix Nielsen, Søren Prehn, and Kim Ritter Wagner.
The BCS Practitioner Series. Prentice-Hall, Hemel Hampstead, , 1992.

That book appears to be out of print. You may be able to buy publisher authorised reprints of the book from:

> http://spd-web.terma.com/Projects/RAISE/faq.html#contact_info
> att.: Mr. Jan Storbank Pedersen

It is hoped that a slight revision of the text may be available over the Internet. The other main reference to RAISE [238]:

The RAISE Method.
Chris George, Anne Haxthausen, Steven Hughes, Robert Milne, Søren Prehn, and Jan Storbank Pedersen.
The BCS Practitioner Series. Prentice-Hall, Hemel Hampstead, UK, 1995.

is now available over the Internet:

> ftp://ftp.iist.unu.edu/pub/RAISE/method_book/

The RSL of the present three-volume series is a "slight extension" of proper RSL. For the variant of RSL which is supported by free tools, see next, is described on the following Internet web page:

> www.iist.unu.edu/newrh/III/3/1/docs/rsltc/RSL.changes/

RSL Tools

Information about down loadable RAISE Tools can be obtained from UNU-IIST:

> http://www.iist.unu.edu/newrh/III/3/1/page.html

---

[20]The information in this and the next section is dated. It is correct as of "year end/year begin" 2004/2005.

[21]UNU-IIST, United Nations University, International Institute for Software Technology, P.O. Box 3058, Macau SAR, China. E-mail: cwg@iist.unu.edu, URL: www.iist.unu.edu

This includes information about free, open-source software for various platforms (Linux, Solaris, DOS, Windows). Includes type checking, pretty-printing, translation to SML and C++.

Information about original RAISE Tools can be obtained from Terma, the company that markets these tools:

`http://spd-web.terma.com/Projects/RAISE/faq.html#tool_support`

Likewise information about tool manuals:

`ftp://ftp.iist.unu.edu/pub/RAISE/tool_manuals/`

10

Atomic Types and Values in RSL

- The **prerequisites** for studying this chapter are that you possess familiarity with ordinary programming language type and value concepts and specific awareness of the mathematical concept of numbers as covered in earlier chapters.
- The **aims** are to introduce the concept of atomic types and values, in particular to introduce the RSL concepts of enumerated types (and their values), and to emphasise the two-faced notion of specific space of RSL specification versus arbitrary spaces of modelled identifiers.
- The **objective** is to teach the reader to choose appropriate atomic types and values as models of simple phenomena and concepts.
- The **treatment** is systematic and semiformal.

Not every phenomenon can be analysed down to a stone, i.e., an atomic thing. But many things can — *and for those we present some modelling principles, techniques and tools.*

Characterisation. By an *atomic value* we mean an entity in whose possible subparts we have no interest. It may have some proper subparts, or it may have none, but all we are interested in is the value itself. ∎

Characterisation. By an *atomic type* we mean a type all of whose values are atomic. ∎

10.1 Introduction

We shall discuss why this chapter brings the material that it does, and why at this place!

10.1.1 Mathematical Versus Enterprise Modelling

Numbers play an important role in everyday life: In budgeting and accounting — i.e., in ordinary reckoning — and in mathematics. Models of physical phenomena are classically expressed in terms of, for example, polynomial, differential and integral equations. The variables of expressions in these equations usually denote numbers. We will not be dealing with traditional, often called applied, mathematics as practiced by all engineers, by operations researchers, by econometricians, etc. Instead we will be teaching principles, techniques and tools. "Our" mathematical specifications will not supplant those of the above-mentioned professionals. We — and you, based on what you learn here — will be applying "our kind" of mathematical specifications to such actual-life phenomena for which classical mathematics have shown to be inadequate or awkward.

Although this chapter is about numbers, we shall, in consequence, not be basing "our kind" of specifications on numbers, but more on "richer" mathematical structures — also not suitably modelled by polynomials, differentials, integrals or other classical mathematical forms of expressions. We shall present principles, techniques and tools for the modelling and for providing software for general enterprises, not conventionally "modellable" by ordinary mathematics.

10.1.2 The "Primitive" Model Building Blocks

In this chapter we shall look at the very basic, you may wish to call them the "primitive", we call them the atomic elements, by means of which our models are built, or upon which they rest. They include numbers: natural numbers, integers and reals — and we discuss why only and exactly those. The elements also include characters and text strings, and what we could refer to as identifiers, or tokens.

Our main use of numbers in modelling, is in modelling quantities. Just as physicists use numbers to quantify weight, speed, etc., so we use numbers to quantify similar and other actual-world phenomena. Our main use of characters, text strings and identifiers is in modelling simple, concrete input/output messages, or respectively in modelling identification of phenomena in the universe of discourse.

10.2 The RSL Numbers

We have already covered, in Chap. 2, the mathematical concepts of numbers. Suffice it here to summarise. There are many kinds of numbers, to wit: natural numbers (**Nat**: $0, 1, 2, \ldots$); integers (**Int**: $\ldots, -2, -1, 0, 1, 2, \ldots$) rationals: consisting of both integers (viz.: i, j) and fractions, $\frac{i}{j}$, for all integers i, j where $j \neq 0$; irrational numbers; real numbers (**Real**), imaginary and complex numbers; and transcendental numbers.

10.2.1 Three Types of Numbers

Without taking into consideration the operations applicable to numbers (Sect. 10.2.2), in RSL we consider just the following three subtypes of all the numbers: the natural numbers, the integers and the reals. The three categories are related as follows:

Nat $\subset$ Int $\subset$ Real

Natural Numbers: Nat

The natural numbers are just the whole numbers larger than or equal to zero: $0, 1, 2, \ldots$.

Integers: Int

The natural numbers are just the whole numbers, positive or negative: $\ldots, -2, -2, 0, 1, 2, \ldots$.

Real Numbers: Real

The real numbers of RSL are those whose numerals (i.e., names) can be written, with or without a minus sign, as a finite sequence of digits before a decimal point, ".", followed by a finite sequence of digits after the decimal point: -987654321.0123456789!

10.2.2 Operations on RSL Numbers

RSL defines the following operations on real numbers:

> **value**
> $+, -, /, *:$ **Real** $\times$ **Real** $\overset{\sim}{\to}$ **Real**
> $<, \leq, =, \neq, \geq, >:$ **Real** $\times$ **Real** $\to$ **Bool**
> $-:$ **Real** $\to$ **Real**
> **abs: Real** $\to \{ |$ r:**Real** $\bullet$ r$\geq$0 $| \}$
> **int: Real** $\to$ **Int**
> **real: Int** $\to$ **Real**
> **axiom**
> $\forall$ n:**Nat** $\bullet$ **abs** $-$n $=$ n $=$ **abs** n

As for all other types, equivalence ($\equiv$) and non-equivalence ($\not\equiv$) are also defined on numbers. The **int** and **real** functions convert a real to the integer nearest 0, or respectively an integer to a real:

int $2.71 = 2$, **int** $-2.71 = -2$, **real** $5 = 5.0$, ...

10.3 Enumerated Tokens

When we wish to speak of typically a finite number of identifiable atomic entities without further describing them, then we turn to the use of enumerated tokens.

10.3.1 Motivation

We believe that Example 2.3 clearly shows the need for a less encoded modelling of finite, usually "small sets" of atomic values where we do not really care what these values are, other than being able to name them individually and distinctly. For this we introduce, as was already done for programming languages, in, for example, Pascal (by Niklaus Wirth [314, 522]), the notion of enumerated tokens.

Example 10.1 *Enumerated Tokens, Playing Cards:* The 52 card set, that is, without the Joker can usually be modelled as:

type
   Suit == club | diamond | heart | spade
   Face == ace | two | three | ... | ten | knight | dame | king
   Card = Suit × Face

The suits are usually shown as: ♣, ◇, ♡ and ♠.   ∎

10.3.2 General Theory

By an enumerated token we understand an atomic value defined in a particular way. Let t and t' be enumerated tokens. Either $t = t'$ (and $t \equiv t'$) or $t \neq t'$ (and $\not\equiv$). The equality (equivalence) and the inequality (nonequivalence) operations are the only ones defined on enumerated tokens.[1]
   A schematic example is in order:

type
   Token == $token_1$ | $token_2$ | ... | $token_n$

is a *variant definition* which defines n atomic values: $token_1$, $token_2$, ..., $token_n$.
   Thus the definition symbol: == signals what we shall call a variant constructor. The type constructor | thus effectively designates a disjoint type union.
   The above variant definition is a shorthand for the following "longhand":

---

[1]In fact these four operations: $=, \equiv, \neq$ and $\not\equiv$, are defined on all values.

type
    Token
value
    $token_1$:Token,
    $token_2$:Token,
    ...
    $token_n$:Token
axiom
    [disjointness of enumerated tokens]
        $token_1 \neq token_2 \wedge ... \wedge token_1 \neq token_n \wedge$
        $token_2 \neq token_3 \wedge ... \wedge token_2 \neq token_n \wedge$
        ...
        $token_{n-1} \neq token_n$

Enumerated tokens, i.e., variant definitions, like the above, thus come with or "generate", an additional axiom: the induction axiom.

The role of the induction axiom is to express that the variant definition designates a model in which there are only and exactly the three enumerated values.

To express this metalinguistically, that is, not as a part of the variant definition, but as one implied, we say: For all predicates p, if p holds for all the enumerated values listed, then p holds for all Tokens:

axiom
    [enumerated token induction]
        $\forall$ p:Token$\rightarrow$**Bool** •
            $p(token_1) \wedge p(token_2) \wedge ... \wedge p(token_n) \Rightarrow \forall$ token:Token • p(token)

Thus, by taking (one) p as:

value
    p: Token $\rightarrow$ **Bool**
    $p \equiv \lambda$ t:Token • $t=token_1 \vee t=token_2 \vee ... \vee t=token_n$

we see that a Token is either $token_1$, or $token_2$, or ..., or $token_n$; that is, only one of those.

10.3.3 Operations on Tokens

Only four operations apply to tokens: equality ($=$) and inequality ($\neq$), equivalence ($\equiv$) and non-equivalence ($\not\equiv$):

type
    Token $==$ a | b | ... | c
value
    $=$: Token $\times$ Token $\rightarrow$ **Bool**

$\neq$: Token $\times$ Token $\rightarrow$ **Bool**
$\equiv$: Token $\times$ Token $\rightarrow$ **Bool**
$\not\equiv$: Token $\times$ Token $\rightarrow$ **Bool**

10.3.4 Enumerated Tokens in Abstract Models

There is a principle of (possible) application to adhere to, there is a technique with which to proceed when having chosen abstraction using enumerated tokens, and there is, in RSL, a tool to apply when carrying out the specification, that is, when considering, respectively choosing to introduce enumerated tokens into an abstract model (i.e., an abstract specification). They (the principle, the technique and the tool) are:

Principles. *Enumerated Tokens:* If a concrete, physically manifest phenomenon or an abstract concept can be characterised by an attribute that can take on (usually only a few) values, where these can all be considered atomic, and among which only the equality and equivalence operations apply, then choose to model these as enumerated tokens.   ∎

Techniques. *Enumerated Tokens:* Identify the one or more attributes of a phenomenon (concept); assign distinct names to their value types; determine the range of values for each enumerated type; ascribe suitably expressive identifiers as names for these values and otherwise apply the tool for modelling enumerated tokens.   ∎

Tools. *Enumerated Tokens:* The RSL language tool for expressing enumerated tokens is the variant definition:

type
    ET == et_1 | et_2 | ... | en_n

The RSL tool, besides expressing equality, for handling enumerated tokens is the **case** construct:

type
    A, B
value
    obs_ET: A $\rightarrow$ ET
    fct, fct_1, fct_2, ..., fct_n: A $\rightarrow$ B
    fct(a) $\equiv$
        case obs_ET(a) **of**
            et_1 $\rightarrow$ fct_1(a), et_2 $\rightarrow$ fct_2(a), ... , et_n $\rightarrow$ fct_n(a)
        end

where fct tests the enumerated token value, say et_i, of an argument a:A, for a given attribute (ET), and invokes an appropriate auxiliary function, say fct_i, to (further) process the argument.

The type A and B, the observer function obs_ET and the auxiliary functions fct_i are assumed..   ∎

10.3.5 Modelling Using Enumerated Tokens

Enumerated Tokens and Finite State Devices

By a finite state device we understand either a finite state automaton, or a finite state machine. In Vol. 2, Chap. 11 we shall introduce the concepts of finite state automata and finite state machines. Each state of such devices is typically labeled, and labels are drawn from a finite alphabet of symbols. These are modelled using the concept of enumerated tokens as introduced in this section.

Example 10.2 *Finite State Automata State Labels:* We present some informal examples:

(1) In an operating system scheduled jobs are either running, queued, waiting for input, idle or other. With each job one can therefore associate its state — as labeled by these enumerated tokens.

type
    Job_Status == running | queued | waiting_for_input | idle | other

(2) An automobile may be in either of the following states: parked, standing still with motor running, driving forwards, driving backwards, or other.

type
    Car_Status == parked | idling | forward | backward | other

(3) An aircraft may be in either of the following states: waiting for maintenance, being maintained, taxiing to departure gate, being serviced (being fueled, loading baggage, boarding passengers, etc.), cleared for take-off, taking off, flying, landing, etc.

type
    Aircraft_Status == wait_maint | under_maint | taxi_dept |
                       | under_service | cleared | take_off | flying | landing

∎

Enumerated Tokens and Linux Commands

Example 10.3 *Linux Command Names:* When specifying the software design for implementing, or the requirements for prescribing the meaning of Linux commands, we need to name them. Some are: cp, emacs, latex, ls, mkdir, mv, rm, rmdir, etc.

type
    Linux_Cmd_Nms == cp | emacs | latex | ls | mkdir | mv | rm | rmdir | ...

∎

10.4 Characters and Texts

Characters and sequences of characters, i.e., texts, form a very concrete type, one we shall not be using much in domain descriptions or requirements prescriptions.

10.4.1 Motivation

For the ordinary use of computers, input data must be read, stored data need be manipulated, and output data must be generated. The input data originally, and the output data finally, are in the form of visualisable marks: alphabetic characters, numeric digits and special symbols (operator symbols, delimiters, etc.). All this is prescribed by computer programs.

The purpose of abstract specification is not to define executable programs but, with respect to software design, to specify classes of these. And with respect to domain descriptions and requirements prescriptions, we need not prescribe concrete input and output, but can abstract these.

Therefore, at high levels of abstractions, we need not make use of RSL's built-in **Char**acter and **Text** data type. But, at close-to-execution level RSL software design specifications, it is useful to have a counterpart to the `character` and `character string` types of ordinary programming languages.

10.4.2 The **Character** and **Text** Data Types

The RSL **Char** and **Text** data types are related to one another, and the **Text** data type is related to the RSL list data type. Meta-linguistically, i.e., "outside" RSL, we can explain the two RSL types:

literals /∗ This is meta RSL ∗/
    $'a'$, ..., $'A'$, ...
type
    Char $\simeq$ {| $'a'$, $'b'$, $'c'$, ..., $'z'$, $'A'$, $'B'$, ..., $'Z'$ |}
    Text $\simeq$ **Char***

value
 c1,c2,...,cn:**Char**
value expressions
 c1=c2 ∨ c1≠c2 ∨ ... ∨ c=$'$a$'$ ∨ c=$'$b$'$ ∨ ...

This is concrete RSL:

value expression explanations or equivalences:

 $"$abra$"$ ≃ ⟨$'$a$'$,$'$b$'$,$'$r$'$,$'$a$'$⟩
 hd $"$abra$"$ = $'$a$'$
 tl tl tl $"$cadabra$"$ = $"$abra$"$
 len $"$abracadabra$"$ = 11
 $""$ ≃ ⟨⟩
 $"$abra$"$^$"$cadabra$"$ = $"$abracadabra$"$
 card inds $"$abracadabra$"$ = **card** {1,2,3,4,5,6,7,8,9,10,11} = 11
 card elems $"$abracadabra$"$ = **card**{$'$a$'$,$'$b$'$,$'$c$'$,$'$d$'$,$'$r$'$} = 5

We refer to our first presentation of the RSL list data type of Example 9.24. Since texts are sequences of characters, texts really are not atomic, but the elements are.

   Above we introduced, without prior explanation, the RSL *sub-typing* construct. If A' is a type (i.e., a type name), then A is the subtype (i.e., the name of the subtype) of A' whose values all satisfy the postulated predicate $P(a)$:

type
 A'
 A = {| a:A' • P(a) |}
value
 P: A' → **Bool**

Thus {| and |} are special forms of set type constructors.

10.5 Identifiers and General Tokens

Identifiers are specially identified "atomic" language quantities, i.e., they "are" syntax. Tokens are identifiable atomic designations, i.e., they "are" atomic semantic quantities.

10.5.1 Identifiers

There are two kinds of identifiers: identifiers used in, for example, RSL specifications (and in programs: variable, label, type and procedure names, etc.), and identifiers that we need again and again in order to model certain phenomena and certain concepts. This section is about identifiers.

RSL Identifiers

In our specifications we need to identify phenomena: types, values, incl. functions, etc., by naming them. Identifiers in, for example, RSL, serve this rôle. RSL identifiers are any string of alphanumeric characters possibly with properly in-fixed underscores and/or suffixed primes:[2]

a, aa, ala, a_la, a1a, abra_ca_dabra, a_1, a', a''

Universe of Discourse Identifiers

Universe of discourse identifiers arise when we model a domain — or some requirements, or some software — in which there is a collection of further unspecified names or identifiers.

Example 10.4 *Universe of Discourse Identifiers:* Some examples of universe of discourse identifiers include names of (i) persons, of (ii) cities, of (iii) product parts (i.e., part numbers), of (iv) patient medical journals, etc., as in some actual, real-life domain. They can also include names of (v) database relations, (vi) relation attributes (i.e., column names) or computing resource names: (vii) pointers to records, (viii) disk segments, or other, as for some requirements prescription, or for some software design.   ■

As far as we are concerned these universe of discourse identifiers need not be given a concrete representation, but can be modelled by any sort about whose elements we may assume that they are "further unanalysed". In Sect. 10.5.3 we shall show how to model such universe of discourse identifiers.

10.5.2 Operations on General Tokens

Only four operations apply to general tokens: equality (=) and inequality ($\neq$), equivalence ($\equiv$) and nonequivalence ($\not\equiv$):

type
    Token
value
    =: Token × Token → **Bool**
    $\neq$: Token × Token → **Bool**
    $\equiv$: Token × Token → **Bool**
    $\not\equiv$: Token × Token → **Bool**

---

[2]For readers with knowledge of the Z specification language, primes are a kind of temporal state operator, hence are not part of identifier names.

10.5.3 General Tokens

By a general token — as distinguished from enumerated tokens (cf. Sect. 10.3) — we understand a further unanalysed atomic quantity. Typically we can think of a sort name standing for an indefinite set of unique general tokens.

Principles. *Unique Universe of Discourse Identifiers:* When an entity, i.e., a set of phenomena, manifests itself, or a concept can best be understood, as a potentially indefinite set of unique atomic and further unanalysed quantities among which there is basically just the equality (and hence also the inequality) operation, and for which no particular representation (i.e., concrete name) is needed, then choose the model concept of general tokens for the abstract specification of these phenomena, respectively this concept.   ∎

Techniques. *Unique Universe of Discourse Identifiers:* Once one or more sets of phenomena or concepts has been chosen for modelling by means of general tokens, then choose appropriate, distinct names as sort names for each of the set of phenomena, respectively for each concept. By not stating any axioms about these sorts values of distinct such sorts, values of different general token sorts are distinct.   ∎

Tools. *Unique Universe of Discourse Identifiers:* To model universe of discourse identifiers we use the concept of general tokens. To model the dynamic issuance of (each time) distinct identifiers we may model as follows: We declare a global variable ids, and an operation get_Id of no arguments. Invocation of get_Id, i.e., get_Id(), amounts to the generation of an identifier that has so far not been issued.

```
class =
      type
[1]   Id
      variable
[2]   ids:Id-set := {}
      value
[3]   get_Id: Unit → read ids write ids   Id
[4]   get_Id() ≡
[5]      let id:Id • id ∉ ids in
[6]      ids := ids ∪ {id};
[7]      id end
      end
```

The keyword **variable** and line [2] above declare an assignable variable of type sets of identifiers and initialise this variable to the empty set of such. The literal **Unit** before the → "announces" that the function get_Id takes no argument.[3] The keyword **write** announces that the function get_Id potentially

---

[3]**Unit** is a type name; () is the only value of type **Unit**.

reads from and is intended to or definitely writes to a variable. The assignment statement prescribes the addition of an, in this case newly generated, identifier.

Elsewhere in the specification — where the above general token definition, with its generator operation, get_Id, is found — one may now invoke the operation:

    ... **let** id = get_Id() **in** ... id ... **end** ...

where the unique identifier id may be used several times: ... id ... .   ■

10.6 Discussion

It is time to review.

10.6.1 General

In this chapter we have introduced the atomic values and types of numbers: natural (**Nat**), integers (**Int**) and reals (**Real**); of enumerated and general tokens; and of characters and texts.

10.6.2 Modelling Atomic Entities

It remains to convey an important issue that we find it is better to mention here, in a summary, where we hope that issue will not be overlooked: When we have to model natural numbers, integers or reals in some universe of discourse, then we model them not by their representation, i.e., numerals, but directly by their semantic values: **Nat**, **Int** and **Real**, respectively. This parallels our similar modelling of Booleans, **Bool**, not by some representation, but by their semantic values.

We emphasize that there is a distinction to be made between using numbers and Booleans, for technical reasons in some specification, and using them to abstract phenomena and concepts of some universe of discourse. In the latter case, instead of describing (or prescribing) representations for each of the aforementioned atomic types, the specifier just uses their semantic value types.

Across many application domains there are many distinct, and even widely different kinds (read: types) of atomic entities. How are we to handle them? The answer was given above.

Principles. *Atomic Entities:* Atomic entities are usually handled as "further un-described" quantities, with no other properties associated with them than distinct actual world entities being modelled as distinct model values. The atomic entity modelling principle finally says: Do not describe specific syntactic representations for atomic entities.   ■

The above was a principle. How does it relate to our formal modelling? That is, how are we to handle the description and formal modelling of atomic entities?

Techniques. *Atomic Entities:* We make the distinction between types and values: Classes of atomic entities are usually modelled by further unspecified sorts. But when the atomic entities do possess such properties as are sufficiently possessed by numbers or characters or by character strings, then we model them so.   ∎

10.7 Exercises

Problem 10.1 below is reminiscent of material in J.H. Conway's book *On Numbers and Games* [159].[4]

Exercise 10.1. *Natural Numbers as Sets.* Let the natural number 0 be represented by the empty set, {}; the natural number 1 by the singleton set whose only member is the empty set, {{}}; and so forth: the natural number n, where n is larger than 0 is thus represented by a singleton set whose only member represents the natural number $n - 1$.

1. Now define an appropriate type, N, for natural number sets as outlined above and two functions, Nat2N and N2Nat. Nat2N takes a natural number and yields its set representation (in N), and N2Nat takes the set representation of a natural number and yields that natural number.
2. Then define simple arithmetic operators of addition and multiplication over N — resorting and without resorting to the use of general addition and multiplication, that is, to addition by other than 1s.

Exercise 10.2. ♣ *Atomic Types in the Transportation Net Domain.* We refer to Appendix A, Sect. A.1, *Transportation Net.*

1. *Segment and Connection Names:* Segments and connections have unique names — but we do not bother as to how they may be represented. Suggest type, that is, names for these names and explain in one or two words of which of the four kinds of atomic types you suggest they should be.
2. *Segment and Net Types:* A transportation net has segments being of either of a definite number of kinds. (You may think of these kinds as representing: public road, toll road, free way, rail line, air corridor or shipping lane.)
   (a) *Concrete Net Types:* Either you decide to model exactly a specific variety, such as just suggested above. Then suggest a suitable atomic type definition for that case.

---

[4]See also [44, 45].

(b) *Abstract Net Types:* Or you decide to model any such variety, say several levels of public roads, or of air corridors, etc. Then suggest a suitable atomic type for that case.

(c) *Nets of One Type:* Now define a predicate that determines whether a transportation net has all of its segments of the same kind — for either of your two models of the previous two items.

3. *Connection Types:* Given that one can observe from a segment its net type, it is reasonable to assume that a connection takes on, as its net type, the sum total, that is, the set of net types of its connected segments.

(a) State the signature of an observer function that determines the net type of any connection.

(b) Express an axiom that must be satisfied by any net, namely that the net type of any connection is commensurate with the net types of its connected segments.

Exercise 10.3. ♣ *Atomic Types in the Container Logistics Domain.*
We refer to Appendix A, Sect. A.2, *Container Logistics.*

Assume that container ships and container terminals can handle a diversity of containers: 20' (twenty feet), 40' (forty feet), and refrigerated such containers. Thus bays on ship and on shore are designated to contain only one specific of these kinds of containers. Suggest a way of modelling this:

1. atomic types (of an appropriate kind),
2. observer functions applicable to containers and to bays and yielding their container type, and
3. a predicate that applies to bays and checks that all stacked containers are of the appropriate kind.

Exercise 10.4. ♣ *Atomic Types in the Financial Service Industry Domain.*
We refer to Appendix A, Sect. A.3, *Financial Service Industry.*

Introduce a notion of credit cards of either one of the following kinds: AEX (American Express), DC (Diners Club), MC (Master Card), or VISA. From credit cards one can observe customer name, a credit card number, and, hidden from view, the number of a credit card account — which is also then a demand/deposit account of the designated customer.

Bank accounts can be of a number of kinds: mortgage (i.e., loan) accounts and demand/deposit accounts. In the latter case, the account is then associated with a set of zero, one or more credit card types and numbers.

Two or more credit cards can be associated with the same, hence shared demand/deposit bank account.

1. What kind of entities are credit cards: atomic or composite?
2. What attributes can be associated with a credit card?
3. Formalise the type of credit cards as a sort,
4. and define suitable observer functions.

5. Augment possibly previously defined types and observer functions related to bank accounts to take into consideration the above rough sketch narrative description. In particular extend the bank type to also include all the credit cards honoured by that bank.

6. Express first in words, i.e., in English, then formally in terms of axioms over bank types the constraints that must hold between the bank accounts of banks and associated credit cards.

11

Function Definitions in RSL

- The **prerequisite** for studying this chapter is that you possess knowledge about the mathematical concepts of numbers, sets, Cartesians and functions as covered in earlier chapters.
- The **aim** is to introduce, in preparation for the following chapters, ways and means of defining functions.
- The **objective** is to start the reader on the road to becoming fluent in defining functions as abstractly as is needed, when needed.
- The **treatment** is systematic and semiformal.

> To express any observation of phenomena and concepts, any operation on or over phenomena and concepts (that may yield "new" such) — in other words, in order to express change — we must apply functions. Hence we must define these functions.

There are a number of ways of defining functions. They are more or less variants of one another. They span a stylistic spectrum from property-oriented to model-oriented. This chapter will elucidate five ways of defining functions. But first we recap the function type.

11.1 The Function Type

Three issues are always relevant when presenting a data type: the means of expressing it (the syntax), the meaning of what is expressed (the semantics), and why we wrote down these expressions in the first place (the pragmatics). We shall cover the first two issues.

11.1.1 Syntax of Function Types

Let A, B stand for any types. Let F name the type of all total functions from A into B and let G name the type of all partial functions from subsets of A into

B. The latter type of functions includes the former type of functions. That is: the space of total functions is included in the space of partial functions.

type A, B
   F = A → B
   G = A $\overset{\sim}{\to}$ B
value
   f: F, g: G

$''$axiom$''$ − i.e., an RSL metalinguistic statement:
   F ⊆ G, i.e., (A → B) ⊆ (A $\overset{\sim}{\to}$ B)

We say that the two clauses, f:F and g:G, represent the *signatures* (the name and type) of the function spaces.

11.1.2 Informal Semantics of → and $\overset{\sim}{\to}$

→ and $\overset{\sim}{\to}$ are infix type operators. Applied to respective types (here the sorts A and B) they "construct" the (type) sets of total functions, respectively partial functions, from A into B.
   We now cover, briefly, five ways of — five sets of RSL language constructs for — defining functions.

11.2 Model-Oriented Explicit Definitions

In model-oriented style of function definition we typically define one function at a time, in a model-oriented manner, and in terms of λ-functions.
   Let $\mathcal{E}(a)$ can be any expression of the specification language being used. $\mathcal{E}(a)$ is intended to yield a value of type B.
   A model-oriented function definition is, schematically:

type
   A, B   f: A → B
value   f ≡ λa:A.$\mathcal{E}$(a), or:
   f: A $\overset{\sim}{\to}$ B   f(a) ≡ $\mathcal{E}$(a)
   f ≡ λa:A.$\mathcal{E}$(a) **pre** $\mathcal{P}$(a)

The first variant, with *f* being partial, requires the pre-condition $\mathcal{P}(a)$.

Example 11.1 *Model-Oriented Explicit Function Definition:* We define a modulo function:

value
    mod: **Nat** $\times$ **Nat** $\overset{\sim}{\to}$ **Nat**
    mod $\equiv$
        λ(m,n):(**Nat**> **Nat**)
          if n=0 **then chaos else**
          if 0<m$-$n$\leq$n **then** m$-$n **else** mod(m$-$n,n)
          end end

The explicit function definition:

type
    A, B
value
    f: A $\to$ B, f $\equiv$ λ a.$\mathcal{E}$(a), etc.

is an instance of the following axiomatic definition:

type
    A, B
value
    f: A $\to$ B,
axiom
    $\forall$ a:A • f(a)$\equiv\mathcal{E}$(a)

11.3 Model-Oriented Axiomatic Definitions

In this style of function definition we typically define one function at a time, in a model-oriented manner, but by a triple of **type/value/axiom** clauses:

type
    A, B, ...
value
    f: A $\overset{\sim}{\to}$ B
    ca:A, cb:B, ..., ca$'$:A, cb$'$:B
axiom
    $\mathcal{R}$(ca,cb), ..., $\mathcal{R}$(ca$'$,cb$'$)
    $\forall$ a:A, b:B •
        $\mathcal{P}_1$(a) $\Rightarrow$ $\mathcal{Q}_1$(a,b)
        $\wedge$ $\mathcal{P}_2$(a) $\Rightarrow$ $\mathcal{Q}_2$(a,b)
        $\wedge$ ...
        $\wedge$ $\mathcal{P}_n$(a) $\Rightarrow$ $\mathcal{Q}_n$(a,b)

ca, cb, ..., ca′, cb′ are usually constant values. Usually their definition (i.e., value identification cum instantiation) is omitted. $\mathcal{R}(ca,cb)$, ..., $\mathcal{R}(ca′,cb′)$ are propositions over constants. The predicate expressions $\mathcal{P}_i(a)$ and $\mathcal{Q}_i(a,b)$ are usually algorithmically expressed, at least to the extent that they do refer to f and some nontrivial operators (and possibly auxiliary functions over A, B, etc.). If f is total then one or more of the $\mathcal{P}_i(a)\Rightarrow$'s are omitted.

Example 11.2 *Two Model-Oriented Axiomatic Definitions:*

- **The modulo function:**

  value
  $\quad$ mod: **Nat** × **Nat** $\overset{\sim}{\to}$ **Nat**
  axiom
  $\quad \forall$ m:**Nat** • mod(m,1) = 0
  $\quad \forall$ m,n:**Nat** • n≠0 $\Rightarrow$
  $\qquad \exists$ q,r:**Nat** • q∗n+r=m $\wedge$ 0≤r≤n−1 $\wedge$ mod(m,n)=r

- **The square root function:**

  value
  $\quad$ sqr: **Real** $\overset{\sim}{\to}$ **Real**
  axiom
  $\quad \forall$ v:**Real** • v > 0.0 $\Rightarrow$ $\exists$ r:**Real** • sqr(v) = r $\wedge$ v∗v = r

∎

The next kind of function definition style differs only by emphasising more property-orientedness than the model-orientedness of the present style. The difference is a matter for discussion and choice.

11.4 Model-Oriented **pre/post**-Condition Definitions

In this style of function definition we typically define one function at a time, in a model-oriented manner, and in terms of a pair of predicates: one characterising function argument values; the other relations between function arguments and corresponding function results. Schematically it syntactically "looks" like:

type
$\quad$ A, B
value
$\quad$ f: A $\overset{\sim}{\to}$ B
$\quad$ f(a) **as** b
$\qquad$ **pre** $\mathcal{P}(a)$
$\qquad$ **post** $\mathcal{Q}(a,b)$

$\mathcal{P}(a)$ and $\mathcal{Q}(a,b)$ are general (usually universally quantified) predicate expressions over (quantified) variables a and b. Note the keyword **as**.

Example 11.3 *Model-Oriented Implicit pre/post-Condition Function Definition:* Yet another form of definition of the modulo function is given:

value
    mod: **Nat** $\times$ **Nat** $\overset{\sim}{\to}$ **Nat**
    mod(m,n) **as** r
      pre $n \neq 0$
      post $\exists$ q:**Nat** $\bullet$ q*n+r=m $\wedge$ $0 \leq r \leq n-1$

∎

The implicit pre/post-condition definition:

type
    A, B
value
    f: A $\overset{\sim}{\to}$ B
    f(a) **as** b **pre** $\mathcal{P}(a)$ **post** $\mathcal{Q}(a,b)$

is an instance of either of the following axiomatic definitions:

type
    A, B
value
    f: A $\overset{\sim}{\to}$ B
axiom
    $\forall$ a:A $\bullet$ $\mathcal{P}(a)$ $\Rightarrow$
      $\exists$! b:B $\bullet$ f(a) = b $\wedge$
      $\mathcal{Q}(a,b)$

type
    A, B
value
    f: A $\overset{\sim}{\to}$ B
axiom
    $\forall$ a:A $\bullet$ $\mathcal{P}(a)$ $\Rightarrow$
      $\exists$ b:B $\bullet$ f(a) = b $\wedge$
      $\mathcal{Q}(a,b)$

The only difference between the above two forms is that one (the one with unique existential quantification) defines a function deterministically, and the other defines it nondeterministically.

We have not shown that many f(a) **as** b **pre** p(a) **post** q(a,b) definitions. However, many will come, including:

Example 13.5's merge function, Example 13.11's int_Call, int_Hang and int_Busy functions, Example 15.6's index function, Example 15.8's sort function, Example 15.10's A_sort and KWIC functions and Example 16.10's retr_G2 function.

11.5 Property-Oriented Axiomatic Definitions

In this style of function definition we typically define one function at a time, usually in a *semi-property-oriented* manner, that is, by some modest use of model-orientedness, and by a triple of **type/value/axiom** clauses:

type
   A, B, ...
value
   f: A $\xrightarrow{\sim}$ B
axiom
   $\forall$ a:A, b:B •
      $\mathcal{P}_1(a) \Rightarrow \mathcal{Q}_1(a,b) \wedge$
      $\mathcal{P}_2(a) \Rightarrow \mathcal{Q}_2(a,b) \wedge$
      ... $\wedge$
      $\mathcal{P}_n(a) \Rightarrow \mathcal{Q}_n(a,b)$

The expressions $\mathcal{P}(a)$ and $\mathcal{Q}(a,b)$ are not algorithmically expressed. If f is total then the $\mathcal{P}_i(a) \Rightarrow$ s are omitted.

Example 11.4 *Two Property-Oriented Axiomatic Function Definitions:*

- **Factorial:**

   value
      factorial: **Nat** $\rightarrow$ **Nat**
      n:**Nat**
   axiom
      n > 1
      factorial(1) = 1,
      factorial(n) = n * factorial(n−1)

- **Fibonacci:**

   value
      fibonacci: **Nat** $\rightarrow$ **Nat**
      n:**Nat**
   axiom
      n > 1
      fibonacci(0) = 1, fibonacci(1) = 1,
      fibonacci(n) = fibonacci(n−1) + fibonacci(n−2)

11.6 Property-Oriented Algebraic Definitions

Here we are usually just given the built-in RSL atomic types (hence semi), the sorts (abstract types) and the signatures (i.e., type) of functions. An axiomatic, property-oriented function definition usually defines both several functions and several sorts — simultaneously. Schematically it syntactically "looks" like:

type
    A, B, C, D, E, F
value
    f: A $\overset{\sim}{\to}$ B, g: C $\overset{\sim}{\to}$ D, ..., h: E $\overset{\sim}{\to}$ F
axiom
    $\mathcal{E}_{p_1}$(f,g,...,h), ..., $\mathcal{E}_{p_k}$(f,g,...,h) [constants]
    $\mathcal{E}_{e_{1_\ell}}$(f,g,...,h) = $\mathcal{E}_{e_{1_r}}$(f,g,...,h) [equations]
    ...
    $\mathcal{E}_{e_{n_\ell}}$(f,g,...,h) = $\mathcal{E}_{e_{n_r}}$(f,g,...,h) ...

where $\mathcal{E}_i$(f,g,...,h) are general expressions involving — usually, but not shown — quantifications of types A, B, C, D, E, and/or F.

    We have shown several axiomatic definitions: Example 8.5 (stacks), Example 8.6 (queues), Example 9.23 (simple sets), and Example 9.24 (simple lists).

Example 11.5 *A Peano Algebra, A Property-Oriented Data Type Definition:* We continue Example 11.4, but now present the two functions in a fully algebraic style. Please refer to the Peano axioms in Example 9.21. They define **Nat**, but we now define arbitrary sum and successor and predecessor (addition, respectively subtraction, by one):

value
    z: **Nat** → **Bool**
    s: **Nat** → **Nat**
    p: **Nat** $\overset{\sim}{\to}$ **Nat**
    sum: **Nat** × **Nat** → **Nat**
    mpy: **Nat** × **Nat** → **Nat**
    fact: **Nat** → **Nat**
    fib: **Nat** → **Nat**

axiom
    ∀ m,n:**Nat** •
        z(n) = n=0,
        p(s(n)) = n,
        p(0) = **chaos**,
        sum(0,n) = n,
        ~z(m) ⇒ sum(m,n)=sum(p(m),s(n)),

> mpy(0,n) = 0, mpy(m,0) = 0,
> mpy(1,n) = n, mpy(m,1) = m,
> $\sim$z(m) $\Rightarrow$ mpy(m,n)=sum(m,mpy(p(m),n)),
> fact(0) = **chaos**, fact(1) = 1,
> $\sim$z(p(n)) $\Rightarrow$ fact(n)=mpy(n,fact(p(n))),
> fib(0) = 1, fib(1) = 1,
> $\sim$z(p(n)) $\Rightarrow$ fib(n)=sum(fib(p(p(n))),fib(p(n)))

Here equality to 0 is assumed a primitive, i.e., given predicate.   ∎

11.7 Summary of RSL Function Definition Styles

Without comments we list the variety of function definition styles covered in this chapter:

1. Model-Oriented Explicit Definitions

   type
     A, B
   value
     f: A $\overset{\sim}{\to}$ B
     f $\equiv$ λa:A.$\mathcal{E}$(a) **pre** .$\mathcal{P}$(a)

     f: A $\to$ B
     f $\equiv$ λa:A.$\mathcal{E}$(a)
         [or − which is the same]
     f(a) $\equiv$ $\mathcal{E}$(a)

2. Model-Oriented Axiomatic Definitions

   type
     A, B
   value
     f: A $\overset{\sim}{\to}$ B
     ca:A, cb:B, ..., ca':A, cb':B
   axiom
     $\mathcal{R}$(ca,cb), ..., $\mathcal{R}$(ca',cb')
     $\forall$ a:A, b:B •
       $\mathcal{P}_1$(a) $\Rightarrow$ $\mathcal{Q}_1$(a,b) $\wedge$
       $\mathcal{P}_2$(a) $\Rightarrow$ $\mathcal{Q}_2$(a,b) $\wedge$
       ... $\wedge$
       $\mathcal{P}_n$(a) $\Rightarrow$ $\mathcal{Q}_n$(a,b)

3. Model-Oriented pre/post-Condition Definitions

   type
     A, B
   value
     f: A $\overset{\sim}{\to}$ B
     f(a) **as** b
       pre $\mathcal{P}$(a)
       post $\mathcal{Q}$(a,b)

4. Property-Oriented Axiomatic Definitions

   type
     A, B, ...
   value
     f: A $\overset{\sim}{\to}$ B
     ca:A, cb:B, ..., ca':A, cb':B
   axiom
     $\mathcal{R}$(ca,cb) $\wedge$
     ... $\wedge$
     $\mathcal{R}$(ca',cb') $\wedge$
     $\forall$ a:A, b:B •
       $\mathcal{P}_1$(a) $\Rightarrow$ $\mathcal{Q}_1$(a,b) $\wedge$
       $\mathcal{P}_2$(a) $\Rightarrow$ $\mathcal{Q}_2$(a,b) $\wedge$
       ... $\wedge$
       $\mathcal{P}_n$(a) $\Rightarrow$ $\mathcal{Q}_n$(a,b)

5. Property-Oriented Algebraic Definitions

type
  A, B, C, D, E, F
value
  f: A $\tilde{\rightarrow}$ B, g: C $\tilde{\rightarrow}$ D, ..., h: E $\tilde{\rightarrow}$ F
axiom
  [constants]

$\mathcal{E}_{p_1}(f,g,...,h)$,
...,
$\mathcal{E}_{p_k}(f,g,...,h)$,
[equations]
$\mathcal{E}_{e_{1_\ell}}(f,g,...,h) = \mathcal{E}_{e_{1_r}}(f,g,...,h)$,
...,
$\mathcal{E}_{e_{n_\ell}}(f,g,...,h) = \mathcal{E}_{e_{n_r}}(f,g,...,h)$

11.8 Discussion

We have shown five styles of defining functions. It is obvious that there is a spectrum of definition styles, from purely algebraic, i.e., property-oriented, to purely algorithmic, i.e., model-oriented explicit function definitions. We leave it to the reader to choose appropriate combinations of these styles.

A function definition, in either of the five styles outlined above, may not uniquely determine exactly one function, i.e., one mathematical value, but the syntax of a function definition may denote a usually infinite set of such mathematical values. This under-specification, or this looseness, may be desirable or not.

11.9 Exercises

♣ **Note:** The three exercises of this chapter are best tackled after you have studied one or more of Chaps. 13–16 on RSL sets, Cartesians, lists and maps!

Exercise 11.1. ♣ *Functions in the Transportation Net Domain.* We refer to Appendix A, Sect. A.1, *Transportation Net.*

As an exercise, try express a function over *Transportation Nets* in some or all of the five styles presented in this chapter.

Hint: Try the following functions: Insert a segment, respectively insert a connection in a transportation net. See Exercise 9.1, items 3 and 4. Be prepared to define these functions in terms of a number of auxiliary functions, including predicates. Describe them loosely, in your own words — rather than attempting a full definition as you have yet to learn about suitable abstract data types with which to define these functions.

Exercise 11.2. ♣ *Functions in the Container Logistics Domain.* We refer to Appendix A, Sect. A.2, *Container Logistics.*

As an exercise, try express a function over *Container Logisticss* in some or all of the five styles presented in this chapter.

Hint: Try the following function: Enter a ship into a container terminal. Be prepared to define this function in terms of a number of auxiliary functions, including predicates. Describe them loosely, in your own words — rather than attempting a full definition as you have yet to learn about suitable abstract data types with which to define these functions.

Exercise 11.3. ♣ *Functions in the Financial Service Industry Domain.* We refer to Appendix A, Sect. A.3, *Financial Service Industry*.

As an exercise, try express a function over *Financial Service Industrys* in some or all of the five styles presented in this chapter.

Hint: Try the following functions: open and close a bank account, deposit and withdraw money into, respectively from a demand/deposit account.

Be prepared to define these functions in terms of a number of auxiliary functions, including predicates. Describe them loosely, in your own words — rather than attempting a full definition as you have yet to learn about suitable abstract data types with which to define these functions.

Property-Oriented and Model-Oriented Abstraction

- The **prerequisite** for studying this chapter is that you are willing to pursue and have the ability to grasp abstractions.
- The **aims** are to discuss the concept of abstraction and to present principles and techniques of abstraction, and to review the notion of property-oriented abstraction, to introduce the concept of model-oriented abstraction, and to relate these two ideas.
- The **objective** is to make the serious reader a professional in the basics of abstract modelling.
- The **treatment** is from systematic to formal.

Characterisation. By an *abstraction* we shall understand a formulation of some phenomenon or concept of some universe of discourse such that some aspects of the phenomenon or concept are emphasised (i.e., considered important or relevant) while others are left out of consideration (i.e., considered unimportant or irrelevant).   ∎

Characterisation. By a *property-oriented abstraction* we shall understand an abstraction of some phenomenon or concept of some universe of discourse such that the abstraction is primarily or solely expressed in terms of logical properties.   ∎

Characterisation. By a *model-oriented abstraction* we shall understand an abstraction of some phenomenon or concept of some universe of discourse such that the abstraction is primarily or solely expressed in terms of mathematical entities such as abstract tokens, sets, Cartesians, lists, functions, etc.   ∎

Abstraction is the act of emphasising certain phenomena and formulating certain concepts as being important, while suppressing other phenomena as not being important. It is a cornerstone of software engineering. Abstraction requires ability to reflect and to seek elegance and beauty. While some aspects of the pursuit of abstraction can be taught, most are learned by osmosis.

The present chapter — in a leisurely manner — discusses and formulates main abstraction and modelling principles and techniques concerning: *abstraction*, *property-oriented abstractions* (an overview of essentials), *model- versus property-oriented abstractions*, and *model-oriented abstractions* (an overview of essentials).

In this chapter we only overview: the rest of these volumes will alternate between giving examples of either of these two alternative styles of modelling as well as of their fusion.

The present chapter thus begins a road of teaching specification which — in view of the next five chapters — could as well be called programming in discrete mathematics. This topic is primarily illustrated in the sections on examples of χ-based abstractions. These sections could as well be named examples of χ-based programming. They are Sects. 13.3 (χ = sets), 14.3 (χ = Cartesians), 15.3 (χ = lists), 16.3 (χ = maps), and 17.2 (χ = functions [i.e., as values]).

Programming in discrete mathematics, is a way in which we ourselves have taught such courses as *Algorithms and Data Structures*.[1] For an early example of what such "rewrites" mean, see Example 16.10.

12.1 Abstraction

In this section we shall cover such issues as modelling, abstraction and specification in general, and abstraction in the form of an essay.

12.1.1 The Issues

The problems to be cursorily addressed in this section are those of models, modelling, abstraction and specification.

Modelling and Models

Modelling is the act of creating models, which include discrete mathematical structures (sets, Cartesians, lists, maps, etc.), and are logical theories represented as algebras. That is, any given RSL text denotes a set of models, and each model is an algebra, a set of named values and a set of named operations on these. Modelling is the engineering activity of establishing, analysing and using such structures and theories. Our models are established with the intention that they "model" "something else" other than just being the mathematical structure or theory itself. That "something else" is, in our case, some

---

[1]Thus we have, for example, had students "rewrite" many graph algorithms in [161] into VDM-SL (rather than, as here, RSL).

part of a reality[2], or of a construed such, or of requirements to[3], or of actual software[4].

Some clarifying observations are in order. We write down models, i.e., we specify them. So a model is represented syntactically by a specification. The meaning of a specification, its semantics, is the model — actually a set of models. The specification establishes, oftentimes, a great number of identifications between a perceived reality (which inherently is and remains elusive and hence informal) and textual parts of the specification — and hence their denoted mathematics. The model is not what it models, only a model of it!

Thus the term model is used in two, closely related senses: The mathematical model denoted by the specification, and that this specification models some phenomena.

12.1.2 Abstraction and Specification

Abstraction relates to conquering complexity of systems description through the judicious use of abstraction, where abstraction, briefly, is the act and result of omitting consideration of (what would then be called) details while, instead, focusing on (what would therefore be called) important facets.

That is, some systems may be thought of as being complex. Many would say that for example (i) the *domain* of railway systems is complex; or that (ii) the set of diverse *requirements* for a number of software packages for (subsystems of) the railway domain is complex; or that (iii) actual *software* systems that cover a reasonably diverse span of computing system-supported railway operations is complex. And, indeed, some descriptions of any of the above (i–iii) may actually be very complex. Such complexity may be inherent, that is, cannot be avoided. Or it may be unintentionally "put into" the descriptions. In the latter case such unintentional complexity could be avoided, we claim, by careful use of abstraction.

On the negative side we often see that descriptions are unnecessarily twisted, long, confused, and thus gives the appearance that the subject being described is complicated. Many such descriptions confuse issues of syntax, semantics and pragmatic nature (hence Sect. 1.6.2). On the positive side, by mastering abstraction we can often present the problem in a way that avoids unnecessary complexity.

12.1.3 An Essay on Abstraction

> Conception, my boy, fundamental brain-work,
> is what makes the difference in all art
>
> *D.G. Rossetti: letter to H. Caine*

---

[2]— as in domain modelling
[3]— as in requirements modelling
[4]— as in software design

Since this is the first chapter where the concept of abstraction — in connection with the modelling of some universe of discourse — is covered, we shall take time and space for a brief essay, essentially by C.A.R. Hoare, on what is meant by abstraction.

"Abstraction as a Fundamental Tool"

In the natural sciences one observes phenomena — and then one abstracts. In programming we create universes, but first abstractly.

The following is from the opening paragraphs of C.A.R. Hoare's: *Notes on Data Structuring* [286].

> Abstraction is a tool, used by the human mind, and to be applied in the process of describing (understanding) complex phenomena. Abstraction is the most powerful such tool available to the human intellect. Science proceeds by simplifying reality. The first step in simplification is abstraction. Abstraction (in the context of science) means leaving out of account all those empirical data which do not fit the particular, conceptual framework within which science at the moment happens to be working. Abstraction (in the process of specification) arises from a conscious decision to advocate certain desired objects, situations and processes as being fundamental; by exposing, in a first, or higher, level of description, their similarities and — at that level — ignoring possible differences.

We can rephrase the above: We consider those similarities which govern prediction and control of future events, i.e., 'meaning', as being fundamental and the differences as trivial. We have then developed — in the process of specification — an abstract concept to cover the set of objects and situations in question. The first requirement in designing a program is to concentrate on relevant features of the situation, and to ignore factors which are believed irrelevant. Abstraction thus implies simplification. That is, we reduce, at each stage of specification, the amount of information — of concepts and their interrelation — which we must hold or manipulate, when considering that situation. Abstraction is thus a relation. We choose the level of simplification and reduction. Our choice is a crucial one. Consider the modelling of some 'real world' phenomenon.

> Its concepts have been reduced to our concepts, i.e., summaries of the characteristics that several specimen have in common. By denoting similarity, our concepts eliminate the bother of enumerating qualities and thus better serve to organise the material of knowledge. They are thought of as mere abbreviations of the items to which they refer. Any use transcending auxiliary, technical summarisation of factual data has been eliminated as a last trace of superstition.

The "lawlessness" of programming is exactly this: Our choice of concepts becomes the tablets of commandments according to which the final program behaves. Their affinity, or to a varying degree lack of any such, to the intended problem is of no concern to the computer — and hence, by the mystique it exerts on certain programmers, also of no concern to them.

12.2 Property-Oriented Abstractions

In Sect. 8.5 (on specification algebras) we introduced the topic of *property-oriented specifications*. And in Sect. 9.6, in the subsection titled *"Property-Oriented Specifications"* we expanded on this topic. It is not a topic to be dispensed with in a few sections. In this section we shall review the idea of *property-oriented specification*. Throughout these volumes we shall repeatedly give examples of property-oriented specifications. In the next section we shall contrast the concept of property-oriented specification to that of *model-oriented specification*. These are two main *paradigms of specification*.

In the following we shall cover three facets of property-oriented specification. These are: (i) **pragmatics**: what is it that we wish to emphasise when choosing the property-oriented specification paradigm; (ii) **syntax**: which are the textual components of a property-oriented specification; and: (iii) **semantics**: what is the meaning of a property-oriented specification.

The concept of *pragmatics*, in the context of descriptions, means roughly: why a linguistic construct was used. The concept of *paradigm*, in the context of descriptions, means roughly: the semantic meanings that are expressible using the linguistic means at disposal — observing, in a sense, those that are not expressible.[5] Thus the two concepts, in the context of descriptions, are related.

12.2.1 Pragmatics of Property-Oriented Specifications

The adjective 'property-oriented' reveals the pragmatics: We choose a property-oriented way of specification when we wish to emphasise (logical) properties — observing that we are not presenting a specific (say a discrete) mathematical model of what we describe. The borderline between property- and model-oriented specifications is not a sharp one. In a loose sense we can speak of "more or less property-oriented", or "more or less model-oriented", or "both

---

[5]Thus we speak of such programming paradigms as the *(i) functional, (ii) imperative, (iii) logic* and *(iv) parallel* programming paradigm. These four programming paradigms individually emphasise (i) functions, their definition, composition and application; (ii) variables, their declaration, initialisation, update, references (pointers) to them (that is, to storage cells), and the manipulations (storage and "chasing" [linking]) of pointers; (iii) truth values, quantification, inference and resolution; respectively (iv) processes, their definition, composition ["in parallel", nondeterministic external or internal choice], synchronisation and inter-process communication.

property- and model-oriented". There are situations, i.e., phenomena in a universe of discourse,[6] which "beg" to be described, i.e., "call for" for being described, or can most "tellingly" be described, in the property-oriented style, others are best described in the model-oriented style, and yet some others in a style "mixing" these![7] It is a purpose of the entirety of these volumes to characterise what these situations are. One main way of delineating when and where the property-oriented specification style should be considered is along the TripTych "divides" of (i) domain: Usually it is a good development choice to try express a domain description primarily or solely through its properties. (ii) Requirements: Usually it is a good development choice to try express requirements primarily or solely through its properties. (iii) Software design: Usually it is a good development choice to try express a software design description primarily or solely by presenting a model. Thus there really are no strict delineations as to when and when not to use the property-oriented specification style. And, as we shall often see, there will be many exceptions.

12.2.2 Syntactics of Property-Oriented Specifications

It is high time to give an example of a pure property-oriented specification. We do that now, then we comment on the textual structure of a typical property-oriented specification. The example is that of modelling *requirements* to a simple telephone exchange system. First we present an informal description, then a formal description. The informal description is here structured so as to "fit" the formal description.

Example 12.1 *Property-Oriented Telephone System Specification:* The example is that of a simple telephone exchange system.

Informal Documentation

We start the informal description by presenting a *synopsis* and its immediate *analysis:*

- **Synopsis:** The simple telephone exchange system serves to efficiently honour requests for conference calls amongst any number of subscribers, whether immediately connectable, whereby they become actual, or being queued, i.e., deferred (or pending) for later connection.

---

[6]By *universe of discourse* we mean "that which we wish to describe". Sometimes our universe of discourse is the domain, some actual part of an actual world, sometimes it is requirements for some software to support actions in that world, and sometimes it is that software, i.e., its design.

[7]The use of the specific words: "beg", "call for", "tellingly" will become obvious from the following.

- **Analysis:** The concepts of subscribers and calls are central: In this example
  we do not further analyse the concept of subscribers. A call is either an
  actual call, involving two or more subscribers not involved in any other
  actual calls, or a call is a deferred call, i.e., a requested call that is not
  actual, because one or more of the subscribers of the deferred call is already
  involved in actual calls. We shall presently pursue the concepts of requested,
  respectively actual calls, and only indirectly with deferred calls.

Types and Values — Informal Description

The structure of the types of interest are first described. We informally describe first the basis types, then their composition. (i) Subscribers: There is
a class (S) of further undefined subscribers. (ii) Connections: There is a class
(C) of connections. A connection involves one subscriber, the 'caller', and any
number of one or more other subscribers, the 'called'. (iii) Exchange: At any
time an exchange reflects (i.e., is in a state which records) a number of requested connections and a number of actual connections (a) such that no two
actual connections share any subscribers, (b) such that all actual connections
are also requested connections, and (c) such that there are no requested calls
that are not actual and share no subscribers in common with any other actual connection. (That is: The actual connections are all that can be made
actual out of the requested connections. This part addresses the efficiency
issue referred to above.) (iv) Requested connections: The set of all requested
connections for a given exchange forms a set of connections. (v) Actual connections: The set of all actual connections, for a given exchange, forms a
subset of its requested connections such that no two actual connections share
subscribers.

In this example we shall also be able to refer to the exchange, later to be
named X, as 'the state' (of the telephone exchange system). We shall later have
a great deal more to say about the concept of state.

Types and Values — Formal Description

type
  S, C, X
value
  obs_Caller: C → S
  obs_Called: C → S-set
  obs_Requests: X → C-set
  obs_Actual: X → C-set

  subs: C → S-set
  subs(c) ≡ obs_Caller(c) ∪ obs_Called(c)

  subs: C-set → S-set
  subs(cs) ≡ ∪ { subs(c) | c:C • c ∈ cs }

The overloaded function name subs stands for two different functions. One observes ("extracts") the set of all subscribers said to be engaged in a connection. The other likewise observes the set of all subscribers engaged in any set of connections. We shall often find it useful to introduce such *auxiliary functions*.

axiom
[1] $\forall$ c:C, $\exists$ s:S •
[2]   s = obs_Caller(c) $\Rightarrow$ s $\notin$ obs_Called(c),

[3] $\forall$ x:X •
[4]   **let** rcs = obs_Requests(x),
[5]   acs = obs_Actual(x) **in**
[6]   acs $\subseteq$ rcs $\wedge$
[7] $\forall$ c,c':C • c $\neq$ c' $\wedge$ {c,c'} $\subseteq$ acs $\Rightarrow$
[8]   obs_Caller(c) $\neq$ obs_Caller(c') $\wedge$
[9]   obs_Called(c) $\cap$ obs_Called(c') = {} $\wedge$
[10] $\sim\exists$ c:C • c $\in$ rcs $\setminus$ acs •
[11]   subs(c) $\cap$ subs(acs) = {} **end**

Let us annotate the above specification. [1] For all connections there exists a subscriber such that [2] the subscriber is a caller, but not a called subscriber. [3] For all telephone exchanges (i.e., telephone exchange states), [4–5] let us observe the requested and the actual connections. [6] The actual ones must also be requested connections, and [7] for any two different actual connections, [8] their callers must be different, [9] the callers and the ones called cannot share subscribers, and [10] there must not be a requested, but not actual connection [11] which could be an actual connection. That is all such connections must have some subscriber in common with some actual connection.

The last two lines above express the efficiency criterion mentioned earlier.

We can express a law that holds about the kind of exchanges that we are describing:

theorem
  $\forall$ x:X •
    obs_Actual(x)={} $\equiv$ obs_Requests(x)={}

The *law* expresses that there cannot be a non-empty set of deferred calls if there are no actual calls. That is, at least one deferred call can be established should a situation arise in which a last actual call is terminated and there is at least one deferred call.

The *law* is a *theorem* that can be *proved* on the basis of the telephone exchange system *axioms* and a *proof system* for *sets*.

Operations:

The following operations, involving telephone exchanges, can be performed:
(i) Request: A caller indicates, to the exchange, the set of one or more other
subscribers with which a connection (i.e., a call) is requested. If the connection
can be effected then it is immediately made actual, else it is deferred and (the
connection) will be made actual once all called subscribers are not engaged in
any actual call. (ii) Caller_Hang: A caller, engaged in a requested call, whether
actual or not, can hang up, i.e., terminate, if actual, and then on behalf of all
called subscribers also, or can cancel the requested (but not yet actual) call. (iii)
Called_Hang: Any called subscriber engaged in some actual call can leave that
call individually. If that called subscriber is the only called subscriber ("left in the
call"), then the call is terminated, also on behalf of the caller. (iv) is_Busy: Any
subscriber can inquire as to whether any other subscriber is already engaged in
an actual call. (v) is_Called: Any subscriber can inquire as to the identities of
all those (zero, one or more) callers who has requested a call with the inquiring
subscriber.

Formal Description

First the signature:

value
　　newX: **Unit** → X
　　request: S × **S-set** → X → X
　　caller_hang: S → X $\overset{\sim}{\to}$ X
　　called_hang: S → X $\overset{\sim}{\to}$ X
　　is_busy: S → X → **Bool**
　　is_called: S → X → **Bool**

The *generator function* newX is an *auxiliary function*. It is needed only to
make the *axioms* cover all *states* of the telephone exchange system. In a sense
it *generates* an empty, that is, an *initial state*. Usually such *empty state
generator functions* are "paired" with a similar *test for empty state observer
function*.
　　Then we get the axioms:

axiom
　　∀ x:X • obs_Requests(x)={} ≡ x=newX(),
　　∀ x:X,s,s′:S,ss:S-**set** •
　　　　∼is_busy(s,newX()) ∧
　　　　s≠s′ ⇒
　　　　　　s ∈ ss ⇒ is_busy(s)(request(s′,ss)(x)) ∧
　　　　　　s ∉ ss ⇒ is_busy(s)(request(s′,ss)(x)) ≡ is_busy(s)(x),
　　　　　　... etcetera ...

We leave the axiom incomplete. Our job was to illustrate the informal and formal parts of a property-oriented specification, not to do it completely.

12.2.3 Semantics of Property-Oriented Specifications

Continuing the line set out in Section 1.6.2, Example 1.7, and continued in Sects. 6.5 and 6.7, we take as the basic assumption that the meaning of a specification, i.e., any expression, is a set of models. Each single model "assigns" (ascribes) to any expression identifier a single value, but "looking" just at the expression, it itself may stand for any of many values, at most as many as there are models of the expression. We shall have much more to say on this issue in these volumes.

12.2.4 Discussion

General

In Sects. 8.5 and 9.6 we started our treatment of property-oriented specifications. This section continues that treatment. In many parts of these volumes we shall return to the issue of property-oriented specifications. The property-oriented specification paradigm is a crucially central specification paradigm.

Why is the present section so short, when we have just stated the importance of property-oriented specification? To that we answer: Taken together with the material in Sects. 8.5 and 9.6 on property-orientedness, not much more methodologically need be said for that concept. And there will be many examples of property-oriented specifications when we proceed in this and following chapters.

Principles, Techniques and Tools

Principles. *Property-Orientedness:* In initial phases and stages of development choose a (primarily) property-oriented style of specification. Or, put differently, when you wish to leave as much implementation freedom as possible for subsequent phases, stages and steps of development choose a property-oriented form of specification.   ∎

Techniques. *Property-Orientedness:* Define sorts (rather than concrete types), introduce (postulate) observer and generator functions, and relate sort values and functions through axioms. Introduce auxiliary functions sparingly, i.e., introduce as few as possible, and then only those that reflect a concept in the relevant universe of discourse.   ∎

Tools. *Property-Orientedness:* Use, for example, the RSL **type, value** and **axiom** constructs.   ∎

12.3 Model Versus Property Abstractions

Section 12.2 reiterated the basic ideas of property-oriented specifications. Section 12.4 and Chaps. 13–17 will cover the basic ideas of model-oriented specifications. The present section will contrast the two specification paradigms.

12.3.1 Representation and Operation Abstraction

Two complementing concepts of *representation* and *operation abstraction* will be introduced. These two complementing concepts of *representation* and *operation abstraction* spring from the *algebraic view* that *a data type is a set of values and a set of operations on these*. We treat these two abstraction principles (representation and operation abstraction) in some isolation from one another. This is possible when we are propagating a basically model-theoretic approach wherein types and instances of objects are defined and constructed separately from the definition of functions involving these objects. The rest of this chapter will mostly treat the concept of *model-oriented representation* and the thereby related *model-oriented operation abstractions*.

In an algebraic specification this separation between presenting models of functions and the values they apply to and result in is not immediately obvious since properties of sorts (i.e., the values) and of operations are defined together, in an "intertwined" manner. The algebraic approach was — so far amply — illustrated earlier in sections: Sects. 8.5, 9.6.5 and 12.2.2.

12.3.2 Property-Oriented Versus Model-Oriented Abstractions

Characterisation. By a *property-oriented abstraction* we basically mean a specification which focuses on properties, i.e., is expressed logically. ∎

Discussion. Among the models satisfying a property-oriented abstraction there may be some that involve such mathematical notions as sets, Cartesians, sequences, maps and functions. ∎

Characterisation. By *model-oriented abstraction* we basically mean a specification in terms of such mathematical notions as sets, Cartesians, sequences (i.e., lists), maps and functions. ∎

Discussion. A logic property may be satisfied by any finite or infinite number of mathematical set, Cartesian, sequence, map or function constructs, including none. These mathematical entities are said to be models of the property-oriented specification. ∎

The Issues

Computers traditionally act by performing specific operations on concrete values, i.e., are operationally concrete and model-oriented. Yet to properly understand *what* is going on, or what is to go on, inside the computer, we necessarily resort to logic. So there seems to be a dichotomy: *How do we reconcile the notions of property- and model-oriented?* Computer programs often must be detailed to a level (of code) which is no longer humanly understandable! So there seems to be a problem: *How do we 'refine' from property- to model-oriented?* So we shall make our first examples of, and show some first principles and techniques for presenting property- and related model-oriented specifications.

Further Characterisations

We present and discuss some informal definitions.

Characterisation. A *property-oriented specification* expresses what is being described in terms of abstract types (sorts) and logic expressions, including axioms. ∎

Discussion. Emphasis is on properties, that is, on what, not on how. ∎

Characterisation. A *model-oriented specification* models what is being described in terms of mathematical entities such as numbers, sets, Cartesians, lists, maps, functions (including predicates) and processes. ∎

Discussion. Emphasis, in model-oriented abstraction, is still on properties, but it is in terms of how a discrete or continuous mathematical construct offers those properties. ∎

In model-oriented descriptions we therefore choose first to describe representation abstraction. In the vernacular, we mean the abstraction of what later in the coding of software become data structures. Then we describe operation abstraction. Later in this section we present both representation and operation abstractions in both property-oriented and model-oriented ways.

12.3.3 Definitions

Characterisation. By *representation abstraction* of [typed] values we mean a specification which does not hint at a particular data (structure) model, that is, which is not implementation-biased. ∎

Discussion. The "most abstract" representation abstraction occurs when we specify a set of values, i.e., a type, as an abstract type, that is, as a sort. ∎

Characterisation. We say that a specification of a (data or a function) value is *implementation-biased* if it foregoes abstraction in favour of some, however rudimentary, notion of realisation.   ∎

Discussion. This last characterisation suffers from vagueness. First, our distinction between "data or function" value is not important. But the distinction is of pedagogical nature: There really is no distinction. By data values "inside the computer" we may think of such things as integers, or vectors of these, or records over integers, character strings and Booleans, just to name a few examples. By function values we correspondingly think of instruction sequences, i.e., of code. But since data values can serve as structures being interpreted by an interpreter, the data value can be considered to represent a function. And vice versa: A function value can be made to represent, say, an infinite list of which one at most need inspect, in any invocation, a finite prefix.   ∎

Characterisation. By *operation abstraction* of functions, i.e., of function values, we mean a specification which does not hint at particular procedural (i.e., algorithmic) means of computing function results.   ∎

12.3.4 Representation Abstraction Examples

We exemplify the two specification styles: property-oriented and model-oriented. At the same time we also exemplify the concept of *representation abstraction*. In Sect. 12.3.5 we then exemplify the corresponding concept of operation abstraction.

Example 12.2 *Telephone Directory — Types:* We focus on the essential properties of a *telephone directory*. We see these as that of the "directory itself" and the "things we can do with it, i.e., to it".

- A telephone directory is seen as an abstract document. Let us name the class of all such telephone directory documents TelDir.
- It lists a finite set of subscribers, say by name, let us call their class for S.
- Each has a finite set of telephone numbers, Tn.

That's all!   ∎

Property-Oriented Representation

In property-oriented models, to repeat, we express properties in terms of sorts, function signatures and axioms relating type values and functions. Sometimes we need define some auxiliary functions. In contrast to classical algebraic specifications our function types allow concrete type expressions. In the examples below these are mostly sets.

Example 12.3 *Telephone Directory: A Property Model, I:* Given a telephone directory, td, we can (thus) observe the set of all its subscribers and the set of all its numbers.

Given a subscriber and a telephone directory we can observe the telephone numbers of that subscriber. And given a telephone number and a telephone directory we can observe the subscribers sharing that number.

In advance of a more systematic treatment in subsequent (set, list, map) sections of this chapter we bring the formalisation below.

type TelDir, S, Tn
value
    obs_Ss: TelDir → S-**set**
    obs_Tns: TelDir → Tn-**set**
    obs_Tns: S → TelDir → Tn-**set**
    obs_Ss: Tn → TelDir → S-**set**

Annotations: The keyword **type** "announces" that the identifiers *TelDir, S* and *Tn* are type names. Since these types are not further explained we refer to them as abstract types, or as sorts. (In property-oriented modelling we almost exclusively use sorts.) *TelDir* shall stand for the set of telephone directories, *S* for the set of subscribers and *Tn* for the set of telephone numbers.

The keyword **value** "announces" that the two identifiers *obs_Ss* and *obs_Tns* denote specific values in the type denoted by the type expression following these names. Since these types are both of the form $A{\to}B$ they are both function values. Here they stand for observers that apply to telephone directories and are intended to extract exactly the set (-**set**) of all subscribers, respectively the set of all the telephone numbers which are listed in the telephone directory — not necessarily all possible subscribers, respectively telephone numbers. ∎

• • •

We continue this (property-oriented) example later when we cover the concept of operation abstraction.

Model-Oriented Representations

In model-oriented specifications, to repeat, we focus on mathematical models of types. Typical mathematical models centre around such mathematical entities as numbers, sets, Cartesians, lists (or sequences) maps, and functions.

Example 12.4 *Telephone Directory: A Model-Oriented Model, I:* In a telephone directory we normally *associate* subscriber information (names etc.) with one or more, i.e., a set of, telephone numbers. The association can be mathematically modelled in a number of ways:

type S, Tn
   TelDir0 = S $\xrightarrow{m}$ Tn-**set**
   TelDir1 = S $\xrightarrow{m}$ Tn*
   TelDir2 = (S × Tn-**set**)-**set**
   TelDir3 = (S × Tn-**set**)*
   TelDir4 = (S × Tn*)*

Annotations: We continue modelling the subscriber and telephone number types as sorts. But we now give several model-oriented, i.e., concrete type proposals for the type of telephone directories.

TelDir0 considers a telephone directory to be a **map** which to each subscriber associates the finite **set** of zero or more telephone numbers that that subscriber is known by.

TelDir1 considers a telephone directory to be a **map** which to each subscriber associates the finite **list** of zero or more telephone numbers that that subscriber is known by.

TelDir2 considers a telephone directory to be a finite **set** of **Cartesian pairs**. Each (pair) pairs a subscriber with the finite **set** of zero or more telephone numbers that that subscriber is known by.

TelDir3 considers a telephone directory to be a finite **list** of **Cartesian pairs**. Each (pair) pairs a subscriber with the finite **set** of zero or more telephone numbers that that subscriber is known by.

Finally, *TelDir4* considers a telephone directory to be a finite **list** of **Cartesian pairs**. Each (pair) pairs a subscriber with the finite **list** of zero or more telephone numbers that that subscriber is known by. ∎

● ● ●

Given the choice between models we may raise a number of questions. Which of the above many possibilities should we choose? Which one of the above "is most abstract"? The answer to both questions is: that depends on the operations we wish to define on telephone directories. We will later return to this question, albeit in other contexts.

How is the property-oriented specification of the telephone directory, TelDir, related to, for example, the model-oriented specification, TelDir0?

Example 12.5 *Telephone Directory: Property- Versus Model-Orientedness:* In this example we indicate (by ~) an answer, one amongst many possible, by also defining, for the model-oriented, i.e., the concrete, types the abstract, postulated observer functions of the property-oriented model.

type
   TelDir0
relations: obs_Ss ~ extract_Ss0, obs_Tns ~ extract_Tns0
value

extract_Ss0: TelDir0 $\rightarrow$ S-set
extract_Ss0(td) $\equiv$ **dom** td

extract_Tns0: TelDir0 $\rightarrow$ Tn-set
extract_Tns0(td) $\equiv$ $\bigcup$ **rng** td

extract_Ss0: Tn $\rightarrow$ TelDir0 $\rightarrow$ S-set
extract_Ss0(tn)(td) $\equiv$ { s | s:S • s $\in$ **dom** td $\wedge$ tn $\in$ td(s) }

extract_Tns0: S $\rightarrow$ TelDir0 $\rightarrow$ Tn-set
extract_Tns0(s)(td) $\equiv$ td(s) **pre** s $\in$ **dom** td

Annotation: With the model-oriented, i.e., the concrete, type definition of
TelDir we can therefore define the *observer* functions. **dom** *td* expresses the
set of definition set elements of the map *td*, and **rng** *td* expresses the set of
range (i.e., codomain) elements of the map *td*. The $\bigcup$ operation[8] represents
distributed union, i.e., an operation that applies to a set of sets and yields
"their" union.   ∎

The two subexamples, the property-oriented and the model-oriented representations of Examples 12.3 and and 12.4 (with Example 12.5 relating them),
illustrated some basic techniques used in property-oriented, respectively in
model-oriented specifications: sorts (or abstract types) versus concrete types,
and observer functions versus explicitly defined (extraction) functions. The
two parts of the continuation of the telephone directory example given below will further illustrate differences between property- and model-oriented
specifications.

12.3.5 Operation Abstraction Examples

Now we cover operation abstractions relating to the two representation abstractions of Example 12.3 and and 12.4's telephone directory example. In
the vernacular: Operation abstraction is an abstraction of what later in the
coding of software become subroutines (procedures, functions).

Example 12.6 *Telephone Directory Operations: Property-Orientedness:* We
define the following operations on telephone directories:

- empty: Create an initial and empty telephone directory.
- enter: Add a new subscriber's telephone number(s) to a telephone directory.
- is_in: Check whether a (potential) subscriber is in a telephone directory:
  true or **false**?

---

[8]The prefix $\bigcup$ operation is not a proper operator of the specification language
RSL, but could easily be.

- look_up: Look up a subscriber's telephone number(s).
- delete: Remove a subscriber from a telephone directory.

Property-Oriented Specification

First we show a property-oriented specification — one that expresses properties in terms of simple predicate and (algebraic) equational axioms.

type
    S, Tn, TelDir
value
    empty: $\rightarrow$ TelDir,
    is_empty: TelDir $\rightarrow$ **Bool**,
    enter: S $\times$ **Tn-set** $\times$ TelDir $\xrightarrow{\sim}$ TelDir
        pre enter(s,tns,td): tns $\neq$ {} $\wedge$ ~is_in(s,td),
    is_in: S $\times$ TelDir $\rightarrow$ **Bool**
    look_up: S $\times$ TelDir $\xrightarrow{\sim}$ Tn-set
        pre look_up(std): is_in(s,td),
    delete: S $\times$ TelDir $\xrightarrow{\sim}$ TelDir
        pre delete(s,td): is_in(s,td)

axiom
    forall s,s':S, tns:Tn-set, td,td':TelDir •
        is_empty(empty()),
        ~is_empty(enter(s,tns,td)),
        ~is_in(s,empty()),
        is_in(s,enter(s,tns,td)),
        s $\neq$ s' $\Rightarrow$ is_in(s,enter(s',tns,td)) = is_in(s,td),
        look_up(s,enter(s,tns,td)) = tns,
        s $\neq$ s' $\Rightarrow$ look_up(s,enter(s',tns,td)) = look_up(s,td).
        delete(enter(s,tns,td)) = td
        s $\neq$ s' $\Rightarrow$ delete(s,enter(s',tns,td)) = delete(s,td).

Annotations: First we present the signature of the empty, is_empty, enter, is_in, look_up and *delete* values.

The first, empty, designates a constant (total) function; empty() designates the empty telephone directory. The remaining also denote functions. Partiality of these is explained wrt. the pre-conditions that must be satisfied for a function application to be defined. The set of telephone numbers entered for a subscriber must be non-empty and the subscriber must not already be in the telephone directory. In order to look_up or delete the phone numbers of a subscriber that subscriber must be in the directory.

Then we give the axioms further defining the properties of these functions. An empty telephone directory is_ indeed empty. A telephone directory into which at least some subscriber has been entered is not empty. No subscriber

is_in an empty directory. A subscriber which has been entered into a directory
is_in that directory. Whether a subscriber, s, is in a directory, which is the
result of having entered another subscriber, s', in a directory td, is the same
as whether subscriber s is in td, and so on for look_up and delete.   ∎

• • •

We refer to empty, enter and delete as *generators*, and to is_empty, is_in and
look_up as *observers*. By means of the empty value and the enter generator
function we can construct all values in TelDir. Therefore we define axioms
for each of the observers — sometimes in terms of the generators. The issue
of whether a set of axioms, as, for example, presented here, is consistent and
complete, i.e., whether they do not define a thing and its opposite and whether
it defines all the things we wish to have defined, will not be dealt with here.
Instead we refer to standard texts on logic [136, 153, 210, 235, 259, 362, 372, 457]
and on Algebraic Semantics [43, 208, 209, 249, 297].

Model-Oriented Specification

After the initial property-oriented specification we now show a model-oriented
specification — one that models operations explicitly.

Example 12.7 *Telephone Directory Operations: Model-Orientedness:* The
signatures are as for the property-oriented axiomatic specification of the operations, except that these now apply to values of the concrete, model-oriented
type TelDir0, and not to values of the abstract, property-oriented sort TelDir.

type
   TelDir0
value
   empty() ≡ [ ]
   is_empty(td) ≡ td = [ ]
   enter(s,tns,td) ≡ td ∪ [s ↦ tns]   **pre** s ∉ **dom** td
is _in(s,td) ≡ s ∈ **dom** td
   look_up(s,td) ≡ td(s)   **pre** s ∈ **dom** td
   delete(s,td) ≡ td \ {s}   **pre** s ∈ **dom** td

                                                          ∎

12.3.6 Discussion

General

Previously we treated property-oriented specification in isolation (cf. Sect. 12.2).
In this section we contrasted property-oriented specifications and model-
oriented specifications. What preliminary conclusions can be drawn? Well,

the ones we can draw are rather superficial. As later examples will show, those of Examples 12.3 and and 12.4 (even with Example 12.5 relating them), respectively Examples 12.6 and 12.7, are too inconclusive.

But we can say this: A sort (that is, an abstract type) specification, i.e., a property-oriented model, sometimes is "unique" in the sense that its types and the structure constraining axioms over these can basically only be expressed in one way given the basic "ingredients" (as here S, Tn and TelDir). On the other hand, a model-oriented specification of "the same", now concrete, types leaves the developer many choices, cf. TelDir0, TelDir1, TelDir2, TelDir3, TelDir4. Somehow it seems easier to say: The abstract type, i.e., the sort, definition is the most abstract one, the one that is less biased.

And then, in the pair of paired examples, Examples 12.3 and 12.4, respectively Examples 12.6 and 12.7, as will indeed be the case in rather many, if not most examples, the operation definitions were "longer" for the property-oriented model than for the model-oriented model. But one should not be lured by the usual brevity of functional operation model-oriented specifications.

The property-oriented axioms both defined the properties of the sorts as well as of the operations, and rather explicitly, we think, express the value and operation properties. As such, property-oriented axioms serve well in proofs of other properties.

The model-oriented specification separated the specification of types (and their values) from the specification of operations. The concrete type definitions imply many properties. These concrete type properties are then found axiomatically expressed in one place: namely where the specification language defines those concrete types (of sets, Cartesians, lists, maps, etc.).

The model-oriented operation definitions, although claimed abstract, could be claimed to "bury" operation properties in the specific, almost "algorithmic" use of specification language constructs, especially the many set, Cartesian, list, maps, etc., operators. Yet the brevity of model-oriented operation specifications and, when used properly, their abstractness, often makes developers select model-oriented specifications in favour of property-oriented specifications.

So, it is too early to "call the game", that is, to say anything definite.

Specific: "What's the Difference Anyway?"

In Example 12.3 we illustrated some observer functions (i.e., observers). They generally apply to values of property-oriented defined abstract types, i.e., sorts, but yield values of model-oriented concrete types (i.e., sets).

So: "what is the difference anyway? " Very simply: Instead of defining the sorts as consisting "exactly" of the model-oriented components as suggested by the observers, we leave the (base, the "interesting") sorts further unspecified. Doing so allows us, later, to join additional observers to the base sorts. We can keep on doing so, as early as from domain descriptions, through requirements prescriptions until software design specifications. This ability leaves the software designer the greatest degree of "freedom".

12.4 Model-Oriented Abstractions

This section serves as a prelude to the next six chapters (Chaps. 13–18).

12.4.1 Ultrashort Overview of the Next Six Chapters

In the next six chapters we cover a number of model-oriented representation and operation abstraction techniques and tools based on:

- Sets   Chap. 13
- Cartesians   Chap. 14
- Lists   Chap. 15
- Maps   Chap. 16
- Functions   Chap. 17
- Types   Chap. 18

In doing so we shall extend the RSL type concept of our primary abstract specification language RSL. Chapter 18 will summarise the RSL type concept. The next six chapter topics will, at the same time, introduce a not inconsiderable number of new RSL language constructs. We have chosen this style of presenting the specification language: commensurate with the pragmatic need for their use in abstraction and modelling — rather than a pedantic style of RSL "reference manual" [236]. Later chapters and sections will augment what we say in the immediately upcoming six chapters. This is because we have decided to tie the introduction of language constructs, whether from RSL or other specification languages, to a conceived need for their use.

12.4.2 Models and Models

Models of Property-Oriented Specifications

Section 12.2.3 outlined the semantics of property-oriented specifications. It was said, then, that the meaning — of what has been, or is being, written down as a property-oriented specification — is a set of models. By that we meant: Either the specification that has been or is being written down has no interpretation (the set of models is empty), or there is exactly one model, or there is a definite or indefinite set of such models. By 'model' we then meant, and shall continue to mean, an interpretation in terms of such constructive mathematical things as Booleans, numbers, characters, text strings, sets, Cartesians, lists, maps and even general functions (in the sense of λ-functions).

Models of Model-Oriented Specifications

Property-oriented specifications are expressed as axioms, i.e., logically. So property-oriented specifications really give no explicit hint at the models they might denote! Model-oriented specifications are expressed "directly": In terms of the mathematical things they are supposed to "be": numbers, characters, text strings, sets, Cartesians, lists, maps and even general functions (in the sense of λ-functions). So model-oriented specifications give all possible — i.e., rather explicit — hints at the models they are meant to denote, hence the name of this type of specification!

12.4.3 Underspecification

The Issue

Characterisation. By an *underspecified identifier* we mean one which for repeated occurrences in a specification text always yield the same value, but what the specific value is, is not knowable. ∎

Example 12.8 *Underspecification (Abstract):* The identifier a in:

value a:A

      ... a ... a ... (a = a) ...

is underspecified. The second line of text ... a ... a ... (a = a) ..., has the same value for a in all occurrences, and hence the test for equality always yields **true**.

    An example of an underspecified function is:

value
    is_prime: **Nat** $\rightarrow$ **Bool**
    is_prime(n) $\equiv$ n=1 $\lor$ (n>2 $\land$ $\sim\exists$ i,j:**Nat** • i>1 $\land$ j>1 $\Rightarrow$ i$\times$j=n)
    f: **Int** $\rightarrow$ **Nat**
axiom
    $\forall$ i:**Int** • is_prime(f(i))

f is specified, to some degree (its type is given). But it is underspecified. An infinity of fs satisfy the axiom, namely all those functions that when applied to any integer generate a prime number! The is_prime predicate is uniquely specified (i.e., is deterministic). ∎

Why Underspecifications?

The simple answer to the "question" above is: Phenomena of the real world (i.e., some domain) are not completely specifiable. If developing a domain description into a requirements prescription, and when refining requirements prescriptions into software designs, the software developer, in agreement with the client ordering the software, is free (at an appropriate stage) to remove underspecification.

12.4.4 Determinism and Nondeterminism

Deterministic Expressions

A piece of specific, say RSL, text may evaluate to one value, or it may evaluate to any one of several values.

Example 12.9 *A Deterministic Expression (Abstract):* Consider the following specification:

value
    f: **Unit** → **Nat**, f() ≡ 7

Function f is deterministic: Always, when invoked, f() returns a predictable result. When invoked multiple times, at various points in some specification text:

    ... f() ... f() ... f() ...

the resulting value is always 7.   ∎

The evaluation of f in Example 12.9 is that it has exactly one value.

Nondeterministic Expressions

Consider, in contrast, a slight modification of Example 12.9:

Example 12.10 *A Non-deterministic Expression (Abstract):* Let the specification now be:

    let n:**Nat** • 5<n<9 **in** n **end**

The expression is nondeterministic. When invoked multiple times, at various points in some specification text:

    ... **let** n:**Nat**•5<n<9 **in** n **end** ...
        let n:**Nat**•5<n<9 **in** n **end** ...
            (**let** n:**Nat**•5<n<9 **in** n **end** =
                let n:**Nat**•5<n<9 **in** n **end**) ...

the resulting value is any one of 6, 7 or 8! In the first line above the expression value may be 8; in the second line the expression value may be 6; and in the third line the expression value may be 7; whereas in the fourth line the expression value may be 8. Sometimes the equality between lines three and four may yield **true**, and sometimes **false**.   ∎

The evaluation of f in Example 12.10 is that it has three possible values. Which one is selected — for various invocations of f — is not predictable: It is nondeterministic.

12.4.5 Why Loose Specifications?

Characterisation. By *looseness* of a specification we mean a specification which features elements of underspecification or nondeterminism.   ∎

The question is now clear enough, given Examples 12.8–12.10. An answer need be considered. It is not the first, and it will not be the last time, in these volumes, that we consider underspecification and nondeterminism.

An answer, one that shall is for the time being, but one that will be elaborated upon, again and again, in these volumes, is as follows: In the world of specific, real-life, actual domains, "things" are not deterministic. Human behaviour is underspecific and nondeterministic, yet we shall have to model human behaviour! Behaviour, even of a number of concurrently operating production processes, is not predictable: Slight deviations from mechanical measurements, even though within tolerances, may cause deviations in production processing times. As a result, two or more production machines may start and/or end their processing before and/or after one another. Yet our production must usually be made robust, and must lead to reasonably predictable products irrespective of such underspecificity and nondeterminism.

Any realistic, abstract specification language must therefore, we claim, facilitate the "free and easy" expression of underspecificity and nondeterminism. It is, in general, the underspecificity that leads to multiple models. In the next Chaps. 13–17 — where we examine the use of the mathematical structures of sets, Cartesians, lists, maps and functions — we shall therefore basically assume that the denotation of any expression is a set of models.

12.4.6 Discussion

General

Ordering of Mathematics

We have briefly listed references to the next six chapters on sets, Cartesians, lists, maps, functions and types. We have chosen to present these mathematical structures in the order listed: sets, which are considered the most basic mathematical structure in our context, then Cartesians, then lists, etc. Each chapter has one or two main examples. Because of the order in which we introduce the mathematical structures we have tried to have the examples make use only of such (mathematical) structures (i.e., types) as have already been introduced at the point of the examples. This means that some examples, certainly those in the earlier sections, may seem a bit contrived and not very abstract. Yet they all model something!

The RSL Language Constructs

In synchrony with the introduction of the mathematical structures (of sets, Cartesians, lists, maps, functions and types) we introduce the corresponding abstract data types of RSL, or, for that matter, VDM-SL or Z. And we likewise introduce a number of other RSL (etc.) language constructs: type union (A|B|...|C) and subtypes ({|a:A•wf_A(a)|}), McCarthy Conditionals (**case e of** p1→e1, p2→e2, ..., _→en **end**), and thereby the notions of *patterns* and their implied bindings. The chapter on types (Chap. 18) introduces further RSL language constructs: variant definitions (A == B|C|...|D), records with constructors and destructors (B == mk_BRec(u:U,v:V,...,w:W)), and so on.

12.5 Principles, Techniques and Tools

Commensurate with Sect. 1.5.1's introduction of methods espousing principles, techniques and tools the next six chapters as well as the rest of these volumes will then enunciate such principles, techniques and tools as they here relate property-oriented versus model-oriented specifications.

For the present chapter we now present its relevant methodological concerns.

12.5.1 Property-Oriented Versus Model-Oriented Specification?

When Property-Orientation?

Principles. *Property-Oriented Specification:* Property-oriented specification is chosen in the earliest phases and stages of development. That is, when, in a sense, the least is known about what is being described. Typically, property-oriented specification is chosen for the earliest stage of domain description, or the earliest stage of requirements prescription. By presenting a property-oriented specification one is telling the reader: This specification has made no design choices as to data and operation representation.   ∎

When Model-Orientation?

Principles. *Model-Oriented Specification:* Model-oriented specification is chosen when commencing design — i.e., in the late phases and stages of development. That is, when, in a sense, sufficient is known about what is being specified to commit concrete data and operation representation. Typically, model-oriented specification is chosen for the later stages of requirements prescription as well as for software design specification.   ∎

12.5.2 Property-Oriented Specification Style

Techniques. *Property-Oriented Specifications:* The basic specification components of a property-oriented specification are those of sorts, i.e., abstract types of function signatures of observers and generators and of axioms relating values of sorts and operations.

scheme POS =
    class
        type
            A, B, ..., C, P, Q, ..., R
        value
            obs_P: A $\to$ P,
            obs_Q: B $\to$ Q,
            ...
            obs_R: C $\to$ R,
            make_A: P $\times$ ... $\to$ A
            make_B: Q $\times$ ... $\to$ B
            ...
            make_C: R $\times$ ... $\to$ C
        axiom
            $\forall$ a:B, b:B, ..., c:C, p:P, q:Q, ..., r:R
            $\mathcal{E}_1(a, b, ..., c, p, q, ..., r)$
            $\mathcal{E}_2(a, b, ..., c, p, q, ..., r)$
            ...
            $\mathcal{E}_m(a, b, ..., c, p, q, ..., r)$
    end

In the above conceptualised, i.e., illustrative, generic but not very specific schema, named POS (for property-oriented specification), a class has been hinted at.

As types, it only has abstract types, i.e., sorts A, B, ..., C, P, Q, ..., and R.

It has some observer functions (typically named: obs_T, where T is one of the type names). The observer functions apply to sort values and yield values of type sorts, or simple sets, Cartesians, lists, etc., but this is not shown.

It has some generator functions (typically named: make_T, where T is one of the sort names). Typically, when only relying on sorts one need define initial values for some of these. This is expressed through the use of suitable generator functions. (One for each type on initial value.) And one must define observer functions which observe whether values of given types are initial. This is expressed through the use of suitable observer functions.

Property-oriented specifications, typically, have some axioms. The schematic expressions $\mathcal{E}_i(a, b, ..., c, p, q, ..., r)$ stand for some predicate. There may be several such. Here m is hinted at. They need not all involve all of the quantified sort values. Some $\mathcal{E}_i(a, b, ..., c, p, q, ..., r)$ may be simple terms usu-

ally involving initial values. Some $\mathcal{E}_i(a, b, ..., c, p, q, ..., r)$ may be equational:
$\mathcal{E}_{j_{k_\ell}}(...) = \mathcal{E}_{j_{k_r}}(...)$ or $\mathcal{E}_{j_{k_\ell}}(...) \equiv \mathcal{E}_{j_{k_r}}(...)$.   ∎

Blending Specification Styles

Oftentimes we find it convenient to use both abstract and concrete types, i.e., sorts and defined types (sets, Cartesians, lists, maps, etc.) in what is essentially still a property-oriented specification. And often we find it convenient to use both property-oriented and model-oriented function definitions, that is, only partially using axioms.

12.5.3 Model-Oriented Specification Style

Techniques. *Model-Oriented Specifications:* The basic specification components of a model-oriented specification are those of defined, i.e., concrete types, of function signatures of analytic and synthetic functions, and of their definition.

scheme MOS =
   class
      type
         $A = ...$
         $B = ...$
         ...
         $C = ...$
      value
         f: $\mathrm{ARG}_f \rightarrow \mathrm{RES}_f$
         $f(\mathrm{arg}_f) \equiv \mathcal{B}_f(\mathrm{argl}_f)$
         g: $\mathrm{ARG}_g \rightarrow \mathrm{RES}_g$
         $g(\mathrm{arg}_g) \equiv \mathcal{B}_g(\mathrm{arg}_g)$
         ...
         h: $\mathrm{ARG}_h \rightarrow \mathrm{RES}_h$
         $h(\mathrm{arg}_h) \equiv \mathcal{B}_h(\mathrm{argl}_h)$
   end

In the above conceptualised, i.e., illustrative, generic but not very specific, schema, named MOS (for model-oriented specification), a class has been hinted at. It has only defined types, i.e., concrete types. (What they are has not been shown. If composite, they could be set, Cartesian, list, map, etc., types.) And it has a number of function definitions: $f, g, \ldots, h$. Each is given a signature: $\mathrm{ARG}_f \rightarrow \mathrm{RES}_f$, etc., where ARG_f and RES_f are type expressions — usually involving Cartesians and functions. And each is given a definition: $g(\mathrm{arg}_h) \equiv \mathcal{B}_g(\mathrm{argl}_g)$, etc. Here arg_g is a list of formal parameter, i.e., argument identifiers. and $\mathcal{B}_g(\mathrm{argl}_g)$ is an RSL expression, that is, a function definition $\mathcal{B}$ody in which the argument identifiers occur free.   ∎

Blending Specification Styles

We sometimes find it convenient to both use concrete and abstract types, i.e., defined types (sets, Cartesians, lists, maps, etc.) and sorts in what is essentially still a model-oriented specification. And we sometimes find it convenient to both use model-oriented and property-oriented function definitions. Thus you may find both axioms and pre/post-specifications also in a model-oriented specification.

12.5.4 Implicit and Explicit Functions

Above we have made a distinction between observer and analytic functions, and between generator and synthetic functions.

The distinction is purely academic, that is, it is one of pragmatic convenience: the notion of observer and generator functions is — in our presentation — a notion that is related to property-oriented specification(s). Whereas the notion of analytic and synthetic functions is a notion that is related to model-oriented specifications. Pairwise, observer and analytic functions are really the same: The former are postulated, and arise out of their signature and the axioms, whereas the latter can be explicitly defined. Pairwise, generator and synthetic functions are really the same: the former are postulated, and arise out of their signature and the axioms, whereas the latter can be explicitly defined.

12.5.5 No Confusion, Please!

> You can't have your cake and eat it too
>
> You can't eat your cake and have it too[9]

Principles. *Not Confusing Property-Oriented and Model-Oriented Specifications:* As the old proverb expresses: You cannot both define types concretely, say:

type
    B, C, D
    A = B × C × D

and postulate observer functions:

value
    obs_B: A → B, obs_C: A → C, obs_D: A → D.

---

[9]From Heywood's A Dialogue Conteynyng Prouerbes and Epigrammes, 1562: "*Wolde ye bothe eate your cake, and haue your cake?*". John Keats quoted it as *Eat your cake and have it*" at the beginning of his poem On Fame in 1816. Franklin D. Roosevelt borrowed it in that latter form for his State of the Union Address in 1940.

But you have concrete, i.e., composite types (and hence values) and extract components values, by explicitly defining functions:

value
    extr_B: A → B
    extr_B(a) ≡ **let** (b,_,_) = a **in** b **end**

Somehow it is like for a man to wear suspenders and a trouser belt: both, at the same time. But, we claim, it is actually worse: It is confusing two issues: abstract and concrete types, or, which is the same, abstract postulated observer functions, and concrete precisely and deterministically defined extraction functions.   ■

12.5.6 A Note on Observer Functions

First Principle: Postulation

What are observer functions? They are postulated. They cannot be defined; they just "exist".

When we postulate a transportation net, N, and from that we postulate that we can observe segments and connections (e.g., street segments and street intersections), S and C, then we are claiming that these observer functions obs_Ss: N → S-set and obs_Cs: N → C-set exist. Certainly, in the domain, i.e., in the reality of street nets, we can, with our own eyes perform these observations. So, observer functions are not defined: "They just exist". But observer functions are bound by constraints. We use axioms to express those constraints.

To say that observer functions are postulated "begs" an answer to the question: By what means can I record the observation? That is: if I cannot define an observer function then how can I compute its value for a given argument? The answer is simple, and it ought be simple: If the thing being observed is a phenomenon, i.e., something that is physically manifest, then *Go look at that thing, and point out ("measure") its observable parts.* If the thing being observed is a concept, i.e., something that only exists in our mind then *Postulate that thing and claim its parts!*

Second Principle: No "Self-reference"

Take another example: When we postulate a transportation net, N, and from that we postulate that we can observe segments and connections (for example, street segments and street intersections), S and C, would it not be nice if we could also, from segments [connections] observe the connections [segments] to which they "attach"? It might be nice, but it would lead to paradoxes, or at least, what we would call undesirable infinite recursive descents!

Let us argue this, but in more generality: Let the following abstract example be given:

type
    A, B
value
    obs_Bs: A → B-**set**
    obs_A: B → A
axiom
    ∀ a:A • ∀ b:B • b ∈ obs_Bs(a) ⇒ obs_A(b) = a

Now what do we mean? It seems we mean that all of a:A is somehow contained in every b:B observable in a:A. But then, which are the bs observable in that contained a? The situation is untenable.

So we edict: we cannot allow the predicate: ∀ a:A • ∀ b:B • b ∈ obs_Bs(a) ⇒ obs_A(b) = a. If we want as to be contained in bs, then they are not the as from which the bs were observed. This resolution is tantamount to allowing, in model-oriented terms:

type
    A = ... × B-**set** × ...
    B = ... × A × ...,

with the recursion of as inside bs ending with empty sets of bs.

Third Principle: Identification

When observing, or, in general modelling composite entities a need may arise for identification of the subentities. This is typically the case in the following (and other) situations.

[1] Set Element Identification

When what is being observed (i.e., modelled) most immediately is thought of as a set:

type
    A, B
value
    obs_Bs: A → B-**set**

then in order to distinguish the individual bs (in B) one is served well by introducing an identification function **obs_Bi**, in fact two (just to make sure!):

type
    A, B, Bi
value
    obs_Bs: A → B-**set**
    obs_Bis: A → Bi-**set**
    obs_Bi: B → Bi

axiom
    $\forall$ a:A •
        card obs_Bs(a) = obs_Bis(a)
        [or, which is the same:]
        $\forall$ b,b':B • {b,b'}$\subseteq$obs_Bs(a) $\wedge$ b$\neq$b'
          $\Rightarrow$ obs_Bi(b) $\neq$ obs_Bi(b').

In fact, as we shall later see, it often "pays off" in modelling to model A as a map from Bi identifier to "the rest of" B:

type
    B, Bi
    A = Bi $\overrightarrow{m}$ B
value
    extract_Bis: A $\rightarrow$ Bi-set
    extract_Bis(a) $\equiv$ **dom** a

We shall introduce maps in Chap. 16.

[2] Fixed Structure Element Identification

When what is being observed (i.e., modelled) most immediately is thought of as a structure of a fixed number of possibly distinct kinds (e.g., types) of entities, then model as a Cartesian. The positions in the Cartesian then serve to identify the components:

type
    B, C, ..., D
    A = B $\times$ C $\times$ ... $\times$ D
value
    a:A
    ... **let** (b,c,...,d) = a **in** $\mathcal{E}$(a,b,c,...,d) **end**

We shall reintroduce Cartesians in Chap. 14.

[3] Sequence Element Identification

When what is being observed (i.e., modelled) most immediately is thought of as a sequence, then model it as a list, and the indices into elements of the list serve to identify.
    We shall introduce lists in Chap. 15.

12.6 Exercises

Exercise 12.1. *Property-Priented and Model-Oriented Abstraction.* Try with a closed book, i.e., without referring back to Page 231 or to Sect. 12.3.2 to formulate our definitions of *abstraction, property-oriented abstraction* and *model-oriented abstraction*. Try formulate in a few words the main difference between *property-oriented abstraction* and *model-oriented abstraction* .

Exercise 12.2. *More on Abstraction.* Try with a closed book, i.e., without referring back to Sect. 12.1.3 (the Essay on Abstraction), to formulate the basic ideas of abstraction.

Exercise 12.3. *Representation and Operation Abstraction.* Try with a closed book, i.e., without referring back to Sect. 12.3.3, to formulate the basic model-oriented ideas of representational and operational abstraction. Contrast this with property-oriented abstraction's treatment of representational and operational abstraction

Exercise 12.4. ♣ *Property-Oriented and Model-Oriented Abstractions in the Transportation Net Domain.* We refer to Appendix A, Sect. A.1, *Transportation Net.*

Sketch two specifications of nets of segments and connections, and of combing (merging, adding) two nets into one net, and of projecting (removing, subtracting) one net from another: one specification being property-oriented (i.e., in terms of sorts, observer functions and axioms), another being model-oriented (i.e., in terms of Cartesians and sets, and in terms of explicit function definitions for merge and project).

Remember: Do not forget (as one usually does in a property oriented specification) to express all the things that do not change.

Sketch: It is early in this volume. So you can only sketch. You still do not have at your disposal all the model-oriented types and their operations. But try anyway!

Exercise 12.5. ♣ *Property-Oriented and Model-Oriented Abstractions in the Container Logistics Domain.* We refer to Appendix A, Sect. A.2, *Container Logistics.*

Sketch type specifications of container ships and container storage areas, and function definitions of unloading containers from a container ship to a container storage area, and of loading containers from a container storage area to a container ship: one set of specifications being property-oriented (i.e., in terms of sorts, observer functions and axioms), another being model-oriented (i.e., in terms of Cartesians and sets, and in terms of explicit function definitions for unload and load). Assume the container unloads to be of one container from a tier (or stack) top position on a container ship to a similar position in a container storage area — where these positions are identified by bay, row and tier (stack) indices. Similarly for loads.

Remember: Do not forget (as one usually does in a property oriented specification) to express all the things that do not change!

Sketch: It is early in this volume. So you can only sketch. You still do not have at your disposal all the model-oriented types and their operations. But try anyway!

Exercise 12.6. ♣ *Property-Oriented and Model-Oriented Abstractions in the Financial Service Industry Domain:* We refer to Appendix A, Sect. A.3, *Financial Service Industry.*

Sketch a type specification of banks, and function specifications of opening and closing accounts, and of depositing into and withdrawing from accounts: one set of specifications being property-oriented (i.e., in terms of sorts, observer functions and axioms), another being model-oriented (i.e., in terms of Cartesians and sets, and in terms of explicit function definitions for open, close, deposit and withdraw).

Assume that the main entities of a bank are: a catalogue, clients, that lists for each bank client their accounts; another catalogue, sharing, which for each account lists the one or more account clients that share the account; and a "state" which to each account associates the balance of that account.

Remember: Do not forget (as one usually does, in a property oriented specification) to express all the things that do not change!

Sketch: It is early in this volume. So you can only sketch. You still do not have at your disposal all the model-oriented types and their operations. But try anyway!

13

Sets in RSL

- The **prerequisite** for studying this chapter is that you possess knowledge of the mathematical concept of sets as introduced in Chap. 3.
- The **aims** are to introduce the RSL abstract data type of sets: the type, the values, and enumeration and comprehension forms of expressing sets, to introduce the RSL set operations, and thus to illustrate the "power" (i.e., expressiveness) of sets by illustrating simple and not so simple examples of phenomena and concepts that can be modelled in terms of sets.
- The **objective** is to set the reader free to choose sets as models of phenomena and concept entities, when appropriate, and to not choose sets when it is not appropriate.
- The **treatment** is semiformal and systematic.

```
A Band of Musicians          A Bevy of Beauties
A Bunch of Crooks            A Crew of Sailors
A Flock of Geese             A Fleet of Ships
A Gang of Outlaws            A Group of People
A Herd of Cattle                A Mop of Hair
A Pack of Dogs           A Posse of Vigilantes
A Pride of Lions          A School of Dolphins
A Suite of Bells             A Swarm of Flies
                            A Volley of Arrows
```

— are all examples of Sets!

Characterisation. By a *set* we shall, loosely, understand an unordered collection of distinct elements (i.e., entities) — something for which it is meaningful to speak about (i) an entity *being a member* of a set (or not) $\in$, (ii) the *union* (merging) of two or more sets into a set (of all the elements of the argument sets) $\cup$, (iii) the *intersection* of two or more sets into a set (of those elements which are in all argument sets) $\cap$, (iv) the *complement* of one set with respect to another set $\setminus$, (v) whether one set is a subset of another set $\subset$

and $\subseteq$, or whether they are equal or not, $=$, resp. $\neq$, and (vi) the cardinality of a (finite) set (i.e., how many members it "contains") **card**, etc.   ∎

We refer to Chap. 3 for a first, reasonably thorough introduction to the mathematical concept of sets. In the present section we shall focus on the means for defining and using set types and sets in the predominant specification language of these volumes: RSL.

13.1 Sets: The Issues

The idea to be illustrated in this section is that of the use of the discrete mathematics concept of sets in abstracting domain, requirements and software phenomena and concepts. Sets offer themselves as an abstraction when a component, s, can best be characterised as a "variable sized" ("flexible")[1] unordered collection[2] $\{a, b, \ldots, c\}$ of otherwise "undistinguished", but distinct components — which one can inspect for element membership ($\in$), to which one can "add" elements ($\cup$), from which one can "subtract" elements ($\setminus$), with respect to which one can form other "common" ("shared") sets ($\cap$), etc.

Sets will become proper components in the modelling of "zillions" of other problems. But sets as the only model-oriented (i.e., as the only discrete mathematical) "device" to "deploy" in abstraction, is a sign of too extreme frugality! That is just our modest opinion.

We refer to the axiom system given for simple sets in Example 9.23.

This chapter is, as are Chaps. 13–17, built up as follows:

- The set data type   (Sect. 13.2)
- Examples of set-based abstractions   (Sect. 13.3)
- Abstracting and modelling with sets   (Sect. 13.4)
- Inductive set definitions   (Sect. 13.5)
- A review of set abstractions and models   (Sect. 13.7)

There are many examples because *before one can write good specifications one must have read and studied many example specifications*. While you may not need to study all of them now, you can return to some later. The chapter ends with a brief discussion.

---

[1]We refer to Sect. 13.6 for an explanation of what really is meant when we say variable-sized or vary.

[2]The foundational nature of sets is revealed in our inability to describe a set by terms we all understand. Here we "fake" a characterisation by, instead, explaining a concept of set by a concept of unordered collection. We could have tried aggregation or structure. And we — and you — would have been no wiser!

13.2 The Set Data Type

We have already, in Example 9.23 covered the mathematical notion of simple sets by presenting an axiom system for sets. We refer the reader to first recall that definition.

13.2.1 Set Types: Definitions and Expressions

Let A stand for a type whose possibly infinite number of elements include $\{a_1, a_2, \ldots, a_n, \ldots\}$.

Types whose values can be considered finite, respectively finite or infinite, sets of A elements can be defined using the suffix **-set**, respectively the **-infset** type power set[3]) operators. See Fig. 13.2.1.

---- Types and Values ----

type	examples
A	$\{a, a_1, a_2, \ldots, a_m, \ldots\}$
F = A-**set**	$\{\{\}, \{a\}, \{a_1, a_2, \ldots, a_m\}, \ldots\}$
S = A-**infset**	$\{\{\}, \{a\}, \{a_1, a_2, \ldots, a_m\}, \ldots, \{a_1, a_2, \ldots\}\}$

Fig. 13.1. Examples

The type forming operator **-set** applies suffix to a type expression, say A, and forms the type of all finite subsets of A. The type forming operator **-infset** applies suffix to a type expression, say A, and forms the type of all finite as well as possibly infinite subsets of A. The **-set** and **-infset** type operators are akin to the power set operator on sets. Note that **-set** and **-infset** apply to type expressions, whereas the power set operator (which is not offered in RSL) applies to sets.

Example 13.1 *A Simple Set Example:* Let fact name the factorial function, then

$$\{fact(1), fact(2), fact(3), fact(4), fact(5), fact(6)\}$$

expresses a simple set of six element, the six "first" factorials!   ∎

---

[3]Other forms of the power set operators are $\wp A$, $\mathcal{B}A$ (where $\mathcal{B}$ refers to Boole, the Irish mathematician), or $_2 A$ (where exponentiation of 2 is meant to be to the power of the cardinality of the set A — which, in turn, is meant to designate the number of different subsets of A, namely the number of elements of $_2 A$).

A-set and A-infset are *set type expressions*. F = A-set and S = A-infset are *set type definitions*. One can see, using metalinguistic notation, i.e., mathematical notation[4] ("outside" RSL), that:

[1] **Bool-set = Bool-infset**, and **Nat-set ⊂ Nat-infset**

Annotations: A is (assumed to be) a type name, i.e,, stands for a type, that is, a set of values — which we do not presently define. The keyword **-set** when applied suffix to a type name denotes the power set operation on a type and makes the type expression A-set denote the type, i.e., the set, of all finite subsets of the type, i.e., the set, A. A-infset correspondingly stands for the (type, i.e., colloquially, the) set of all finite and (possibly) infinite subsets of A. (There will only be the possibility of infinite subsets of A if A itself is an infinite (type) set.) The type names F and S are then made to name these respective sets by the respective type equations. A may be a 'sort', i.e., an 'abstract type' which has just been named but not given a model in terms of something else, as has F and S. These latter are, in contrast, called 'concrete types'. The keyword **type** tells us that the definitions which follow are type definitions.

13.2.2 Set Value Expressions

There are several forms of set valued expressions: enumerations, comprehensions and operator/operand expressions.

Set Enumerations

There follows, in the right half of the above expressions, examples of enumerated set expressions: an empty set, a singleton set, a finite set of m elements. The use of ellipses (. . .) is metalinguistic, i.e., not part of our RSL notation. It is used only to signal to you, the reader, that we wish to exemplify an arbitrary set of m elements. If we were to enumerate a specific set of m (for example, for $m = seven$) elements, then we would have to list all seven elements by their names (or some expressions).

Sets are finite or infinite aggregations, collections, or structures of distinct individuals. Sets are considered variable-sized, or flexible in that the number of their elements may vary. Curly braces: "{", "}", and commas: ",", are set value forming. A set may contain no (i.e., zero) elements (the empty set {}). Another set may contain just one element (singleton sets $\{a_i\}$, $\{a_j\}$, . . . , $\{a_k\}$), and so forth. A given (say, finite) set, of course, has a specific cardinality (number of elements). But one may form a set from two sets resulting in a set with cardinality being the number of distinct elements in the two sets. Or one may remove an element from a nonempty set, resulting in a set with cardinality one lower.

---

[4]The metalinguistics of formula [1] is that we use the infix equality and the proper subset operators (=, resp. ⊂) between type expressions.

Let e, e1, e2, ..., en[5] be expressions that deterministically or nondeterministically evaluate to not necessarily distinct values (v, v1, v2, ..., vn) of some type A, and let ei, ej be expressions which deterministically or nondeterministically evaluate to integer values, say vi, vj, then the following are examples of *set value expressions:*

[1] {}, {e}, ..., {e1,e2,...,en}
[2] {ei..ej}

The above expressions, in [1], left to right, denote the single model of the empty set of no elements; a set of models of singleton sets of one element values (any value will do!), etc.; respectively a set of models of sets of not necessarily n distinct element values, since some ei, ej for different i, j may evaluate to the same value. The range set expression (of line [2]) denotes a set of models each being a (dense) set of integers lying in the range between, and inclusive, vi and vj. If vi>vj, then the integer set is empty. For each model the above expressions have a specific, determinate value. Notice, hence, our distinction between *denotations*, in terms of models (set of mathematical structures), and *values*, in terms of mathematical entities.

This is an important distinction — and it is to be kept in "vigilant" mind throughout these volumes.

We call the above, [1–2], *explicit enumeration* of set values. We call the second line example, [2], {ei..ej} an *integer range expression*. Later (paragraph **Set Comprehension** in this section) we shall show an implicit enumeration of set values in the form of set comprehension (i.e., comprehended set expressions). We use explicit set enumeration expressions when we wish to explicate specific, always finite, and usually "small" sets. We use comprehended set expressions when we wish to implicitly specify (i.e., 'implicate'), possibly infinite, sets characterised by some predicate.

Set Value Operator/Operand Expressions

Sets come, in RSL, with the usual operations listed below. ∈ is taken to stand for a primitive, i.e., as an inexplicable operation, the set membership operation.

---

[5]In the rest of these volumes we shall use the following naming convention: Identifiers starting with e (and often "suffixed" or indexed (subscripted) by some alphanumeric characters) stand for *expressions*. Identifiers starting with v (and often suffixed or indexed (subscripted) by some alphanumeric characters) stand for *values*. Values are definite, in the sense that a value is a specific thing. Expressions may be constant expressions, i.e., evaluate, in any context (and state) to one and the same value, or expressions may be variable expressions, i.e., evaluate, in different contexts (and states) to different values.

Set Operation Signatures and Examples

We explain the formulas and expressions of Fig. 13.2.2. The keyword **value** tells us that the definitions which follow are value definitions. In all of the below we assume that the operations, wherever applicable, apply to set values. The 13 lines that follow are extra- (or meta-) linguistic, i.e., outside RSL. They are used here to present RSL set constructs. In particular they are meant to express that there are 13 given (i.e., "built-in") set operators: ∈, the membership operator (*is an element member of a set,* **true** *or* **false***?*); ∉, the non-membership operator (*is an element not a member of a set,* **true** *or* **false***?*); ∪, the infix union operator (when applied to two sets expresses the set whose members are in either or both of the two operand sets).

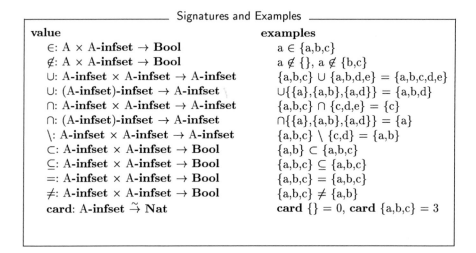

—————— Signatures and Examples ——————

value	**examples**
∈: A × A-**infset** → **Bool**	a ∈ {a,b,c}
∉: A × A-**infset** → **Bool**	a ∉ {}, a ∉ {b,c}
∪: A-**infset** × A-**infset** → A-**infset**	{a,b,c} ∪ {a,b,d,e} = {a,b,c,d,e}
∪: (A-**infset**)-**infset** → A-**infset**	∪{{a},{a,b},{a,d}} = {a,b,d}
∩: A-**infset** × A-**infset** → A-**infset**	{a,b,c} ∩ {c,d,e} = {c}
∩: (A-**infset**)-**infset** → A-**infset**	∩{{a},{a,b},{a,d}} = {a}
\: A-**infset** × A-**infset** → A-**infset**	{a,b,c} \ {c,d} = {a,b}
⊂: A-**infset** × A-**infset** → **Bool**	{a,b} ⊂ {a,b,c}
⊆: A-**infset** × A-**infset** → **Bool**	{a,b,c} ⊆ {a,b,c}
=: A-**infset** × A-**infset** → **Bool**	{a,b,c} = {a,b,c}
≠: A-**infset** × A-**infset** → **Bool**	{a,b,c} ≠ {a,b}
card: A-**infset** $\xrightarrow{\sim}$ **Nat**	**card** {} = 0, **card** {a,b,c} = 3

Fig. 13.2. Set operations

∪, the distributed prefix union operator (when applied to a set of sets expresses *the set whose members are in some of the sets of the operand set*); ∩, the infix intersection operator (expresses *the set whose members are in both of the two operand sets*); ∩, the distributed prefix intersection operator (when applied to a set of sets expresses *the set whose members are in all of the sets of the operand set*); \, the set complement (or set subtraction) operator (expresses *the set whose members are those of the first operand set which are not in the second operand set*); ⊂, the proper subset operator (*are the members of the first operand set all members of the second operand set, and are there members of the second operand set which are not in the first operands set,* **true** *or* **false***?*); ⊆, the subset operator (as for proper subset, but allows equality of the two operand set to be **true**); =, the equal operator (*are the two operand sets the same,* **true** *or* **false***?*); ≠, the not equal operator (*are* *the two operand sets different,* **true** *or* **false***?*); and **card**, the cardinality operator (*"counts" the number of elements in the presumed finite operand set*). ∪ and ∩ are called overloaded operators. They apply to pairs of sets as well as to possibly infinite sets of sets.

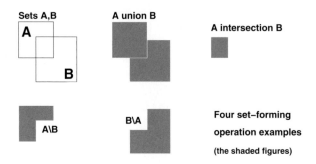

Fig. 13.3. Four set-forming operations

In Fig. 13.3 the text 'union' (respectively 'intersection') stands for the mathematical operator ∪ (respectively ∩).

Mathematical Meaning of the Set Operators

We define the meaning of the set operators. ∈ is a primitive (given, assumed) operation:

value
$$s' \cup s'' \equiv \{\, a \mid a{:}A \bullet a \in s' \lor a \in s'' \,\}$$
$$\cup\, ss \equiv \{\, a \mid a{:}A \bullet \exists\, s{:}A\text{-}\mathbf{set} \bullet s \in ss \Rightarrow a \in s \,\}$$
$$s' \cap s'' \equiv \{\, a \mid a{:}A \bullet a \in s' \land a \in s'' \,\}$$
$$\cap\, ss \equiv \{\, a \mid a{:}A \bullet \forall\, s{:}A\text{-}\mathbf{set} \bullet s \in ss \Rightarrow a \in s \,\}$$
$$s' \setminus s'' \equiv \{\, a \mid a{:}A \bullet a \in s' \land a \notin s'' \,\}$$
$$s' \subseteq s'' \equiv \forall\, a{:}A \bullet a \in s' \Rightarrow a \in s''$$
$$s' \subset s'' \equiv s' \subseteq s'' \land \exists\, a{:}A \bullet a \in s'' \land a \notin s'$$
$$s' = s'' \equiv \forall\, a{:}A \bullet a \in s' \equiv a \in s'' \equiv s \subseteq s' \land s' \subseteq s$$
$$s' \neq s'' \equiv s' \cap s'' \neq \{\}$$

card s ≡
    if s = {} **then** 0 **else**
    let a:A • a ∈ s **in** 1 + **card** (s \ {a}) **end end**
    pre s /∗ is a finite set ∗/
card s ≡ **chaos** /∗ tests for infinity of s ∗/

The above definition is not in RSL. Instead it is in "ordinary" mathematics. It relies on logic and set comprehension as already understood. If we claimed it was self-referentially defined, i.e., in RSL, then any meaning one would assign to, for example, the logic connectives and quantification would be OK, and one would get a new meaning each time!

Set Comprehension

We finish this terse overview of the RSL set data type by illustrating *set comprehension*. To do so we introduce a sort B and the concrete types of predicates (P) over A and functions (Q) from A into B. (It is enough that the q:Q functions are partial, but defined (over a:A) whenever (for p:P) p(a) is **true**.) Now the "function" *comprehend* illustrates the idea of set comprehension: *We define the set of all those q(a) for which a is of type A such that (•) a is in (argument) set s and the predicate p(a) holds.*
    Concretely we may express:

Example 13.2 *A Simple Set Example:* Let fact name the factorial function, then

$$\{fact(i)|i:\mathbf{Nat} \bullet i \in \{1..6\}\}$$

expresses a simple set of six elements, the first six factorials!   ∎

type
    A, B
    P = A → **Bool**
    Q = A $\overset{\sim}{\to}$ B
value
    comprehend: A-**infset** × P × Q → B-**infset**
    comprehend(s,$\mathcal{P}$,$\mathcal{Q}$) ≡ { $\mathcal{Q}$(a) | a:A • a ∈ s ∧ $\mathcal{P}$(a) }

The texts $\mathcal{Q}$(a) and $\mathcal{P}$(a) need not be invocations of functions $\mathcal{Q}$, respectively $\mathcal{P}$, but can be any B-valued respectively **Bool**-valued expression over the free variable a. $\mathcal{P}$(a) must, additionally, be deterministic in order to evaluate to **true**.
    We use comprehend set expressions when we wish to implicitly specify (i.e., 'implicate'), possibly infinite, sets, characterised by some function, q, and some predicate, p.
    Set comprehension, as do list and map comprehension (to be introduced in forthcoming chapters), expresses a form of 'homomorphic' principle: Functions over composite structures being expressed as a(nother) function over the (first) function applied to all immediate constituents of the composite structure. We refer to Sect. 8.4.4 for a first enunciation of the (homo)morphism concept.
    The general syntactic form of *comprehended set expressions* is

    { <value_expr> | <typings> • <bool_expr> }

where the • <bool_expr> } part is optional.

Sets — Determinism and Nondeterminism Revisited

Since set enumeration and range expressions in general denote sets of models of sets; and since set operands of set operator/operand expressions in general apply to evaluation within such models, we can expect that the denotation of set operator/operand expressions, and of comprehended set expressions likewise denote sets of models of sets or such other appropriate values (Booleans, natural numbers) as are the result types of the set operators. It is important to keep this in mind throughout!

Example 13.3 *Nondeterministic Sets (Abstract):* Let expressions e_1, e_2, and e_3, denote the set of models:
$$\{v_{1_1}, v_{1_2}\}, \{v_{2_1}, v_{2_2}, v_{2_3}\}, \text{ and } \{v_3\},$$
respectively. Then the set expression $\{e_1, e_2, e_3\}$ denote the set of models:
$$\{\{v_{1_1}, v_{2_1}, v_3\}, \{v_{1_2}, v_{2_1}, v_3\}, \{v_{1_1}, v_{2_2}, v_3\}, \{v_{1_2}, v_{2_2}, v_3\}, \{v_{1_1}, v_{2_3}, v_3\},$$
$$\{v_{1_2}, v_{2_3}, v_3\}\}$$
Any one of these, viz., $\{v_{1_1}, v_{2_3}, v_3\}$, is a value of $\{e_1, e_2, e_3\}$.   ∎

Sets — Models, Values and the ≡ Operation

A specification, all of it, denotes a set of models. The evaluation of a specification, all of it, takes place in exactly one of these models. Which one is chosen, if there is more than one model in the set, we cannot specify.

Equality, =, of set expressions is **true** if the chosen model possesses appropriate set element values, otherwise **false:**

$$\{e1, e2, ..., en\} = \{e, e', ..., e''\}$$

is **true** if both expressions evaluate, in the chosen model, to sets of the same number of values, and such that the sets of these values are the same, otherwise **false.** To express that we wish equality to hold for all models we use the ≡ operator:

$$\{e1, e2, ..., en\} \equiv \{e, e', ..., e''\}$$

is **true** if for all models the set values are equal.

13.2.3 Set Binding Patterns and Matching

We shall here consider the RSL construct of *set binding patterns* and the *set matching* concept. We shall later deal with these concepts in other contexts: Sects. 14.4.1, and 14.4.2 for Cartesians, 15.2.3 for lists and 16.2.3 for maps.

By a 'set **let** decomposition *binding pattern*' we understand a construct basically of the following form:

type
   A, B = **A-set**
value
   ... **let** {a} ∪ b = e **in** ... **end** ...
   post e = {a} ∪ b ∧ b = e \ {a}

Here it is (somehow) known that e is a nonempty set. {a} ∪ b is the binding pattern. The understanding of **let** {a} ∪ b = e **in** ... **end** is that e is a set expression with nonempty value, say v; that the free identifier a is *bound* to an arbitrary member of v; and that the free identifier b then is *bound* to the remainder of v, that is a possibly empty set without a.

Example 13.4 *Set Pattern:* We show a very simple example of the use of set binding patterns — leaving its "encoding" to the reader:

value
   sum: **Nat-set** → **Nat**
   sum(ns) ≡
      if ns={}
         then 0
         else
            let {n} ∪ ns′ = ns **in**
            n + sum(ns′)
      end end

■

The general form of a set binding pattern definition is:

   let { binding_pattern } ∪ id = set_expr
   in body_expr **end**

Here binding_pattern is a simple expression with only free identifiers, id is an identifier, and set_expr is a set-valued expression which evaluates to at least one element of a kind that 'matches' the binding_pattern. Which forms binding_pattern may take, and what 'matching' means will be dealt with, in Sect. 19.6. We shall introduce similar specification language binding pattern constructs for Cartesians, lists and maps.

13.2.4 Nondeterminism

In the typing construct and in the set decomposition construct:

   let a:A • P(a) **in** ... **end**
   let {a} ∪ s = set **in** ... **end**

the selection of the a value is *nondeterministic*. Nondeterminism is an important abstraction mechanism. It expresses that we abstract from the specific choice: Any, or almost any, will do!

13.3 Examples of Set-Based Abstractions

This section "matches" Sections 14.3, 15.3, 16.3, and 17.2. They all give small examples of set, Cartesian, list, map and function-based specifications. They are meant as class room examples.

13.3.1 Representation I

Example 13.5 *Equivalence Relation cum Partitioning:* Let A denote any finite set of (simple) values. An equivalence relation over A is a set of disjoint sets of A elements which together "span" all of A. Such an equivalence relation is also called a partitioning of A. Given an equivalence relation, q, over A, and two elements, a and a′ of A such that a and a′ belong to different elements (also called classes) s, and s′ of q, merge those two classes into one in q′, leaving all other classes of q unchanged in q′.

type
    A
    Q′ = (A-**set**)-**set**
    Q = {| q:Q′ • wf_Q(q) |}
value
    sas:A-**set**
    wf_Q: Q′ → **Bool**
    wf_Q(q) ≡
      ∪ q = sas ∧
      ∀ s,s′:A-**set** • s≠s′ ∧ {s,s′}⊆q ⇒ s ∩ s′={}

    merge: A × A × Q → Q
    merge(a,a′,q) **as** q′
    pre ∃ s,s′:S•s≠s′∧ {s,s′}⊆q∧ a ∈ s∧ a′isin s′
    post (∀ s:S•s ∈ q∧ s ∩{a,a′}={} ⇒ s ∈ q′) ∧
           (∀ s,s′:S•{s,s′}⊆q∧ a ∈ s∧ a′isin s′ ⇒
                s ∪ s′ ∈ q′)
    assert:
      card q = **card** q′ + 1 ∨
      ∃ s,s′:S • q ∩ q′ = {s,s′} ∧ a ∈ s ∧ a′ ∈ s′

We refer to Examples 15.3 and 16.4. ∎

13.3.2 File Systems I

This is the first in a series of models of what, with an overbearing mind, we could call *file systems*. Other models are presented in Examples 14.2 (Cartesians), 15.6 (lists) and 16.8 (maps).

Example 13.6 *A Set-Oriented File System:* A file system consists just of an unordered, non-void collection of distinct information. Information is itself an unordered, nonempty collection of distinct data.

A file system user can (i) create a void file system of no information; can (ii) insert information not already in the file system; can (iii) inquire whether some information is in the file system; can (iv) get the set of all the information ("informations") that each contain some specific data; can (v) delete some given data from given information; can (vi) delete all the information that contains some given data; and can (vii) update all that information which contain some given data by replacing this data with some other given data.

type
   D
   I = D-**set**
   B = I-**set**
examples
   d, d', ..., d'':D
   i:{}, i':{{d}}, i'':{{d,d'},{d,d''},{d',d''},...}
   b:{{{d}},{{d'}},{{d''}},{{d,d'}},{{d,d'},{d,d''},{d',d''}}}

Updating all the information in b that contains d with d' results in:

   b:{{{d'}},{{d''}},{{d'},{d',d''}}}

value
   void: **Unit** → B
   void() ≡ {}

   insert: I → B $\overset{\sim}{\to}$ B
   insert(i)(b) ≡ b ∪ {i} **pre** i ∉ b

   is_in: I → B → **Bool**
   is_in(i)(b) ≡ i ∈ b

   get: D → B → I-**set**
   get(d)(b) ≡ { i | i:I • i ∈ b ∧ d ∈ i }

   del_spec: D × I → B $\overset{\sim}{\to}$ B
   del_spec(d,i)(b) ≡
      {i'|i':I•i'isin b∧d∉ i'}∪{i'\{d}|i':I•i'isin b∧d ∈ i'∧i=i'}
      pre d ∈ i

   del_all: D → B $\overset{\sim}{\to}$ B
   del_all(d)(b) ≡

{i'|i':I•i'isin b∧d∉ i}∪{i'\{d}|i':I•i'isin b∧d ∈ i'}

update: D × D → B $\overset{\sim}{\to}$ B
update(od,nd)(b) ≡
     {i'|i':I•i'isin b∧od∉ i}∪{i'\{od}∪{nd}|i':I•i'isin b∧d ∈ i'}

■

13.3.3 Representation II

Example 13.7 *Coarsest Partitioning:* We refer to an earlier example: Example 13.5. Let there be given a sort A of further unspecified elements. Let q be a set of sets of A elements. These sets may overlap. A coarsest partitioning p is the smallest equivalence relation over A, that is, a set of disjoint sets of A elements, such that each of these sets is contained in some set element of q and such that all A elements of q are in some set of p.

type
     A, Q = (A-**set**)-**set**, P' = Q
     P = {| p:P' • wf_P(p) |}
value
     wf_P: A-**set** → **Bool**
     wf_P(p) ≡ ∀ ma,ma':A-**set** • ma≠ma' ∧ {ma,ma'} ⊆ p ⇒ ma ∩ ma' = {}
     cp: Q → P
     cp(q) ≡
         if ∃ ma,ma':A-**set** • ma≠ma' ∧ ma ∩ ma' ≠{}
             then
                 let ma,ma':A-**set** • ma≠ma' ∧ ma ∩ ma' ≠{}
                 in cp((q \ {ma,ma'}) ∪ {ma ∩ ma',ma \ ma',ma'\ma} \ {})
                 end
             else q
         end

■

The fact that the function cp, defined in Example 13.7, actually "computes" the coarsest partitioning, that is, produces a result which satisfies wf_P, transpires from the termination criterion for cp. But whether cp ever reaches a value of its input argument that satisfies the termination criterion requires a proof.

13.4 Abstracting and Modelling With Sets

This section "matches" Sections 14.4, 15.4, 16.4 and 17.3. They all give larger examples of set, Cartesian, list, map and function abstractions and models. They are meant as self-study examples.

The purpose of this section is to introduce *techniques* and *tools* for model-oriented specifications primarily based on sets. Among the *set modelling principles, techniques* and *tools* are (1) *Subtyping:* Sometimes a type definition defines "too much"; a type constraining (*well-formedness, invariant*) predicate technique can therefore be applied. (2) **pre/post**-*conditions:* function abstraction in terms of **pre**- and **post**-*conditions.* (3) *"Input/Output/Query" functions:* Identification of main functions according to their *signature.* (4) *Auxiliary functions:* Decomposition of function definitions into "smallest" units. The *principles* and *techniques* reoccur for Cartesians, lists and maps in Sect. 14.4, 15.4 and 16.4.

13.4.1 Modelling Networks

In Example 16.7 we show models of tree-like hierarchies — such as we saw in, for example, feudal, central European states in the past, and such as we see in conventionally organised company structures. In the next example we model instead the flat "group of persons"-centered and connected networks as seen in especially rural Chinese societies, not only of the past [499].

Example 13.8 *Chinese Societal Nets:*

Narrative of Flat Networks:

Let c:C stand for a citizen value c being an element in the type C of all such. Let g:G stand for any (group) of citizens, respectively the type of all such. Let s:S stand for any set of groups, respectively the type of all such. Two otherwise distinct groups are related to one another if they share at least one citizen, the liaisons. A network n:N is a set of groups such that for every group in the network one can always find another group with which it shares liaisons.

Formalisation of Flat Networks

Solely using the set data type and the concept of subtypes, we can model the above:

type
 C
 G′ = C-**set**, G = {| g:G′ • g≠{} |}
 S = G-**set**
 L′ = C-**set**, L = {| ℓ:L′ • ℓ≠{} |}
 N′ = S, N = {| s:S • wf_S(s) |}

value
    wf_S: S $\rightarrow$ **Bool**
    wf_S(s) $\equiv \forall$ g:G • g $\in$ s $\Rightarrow \exists$ g':G • g' $\in$ s $\land$ share(g,g')
    share: G$\times$G $\rightarrow$ **Bool**
    share(g,g') $\equiv$ g$\neq$g' $\land$ g $\cap$ g' $\neq$ {}
    liaisons: G$\times$G $\rightarrow$ L
    liaisons(g,g') = g $\cap$ g' **pre** share(g,g')

Annotations: L stands for proper liaisons (of at least one liaison). G', L' and N' are the "raw" types which are constrained to G, L and N. {| binding:type_expr • bool_expr |} is the general form of the subtype expression. For G and L we state the constraints "in-line", i.e., as direct part of the subtype expression. For N we state the constraints by referring to a separately defined predicate. wf_S(s) expresses — through the auxiliary predicate — that s contains at least two groups and that any such two groups share at least one citizen. liaisons is a "truly" auxiliary function in that we have yet to "find an active need" for this function!

Narrative of Hyper-networks

A society, m:M, can be viewed as consisting of two or more (i.e., multiple) networks. As before, every network, n:N, in the set m of multiple networks, has each of its groups relate to at least one other, different group of that network. For a society it may or may not be that two or more distinct networks have respective groups which share *emissaries*, i.e., citizens, with one another. And, for a society it may or may not be that two or more distinct networks have identical groups, etc.!

Formalisation of Hyper-networks

type
    M' = N-**set**
    M = {| m:N' • **card** m > 1 |}
value

                                                                   ■

13.4.2 Modelling Pseudo-hierarchies

We cannot illustrate anywhere reasonable uses of models based entirely on sets. In the next examples we additionally assume the Cartesian data type — as introduced in Sect. 6.6.

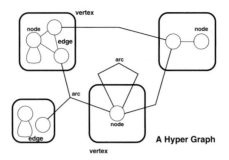

Fig. 13.4. An example hyper-graph

Example 13.9 *Graphs: Simple and Hyper:*

Narrative of Simple Graphs

A graph, g:G, consists of a set of uniquely labelled nodes n:N, and a set of
unlabelled multi-edges, e:E. A multi-edge is ("thought of", i.e., modelled as)
a set of one or more (i.e., always as a nonempty set of) nodes: If an edge
is (modelled as) a singleton set, then the edge is said to "loop" from that
labelled node only back to itself. If an edge is (modelled as) a set of two or
more nodes, then the edge is said to "connect" those nodes, including "loops".
Nodes of edges of a graph must be nodes of the graph.

Formalisation of Simple Graphs

type
    N
    E′ = N-set
    E = {| ns:E′ • ns ≠ {} |}
    G′ = N-set × E-set
    G = {| (ns,es):G′ • ∪ es ⊆ ns |}

Annotations: The E′ constraining predicate, ns≠{}, expresses that an edge is
not void. G′ expresses that a (potentially ill-formed) graph is modelled as a
Cartesian pair of nodes and edges. The G′ constraining predicate expresses
that all nodes of edges are nodes of the graph.

Narrative of Hyper-graphs

A hyper-graph, h:H, is a graph with vertices and arcs, where simple graphs
have nodes and edges, respectively. More specifically, vertices, v:V, are simple
graphs — as defined above — such that no two vertices have nodes in common.
Arcs, a:A, are sets of one or more nodes, such that all nodes belong to different
vertices. Figure 13.4 attempts to illustrate a hyper-graph.

Formalisation of Hyper-Graphs

type
  V = G
  A = N-set
  H′ = V-set × A-set
  H = {| h:H′ • wf_H(h) |}
value
  wf_H: H′ → **Bool**
  wf_H(vs,arcs) ≡ wf_vertices(vs,_) ∧ wf_arcs(vs,arcs)

Annotations: V: A vertex is a graph, as defined earlier, and can thus be assumed well-formed. A: An arc is a set of nodes. H′, H: A hyper-graph has its vertices well-formed ("in isolation"), and its arcs well-formed with respect also to vertices. (Note the use of the *wildcard* (_) as a "don't care" argument in the invocation (above) and the definition (next) of wf_vertices. One could instead just have used the vs argument in a more narrowly typed function. We have, perhaps arbitrarily, decided to keep the type as chosen, in order to signal, through the wildcard (_), that the specific constraints apply only to part of the graph!)

value
  wf_vertices: H′ → **Bool**
  wf_vertices(vs,_) ≡
    ∀ v,v′:V • {v,v′}⊆vs ⇒ wf_ns(ns(v),ns(v′))

  wf_arcs: H′ → **Bool**
  wf_arcs(h) ≡ wf_arcs_ns(h) ∧ wf_links(h)

  ns: V → N-set, ns(nodes,_) ≡ nodes
  ns: V-set → N-set,
  ns(vs) ≡ ∪{ns(v)|v:V•v ∈ vs}

Annotations: wf_vertices: Vertices are well-formed if their nodes are well-formed. wf_arcs: Arcs are well-formed if they are well-formed wrt. nodes of vertices and they link properly. ns is an overloaded auxiliary function: It applies both to vertices and to sets of vertices. It yields their nodes.

  wf_ns: N-set × N-set → **Bool**
  wf_ns(ns,ns′) ≡ ns≠ns′ ⇒ ns ∩ ns′ = {}

  wf_arcs_ns: H′ → **Bool**,
  wf_arcs_ns(vs,arcs) ≡ arcs ⊆ ns(vs)

  wf_links: H′ → **Bool**
  wf_links(vs,arcs) ≡

$$\forall \ n,n':N,v:V \ \bullet$$
$$\{n,n'\}\subseteq arcs \wedge v \in vs \wedge \{n,n'\}\subseteq nodes(v) \Rightarrow n=n'$$

Annotations: wf_ns: Node sets of hyper-graph vertices are well-formed if, when they are distinct, they share no nodes in common. wf_arcs_ns: Well-formedness of arcs wrt. nodes of vertices holds if arcs mention only nodes of vertices. wf_links: Well-formedness of links expresses that no two distinct nodes of an arc belong to the same vertex, or vice versa: Each node of an arc belongs to a distinct vertex. ∎

The two previous examples illustrated several ideas: (1) Seemingly complex concepts can be modelled in simple terms, using sets and Cartesians. (2) Social sciences concepts (here of citizen-brokered community networks and society-brokered interactions between networks) can be captured abstractly. It remains to show a number of "interesting" functions on such networks and interactions, that is, to use formalisation to create formal, social sciences theories. (3) Graphs and hyper-graphs are mathematical concepts that relate to the social sciences concepts of citizen networks, etc. (4) Well-formedness constraints (needed to express appropriate subtypes) can and should be decomposed into "smallest" parts — with some of these suitably being defined in terms of auxiliary functions.

Some Ancillary Remarks: The formal, social sciences theories suggested above would certainly make use of many such auxiliary concepts. "Jotting" them down, as was liaisons (Example 13.8), is part of the research into such a theory: The formaliser's mind "roams in uncharted territory". Sometimes the formulation of such seemingly auxiliary concepts takes on a life of its own and become crucial components of an emerging theory. These last remarks are true not just for the above example of a possible social sciences theory, but for any domain or requirements or software design theory we might contemplate!

The next example will adopt a slightly different style of presentation.

13.4.3 Modelling a Telephone System

We give an example which illustrates sets and Cartesians. It differs slightly from that of the property-oriented model of a telephone exchange system, Example 12.1. In the example below we do not make any distinction between callers and called. This simplifies several matters.

The example is "borrowed" — in edited form — from J.C.P. Woodcock and M. Loomes' book *Software Engineering Mathematics* [534].

Example 13.10 *Telephone System, I:* The presentation is in two parts: The present example and Example 13.11. Each part will alternate between narratives and formalisations.

Narrative of *the State*

There are the notions of:

- subscribers, s:S;
- connections, c:C, between two or more subscribers;
- actual, a:A, and
- requested, r:R, connections between two or more subscribers;
- and a telephone exchange system, x:X, with actual and requested connections such that all actual connections are requested.

Formalisation of *the State*

type
   S
   $C = \{| \text{ ss } | \text{ ss:S-set} \bullet \textbf{card } ss \geq 2 |\}$
   $R = \text{C-set}$
   $A = \text{C-set}$
   $X = \{| \text{ (r,a) } | \text{ (r,a):R} \times \text{A} \bullet a \subseteq r \wedge \bigcap a = \{\} |\}$

where $\bigcap$ is the distributed intersection operator. $\bigcap a = \{\}$ expresses that no two connection elements of a share subscribers. That is, no subscriber participates in more than one actual call. We may consider $x{:}X$ to represent the state notion of this system.

    An example may be warranted:

value
   a,b,c,d,e,f,g,h,k:S
   x:X
axiom
   $x = (\{\{a,b,c\},\{d,e\},\{f,g\},\{g,h,k\}\},\{\{a,b,c\},\{d,e\},\{g,h,k\}\})$

Narrative of *Efficient States*

There is a notion of telephone exchange system efficiency, a constraint that governs its operation, hence the state, at any one time. The efficiency criterion says that all requested calls that can actually be connected are indeed connected:

Formalisation of *Efficient States*

value
   eff_X: $X \xrightarrow{\sim} \textbf{Bool}$
   eff_X(r,a) $\equiv \sim\exists \, a'{:}A \bullet a \subset a' \wedge (r,a') \in X$

Narrative of *Subscriber Actions*

Now there is the notion of subscriber actions: making a (possibly multi-party) call, terminating (hanging up on) a call and inquiring whether a line is busy. Let us model them as if they were the denotation of commands "being executed" in a state x:X.

Formalisation of Action Types

type
>   Cmd = Call | Hang | Busy
>   Call' == mk_Call(p:S,cs:C)
>   Call = {| c:Call' • **card** cs(c) ≥ 1 }
>   Hang == mk_Hang(s:S)
>   Busy == mk_Busy(s:S)

cs selects the *C* part of a *Call*.   ∎

An Aside on Type Union and Variant Records

This seems to be one of the first times, in these volumes, that we are using the two type constructors | and mk_Id. | as in A|B and mk_Id as in mk_Id(r:R,s:S,...,t:T). (Here A and B are any type expressions and Id, in fact mk_Id, can be any identifier. R, S, ..., and T are any type expressions.) So let us explain further. (We simplify the case for mk_Id(s_r:R,s_s:S,...,s_t:T) into just mk_A(s_a:A) and mk_B(s_b:B).)

- The informal, intuitive idea is first that we wish to express the type union of two types — and A|B is our means for doing so.
- Then we may be in the situation that the two types A and B "overlap": i.e., have values in common.
- So we cannot write A|B, but instead we write A' | B', and define A' and B' as A' == mk_A(s_a:A), respectively B' == mk_B(s_b:B).
- Now, as we shall later explain, more formally, the two types (A' and B') designate disjoint sets.
- s_r, s_s, ..., s_t, s_a and s_b are called selector functions.

In order to be systematic, safeguarding against possible overlapping of types, and to otherwise be able to exploit some pattern decomposition features of our main specification language (RSL), we extend this disjoint union construction to all alternatives of the union construction, as in the example above. We call the construction V == mkA(a:A) | mkA(a:A,b:B) | mkA(b:B,a:A), etc., a record variant construction. In Sect. 10.3 we illustrated the use of variant definitions in connection with enumerated token definitions. Section 18.4 covers variant record types. Section 18.5 covers union types.

Example 13.11 *Telephone System, II:* We continue Example 13.10.

Narrative: *Multi-party Call*

A multi-party call involves a (primary, *s*) caller and one or more (secondary, *ss*) callees. Enacting such a call makes the desired connection a requested connection. If none of the callers are already engaged in an actual connection then the call can be actualised. A multi-party call cannot be made by a caller who has already requested other calls.

Formalisation of Multi-party Call

We define the meaning of making a multi-party call in two ways: By means of a **pre/post**-definition, and explicitly:

value
    int_Call: Call $\overset{\sim}{\to}$ X $\overset{\sim}{\to}$ X
    int_Call(mk_Call(p,cs))(r,) **as** (r′,a′)
    pre p $\notin \bigcup$ r
    post r′ = r $\cup$ {{p} $\cup$ cs} $\wedge$ eff_X(r′,a′)

    int_Call(mk_Call(p,cs))(r,a) $\equiv$
        let r′ = r $\cup$ {{p} $\cup$ cs},
            a′ = a $\cup$ **if** ({{p} $\cup$ cs} $\cap \bigcup$ a) = {}
                    then {{p} $\cup$ cs} **else** {} **end in**
    (r′,a′) **end**
    pre p $\notin \bigcup$ r

The above **pre/post**-definition (of int_Call) illustrates the power of this style of definition. No algorithm is specified, instead all the work is expressed by appealing to the invariant!

Narrative: *Call Termination*

It takes one person, one subscriber, to terminate a call.

Formalisation of Call Termination

value
    int_Hang: Hang $\to$ X $\overset{\sim}{\to}$ X
    int_Hang(mk_Hang(p))(r,a) **as** (r′,a′)
        pre existS c:C • c $\in$ a $\wedge$ p $\in$ a
        post r′ = r \ {c|c:C • c $\in$ r $\wedge$ p $\in$ c} $\wedge$ eff_X(r′,a′)

    int_Hang(mk_Hang(p))(r,a) $\equiv$

> **let** $r' = r \setminus \{ c \mid c{:}C \cdot c \in a \land p \in c \}$,
> $a' = a \setminus \{ c \mid c{:}C \cdot c \in r \land p \in c \}$ **in**
> **let** $a'' = a' \cup \{ c \mid c{:}C \cdot c \in r' \land c \cap a' = \{\} \}$ **in**
> (r', a'') **end end**
> **pre** existS $c{:}C \cdot c \in a \land p \in a$

The two ways of defining the above int_Hang function again demonstrate the strong abstractional feature of defining by means of **pre/post**-conditions.

Narrative: *Subscriber Busy*

A line (that is, a subscriber) is only 'busy' if it (the person) is engaged in an actual call.

Formalisation of Subscriber Busy

value
    int_Busy: $S \to X \overset{\sim}{\to}$ **Bool**
    int_Busy(mk_Busy(p))(_,a) **as** b
        pre true
        post if b **then** $p \in \bigcup a$ **else** $p \notin \bigcup a$ **end**

    int_Busy(mk_Busy(p))(_,a) $\equiv p \in \bigcup a$

Here, perhaps not so surprisingly, we find that the explicit function definition is the most straightforward.   ∎

13.5 Inductive Set Definitions

We wish to illustrate the use of recursive and, in general, inductive definitions. In this chapter for sets. In subsequent chapters for Cartesians, lists and maps.

13.5.1 Inductive Set Type Definitions

Is it allowed to specify:

type
    S = S-**set**?

The answer is no. For technical reasons.

Let us try to understand this answer.

First let us try imagine what could be a solution to the above type definition. One proposal is:

$\mathcal{S}$: {{}, {{}}, {{},{{}}}, {{},{{}},{{},{{}}}}, ... },

where the set elements indicated by the ... 's are all to be finite or infinite sets whose elements are "drawn" from "the aforementioned". Not very useful you may say. Let $\mathcal{S}$ be the set indicated above. Is it itself a member of $\mathcal{S}$? Obviously no. That would lead to the classical paradox: *"Is the set of all sets an element of that set ?"*. The cardinality of the class of values of type S of the left-hand side must be equal to cardinality of the class of values of type S-set of the right-hand side. Obviously they are not. So we reject this kind of recursive set type definition.

So we use this example as a pragmatic reason for not getting involved in paradoxes.

But we may need some kind of inductive set definition. Let us try this one:

type
    E
    S = mS-**set**
    mS = Es | Ss
    Es == mkE(e:E)
    Ss == mkS(s:S)

Now an example element, s, of S expressed outside the RSL notation would be:

value
    $\mathcal{S}$ = ∪{es|es:Es-**set**} ∪ ∪{mss|mss:mS-**set**•mss⊆$\mathcal{S}$}

Is the above mathematical definition of $\mathcal{S}$ allowed? Yes, in mathematics, but not in RSL. In mathematics a foundation for RSL can be given in which the recursive type definition of mS makes sense. The recursive equation in $\mathcal{S}$ is, in RSL, any fixpoint of the equartion, i.e., a set, σ, which when replacing $\mathcal{S}$ in the equation satisfies that equation. The fact that σ may be infinite should not bother us: We are specifying, not computing. So we conclude: Recursive definitions of sets must have built into them a variant, a "boot strap". The variant serves to get the generation of proper set values started and serves to avoid seemingly meaningless void values.

We shall introduce the variant record **type** mS == mkE(se:E) | mkS(ss:S), shown above, in Chap. 18.

13.5.2 Inductive Set Value Definitions

We illustrate the use of inductive definitions of set values — mostly in the form of set comprehensions. At the end of the below example we also show a recursive function definition over sets.

Example 13.12 *Purely Sort- and Set-Based Model of Networks:* A network consists of uniquely identified segments and uniquely identified connectors. From a segment one can observe the identities of the exactly two connectors that the segment is delimited by. And from a connector one can observe the set of identities of segments connected to the connector.

type
    N, S, Si, C, Ci
value
    obs_Ss: N → S-**set**
    obs_Cs: N → C-**set**
    obs_Si: S → Si
    obs_Sis: C → Si-**set**
    obs_Ci: C → Ci
    obs_Cis: S → Ci-**set**
axiom
    ∀ s:S • **card** obs_Cis(s) = 2
value
    xtr_Cis: S-**set** → Cis-**set**
    xtr_Cis(ss) ≡ ∪{obs_Cis(s)|s:S•s ∈ ss}

    xtr_Cis: N → Ci-**set**
    xtr_Cis(n) ≡ xtr_Cis(obs_Ss(n))

An acyclic route is a set of segments such that any segment of the route connects to one or two segments in the route, one if the segment is a first or a last of the route and two if it is "in-fixed" between two other segments of the route, and such that no in-fixing, but not explicitly represented, connector is implied more than at most once. gen_Rs when applied to a net generates the possibly infinite set of all routes of a network. To define genRs we need define a number of auxiliary functions, incl. predicate.

type
    R′ = S-**set**
    R = {| r:R′ • wfR(r) |}
value
    genRs: N → R-**set**
    genRs(n) ≡ {r|r:R•r⊆obs_Ss(n)}

    Ci_deg: Ci × R′ → **Nat**
    Ci_deg(ci,r) ≡ **card**{ s | s:S • s ∈ r ∧ ci ∈ obs_Cis(s)}

    wfR: R′ → **Bool**
    wfR(r) ≡
        card r = 1 ∨

$$\exists \; ci,ci':Ci, \; s:S \bullet s \in r \land \{ci,ci'\} = obs\_Cis(s) \land$$
$$Ci\_deg(ci,r){=}1 \land Ci\_deg(ci',r){=}2 \land wfR(r\backslash\{s\})$$

∎

13.6 A Comment on Varying Sets

In the beginning of Sect. 13.1 we made a footnote reference to the present section. It concerned the term varying sets. We now make precise what we mean by that term.

What we mean is roughly the following, explained in two ways. Let v_s be an assignable variable. Let its value range over sets. Assignment to v_s may result in there being, at one time, no elements in the variable value, i.e., the set is empty; while at another time an assignment may add or remove any number of set elements to the set variable.

type
    A
variable
    v_s:A-**set** := {}
value
    g: A-**set** → **Unit**
    g(set) ≡
        ...
        v_s := set; ...
        let a:A • a ∉ v_s **in** v_s := v_s ∪ {a}; ... **end**; ...
        let a:A • a ∈ v_s **in** v_s := v_s \ {a}; ... **end**; ...
        v_s := set; ...
        v_s := {}; ...
        ...

The above was an explanation given in terms of an imperative, i.e., an assignment language.

An explanation given in terms of a functional programming style would, for example, run as follows. Let there be given a function definition:

type
    A, B
value
    f: A-**set** → **Nat**
    f(set) ≡
        if set={} **then** 0 **else let** a:A • a ∈ set **in** 1+f(set\{a}) **end end**

The argument **set** designates a set. For recursive invocations of f the set **set** takes on "varying" values. Initially there may be 5 elements. In successive invocations there will be 4, 3, 2, 1 and then, finally 0 elements. Incidentally, the function f is the same as the **card**inality function for finite set arguments.

13.7 Principles, Techniques and Tools

Based on this chapter on the set data type, its definition and its many examples, we shall now enunciate principles, techniques and tools of abstraction and modelling.

Principles. *Set Abstraction and Modelling:* If and when a model-oriented abstraction has been chosen, then set abstraction is chosen if a reasonable number of the following characteristics can be identified as properties of the phenomena being modelled: (i) the abstract structure of the composite components being modelled consists of an unordered collection of not necessarily uniquely named, but otherwise distinct, subcomponents (constituent phenomena or concepts)) (ii) whose number is not fixed, i.e., may vary, that is, (iii) to which new, distinct subcomponents may be joined; (iv) from which existing subcomponents may be removed; (v) where one may inquire about "containment" relations between modelled phenomena (concepts); (vi) where one may compose other such phenomena (concepts) from similar such phenomena (concepts) (vii) or decompose into "smaller" such phenomena (concepts); and (viii) where one may inquire whether the phenomena (concepts) contain a given constituent phenomenon (respectively concept). ■

Other model choices may be chosen (viz.: lists, maps), but they will often need to be manipulated using set operations.

Techniques. *Set Abstraction and Modelling:* We refer to initial paragraphs of Sect. 13.4 for a listing of some of the techniques used when abstracting using sets. More specifically: A number of set-oriented techniques are offered: (ix) Observer functions usually "extract" sets; (x) the various set operations apply to appropriate modelling instances: (x.1–.3) Union, intersection and set complement apply to models of "all", "shared", respectively "some, except" instances of a phenomenon possessed by two or more sets of phenomena, (x.4–.5) subset, equality and inequality apply to models of "contained", "the same", respectively "definitely not the same", instances of a phenomenon possessed by two or more sets of phenomena; (x.6) cardinality applies to models of "how many" instances of a phenomenon; (xi–xii) set enumeration and set comprehension apply to the expression of the construction of an instance of an otherwise set modelled phenomenon. These are just some of the more "important" techniques. ■

Tools. *Set Abstraction and Modelling:* If abstraction and modelling using the set data type has been chosen, then the tool can either be the RSL, the VDM-SL, the Z, or, for example, the B specification language. ■

Please compare the present section to Sections 15.6 (lists) and 16.6 (maps).

13.8 Discussion

We have outlined the set data type. And we have enunciated principles for when to deploy set abstraction, to mention some of the techniques that follow from such a choice, and to identify some of the set abstraction specification language tools available. Sets constitute "the basic workhorse" of model-oriented abstraction and modelling. In Chapters 15 and 16 we introduce the list and the map data types. We shall then see how sets reappear in the expression of the set of all indices, respectively elements of a list, and the definition, respectively the range sets of maps.

13.9 Bibliographical Notes

We refer to the following seminal works on set theory: [46, 211, 230, 258, 273, 394, 491, 500, 505].

13.10 Exercises

Exercise 13.1. *Set Types.* This exercise helps to develop your skills in manipulating sets. It is certainly not one of abstraction.

1. List the elements of **Bool-set** and **Bool-infset**.
2. List some of the elements of **Nat-set**, respectively **Nat-infset.**

Exercise 13.2. *Simple Number Sets, I.* This exercise also helps to develop your skills in manipulating sets. It is really not one of abstraction.

You are to formally specify sets, sns:SNS, of sets, ns:NS, of natural numbers such that each set, ns, in a set sns contains a dense set of numbers from and including 0 to and including one less than the cardinality of that set (ns), and such that sns contains all the sets ns_0, ns_1, up to and including ns_{n-1}, where n is the cardinality of sns.

Exercise 13.3. *Simple Number Sets, II.* This exercise continues that of Exercises 13.2. You are now to formally define operations:

1. that join a "next higher number" to a set of sets of numbers,
2. and that remove a "highest numbered" such set.

That is, if sns is the set $\{\{0\}, \{0,1\}, \{0,1,2\}\}$,

- then adding a "next higher number" to sns yields the set $\{\{0\}, \{0,1\}, \{0,1,2\}, \{0,1,2,3\}\}$,
- and removing a "highest numbered" such set yields the set $\{\{0\}, \{0,1\}\}$.

Exercise 13.4. *More on Networks.* We refer to Example 13.8. This exercise is intended to open your eyes to rather unconventional applications: basically, the one here is taken from the social sciences!

1. Define functions, citizens, which, for any network, n:N, respectively for any society, m:M, yields all its citizens.
2. Define a function, hermits, which, for any set of groups, s:S, yields all its hermits, i.e., citizens whose group includes only themselves and who are not liaisons.
3. Define a function, isolated, which, for any society, m:M, yields all those citizens who are citizens belonging to only one network.
4. Define a function, individualists, which, for any society, m:M, yields the set of all those citizens who only belong to one network.
5. Define a function, emissaries, which, for any society, m:M, yields all those citizens who are emissaries.
6. Define functions, ordinary, which, for any network, n:N, respectively for any society, m:M, yield all those citizens who are not liaisons, respectively neither liaisons nor emissaries.

We advise the exercise solver to wait tackling these next three exercises till after having studied the next chapter (on Cartesians). Then you will be better equipped to solve the exercises in a meaningful way.

Exercise 13.5. ♣ *Sets in the Transportation Net Domain.* We refer to Appendix A, Sect. A.1, *Transportation Net.*

We assume the following properties of transportation nets: they consist of sets of Segments[6] and sets of Connections. Segments can be modelled as Cartesians containing a unique Segment Identifier, a Segment Name, a Segment Length, the directions in which traffic may flow along the segment, modelled, for example as a set of zero, one or two pairs of Connection Identifiers, where these latter are thought of as identifying the Connections at either end of the Segment Connections can be modelled as Cartesians containing a unique Connection Identifier, a Connection Name, and the Identifiers of Segments incident upon (and/or emanating from) the Connection.

1. Define the sorts Segment Identifier, Segment Name, and Connection Identifier,
2. Define the concrete types of Nets, Segments and Connections.
3. Define a predicate function, wf_N, which tests whether a given Net is well-formed wrt. the following: (i) all Segments of a Net have unique Segment Identifiers; (ii) all Connections of a Net have unique Connection Identifiers; and (iii) for each Segment of a Net its Connection Identifiers are those of actual Connections of the Net.

---

[6]By using capital letters we indicate a possible type name.

4. Define a function, is_Route, which tests whether a given subset of segments are sequentially connected.
5. Define a function, is_Circular_Route, which tests whether a given Route is circular.
6. Define a function, is_Line, which tests whether a given Route has all of its Segments having the same Segment Name, and that it is then non-circular.
7. Define a function, all_non_Circular_Routes, which generates all non-circular Routes of a Net.
8. Define a function, all_Lines, which generates all Lines of a Net.
9. Define a function, Route_Length, which computes the length of a Route.

Exercise 13.6. ♣ *Sets in the Container Logistics Domain.* We refer to Appendix A, Sect. A.2, *Container Logistics.*

Assume that a Line is a set of Container Ship Terminal Visits, where each Container Ship Terminal Visit is a triple of Container Terminal Names: The Names of the previous, the present, and the next Container Terminals. Assume that there is a set, all shipping routes, of Shipping Routes: A Shipping Route is a pair: The Name of a Container Ship, and a Line. Assume that a Waybill is a set of Container Terminal Visits, where each Container Terminal Visit is a triple of a "from" Container Terminal Name, a Name of a Container Ship, and a "to" Container Terminal Name. Let there further be given a type, Seven Seas, of Container Terminal Names.

1. Define the types of Seven Seas, Line, Container Ship Terminal Visit, All Shipping Routes, Shipping Route, Waybill, and Container Terminal Visit.
2. Define a predicate, wf_Single_Line, which tests that a Line, i.e., the set of Container Ship Terminal Visits, form a simple cyclic sequence: That is, that one Container Ship Terminal Visit connects to a next, with a last connecting back to a first:

$$\{(n_6, n_1, n_2), (n_1, n_2, n_3), (n_2, n_3, n_4), (n_3, n_4, n_5), (n_4, n_5, n_6), (n_5, n_6, n_1)\}$$

Any Container Terminal can serve as a last, etc. Figure 13.5 shows, at top, such a line.

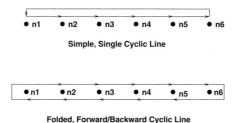

Simple, Single Cyclic Line

Folded, Forward/Backward Cyclic Line

Fig. 13.5. Two lines

3. Define a predicate, wf_Folded_Line, which tests that a Line, i.e., the set of Container Ship Terminal Visits, form a simple sequence followed by a reverse sequence:

$$\{(n_2, n_1, n_2), (n_1, n_2, n_3), (n_2, n_3, n_4), (n_3, n_4, n_5),$$

$$(n_4, n_5, n_6), (n_5, n_6, n_5), (n_5, n_4, n_3), (n_4, n_3, n_2)\}$$

Figure 13.5 on the page before shows, at bottom, such a line.

4. Given any Waybill value and any All Shipping Routes value, define a predicate, wf_Way_Bill, which checks that there is a suitable set of Lines that can convey the Container according to a Waybill.

Exercise 13.7. ♣ *Sets in the Financial Service Industry Domain.* We refer to Appendix A, Sect. A.3, *Financial Service Industry*.

From a bank one can observe the amount of cash that the bank possesses. From a bank once can observe the names of all the clients of that bank. From a bank once can observe the set of all its account numbers. From a bank and given a client name one can observe that client's set of one or more bank account numbers. From a bank and given an account number one can observe which clients (by their client names) share that account number. From a bank and given an account number one can observe the balance on the designated account.

1. Define the sorts of entities mentioned above.
2. Define the signature of the observer functions mentioned above.

The set of bank account numbers of a bank must be the same whether one observes these directly from the bank, or observes them through the set of all client names (acct_nos). The set of client names of a bank, must be the same whether one observes these directly from the bank, or observing them through the set of all account numbers (cli_nms).

3. Please formulate appropriate predicates for the two constraints expressed above.
4. Can you think of other constraints?

The following simple operations can be performed on a bank:

5. *Open an account:* A client opens an account by presenting a client name. In return the client obtains a new, fresh, hitherto unused account number. The balance is set to 0. The account is not shared with other clients.
6. *Deposit into an account:* A client presents an amount of cash to the bank to be added to an account whose number is also presented to the bank. The amount of cash in the bank is incremented with the presented amount.
7. *Withdraw from an account:* A client presents a request to withdraw a stated amount of cash from the bank by subtracting it from an account whose number is also presented to the bank. The amount of cash in the bank is decremented with the requested amount.

8. *Close an account:* A client closes an account by presenting an account number (owned by that client). As a result the account is closed. If the balance is positive then the closure also amounts to a withdrawal of cash. If the account balance is negative then the closure also amounts to a prior deposit of cash.

Please state appropriate pre/post-conditions on the bank for:

5 the open transaction,
6 the deposit transaction,
7 the withdraw transaction and
8 the close transaction.

Can you think of an invariant over bank cash and bank account balances?

9. Please formalise it!

Cartesians in RSL

- The **prerequisite** for studying this chapter is that you possess knowledge of the mathematical and the RSL concepts of sets and Cartesians as covered in earlier chapters (Chaps. 3–4 and 13).
- The **aim** is to introduce the RSL concept of Cartesians, also known in programming languages as records or structures.
- The **objective** is to help set the reader free to choose Cartesian abstractions when appropriate, and to not choose Cartesians when they are not appropriate.
- The **treatment** is semiformal and systematic.

Characterisation. By a *Cartesian* we understand, loosely, a fixed grouping (i.e., aggregation) of a number of not necessarily distinct entities such that it is meaningful to speak of (i) the composition of these entities, e_i, into a Cartesian, $(e_1, e_2, \ldots, e_n)$, of (ii) the decomposition of a Cartesian, c, into its components: **let** $(id_1, id_2, \ldots, id_n) = c$ **in** ... **end**, and of (iii) comparisons between Cartesians $(=, \neq)$. ∎

Cogito ergo sum

René Descartes, 1596–1650

We know of René Descartes from our first school days: the division of the plane into X and Y (Cartesian) coordinates is attributed to him [186]. And we know of Cartesians, such as we shall think of them from programming languages, as records, or structures. We refer to Sect. 6.6 for an early introduction to Cartesians.

14.1 Cartesians: The Issues

The idea illustrated in this chapter is the use of the discrete mathematics concept of Cartesians in abstracting domain, requirements and software phenomena and concepts. Cartesians offer themselves as an abstraction when a component k can best be characterised as a fixed composition, i.e., grouping of not necessarily distinct components $(a, b, \ldots, c)$, and where the order of appearance in the grouping is arbitrarily chosen (but then fixed). The section will just give a single example — as Cartesians become proper components in the modelling of "zillions" of other problems. That is: Cartesians, as such, as the only model-oriented (i.e., discrete mathematical) "device" — even when used together with sets — to "deploy" in abstraction is a sign of too extreme a frugality![1]

This chapter is, as are Chaps. 13–17, built up as follows:

- The Cartesian data type   (Sect. 14.2)
- Examples of Cartesian-based abstractions   (Sect. 14.3)
- Abstracting and modelling with Cartesians   (Sect. 14.4)
- Inductive Cartesian definitions   (Sect. 14.5)
- A review of Cartesian abstractions and models   (Sect. 14.6)

There are many examples because *before one can write good specifications one must have read and studied many example specifications*. While you may not need to study all of them now, you can return to some later. The chapter ends with a brief discussion.

14.2 The Cartesian Data Type

We shall treat the following as separate issues: types and type expressions, value expressions, binding patterns and matching, and operations on Cartesians.

14.2.1 Cartesian Types and Type Expressions

Cartesian types are products (groupings, aggregations, structures) of two or more types,

─────────────────── Types and Values ───────────────────

type	examples /* all subscripted a, b, cs: values */
A, B, ..., C	$a1,..,a\alpha,..,b1,..,b\beta,..,c1,..,c\gamma,...$
$A \times B \times ... \times C$	$(a1,b1,..,c1),(ai,bj,..,ck),...$
$K = A \times B \times C$	k: $(a1,b1,c1),(ai,bj,ck),...$
$K' = (A \times B \times C)$	k': $(a1',b1',c1'),(ai',bj',ck'),...$
$K2 = A \times B$	k2: $(ai,bj),..,(ak,b\ell),..$
$K3 = A \times B \times C$	k3: $(ai,bj,ck),..,(a\ell,bm,cn),..$

───

[1]But that is, of course, just an opinion. For concrete programming one can come a very long way, in fact all the way, as was proven by the programming language Lisp [370], in which there are just two data type values: Atoms and pairs, i.e., Cartesians, the latter of any of these two values.

Let A, B, ..., C stand for types whose possibly infinite numbers of elements include the values $\{a_1, a_2, \ldots, a_\alpha, \ldots\}$, $\{b_1, b_2, \ldots, b_\beta, \ldots\}$, respectively $\{c_1, c_2, \ldots, c_\gamma, \ldots\}$. Types whose values can be considered finite groupings of A, then B, etc., finally C, elements can be defined using the × (Cartesian product) type operators.

Example 14.1 *A Simple Cartesian Example:* Let fact name the factorial function, then

(fact(1),fact(2),fact(3),fact(4),fact(5),fact(6))

expresses a simple Cartesian of six elements, the first six factorials!   ∎

The ellipses (...) in the type expression A × B × ... × C make it metalinguistic, that is, outside ("above" or "about") the language, here RSL, which is being explained. Ellipses occurring in our expressions should signal to the reader that we are presenting a generic metalinguistic expression.

Cartesians are thus formed from the use of the × type constructor operation. Hence Cartesian values consist of groupings of a definite number of values — where the definite number is at least two. Examples K, K', K2, K3 are not metalinguistic. K defines, or the type expression A × B × C expresses, the type of Cartesian groupings of values of respective type. K' defines, or the type expression (A × B × C) expresses, the same as K! That is, parenthesization at this "outermost" level "adds nothing new". K3 defines exactly the same as does K (and K'). So one cannot distinguish between values of these three (identical) types. When this is needed we need to deploy extra notational "machinery".

To see the consequences, let us examine a few type expressions.

For the sake of reference in the subsequent explanatory text, we have defined (i.e., named) the types (previously only expressed [i.e., as expressions]):

type
    A, B, C
    G0 = A × B × C
    G1 = (A × B × C)
    G2 = (A × B) × C
    G3 = A × (B × C)

Brackets, "(" and ")" are used in type expressions, as an abbreviation, only to "break" the priority of the × operator, and thus to avoid having to define auxiliary types:

type
    G2 = AB × C
    AB = A × B
    G3 = A × BC

BC = B × C

To the individually defined types there correspond many examples:

a, a′, a″, .., b, b′, .., b″, c, c′, .., c″ /∗ values ∗/
g0: (a,b,c), g0′: (a′,b′,c′), .., g0‴: (a″,b,c′)
g1: (a,b,c), g1′: (a′,b′,c′), .., g1‴: (a″,b,c′)
g2: ((a,b),c), g2′: ((a′,b′),c′), .., g2‴: ((a″,b),c′)
g3: (a,(b,c)), g3′: (a′,(b′,c′)), .., g3‴: (a″,(b,c′))

We have shown many examples with single, double, triple quotes and indices so as to avoid defining, for now, mathematically, the general case. We believe these examples exhaust the possible cases.

14.2.2 Cartesian Value Expressions

Any identifier may denote a Cartesian. The only "operation" that results in Cartesian values is that of grouping: $(a, b, \ldots, c)$ where $a, b, \ldots$, and c are any expressions denoting any kind of value. This operation has already been amply illustrated earlier, but for the sake of systematic treatment we summarise.

Cartesian value expressions are expressions whose values are Cartesians. Specific Cartesian value formation is achieved, in RSL, through the use of the Cartesian value *constructors*: "(", "," and ")". Let e1, e2, ..., en be any *value expressions*,[2] then the second line of the **type** clause below, and the first line of the **value** clause:

type
    A, B, ..., C
    A × B × ... × C
value
    ... (e1,e2,...,en) ...

(the use of ellipses is metalinguistic) are respectively a *Cartesian type expression*, and a *Cartesian valued expression* with (e1,e2,...,en) indicating an explicit Cartesian enumeration. The type expression denote models and have values from these models. Mathematically, i.e., not expressed in the RSL notation, and referring only to values of respective types (or sorts) A, B, ..., C we can define the meaning of A × B × ... × C as:

---

[2] We remind the reader that in the rest of these volumes we shall use the following naming convention: Identifiers starting with e (and often "suffixed" or indexed (subscripted) by some alphanumeric characters) stand for *expressions*. Identifiers starting with v (and often suffixed or indexed (subscripted) by some alphanumeric characters) stand for *values*. Values are definite, in the sense that a value is a specific thing. Expressions may be constant expressions, i.e., evaluate, in any context (and state) to one and the same value, or expressions may be variable expressions, i.e., evaluate, in different contexts (and states) to different values.

$$\{(a_i, b_j, \ldots, c_k) \mid a_i : A, b_j : B, \ldots, c_k : C\}$$

The $A, B, \ldots, C$ all refer to a same model which associates A with A, etcetera. There might be different models for the specification in which the above type expression occurs. But a specific, albeit an arbitrary, one is chosen for the evaluation of all RSL constructs.

14.2.3 Cartesian Operations, I

First we show the *decomposition* operation. From Cartesian gi values, and using the RSL **let ... in ... end** construct, we decompose into defined A, B, C values named by the respective ai, bj, ck, etc., identifiers.

> **let** (a1,b1,c1) = g0″, (a1′,b1′,c1′) = g1″ **in** .. **end**
> **let** ((a2,b2),c2) = g2″ **in** .. **end**
> **let** (a3,(b3,c3)) = g3″ **in** .. **end**

Then we show the *composition* operation: From respective ai, bj, ck, etc., values we compose into defined Cartesian Gi values named by the respective gi, etc., identifiers.

> **let** g0″ = (a1,b1,c1), g1″ = (a1′,b1′,c1′) **in** ... **end**
> **let** g2″ = ((a2,b2),c2) **in** ... **end**
> **let** g3″ = (a3,(b3,c3)) **in** ... **end**

14.2.4 Cartesian Binding Patterns and Matching

So composition into Cartesians and decomposition (*matching* and *binding*) with respect to Cartesians are two major operations related to Cartesians. The use of the RSL **let ... in ... end** construct in decompositions thus showed the use of *binding patterns*:

let (a,b,c) = g1,
    ((a,b),c) = g2,
    (a,(b,c)) = g3 **in** ... **end**

All three cases show *binding patterns* to the left of the '=' symbol. All the a's, b's, and c's are identifiers. They are bound to values as a result of the decomposition process. We refer to a more systematic treatment of *patterns, matching,* and *binding* in subsections of Sect. 14.4.1 (*Cartesian Patterns* and *Cartesian Patterns, Fitting and Binding*) and in Sect. 14.4.2. We have earlier (Sect. 13.2.3) covered these concepts for set binding-pattern, and we shall later deal with these concepts in additional contexts: Sect. 15.2.3 for lists, and Sect. 16.2.3 for maps.

14.2.5 Cartesian Operations, II

In Sect. 14.2.3 we introduced the decomposition of Cartesians, which one may consider an operation on Cartesians. The only other operations on Cartesians are equality, $=$, and equivalence, $\equiv$; they are defined between any typed, non-function value in RSL.

type
    A, B, C, ...
    $G = A \times B \times ... \times C$
value
    $=, \equiv:\ G \times G \rightarrow$ **Bool**
axiom
    $\forall\ (a,b,...,c),(a',b',...,c'):G \bullet ((a,b,...,c) = (a',b',...,c'))$
       $\equiv (a = a') \wedge (b = b') \wedge ... \wedge (c = c')$

The above is true, provided that none of the A, B, ..., C contain (non-map) functional values. That is, they may contain finite or infinite sets, finite or infinite lists, finite or infinite maps, and Cartesians over nonfunctional values.

14.3 Examples of Cartesian Abstractions

This section "matches" Sections 13.3, 15.3, 16.3, and 17.2. They all give examples of set, Cartesian, list, map and function-based specifications. They are meant as "drill", i.e., class lecture, examples.

14.3.1 File Systems II

This is the second in a series of models of what we could call *file systems*. Other models are presented in Examples 13.6 (sets), 15.6 (lists [and Cartesians and sets]), and 16.8 (maps [and records]). See also Exercise 16.11.

Example 14.2 *Another File System:* A simple file system consists of a set of records. A record is a pair of keys (k:K) and sets ($\{d,d',...,d''\}$) of data (s:D, etc.). No two otherwise distinct records have the same key.

type
    K, D
    $R = K \times D\text{-set}$
    $B' = R\text{-set}$
    $B = \{|\ b:B' \bullet wf\_B(b)\ |\}$
value
    $wf\_B:\ B' \rightarrow$ **Bool**
    $wf\_B(b) \equiv \forall\ (k,ds),(k',ds'):R \bullet k=k' \Rightarrow ds=ds'$

A file system user wishes to perform the following operations: (i) Create an empty file system. (ii) Inquire whether a file system is empty. (iii) Inquire whether a given key is that of a record in the file system. (iv) Insert a new record in the file system, such that no record already in the file system has the same key as the record to be inserted. (v) Given a key, select the data set of the record (if present) with that key. (vi) Given a key, remove the record (if present) with that key.

value

    create: $\to$ B, create() $\equiv$ {}

    is_empty: B $\to$ **Bool**, is_empty(b) $\equiv$ b={}

    is_inB: K $\to$ B $\to$ **Bool**

    is_inB(k)(b) $\equiv$ $\exists$ (k',ds'):R • (k',ds') $\in$ b $\wedge$ k=k'

    insert: R $\to$ B $\overset{\sim}{\to}$ V

    insert(k,ds)(b) $\equiv$ b $\cup$ {(k,ds)}

      pre $\sim$is_inB(k)(b)

    select: K $\to$ B $\overset{\sim}{\to}$ D-set

    select(k)(b) $\equiv$ **let** (k',ds):R • k=k' $\wedge$ (k',ds) $\in$ b **in** ds **end**

      pre is_inB(k)(b)

    remove: K $\to$ B $\overset{\sim}{\to}$ B

    remove (k)(b) $\equiv$ **let** (k',ds):R • k=k' $\wedge$ (k',ds) $\in$ b **in** b \ {(k',ds)} **end**

      pre is_inB(k)(b)

■

14.3.2 Kuratowski: Pairs as Sets

Example 14.3 *Pairs as Sets:* Pairs (a_1, a_2) of distinct simple entities can be represented as sets: $\{a_1, \{a_1, a_2\}\}$. Allow also a_2 to be a pair: (a_{2_1}, a_{2_2}) then its representation is $\{a_1, \{a_1, \{a_{2_1}, \{a_{2_1}, a_{2_2}\}\}\}\}$. That is, we now allow pairs to be either pairs of distinct simple elements, or of a first simple element and a pair. We still assume, but do not formally specify, distinctness of A elements (of simple pairs).

type

    A

    P' = A $\times$ Q

    P = {| p:P' • wf_P(p){} |}

    Q = A | P

    S' = R-set

    R = A | S

    S = {| s:S' • wf_S(s) |}

value

wf_P: P′ → A-set → **Bool**
wf_P((a,q))(as) ≡
    a ∉ as ∧
    case q **of**
        (_,_) → wf_P(q)({a}∪as),
        _ → **true**
    end

wf_S: S′ → **Bool**
wf_S(s) ≡
    card s = 2 ∧
    case s **of**
[1]   {a,{a,{b,r}}} → wf_S({b,r}),
[2]   {a,{a,b}} → **true**,
[3]   _ → **false**
    end

Notice, in wf_P, the sequential use of binding patterns to "detect" whether an argument to wf_P is a pair (i.e., a Q value) or not. Wildcards are used in order to signal to the reader that the particular values are irrelevant. Sequentiality of the **case** construct evaluation means that the argument to wf_P is matched first with a pair, then with "whatever". Notice, similarly, in wf_S, the particular (perhaps a bit "tricky") sequential use of binding patterns to "detect" whether an s is [2] a simple pair, [1] a possibly well-formed (but more composite) pair or [3] not a pair. Given a set representation of pairs, as defined above, we can find its pair of ordered elements:

value
    first: S → A
    first(s) ≡ **let** a:A, s′:S • s = {a,s′} **in** a **end**
    secnd: S → R
    secnd(s) ≡ **let** a:A, s′:S • s = {a,s′} **in** s′ **end**

Given a an arbitrary pairing, as defined above, we can construct its set representation. And given a set representation of pairs, as defined above, we can reconstruct its ordered pairing of elements:

value
    P2S: P → S
    P2S(p) ≡
        case p **of**
            (a,(a,q)) → {a,{a,Q2R(q)}}, (a,a′) → {a,{a,a′}}
        end
    Q2R: Q → R
    Q2R(q) ≡ **case** q **of** (a,q′) → P2S(a,q′), a → a **end**

Observe the need for an auxiliary function, Q2R, to handle a "special" case. Similarly wrt. S2P:

S2P: S → P
   case p **of**
      {a,{a,r}} → (a,R2Q(r)), {a,a′} → (a,a′) **end**
R2Q: R → Q
R2Q(r) ≡
   case r **of** {a,{a,r′}} → (a,S2P(r′)), a → a **end**

Observe the various ways in which we have syntax-formatted, i.e., laid out the formula texts, line-wise: Sometimes on one, sometimes spread out over several lines.

    Exercise 14.2 generalises the above problem to that of allowing non-distinct A elements in simple pairs.   ■

14.4 Abstracting and Modelling with Cartesians

This section "matches" Sections 13.4, 15.4, 16.4, and 17.3. They all give larger examples of set, Cartesian, list, map, respectively function abstractions and models. They are meant as self-study examples.

    The purpose of this section is to introduce *techniques* and *tools* for model-oriented specifications primarily based on Cartesians. Among the *Cartesian modelling principles, techniques* and *tools* are: (1) *Subtyping:* Sometimes a type definition defines "too much": a type-constraining (*well-formedness, invariant*) predicate technique can therefore applied. (2) **pre/post**-*conditions:* Function abstraction in terms of **pre**- and **post**-*conditions*. (3) *"Input/-Output/Query" functions:* identification of main functions according to their *signature.* (4) *Auxiliary functions:* decomposition of function definitions into "smallest" units. The *principles* and *techniques* reoccur, for sets, lists and maps in Sections 13.4, 15.4 and 16.4.

14.4.1 Modelling Syntactic Structures

A structure, like a set, a Cartesian grouping, a list or a map, is syntactic if its representation, like the above, has a meaning which may be another structure, but whose semantic components are (rather) different from the syntactic components. We shall give a somewhat "primitive" and "not very abstract" example of the syntax and semantics of a simple imperative programming language. We say "primitive" and "not very abstract" since we can later demonstrate more realistic, as well as "more abstract" programming language examples. Thus the examples of this section, since they necessarily have to make use only of such structured values as sets and Cartesians, are not really exemplifying abstractions, only modelling!

Example 14.4 *Syntax of a Simple Computer Language, Part I:*

Narrative — Syntactic (Cartesian) Categories

(i) A computer program, m:M, contains a procedure name pn, a procedure statement label, ln, and a set of uniquely named procedures, ps, such that the procedure name is one of a procedure in the program set, ps, of procedures. (ii) A procedure has a name and otherwise contains a set of uniquely labelled statements, such that the labels of goto statements of the procedure (see (xi) below) are labels of statements of that procedure, and such that procedure names and labels of procedure invocation statements (see (xiv) below) are those of procedures of the program and their sets of labelled statements. (iii) A labelled statement contains a label and a statement. (iv) A label is a further un-analysed quantity. (v) A statement is either an assignment, or a conditional, or a goto, or a procedure call, or an exit statement. (vi) An assignment contains a variable and an expression. It also designates a continuation, i.e., the label of a next statement to be interpreted after interpretation of the present assignment statement. (vii) A variable is a further un-analysed quantity. (viii) An expression is a further un-analysed quantity. (See, however, Exercise 14.5 for a thorough analysis (cum discussion) of analysed expressions.) (ix) A conditional contains one expression, the test expression, and two (continuation) labels, the consequence label and the alternative label. (x) A goto statement contains a label. (xi) A procedure call contains a procedure name and a statement label. It also designates a continuation, i.e., the label of a next statement to be interpreted after interpretation of the present call statement. (xii) An exit statement is a further un-analysed quantity. (xiii) The "further un-analysed" procedure name, variable, statement label and exit quantities are all distinct sets (i.e., cannot be confused).   ∎

An Aside—The Union Type Operator: |

To formalise the type of statements which consist of various, i.e., alternative (|) kinds, assignment, conditionals, etc., we introduce here the type constructor |. Let A, B, ..., C stand for arbitrary types.

type
    A, B, ..., C
    U = A | B | ... | C

U is defined to be the type whose values are the union of all the values of respective types A, B, ..., C.

Another Aside — Cartesian Text Types

By {"text_1,text_2,...,text_n"} we understand the finite type whose elements are just the strings of text listed.

Example 14.5 *Syntax of a Simple Computer Language, Part II:*

Formalisation — Syntactic (Cartesian) Categories

type
    Pn, Ln, V, E
    $M' = (Pn \times Ln) \times$ P-set
    $M = \{| \ m{:}M \bullet wf\_M(m) \ |\}$
    $P = Pn \times (Ln \times S)$-set
    S = Asgn | Cond | Goto | Call | Exit
    $Asgn = \{"asgn"\} \times (V \times E) \times Ln$
    $Cond = \{"cond"\} \times (E \times Ln \times Ln)$
    $Goto = \{"goto"\} \times Ln$
    $Call = \{"call"\} \times (Pn \times Ln) \times Ln$
    $Exit = \{"exit"\}$

Annotations: (xiv) The wf_M subtyping predicate is hinted at in the narrative above. It is further narrated (See items (xv–xxix)), as well as also formally defined. (xv) The individual statements are "singled" out by the text markers' shown.

Formalisation — Well-formedness (of Cartesians)

value
    wf_M: $M' \rightarrow$ **Bool**
    wf_M((pn,ln),ps) $\equiv$
        wf_Call((pn,ln),ln)($\{ln\}$)(ps) $\land$ $\forall$ p:P $\bullet$ p $\in$ ps $\Rightarrow$ wf_P(p)(ps)

    wf_Call: $(Pn \times Ln) \times Ln \rightarrow$ Ln-set $\rightarrow$ Pn-set $\rightarrow$ **Bool**
    wf_Call((pn,ln),ℓ)(ls)(ps) $\equiv$
        $\ell \in$ ls $\land$ $\exists$! (pn',lss):P $\bullet$ (pn',lss) $\in$ ps $\land$ pn'=pn $\Rightarrow$ ln $\in$ labels(lss)

    wf_P: $Pn \times (Ln \times S)$-set $\rightarrow$ P-set $\rightarrow$ **Bool**
    wf_P(_,lss) $\equiv$
        let lns = labels(lss) **in**
        $\forall$ (ln,s):(Ln $\times$ S) $\bullet$ (ln,s) $\in$ lss $\Rightarrow$ wf_S(s)(lns)(ps) **end**

    labels: $(Ln \times S)$-set $\rightarrow$ Ln-set
    labels(lss) $\equiv$ { ln:Ln | (ln',s):(Ln $\times$ S) $\bullet$ (ln',s) $\in$ lss $\land$ ln'=ln }

A Detour: The RSL "case" Construct

Functions that apply to constructs that are values of a type which is a union of types usually need "to be able to *discriminate* between these values on the basis solely of their type". The following generic example illustrates the point being made:

type
    A, B
    $U = A \mid (U \times U) \mid (U \times U \times U) \mid ...$
value
    f: $U \to B$, g: $A \to B$, $\oplus$: $B \times B \to B$
    $f(u) \equiv$
        case u **of:**
            $(u',u'',u''') \to f(u')\oplus(f(u'')\oplus f(u'''))$
            $(u',u'') \to f(u')\oplus f(u'')$
            _ $\to$ g(u) **end**

The RSL **case** construct is here used in such a way as to first discriminate whether an argument value is a triple, then whether it is a pair, and finally the wildcard case, _, whether it is just a simple A value. Ignore the expressions to the right of the $\to$'s. The value of expression u of the infix **case of** operand — whose other operand is the list, from top to bottom, of the patterns — is compared, successively to elements of this (text vertical, top-to-bottom) list of patterns. When a fit can be made, then the value of the corresponding right-hand-side expression becomes the value of the **case** construct in the context of the fit.

    The RSL **case** construct has the general syntax and informal evaluation scheme:

    ⟨ case_clause ⟩ ::=
        case ⟨ value_expr ⟩ **of**
            ⟨ pattern ⟩ $\to$ ⟨ value_expr ⟩,
            ... ,
            ⟨ pattern ⟩ $\to$ ⟨ value_expr ⟩,
            _ $\to$ ⟨ value_expr ⟩
        end

where the wildcard line, _ $\to$ ⟨value_expr⟩, is optional. Evaluating the **case** construct proceeds as follows: First the ⟨value_expr⟩ of the "opening" **case** ⟨value_expr⟩ **of** line is evaluated. Let its value be v. Then v is attempted to be *fitted* to ⟨pattern⟩.

Cartesian Patterns

We explain the concept of *Cartesian pattern:* A *Cartesian pattern* is a grouping of two or more *constants* (i.e., literals), *identifiers* and *patterns.* (The value of v is correspondingly a Cartesian of two or more values.) We shall later introduce list, name and record patterns.

Cartesian Patterns, Fitting and Binding

We explain the concept of *Cartesian fitting*: A value fits a literal if it is equal to the designated literal value. Any value fits, and is *bound* to, a pattern identifier. The context, alluded to above is enriched by the mapping of the pattern identifier to the value.

If a pattern is a grouping of n elements (*constants, identifiers* or *patterns*) then v must be a Cartesian of n values. One-by-one a fit must be made between components of the pattern and of the value, "left to right". If all can be fitted, then a fit has been achieved. Component identifiers of the pattern are bound to corresponding component values — thus further enriching the context. We shall later introduce list, name and record fittings.

· · ·

If v can be fitted then the corresponding line's ⟨ value_expr ⟩ is evaluated in the enriched context, and its value is then the value of the entire **case** construct — whose evaluation is thereby ended. If v cannot be fitted, then the second line, ⟨ pattern ⟩ → ⟨ value_expr ⟩, is evaluated. And so forth, until either no fit has been made, or the optional, "catch-all" *wildcard* line, _ → ⟨ value_expr ⟩, is encountered. The value of its ⟨ value_expr ⟩, in this situation, becomes the value of the **case** construct.

Bindings (i.e., contexts) made during individual fit attempts are lost between attempts and upon termination of evaluation.

End of the RSL **case** *Construct Detour*

Example 14.6 *Syntax of a Simple Computer Language, Part III:* We are now ready to express statement well-formedness:

wf_S: S → Ln-set → P-set → **Bool**
wf_S(s)(lns)(ps) ≡
    case s **of**
        ("assign",(v,e),ℓ) → ℓ ∈ lns,
        ("cond",(e,ln,ln')) → {ln,ln'} ⊆ lns,
        ("goto",ln) → ln ∈ lns,
        ("call",(pn,ln),ℓ) →
            wf_Call((pn,ln),ℓ)(ps),
        "exit" → **true**
    end

Annotations: By syntactic well-formedness we mean that a larger syntactic category is constrained to a subtype. Later semantic functions assume syntactic well-formedness, i.e., that syntactic values lie within properly constrained subtypes. (xvi) wf_M: A program is well-formed if its intended invocation (i.e., call) is well-formed and if all of its defined procedures are well-formed *in the context of this syntactic set of procedures.* (xvii) wf_Call: A call is well-formed if its intended invocation names a program defined procedure and, within it, it labels a statement. (xviii) wf_P: A procedure is well-formed if all its contained statements are wellformed *in the context of the procedure statement labels and the program set of procedures.* (xix) wf_Asgn: An assignment statement is well-formed if its continuation label is defined, *i.e., is in the context of the (current) procedure's statement labels.* That is, we presently, in this simple example, ignore well-formedness of variables and expressions *in whatever context!* (xix) wf_Cond: A conditional statement is well-formed if the consequence and the alternative labels are defined, *i.e., in the context of the (current) procedure's statement labels.* (xx) wf_Goto: A goto statement is well-formed if its label is in the label set *context* component. (xxi) wf_Stop: A stop statement is always well-formed. (xxii) labels: The set of labels (label names) are yielded by this function.   ∎

14.4.2 Cartesian "let ... in ... end" Bindings

From Sections 13.2.3 and 14.2.1 onwards we have used set, respectively Cartesian patterns in the RSL **let ... in ... end** constructs. And as from Sect. 14.4.1 we defined Cartesian patterns. The purpose of this little injected paragraph is only to make sure that we are talking about the same linguistic idea introduced for the same pragmatic purpose: to *decompose* Cartesian values, i.e., to *fit* such to Cartesian patterns, and to *bind* pattern identifiers to the Cartesian value's component values. In later sections we have shall further introduce similar pattern constructs, and decomposition (i.e., fitting) and binding concepts for lists, maps, and other RSL constructs.

14.4.3 Modelling Semantic Structures

Example 14.7 *A Mechanical Semantics for the Simple Computer Language:*

Narrative — Semantic Types

Variables and storage. Variables designate values *"in the computer storage"*. To model this fact — and given that we have so far only "officially" learned about sets and Cartesians as the only structured values — we model storage as a set of variable-value associations. A variable-value association is a pair consisting of a variable and a value. No two otherwise distinct associations of a computer storage have the same variable part and different value parts.

On intuition and concept analysis. We rely on your intuition of what is normally understood by the anthropomorphic term *program execution*, namely: computer processing of programs. We are about to systematically describe the notion of such concepts as processing of programs as data. But first we need some intuition and some analysis of the concepts resulting from such intuition.

A piece of good advice is to always start a systematic narration by the enunciation of intuitions and their analyses.

Program Points

At any point during execution, the computer is interpreting a specific statement of a specific procedure. We can thus model a program point by the pair of procedure name and statement label, respectively.

Termination of the interpretation of most statements occurs with the establishment of the next program point, which is that of the present procedures' name and the designated statement continuation label. Invocation of procedures, i.e., the interpretation of the "called" procedure, when finished, must "return" to end the interpretation of the calling statement, which is that of continuing with that calling statement's designated continuation statement.

The effect of statement interpretation is generally to change the computer state. But what exactly is this state — which we shall henceforth call a configuration? Well, for one, it must include some variable value associations so that we can update variable values as a result of assignment statement interpretation, and find these values during expression evaluation. Then we must somehow record the current and next program point. Since invocation of procedures may be indefinitely "nested", we may expect some sort of stacking and un-stacking of program points.

To express the meaning of a program we therefore introduce the notion of a configuration.

Configurations

A configuration is a pair consisting of a program pointer stack and a storage.

Program Pointer Stacks

The program pointer stack is either void, modelled here as the character string "empty", or is a pair whose first element is a program pointer, i.e., a pair consisting of a procedure name and a statement label, and whose other element is a program pointer stack.

Formalisation — Semantic Types

type
  VAL
  STG$'$ = (V × VAL)-**set**
  Σ = {| stg:STG$'$ • wf_STG(stg) |}
  Θ = {$''$empty$''$} | ((Pn×Ln) × Θ)
value
  wf_STG: STG$'$ → **Bool**
  wf_STG(stg) ≡
    $\forall$ (v,val),(v$'$,val$'$):(V×VAL) •
        {(v,val),(v$'$,val$'$)} ⊆ stg ⇒ (v=v$'$ ⇒ val=val$'$)

VAL is the semantic type of values.

Narrative — Computer Program Interpretation

Let ((pn,ln),ps) be the program. Computer program interpretation starts with
a possibly empty storage and a void program pointer stack. Computer program
interpretation then goes on to stack the pair (pn,ln) on top of the program
pointer stack. Now the interpreter enters an indefinite sequence of statement
interpretations. Each statement interpretation starts by identifying the procedure and statement being interpreted. This is done on the basis of the top
element of the program pointer stack. Then it interprets this statement.

If it is an assignment statement then an appropriate expression evaluation
takes place and storage is updated for the given variable. Then the top program point has its label component changed to reflect the continuation. If it is
a conditional statement an appropriate test expression evaluation takes place
first. Then the top program point has its label component changed to reflect
the continuation: If the test expression value yielded is **true** the consequence
label is chosen, otherwise the alternative. Etcetera. We leave it to the reader
to decipher the formalisation that follows!

Formalisation — Semantic Functions

value
  int_M: M $\overset{\sim}{\rightarrow}$ Σ
  int_M((pn,ln),ps) ≡ int_S((pn,ln),$''$empty$''$)({})(ps)

  int_S: Θ → Σ → P-**set** → Σ
  val_E: Expr → Σ → VAL

Interpreting the program is the same as interpreting a statement with the
program program point (of the only program pointer stack element) and with
an empty storage.

int_S and val_E name the operational statement interpretation, respectively the simple expression evaluation functions.

int_S$(\theta')(\sigma)$(ps) $\equiv$
    case θ' **of**
        $''$empty$''$ $\to \sigma$,
        $((pn,ln),\theta) \to$
            let s = find_S(ln)(find_P(pn)(ps)) **in**
            case s **of**
                $(''$assign$'',(v,e),\ell) \to$
                    let val = val_E(e)(σ) **in**
                    let σ' = update(v,val)(σ) **in**
                    int_S$((pn,\ell),\theta)(\sigma')$(ps) **end end**,
                $(''$cond$'',(e,ln,ln')) \to$
                    let test = val_E(e)(σ) **in**
                    let ℓ = **if** test **then** ln **else** ln$'$ **end in**
                    int_S$((pn,\ell),\theta)(\sigma)$(ps) **end end**,
                $(''$goto$'',ln') \to$
                    int_S$((pn,ln'),\theta)(\sigma)$(ps),
                $(''$call$'',(pn',ln'),\ell) \to$
                    Int_S$((pn',ln'),((pn,\ell),\sigma))(\sigma)$(ps),
                $''$exit$''$ $\to$ Int_S$(\theta)(\sigma)$(ps)
    end end end

Observe how an exit prescribes procedure termination.

value
    update: V $\times$ VAL $\to \Sigma \to \Sigma$
    update(v,val)(σ) $\equiv$
        let (v',val'):(V$\times$VAL) $\bullet$ v=v$'\wedge(v',val') \in \sigma$ **in**
        $\sigma \setminus \{(v,val')\} \cup \{(v,val)\}$ **end**

    find_P: Pn $\to$ P-set $\to$ (Ln $\times$ S)-set
    find_P(pn)(ps) $\equiv$
        let (pn$'$,lss):(Pn$\times$(Ln$\times$S)-set) $\bullet$ (pn$'$,lss) $\in$ ps $\wedge$ pn=pn$'$ **in** lss **end**
        assert: /* predicate true; guaranteed by wf_M */

    find_S: Ln $\to$ (Ln$\times$S)-set $\to$ S
    find_S(ln)(lss) $\equiv$
        let (ln$'$,s):(Ln$\times$S)-set $\bullet$ (ln$'$,s) $\in$ lss $\wedge$ ln=ln$'$ **in** s **end**

We remind the reader that the above example is not an example of abstraction, but only of modelling. In Chap. 20 we shall show what we mean by more proper abstractions of storage, stacks, and contexts (environments), as well as of the semantic interpretation functions.

14.4.4 Cartesians: A First Discussion

Before going on to distill some of the essence of the above examples wrt. Cartesian abstraction and modelling principles, techniques and tools, what can we otherwise, so far, conclude from this section of Cartesian abstraction and modelling examples? We can conclude that the introduction of Cartesians is essentially based on a pragmatic desire to group things in two or more components — as somehow belonging together. And that since we wished to thus compose one kind, i.e., one type, of values as, say, pairs, to group other kinds, i.e., another type, of values as, say, triples, etc., was not far behind! Hence we arrived at the need for (i) *union types*, the **case ... of ... end** construct (known also as the McCarthy conditional), the *pattern* construct and hence the related *fitting* and *binding* concepts.

14.5 Inductive Cartesian Definitions

14.5.1 Inductive Cartesian Type Definitions

Suppose we wanted to define:

type
    C = C × C

What would that mean? Well, I do not know! Somehow I can not get started on enumerating Cartesian elements of C. The problem is, that there is no "boot strap". So we introduce a "boot strap", B, and a means of terminating the recursion:

type
    B
    C = BorC × BorC
    BorC == mkB(sb:B) | mkC(sc:C)

The alternative boc:BorC can be either a b:B or a mkc:mkC(c1,c2). B is assumed not to contain c:BorCs. And now we can suggest the following set of type C value:

$$\mathcal{C}\text{: } \{(b,b')|b,b':B\} \cup \{(c',c'')|c',c'':BorC \bullet \{c',c''\}\subseteq\mathcal{C}\}$$

We remind the reader that the above definition of $\mathcal{C}$ was a definition in mathematics, not a definition in RSL.

That looks fine, so we conclude:

Recursive definitions of Cartesians must have built into them a variant, a "boot strap". The variant serves to get the generation of proper Cartesian values started, and serves also to stop an infinite regression.

14.5.2 Inductive Cartesian Value Definitions

Example 14.8 *Cartesian and Set-Based Model of Networks:* We rephrase
the solution of Example 13.12.

We introduce a concept of path. A path is a triple of a connector identifier,
c_{i_1}, a segment identifier, s_i, and a connector identifier, c_{i_2}, such that the
two distinct connector identifiers $\{c_{i_1} c_{i_2}\}$, are the connector identifiers of the
segment identified by s_i.

A route is now a set of paths such that either there is just one path in the
route, or for more than one path in the route there is an end[3] segment, that
is, a segment one of whose connector identifiers is not is not one of another
segment in the path, such that the other connector identifier of that end
segment is one of another segment of the path, and such that the remaining
path is well-formed.

type
　　$P' = Ci \times Si \times Ci$
　　$P = \{| \ p{:}P' \bullet \exists \ n{:}N \bullet wfP(p)(n) \ |\}$
value
　　wfP: $P' \to N \to$ **Bool**
　　$wfP(ci1,si,ci2)(n) \equiv \exists \ s{:}S \bullet s \in obs\_Ss(n) \wedge \{ci1,ci2\}=obs\_Cis(s) \wedge si=obs\_Si(s)$

Notice that we must indicate some net in the context of which we can express
well-formedness of paths. From a net we can generate the set of all paths:

　　gen_Ps: $N \to$ **P-set**
　　$gen\_Ps(n) \equiv \{ \ p \mid p{:}P' \bullet wfP(p)(n) \ \}$

Now we can define routes:

type
　　$R' =$ **P-set**
　　$R = \{| \ r{:}R' \bullet wfR(r) \ |\}$

value
　　Ci_deg: $Ci \times R' \to$ **Nat**
　　$Ci\_deg(ci,r) \equiv \mathbf{card}\{(ci',si,ci'')|(ci',si,ci''){:}P \bullet (ci',si,ci'') \in r \wedge ci \in \{ci',ci''\}\}$

　　$wfR(r) \equiv$
　　　　$\mathbf{card} \ r = 1 \ \vee$
　　　　$\exists \ ci,ci'{:}Ci,si{:}Si \bullet (ci,si,ci') \in r \ \wedge$
　　　　　　$Ci\_deg(ci,r) = 1 \wedge Ci\_deg(ci',r) = 2 \wedge wfR(r \backslash \{(ci,si,ci')\})$

　　　　　　　　　　　　　　　　　　　　　　　　　　　　　　　　　■

The next example illustrates recursive value definition.

Example 14.9 *Transitive Closure:* We introduce a concept of line. That concept of line is an extension of the concept of path. Where a path is just a Cartesian encoding of one of the ways through a segment in the form of a triple: the segment identifier (say in the middle) and the identities of the from and to connectors at respective ends of the segment, a line is a similar Cartesian encoding of the transitive closure over paths. Since we arbitrarily decided that paths be identified also by their segment identifiers we have to construct new unique segment identifiers for lines.

A line, ℓ, is a triple: $(\ell_{c_{fst}}, \ell nm, \ell_{c_{lst}})$, of two line connector identifiers (a first and a last connector identifier), and a line name. A path, (c_{i_1}, s_i, c_{i_2}), is a line. In (c_{i_1}, s_i, c_{i_2}) c_{i_1} and c_{i_2}, respectively, are the first and last connector identifiers, and s_i is the line identifier (or name). If ℓ and ℓ' are lines: $(\ell_{c_{fst}}, \ell n_j, \ell_{c_i})$ and $(\ell_{c_i}, \ell n_k, \ell_{c_{lst}})$ such that the last connector identifier of ℓ, ℓ_{c_i}, is also the first connector identifier of ℓ' then $(\ell_{c_{fst}}, \text{comp}(\ell n_j, \ell n_k), \ell_{c_{lst}})$ is a line. comp is a function which composes distinct segment identifiers into unique segment identifiers. decomp is the inverse of comp:

value
    comp: Si × Si → Si
    decomp: Si → Si × Si
axiom
    $\forall$ si,si':Si • si≠si' $\Rightarrow$ decomp(comp(si,si'))=(si,si')

If, in a network, there is a path (i.e., a line) from the connector identified by c_f to the connector identified by c_i, and another connector identified by c_i to the connector identified by c_t, then in the transitive closure (wrt., lines) of that network we say that there is a line from connector c_f to connector c_t. More generally, if in a network there is a line from the connector identified by c_f to the connector identified by c_i, and from the other connector identified by c_i to the connector identified by c_t, then, in the transitive closure (wrt., lines) of that network we say that there is a line from the connector identified by c_f to the connector identified by c_t. Thus the concept of line is almost similar to the concept of path. Given a network we can compute its transitive closure wrt. lines.

type
    L = Ci × Si × Ci
value
    closure: N → L-set
    closure(n) ≡
        let ps = gen_Ps(n) **in**
        let clo = ps ∪ {(cf,comp(sf,st),ct) |
                    (cf,sf,ci),(ci',st,ct):L•{(cf,sf,ci),(ci',st,ct)}⊆clo∧ci=ci'} **in**
        clo **end end**

We assume that nets are finite, that is, that their numbers of segments and connectors are finite. Hence the set clo is finite.

closure expresses its result, clo, inductively. Think of solving the recursive equation clo = ps ∪ { (cf,comp(sf,st),ct) | (cf,sf,ci),(ci′,st,ct):L • {(cf,sf,ci),(ci′,st,ct)}⊆clo ∧ ci=ci′} iteratively. Initially there is just the contribution of ps to clo. In a second iteration the clo in the body of the set comprehension is ps, so it now contributes to forming lines that span two paths. For each iteration, i, lines that span i paths are generated. At some iteration, n, where n is at most the number of connections in the network (i.e., nodes in a graph), no more lines are contributed to clo. The recursive equation in clo is solved: the smallest set, γ, has been found such that when replacing clo by γ in the equation it satisfies that equation. γ is a fix point solution to the equation.[4]

∎

14.6 Discussion

14.6.1 General

We have outlined the Cartesian data type. And we have tried to (i) enunciate principles for when to deploy Cartesian abstraction, to (ii) list some of the techniques that follow from such a choice and (iii) to identify some of the Cartesian abstraction specification language tools today available. Cartesians constitute "another basic workhorse" of model-oriented abstraction and modelling. We shall later see how the record data type extends, and enriches the simple concept of Cartesians brought forward in the present chapter.

14.6.2 Principles, Techniques and Tools

Principles. *Cartesians:* If and when a model-oriented abstraction has been chosen, then Cartesian abstraction is chosen if the following characteristics can be identified as properties of the phenomenon or concept being modelled: (i) The abstract structure of the composite components being modelled consists of an ordered collection of not necessarily uniquely named, but otherwise distinct subcomponents (constituent phenomena or concepts); (ii) whose number is fixed, i.e., constant; (iii) where one may thus decompose into constituent such subphenomena, respectively subconcepts; and (iv) where a need to express the composition into the overall abstraction occurs naturally.   ∎

Principles. *Cartesians:* We mention, at this early stage in these volumes, two specific principles of when to choose Cartesians as a basis for abstract

---

[4]Since, in RSL, we must reckon with nondeterminism, that is, many models of our specifications, the semantics of RSL is designed to allow all fix points of recursive definitions.

modelling. (v) *Semantic configurations* are usually compositions of semantic concepts referred to as configurations: contexts and states, treated in Vol. 2, Chap. 4. Configurations are typically modelled as Cartesians. This was already enunciated above, under General Principles. We also refer to Example 14.7 (specifically 'Configuration'). (vi) *Syntactic Structures:* Compositions of syntactic concepts are "classically" modelled as Cartesians. This was amply illustrated in Examples 14.4–14.6. We shall often illustrate the deployment of the above specific principles.   ∎

Techniques. *Cartesians:* We refer to initial paragraphs of Sect. 14.4, for a listing of some of the techniques (1–4) used when abstracting using Cartesians. More specifically, just a few Cartesian-oriented techniques are offered: (vii) observer functions occassionally "extract" groupings (i.e., Cartesians). (viii) Otherwise the simple, explicit, parenthesised grouping expressions serve to express composition, (ix) and the simple **let**-style decomposition clauses serve to express analysis into components.   ∎

Tools. *Cartesians:* If abstraction and modelling using the Cartesian data type has been chosen, then the tool can either be the RSL, the VDM-SL, the Z or, for example, the B specification language.   ∎

14.7 Exercises

Exercise 14.1. *Simple Cartesian Types.* This exercise helps to develop your skills in manipulating Cartesians. It is not one of abstraction.

1. List the elements of
   (a) **Bool×Bool** and
   (b) **Bool×Bool×Bool**.
2. List some of the elements of **Nat×Bool**

Exercise 14.2. *Set Representations of General Cartesian Pairs.* We refer to Example 14.3. In that example all **A** elements we assumed distinct — yet no well-formedness predicate was defined for checking that. If two elements of a simple pair, (a, a), are identical then the assumed set representation $\{a, \{a, a\}\}$ "collapses" into $\{a, \{a\}\}$. Now, accepting this, that is, accepting non-distinct **A** elements, redefine the functions P2S and S2P, etcetera.

Exercise 14.3. *Lisp-like Lists.* A pair can model a simple list of two ordered elements: $(a, b) = \langle a, b \rangle$. A list of three elements $\langle a, b, c \rangle$ can be modelled as the pair $(a, (b, c))$, and so forth: $\langle a, b, c, d \rangle = (a, (b, (c, d)))$, etc. To complete the description of these, as we shall call them, "pair lists", we allow for the empty list, (), and the list of just one element, (a).

1. Formalise the type of "pair lists".

2. Define the operations of
   (a) Creating an empty "pair list",
   (b) checking that a "pair list" is empty,
   (c) concatenating simple elements to the front, respectively back of a "pair list",
   (d) obtaining the first, respectively the last, (simple elements) of a "pair list",
   (e) obtaining the list of all simple elements of a "pair list", but the first, respectively the last.

Exercise 14.4. *Binary, Sorted and Balanced Trees.* This exercise helps to finally develop your skills in manipulating Cartesians — while also introducing you to the important computing science notions of *binary, sorted and balanced trees.* It is not one of abstraction.

A binary tree consists of a root and left and right subtrees. A subtree is either a leaf or a binary tree. Roots consists of pairs of integers (the root index) and text. A leaf is a root (thus with a leaf index). (Texts are considered not to contain integers!) A tree is sorted (or ordered) if the integer of the left subtree root is less than the integer of the tree root, and if the integer of the right subtree root is larger than the integer of the tree root.

1. Define the type of binary trees.
2. Define the type of sorted binary trees.

The next concepts are defined only for ordered (i.e., sorted) binary trees.

Let t be a proper, non-leaf tree and $(\ell t, (i, \tau), rt)$ its representation. If ℓt is a proper tree, $(\ell\ell t, j, r\ell t)$, then (i, j) is a branch of t, and $\{(i,j)\}$ is a path of length 1 in t. If ℓ is a leaf, (k, τ), then (i, k) is a branch, etc. If p is a path of proper tree ℓt, then $\{(i, j)\} \cup p$ is a path of t. The empty path is modelled by the empty set $\{\}$. It is always a path of any tree: from its root to itself!

3. Define the type of the above sketched trees.
4. Argue, i.e., reason informally, that if a tree is sorted, then a nonempty path contains of a set of integers of cardinality one higher than the number of pairs in the path.
5. Argue also that if the path set contains two or more branches then for any branch (i, j) one can find exactly one other branch $(j, \_)$, where the wildcard "$\_$" stands for some integer.
6. Argue, finally, that if a tree is sorted, then the cardinality of a path denotes its length.

A binary tree t is balanced if all paths from the root of t to its proper leaves differ by at most one.

7. Define the type of trees sketched above.
8. Define functions which generate the set of all paths of a tree, which compute the length of a path, the maximum depth of a tree: the length of its longest path, and the set of all root indexes of a tree.

9. Define predicates which tests whether a binary tree as defined is sorted, respectively balanced.

A binary tree path traversal is a visit to the nodes of a tree in one of any six ways: pre-order, postorder or in-order; and either left-to-right or right-to-left. In a left-to-right traversal of any tree, left subtrees are visited before right subtrees of that tree. In a pre-order roots of subtrees are visited when first encountered. For post-order, they are visited when last encountered. For in-order, they are visited when encountered after the first traversal of a subtree. Encountering means: A traversal of any tree "starts" at the root of that tree. Then it encounters that tree's root first time. After having visited, say, the left subtree, if any, it reverts to "that root", for the second time, and again reverts to it, for the last time when it has traversed the other (here the right subtree).

10. Define six functions
    (a) pre-ltr, pre-order, left-to-right
    (b) in-ltr, in-order, left-to-right
    (c) pst-ltr, post-order, left-to-right
    (d) pre-rtl, pre-order, right-to-left
    (e) in-rtl, in-order, right-to-left
    (f) pst-rtl, post-order, right-to-left
    which each yields the text of roots during the respective traversals

Exercise 14.5. *Simple Expression Language.* This exercise is not one of abstraction, but only of modelling. It is included in order to show you how little we need in order to tackle seemingly complex structures.

We refer to Examples 14.4–14.6 and 14.7. Those examples referred to an expression language and its evaluation. This exercise is about that expression language!

We narrate

(a) first the syntax of the simple expression language,
(b) then the semantic types,
(c) and finally how expressions can be evaluated.

(a) **Syntactic categories:** An expression is either a [i] constant, a [ii] variable, a [iii] prefix, an [iv] infix or a [v] suffix expression. [i] A constant is either a Boolean or a real number. [ii] A variable is a further un-analysed quantity. [iii] A prefix expression is a pair consisting of a [vi] prefix operator and an expression. [iv] An infix expression is a triple consisting of two expressions and an [vii] infix operator. A [v] suffix expression is a pair consisting of an expression and a [viii] suffix operator. Operators are simple text strings. The following are [vi] prefix operators: "negation" and "minus". The following are [vii] infix operators: "and", "or", "imply", "add", "subtract", "multiply" and "division". The following is the only [viii] suffix operator: "factorial".

1. Define the types of the above-sketched syntactic categories.

(b) **Semantic types**: [ix] The value of an expression is either a Boolean or a real. [x] A state is needed to evaluate an expression containing variables. A state is here considered to be a set of pairs of variables and their values. No two otherwise distinct state pairs have the same first variable component.

2. Define the types of the above-sketched semantic categories.

(c) **Expression evaluation**: To evaluate an expression the evaluator takes two arguments: a syntactic and a semantic, i.e., an expression and a state. [i] A constant expression has the value of the constant. [ii] A variable expression has the value by which it is recorded in the state. If it is not recorded then the **chaos** value is yielded. Pre-, in- and suffix expressions first have their operand expression values evaluated. [iii] If the prefix operator of a prefix expression is "negation", then the value is the negation of the operand expression value — which is assumed to be a Boolean, otherwise **chaos** is yielded, etc. [iv] The value of an infix expression is the conjunction of the operand expression values if the infix operator is "and", etc. Operators "and", "or" and "imply" require Boolean values, otherwise **chaos** is yielded, etc. Division by zero yields **chaos.** [v] The value of a suffix expression is the factorial of the operand expression value (real) if the suffix operator is "factorial" .

"Etc." above means: Please add the "missing" narration.

3. Define the semantic expression evaluation function.

Observe that evaluation dynamically tests operand values. And observe that all functions are strict.

Exercise 14.6. ♣ *Cartesians in the Transportation Net Domain:* We refer to Appendix A, Sect. A.1, *Transportation Net.* We also refer to Exercise 13.5.

Define the Cartesian types of as many phenomena and concepts in the *Transportation Net* domain that you think should be so modelled.

Exercise 14.7. ♣ *Cartesians in the Container Logistics Domain.* We refer to Appendix A, Sect. A.2, *Container Logistics.* We also refer to Exercise 13.6.

Define the Cartesian types of as many phenomena and concepts in the *Container Logistics* domain that you think should be so modelled.

Exercise 14.8. ♣ *Cartesians in the Financial Service Industry Domain.* We refer to Appendix A, Sect. A.3, *Financial Service Industry.* We also refer to Exercise 13.7.

Define the Cartesian types of as many phenomena and concepts in the *Financial Service Industry* domain that you think should be so modelled.

15

Lists in RSL

- The **prerequisite** for studying this chapter is that you possess knowledge of the mathematical concepts of sets and Cartesians as introduced in earlier chapters.
- The **aims** are to introduce the RSL abstract data type of lists: The type, the values, and enumeration and comprehension forms of expressing lists, and to illustrate the expressiveness of lists by illustrating simple and not so simple examples of phenomena and concepts that can be modelled in terms of lists.
- The **objective** is to set the reader free to choose lists as models of phenomena and concept entities, when appropriate, and to not choose lists when doing so is not appropriate.
- The **treatment** is semiformal and systematic.

> For so work the honey-bees,
> creatures that by a rule in nature,
> teach the act of order.
>
> *William Shakespeare, 1564–1616 [412]*
> *King Henry the IV, Part V, Chorus, ii, 163*

> The only liberty I mean,
> is a liberty connected with order;
> that not only exists along with order and virtue,
> but which cannot exist at all without them.
>
> *E. Burke, 1729–1797 [412]*
> *Speech at his arrival at Bristol, 13 Oct. 1774*

Characterisation. *List:* By a *list* we shall mean the same as by a *sequence*, or *tuple:* an ordered, i.e., an indexed (or indexable), grouping of zero, one or more — not necessarily distinct entities — all being of a common type, i.e., of a type that can be named. Furthermore, for the "thing" to be classified as a list it must be meaningful to speak of such list operations as the head, **hd,**

the tail, **tl,** the distinct elements, **elems,** the set of all the indices, **inds,** the **length,** and of selecting an i'th element of a list $\ell(i)$, of concatenating, ⌢, two lists, and of inquiring whether two lists are equal (not equal), $=(\neq)$.   ∎

15.1 Issues Related to Lists

The idea to be illustrated in this section is that of the use of the discrete mathematics concept of lists in abstracting domain, requirements and software phenomena and concepts. Other terms used in lieu of lists are: sequences or tuples. Lists offer themselves as an abstraction when a component q can best be characterised as an "ordered set", a "variable-sized" (i.e., "flexible") arrangement $\langle a, b, \ldots, c \rangle$ of possibly "repeated" components. Sets, Cartesians and lists, as such, as the only model-oriented (i.e., discrete mathematical) "devices" to "deploy" in abstraction, is a sign of some frugality. But it is, in most cases, better, we claim, than just sets! As a programming data type lists go a long way!

We refer to the axiom system given for simple lists in Example 9.24 (as from Page 193).

This chapter is, as are Chaps. 13–17, built up as follows:

- The list data type   (Sect. 15.2)
- Examples of list-based abstractions   (Sect. 15.3)
- Abstracting and modelling with lists   (Sect. 15.4)
- Inductive list definitions   (Sect. 15.5)
- A review of list abstractions and models   (Sect. 15.6)

There are many examples because *before one can write good specifications one must have read and studied many example specifications.* While you may not need to study all of them now, you can return to some later. The chapter ends with a brief discussion.

15.2 The List Data Type

We have already, in Chapter 9's Example 9.24 (Pages 193–194) covered the mathematical notion of simple lists by presenting an axiom system for lists. We urge the reader to first recall that definition.

15.2.1 List Types

Let A stand for a type whose possibly infinite number of elements include $\{a_1, a_2, \ldots, a_n, \ldots\}$.

Types whose values can be considered finite, respectively finite or infinite lists of A elements can be defined using the suffix * and $^\omega$ type operators, respectively:

type	examples
A	$\{a,a1,a2,...,am,...\}$
$F = A^*$	$\{\langle\rangle, \langle a\rangle, ..., \langle a1,a2,...,am\rangle, ...\}$
$L = A^\omega$	$\{\langle\rangle, \langle a\rangle, ..., \langle a1,a2,...,am\rangle, ..., \langle a1,a2,...,am,... \rangle, ...\}$

We refer to examples above right. They correspond, line for line, to the sort, finite list, respectively infinite list type definitions above left.

The expressions A^* and A^ω are *list type expressions*

Example 15.1 *A Simple List Example:* Let fact name the factorial function, then

$$\langle \text{ fact}(1),\text{fact}(2),\text{fact}(3),\text{fact}(4),\text{fact}(5),\text{fact}(6) \rangle$$

expresses a simple list of six elements, the first six factorials!   ∎

15.2.2 List Value Expressions

Lists are finite or infinite, ordered aggregations of not necessarily distinct individuals. Lists are considered variable-sized, or flexible in that the number of their elements may vary.[1] One list may contain 0 elements (the empty list $\langle\rangle$). Another list may contain just one element (singleton lists $\langle a_i\rangle$, $\langle a_j\rangle$, ..., $\langle a_k\rangle$). And so forth. A given (say, finite) list, of course, has a specific length. But one may form another list from two lists forming a list with cardinality the sum of the two lengths. Or one may remove an element from a non-empty list forming a list with length one lower. All this while the list value remains of some given type.

List Enumerations

Let e, e1, e2, ..., en[2] be expressions that deterministically or nondeterministically evaluate to not necesarily distinct values (v, v1, v2, ..., vn) of some type A, and let ei, ej be expressions which deterministically or nondeterministically evaluate to integer values, say vi, vj, then the following are examples of *list value expressions*, in particular *list enumerations*, respectively a *ranged list expression*:

---

[1] We refer to Footnote 1 and to Sect. 13.6 for a clarification of what we mean by variable-sized, flexible and vary.

[2] We remind the reader that in the rest of these volumes we shall use the following naming convention: Identifiers starting with e (and often "suffixed" or indexed (subscripted) by some alphanumeric characters) stand for *expressions*. Identifiers starting with v (and often suffixed or indexed (subscripted) by some alphanumeric characters) stand for *values*. Values are definite, in the sense that a value is a specific thing. Expressions may be constant expressions, i.e., evaluate, in any context (and state) to one and the same value, or expressions may be variable expressions, i.e., evaluate, in different contexts (and states) to different values.

⟨⟩, ⟨e⟩, ..., ⟨e1,e2,...,en⟩
⟨ ei .. ej ⟩

The first line, left to right, denotes the single model of the empty list of no elements, a set of models of singleton lists of one element values (any value will do!), etc., ..., respectively a set of models of lists, all of n, not necessarily distinct, element values. The second line list expression denotes a set of models, each being a list of successive integers lying between, and inclusive, vi and vj. If vi>vj, then the integer list is empty.

For each model the above expressions have a specific, value — that may be nondeterministic for reasons not immediate from the above, cf. Sect. 12.4.4.

Syntactically an extended BNF grammar for the explicit list expressions follows:

<exp_list_enum> ::=
        <sim_list_enum>
        | <list_rang>
<sim_list_enum> ::=
        ⟨ <val_expr> , ... , <val_expr> ⟩
<list_rang> ::=
        ⟨ <val_expr> .. <val_expr> ⟩

The list comma-separated list of value expressions may be empty, or just have one element — in which case there are no separating commas.

Please observe the distinction between the ⟨'s and ⟩'s — serving as list pointed brackets, i.e., as terminal symbols — and <'s and >'s serving as BNF grammar delimiters.

Later we shall show an implicit enumeration of list values in the form of list comprehension (i.e., comprehended list expressions).

List Value Operator/Operand Expressions

We first present the list operator/operand expressions semi-formally, only explaining the operator meanings informally. Then we informally explain these meanings operationally.

Operator Signatures and Informal Meaning:

In general, a number of operators can be used to inspect properties of list values, respectively "construct" list values:

value
    hd: $A^\omega \overset{\sim}{\to} A$
    tl: $A^\omega \overset{\sim}{\to} A^\omega$
    len: $A^\omega \overset{\sim}{\to}$ **Nat**
    inds: $A^\omega \to$ **Nat-infset**
    elems: $A^\omega \to$ A-**infset**
    .(.): $A^\omega \times$ **Nat** $\overset{\sim}{\to} A$
    ⁀: $A^* \times A^\omega \to A^\omega$
    =: $A^\omega \times A^\omega \to$ **Bool**
    ≠: $A^\omega \times A^\omega \to$ **Bool**

examples /∗ the a, b, c, d: are values ∗/
    hd⟨a1,a2,...,am⟩=a1
    tl⟨a1,a2,...,am⟩=⟨a2,...,am⟩
    len⟨a1,a2,...,am⟩=m
    inds⟨a1,a2,...,am⟩={1,2,...,m}
    elems⟨a1,a2,...,am⟩={a1,a2,...,am}
    ⟨a1,a2,...,am⟩(i)=ai
    ⟨a,b,c⟩⁀⟨a,b,d⟩ = ⟨a,b,c,a,b,d⟩
    ⟨a,b,c⟩=⟨a,b,c⟩
    ⟨a,b,c⟩ ≠ ⟨a,b,d⟩

We refer to finite lists only examples above right. They correspond, line for line, to the operation signatures above left.

Operational, Informal Definition of List Operations:

Although we have already introduced lists, axiomatically, in Example 9.24 (as from Page 193), we shall now present another "definition", an operational one. As such it is basically bound to fail since we wish to deal also with infinite lists and we cannot meaningfully speak of the length of an infinite list. Let us anyway try — thereby stepping outside the realm, for a moment, of formally correct formulations. **chaos** is yielded for the length of an infinite list.

    Relying on the longish annotation of the RSL set data type (Sect. 13.2.2 on page 268) we can now bring a shorter, informal description of the RSL list data type.

    The list operators (i–v) **hd, tl, len, inds** and **elems** express (i) yielding the head element of non-empty lists, (ii) yielding the list of list elements other than the head of the argument list (also only of non-empty lists), (iii) the length of a finite list, (iv) the index set, from 1 to the length of the list (which may be empty in which case the index set is also empty, or may be infinite, in which case the result is **chaos**), and (v) the possibly infinite set of all distinct elements of the list. (vi) Indexing with a natural number, i, larger than 0 into a list larger than or equal to i yields its i'th element. (vii) ⁀ concatenates its two operand lists into one list, first the elements of the first, finite length operand list, and then the elements of the second, possibly infinite length operand list, and in their respective order. (viii–ix) = and ≠ compares two operand lists for equality, element-by-element, respectively for the occurrence of at least one deviation!

    We now informally define the meaning of the list operators model-theoretically. Not in RSL, but in some "similar" mathematical notation which is assumed understood.

    hd (head) and **tl** (tail) are assumed primitive operations. So is is_finite_list.

value
    is_finite_list: $A^\omega \to$ **Bool**

len q ≡
  case is_finite_list(q) **of**
    true → **if** q = ⟨⟩ **then** 0 **else** 1 + **len tl** q **end**,
    false → **chaos end**

inds q ≡
  case is_finite_list(q) **of**
    true → { i | i:**Nat** • 1 ≤ i ≤ **len** q },
    false → { i | i:**Nat** • i≠0 } **end**

elems q ≡ { q(i) | i:**Nat** • i ∈ **inds** q }

q(i) ≡
  if i=1
    then if q≠⟨⟩ **then let** a:A,q':Q • q=⟨a⟩^q' **in** a **end else chaos end**
    else q(i−1) **end**

fq ^ iq ≡
  ⟨ **if** 1 ≤ i ≤ **len** fq **then** fq(i) **else** iq(i − **len** fq) **end**
    | i:**Nat** • **if len** iq≠**chaos then** i ≤ **len** fq+**len end** ⟩
  pre is_finite_list(fq)

iq' = iq'' ≡ **inds** iq' = **inds** iq'' ∧ ∀ i:**Nat** • i ∈ **inds** iq' ⇒ iq'(i) = iq''(i)
iq' ≠ iq'' ≡ ~(iq' = iq'')

Notice (i) that we have made use of an undefined predicate: is_finite_list which applies to both finite and infinite lists; (ii) that **len** is defined both recursively and in terms of **tl** — for infinite lists that wouldn't work: instead we rely on **len** q = **chaos**; (iii) that **inds** is defined in terms of **len** for finite lists, otherwise it is just the non-zero natural numbers; (iv) that **elems** is defined in terms of **inds**; (v) that ^ is defined in terms **len**; and (vi) that = is defined in terms of **inds**.

List Comprehension

List comprehension, in general, usually applies to a list, l, of elements of type, say A. Comprehension then results in a list, say, of type B elements.

These latter elements, q(l(i)), derive from such l elements, l(i), which satisfy some predicate, p(l(i)). The order of the resulting elements, q(l(i)) follows the natural ordering of indices (i) **in** the given range expression.

Example 15.2 *A Simple List Example:* Let fact name the factorial function, then

⟨ fact(i) | i **in** ⟨1..6⟩ ⟩

expresses a simple list of six elements, the first six factorials!   ∎

type
    A, B, P = A → **Bool**, Q = A $\overset{\sim}{\to}$ B
value
    comprehend: A^ω × P × Q $\overset{\sim}{\to}$ B^ω
    comprehend(lst,$\mathcal{P}$,$\mathcal{Q}$) ≡
      ⟨ $\mathcal{Q}$(lst(i)) | i **in** ⟨1..**len** lst⟩ • $\mathcal{P}$(lst(i)) ⟩

The text $\mathcal{P}$(lst(i)) need not be an invocation of a predication function, but can be any Boolean value expression. It must, however, be deterministic in order to evaluate to **true.** The text $\mathcal{Q}$(lst(i)) can similarly be any expression, even a nondeterministic one. Nondeterminism gives rise to the list comprehension expression denoting several models. We use comprehended list expressions when we wish to implicitly specify (i.e., 'implicate'), possibly infinite, lists, characterised by some $\mathcal{P}$ and some $\mathcal{Q}$.

    List comprehension, as does set and map comprehension, expresses a form of 'homomorphic' principle: Functions over composite structures being expressed as a(nother) function over the (first) function applied to all immediate constituents of the composite structure. We refer to Sect. 8.4.4 on page 132 for a first enunciation of the homomorphism concept.

    The general syntactic form of comprehended list expressions follows:

    <list_comp> ::=
      ⟨ <value_expr> | <binding> **in** <list_expr> • <bool_expr> ⟩

where the • <bool_expr> part is optional. Please observe the use of BNF delimiters < and > versus the use of list pointed brackets: ⟨ and ⟩.

15.2.3 List Binding-Patterns and Matching

We have earlier dealt with the concepts of *binding-patterns* and *matching,* starting Page 271 for sets, and Page 306 (and Page 308) for Cartesians. We shall here consider the construct of *list patterns*, and the *list matching* and *binding* concepts. We shall later take these ideas up for *maps*, starting Page 355.

    By a list **let** decomposition *binding-pattern* we understand a construct basically of the following form (line [4]):

[1] **type**
[2]   A, B = A^*
[3] **value**
[4]   ... **let** ⟨a⟩⌢b = e **in** ... **end** ...
[5]   **post** e = ⟨a⟩⌢b, i.e., a = **hd** e ∧ b = **tl** e

⟨a⟩⌢b is the binding-pattern. Here it is (somehow) known that e is a non-empty list of A elements. The understanding of **let** ⟨a⟩⌢b = e **in** ... **end** is that e is list expression with non-empty value, say v, that the free identifier a is *bound* to the head of v, and that the free identifier b is bound to the possibly empty list tail of v.

We show a very simple example of the use of list patterns — leaving its "encoding" to the reader:

value
   sum: **Nat*** → **Nat**
   sum(ns) ≡
      if ns=⟨⟩
         then 0
         else
            let ⟨n⟩⌢ns' = ns **in**
            n + sum(ns')
      end end

15.2.4 Lists: Determinism and Nondeterminism Revisited

The remarks made earlier, for sets, in Sect. 13.2.2, Page 271, apply, inter alia, to lists also: Since list enumeration and range expressions, in general denote sets of models of lists, and since list operands of list operator/operand expressions in general apply to evaluation within such models, we can expect that the denotation of list operator/operand expressions, and comprehended list expressions likewise denote sets of models of lists or such other appropriate values (Booleans, natural numbers) as are the result types of the list operators.

It is important to keep this in mind throughout!

15.3 Small Examples of List-Based Abstractions

This section "matches" 13.3, Sections 14.3, 16.3, and 17.2. They all give small examples of set, Cartesian, list, map and function-based specifications. They are meant as "drill", i.e., class lecture examples.

15.3.1 Representations

Example 15.3 *Simple List Representation of Equivalence Relations:* We refer to Example 13.5 on page 273. Let A be a type, and let ns be a set of values of type A. A list representation of equivalence relations over set of A elements is now to be a list of (element wise disjoint) lists of (thus distinct) A elements. The set-oriented equivalence relation $\{\{a, b\}, \{c, d, e\}\}$ thus could have, for example, the following list-oriented representation $<< e, d, c >, < b, a >>$. As for Example 13.5 on page 273, we now formalise the above.

type

   A

   $P' = (A^*)^*$

   $P = \{| \ p{:}P' \bullet \text{wf\_P}(p) \ |\}$

value

  sas:A-**set**

  wf_P: $P' \to$ **Bool**

  wf_P(p) $\equiv$

     sas = $\cup$ { **elems**(p(i)) | i **in** $\langle 1 .. \textbf{ len } p \rangle$ } $\wedge$

     $\forall$ i:**Nat** $\bullet$ {i,i+1}$\subseteq$**inds** p $\Rightarrow$ **elems** p(i) $\cap$ **elems** p(i+1)

  merge: $A \times A \times P \to P$

  merge(a,a',p) $\equiv$

     $\langle$ p(i) | i **in** $\langle 1..\textbf{len } p\rangle \bullet$ {a,a'} $\cap$ **elems** p(i) = {} $\rangle$

     $\widehat{\ }\langle$ p(i)$\widehat{\ }$p(j) | i,j **in** $\langle 1..\textbf{len } p\rangle \bullet$ a $\in$ **elems** p(i) and a' $\in$ **elems** p(j) $\rangle$

     pre $\exists$ i,j:**Nat** $\bullet$ i$\neq$j $\wedge$ {i,j}$\subseteq$**inds** p $\wedge$ a $\in$ **elems** p(i) and a' $\in$ **elems** p(j)

We refer to Exercise 15.3 on page 344, and to Example 16.4 on page 357 for yet other representations of equivalence relations. ∎

15.3.2 Stacks and Queues

Example 15.4 *Stacks:* We have already, in Chapter 8's Examples 1 on page 129, 8.3 on page 131 and 8.5 on page 134 covered the computing science notion of stacks by presenting an algebraic definition of stacks. We urge the reader to recall Example 8.5 on page 134.

    On the background of Example 8.3 on page 131 we therefore present:

type

   E, S = E*

value

  empty: $\to$ S, empty() $\equiv \langle\rangle$

  is_empty: S $\to$ **Bool**, is_empty(s) $\equiv$ s=$\langle\rangle$

  push: E $\to$ S $\to$ S, push(e)(s) $\equiv \langle$e$\rangle\widehat{\ }$s

  top: S $\overset{\sim}{\to}$ E, top(s) $\equiv$ **hd** s **pre**: $\sim$is_empty(s)

  pop: S $\overset{\sim}{\to}$ S, pop(s) $\equiv$ **tl** s **pre**: $\sim$is_empty(s)

One observes a "shorter" definition above as compared to Example 8.3 on page 131. ∎

Example 15.5 *Queues:* We have already, in Chapter 8's Example 2 on page 129 and Example 8.6 on page 135 (for the latter, see Pages 135–136) covered the computing science notion of queues by presenting an algebraic definition of queues. We refer the reader to recall that definition.

On the background of Example 8.6 on page 135 we therefore present:

type
    E, Q = E*
value
    empty: → Q, empty() ≡ ⟨⟩

    is_empty: Q → **Bool**
    is_empty(q) ≡ q=⟨⟩

    enq: E → Q → Q
    enq(e)(q) ≡ q^⟨e⟩

    deq: Q $\overset{\sim}{\to}$ Q × E
    deq(s) ≡ (**tl** q,**hd** q) **pre**: ~is_empty(q)

One observes a "shorter" definition above as compared to Example 8.6.   ∎

15.3.3 File Systems III

This is the third in a series of models of what, with an overbearing mind, we could call *file systems*. Other models are presented in Examples 13.6 on page 274 (sets), 14.2 on page 300 (Cartesians [and sets]), and 16.8 on page 366 (maps [and records]). See also Exercise 16.11 on page 390.

Example 15.6 *A Sequential File System:*
    A file system is a sequence of uniquely named files. Each file is a sequence of records. Each record has three components: A key, a time stamp, and a set of data. On time stamps we assume an ordering relation, say $\mathcal{O}$, such that if $\mathcal{O}(t, t')$ then time t is strictly before time t'. No two otherwise distinct records of a file where these two records has the same key, has the same time stamp. Records occur in the sequence of "older" records "last" in the list, "youngest" record at the front. File names, keys and time stamps are further unanalysed quantities.

type
    Fn, K, T, D
    FS′ = (Fn × F)*, FS = {| fs:FS′ • wf_FS(fs) |}
    F′ = R*, F = {| b:F′ • wf_F(f) |}
    R = K × T × D-**set**
value
    $\mathcal{O}$: T × T → **Bool**

    wf_FS: FS′ → **Bool**

wf_FS(fs) ≡
  ∀ i,j:**Nat** • {i,j}⊆**inds** fs ∧ i≠j ⇒
    let (fn,)=fs(i),(fn',)=fs(j) **in** fn≠fn' **end**

wf_F: F' → **Bool**
wf_F(f) ≡
  ∀ i,j:**Nat** • {i,j}⊆**inds** f ∧ i<j ⇒
    let (k,t,ds) = f(i), (k',t',ds') = f(j) **in**
    t=t' ∨ 𝒪(t,t') ∧ k=k' ⇒ 𝒪(t,t') **end**

Operations on a file system, such as defined above, include: (i) Creating an
initially empty file system; (ii) creating an initially empty named file in the file
system; (iii) adding a record to a named file of the file system; (iv) getting all
the records, of a named file, and having a given key; (v) deleting the record,
of a named file, having a given key and a specific insertion time. Etc. We leave
it to the reader to decipher the formulas below.

value
  empty: → FS
  empty() → ⟨⟩

  crea: Fn × FS $\overset{\sim}{\to}$ FS
  crea(fn)(fs) ≡ ⟨(fn,⟨⟩)⟩⌢fs   **pre** fn ∉ file_names(fs)

  re_crea: Fn × F × FS $\overset{\sim}{\to}$ FS
  re_crea(fn)(f)(fs) ≡ ⟨(fn,f)⟩⌢fs   **pre** fn ∉ file_names(fs)

  file_names(fs) ≡ {fn|i:**Nat**•i ∈ index fs∧**let** (fn',f')=fs(i) **in** fn'=fn **end**}

  index: Fn → FS $\overset{\sim}{\to}$ **Nat**
  index(fn)(fs) **as** i
    post ∃ j:**Nat** • j ∈ **inds** fs ∧ **let**(fn',)=fs(j) **in** fn=fn' ∧ i=j **end**
    pre fn ∉ file_name(fs)

  get_file: Fn → FS → **Nat** × F
  get_file(fn)(fs) ≡
    let i:**Nat** • index(fn)(fs), (fn',f) = fs(i) **in** (i,f) **end**
    pre fn ∉ file_name(fs)

  add: R × Fn → FS → FS
  add(r,fn)(fs) ≡
    let (i,f) = get_file(fn)(fs) **in**
    ⟨(fn,⟨r⟩⌢f)⟩ ⌢ ⟨ fs(k) | k **in** ⟨1..len fs⟩ • k≠i ⟩ **end**
    pre: fn ∉ file_name(fs)
    assert: fn=fn'

get: K × Fn → FS → R-set
get(k,fn)(fs) ≡
    let (i,f) = get_file(fn)(fs) **in**
    { f(j) | j **in** ⟨1..**len** fs⟩ • **let** (k′,,) = f(j) **in** k = k′ **end** } **end**
    pre: fn ∉ file_name(fs)

del: K × T × Fn → FS $\overset{\sim}{\to}$ FS
del(k,t,fn)(b) ≡
    let (i,f) = get_file(fn)(fs) **in**
    ⟨ f(j) | j **in** ⟨1..**len** fs⟩ • **let** (k′,t′,)=f(j) **in** ~(k=k′ ∧ t=t′) **end** ⟩
    ⌢⟨ fs(k) | k **in** ⟨1..**len** fs⟩ • k≠i ⟩ **end**
    pre: fn ∉ file_name(fs) ∧ ∃ j:**Nat** • **let** (k′,t′,)=f(j) **in** k=k′ ∧ t=t′ **end**

■

15.3.4 Sorting Algorithms

This section, on sorting algorithms, as the title reveals, exemplifies the use
of the model-oriented features of the RSL (and for that matter any similar
model-oriented specification language [VDM-SL, Z or other]) as a list-oriented
programming language.

    There are many classical sorting algorithms: *exchange sort: bubble, shaker,
shell, insertion sort (straight and binary), merge sort, partition sort (Quicksort), selection sort (straight, heap)*. These will be the subject of assignments.
See Exercises 15.6–15.13 (bubble, heap, insertion (straight and binary), merge,
(straight) selection, shaker, shell and quicksort).

    But first: *When is a list sorted?*

Example 15.7 *When is a list sorted?:* Let us assume an abstract type, A,
of further unspecified values, between which an ordering relation, O, holds.
Now is_sorted holds of a list, with possibly multiple occurrences of identical
elements, if any adjacent pair of elements are ordered. And is_sorted_wrt holds
between a pair of such lists, if the first list is ordered, as defined above, and
if the number of distinct A elements in the two lists are the same for all such
A elements.

type
    A, L = A*
value
    O: A × A → **Bool**
    is_sorted: Q → **Bool**
    is_sorted(q) ≡ ∀ i:**Nat** • {i,i+1}⊆**inds** q ⇒ O(q(i),q(i+1))

    is_sorted_wrt: Q×Q → **Bool**

is_sorted_wrt(q',q'') ≡
  is_sorted(q') ∧ ∀ a:A • a ∈ **elems** q' ∪ **elems** q'' ⇒
    card{i|i:**Nat** • i ∈ **inds** q'∧a=q'(i)} =
    card{i|i:**Nat** • i ∈ **inds** q''∧a=q''(i)}

theorem:
  is_sorted_wrt(q',q'') ⇒ **len** q'=**len** q'' ∧ **elems** q'=**elems** q''

When we have covered the map data type, we can, in Example 16.3 on page 356, give another formulation of the is_sorted_wrt predicate.

Example 15.8 *Pre/Post Defined Sorting:* Any sorting algorithm, when applied to an argument q, must yield a result q', such that is_sorted_wrt(q,q').

type
  A, Q = A*
value
  sort: Q → Q
  sort(q) **as** q'
    post is_sorted_wrt(q,q')

15.4 Abstracting and Modelling with Lists

This section "matches" Sections 13.4, 14.4, 16.4, and 17.3. They all give larger examples of set, Cartesian, list, map and function abstractions and models. They are meant as self-study examples.

The purpose of this section is to introduce *techniques* and *tools* for model-oriented specifications primarily based on lists. Among the *list modelling principles, techniques* and *tools* are: (1) *Subtyping:* Sometimes a type definition defines "too much": A type constraining (*well-formedness, invariant*) predicate technique can therefore applied. (2) **pre/post** *conditions:* Function abstraction in terms of **pre** and **post** *conditions.* (3) *"Input/Output/Query" functions:* Identification of main functions according to their *signature.* (4) *Auxiliary functions:* Decomposition of function definitions into "smallest" units. The *principles* and *techniques* re-occur, for sets, Cartesians and maps in Sects. 13.4, 14.4 and 16.4.

15.4.1 Modelling Books Using Lists

Example 15.9 *Textual Documents:*

A Narrative of Entities

(i) A textual document consists of some front matter (a title, author, date, etc.) and a non-empty sequence of named sections. (ii) We do not define what is meant by title, author, date, etc. (iii) A section consists of a display line title and a possibly empty sequence of paragraphs and a possibly empty sequence of subsections, such that at least one of these two components is non-empty. (iv) A subsection consists of a display line title and a possibly empty sequence of paragraphs and a possibly empty sequence of subsubsections, such that at least one of these two components is non-empty. (v) A subsubsection consists of a display line title and a non-empty sequence of paragraphs. (vi) A paragraph consists of a non-empty sequence of sentences. (vii) A sentence consists of words and punctuation marks put into a further undefined sequence. (vii) A display line title consists of a sequence of words.

Formalisation

type
    Tit, Aut, Dat, Sen, Wor, PuM

    Doc = Fro $\times$ Sec*
    Fro = Tit $\times$ Aut $\times$ Dat $\times$ ...
    Sec = Dis $\times$ Par* $\times$ Sub*
    Sub = Dis $\times$ Par* $\times$ SuS*
    SuS = Dis $\times$ Par*
    Par = Sen*
    Dis = Wor*
value
    obs_Wseq: Sen $\rightarrow$ Wor*

An Operations Narrative

(viii) A Dewey Decimal Numeral is a sequence of one or more natural numbers (separated by periods — from which we, naturally, abstract). (ix) Any section, subsection and subsubsection can be identified by a Dewey Decimal Numeral. (x) The Dewey Decimal Numeral of the first section of a document is 1, of the second section it is 2, etc. (xi) The Dewey Decimal Numeral of the jth subsection of the ith section of a documents is i.j — etc. (xii) The Dewey Decimal Numeral of the kth subsubsection of the jth subsection of the ith section of a document is i.j.k — and here our numbering stops. (xiii) A document table of contents is a list of pairs of Dewey Decimal Numerals and display lines. (xiv) gen_TOC is a function which applied to a document produces "its" table of contents.

Formalisation

Left as Exercise 15.14.   ∎

15.4.2 Modelling "KeyWord-In-Context, KWIC"

We refer to an extensive and, we think, illustrative example in Sect. 15.4.2. This example also illustrates some analysis techniques.

Example 15.10 *KWIC: KeyWord-In-Context:*
This example subsection has several subparts, and otherwise presents the problem in a more pedantic style than were the examples above. First we are given a problem formulation. We then, very briefly, analyse this given formulation. From the informal formulation and, as a result of the analysis, we (informally, yet somehow) systematically 'derive'[3] our formal model. Finally we discuss our particular model and variants thereof. The purpose of this example illustration is then to show some of the aspects of going from a fixed problem formulation (given a priori) to models, and the problems posed by such oftentimes incomplete (or, but not in this case, inconsistent) informal formulations. The problem is taken from [6].

The Given Problem:

We are given the following informal, English language program specification:

"Consider a Program which generates a KWIC (KeyWord-In-Context) index.
A title is a list of words which are either **significant** or **non-significant**.
A rotation of a list is a cyclic shift of words in the list, and a **significant rotation** is a rotation in which the first word is significant.
Given a set of titles and a set of non-significant words, the program should produce an alphabetically sorted list of the significant rotations of titles"

An example of input and output is then given:

Input:
   Titles:
      THE THREE LITTLE PIGS.
      SNOW WHITE AND THE SEVEN DWARFS.

Non-significant Words:
> THE, THREE, AND, THE, SEVEN

Output:
> DWARFS, SNOW WHITE AND THE SEVEN
> LITTLE PIGS. THE THREE
> PIGS. THE THREE LITTLE
> SNOW WHITE AND THE SEVEN DWARFS.
> WHITE AND THE SEVEN DWARFS. SNOW

Discussion of Informal Problem Formulation:

We now analyse the problem statement. The point of our analysis is to isolate concepts, discover incompletenesses and/or inconsistencies, etc.

(1) The informal problem formulator already isolated some concepts; these appear (by our choice) italicised in the text. Other concepts potentially useful in, or for, our further work are: list, word, cyclic shift, first, set, and alphabetically sorted.

(2) Some concepts are problem-oriented: title, words, significant, and non-significant. Other concepts are more abstract, explication-oriented: list, rotation, (equal to) cyclic shift, first, set, and [alphabetically] sorted. (Our modelling will basically centre around, or express, but not necessarily all of, these concepts.)

(3) The descriptive paragraph does not deal with punctuation marks; period (".") is not isolated as a concept, but it occurs, as a marker, in the rotations. Also: Words are not further explained. We take these to consist of letters. And we assume some given alphabetical order of, or among, both upper and lower case letters. Blanks appear, but nothing is said about their relation to the ordering of titles.

(4) Nothing is said about duplicate occurrences in the input or output. The input title "XXX XXX" might thus give rise to, e.g., two output rotations!

(5) Finally nothing is said about the concrete input and output presentation: Carriage returns, new lines; respectively single or multiple column printing, and display and the ordering within multiple columns: whether by row or by column. Etc.

Program Assumptions: In order to proceed into a modelling step we make the following assumptions:

(6) We ignore punctuation marks — but keep the title termination period as a "wrap-around-marker", one that designates where a title ends.

(7) We assume 'alphabetic sorting' (see the o function below) to apply to all of the text of a title.

(8) We omit multiple (duplicate) occurrences of [rotated] titles in the output, that is: we list (generate) only one copy.

Model Decisions: Our modelling will be based on the following decisions:

(9) We assume a type of further unidentified characters from which we define titles (which do not include blanks) and strings (which includes blanks); we assume a character ordering relation from which we define title and string ordering relations.

(10) We do not abstract away blanks — since blanks (and, in general, punctuation marks) are needed to delineate words.

(11) We abstract, as suggested by the informal formulation, both the presentation of input and output. (This issue will be a pressing one the 'closer' we get to a realization — and should, we seriously believe, be specified, in detail, before implementation is properly begun.)

Some Auxiliary Functions:

type
   Char
value
   o: **Char** × **Char** → **Bool**
   $o(c1,c2) \equiv$ **true** /* if c1 is before c2 else */ **false**
type
   Word = **Char***
   Title = Word*
   String = (Word |{blank})*
axiom
   blank $\notin$ **Char**

value
   o: Title × Title → **Bool**
   $o(t1,t2) \equiv o(ctts(t1),ctts(t2))$

   ctts: Title → String
   $ctts(t) \equiv$ **tl** c $\langle\langle$blank$\rangle$^t(i) | i$ **in** $\langle 1..$**len** t$\rangle\rangle$

   c: String* → String
   $c(sl) \equiv$ **if** sl=$\langle\rangle$ **then** sl **else** **hd** sl $^\frown$ c(**tl** sl) **end**

   o: String × String → **Bool**
   $o(s1,s2) \equiv$
      if s1=$\langle\rangle$ ∧ s2=$\langle\rangle$ **then** **true** **else**
      if s1=$\langle\rangle$ ∨ o(**hd** s1,**hd** s2) **then** **true** **else**
      if s2=$\langle\rangle$ ∨ o(**hd** s2,**hd** s1) **then** **false** **else**
      o(**tl** s1,**tl** s2) **end end end**

Since we ignore punctuation marks, including end-of-title marker, such marks will not be modelled either.

The major model decision is that of giving a model, in particular one in the style that these volumes advances.

Model:

The presentation of the model will follow, in sequence, the way in which it was derived. That is: we decide, in a first, successful, attempt to model first some of the individual concepts outlined or *italicised* above. Then we bring all aspects together in the specification of the input/output types and the one, major program function (that is: the specification of the program itself). Finally we specify the auxiliary functions introduced by the major program specification.

In this example the modelling of the auxiliary concepts turned out to be of direct use in the subsequent [main] model.

Auxiliary Notions: "A rotation of a list is a cyclic shift of the words in the list":

value
    Rotations: Title $\rightarrow$ Title-**set**
    Rotations(t) $\equiv$
        { rot(t,i) | i:**Nat** • i $\in$ **inds** t }

    rot: Title $\times$ **Nat** $\rightarrow$ Title
    rot(t,i) $\equiv$
        $\langle t(j)|j$ **in** $\langle 1..\text{len } t\rangle\rangle^\frown \langle t(k)|k$ **in** $\langle 1..i-1\rangle\rangle$

We need select a "first word":

value
    First: Title $\rightarrow$ Word
    First(t) $\equiv$ **hd** t **pre** t $\neq \langle\rangle$

We need identify "is significant" (wrt. a set of non-significant words):

value
    Is_significant: Title $\times$ Word-**set** $\Rightarrow$ **Bool**
    Is_significant(t,ws) $\equiv$ First(t) $\notin$ ws

We choose to model "alphabetical sort", rather than "is alphabetically sorted" — leaving the latter as a variant exercise:

value
    A_sort: Title-**set** $\rightarrow$ Title*
    A_sort(ts) **as** ql
        pre true
        post elems ql = ts $\wedge$ **len** ql = **card elems** ql $\wedge$ aO(ql)

The **post** condition ensures that all (rotated) titles in the set, and only such, appear in the title output list; and that there are no duplicates.

value
    aO: Title* $\to$ **Bool**
    aO(ql) $\equiv \forall$ i,j:**Nat** • {i,j} $\subseteq$ **inds** ql $\wedge$ i$<$j $\Rightarrow$ o(ql(i),ql(j))

Types: "Given a set of titles and a set of non-significant words":

type
    Input = Title-**set** $\times$ Word-**set**

"the program should produce a ... list ... of titles":

type
    Output = Title*

The Main Function: is expressed as: "Produce an alphabetically sorted list of the significant rotations of titles":

value
    KWIC: Input $\to$ Output

Again we choose to express the definition of KWIC in terms of a pair of **pre/post** conditions:

value
    KWIC(i) **as** o
    pre true
    post Significant_Rots(i,o) $\wedge$ aO(o) $\wedge$ No_Duplicates(o)

Auxiliary Functions: We need some auxiliary functions:

value
    Significant_Rots,All_Rots,Only_Rots:
        Input$\times$Output $\to$ **Bool**

    Significant_Rots(i,o) $\equiv$ All_Rots(i,o) $\wedge$ Only_Rots(i,o)

    All_Rots((ts,ns),o) $\equiv$
        $\forall$ t:Title • t $\in$ ts $\wedge$ $\forall$ t$'$:Title •
            t$'$ $\in$ Rotations(t) $\wedge$ Significant(t$'$,ns) $\Rightarrow$ t$'$ $\in$ **elems** o

Only_Rots((ts,ns),o) ≡
    ∀ t':Title • t' ∈ **elems** o ∧ ∃!t:Title •
        t' ∈ ts ∧ t' ∈ Rotations(t') ∧ Is_Significant(t',ns)

No_Duplicates: Title* → **Bool**
No_Duplicates(o) ≡ **card elems tl = len tl**

The All-Rots predicate checks that the output contains all significant rotations implied by input. The Only-Rots predicate checks that the output does not contain other such rotations: Observe that although we defined it, we never actually found a need for deploying the A-Sort function. Such "things" happen when modelling bottom-up, configurationally ! ∎

15.5 Inductive List Definitions

15.5.1 Inductive List Type Definitions

Suppose we wanted to define:

type
    L = L*.

What would that mean ? Here is an attempt:

value
    $\mathcal{L}$: {⟨⟩,⟨⟨⟩,⟨⟩,...,⟨⟩⟩, ..., ⟨⟨⟩,⟨⟨⟩⟩,...,⟨⟨⟨⟩⟩⟩⟩, ...}

The cardinality of the class of values of type L of the left-hand side must be equal to the cardinality of the class of values of type L of the right-hand side. Obviously it is not. So we reject this kind of recursive set type definition.

Following the lines of earlier recursive type definitions we reformulate the above problematic type equation into:

type
    B
    L = BoL*
    BoL = mB | mL
    mB == mkB(sb:B)
    mL == mkL(sl:L)

and would correspondingly get, in some :

value
    $\mathcal{L} = \{\langle \ell_1, \ell_2, ..., \ell_n \rangle |$
        $\ell_i \in \{mkB(b)|b:B\} \cup \{mkL(\langle \ell_x, \ell_y, ..., \ell_z \rangle)|\ell_x, \ell_y, ..., \ell_z \in \mathcal{L}\}\}$

That looks fine, so we conclude:

Recursive definitions of lists must have built into them a variant, a "boot strap". The variant serves to get the "generation" of proper list values started, and serves to avoid seemingly meaningless "empty" values.

15.5.2 Inductive List Value Definitions

Example 15.11 *List, Cartesian and Set-Based Model of Networks:* We rephrase the solution of Example 14.8. That example was itself a rephrasing of Example 13.12

We model routes as finite sequences of paths.

type
  $R' = (Ci \times Si \times Ci)^*$
  $R = \{| \ r{:}R' \bullet wfR(r) \ |\}$
value
  wfR: $R' \to$ **Bool**
  wfR(r) $\equiv$
    len r>0 $\wedge$
    $\forall$ i:**Nat** $\bullet$ $\{i,i+1\} \in$ **inds** r $\Rightarrow$
      let (ci,si,ci')=r(i),(ci'',si',ci''')=r(i+1) **in** ci'=ci'' **end** $\wedge$
    let (c1,_,_)=r(1),(_,_,cin)=r(**len** r) **in** c1$\neq$cn **end**

First some auxiliary functions:

  Ci_deg: $Ci \times R' \to$ **Nat**
  Ci_deg(ci,r) $\equiv$
    card$\{i|i{:}$**Nat**$\bullet i \in$ **inds** r$\wedge$**let** (ci',_,ci'')=r(i) **in** ci $\in\{$ci',ci''$\}$ **end**$\}$

  xtr_Cis: $R' \to$ Ci-**set**
  xtr_Cis(r) $\equiv$ $\{$ci$|$(ci',_,ci''):P,ci:Ci$\bullet$(ci',_,ci'')$\in$ **elems** r$\wedge$ci $\in\{$ci',ci''$\}\}$

value
  fst_Ci: $R' \to Ci$
  fst_Ci($\langle$ci,_,_$\rangle$^r) $\equiv$ ci

  lst_Ci: $R' \to Ci$
  lst_Ci(r^$\langle$_,_,ci$\rangle$) $\equiv$ ci

  no_mps_Ci: $R \to$ **Bool**
  no_mps_Ci(r) $\equiv$ $\forall$ ci:Ci$\bullet$ci $\in$ xtr_Cis(r) $\Rightarrow$ Ci_deg(ci,r)$\leq$2

The set of all acyclic routes is defined by:

gen_Rs: N → R-**set**
gen_Rs(n) ≡
   let ps = gen_Ps(n) **in**
   let ars =
      {⟨p⟩|p:P•p ∈ ps}
      ∪{r⌢r′|r,r′:R•{r,r′}⊆ars∧lst_Ci(r)=fst_Ci(r′)∧no_mps_Ci(r⌢r′)} **in**
   ars **end end.**

15.6 A Review of List Abstractions and Models

Principles. *Lists:* When a model-oriented abstraction has been chosen, then list abstraction may be chosen if a reasonable number of the following characteristics can be identified as properties of the phenomena or concepts being modelled: (i) The abstract structure of the composite components being modelled consists of an ordered collection of not necessarily distinct subcomponents (constituent phenomena or concepts), (ii) whose number is not fixed, i.e., may vary, i.e., (iii) to which new, distinct subcomponents may be joined — typically at either end of lists; (iv) from which existing subcomponents may be removed — typically at either end of lists; and (v) where one may compose other such phenomena or concepts from similar such phenomena, respectively concepts.   ∎

Principles. *Lists:* We mention, at this early stage in these volumes, two specific principles of when to choose lists as a basis for abstract modelling. (vi) *Semantics of Imperative Languages:* As illustrated in Examples 14.4–14.6 and Example 14.7, the semantics of an imperative[4] program is expressed as a sequence of state transitions, with this sequence being afforded by the iterated interpretation of statements. (vii) *Syntactic Structures:* The sequence of interpretation of statements mentioned above is then facilitated by the modelling of central structures of imperative programs as lists of statements.[5] That is, the former "specific principle" is more conceptual. Its modelling consequences are to be found in the structuring of the function definitions which express the semantics.[6]

We shall later have opportunity to illustrate the deployment of the above specific principles.   ∎

---

[4]An imperative program is a syntactic structure the elaboration of whose components, i.e., statements, causes changes to a state. Each pair of conjoined statements, so-to-speak, express: *First do this, then do that!* Truly an imperative. C++ and Java are examples of imperative programming languages.

[5]Although that was not done in Examples 14.4–14.6 and Example 14.7.

[6]And that indeed was done in Example 14.7: Sequential iteration.

Techniques. *Lists:* We refer to initial paragraphs of Sect. 15.4 for a listing (1–4) of some of the techniques used when abstracting using sets.

More specifically: A number of list-oriented techniques are offered: (viii) Observer functions sometimes "extract" lists; (ix) the various list operations apply to appropriate modelling instances: (x.1) Concatenation applies to models of "all", "shared", respectively "some, except" instances of a phenomenon (a concept) possessed by two or more sets of phenomena (respectively concepts), (x.2–4) head, tail and indexing apply to models of "the first" instance, "the remaining" instances, respectively "some specific" instance, of a phenomenon (concept) possessed, (x.5) length applies to models of "how many" instances of a phenomenon (concept), (x.6–7) with elements and indices being mere technical operations; (xi–xii) list enumeration and list comprehension apply to the expression of the construction of an instance of an otherwise list modelled phenomenon (or concept).

These are just some of the more "important" techniques.   ∎

Tools. *Lists:* If abstraction and modelling using the list data type has been chosen, then the tool can either be the RSL, the VDM-SL, the Z, or, for example, the B specification language.   ∎

Please compare the present section to those of Sections 13.7 (sets) and 16.6 (maps).

15.7 Lists: A Discussion

We have outlined the list data type. And we have tried to (i) enunciate principles for when to deploy list abstraction, to (ii) mention some of the techniques that follow from such a choice, and to (iii) identify some of the list abstraction specification language tools today available. Lists constitute "another basic workhorse" of model-oriented abstraction and modelling.

15.8 Exercises

Exercise 15.1. *Simple List Types.* This exercise is intended to help develop your basic skills in manipulating lists. It is certainly not one of abstraction.

List the elements of A^* and A^ω.

List some of the elements of Nat^*, respectively Nat^ω.

Exercise 15.2. *List Representation of Sets.* The present problem intends to exercise your skills in manipulating sets and lists — and to put the ideas of refinement and abstraction functions into your repertoire of software development techniques.

Given the type definition $L = A\text{-set}$ where A is some trivial sort.

Suggest a representation of finite sets as finite lists; express a well-formedness predicate on such "set" lists; and define, as proper functions, the set operators, ∪, ∩, \, ⊆, ⊂, and **card**, on the "set" list representations; and argue, informally, that your functions maintain the "set" list well-formedness predicate.

Exercise 15.3. *List Representation of Equivalence Relations.* We refer to Examples 13.5 on page 273 and 15.3. Let a list representation of an equivalence relation be that of a a pair: A list of indices into the pair-list (being described presently), and a list of pairs. Each pair contains a distinct element of the type being partitioned, and an index to an arbitrary next (or the same) pair. The indices designate circular, disjoint lists. The equivalence relation $\{\{a, b\}, \{c, d, e\}\}$ may thus be represented as the pair $(< 1, 5 >, < (d, 4), (a, 5), (e, 1), (c, 3), (b, 2) >)$. (i) Formalise this type, (ii) express, formally, well-formedness of such pair-list representations, and (iii) define the list-oriented **merge** operation. We also remind the reader of Example 16.4.

Exercise 15.4. *List Representation of Stacks.* The present problem further intends to exercise your skills in manipulating sets and lists, and in understanding stacks — and to put the ideas of refinement and abstraction functions into your repertoire of software development techniques.

Define an abstract data type 'stack' with the "usual" operations, but allowing only for a maximum size stack.

Exercise 15.5. *List Representation of Queues.* The present problem intends to exercise your skills in manipulating sets and lists and in understanding queues — and to put the ideas of refinement and abstraction functions into your repertoire of software development techniques.

Define an abstract data type 'queue' with the "usual" operations, but allowing only for a maximum size queue.

Exercise 15.6. *Bubble Sort.* Find, in some textbook, a description, in some language, whether natural or a programming language, of the bubble sort algorithm, and reformulate that algorithm in RSL.

Exercise 15.7. *Heap Sort.* Find, in some textbook, a description, in some language, whether natural or a programming language, of the heap sort algorithm, and reformulate that algorithm in RSL.

Exercise 15.8. *Insertion Sort.* Find, in some textbook, a description, in some language, whether natural or a programming language, of the insertion sort algorithm, and reformulate that algorithm in RSL.

Exercise 15.9. *Merge Sort.* Find, in some textbook, a description, in some language, whether natural or a programming language, of the merge sort algorithm, and reformulate that algorithm in RSL.

Exercise 15.10. *Selection Sort.* Find, in some textbook, a description, in some language, whether natural or a programming language, of the selection sort algorithm, and reformulate that algorithm in RSL.

Exercise 15.11. *Shaker Sort.* Find, in some textbook, a description, in some language, whether natural or a programming language, of the shaker sort algorithm, and reformulate that algorithm in RSL.

Exercise 15.12. *Shell Sort.* Find, in some textbook, a description, in some language, whether natural or a programming language, of the shell sort algorithm, and reformulate that algorithm in RSL.

Exercise 15.13. *Quicksort.* Find, in some textbook, a description, in some language, whether natural or a programming language, of the quicksort algorithm, and reformulate that algorithm in RSL.

Exercise 15.14. *Formalisaton of Books.* We refer to Example 15.9. Please formalise the notion of books, table of contents and a function which generates tables of contents from books. Please sketch how one might be able to provide page numbering?

Exercise 15.15. ♣ *Lists in the Transportation Net Domain.* We refer to Appendix A, Sect. A.1, *Transportation Net.*

Further Reference: The description which follows is a rewording of the description given in Exercise 13.5 on page 290. Should you find, when reading the below description, that some information necessary to solve the problem is missing, then please consult Exercises 13.5 and 14.6.

Let us assume that transportation net segments are modelled by Cartesians "containing" (i) the unique segment identifier, (ii) the set of the two or one connection identifiers (or names) of the connections between which the segment "spans", (iii) the "route" name [road name for road nets, etc.], (iv) the segment length, and (v) possibly some more attributes [albeit all "lumped" into one component]. Let us similarly assume that connections (connectors) are likewise modelled by Cartesians "containing"(1) the unique connection identifier, (2) a set of unique segment identifiers (of those segments incident upon (i.e., emanating from) the connection, and (3) possibly some more attributes [albeit all "lumped" into one component].

Now model a concept of a path as a sequence of zero, one or more segments such that adjacent segments in the sequence (i.e., in the list) share connection identifiers.

Finally model a transportation net as a pair of sets of segments and sets of connections.

1. Define the types of nets, segments, connections, and paths.

2. Define a well-formedness predicate which tests whether a net is well-formed.

3. Define a well-formedness predicate which tests whether a segment is well-formed wrt. a net.

4. Define a well-formedness predicate which tests whether a connection is well-formed wrt. a net.

5. Define a well-formedness predicate which tests whether a path is well-formed wrt. a net.

6. Define a predicate which tests whether a path is a cyclic path.

7. Define a function which given a well-formed net generates all finite length non-cyclic (and well-formed) paths of the net.

8. Define a function which given two distinct connection identifiers finds the set of all (well-formed) paths between them.

9. Define a function which given two distinct connection identifiers finds the set of (one or more) shortest (well-formed) paths between them.

Exercise 15.16. ♣ *Lists in the Container Logistics Domain.* We refer to Appendix A, Sect. A.2, *Container Logistics*.

Further Reference: The description which follows is a rewording of the description given in Exercise 13.6 on page 291. Should you find, when reading the below description, that some information necessary to solve the problem is missing, then please consult Exercises 13.6 and 14.7.

Let us assume three kinds of lists: (1) 'Container routes', (2) 'actual sailing plans', and (3) 'container way-bills', and two kinds of sets: A set, (4) 'lines', of 'actual sailing plans', and a set, (5) 'seven-seas', of names of (all known) container terminals.

(1) A 'container route' is merely a "cyclic sequence" of names of container terminals. (A 'container route' stands for a number of 'actual sailing plans'.) An adjacent pair of (container terminal) names in a sequence expresses that some container ship sails non-stop between the named container terminals. A "cyclic sequence" (of container terminal names) is a sequence where the pair of the last and the first container terminal name expresses that some container ship sails non-stop between the named container terminals.

(2) An 'actual sailing plan' is a sequence of 'records of (past, present, or future) visits of a container ship to container terminals'. A 'record of a visit to a container terminal' can be thought of as a Cartesian. It may typically contain the following information: (i) a container terminal name, (ii) [relative] arrival time, (iii) [relative] departure time, and (iv) frequency of visits [the related concepts of 'relative' and 'frequency' are presently left further unexplained].

(3) A 'container way-bill' is a sequence of 'records of (past, present, or future) visits of a container to container terminals': Exactly and only those container terminals where the container is loaded and unloaded (including transferred between container ships), via respective container storage areas. The 'records of visits of a container to container terminals' also inform about

arrival and departure times at terminals, and the names of the container ships on which the container is to be conveyed.

1. Define the concrete types of 'container route', 'actual sailing plan', 'container way-bill', 'lines', and 'seven-seas'.
2. Define a predicate, wf_CR, which tests that a 'container route' value is well-formed wrt. a 'seven-seas' value.
3. Define a predicate, wf_ASP, which tests that an 'actual sailing plan' value is well-formed wrt. a 'container route' value.
4. Define a predicate, wf_ASP, which tests that an 'actual sailing plan' value is well-formed wrt. a 'lines' value.
5. Define a function, gen_Routes, which applies to any well-formed 'lines' value and generates the set of all routes. A 'route' is defined as a sequence of 'container terminal names' such that any adjacent pair of names in the sequence is visited by some container ship, i.e., are on an 'actual sailing plan' — hence in an 'actual sailing plan' of the 'lines' argument.
6. Define a predicate, wf_WB, which tests that a 'way-bill' value is well-formed wrt. a 'lines' value.
7. Define a function, gen_WBs, which, given a pair of 'container terminal names' and a 'lines' argument, generates the (possibly empty) set of 'way-bills".
8. Consider Bays to be lists of Rows, Rows to be lists of Stacks, and Container Stacks to be lists of Containers. Now redefine appropriate load and unload functions.

Exercise 15.17. ♣ *Lists in the Financial Service Industry Domain.* We refer to Appendix A, Sect. A.3, *Financial Service Industry.*We also refer to above Exercises 15.15 and 15.16.

You are to formulate yourself some narrative and formalisations of phenomena and concepts of the *Financial Service Industry* domain for which lists may come in as a suitable abstraction. Please also consult Exercises 13.7 and 14.8.

Maps in RSL

- The **prerequisite** for studying this chapter is that you possess knowledge of the mathematical concepts of sets, Cartesians and lists as introduced in earlier chapters.
- The **aims** are to introduce the RSL abstract data type of maps: the map type expression, the map value expressions, enumeration and comprehension forms of expressing maps, and operations over maps, as well as to illustrate the expressiveness of maps by illustrating simple and not so simple examples of phenomena and concepts that can be modelled in terms of maps.
- The **objective** is to set the reader free to choose maps as models of phenomena and concept entities, when appropriate, and to not choose maps when doing so is not appropriate.
- The **treatment** is from systematic to semiformal.

Characterisation. By a *map* we shall intuitively understand a somehow enumerable set of pairs[1] of distinct argument result values, such that it is meaningful to speak of operations involving maps such as applying a map to an argument, $m(a)$, merging two otherwise distinct maps, $\cup$, overriding one map by another, $\dagger$, restricting one map by the definition set of another, $\backslash$, restricting one map to the definition set of another, $/$, inspecting the definition set of a map, **dom**, inspecting the range set of a map, **rng**, composing two suitable maps, $\circ$, and comparing two maps for equality (inequality), $= (\neq)$. ∎

Map me no maps, sir, my head is a map, a map of the whole world.
H. Fielding, 1707–1754, Rape upon Rape

---

[1] By the hedge "somehow" we mean that it is possible to either explicitly list the pairs, or to characterise the set of pairs through some suitable predicate.

16.1 The Issues

The idea to be illustrated in this section is the use of the discrete mathematics concept of maps in abstracting domain, requirements and software phenomena and concepts. Other terms used in lieu of maps are relations or (enumerable definition set) functions. Maps offer themselves as an abstraction when a component can best be characterised as a set of uniquely identified (other) components. The section gives a few more examples.

> Maps are a major "workhorse" in model-oriented abstraction.

This chapter is, as are Chaps. 13–17, built up as follows:

- The map data type   (Sect. 16.2)
- Examples of map-based abstractions   (Sect. 16.3)
- Abstracting and modelling with maps   (Sect. 16.4)
- Inductive map definitions   (Sect. 16.5)
- A review of map abstractions and models   (Sect. 16.6)

There are many examples because *before one can write good specifications one must have read and studied many example specifications*. While you may not need to study all of them now, you can return to some later. The chapter ends with a brief discussion.

16.2 The Map Data Type

Chapter 6 covered the subject of mathematical functions. Maps are special kinds of functions. Normally, for general functions, one cannot compute their definition sets (i.e., the set of values for which the function is defined), and hence not their image (or range) sets. Maps are distinguished by exactly being functions having the property that their definition set, and hence their range sets, can be computed. In domain descriptions we need not compute all such definition sets, but we need be able to express a predicate that delineates the definition set. Since this is so, the map data type comes further "equipped" with a number of other operations on maps.

The map data type has the following facets: (i) The map type (syntactically the map values, semantically the map type expressions and the map type definitions); (ii) the map values (a semantic concept); and (iii) the map value expressions (the syntactic counterpart of the semantic map value concept).

16.2.1 Map Types: Definitions and Expressions

Types whose values are total or partial functions, or are maps, can be defined using the type operators $\rightarrow$ and $\overset{\sim}{\rightarrow}$, respectively $\overrightarrow{m}$. On total and partial functions only a few operations are provided for (in RSL): (i) the function abstraction (λ), (ii) the function application ("$\bullet(\bullet)$") and (iii) the function composition (°) operations. In contrast, although maps are also functions, they are definition set enumerable functions on which a larger number of operations can (therefore) be defined. That is: One can enumerate the definition set. They can be defined exactly because the definition set, the arguments for which the function, i.e., the map, is defined, is computable.

Let A and B stand for arbitrary types whose possibly infinite number of element values include a1, a2, ..., am, ..., respectively b1, b2, ..., bn, ... Types whose values can be considered finite or infinite, definition set enumerable maps from A elements to B elements, can be defined using the infix $\overrightarrow{m}$ type constructor:

type A, B
  M = A $\overrightarrow{m}$ B

The expression A $\overrightarrow{m}$ B is a *map type expression*.

Let us illustrate elements of some map type ([1]): In the expressions below ([2]) the possibly decorated a's and the b's denote single values.

[1] A $\overrightarrow{m}$ B
[2] [], [a↦b], ..., [a1↦b1,a2↦b2,...,a3↦b3],

The expression [ ] designate the empty map. The expression [a↦b] stands for the singleton map that maps a into b. The expression [a1↦b1, a2↦b2, ..., a3↦b3] stands for the map which (possibly nondeterministically) maps respective, distinct ai into corresponding (not necessarily distinct) bi.

Example 16.1 *A Simple Map Example:* Let fact name the factorial function, then

$$[1↦\text{fact}(1),2↦\text{fact}(2),3↦\text{fact}(3),4↦\text{fact}(4),5↦\text{fact}(5),6↦\text{fact}(6)]$$

expresses a simple map of six element, the natural numbers one to six, mapping into their respective factorials.   ∎

16.2.2 Map Value Expressions

For sets and lists there were three kinds of explicit set-forming, respectively list-forming, expressions: enumerative, ranged expressions and comprehended expressions. For maps there are only enumerative and comprehended map expressions.

Map Enumerations

Let ae, ae1, ae2, ..., aen, be expressions that denote not necessarily distinct values of type A, and let be, be1, be2, ..., ben be expressions that denote not necessarily distinct values of type B. Then the following are examples of *explicit map value expressions*, in particular *enumerative map expressions:*

[], [ae↦be], ..., [ae1↦be1,ae2↦be2,...,aen↦ben]

The formula line above, left to right, denotes the single model of the empty map of no elements, a set of models of singleton maps of one element definition sets, etc., respectively a set of models of maps, all of n map pairs vai into vbi. For each model the above expressions have a specific, value, which may be nondeterministic for reasons not immediately clear from the above, cf. Sect. 12.4.4. Or it may be nondeterministic for reasons covered next.

Deterministic and Nondeterministic Map Values

If two or more aei, aej expressions evaluate to the same A value, then the map is said to be *nondeterministic*, otherwise it is said to be *deterministic*. A deterministic map, like a deterministic function, yields unique results for definition set, i.e., argument values. A nondeterministic map, like a nondeterministic function, nondeterministically yields some result value for some or all definition set argument values.

Let a, a′, ..., a″, b, b′, ..., b″ stand for distinct type A and type B values, respectively, then:

[a↦b,a′↦b′,...,a″↦b″]

stands for a deterministic map, while

[a↦b,a↦b′,...,a↦b″]

stands for the nondeterministic map which, when applied to a, either yields b, or b′, or ..., b″, nondeterministically. The idea of a nondeterministic map is not to be confused with a map expression that denotes a set of models.

Map Operator/Operand Expressions

First we present the map operator/operand expressions semiformally: presenting the formal signature of the map operations and giving, informally, a metalinguistic[2] example for each operation. Instead we pretend to give something that you may informally take to be a kind of axioms.

Map Operation Signatures and Examples

There are eleven map value related operations: •(•), **dom, rng**, †, ∪, \, /, =, ≠, ≡ and °.

---

[2]This example is metalinguistic because we cannot give the semantics of RSL in RSL, and because we use ellipses (...).

value

- $(\bullet)$: $M \to A \overset{\sim}{\to} B$, $m(ai) = bi$

    dom: $M \to A\text{-}\mathbf{infset}$ [domain of map]
    $\quad$ **dom** $[a1 \mapsto b1, a2 \mapsto b2, ..., an \mapsto bn] = \{a1, a2, ..., an\}$

    rng: $M \to B\text{-}\mathbf{infset}$ [range of map]
    $\quad$ **rng** $[a1 \mapsto b1, a2 \mapsto b2, ..., an \mapsto bn] = \{b1, b2, ..., bn\}$

    $\dagger$: $M \times M \to M$ [override extension]
    $\quad [a \mapsto b, a' \mapsto b', a'' \mapsto b''] \dagger [a' \mapsto b'', a'' \mapsto b'] = [a \mapsto b, a' \mapsto b'', a'' \mapsto b']$

    $\cup$: $M \times M \to M$ [merge $\cup$]
    $\quad [a \mapsto b, a' \mapsto b', a'' \mapsto b''] \cup [a''' \mapsto b'''] = [a \mapsto b, a' \mapsto b', a'' \mapsto b'', a''' \mapsto b''']$

    $\backslash$: $M \times A\text{-}\mathbf{infset} \to M$ [restriction by]
    $\quad [a \mapsto b, a' \mapsto b', a'' \mapsto b''] \backslash \{a\} = [a' \mapsto b', a'' \mapsto b'']$

    $/$: $M \times A\text{-}\mathbf{infset} \to M$ [restriction to]
    $\quad [a \mapsto b, a' \mapsto b', a'' \mapsto b''] / \{a', a''\} = [a' \mapsto b', a'' \mapsto b'']$

    $=, \neq$: $M \times M \to \mathbf{Bool}$

    $\circ$: $(A \underset{\widetilde{m}}{\to} B) \times (B \underset{\widetilde{m}}{\to} C) \to (A \underset{\widetilde{m}}{\to} C)$ [composition]
    $\quad [a \mapsto b, a' \mapsto b'] \circ [b \mapsto c, b' \mapsto c', b'' \mapsto c''] = [a \mapsto c, a' \mapsto c']$

Meaning of Map Operators

The first line above, $\bullet(\bullet)$, expresses that functions and maps can be applied to arguments. The prefix operators **dom** and **rng** denote "taking" the definition set values (i.e., the domain[3]) of a map (the **a** values for which the map is defined), respectively the range of a map (the corresponding **b** values for which the map is defined). The infix operators $\dagger$, $\cup$, and $/$, when applied to two operands, denote the map which is like an override of the first operand map by all or some "pairings" of the second operand map, the merge of two such maps, the map which is a restriction of the first operand map to the elements that are not in the second operand set, respectively the map which is a restriction of the first operand map to the elements of the second operand set. The infix operators $=$ and $\neq$, when applied to two maps, compare these for equality, respectively inequality.

To explain composition ($\circ$) of two maps, mostly in terms of map comprehension, we introduce two map domains, M and N, such that the range of m:M operand maps fall within the domain of n:N operand maps.

We explain, operationally, some of the map operations. We assume that **dom** and $\bullet(\bullet)$ are primitive operations.

value
$\quad$ **rng** $m \equiv \{ m(a) \mid a{:}A \bullet a \in \mathbf{dom}\ m \}$

---

[3]Note that the term 'domain' is used here in a sense which is different from that of 'domain' used in the context of domain engineering, requirements engineering and software design. Observe further the danger of misinterpreting the term 'application' in 'application domain' as that of applying some function or map!

m1 † m2 ≡
  [a↦b | a:A,b:B •
    a ∈ **dom** m1 \ **dom** m2 ∧ b=m1(a) ∨ a ∈ **dom** m2 ∧ b=m2(a)]

m1 ∪ m2 ≡ [a↦b | a:A,b:B •
        a ∈ **dom** m1 ∧ b=m1(a) ∨ a ∈ **dom** m2 ∧ b=m2(a)]

m \ s ≡ [a↦m(a) | a:A • a ∈ **dom** m \ s]
m / s ≡ [a↦m(a) | a:A • a ∈ **dom** m ∩ s]

m1 = m2 ≡
  dom m1 = **dom** m2 ∧ ∀ a:A • a ∈ **dom** m1 ⇒ m1(a) = m2(a)
m1 ≠ m2 ≡ ~(m1 = m2)

m°n ≡
  [a↦c | a:A,c:C • a ∈ **dom** m ∧ c = n(m(a))]
  pre rng m ⊆ **dom** n

Map Comprehension

Just as for sets and lists, we can either explicitly enumerate finite maps, or
we can implicitly comprehend possibly infinite maps.

Example 16.2 *A Simple Map Example:* Let fact name the factorial function,
then

  [i ↦ fact(i) | i:**Nat** • i ∈ {1..6}]

expresses a simple map of six element, the natural numbers 1 to 6, mapping
into their respective factorials.   ■

Let A, B, C and D denote arbitrary types, and let $\mathcal{F}(a)$ and $\mathcal{G}(b)$ stand for
arbitrary expressions that applies to A, respectively B, values, and evaluate to
C, respectively D values. That is, $\mathcal{F}$ and $\mathcal{G}$ may be viewed as functions from
A into C, and B into D. Finally let $\mathcal{P}(a)$ stand for a predicate expression over
A. Then:

type
  A, B, C, D
  M = A $\overrightarrow{m}$ B
  $\mathcal{F}$:F = A $\overset{\sim}{\to}$ C
  $\mathcal{G}$:G = B $\overset{\sim}{\to}$ D
  $\mathcal{P}$:P = A → **Bool**

value
   comprehend: $M \times F \times G \times P \to (C \underset{m}{\to} D)$
   comprehend$(m,\mathcal{F},\mathcal{G},\mathcal{P}) \equiv$
     $[\ \mathcal{F}(a) \mapsto \mathcal{G}(m(a))\ |\ a{:}A \bullet a \in \mathbf{dom}\ m \wedge \mathcal{P}(a)\ ]$

is a schematic example of a map comprehension expression. It maps, for those a in the domain of a given map m which satisfy a given predicate $\mathcal{P}$, $\mathcal{F}(a)$ into $\mathcal{G}(m(a))$. The resulting map may be nondeterministic or deterministic independent of whether the argument is deterministic or not. It all depends on some or all of the arguments m, $\mathcal{F}$, $\mathcal{G}$ and $\mathcal{P}$.

    The text $\mathcal{P}(a)$ need not be an invocation of a predicate function, but can be any Boolean-valued expression. It must, however, be deterministic in order to evaluate to **true.**

    We use comprehended map expressions when we wish to implicitly specify (i.e., implicate) possibly infinite maps characterised by some functions $\mathcal{F}$ and $\mathcal{G}$ and some predicate, $\mathcal{P}$.

    Map comprehension, as do set and list comprehension, expresses a form of homomorphic principle: Functions over composite structures being expressed as a(nother) function over the (first) function applied to all immediate constituents of the composite structure. We refer to Sect. 8.4.4 for a first enunciation of the '(homo)morphism' concept.

    The general syntactic form of comprehended map expressions follow:

   <map_comp> ::=
      [<value_expr> $\mapsto$ <value_expr> | <typings> $\bullet$ <bool_expr>]

where the $\bullet$ <bool_expr> part is optional.

16.2.3 Map Binding Patterns and Matching

Earlier we dealt with the concepts of *binding pattern*, *matching* and *binding*, Sect. 13.2.3, for sets, Sects. 14.4.1–14.4.2, for Cartesians, and Sect. 15.2.3 for lists. We shall here consider the construct of *map binding patterns* and the *map matching* and *binding* concepts.

    By a map **let** decomposition *binding pattern* we understand a construct basically of the following form, line 4 below:

type
   A, B, C = A $\underset{m}{\to}$ B
value
   ... **let** $[a \mapsto b] \cup c = e$ **in** ... **end** ...
   post $e = [a \mapsto b] \cup c$, i.e.: $c = e \setminus \{a\} \wedge b = c(a)$

Here it is somehow known that e is a nonempty map. The understanding of **let** $[a \mapsto b] \cup c = e$ **in** ... **end** is that e is map expression with nonempty value, say v, that the free identifier a is *bound* to an arbitrary member of the definition set of v, that the free identifier b is bound to $v(a)$, and that the free identifier c then is *bound* to the remainder of v, that is, a (possibly empty) map without $[a{\mapsto}b]$.

We show a very simple example of the use of set patterns — leaving its decoding to the reader

value
    sum: $(\mathbf{Nat} \xrightarrow{m} \mathbf{Nat}) \to \mathbf{Nat}$
    sum(m) $\equiv$
      if m=[]
        then 0
        else
          let $[a{\mapsto}b] \cup m' = m$ **in**
          $a + b + \text{sum}(m')$
      end end

16.2.4 Nondeterminism

In the map decomposition construct:

    let $[a{\mapsto}b] \cup m = \text{map}$ **in** ... **end**

the selection of the definition set value a is *nondeterministic*. Nondeterminism is an important abstraction mechanism. It expresses that we abstract from the specific choice: Any, or almost any, will do!

16.3 Examples of Map-Based Abstractions

This section "matches" Sections 13.3, 14.3, 15.3, and 17.2. They all give small examples of set, Cartesian, list, map and function-based specifications. They are meant as class lecture examples.

16.3.1 Sorting

Example 16.3 *When Is One List Sorted wrt. Another?:* First we introduce the notion of bijective index maps. A bijective index map is a map from natural numbers into natural numbers, such that the definition and the range sets of these maps are identical, and such that the definition set is the dense set of natural numbers from 1 into the number of elements in the dense sets (when they are nonempty). The idea is that the index map-elements "mimic" indices of a list.

type
  A, Q = A*
  M' = **Nat** $\overrightarrow{m}$ **Nat**
  M = {| m:M' • bijection(m) |}
value
  bijection: M' → **Bool**
  bijection(m) ≡
    dom m = **rng** m = {1..**card dom** m}

  is_sorted_wrt: Q × Q → **Bool**
  is_sorted_wrt(q,q') ≡
    len q = **len** q' ∧ is_sorted(q) ∧
    ∃ m:M • **dom** m = **inds** q ∧
      ∀ i:**Nat** • i ∈ **dom** m ⇒ q(i) = q'(m(i))

∎

16.3.2 Equivalence Relations

Example 16.4 *Simple Map Representation of Equivalence Relations:* We refer to Examples 13.5 and 15.3.

We shall outline a map representation of equivalence relations. Let A be the type on subsets of which we may wish to record some equivalence relation. Let M be any bijective map from A to A. Let the map [d ↦ c, b ↦ a, e ↦ d, a ↦ b, c ↦ e] represent the equivalence relation {{a, b}, {c, d, e}} over the set {a, b, c, d, e}. It can thus be shown that any bijective map records an equivalence relation over its definition set (which, obviously, equals its range set. The function retr_Q takes a bijective map and retrieves a set representation of an equivalence relation.

type
  M' = A $\overrightarrow{m}$ A,   M = {| m:M' • **dom** m = **rng** m |}
value
  retr_Q: M → Q
  retr_Q(m) ≡ {get_eq(a,m) | a:A • a ∈ **dom** m}
    comment:
        different a's that get the same equivalence class
        have these classes reduced to one in the result

  get_eq: A × M $\overset{\sim}{\rightarrow}$ A-**set**
  get_eq(a,m) ≡
    let ns = {a}∪{b | b:A • ∃ c:A•c ∈ ns ∧ b=m(a)} **in** ns **end**
    pre a ∈ **dom** m

  merge: A × A × M $\overset{\sim}{\rightarrow}$ M

merge(a,b,m) ≡
    [c ↦ m(c) | c:A • c ∈ **dom** m ∧ c ∉ {a,b}] ∪ [a ↦ b , m(b) ↦ m(a)]
    pre a≠b ∧ {a,b}⊆**dom** m ∧ a ∉ get_eq(b,m)

∎

16.4 Abstracting and Modelling with Maps

This section "matches" Sections 13.4, 14.4, 15.4, and 17.3. They all give larger examples of set, Cartesian, list and function abstractions and models, which are meant as self-study examples.

The purpose of this section is to introduce *techniques* and *tools* for model-oriented specifications primarily based on maps. Among the *map modelling principles, techniques* and *tools* are (1) *subtyping:* Sometimes a type definition defines "too much". A type constraining (*well-formedness, invariant*) predicate technique can therefore applied. (2) **pre/post**-*conditions:* function abstraction in terms of **pre**- and **post**-*conditions.* (3) *"Input/Output/Query" functions:* Identification of main functions according to their *signature.* (4) *Auxiliary functions:* Decomposition of function definitions into "smallest" units. The *principles* and *techniques* reoccur, for sets, Cartesians and lists in Sections 13.4, 14.4 and 15.4.

We present five kinds of examples: *graphs, structured tables, hierarchies, relational databases* and *pointer-based data structures.*

16.4.1 Graphs

We show an example graph (Fig. 16.1).

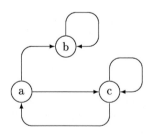

Fig. 16.1. An example directed graph

Example 16.5 *Graphs:* A directed graph consists of nodes and arcs. An arc always "connects" two nodes. "Connection" is a function, here a map, from nodes to sets of nodes. Thus, if, in a directed graph with nodes a, b and c, directed arcs connect a to b and c, b to itself only, and c to a and itself, then:

$$[a \mapsto \{b, c\}, b \mapsto \{b\}, c \mapsto \{a, c\}]$$

is a model of the graph of Fig. 16.1.

Let nodes of graphs be distinctly labelled. Let labels belong to type A, then a concrete, yet representationally abstract type of graphs, G, is:

type
$$G' = A \twoheadrightarrow A\text{-set}$$

What if a node a of a graph g has no arcs (directed edges) emanating from it — how is it modelled in g:G? Then we could choose it to not appear in the definition set of g, but it will appear in one or more range elements — namely for those nodes from which arcs are incident upon a. But what if a node s is isolated in g, i.e., has no arcs leading into it (in-degree 0) and no arcs leading out from it (out-degree 0); how is it to be modelled in g? The answer is: It cannot if we choose the modelling principle of the previous sentence, that is, positive, nonzero in-degree nodes of out-degree 0 appear only in range elements of g. Therefore we sharpen our modelling. Out-degree 0 nodes a in g map into empty sets. Thus all nodes in range elements of g must also be in the definition set of g:

$$G = \{|\ g\ |\ g:G' \cdot \bigcup \text{rng } g \subseteq \text{dom } g\ |\}$$

We have now modelled the type of all directed graphs. Here it is assumed that no two or more directed edges emanate (from) and are incident upon (pairwise) the same nodes.

We now wish to operationally abstract a number of functions on graphs. To find all the nodes reachable through one or more *steps* from a given node a in a given graph g, we define a function Nodes. A "step" from a is any node b connected to a by an edge directed from a to b. Two steps from a is any node c connected by a directed edge from any node b which is reachable in one step from a.

Here we give an *inductive* function definition:

Nodes: $A \times G \rightarrow A\text{-set}$
Nodes(a,g) $\equiv$
    let nodes = g(a) $\cup$ { a' | a':A $\cdot \exists$ a'':A $\cdot$ a'' $\in$ nodes $\wedge$ a' $\in$ g(a'') }
    in nodes **end**

To find out whether a graph is acyclic, i.e., whether any node can be reached in one or more steps from itself, we define a function isAcyclic. The function is to be a predicate which yields truth if no such node exists, falsity otherwise. We use Nodes in the definition of isAcyclic. We do so since a graph is cyclic if some node a is in the set of nodes Nodes(a,g) reachable from a:

isAcyclic: G → **Bool**
isAcyclic(g) ≡ ∀ a:A • a ∈ **dom** g ⇒ a ∉ Nodes(a,g)

The function Nodes produces the set of nodes reachable from a node a, in a graph g whether or not this graph is acyclic, i.e., independent of possible cycles from a, in the direction of arrows, to g.   ∎

16.4.2 Structured Tables

A *table* is like a *relation*. It consists of a finite number of zero, one or more *entries*. Each entry consists of one or more, but a finite number of *fields*. Each field contains a *value*. Let a table have entries of say n fields (*positions* 1 through n), where n is larger than 1. In:

type
    A, C
    B = A-**set**
    B = ... × A × ...
    B = A*
    B = A ⇸ C
    B = C ⇸ A
    ...

If *type* B is one of the alternatives, or, more generally (than hinted at above), some *discrete type*[4] otherwise involving type A, then we say that B is *commensurate* with A. Let entry field values in, for example, field (position) i be of a type commensurate with the type of entry field values of field (position) j, where i≠j. Then we may say that one entry field value *refers* to (or *implies*) one or more other entries. If values contained in one entry implies other entries, then we say that the **table is structured**.

Examples follow.

Example 16.6 *Bill of Materials:*

Narrative — Types

A *simple bill of materials* is a table. Each entry in this table has two parts: a part-number,[5] p, in the type *Pn* of part numbers, and a possibly empty

---

[4]A discrete type "contains" no functions.

[5]Part numbers are not necessarily numbers, but rather general (spare) part identification "numbers".

set of part numbers. If the set is empty the part number p is said to be an elementary, i.e., a noncomposite part (consisting only of itself!). If the set is nonempty, i.e., $\{p_1, p_2, \ldots, p_n\}$ (for $n \geq 1$), then p is said to be composite — consisting of the immediate, or constituent parts $p_1, p_2, \ldots,$ and p_n. Such constituent parts must all be recorded in the simple bill of materials. Constituent parts of p, or constituent parts of constituent parts of p, etc., cannot themselves consist of part p. That is, no part can be recursively constructed. We abstract the type of simple bill of materials by a map from part numbers to sets of part numbers.

Formalisation — Types

type
    BOM_0$'$ = Pn $\underset{m}{\rightarrow}$ Pn-set
    BOM_0 = {| bom | bom:BOM_0$'$ • inv_BOM_0(bom) |}

We have now given an abstract model of a simple bill of materials type. For the sake of illustration we express a "typical" **bom**:

$$\text{bom} : [\; p_1 \mapsto \{p_a, p_b, \ldots, p_c\},$$
$$p_2 \mapsto \{p_d, p_b, \ldots, p_f\}, \ldots$$
$$p_a \mapsto \{\},$$
$$p_b \mapsto \{p_x, p_y\}, \ldots$$
$$p_x \mapsto \{\},$$
$$p_y \mapsto \{\}]$$

Narrative — Invariant

Well-formedness amounts to all constituent parts are recorded, and none is recursively defined.

Formalisation — Invariant

value
    inv_BOM_0(bom) ≡
(1)   ∀ pns:Pn-set • pns ∈ **rng** bom ⇒ pns ⊆ **dom** bom ∧
(2)   ∀ p:P • p ∈ **dom** bom ⇒ p ∉ sub_Pns(p,bom)

    sub_Pns: Pn × BOM_0 $\overset{\sim}{\rightarrow}$ Pn-set
    sub_Pns(p,bom) ≡
(3)   { sp | sp:Pn • depends_on(p,sp,bom) }
(4)   **pre** p ∈ **dom** bom

    depends_on: Pn × Pn × BOM_0 $\overset{\sim}{\rightarrow}$ **Bool**

depends_on(pn,sp,bom) ≡
(5)   sp ∈ **dom** bom(pn) ∨
(6)   ∃ p:Pn • (p ∈ **dom** bom(pn) ∧ depends_on(p,sp,bom))
(7)   **pre** pn ∈ **dom** bom

Annotations: We say that a definition set part number represents a defining occurrence and that a range set of part numbers represent using occurrences of these. (1) If a set of part numbers is used in the table, then they are all defined by the table. (2) If a part number is defined in the table, then it is not used (i.e., defined) recursively. (3) Subsidiary part numbers of a part number p are those that can depend on p in the table. (4) p must be in the table. (5) For a part number sp to depend on a part number pn, either sp must be in the immediately used set of part numbers bom(pn), (6) or there must exist a part number p that is in the using set of part numbers bom(pn) and such that p depends on sp. (7) The "depends on" part number must be in the table.   ∎

Observe that the above definitions of sub_Pns and depends_on represents another way of expressing acyclicity of a graph using Nodes and isAcyclic. It is obvious that the bill_of_materials type is tantamount to a model of graphs!

Other examples of structured tables are compiler dictionaries, operating system directories, and so on. We shall have occasion to see many forms of structured tables in the rest of these volumes.

16.4.3 Hierarchies

Hierarchy:
A body of things ranked in grades, orders, or classes,
one above another
The Shorter Oxford English Dictionary [350] (1643)

There seems to be an obsession, predominantly, it seems, amongst intellectually weak people, politicians and managers especially, to view the world hierarchically — usually with themselves at the top. Most of us tend, since the time of Aristotle (384–322 BC) it seems, to organise our world of documents hierarchically, so much so that now most computing filing systems offer basically hierarchically structured means of access called *directories*. We shall next study a variety of "abstract, generic" hierarchical structures. Their essence is their treelike nature, with *roots* and *branches*.

Concrete phenomena whose structure resembles such trees or similar to hierarchies include books — with the book itself as the root, its various chapters as immediate subtrees, their sections as subtrees of chapter subtrees, etcetera. This can continue down to a usually *definite depth*, achieved at plain texts within subsubsections, or within possible paragraphs, subparagraphs, and even within their maximum depth enumerations (as in these volumes).

Plain text forms *tree leaves*. We normally explain a *leaf* to be a possibly annotated (as for the text) *empty tree*.

Another example is the *organisational structure* — here represented in terms of the staff — of an *enterprise*: a bureaucracy, a company or a hospital. At the top, *"at the root"*, there is the top executive, then follows line management, usually layered in several levels, i.e., hierarchically, then "floor" management with their charge, the "workers", as the leaves, *"at the bottom"!* The above text represented a part analysis of the abstract concept of hierarchy. The analysis was carried out on, i.e., wrt. concrete, "manifestable" phenomena. We are therefore ready to begin a more systematic, but now abstract, treatment.

Example 16.7 *Hierarchies:*

Narrative — Hierarchies

A hierarchy has a root and otherwise consists of zero, one or more distinctly labelled subhierarchies. A root is a further unanalysed quantity. A subhierarchy is a hierarchy. A subhierarchy label is a further unanalysed — albeit, most likely, different kind of quantity.

Formalisation — Hierarchy:

type
  A, B
  AH == cR(sa:A,sh:mH)^6
  mH == cH(sm:(B $\overrightarrow{m}$ AH))
value
  a,a′,...,a″:A, b,b′,...,b″:B, h,h′,...,h″:mH
examples
  h1: cR(a,cH([ ]))
  h2: cR(a,cH([b′↦h′,...,b″↦h″]))
  h3: cR(a,cH([b′↦cR(a′,cH([ ])),...,b″↦cR(a″,cH([b↦h,...,b‴↦h‴]))]))

Annotations. (i) A stand for the further unanalysed root type. (ii) B stand for the further unanalysed branch type. (iii) AH stand for the defined type of Cartesian pairs of A and mH entities. (iv) mH stand for the defined type of maps from B entities to AH entities.

Observations. Nothing was said about the following possibilities: (iv) Can two or more (immediate) subhierarchies of a given hierarchy have identical roots? (v) Can any two branches along a path, i.e., a sequence of "connected" branches, have identical labels? (vi) What, exactly do we mean by immediate

---

^{6}The explanation, here, of "==" variant record definitions, ahead of their proper, formal introduction, was first briefly explained in Sect. 13.4.3. Sects. 18.4 and 18.5 will further deal with record and union types. We will here give a brief "recap".

subhierarchy of a hierarchy? (vii) And what, exactly do we mean by paths? To
this we turn next.

Narrative — Paths

Let there be given a hierarchy. A label, ℓ_1, (from the root of the hierarchy to
the root of a possibly empty subhierarchy, said to be labelled by ℓ_1) is a path.
A path is, in general, a sequence, $\langle \ell_1, \ell_2, \ldots, \ell_i, \ell_{i+1}, \ldots, \ell_n \rangle$, of one or more
labels, ℓ_j, such that each ℓ_j is the label of a subhierarchy for all j, and such
that if $\langle \ell_1, \ell_2, \ldots, \ell_i \rangle$ is a path of the hierarchy, and ℓ_{i+1} is a label of the root
of a subhierarchy labelled by ℓ_i, then $\langle \ell_1, \ell_2, \ldots, \ell_i, \ell_{i+1} \rangle$ is also a path of the
given hierarchy.

Formalisation — Paths

type
 $P = B^*$
value
 gen_Ps: AH $\rightarrow$ P-set
 gen_Ps(cR(a,m)) $\equiv$
  case m **of**
   cH([ ])$\rightarrow$\{$\langle\rangle$\},
   cH(m)$\rightarrow$∪\{$\langle b\rangle\widehat{\ }$p|b:B,p:P•b $\in$ **dom** m∧(p=$\langle\rangle$∨p $\in$ gen_Ps(m(b)))\}
  end

Annotations. Paths are sequences of labels. If a hierarchy is empty, then
it contains just the empty path; else a path consists of a prefix and a suffix
whose first label (the prefix) is any label of a subhierarchy and any path
(including no path, i.e., the empty path) of that subhierarchy. The possibility
of "any path" allows for paths not necessarily ending up at leaves of the given
hierarchy. ∪ expresses the distributed set union.

Narrative — Path Operations

Given a hierarchy and a path, we wish to ascertain whether the latter is a
path of the former. If so we wish to "access" the subhierarchy designated by
the path. And we may wish to delete the designated hierarchy, or we may
wish to replace it by another subhierarchy.

Formalisation — Path Operations

value
 wf_P_in_H: P $\times$ AH $\rightarrow$ **Bool**
 wf_P_in_H(p,h) $\equiv$ p $\in$ gen_Ps(h)

 Access: P $\times$ AH $\overset{\sim}{\rightarrow}$ AH

Access(p,cR(a,cH(m))) ≡
    if p=⟨⟩ **then** cR(a,cH(m)) **else** Access(**tl** p,m(**hd** p)) **end**
    pre wf_P_in_H(p,cR/a,cH(m))

value
    Delete: P × AH $\overset{\sim}{\to}$ AH
    Delete(p,cR(a,cH(m))) ≡
      if p=⟨⟩
        then cR(a,cH([ ]))
        else
            let cH(m') = m(**hd** p) **in**
            let mh = cH([b'↦m'(b')|b':B•b' ∈ **dom** m'∧b'≠**hd** p]
                          ∪[**hd** p↦Delete(**tl** p,m'(**hd** p))]) **in**
            cR(a,mh) **end end**
      end
      pre wf_P_in_H(p,cR(a,cH(m)))

value
    Replace: P × AH × AH $\overset{\sim}{\to}$ AH
    Replace(p,cR(a,cH(m)),sh) ≡
      if p=⟨⟩
        then cR(a,sh)
        else
            let cH(m') = m(**hd** p) **in**
            let mh = cH([b'↦ m'(b')|b':B•b' ∈ **dom** m'∧b'≠**hd** p]
                      ∪[**hd** p↦Replace(**tl** p,m'(**hd** p),sh)]) **in**
            cR(a,mh) **end end**
      end
      pre wf_P_in_H(p,cR(a,cH(m)))

Annotations. The empty path deletes only the hierarchical part, by voiding it, not the A component of its root. A proper subhierarchy is selected. All the proper sub-subhierarchies that are not selected by the prefix label of the path are left unchanged. Only the sub-subhierarchy selected by the prefix label of the path is changed. The delete operation proceeds as from the sub-subhierarchy and wrt. the suffix path.

    The replace operation follows the structure of the delete operation.   ■

Notice how a recursively defined data structure (i.e., type) results in recursively defined operations. Notice also that we could probably find a generic function Generic that traverses the hierarchy as do both Delete and Replace, but which is given different arguments for effecting deletes, respectively replacements. To define this function is left as a standard exercise for parameterised higher-order functional programming.

16.4.4 Relational File Systems (IV) and Databases

This is the fourth in a series of models of what we could call *file systems*. Other models are presented in Examples 13.6 (sets), 14.2 (Cartesians and sets), and 15.6 (lists, Cartesians and sets). See also Exercise 16.11.

The next two examples resemble each other. The first, Example 16.8, purports to be that of a simple, "classical" file system. While the second, Example 16.9, purports to be that of a simple, "classical" relational database system. Observe their rather similar types. Observe also the use of record type definitions of VALues. Record type definitions were first informally introduced in Sect. 13.4.3, and will be formally covered in Sect. 18.4. And finally observe the use of subtype definition, of FILE. Subtype definitions were already introduced informally in Sect. 13.7, and will be formally covered in Sect. 18.8.

Example 16.8 *A File System:* A file system consists of a set of uniquely named files. Each file consists of a set of uniquely "keyed" records. All records of a given file have the same number of "correspondingly" typed and uniquely named field values.

type
>   Fn, An, Key
>   FS = Fn $\rightarrow$ FILE
>   FILE$'$ = Key $\overrightarrow{m}$ REC
>   FILE = {| file:FILE$'$ • wf_FILE(file) |}
>   REC = An $\overrightarrow{m}$ VAL
>   VAL = Integer | Boolean | Textstring
>   Integer == mk_Integer(i:**Int**)[7]
>   Boolean == mk_Boolean(b:**Bool**)
>   Textstring == mk_Textstring(s:**Text**)
>   Kind == integer | Boolean | string

Notice the use of the variant record way of defining types. In Fig. 16.2 we contrast two ways of defining union of types. To the left the union (|) of types B, C, ... and D is discriminated, that is, one can distinguish the types. To the right one cannot.

The latter (to the right), in effect, makes the types B, C, ..., D identical. The former (to the left) makes them distinct by virtue of distinct constructor names: mk_β, mk_γ, ..., mk_δ. These names are allowed to be, or to contain, the same type name as appears on the left-hand side of the corresponding type definition. We shall say no more on constructor types for the moment.

---

[7]Again we use the variant type construction. See footnote 6.

Fig. 16.2. Discriminate and indiscriminate union, |, of types.

type	**type**
X, Y	X, Y
A = B | C | ... | D	A = B | C | ... | D
B == mk_β(x:X,y:Y)	B = X × Y
C == mk_γ(f:X,y:Y)	C = X × Y
...	...
D == mk_δ(x:X,g:Y)	D = X × Y

Any two records of the same file must have values of the same type for the same attribute name. This type constraint (i.e., subtype condition) is defined below:

value
  wf_FILE: FILE$'$ → **Bool**
  wf_FILE(file) ≡
    ∀ r,r$'$:REC •
      dom r=**dom** r$'$∧∀ a:An•a ∈ **dom** r=type_of(r(a))=type_of(r$'$(a))

  type_of: VAL → Kind
  type_of(v) ≡
    case v **of**
      mk_Integer(ij) → integer,
      mk_Boolean(tf) → Boolean,
      mk_Textstring(cs) → string
    end

We leave as an exercise (Exercise 16.11) to formally specify a number of operations on the above file system.   ∎

Example 16.9 *Relational Database System:* A relational database system, sys:SYS, has two components: a schema, sch:SCH, defining the type of all database relations; and the database, rdb:RDB.

  The relational database, rdb:RDB, can be characterised as follows: rdb:RDB consists of a number of uniquely identified, r:R, relations, rel:REL, where a relation rel:REL consists of a set of identically attributed tuples, tpl:TPL. Each tuple, tpl:TPL, has a distinct number of differently named attributes, a:A, and, for each attribute, there is its value, v:VAL.

  Values are either integers, reals or character strings. Thus values are of types **integer**, **realno**, **string**, respectively. Given a value we can deduce its type. The relational schema, sch:SCH, defines the types of relation attributes, and can be characterised as follows: For each relation, named r:R, there is defined the type for each of the attributes.

type
  R, A
  SYS′ = SCH × RDB, SYS = {| sys:SYS′ • wf_SYS(sys) |}
  SCH = R $\overrightarrow{m}$ TplTyp
  TplTyp = A $\overrightarrow{m}$ Typ
  Typ == integer | realno | text
  RDB = R $\overrightarrow{m}$ REL
  REL′ = TPL-**set**, REL = {| rel:REL′ • wf_REL(rel) |}
  TPL = A $\overrightarrow{m}$ VAL
  VAL == mk_int(i:**Int**)
       | mk_real(r:**Real**)
       | mk_txt(txt:**Text**)

We model values as a type of three disjoint types, disjointness afforded by the use of the distinctly named type record constructors mk_int, mk_real, and mk_txt. For disjointness of record types, see Sect. 18.4 (specifically the paragraph on *Records: Constructors and Destructors*).

value
  typ: VAL → Typ
  typ(v) ≡
    case v **of**
      mkint(i) → integer,
      mkreal(r) → realno,
      mktxt(txt) → text
    end

  wf_SYS: SYS′ → **Bool**
  wf_SYS(sch,rdb) ≡
    wf_RDB(rdb) ∧ **dom** rdb ⊆ **dom** sch
    ∀ r:R • r ∈ **dom** rdb ⇒ wf_TPLs(sch(r),rdb(r))

  wf_RDB: RDB′ → **Bool**
  wf_RDB(rdb) ≡ ∀ r:R • r ∈ **dom** rdb ⇒ wf_REL(rdb(r))

  wf_REL: REL → **Bool**
  wf_REL(rel) ≡
    ∀ t,t′:TPL • {t,t′}⊆rel ⇒ **dom** t = **dom** t′ ∧
      ∀ a:A • s ∈ **dom** t ⇒ typ(t(a))=typ(t′(a))

  wf_TPLs: TplTyp × REL → **Bool**
  wf_TPLs(tt,rel) ≡

> rel={} ∨
> **let** t:TPL • t ∈ rel ⇒ ∀ a:A • a ∈ **dom** t ⇒ tt(a)=typ(t(a)) **end**
> **assert:**
>   ∀ t:TPL • t ∈ rel ⇒ tt(a)=typ(t(a))
>
>   ■

16.4.5 Complex Pointer Data Structures

Complex, usually implementation-oriented, data structures, such as we are used to in imperative programming languages like PL/I, Pascal, C++, etcetera, and data structures like linked lists, graphs and trees were implemented using *references, pointers, links, addresses* (all are synonymous names), or concepts having similar connotations. They were all justified by the imperative programming language notion of storage, with storage being understood as having locations which contained values, with *references, pointers, links, addresses*, etc., being allowed as *first class* values.

The next examples illustrates the point being made above.

Example 16.10 *Pointer-Based Data Structures: Development:*
This is a metaexample! After the text below we present Examples 16.11–16.20, which substitute for this example!

Next we show a number of related examples. They illustrate, besides extensive use of map abstractions (as well as models using sets, Cartesians and lists), such development concepts as *reification, retrieve functions,* (or *abstraction functions*) and *injection relations*. The examples also illustrate the need for defining appropriate *well-formedness predicates*. These will be illustrated in Examples 16.22–16.30.   ■

Our first in a long series of 10 examples (Examples 16.11–16.20) is informal. It exemplifies the representation of a graph in terms of what are known as adjacency lists.

Example 16.11 *Pointer Data Structure Graphs — Reification:* Figure 16.3 diagrams a "classical" way of representing graphs. The emphasis is on the adjacency chain model of graphs.

Transforming, as it were, the "abstract" graph picture in the left part of Fig. 16.3, into the "concrete" data structure in the right part of Fig. 16.3, is referred to as *reification. Reification* is a major technique for developing abstract specifications into concrete designs. Other terms are *data structure transformation* and *concretisation.*

The triplet and doublet boxes designate some form of *record values.* The arrows designate storage addresses (i.e., pointers). The **Sentinel** part of Fig. 16.3 on the next page represents a declared, named variable.

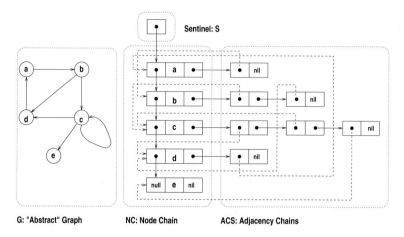

Fig. 16.3. Abstract and concrete graphs

We consider the *node chain* and *adjacency chain* parts of Fig. 16.3 to reflect the "layout" of typically dynamically allocated storage, i.e., unnamed storage.[8]

In the following we shall slowly introduce a series of models of graphs, which will lead to the above model in such a way as to facilitate reasoning about its correctness. ∎

We now embark on a list of development steps. Eventually we will reach a formalisation of the adjacency list representation just exemplified informally. We start by representing each node and its adjacency list as a pair: a node and its immediate, i.e., adjacent successors.

Example 16.12 *Map/Set Graphs:* First we recall, as G0 (next), a simple model of graphs. The range sets of nodes are called the adjacency sets.

type
  N
  G0 = N $\overrightarrow{m}$ N-set
value
  a,b,c,d,e : N

---

[8]By dynamically allocated storage is understood a storage some of whose locations (i.e., storage cells) are set aside for storing values. Such "setting aside" is typically the result of program clauses that explicitly prescribe the creation of such cells. Typically such a clause may have the syntactical form: allocate with type t — which as an expression yields a pointer value. (The terms allocate, with and type are keywords. The identifier t is (assumed to be) a type name.) Graph data structures, as here, with an unknown number of nodes and edges, are typical candidates for dynamically allocated storage representations.

g0:G0
axiom
  [all nodes are distinct]
    card{a,b,c,d,e}=5
  [graph is a constant]
    g0=[a↦{b},b↦{c,d},c↦{c,d,e},d↦{a},e↦{}]

The cardinality predicate expresses that nodes a,b,c,d,e are distinct. The g0=... predicate expresses that g0 is bound to a specific g0 value, not, as in g0:G0, to an arbitrary G0 value.

We also show, above, the particular value of g0 for the graph shown in the left-hand side of Fig. 16.3. We omit expression of well-formedness.   ∎

Instead of modelling immediate successors as a set, we now represent them as lists.

Example 16.13 *Map/List Graphs:* We recast model G0 into G1, in which adjacency sets have become adjacency chains.

type
  N
  G0 = N $\overrightarrow{m}$ N-set
  G1 = N $\overrightarrow{m}$ N*
value
  a,b,c,d,e : N
  g1 : G1
axiom
  [∀ nodes are distinct]
    card{a,b,c,d,e}=5
  [graph is a constant]
    g1=[a↦⟨b⟩,b↦⟨c,d⟩,c↦⟨c,d,e⟩,d↦⟨a⟩,e ↦⟨⟩]

value
  wf_G1: G1 → **Bool**
  retr_G0: G1 $\overset{\sim}{\rightarrow}$ G0
  retr_G0(g1) ≡ [n↦**elems**(g1(n1))|n:N•n ∈ **dom** g1]

Again we omit expression of well-formedness. retr_G0 is a function which *retrieves* well-formed G0 values from well-formed G1 values.   ∎

In the next step, instead of modelling the set of all pairs of nodes and adjacency lists as a map from nodes to lists, we model it as a list of pairs.

Example 16.14 *Embedded List Graphs:* We recast model G1 into G2, in which the node map has become a node chain.

type
    N
    $G1 = N \underset{\overrightarrow{m}}{} N^*$
    $G2 = (N \times N^*)^*$
value
    a,b,c,d,e : N
    g2 : G2
axiom
    [∀ nodes are distinct]
        card{a,b,c,d,e}=5
    [graph is a constant]
        g2 =
            ⟨ a ↦ ⟨b⟩, b ↦ ⟨c,d⟩, c ↦ ⟨c,d,e⟩, d ↦ ⟨a⟩, e ↦ ⟨⟩ ⟩

value
    wf_G2: G2 → **Bool**
    retr_G0: G2 $\overset{\sim}{\to}$ G1
    retr_G1(g2) ≡
        ⟨ **let** (n,nl)=g1(i) **in**
            (n,⟨nl(j) | j:**Nat** • 1≤j≤len nl ⟩) **end**
            | i:**Nat** • 1≤i≤len g2⟩

retr_G1 is a function which *retrieves* well-formed G1 values from well-formed G0 values.   ∎

In the next step, as an illustration, we represent the list of pairs of nodes and node lists, as a map, now from natural number encodings of (source) nodes (i.e., their names), into a pair: the node and a map from natural number encodings of (adjacent, i.e., target) nodes into their node (names).

Example 16.15 *Cartesian/Index Map Graphs:* We now observe that lists, in general, can be thought of as functions from their indices into their elements. Hence we recast model G2 into G3, in which the node and adjacency chains (which were modelled as lists) have become index maps.

type
    N
    $G2 = (N \times N^*)^*$
    $G3 = \mathbf{Nat} \underset{\overrightarrow{m}}{} (N \times (\mathbf{Nat} \underset{\overrightarrow{m}}{} N))$
value
    a,b,c,d,e : N
    g3 : G3

axiom
    [all nodes are distinct]
      card{a,b,c,d,e}=5
    [graph is a constant]
      g3 =
          [1 ↦ (a,[1↦b]),
            2 ↦ (b,[1↦c,2↦d]),
            3 ↦ (c,[1↦c,2↦d,3↦e]),
            4 ↦ (d,[1↦a]),
            5 ↦ (e,[])]

value
    wf_G3: G3 → **Bool**
    inj_G3: G2 → G3
    inj_G3(g2) ≡
      [i ↦ **let** (n,nl) = g2(i) **in** (n,[j ↦ nl(j) | j:**Nat** • j ∈ **inds** nl]) **end**
        | i:**Nat** • i ∈ **inds** g2]

    retr_G2: G3 $\overset{\sim}{\to}$ G2
    retr_G2(g3) **as** g2
      pre wf_G3(g2)
      post g3 = inj_G3(g2)
    assert:
      ∀ g2:G2 • retr_G2(inj_G3(g2))=g2 ∧
      ∀ g3:G3 • inj_G3(retr_G2(g3))=g3 ∧
      retr_G2°inj_G3 = λx.x = inj_G3°retr_G2

inj_G3 is a function which *injects* well-formed G2 values into well-formed G3 values. retr_G2 is a function which *retrieves* well-formed G2 values from well-formed G3 values. The composition of the two functions, retr_G2 and inj_G3, (in any order) yields the *identity function*. ∎

Instead of relying on list indices and on the ordering of natural numbers we introduce pointers as we know them from classical storage models.

Example 16.16 *Cartesian/Pointer/Map/List Graphs:* We now "equate" the indices with locations of storage, or would like to do so. But doing so directly, without any precaution, might give us problems such as: (i) first, the indices of the various adjacency chain "storage parts" (may) coincide, i.e., designate "overlapping" adjacency storages. (ii) Second, they also "overlap" with the node chain "storage part". By overlap we mean that a designated value (may) partly or fully "occupy" the same storage locations. (iii) Third, the indices always started with index 1, and we must, in general, be prepared to model arbitrary storage allocations. Hence we introduce a notion of anonymous storage addresses, i.e., pointers.

We first reify the node chain map. Index pointers "carry" with them an ordering. Anonymous pointers are assumed not to have an ordering. Hence we need two things: to indicate which is a first node of a node chain, and to indicate, for each node in a node chain, which is "the next" node. A sentinel, OP, component of G4 designates a possible first node. A next node pointer, OP, component of each node designates a possible next node.

type
  N, P
  $G4 = OP \times (P \underset{m}{\rightarrow} (OP \times N \times N^*))$
  OP = null | P
value
  a,b,c,d,e : N
  p_a, p_b, p_c, p_d, p_e : P
  g4 : G4
axiom
  card$\{p_a, p_b, p_c, p_d, p_e\}$=5,
  g4=$(p_a,$
      $[p_a \mapsto (p_b, a, \langle b \rangle),$
      $p_b \mapsto (p_c, b, \langle c, d \rangle),$
      $p_c \mapsto (p_d, c, \langle c, d, e \rangle),$
      $p_d \mapsto (p_e, d, \langle a \rangle),$
      $p_e \mapsto (null, e, \langle \rangle),])$

The combination of sentinel and next node pointers must designate a linear chain. We leave, in Example 16.26 the expression of well-formedness. Note how null pointers terminate a node chain. ∎

We augment the model to include proper records: For source nodes these structures record the next node by a pointer, the name of the source node and a pointer to the first, if any, successor node. Successor nodes are also represented as records. They record the name of the successor node and a pointer the another adjacent node. Storage now contains a sentinel pointer to a possibly first, arbitrarily chosen node, otherwise maps pointer to source node records.

Example 16.17 *Cartesian/Pointer/Embedded Map Graphs:* Next we reify the adjacency chains (which were modelled as lists). Each node of a node chain contains ("sentinels", as a verb) a possible link to a first edge. Next edge links analogous to next node pointers. Each edge chain is to remain a proper part of a node chain node element.

type
  N, P, L
  $G5 = OP \times (P \underset{m}{\rightarrow} NR)$

$NR = OP \times N \times (OL \times (L \underset{m}{\rightarrow} ER))$
$ER = N \times OL$
$OP = null \mid P$
$OL = nil \mid L$

value

$p_a, p_b, p_c, p_d, p_e : P$
$\ell_{b_a}, \ell_{c_b}, \ell_{d_b}, \ell_{c_c}, \ell_{d_c}, \ell_{e_c}, \ell_{a_d} : L$
$g5 : G5$

axiom

$[\; \forall \text{ pointers are distinct }]$
  $\mathbf{card}\{p_a, p_b, p_c, p_d, p_e\} = 5$
$[\text{ links } \mathbf{of} \text{ each adjacency list are distinct }]$
  $\mathbf{card}\{\ell_{c_b}, \ell_{d_b}\} = 2, \; \mathbf{card}\{\ell_{c_c}, \ell_{d_c}, \ell_{e_c}\} = 3$
$[\text{ graph} \equiv \text{a constant }]$
  $g5 =$
    $(\; p_a,$
      $[\; p_a \mapsto (p_b, a, (\ell_{b_a}, [\ell_{b_a} \mapsto (a, nil)])),$
        $p_b \mapsto (p_c, b, (\ell_{c_b}, [\ell_{c_b} \mapsto (c, \ell_{d_b}), \ell_{d_b} \mapsto (d, nil)])),$
        $p_c \mapsto (p_d, c, (\ell_{c_c}, [\ell_{c_c} \mapsto (c, \ell_{e_c}), \ell_{d_c} \mapsto (d, \ell_{e_c}), \ell_{e_c} \mapsto (e, nil)])),$
        $p_d \mapsto (p_e, d, (\ell_{a_d}, [\ell_{a_d} \mapsto (a, nil)])),$
        $p_e \mapsto (null, e, (nil, [\,]))\;]\;)$

The stepwise development continues in the next examples.

Example 16.18 *Cartesian/Pointer/Distinct Map Graphs:* We now partly factor adjacency chains out from node chain node elements into a separate adjacency chains "storage", i.e., one shared by all adjacency chains.

type
  N, P, L
  $G6 = OP \times (P \underset{m}{\rightarrow} NR) \times (L \underset{m}{\rightarrow} ER)$
  $NR = OP \times N \times OL$
  $ER = P \times OL$
  $OP = null \mid P$
  $OL = nil \mid L$
value
  $p_a, p_b, p_c, p_d, p_e : P$
  $\ell_{b_a}, \ell_{c_b}, \ell_{d_b}, \ell_{c_c}, \ell_{d_c}, \ell_{e_c}, \ell_{a_d} : L$
  $g6 : G6$

axiom
[∀ pointers are distinct]
  card$\{p_a,p_b,p_c,p_d,p_e\}$=5
[∀ links are distinct]
  card$\{\ell_{b_a},\ell_{c_b},\ell_{d_b},\ell_{c_c},\ell_{d_c},\ell_{e_c},\ell_{a_d}\}$=7
[graph g6 ≡ a constant]

g6 =
  (p_a,
  [$p_a \mapsto (p_b,a,\ell_{b_a})$,
    $p_b \mapsto (p_c,b,\ell_{c_b})$,
    $p_c \mapsto (p_d,c,\ell_{c_c})$,
    $p_d \mapsto (p_e,d,\ell_{a_d})$,
    $p_e \mapsto (null,e,nil)$],
  [$\ell_{b_a} \mapsto (a,nil)$,
    $\ell_{c_b} \mapsto (c,\ell_{d_b})$,
    $\ell_{d_b} \mapsto (d,nil)$,
    $\ell_{c_c} \mapsto (c,\ell_{e_c})$,
    $\ell_{d_c} \mapsto (d,\ell_{e_c})$,
    $\ell_{e_c} \mapsto (e,nil)$,
    $\ell_{a_d} \mapsto (a,nil)$])

■

Example 16.19 *Record/Pointer/Shared Map Graphs:* We next "fold" the two "storages" into one: merging the node chain storage with the common adjacency chains storage. Thus we no longer distinguish between node pointers and edge links; all are pointers.

type
  N, P
  G7 = OP × (P $\overrightarrow{m}$ (NR|ER))
  NR == mkNR(p:OP,n:N,ol:OL)
  ER == mkER(p:P,ol:OL)
  OP == null | mkP(p:P)
  OL == nil | mkL(p:P)

value
  $p_a,p_a,p_a,p_a,p_a,p_{b_a},p_{b_a},p_{b_a},p_{b_a},p_{b_a},p_{b_a}$: P
  g7 : G7
axiom
  [∀ pointers are distinct]
    card$\{p_a,p_b,p_c,p_d,p_e,p_{b_a},p_{c_b},p_{d_b},p_{c_c},p_{d_c},p_{e_c},p_{a_d}\}$=12

[graph ≡ a constant]
  g7 = (p_a,
      [p_a ↦ mkNR(mkP(p_b),a,mkL(p_{b_a})),
        p_b ↦ mkNR(mkP(p_c),b,mkL(p_{c_b})),
        p_c ↦ mkNR(mkP(p_d),c,mkL(p_{c_c})),
        p_d ↦ mkNR(mkP(p_e),d,mkL(p_{a_d})),
        p_e ↦ mkNR(null,e,nil),
        p_{b_a} ↦ mkER(a,nil),
        p_{c_b} ↦ mkER(c,mkL(p_{d_b})),
        p_{d_b} ↦ mkER(d,nil),
        p_{c_c} ↦ mkER(c,mkL(p_{e_c})),
        p_{d_c} ↦ mkER(d,mkL(p_{e_c})),
        p_{e_c} ↦ mkER(e,nil),
        p_{a_d} ↦ mkER(a,nil)])

■

And finally we are satisfied!

Example 16.20 *Cartesian/Pointer/Shared Map Graphs:* Finally we remove the record constructors from node and edge elements, and from next node addresses and next edge addresses.

type
  N, P
  G8 = OP × (P $\overrightarrow{m}$ (NR|ER))
  NR = OP × N × OL
  ER = P × OL
  OP = null | P
  OL = nil | P

value
  p_a,p_a,p_a,p_a,p_a,p_{b_a},p_{b_a},p_{b_a},p_{b_a},p_{b_a},p_{b_a},p_{b_a} : P
  g8 : G8
axiom
  [∀ pointers are distinct]
    card{p_a,p_b,p_c,p_d,p_e,p_{b_a},p_{c_b},p_{d_b},p_{c_c},p_{d_c},p_{e_c},p_{a_d}}=12

  [graph ≡ a constant]
    g8 =
      (p_a,
      [p_a↦(p_b,a,p_{b_a}),
        p_b↦(p_c,b,p_{c_b}),
        p_c↦(p_d,c,p_{c_c}),

$$p_d \mapsto (p_e, d, p_{a_d}),$$
$$p_e \mapsto (\text{null}, e, \text{nil}),$$
$$p_{b_a} \mapsto (a, \text{nil}),$$
$$p_{c_b} \mapsto (c, p_{d_b}),$$
$$p_{d_b} \mapsto (d, \text{nil}),$$
$$p_{c_c} \mapsto (c, p_{e_c}),$$
$$p_{d_c} \mapsto (d, p_{e_c}),$$
$$p_{e_c} \mapsto (e, \text{nil}),$$
$$p_{a_d} \mapsto (a, \text{nil}) \,])$$

■

Discussion

Examples 16.11–16.20 illustrated the conversion of (G0) general maps and sets, in steps of *reification*, (G1) into general maps and lists; (G2) these into lists of lists; (G3) these "back" into index maps, index pointers and lists; (G4) these into anonymous pointer maps, Cartesians and lists; (G5,G6,G7) these into anonymous pointer maps and Cartesians — of varying degrees of "generality" while, in G7, illustrating records ("tagged storage values"); and (G8) finally illustrated a basically "untagged" storage model. The *reifications* of this example were supported by *retrieve functions*, or, as they are also called, *abstraction functions*, as well as *injection functions*. Usually these are not functions, but *injection relations*: To an abstract value there usually correspond several, "equally valid" concrete, i.e., *reified*, values.

We refer to the discussion found at the end of the next examples.

16.4.6 Well-formedness of Data Structures

Example 16.21 *Pointer-Based Data Structures: Well-formedness:*
This is a metaexample. After the text below we present Examples 16.22–16.30.

We shall present well-formedness for all steps of development in the form of a sequence of examples. In initial steps expressing the well-formedness criteria is relatively simple and easy. For the pointer- and link-based realisations the expression of well-formedness is not so straightforward. The reason for this is immediate: Pointers (etc.) designate paths through the concrete data structure, and these paths may merge or "loop", whereas, for this case, the node chain next pointers and the adjacency chain next pointers must form lists. To express that logically and precisely, informally and formally, without resorting to "graph vertex marking" algorithms, is not that easy.   ■

Example 16.22 *Well-formed G0 Graphs:* See Example 16.12 for an example value. All range node names must be in the definition set of the map.

type
  N
  G0 = N $\overrightarrow{m}$ N-set
value
  wf_G0: G0 → **Bool**
  wf_G0(g0) ≡ ∪ **rng** g0 ⊆ **dom** g0

∎

Example 16.23 *Well-formed G1 Graphs:* See Example 16.13 for an example value. All elements of range lists (i.e., the adjacency chains) must be in the definition set (i.e., the node chain) of the map.

type
  N
  G1 = N $\overrightarrow{m}$ N*
value
  wf_G1: G1 → **Bool**
  wf_G1(g1) ≡ ∪{**elems**(g1(n))|n:N•n ∈ **dom** g1}⊆**dom** g1

∎

Example 16.24 *Well-formed G2 Graphs:* See Example 16.14 for an example value. All adjacency chain (list) elements must be in the set of elements formed by the first element of all pairs (i.e., the node chain).

type
  N
  G2 = (N × N*)*
value
  wf_G2: G2 → **Bool**
  wf_G2(g2) ≡
    ∪{**elems**(nl)|(,,nl):(N×N*)•(n,nl)∈ g3}
    ⊆ ∪{n|(n,nl):(N×N*)•(n,nl)∈ g3}

∎

Example 16.25 *Well-formed G3 Graphs:* See Example 16.15 for an example value. All node chain index maps and all adjacency chain index maps (if nonempty) must have dense definition sets starting with 1. All range elements of adjacency chain maps must be in the set of elements formed by the first elements of all range elements of the node chain map.

type
  N
  G3 = **Nat** $\overrightarrow{m}$ (N × (**Nat** $\overrightarrow{m}$ N))
value
  wf_G3: G3 → **Bool**
  wf_G3(g3) ≡
    dom g3 = {1..**card dom** g3}∧
    ∀ (n,m):(N × (**Nat** $\overrightarrow{m}$ N))•(n,m)∈ **rng** g3
      ⇒ **dom** m = {1..**card dom** m}

∎

Example 16.26 *Well-formed G4 Graphs:* See Example 16.16 for an example value. The node chain designated by the sentinel and the next node pointers must be linear and include exactly all range elements. The set of all node names contained in the adjacency chains of the third component of each node chain element must be in the set of node names formed by the second node chain element.

type
  N, P
  G4 = OP × (P $\overrightarrow{m}$ (OP × N × N*))
  OP = null | P
value
  wf_G4: G4 → **Bool**
  wf_G4(s,m) ≡ ... see Exercise 16.1 ...

∎

Example 16.27 *Well-formed G5 Graphs:* See Example 16.17 for an example value. The node chain designated by the sentinel and the next node pointers must be linear and include exactly all range elements. The set of all node names contained in the adjacency chain map edge elements of the third component of each node chain element must be in the set of node names formed by the second node chain element.

type
  N, P, L
  G5 = OP × (P $\overrightarrow{m}$ NR)
  NR = OP × N × (OL × (L $\overrightarrow{m}$ ER))
  ER = N × OL
  OP = null | P
  OL = nil | L

value
  wf_G5: G5 → **Bool**
  wf_G5(s,m) ≡ ... see Exercise 16.1 ...

Example 16.28 *Well-formed G6 Graphs:* See Example 16.18 for an example value.

type
  N, P, L
  G6 = OP × (P ⇸ NR) × (L ⇸ ER)
  NR = OP × N × OL
  ER = P × OL
  OP = null | P
  OL = nil | P
value
  wf_G6: G6 → **Bool**
  wf_G6(s,nm,am) ≡ ... see Exercise 16.1 ...

Example 16.29 *Well-formed G7 Graphs:* See Example 16.19 for an example value.

type
  N, P
  G7 = OP × (P ⇸ (NR|ER))
  NR == mkNR(p:OP,n:N,ol:OL)
  ER == mkER(p:P,ol:OL)
  OP == null | mkP(p:P)
  OL == nil | mkL(p:P)
value
  wf_G7: G7 → **Bool**
  wf_G7(s,m) ≡ ... see Exercise 16.1 ...

Example 16.30 *Well-formed G8 Graphs:* See Example 16.20 for an example value.

type
  N, P
  G8 = OP × (P ⇸ (NR|ER))
  NR = OP × N × OL

$$ER = P \times OL$$
$$OP = null \mid P$$
$$OL = nil \mid P$$
value
$\quad$ wf_G8: G8 $\rightarrow$ **Bool**
$\quad$ wf_G8(s,m) $\equiv$ ... see Exercise 16.1 ...

$\blacksquare$

Discussion

As for the "prerequisite" examples (Examples 16.11–16.20), the present examples (Examples 16.22–16.30) illustrated many facets of development: The need for and techniques of expressing *constraints* (i.e., *invariants, well-formedness*) over data structures; *stepwise development*; and *explorative* (nearly the same, here, as *experimental*) development. The last concept, *explorative development*, may warrant a few comments. It is sometimes not so easy, i.e., relatively quick or obvious, to find a most suitable next step or stage of development. Exploring and experimenting with different ways of development and its expression, and doing this also formally, is, oftentimes, a good way of "discovery". Thus we explore different reifications, while experimenting with their expression.

There is a final, important observation to make. We have not shown any of the *operations* that may otherwise use or change the node and adjacency chain data structure. In particular the latter are of interest — to really justify our heavy investment, in this long example (and its predecessor examples): *Adding nodes* to a graph means adding node records and preparing for an adjacency list, and *adding edges* to a graph means adding edge records, while maintaining the invariance of the data structure "between" the "additions" of nodes and edges; similarly for *removing nodes* and *edges nodes*. It is thus we see that well-formedness criteria are also constraints, or, better, are invariants of the respective data structures.

16.4.7 Discussion

Let us now distil some of the essence of the above examples wrt. map abstraction and modelling principles, techniques and tools. More will follow in Sect. 16.6. Maps form a major model-oriented tool for abstraction and modelling. "Classical" discrete mathematics structures, as well as "classical" algorithmic data structures, often find their most immediate abstraction in terms of maps. We typically model "fragments" of dynamically allocated storage as explicit maps from addresses (pointer, links) to values. Usually conventional, imperative programming languages "hide" the storage structures: Addresses are not always allowed as values, i.e., they are not always "first-class values"[9]. Here we open up for, and delineate — cum identify — specific, relevant parts of the storage that one needs to consider for a specific data structure (cf. Examples 16.12–16.30). In a later step of implementation we can then merge this fragment with other such fragments, and merge all these together with storage for explicitly declared and named variables. Operations — and we have not seen so many in the examples referred to above — which change a data structure must be seen to preserve defined well-formedness criteria, i.e., invariants over these.

16.5 Inductive Map Definitions

16.5.1 Inductive Map Type Definitions

Let

type
  $M = M \overrightarrow{m} M$.

A naive model, $\mathcal{M}$, of M could be

$$\mathcal{M}: \{[\,],[[\,]\mapsto[\,]],[[\,]\mapsto[[\,]\mapsto[\,]]],[[[\,]\mapsto[\,]]\mapsto[\,]],...\}$$

From a pragmatic viewpoint the definition $M = M \overrightarrow{m} M$ is quite meaningless. For an equation of the above kind to make mathematical sense it must be the case that the cardinality of the class of values of type M of the left-hand side must be equal to the cardinality of the class of values of type M of the right-hand side. Obviously this is not the case. So we reject this kind of recursive type definition.

  Some possibly desirable variants are:

type
  A, B
  $Ma = A \overrightarrow{m} Ma$
  $Mab = A \overrightarrow{m} (B|Mab)$

The above are just hypothetical structures.

  To avoid problems we formulate these instead as:

type
  A, B
  $M = A \overrightarrow{m} Ma$
  $Ma == mkM(sm:M)$

---

[9]By a 'first-class value' we mean one which, in the context of ordinary, imperative programming languages, is allowed to serve as a value in any context: as one that can be assigned to a variable, as a constant, as a parameter to a procedure invocation, etcetera.

respectively:

type
    A, B
    M = A $\xrightarrow{m}$ Mab
    Mab == mkB(sb:B) | mkM(sm:M)

Now RSL guarantees sensible models of these concrete type definitions.

16.5.2 Inductive Map Value Definitions

Example 16.31 *Map-, List-, Cartesian- and Set-Based Model of Networks:*
We rephrase the solution of Example 15.11. That example was itself a rephrasing of Example 14.8, which, in turn, was a rephrasing of Example 13.12.
    We now present a rather concrete model of networks:

type
    Si, Ci, Sn, Cn, S_Misc, C_Misc
    Len = **Real**
    S = Sn × Len × S_Misc
    C = Cn × C_Misc
    N' = Ss × Cs × G
    N = {| n:N' • wfN(n) |}
    Ss = Si $\xrightarrow{m}$ S
    Cs = Ci $\xrightarrow{m}$ C
    G' = Ci $\xrightarrow{m}$ (Si $\xrightarrow{m}$ Ci)
    G = {| g:G' • wfG(g) |}

The model separates networks into three parts: One part that defines segments. Think of this part as a relation, Segments, in a relational database. Each tuple has a unique key, si:Si, and otherwise contains the segment name, the segment length and some additional segment attributes. Another part that defines connections. Think of this part as a relation, Connectors, in a relational database. Each tuple has a unique key, ci:Ci, and otherwise contains the connector name and some additional connector attributes. A third part, the graph part, defines how connectors (identified by their unique connector identifiers) connect to other connectors via segments (identified by their unique connector and segment identifiers). The well-formedness of these graphs is left as an exercise. We refer to Example 16.5.
    Given a graph we can, as illustrated in Example 14.9, express its closure with respect to lines.

type
    G' = Ci $\xrightarrow{m}$ (Si $\xrightarrow{m}$ Ci)
    G = {| g:G' • wfG(g) |}

value
   closure: G → G
   closure(g) ≡
      let clo =
         [ci ↦ [si ↦ ci′
         | si:Si,ci′:Ci •
           ∧ (si ∈ **dom** g(ci)∧ci′=(g(ci))(si))∨
             (∃ si′,si″:Si,ci″:Ci •
                si′ ∈ **dom** clo(ci)∧ci″=(clo(ci))(si′)∧si″ ∈ **dom**(clo(ci″))∧
                ci′=(clo(ci″))(si″)∧si=comp(si′,si″))]
         | ci:Ci • ci ∈ **dom** g] **in**
      clo **end**

The well-formedness of networks is defined by:

value
   wfN: N → **Bool**
   wfN(ss,cs,g) ≡
      dom cs = **dom** g ∧
      dom ss = ∪{**dom**(g(ci))|ci:Ci•ci ∈ **dom** g} ∧
      dom g = ∪{**rng**(g(ci))|ci:Ci•ci ∈ **dom** g} ∧
      wfG(g)

Line by line: all connectors identified in the graph are defined as connectors;
all segments identified in the graph are defined as segments; and no isolated
connectors.

    For every edge (that is, a segment identified by si) from connector identified
by ci to connector identified by ci′ there is also an edge in the reverse direction
(from (g(ci))(si) to ci) with the same segment identifier. And there are only
such edges.

   wfG: G → **Bool**
   wfG(g) ≡
      ∀ ci:Ci • ci ∈ **dom** g ⇒
         ∀ si:Si • si ∈ **dom** g(ci) ⇒
           let ci′ = (g(ci))(si) **in**
           si ∈ **dom**((g(ci))(si)) ∧ ci=(g(ci′))(si) **end**

The last line of wfG expresses that an edge in the graph goes both ways: If
from c_i one can reach s_j (namely $s_j ∈$ **dom** $g(c_i)$), and from s_j, one can reach
c_k (namely $(g(c_i))(s_j) = c_k$), then, vice versa, one can, in g from c_k reach the
same s_j and, from it, c_i.

    We can convert the above graphs to those of Example 16.4.1.

type
   Gs′ = Ci $\overrightarrow{m}$ Ci-**set**

$$Gs = \{| \ gs{:}Gs' \bullet \textbf{dom} \ gs = \cup \ \textbf{rng} \ gs \ |\}$$

value
  conv: $G \rightarrow Gs$
  conv(g) $\equiv$
    $[\ ci{\mapsto}\{ci'|ci'{:}Ci,si{:}Si{\bullet}si \in \textbf{dom} \ g(ci)\wedge ci'{=}(g(ci))(si)\}|ci{:}Ci{\bullet}ci \in \textbf{dom} \ g\ ]$

Now the Nodes function of Example 16.4.1 — slightly reformulated:

  Nodes: $Ci \times G \rightarrow Ci{\text{-}}\textbf{set}$
  Nodes(ci,g) $\equiv$
    let gs=conv(g) **in**
    let nodes=gs(ci) $\cup\{ci'|ci'{:}Ci{\bullet}\exists \ ci''{:}Ci{\bullet}ci'' \in$ nodes$\wedge ci' \in$ gs(ci''$)\}$ **in**
    nodes **end end**,

can be re-expressed as:

value
  Nodes: $Ci \times G \rightarrow Ci{\text{-}}\textbf{set}$
  Nodes(ci,g) $\equiv$ **let** gs = conv(closure(g)) **in** gs(ci) **end**.

■

16.6 A Review of Map Abstractions and Models

We have already, at various points above, discussed a number of abstraction and modelling principles, techniques and tools, notably in the discussion parts of Examples 16.12–16.30, and the separate discussion section immediately following Example 16.30.

Principles. If and when a model-oriented abstraction has been chosen, then map abstraction may be chosen if a reasonable number of the following characteristics can be identified as properties of the phenomena or concepts being modelled: (i) the abstract structure of the composite components being modelled is an enumerable function, i.e., consists of an unordered collection of uniquely named, but not necessarily distinct subcomponents (constituent phenomena or concepts), (ii) whose number is not fixed, i.e., may vary, (iii) to which new, distinctly identified subcomponents may be joined; (iv) from which existing subcomponents may be removed — again based on given identifications; and (v) where one may compose other such phenomena from similar such phenomena.   ■

Principles. A number of "standard" uses of the map type in abstraction and modelling can be identified: (vi) The concepts of configurations, i.e., contexts and states, such as conceptualised from actual phenomena in some domains, are usually modelled, individually, as maps.[10] (vii) The concepts of data structures such as graphs, tables, hierarchies, file systems, databases, etc., as amply shown in Sect. 16.4, have as their basic model those of maps. ∎

Principles. *Type Invariance:* We have, in this section on maps seen a systematic use of well-formedness predicates on types. Reference can be made to Example 16.7 (wf_P_in_H), Example 16.8 (wf_FILE), and Example 16.9 (wf_FILE, wf_RDB, wf_TPLs, and wf_REL). A choice has, in most cases, to be made between simplicity (including ease of understanding) of type expressions, and simplicity (including ease of understanding) of well-formedness predicates. We shall have occasion, throughout these volumes, to invoke this principle, again and again. ∎

Principles. *Types Versus Values:* We have seen in several examples the need for recording types of values, and the need, therefore, for defining type observation functions. This leads us to the enunciation of a principle: For systems of data collections, files, databases and, as we shall see later, other such aggregations, it is prudent to introduce a type definition (schema) facility, as illustrated in Example 16.9. Following this principle implies also defining related type observation cum type extraction functions; and, as mentioned above, also implies descriptions of well-formedness predicates involving these functions. ∎

Principles. *Pointer-Based Data Structures:* In Examples 16.16–16.20 we have seen the use of maps to model specific properties of storages: namely the concept of pointers (links, addresses). Here the association to values, in the map ranges, are from identifiers that stand for such pointers (links, addresses). Whereas the identifiers of phenomena-related context and state maps usually "mimic" phenomena, i.e., "user" names, in the domain, pointers are pure concepts, pure abstractions. ∎

Techniques. We refer to initial paragraphs of Sect. 16.4 for a listing (1–4) of some of the techniques used when abstracting using maps. More specifically,

---

[10] Both concepts: contexts and states, associate varying numbers of identifiers to more or less static constants, respectively (temporally, i.e., dynamically) varying values. In a much later chapter (Vol. 2, Chap. 4), we shall treat the concept of configurations, contexts and states in detail. For now suffice it to say that some universe of discourse, i.e., some domain, usually exhibits a state notion: something that may consist of either a fixed or a varying number of components, each of which possesses one or more attributes whose values change. Such domains usually also exhibit a context notion: something that may consist of either a fixed or a varying number of components, each of which possesses one or more attributes whose value — for all intents and purposes do not change. Of course: in actual system phenomena there is a spectrum from contexts to states. But our point here is: We model association of identifiers to values by means of maps.

a number of map-oriented techniques are offered. The various map operations apply to appropriate modelling instances: (viii–xii) map union, override, composition and the two map restriction operations apply to models of "all", "new", "new", respectively "some, except" (twice) instances of a phenomenon possessed by two or more sets of phenomena, (xiii) application applies to the modelling of selection (choice), (xiv–xv) with definition set (i.e., **domain**) and range (**rng**) set being more technical operations; (xvi–xvii) map enumeration and map comprehension apply to the expression of the construction of an instance of an otherwise list modelled phenomenon.

These are just some of the more important techniques.   ∎

Tools. If abstraction and modelling using the map data type has been chosen, then the tool can either be the RSL, the VDM-SL, the Z, or, for example, the B specification language.   ∎

Please compare the present section to Sects. 13.7 (sets) and 15.6 (lists).

16.7 Maps: A Discussion

We have outlined the map data type. And we have enunciated principles for when to deploy map abstraction, mentioned some of the techniques that follow from such a choice, and identified some of the list abstraction specification language tools today available. Maps constitute *the* main workhorse of model-oriented abstraction and modelling.

16.8 Exercises

Exercise 16.1. *Well-formedness of Graph Models.* We refer to Examples 16.26–16.30. Complete the definition of the wf_Gi for i=4,5,6,7,8.

• • •

In the next exercises we refer to labels. Labels are further unspecified comparable quantities. By comparable mean that they can be tested for "being the same", i.e., for equality. In Exercises 16.2–16.9 we ask you to not formalise your definitions, but simply to express them in a concise (i.e., short and precise) manner and in English.

Exercise 16.2. *Finite Root-Labelled Trees.* Please define in English a concept of finite trees for which all roots are labelled — and such that no two 'immediate', but otherwise 'distinct' subtrees of a tree have 'identically labelled' roots but branches are unlabelled. Suggest yourself what we might mean by 'immediate', 'distinct', and 'identical labels'.

Exercise 16.10 item 1 takes up where the present exercise leaves off: namely asking you to formalise the problem solution.

• • •

Figure 16.4 illustrates the kind of labelled trees referred to in Exercises 16.2–16.4.

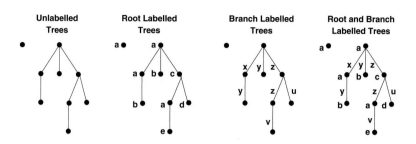

| Unlabelled Trees | Root Labelled Trees | Branch Labelled Trees | Root and Branch Labelled Trees |

Fig. 16.4. Unlabelled and labelled trees

Exercise 16.3. *Finite Branch-Labelled Trees.* Please define in English a concept of finite trees for which all branches (the things that connect a root of a tree with the roots of its immediate subtrees) are labelled — and such that no two branches incident upon immediate subtrees of a tree are identically labelled. Exercise 16.10 item 2 takes up where the present exercise leaves off: namely asking you to formalise the problem solution.

Exercise 16.4. *Finite Root- and Branch-Labelled Trees.*

Please define in English a concept of finite trees for which all roots and all branches, that is, the things that connect a root of a tree with the roots of its immediate subtrees are labelled — and such that all roots of the subtrees of any tree have distinct labels, and such that no two branches emanating from a root (to the root of a subtree) are identically labelled.[11] Do you need to maintain distinctness of root labels of the subtrees of a root and branch labelled tree? Explain your answer.

Exercise 3 item 1 takes up where the present exercise leaves off: namely asking you to formalise the problem solution.

Exercise 16.5. *Distinctly Labelled Trees.* The problem formulation is as for Exercise 16.4, only now it is required that no two root labels are the same and that no two branch labels are the same and that root and branch labels also differ.

Exercise 4 item 1 takes up where the present exercise leaves off: namely asking you to formalise the problem solution.

---

[11] Please observe that this last part of the sentence, namely "and such that no two branches emanating from a root (to the root of a subtree) are identically labelled" is meant to express exactly the same as the sentence "and such that no two branches incident upon immediate subtrees of a tree are 'identically labelled'". The latter was used in the previous exercise formulation (i.e., in Exercise 16.3).

Exercise 16.6. *Forest of Trees.* Based on Exercises 16.2–16.5 define in English a concept of forest as consisting of a finite number of trees, unlabelled, or labelled one way or another, but such that no two labels of any two somehow labelled trees are identical. Does Fig. 16.4 "portray" such a forest? Explain your answer.

Exercise 16.10 item 5 takes up where the present exercise leaves off: namely asking you to formalise the problem.

Exercise 16.7. *Finite Node-Labelled Graphs.* Please define in English a concept of oriented graphs for which all nodes are distinctly labelled.

Exercise 16.10 item 6 takes up where the present exercise leaves off: namely asking you to formalise the problem solution.

Exercise 16.8. *Finite Edge-Labelled Graphs.* Please define in English a concept of oriented graphs for which all edges between any given pair of (in this exercise, unlabelled) nodes are distinctly labelled.

Exercise 16.10 item 7 takes up where the present exercise leaves off: namely asking you to formalise the problem solution.

Exercise 16.9. *Finite Node- and Edge-Labelled Graphs.* Please define in English a concept of oriented graphs for which all nodes are distinctly labelled, and for which all edges between any given pair of (in this exercise, now labelled) nodes are distinctly labelled.

Exercise 16.10 item 8 takes up where the present exercise leaves off: Namely asking you to formalise the problem solution.

• • •

We now turn to the reformulation of above exercise problems 16.2–16.9 into exercise problem 16.10 items 1–8. We now ask for formal map-based solutions to the same questions!

Exercise 16.10. *Tree and Graph Structures.* We refer to Exercises 16.2–16.9. In the present exercise you are to formally define the concrete types and possibly applicable well-formedness predicates for:

1. Finite Root-Labelled Trees	cf. Exercise 16.2
2. Finite Branch-Labelled Trees	cf. Exercise 16.3
3. Finite Root- and Branch-Labelled Trees	cf. Exercise 16.4
4. Distinctly Labelled Trees	cf. Exercise 16.5
5. Forest of Trees	cf. Exercise 16.6
6. Finite Node-Labelled Graphs	cf. Exercise 16.7
7. Finite Edge-Labelled Graphs	cf. Exercise 16.8
8. Finite Node- and Edge-Labelled Graphs	cf. Exercise 16.9

Exercise 16.11. *File System Operations.* You are referred to Example 16.8. Please read it carefully.

- For the file system defined in Example 16.8 you are to first define a notion of initial record values.
  - ⋆ 0 is the initial field value of type `integer`.
  - ⋆ **false** is the initial field value of type `Boolean`.
  - ⋆ "" is the initial field value of type `string`.
  - ⋆ Any key is an initial key.

  An initial record is any record that maps a number of field names in An into only initial field values.
- Specify formally initial records.
- Then formally specify the following operations:
  1. *Create empty file system:* Create an initially empty file system, i.e., a file system of no files.
  2. *Create initial file:* For any file system create a file of a given, unused file name associated to a file of just one given initial record.
  3. *Write a record to a file of a file system:* Given a file system, given a file name of a file of that system, and given a record which if joined to the named file will leave it well-formed. Writing this record to the named file will join it to the file and assign it an unused key which, besides the updated file system, is (hence also) yielded.
  4. *Read a record of a file of a file system:* Given a file system, given a file name of a file of that system, and given a key of that file, yield an unchanged file system and the record of the named file having the given key.
  5. *Delete a record of a file of a file system:* Given a file system, given a file name of a file of that system, and given a key of that file, yield a changed file system in which only the designated record has been deleted. One cannot delete an initial record. (Note there may be many initial records, one of which will necessarily have the initial key.)
  6. *Delete a file of a file system:* Obvious, is it not?

Exercise 16.12. ♣ *Maps in the Transportation Net Domain.* We refer to Appendix A, Sect. A.1, *Transportation Net.* We also refer to Exercises 13.5, 14.6 and 15.15.

You are to formulate yourself some narrative and formalisations of phenomena and concepts of the *Transportation Net* domain for which maps may come in as a suitable abstraction.

Exercise 16.13. ♣ *Maps in the Container Logistics Domain.* We refer to Appendix A, Sect. A.2, *Container Logistics.* We also refer to Exercises 13.6, 14.7 and 15.16.

You are to formulate yourself some narrative and formalisations of phenomena and concepts of the *Container Logistics* domain for which maps may come in as a suitable abstraction.

Exercise 16.14. ♣ *Maps in the Financial Service Industries Domain.* We refer to Appendix A, Sect. A.3, *Financial Service Industry*. We also refer to Exercises 13.7, 14.8 and 15.17.

You are to formulate yourself some narrative and formalisations of phenomena and concepts of the *Financial Service Industry* domain for which maps may come in as a suitable abstraction.

Higher-Order Functions in RSL

- The **prerequisite** for studying this chapter is that you are, by now, reasonably fluent in the definition and use of functions such as introduced in earlier chapters.
- The **aims** are to introduce the use of higher-order functions in function definitions, or, put differently, to introduce the concept of functional data abstractions, i.e., modelling phenomena and concepts as higher-order functions.
- The **objective** is to ensure that the reader has a firm foundation in the area of function abstractions.
- The **treatment** is semiformal and systematic.

> It is my function
> to make sure that the function
> is functioning
>
> *Mr. NN, Manager of Hotel Functions*[1]

We refer to Chap. 6 for a first, reasonably thorough introduction to the mathematical concept of functions, and to Chap. 11 for the function concept such as it is provided for in RSL. In the present section we shall focus on the means for defining and using function types and functions in the predominant specification language of these volumes, RSL.

17.1 Functions: The Issues

The idea to be illustrated in this section is the use of the discrete mathematics concept of functions in abstracting domain, requirements and software phenomena and concepts. We can hardly express anything without using functions. We often abstract a concept as a function, and we define this function

---

[1] A play on three different meanings of the term 'function' is intended: *job, event,* and *"that it works"*.

in terms of other functions (which are then defined separately). The former, abstraction of concepts as functions, has been illustrated repeatedly up till now, and much more is to come. The latter, defining abstracted functions in terms of other functions, will be illustrated in this chapter and in Vol. 2, Chap. 3, Sect. 3.3.3 on denotational semantics.

This chapter is built up, as are Chaps. 13–16, and relies on material about:

- The function data type   (Sect. 11.1)
- Means of function definition   (Sects. 11.2–11.6)

and otherwise complements Chap. 11 with new material:

- Examples of function-based abstractions   (Sect. 17.2)
- Abstracting and modelling with functions   (Sect. 17.3)
- Inductive function definitions   (Sect. 17.4)
- A review of function abstractions and models (Sect. 17.5)

There are many examples because *before one can write good specifications one must have read and studied many example specifications.* So you may not need to study all of them now, but can, perhaps, return to some later.

The chapter ends with a brief discussion.

17.2 Examples Using Function-Based Abstractions

This section "matches" Sects. 13.3, 14.3, 15.3, and 16.3. They all give small examples of set, Cartesian, list, map and function-based specifications. They are meant as class lecture examples.

A function-based abstraction is a specification which uses or deploys functions as entities. In the vernacular, functions as data. In "practice" a common technique is here to pass functions f as arguments to other functions g. The body of the latter, g, may then apply the argument function f to some other values. Different invocations of g may then be given different arguments: $f, f', f'', \ldots$, resulting, usually, in different results.

17.2.1 Functionals

A *first-order functional* (FOF) is here defined to be a function which takes functions as arguments and yields non-function values as results. A *higher-order functional* (HOF) is here defined to be a function which takes functions as arguments and yields function values as results. Two conceptual examples are in order:

Example 17.1 *First-Order Functionals:*

```
type
    FOF = Int → Nat
value
    square: FOF, square(i) ≡ i∗i
    cube: FOF, cube(i) ≡ square(i)∗i
    quad: FOF, quad(i) ≡ first_order_f(i)(square°square)
    first_order_f: Int → FOF → Nat
    first_order_f(i)(f) ≡ f(i)
assert:
    first_order_f(3)(square) = 9
    first_order_f(3)(cube) = 27
    first_order_f(3)(quad) = 81
```

Note the use of the function composition operation °.

Example 17.2 *Higher-Order Functionals:*

```
type
    HOF = FOF → FOF
value
    double: HOF, double(f) ≡ f°f
    triple: HOF, triple(f) ≡ f°f°f
    penta: FOF, penta(i) ≡ double°triple
assert:
    penta(f)(i) = first_order_f(i)(f°f°f°f°f)
```

17.2.2 Discussion

Examples 17.1 and 17.2 were just "academic", conceptual, in that they illustrate a "coding" technique. We shall later have occasion to illustrate the use of functionals.

17.3 Abstracting and Modelling With Functions

This section "matches" Sects. 13.4, 14.4, 15.4 and 16.4, all give larger examples of set, Cartesian, list and map abstractions and models. They are meant as self-study examples.

17.3.1 Concepts as Functions

In Sect. 17.1 we said: *We often abstract a concept as a function, and we define this function in terms of other functions (which are then defined separately).* We will now exemplify this claim.

Example 17.3 *A Simple Programming Language:*
    The programming language to be illustrated is an imperative language. The imperative programming concepts are those of binding and storage; that is, of definable (named constants) and assignable variables (having names denoting locations and having a storage which map locations to values), i.e., an assignment. Linguistically — speaking, for the remainder of the present paragraph, about syntax — and in order to talk about bindings and variables, we postulate a small programming language. Its programs are simple blocks. A program is a block. Blocks consist of variable declarations and a finite sequence of simple statements. Statements are either blocks or are simple assignment statements. A declaration introduces a variable by a name. An assignment statement has two parts: a "left-hand side" variable and a "right-hand side" expression. Expressions are either just variables, or ..., i.e., we do not further detail the syntax of other kinds of expressions. We illustrate the syntactic modelling of the programming language concepts of binding and allocation, and of programs, block, assignments, variables and expressions as mathematical function.

Syntactic Types

type
    V
    P == mk_P(b:B)
    B == mk_Blk(vs:V-**set**,sl:S*)
    S = A | B
    A == mk_Asg(lhs:V,rhs:E)
    E == mk_Var(v:V) | ...

We remind the reader about union types and variant records — used above in the definitions of S, respectively of P, B, A and E — as first briefly explained in Sect. 13.4.3.
    Programs have been made variant records in order to be able, later, to write a semantic function which accept P|B type arguments. Sections 18.4 and 18.5 covers record and union types.
    Blocks form a scope for binding variables to locations.

Semantic Types:

The semantic types are:

type
  L, VAL
  ENV = V $\overrightarrow{m}$ L
  STG = L $\overrightarrow{m}$ VAL

The meaning, i.e., semantics, of programs, blocks, (assignment) statements, variables and expressions is: Variables designate locations. Expressions designate values. Given a storage a location designates a variable. An assignment statement designates that the location of the left-hand side variable be associated with the value of the right-hand side expression. A sequence of assignment statements designates a change of storage resulting from obeying the designations of the individual assignment statements of the list in the order listed. A block designates a change of storage as designated by its statement list except that the storage being changed and the changed storage have the same locations. Thus the new, fresh locations designated by the variable declarations of a block are only valid "within the scope of that block". More operationally, i.e., explaining the semantics operationally, rather than through designations, we speak of a locus of program points: Each statement designates a program point. Execution, by an interpreter (i.e., a machine), according to the prescriptions of a program, starts by entering a block and continues by ordered elaboration, first of variable declarations, then of the statement list. Upon block entry the first program point is that of the variable declarations. They are elaborated, their elaboration leads to the allocation of fresh, new locations, one distinct for each variable. An environment, i.e., a context, say, a table, is set up. It associates with each block variable (v) its location (l). A storage, i.e., a state ($n\sigma$), is similarly set up: To each freshly allocated location it associates some initial, default value (?). Then the storage (σ) of the surrounding block is "added", conjoined to that ($alloc(ls)[]$) of the local block (to become $n\sigma$), and the environment of the local block ($bind(vs,ls)[]$) inherits that of the surrounding block (ρ), but overrides variable names of the surrounding block, if redefined in the local block (to become $n\rho$). The initial, "outermost" block is elaborated in a predefined environment (ρ_o), and in a corresponding predefined storage (σ_o). Now we are ready to show the semantic elaboration functions.

Semantic Elaboration Functions

Main semantic function signatures:

value
  M: (P|S) → ENV → STG → STG
  I: S* → ENV → STG → STG
  Val: E → ENV → STG → VAL

Main semantic function definitions:

$$M(mk\_P(mk\_B(vs,sl)))\rho_o\sigma_o \equiv I(mk\_B(vs,sl))\rho_o\sigma_o$$
$$M(mk\_A(v,e))\rho\sigma \equiv \sigma \dagger [\rho(v){\mapsto}Val(e)\rho\sigma]$$

$M(mk\_B(vs,sl))\rho\sigma \equiv$
    let ls = obtain(**card** vs)(σ) **in**
    let nσ = $\sigma \cup$ alloc(ls)[ ], nρ = $\rho \dagger$ bind(vs,ls)[ ] **in**
    (I(sl)(nρ)(nσ) \ ls) **end end**

$I(sl)\rho\sigma \equiv$ **if** sl = $\langle\rangle$ **then** σ **else** $I(\mathbf{tl}\ sl)(\rho)(M(\mathbf{hd}\ sl)\rho\sigma)$ **end**

$Val(mk\_Var(v))\rho\sigma \equiv \sigma(\rho(v))$

Auxiliary semantic functions:

value
    obtain: **Nat** $\to$ Σ $\to$ L-set
    obtain(n)(σ) $\equiv$
        let ls:L-set • ls $\cap$ **dom** σ = {} $\wedge$**card** ls=n **in** ls **end**

    alloc: **L-set**$\to$ STG $\to$ STG
    alloc(ls)σ $\equiv$
        if ls = {} **then** σ **else**
        let l:L • l $\in$ ls **in** alloc(ls \ {l})($\sigma \cup [l \mapsto ?]$) **end end**

    bind: **V-set** $\times$ **L-set** $\to$ ENV $\to$ ENV
    bind(vs,ls)ρ $\equiv$
        if vs = {} **then** ρ **else**
        let v:V,l:L • v $\in$ vs $\wedge$ l $\in$ ls **in**
        bind(vs \ {v},ls \ {l})($\rho \cup [v \mapsto l]$) **end end**

Denotations as Higher-Order Functions

Now we can conclude:

- The semantic functions, M, I and Val are of higher-order. That is, they are functions from values of syntactic types into functions over values of semantic types:

type
    M: (P|S) $\to$ ENV $\to$ STG $\to$ STG
    I: S* $\to$ ENV $\to$ STG $\to$ STG
    Val: E $\to$ ENV $\to$ STG $\to$ VAL

- Programs are functions from [initial] environments — which are themselves a kind of functions — state (i.e., storage) to state changing functions.

- So are statements and statement lists. Thus syntactic programs and syntactic statements denote higher-order functions, and these are defined in terms of other functions.
- Expressions denote functions from environments to functions from storages — which, lest we should forget to say it, are themselves a kind of functions (i.e., maps) — to values. Thus syntactic expressions denote such functions.
- Thus a simple variable name denotes a function from environment to a function from storages to values!

These denoted functions can be determined at compile time. They are then applied to appropriate environments and storages at run time to yield designated values and storages.

∎

17.3.2 Operator Lifting

The notion of operator lifting should, finally, bring home the idea of modelling concepts in terms of higher-order functions.

By an operator we understand a function, typically from B into C:

type
   B, C
   O: B $\rightarrow$ C

By lifting an operator we mean that of abstracting its functionality into, for example:

type
   A
   L: A $\rightarrow$ B $\rightarrow$ C

We saw in Example 17.3 how we could view the meaning of programming constructs at various levels of abstraction: Given an environment (A), statements denoted storage (B) to storage (C) changing functions (B $\rightarrow$ C), which could then be lifted into: A $\rightarrow$ B $\rightarrow$ C.

Examples of Operator Lifting

We give two examples: lifting classical Boolean connectives, and lifting compositions of defined maps. The first is brief, and illustrates the idea. The other is long, and illustrates an important specification programming technique.

Example 17.4 *Time-Lifted Boolean Functions:* The RSL connectives $\wedge, \vee$, and operators $+, *$, etcetera, can be overloaded. That is: they have an already defined meaning on Booleans, respectively integers (reals, natural numbers), but can be given meaning wrt. to other types.

Let variables u, v, w denote functions from time into Booleans:

type
    B = T → **Bool**
value
    u,v,w:B

Now we extend the meaning of the Boolean connectives to range over arguments of type B as follows:

value
    ∼: B → B, (∼(u)) ≡ ∼λ t:T.(u(t))
    ∧: B × B → B, u ∧ v ≡ λ t:T.(u(t)∧v(t))
    ∨: B × B → B, u ∨ v ≡ λ t:T.(u(t)∨v(t))
    ⇒: B × B → B, u ⇒ v ≡ λ t:T.(u(t)⇒v(t))
    =: B × B → B, u = v ≡ λ t:T.(u(t)=v(t))

Here the two leftmost uses (to the left of ≡) of the connectives, respectively operators, designate the lifted functionals, whereas the rightmost usage (to the right of ≡) designates the "old" operations.   ∎

Example 17.5 *Table-Lifted PartsExplosion Functions:*   We refer to Example 16.6.

Narrative and Analysis: Types

Instead of recording just the part identification numbers of constituent parts of composite parts, as was done in Example 16.6, we wish to record, in any bill of materials, bom, also the number of occurrences of these constituent parts in any such composite part. Informally you may think of a bom concretely as a table with two columns, where each entry is a row. The first part of an entry contains the part number. The second part of an entry contains either nothing, if the described part is elementary (as are p_4, p_5, p_6), or it consists of a two-column subtable with n entries, i.e., rows if there are n distinct constituent parts. Each row in this subtable has two elements. These record the part number of constituent parts, and the number of occurrences of that part in the composite part (Fig. 17.1).

We abstract the class of the tables shown in Fig. 17.1 in the form of maps from part numbers to part information (second column item), with part information either being a map from (constituent part) part numbers to (natural) numbers (of occurrences of constituent parts in the corresponding composite part), or being an empty such map in the case the column one item is elementary. Thus:

Part Number	Part Information	
p_1	p_{1_1}	n_{1_1}
	p_{1_2}	n_{1_2}
	...	...
	p_{1_n}	n_{1_n}
p_2	p_{2_1}	n_{2_1}
	p_{2_2}	n_{2_2}
	...	...
	p_{2_m}	n_{2_m}
p_3	p_a	n_a
	p_b	n_b
p_4		
p_5		
p_6		
...		

Fig. 17.1. Part number table

$$[p_1 \mapsto [p_{1_1} \mapsto n_{1_1}, p_{1_2} \mapsto n_{1_2}, \ldots, p_{1_n} \mapsto n_{1_n}],$$
$$p_2 \mapsto [p_{2_1} \mapsto n_{2_1}, p_{2_2} \mapsto n_{2_2}, \ldots, p_{2_m} \mapsto n_{2_m}],$$
$$p_3 \mapsto [p_a \mapsto n_a, p_b \mapsto n_b],$$
$$p_4 \mapsto [\,], p_5 \mapsto [\,], p_6 \mapsto [\,], \qquad \ldots]$$

is the mathematical designation of the above table. We justify this choice of
abstraction by recalling that each part is described only (or exactly) once,
and that so is the case for constituent parts.

Formalisation: Types

type
    BOM = Pn $\xrightarrow{\sim_m}$ TBL
    TBL = Pn $\xrightarrow{\sim_m}$ **Nat**

The above names and defines the concrete type of this kind of more informative bill of materials. Again we need a well-formedness criterion. In fact, we
see that:

inv_BOM: BOM → **Bool**
inv_BOM(bom) ≡ inv_BOM_0(abs_BOM_0(bom))

abs_BOM_0: BOM → BOM_0
abs_BOM_0(bom) ≡
    [p $\mapsto$ **dom** bom(p) | p:Pn • pn ∈ **dom** bom]

BOM_0 was defined in Example 16.6; inv_BOM_0, likewise.

The argument to inv_BOM is a "retrofit construction" (retrieval, abstraction) of a BOM_0 object from a BOM object! That is, well-formedness of BOM objects is independent of the "occurrence number" information! The retrieve function abs_BOM_0 considers the type BOM to be a concretisation of the BOM_0 type.

Narrative: Operations

We next turn to illustrating a rather complicated function on this new kind of bill of materials. The idea of this function, which we shall call Parts_Explosion, is, for a given part number, p, and a bom in which it is recorded, to yield a table which lists all the elementary parts it contains, together with their (sum-)total number of occurrences. We first illustrate the problem. Let the below forest (of trees) record parts relevant to some parts "explosion" (say from p) (Fig. 17.2).

Fig. 17.2. An example part number table

In words: part p consists of n_1 parts p_1, n_2 parts p_2, ..., n_k parts p_k. The constituent part p_1 consists, in turn, of m_2 parts p_2, m_3 of p_3, ..., m_k of p_k, etc. Thus for one part p we find, by (what we here consider to be a self-explanatory) tree-substitution, an unfolded tree of parts and their number of occurrences (Fig. 17.3 on the facing page).

In this example it is assumed that all other parts, e.g. p_3, p_k are elementary. From the tree we see that p consists of $n_1 \times m_2 \times l_3 + n_1 \times m_3 + n_2 \times l_3$ copies of part p_3, and $n_1 \times m_2 \times l_k + n_1 \times m_k + n_2 \times l_k + n_k$ copies of part p_k. (Since parts are not recursively defined it is always possible to perform this suggested tree-substitution.) Our result table will then, illustratively, look like the table shown in Fig. 17.4.

We abstract these result tables in the form of tables (tbl:TBL). The problem now is to define the Parts_Explosion function:

value
    Parts_Explosion: Pn × BOM → TBL

From the above "tree" drawing we observe two things: first that the parts explosion applied at the root (p) of the (entire) tree, for $n = 1$, is the same

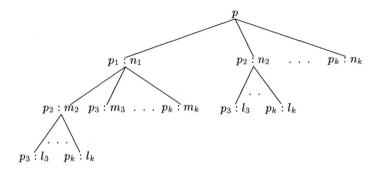

Fig. 17.3. Expanded part number tree

p	
p_3	np_3
p_k	np_k
$\vdots$	$\vdots$

Entries computed as follows:

$$np_3 = n_1 \times m_2 \times l_3 + n_1 \times m_3 + n_2 \times l_3$$

$$np_k = n_1 \times m_2 \times l_k + n_1 \times m_k + n_2 \times l_k + n_k$$

$$\ldots = \ldots$$

Fig. 17.4. Result table

(kind of) parts explosion which is to be applied at respective subtree roots (p_i) for $n = n_i$. Then, in order to construct the tree, and therefore any subtree, all we need is its root label, p, respectively p_i. In fact we (decide to) never construct this tree (or subtrees).

The algorithmic idea of our putative Parts_Explosion function definition is now the following: We define Parts_Explosion in terms of an *auxiliary* function (Exp, for Explosion) which in the general case, while computing the table for some part, "sweeps", left-to-right, across the subtrees, accumulating a partial result table, tbl. The subtrees to be swept across are fully recorded in a subtable. For part p this subtable is bom(p). In general we refer to it as trees. We refer now to Fig. 17.5. The sweep now consists of arbitrarily selecting subtable trees. At some stage of the sweep, or explosion, some such subtrees have all been inspected, and their contribution, tbl, to the final result has been computed.

At this stage we select subtree with root p, i.e., we select part p for explosion. The result of combining the explosion of p with the hitherto accumulated partial result, tbl, we call tbl'. This new result, tbl', is then used as input in the remaining explosion of remaining subtrees. These are trees with subtree p removed, i.e., trees $\setminus \{p\}$. Once there are no more subtrees to be exploded, the accumulated and forwarded partial result becomes the final result.

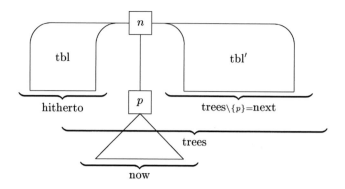

Fig. 17.5. A parts "explosion" computation state

We note that the hitherto accumulated partial result, **tbl**, is merged with the result of the explosion of p, with this merge taking place while p is being exploded. We could instead compute the explosion of p fully, and then merge.

The **Explosion** function thus requires the following four arguments: (i) **trees**, i.e., a description, obtained (previously) from **bom**, of the subtrees to be "exploded" (now and next); (ii) a multiplier, n, which denotes the count of the part being exploded; (iii) the partial result, **tbl**; and (iv), as a global variable (constant), the entire bill of material: **bom**. Since the latter is used only for reference, and not changed, we choose the following type clause for **Explosion**:

value
    Exp: (Pn $\overrightarrow{m}$ **Nat**) × **Nat** × TBL → (BOM → TBL)

    Parts_Explosion(p,bom) ≡ Exp(bom(p),1,[ ])(bom) **pre**: p ∈ **dom** bom

    Exp(trs,n,tbl)(bom) ≡
1.   **if** trs = [ ]
2.   **then** tbl
3.   **else**
4.   **let** p:Pn ∈ **dom** trs **in**
5.   **let** tbl′ =
6.   **if** bom(p)=[ ]
7.   **then**
8.   **if** p ∈ **dom** tbl
9.   **then** tbl † [p ↦ tbl(p) + n∗trs(p)]
10.   **else** tbl ∪ [p ↦ n∗trs(p)] **end**
11.   **else**
12.   Exp(bom(p),n∗trs(p),tbl)(bom) **end in**
13.   Exp(trs \ {p},n,tbl′)(bom) **end end end**

Annotation:

If the part to be exploded is the empty part, i.e., has been all "exploded", then the so-far accumulated result table, is yielded, (2.).

Otherwise, (3.), a subpart, p, is selected (4.) for explosion. If it itself is elementary (6.), then its contribution to the so-far accumulated (partial) result is computed and merged (9-10.) with that result. Otherwise (11.) the contribution of the explosion, of the subpart p, is merged with the so far accumulated result. The so-far plus now accumulated (partial) result (tbl') is then used (13.) when exploding the remaining subparts.

Discussion

Could we have defined Parts_Explosion by means of a **pre/post** pair of conditions? We believe not as descriptively! Let us analyse why we give this answer, but first what the answer says.

First our negative answer says that sometimes, as we believe it to be in this case, functions are more tellingly defined explicitly (and hence prescriptively) than descriptively (axiomatically, or by means of a **pre/post** pair). When so is (indeed) the case, we see that the borderline between prescriptive and descriptive somehow crumbles. We might have believed that prescriptive definitions, by being more algorithmic, were also less transparent, i.e., harder to read and understand, than were descriptive definitions. We might, as a corollary, also have believed that one could always define functions descriptively as easily as defining the same functions prescriptively.

Now why might these claims be true? Could it be that our problem is itself an operationally concrete one, rather than an abstract one? In descriptive definitions we express properties, rather than explicit, computed results.

In the case of the Parts_Explosion function this seems so: The problem is operational. We are indeed asked to compute a functional result and not to maintain or express a property.

Narrative: Lifted Functions

Next we show a way of simplifying the above Parts_Explosion and Expr function definitions by definining so-called 'lifted' functions. In reference to our remark above: The present Parts_Explosion and Expr function definitions may not seem very abstract, the parts, parts_of_Pn and parts_of_TBL function definitions next could be claimed to be more abstract!

Formalisation: Lifted Functions

value
   +: TBL × TBL → TBL
   $t + t' \equiv [\,p \mapsto c(p,t)+c(p,t')\,|\,p{:}Pn{\bullet}p \in \mathbf{dom}\ t \cup \mathbf{dom}\ t'\,]$

   *: **Nat** × TBL → TBL

$n * t' \equiv [\,p\mapsto n*t(p)|p{:}Pn\bullet p \in \textbf{dom } t\,]$

c: Pn × TBL → **Nat**
c(p,t) ≡ **if** p ∈ **dom** t **then** t(p) **else** 0 **end**

parts: Pn × BOM $\overset{\sim}{\to}$ TBL
part(p,bom) ≡ parts _of_Pn(p,bom) \ {p}
  pre p ∈ **dom** bom

value
  parts_of_Pn: Pn × BOM → TBL
  parts_of_Pn(p,bom) ≡
    let t = bom(p) **in**
    if t = [] **then** [p↦ 1] **else** parts _of_TBL(bom(p),bom) **end end**
  pre p ∈ **dom** bom

  parts_of_TBL: TBL × BOM → TBL
  parts_of_TBL(t,bom) ≡
    if t = [] **then** []
    else
      let p:Pn • p ∈ **dom** t **in**
      t(p) * parts_of_Pn(p,bom) + parts_of_TBL(t \ {p},bom)
    end end
  pre dom t ⊆ **dom** bom

■

17.4 Inductive Function Definitions

17.4.1 Inductive Function Type Definitions

In the λ-calculus everything is a function. Thus it is natural to think of D of the type:

type
  D = D → D

as modelling λ-functions. In RSL this is not possible. The RAISE specification language design decision was made to cope with looseness, nondeterminism, concurrency, and several other desirable language properties. Therefore it would have made a number of RSL language constructs and their use somewhat awkward if definitions like D = D → D should also be possible. It prevents users of RSL from defining certain kinds of common programming language constructs — such as procedures that take procedures as arguments, sets of mutually recursive procedure definitions, etc. That restriction was deemed acceptable by the language designers. RAISE was and is to be used more for application-oriented domains than for sophisticated programming or specification language constructs. Solution to the recursive type definition, $D = D \to D$, was first provided by Dana Scott [251, 458–462, 464, 466–468].

17.4.2 Inductive Function Value Definitions

Chapters 12–16 abound with recursive function definitions; Chap. 11 outlined various styles of function definitions, incluing recursive definitions; and Chap. 7 dealt with the meaning of recursive function definitions.

17.5 Review of Function Abstractions and Models

Principles. *Functions as Denotations:* The most overriding principle is that of *"always looking for the function being denoted by some syntactic structure"*.   ∎

The above principle was illustrated in Example 17.3.

Principles. If and when a model-oriented abstraction has been chosen, then function abstraction may be chosen if a reasonable number of the following characteristics can be identified as properties of the phenomena being modelled:

(i) The abstract structure of the composite components being modelled as an ordinarily definable function, i.e., one whose range elements can be functionally based on definition set elements;

(ii) whose number is not otherwise easily enumerable;

(iii) and a common operation is that of determining functional relationships.

The basic principle for choosing among the many styles of function definition, outlined in Chap. 11, is simple:

(iv) Choose property-oriented (axiomatic, algebraic and possibly implicit pre/post) styles "early" in development, that is, for the domain description and requirements definition phase. And choose the model-oriented, explicit function definition style for the later stages of requirements definition and the software design phase.

(v) In addition, judicious use of carefully developed lifted functions can significantly help express suitable abstractions.   ∎

Techniques. *Functions:* We have shown, in Chap. 11, a number of function definition styles. They reflect a spectrum from axiomatic and algebraic, via pre/post implicit, to explicit, algorithm-like, definitions of functions. The techniques that go with the property-oriented styles are those of property-oriented abstractions, and those of the model-oriented styles are those, obviously, of model-oriented abstractions. Make sure, however, only to tackle such algorithm-like definitions which reflect complexity, i.e., algorithm efficiency concerns during the latter software design stages and steps. Seriously consider using function lifting when defining functions over complex, typically recursive data structures.   ∎

Tools. *Functions:* If abstraction and modelling using the function data type has been chosen, then the tool can either be the RSL, the VDM-SL, the Z, or, for example, the B specification language.   ∎

17.6 Discussion

Functions are, obviously, the main means of defining any dynamics, any operations, manipulations, etc., of manifest (domain) as well as conceptual (domain, requirements and software) concepts. This is not surprising to the ordinary programmer, who is used to defining procedures, routines, subroutines, methods, etc. What is additional here are the concepts of functions as values, and hence as parameters (i.e., arguments), and function lifting.

These volumes will only have succeeded they teach its readers to think of domain phenomena and concepts, and of requirements and software concepts as functions. We shall have many opportunities in the rest of these volumes to propagate the principle of thinking denotationally, that is, of syntactic structures denoting mathematical functions.

17.7 Exercises

Exercise 17.1. *A Subroutine Library.* A subroutine library is a simple set of uniquely named functions. Each function, besides its name, has a pair of type lists: one designating arity and types of subroutine arguments, the other the arity and types of subroutine results. Finally, each such function signature is associated with a function, typically from states and argument values to states and result values. Assume, for simplicity, all argument and all result values to be of simple scale type, say reals, integers, Booleans and text strings of characters. Functions, when applied, are applied in the current state, and functions when elaborated may change that current state.

1. Define the type of subroutine libraries, considering also possible well-formedness (i.e., subtypes).

Postulate, i.e., assume, the existence of the functional subroutine values. Now define the following operations on subroutine libraries:

2. Insert a new subroutine (please consider well-formedness).
3. Inquire as to the signature of a named subroutine.
4. Apply a list of argument values to a named subroutine — checking first that the type of the argument values matches the type given in the signature for that function.
5. Delete a subroutine.

Above it was (perhaps) assumed that no one function name could be defined with more than one signature. Now allow a function name to be 'overloaded', that is: The same function name may have two or more signatures but they must differ in the arity and/or type of the arguments.

6. Restate, if needed, your answer to part 1 above.
7. Refine, if needed, your answers to 2–5 above.

Part IV

SPECIFICATION TYPES

The previous chapters have now covered sufficient material on types for us to summarise (Chap. 18). Although type theory may, by 2005, be the grandest contribution computer science has made to mathematics, we shall refrain from covering the theoretically more exciting aspects of type theory. Instead we refer to a few books: $[1, 282, 424, 443, 532]$. Dana Scott provided the basic research that cast classical λ-calculus in a proper mathematical (i.e., type theoretic) setting, and thereby provided a basis for a mathematical understanding of types: $[251, 458\text{–}462, 464, 466\text{–}468]$.

Types in RSL

- The **prerequisite** for studying this chapter is that you have read the previous many chapters and that you desire a summary, comprehensive treatment of the RSL type system.
- The **aims** are to summarise and complete the coverage of the type constructs, that is, expressions and definitions of RSL, to introduce the type concepts of record constructors and destructors, union types, variant types, short record type definitions, and subtypes and to illustrate the versatility of the RSL type system on "actual computing world" examples.
- The **objective** is to help ensure that the reader is put firmly on the road to being a professional in perhaps the most crucial area of specification engineering, namely defining and using types.
- The **treatment** is from systematic to semiformal.

> The Republican form of Government is the highest form of government; but because of this it requires the highest type of human nature — a type nowhere at present existing.
>
> *Herbert Spencer 1820–1903 Essays (1891)* Vol. III, P.478, `The Americans`

"Back-of-the-envelope" sketching of types, for well-nigh any universe of discourse, can be considered like the house architect's similar sketches of an opera building, a private villa or a community centre. The ease with which it is done, and done so that the result is pleasing, has utility, and is fit for purpose, is the hallmark of a great software engineer, or respectively of a great architect.

We refer to Chap. 5 for a first introduction to the concept of types.

18.1 The Issues

The above quotation expresses one of the issues of types we shall have to deal with: Existence! (i) We often designate manifest things. (ii) But we express collections of these by expressing types. (iii) Our type expressions are not these collections, only abstractions thereof!

We will briefly discuss the importance of statements (i–iii) above. (i) When modelling domains we designate, we point to real, actual occurrences of things: (a) Mister Goldsmith, (b) Missus Goldsmith's rusty Raleigh bicycle, and (c) Mister and Missus Goldsmith's two ponies 'The Spirit' and 'The Flight'. (ii) But we abstract them as values of type (A) Person, (B) Bicycle and (C) Animal (or Horse). (iii) The values by which we speak of the actual Mister Goldsmith, the manifest things, these values are only abstractions of the real things. (iv) And there is even the problem of some definitions not having any, however abstract, mathematical models. By that we mean: Some type expressions, some type definitions, make no sense, viz.: the set of all winged horses, from poetic, daily parlance; and the 'collection', as a type, of all functions from functions into functions.

Issues other than mere concrete or abstract existence are: (v) *Choice between abstract and concrete types:* sorts versus model-oriented types (i.e., abstract versus concrete types). (vi) *Choice of model-oriented representational abstraction:* set, Cartesian, list, map and function types; and finite or infinite sets, lists and maps. (vii) *Choice between simplicity of "nearest, closest" type versus complexity of defining "exactly fitting" subtype.*

Again we comment briefly on items (v–vii). (v) We normally choose abstract types in earlier parts of development, thereby being abstract and leaving room for addition of axiomatically characterised observer and generator functions. We often find that later stages of development — first requirements, then software design — bring about the desire to introduce further properties of types than first needed. (vi) Once "the road to using" model-oriented specifications has been entered, the developer will derive much benefit from using map and function types. They often capture essential properties and are simple to grasp, hence reasonably abstract. Set types are seldom seen, but using sets in handling definition sets and ranges of maps, and in handling index sets and elements of lists is an efficient means of expressing properties abstractly — in an expressive, reasonably understandable style. (vii) *Choice between simplicity of "nearest, closest" type versus complexity of defining "exactly fitting" subtype:* When choosing a model-oriented, i.e., concrete type, we may choose, just for the sake of argument, to represent a type of binary trees as hierarchical maps, each with exactly two definition set elements (i.e., hierarchies as dealt with in Example 16.7), rather than as a recursively defined Cartesian type (as posed in Exercise 14.4). These and related issues will be further dealt with in this chapter, and in the remaining parts of these volumes.

18.2 Type Categories

There are (semantically speaking) different kinds of types. For each of these kinds there are (syntactically speaking, different) forms of expressions and definitions. There are abstractly and concretely defined types.

18.2.1 Abstract Types: Sorts

The developers have available any abstract base type, i.e., sort, they choose to start with! The previous chapters and their examples made liberal use of sorts. Sorts are usually type abstractions of oftentimes rather complex values. What these value (i.e., component) types are is then revealed through the introduction, by the developer, of observer (and generator) functions. Initially, i.e., when starting out a long line of phases[1], stages[2] and steps[3] of development, in other words, when initially choosing sorts, the specifier is relieved of having to find a "most suited" model-oriented type.

18.2.2 Concrete Types

In parts of domain descriptions, in requirements prescriptions, and certainly in software design stages and steps of development, one must eventually and increasingly turn to models based on model-oriented, i.e., concrete types.

The *concrete types* are those whose elements may be (i) Booleans (**Bool**), (ii) integers (**Int**), (iii) natural numbers (**Nat**), (iv) reals (**Real**), (v) characters (**Char**), (vi) texts (**Text**), (vii) sets, (A-[**inf**]**set**), (viii) Cartesians (A×B×...×C), (ix) lists (A*, A$^\omega$), (x) maps (A $\twoheadrightarrow$ B) (xi) or are total and/or partial functions (A→B, A$\overset{\sim}{\to}$B).

(xii) Finally we have the types whose elements are either of two or more of Booleans, or integers, or numbers, or sets, or Cartesians, or functions:

type
    U = D | E | ... | F

that is, that are *union types*. In this section we shall, more systematically, explain the *union type*, and many additional type concepts.

---

[1]Phases: domain, requirements and software design.

[2]Stages: major "re-specifications", for the purposes of enriching (detailing) a specification. Stages "turn" BIG LIES, successively into Smaller Lies, finally into truth! That is, the big lies are gross simplifications of what is being specified, and the smaller lies add actual properties needed in order to approach reality.

[3]Steps: minor refinements or transformations of specifications within stages.

18.2.3 Discussion

With types a number of questions arise: Are there other types than the ones introduced so far? (xiv) How do we express and define types, including union types? (xv) Given a value, what means do we have for determining its type? (xvi) For any concrete *type expression* or any concrete *type definition* can we expect it always to denote something sensible, something we had in mind? These and other issues are the topics of the next sections.

Indeed, there are some types, in addition to union types, that we would like to either reintroduce or to enlarge our previous coverage of, and/or to more properly introduce: the enumerated token types (Chap. 10) and record types (Sect. 13.4.3 and Exercise 16.8). They are respective cases of the more general concepts of *variant record definitions*. Next we explain these three kinds of type expressions and definitions: Variant type definitions, union type expressions and short record type definitions. The latter two are related to variant types.

18.3 Enumerated Token Types Revisited

By an *enumerated token type*, also referred to as a constructed constant names type, we understand a type defined as follows:

type
    A == a1 | a2 | ... | an.

where the distinct identifiers a1, a2, ..., an are not defined elsewhere in the specification at hand. The definition of A, using the special *variant type constructor* ==, as well as the *union type constructor* |, is short for the following *sort* and value definitions, and the axioms:

type
    A
value
    a1:A, a2:A, ..., an:A
axiom
    [disjointness: A values]
        [informal: $\forall$ i,j:**Nat** • $0 < i,j \leq n$]
            $i \neq j \Rightarrow ai \neq aj$

Example 18.1 *Enumerated Types: Operators, Playing Cards and the Compass:* The enumerated — constant values — type can thus be used to define such things as a known set of operators of a programming language, cf. our earlier use of text strings, in Examples 14.4 to 14.7:

type
    MOp == minus | factorial | abs | not | ...
    DOp == add | sub | mpy | div | mod | and | or | imply | ...

the known set of playing card suit and face values:

type
    Suit == club | diamond | heart | spade
    Face == ace | two | ... | ten | knight | queen | king

or the "compass corners" of the world:

type
    Corner == east | west | north | south

Two kinds of axioms are needed in order to ensure a consistent meaning of constant constructors: disjointness of enumerated values (see axiom above) and an induction axiom:

type
    A == a1 | a2 | ... | an
axiom
    [induction]
    $\forall$ p:(A$\rightarrow$**Bool**) •
        (p(a1) $\wedge$ p(a2) $\wedge$ ... $\wedge$ p(an)) $\Rightarrow$ $\forall$ a:A • p(a)

The purpose of the induction axiom is to express that **A** only contains the explicitly enumerated values.

18.4 Records: Constructors and Destructors

Records are like Cartesians, only a little bit different!

18.4.1 General

Examples 14.4 to 14.7 illustrated the use of Cartesians and union types in defining a type of language constructs.

In general we can use the variant type definition to define composite, or as they will be called here, record types.

type
    A, B, ..., C
    K == k1(sa:A) | k2(sa:A,sb:B) | kn(sa:A,sb:B,sc:C) | ...

(where we think of A, B, ..., C as sorts). The identifiers k1, k2, ..., kn stand for distinct *record constructor functions* (*record constructors* or just *constructors*). The identifiers sa, sb, ..., sc (that are the same in the various alternatives, but could be a mix of some being the same and the rest, obviously, being distinct), denote and are distinct (possibly overloaded) *record destructor functions*. We also refer to these as just *record field selectors*, *record destructors* or just *destructors*.

Constructors and destructors can be used to compose, respectively decompose record values. To express the idea of the constructor (composition) and destructor (decomposition) functions, we present the full definitions (of which the above is an abbreviation):

type
    A, B, ..., C, K
value
    k1: A→K, k2: A×B→K, kn: A×B×C→K, ...
    sa: K→A, sb: K→B, sc: K→C, ...
axiom
    [disjointness of K values]
    ∀ av:A, bv:B, ..., cv:C •
        k1(av) ≠ k2(av,bv) ∧ k1(av) ≠ k3(av,bv,cv) ∧
        ... ∧ av = sa(k1(av)) = sa(k2(av,bv)) = sa(k3(av,bv,cv)) ∧
        ... ∧ bv = sb(k2(av,bv)) = sb(k3(av,bv,cv)) ∧
        ... ∧ cv = sc(k3(av,bv,cv)) ...

18.4.2 Variant Record Value Induction Axioms

Non-recursive Record Type Definitions

We have exemplified axioms governing the disjointness of values defined by a variant definition. But an induction axiom is needed in order to remove "junk", that is, undesirable, unintended, values from the defined types. For the (simple) record type definition (below) we need:

axiom
type
    A, B, ..., C
    K == k1(sa:A)|k2(sa:A,sb:B)|kn(sa:A,sb:B,sc:C)
value
    k1: A→K, k2: A×B→K, kn: A×B×C→K
axiom
    [induction]
        ∀ p:K→**Bool**, av:A,
            (p(k1(av)) ∧ p(k2(av,bv)) ∧ p(k3(av,bv,cv)) ⇒ ∀ k:K • p(k))
              ⇒ (∀ k:K • p(k))

Recursive Record Type Definitions

For recursively defined record types, disjointness and induction axioms, for example, become:

type
    A
    R == empty | rec(sa:A,sr:R)
axiom
    [disjointness: R values]
      ∀ av:A, rv:R • empty ≠ rec(av,rv) ∧
        sa(rec(av,rv))=av ∧ sr(rec(av,rv))=rv
    [induction, no junk]
      ∀ p:R→**Bool** • p(empty) ∧ (∀ av:A, rv:R • p(rv) ⇒ p(rec(av,rv)))
        ⇒ ∀ rv:R • p(rv)

18.4.3 An Example

One of the standard uses of the union and variant record type definition capability is that of defining syntactic structures such as found in programming languages. Another is that of defining different kinds of data structure values. We exemplify the former.

Example 18.2 *Cartesian vs. Record Variant Types:* We give an example of the use of record types. The example really only rephrases parts of Examples 14.4 to 14.7. We show, for comparison, the Cartesian and record type models of the syntax (cf. Example 14.5):

type
    Pn, Ln, V, E
    M' = (Pn × Ln) × P-set
    M = {| m:M • wf_M(m) |}
    P = Pn × (Ln × S)-set
    S = Asgn | Cond | Goto | Call | Stop
    Asgn = {"asgn"} × (V × E) × Ln
    Cond = {"cond"} × (E × Ln × Ln)
    Goto = {"goto"} × Ln
    Call = {"call"} × (Pn × Ln) × Ln
    Stop = {"stop"}

type
    Pn, Ln, V, E
    M' = (Pn × Ln) × P-set
    M = {| m:M • wf_M(m) |}
    P = Pn × (Ln × S)-set
    S == Asgn(ve:V,e:E,l:Ln)
      | Cond (e:E,cl:Ln,al:Ln)
      | Goto(l:Ln)
      | Call(pn:Pn,cl:Ln,rl:Ln)
      | stop

We compare the control structures of the two well-formedness functions (cf. Example 14.6):

wf_S(s)(lns)(ps) ≡
  cases s **of**
    ("assign",(v,e),ℓ) → ...,
    ("cond",(e,ln,ln')) → ...,
    ("goto",ln) → ...,
    ("call",(pn,ln),ℓ) →
      ...,
    "stop" → ...,
  end

wf_S(s)(lns)(ps) ≡
  cases s **of**
    Asgn((v,e),ℓ) → ℓ∈ lns,
    Cond(e,ln,ln') → {ln,ln'} ⊆ lns,
    Goto(ln) → ln ∈ lns,
    Call(pn,ln,ℓ) →
      wf_Call((pn,ln),ℓ)(ps),
    stop → **true**
  end

18.5 Union Type Definitions

The union type concept was introduced in Sect. 13.4.3 in Example 13.10's subsection on *An Aside on Type Union and Variant Records*) and illustrated in that example's definition of Cmd's, subsection on *Formalisation of Action Types*. Another explanation of the union type was also given in Sect. 14.4.1's subsection *An Aside: The Union Type Operator*, |. Other union type definitions were given in Example 14.3's definitions of Q, R and S, in Example 14.7's definition of Θ (subsection *Formalisation — Semantic Types*), in Example 16.8's definition of VAL, in Examples 16.17's and 16.18's definitions of OP and OL, and in Example 17.3's definition of S^4.

In general, the 'shorthand':

type
  A = B | ... | C

where B and C are identifiers, is, theoretically, intended to mean:

type
  A == A_from_B(A_to_B:B) | ... | A_from_C(A_to_C:C)

The shorthand implicitly defines a set of constructors (from A_from_B to A_from_C) and destructors (from A_to_B to A_to_C). If you think their names too cumbersome, then you are free to use the full definitional facility offered by the record variant definition. Constructors are sometimes called injector functions. Destructors are correspondingly called projector functions.

Thus, if you define:

---

[4]We present all these references so that you may go back and recapitulate the uses of record type definitions. Doing so, "going back", the reader will, we strongly believe, more easily grasp the ideas.

type
    A = B | C | ...
    B == mk_beta(sel_b:B)
    C == mk_gamma(sel_c:C)
    ...

then you avoid:

type
    A == A_from_B(A_to_B:B) | A_from_C(A_to_C:C) | ...

mk_beta and sel_b "replaces" A_from_B, respectively A_to_B; etcetera.

18.6 Short Record Type Definitions

Defining:

type
    B, ..., C
    A == mk_alpha(sel_beta:B,...,sel_gamma:C)

can be abbreviated by the short record type definition:

type
    B, ..., C
    A :: sel_beta:B ... sel_gamma:C

18.7 Type Expressions, Revisited

A schematic syntax for the syntactic category of all type expressions can now be summarised:

type
    [1] **Bool**,   [10] A*,
    [2] **Int**,   [11] A$^\omega$,
    [3] **Nat**,   [12] A $\underset{m}{\rightarrow}$ B,
    [4] **Real**,   [13] A → B,
    [5] **Char**,   [14] A $\overset{\sim}{\rightarrow}$ B,
    [6] **Text**,   [15] (A),
    [7] **A-set**,   [16] A | B | ... | C,
    [8] **A-infset**,   [17] mk_id(sel_a:A,...,sel_b:B),
    [9] A × B × ... × C,   [18] sel_a:A ... sel_b:B.

where A, B, ..., C can be any of the expressions [1–16].
    The meaning of these type expressions has been explained earlier.

18.8 Subtypes

Thus there is one type expression in addition to those ([1–18]) summarised in Sect. 18.7. It is the subtype expression. The type expression:

$$\{|\ b{:}B \bullet \mathcal{P}(b)\ |\}$$

usually occurs in connection with type definitions:

type
    $A = \{|\ b{:}B \bullet \mathcal{P}(b)\ |\}$

and is a subtype expression. It defines A to be the type of those b in a usually "larger"[5] type B, but for which the predicate $\mathcal{P}(b)$ holds.

The general form of subtype expressions is:

$$\{|\ <\text{binding}> : <\text{type\_expression}> \bullet <\text{Boolean\_valued\_expression}>\ |\}$$

The structure of the **binding** must 'match' the structure of the values of type **type_expression**.

18.9 Type Definitions, Revisited

Throughout we have exemplified type definitions. It is time to summarise. We now present a set [1–5] of example forms of type definitions. So, what follows is not an RSL set of type definitions as one would find them in an RSL **type** clause, but 'concrete' such type equations. The **Type_names** are the left-hand side of the type equations. The =, == or :: are the type "equation" symbols. And the rest, to the right, or after the equation symbols, are concrete examples of the kind of type expressions that are special to 'union type', 'record type' and 'subtype' types.

[1] Type_name =
        Type_expr /* without | s or subtypes */
[2] Type_name =
        Type_expr_1 | Type_expr_2 | ... | Type_expr_n
[3] Type_name ==
        mk_id_1(s_a1:Type_name_a1,...,s_ai:Type_name_ai) |
        ... |
        mk_id_n(s_z1:Type_name_z1,...,s_zk:Type_name_zk)
[4] Type_name :: sel_a:Type_name_a ... sel_z:Type_name_z
[5] Type_name = {| v:Type_name' • $\mathcal{P}$(v) |}

---

[5]Type X is said to be a type "larger" than type Y if all values of type Y are also values of type X, and there are values of type X which are not of type Y. In other words Y is a subtype of X.

where a form of [2–3] is provided by the combination:

Type_name = A | B | ... | Z
A == mk_id_1(s_a1:A_1,...,s_ai:A_i)
B == mk_id_2(s_b1:B_1,...,s_bj:B_j)
...
Z == mk_id_n(s_z1:Z_1,...,s_zk:Z_k)

The meaning of type definitions has been explained in all the previous chapters where new types were introduced.

18.10 On Recursive Type Definitions

We refer to Sects. 13.5.1, 14.5.1, 15.5.1, 16.5.1 and 17.4.1 for discussions on the issue of defining types recursively. Dana Scott provided the basic research that now serves as the theoretical setting for our understanding of types: [251, 458–462, 464, 466–468].

18.11 Discussion

18.11.1 General

We have reviewed and extended the concept of types. Chapters 13–16 formally introduced the set, Cartesian, list and map types, while also informally making use of union, enumerated and record types. These latter have now been formally introduced.

18.11.2 Principles, Techniques and Tools

> A picture is worth a thousand words.
> And a type system is worth a zillion pictures.
>
> *Anonymous*

Principles. Four fundamental ideas of *types* are those (i) of abstract classification, of (ii) distinguishing between syntactic and semantics types, of (iii) sketching type structures as a first development activity and of (iv) abstract data structure designs.

By forcing distinctness of types, by introducing subtypes and by being able to formulate well-formalness constraints over types, one is able to establish a type system, i.e., a set of types. By judicious use of abstraction, that is, through the use of both abstract and concrete types, sketching a type system is something that can be done rather quickly by the reasonably trained developer.

Methodologically the main principles are (1) to design types for all semantic entities of interest first and (2) to initially choose sorts. ∎

Discussion. Very many software engineers draw diagrams which picture an instantiation of a value of a given type, usually a composite one. Defining a system of types is a way to draw zillions of pictures. The shortcomings of drawing instantiations of values is that one usually has to draw families of diagrams. It then becomes hard to discuss whether to choose one kind of type rather than another kind. We find that defining type systems enable us to conduct far more mature and concise discussions concerning alternative choices of types. The techniques and tools for constructing types allow the developer to rapidly sketch a type system. Should discussions with colleagues lead to a desire for another type structure then even sweeping changes can be effected rapidly.   ▪

Techniques. Two contrasting approaches to the design of *type* systems exist. They are the property-oriented and the model-oriented. In the former approach one postulates sorts, then the function signatures of usually primitive or simple operations over these sorts, and finally axioms that relate the values of the sorts and the operations. In the model-oriented approach one designs concrete, albeit abstract model-oriented types. Functions are fully defined and their definition helps the developer to test the usefulness of a type abstraction.   ▪

Tools. The RSL *type* definition constructs, including definition of sorts and concrete types, subtypes and well-formedness constraints, that is, predicates, over types, form the basic tools.   ▪

18.12 Bibliographical Notes

In the interlude, Part IV, just before this chapter, we mentioned these books: [1, 282, 424, 443, 532]. They, in various ways, cover types in programming languages, both the practical ones that you apply when programming, as well as the mathematical meanings of these types, that is, the theoretical ones you normally do not have to bother about. I, myself, find [1, 424, 443] particularly useful. As remarked just above (Sect. 18.10) Dana Scott provided the basic research that now serves as the theoretical setting for our understanding of types: [251, 458–462, 464, 466–468].

18.13 Exercises

Exercise 18.1. ♣ *A Summary Type System for Transportation Nets.* We refer to Appendix A, Sect. A.1, *Transportation Net.* We also refer to Exercises 13.5 14.6, 15.15 and 16.12.

Summarise your work, so far, on abstract and concrete types for *Transportation Nets* by presenting a suitable sort-, map-, list-, Cartesian- and set-based type system for *Transportation Nets*.

Indicate appropriate subtypes, variant types, and well-formedness predicates. If defined earlier, then refer to these latter predicates.

Exercise 18.2. ♣ *A Summary Type System for for Container Logistics.* We refer to Appendix A, Sect. A.2, *Container Logistics.* We also refer to Exercises 13.6 14.7, 15.16 and 16.13.

Summarise your work, so far, on abstract and concrete types for *Container Logistics* by presenting a suitable sort-, map-, list-, Cartesian- and set-based type system for *Container Logistics.*

Indicate appropriate subtypes, variant types, and well-formedness predicates. If defined earlier, then refer to these latter predicates.

Exercise 18.3. ♣ *A Summary Type System for Financial Industries.* We refer to Appendix A, Sect. A.3, *Financial Service Industry.* We also refer to Exercises 13.6 14.7, 15.16 and 16.13.

Summarise your work, so far, on abstract and concrete types for *Financial Service Industries* by presenting a suitable sort-, map-, list-, Cartesian- and set-based type system for *Financial Service Industries.*

Indicate appropriate subtypes, variant types, and well-formedness predicates. If defined earlier, then refer to these latter predicates.

Part V

SPECIFICATION PROGRAMMING

On Specification Programming

Characterisation. By *specification programming* we understand a style of specification (resp. programming) which "borders" on programming (resp. specification). ∎

Specification programming is neither very abstract nor algorithmic.

In this part, i.e., in Chaps. 19–21, we illustrate a spectrum of specification programming which spans from applicative (Chap. 19), i.e., functional, via imperative (Chap. 20), i.e., with assignable variables and statements, to parallel specification programming (Chap. 21), i.e., with processes and process synchronisation and inter-communication.

Thus we shall review, in Chap. 19, much of the RSL language constructs already covered (while adding a few). We shall, in Chap. 20, introduce the imperative constructs of RSL: assignable variable declarations, assignment statements, iterative and loop statements, etc. Finally, in Chap. 21, we shall introduce the parallel constructs of RSL: processes, process input expressions and output statements, channels, and the parallel, nondeterministic internal (choice), and nondeterministic external (choice) composition of processes. In this respect, the RSL, which the reader has been introduced to so far, is extended with basic constructs of Hoare's calculus for expressing Communicating Sequential Processes, CSP [288, 448, 456].

On Problems and Exercises

Most problem formulations of Part V ask for solutions that contain both a property-oriented solution and a model-oriented solution along the lines of the next three chapters.

Exercises 19.1, 20.1, and 21.9 form one set of related exercises. So do Exercises 19.2, 20.2, and 21.10. And so do Exercises 19.3, 20.3, and 21.11. They all illustrate programming more than abstract modelling. They are all intended to develop your skills in large-scale specification programming. In contrast, Exercises 21.2, 21.3, 21.4, 21.5, 21.6, 21.7, and 21.8, call for reasonably abstract RSL/CSP modelling of producer/consumer buffers, client/server and UNIX pipes. These latter exercises are intended to develop your skills in small-scale elegance when modelling these latter kinds of computing systems concepts.

19

Applicative Specification Programming

- The **prerequisites** for studying this chapter are that you have understood most, if not all, of what has been covered in previous chapters.
- The **aims** are to summarise the applicative features of RSL already given, to introduce additional applicative features of RSL, to bring a detailed model of bindings, their types, patterns and matchings (Sect. 19.6), and to illustrate more comprehensive uses of the applicative subset of RSL, thus exemplifying additional modelling ideas.
- The **objective** is to make the reader fluent in applicative specification programming.
- The **treatment** is systematic.

In this chapter we shall summarise the applicative constructs of the specification notation (RSL). The term 'applicative' (as prefix to 'programming') derives from 'function application'. The main distinguishing property of *applicative programming* is that of *defining, applying* and *composing functions*. Therefore the term 'functional' is often used in lieu of the term 'applicative', hence *functional programming* [51,175,225,261,278,380,389,433,498,502,520].

The main distinguishing property of all expressions, be they arithmetic, Boolean, set, Cartesian, list, or map expression is their operator/operand structure, and hence that they involve function applications.

Characterisation. By *applicative programming* we shall understand programming with functions, that is, programming where functions are first-class citizens, where function application is a core notion, and where there are no concept of storage, that is, assignable variables, nor of concurrency. ∎

Discussion. We resort to characterising *applicative programming* also by what it is not: it is not programing with assignments, hence there is no notion of statements. Also it is not programing with processes, hence there is no notion of concurrency. ∎

Characterisation. By *function programming* we mean the same as applicative programming.   ∎

Characterisation. By *applicative specification programming* we shall understand an abstract, property-oriented form of *applicative programming*, one in which we deploy abstract types and so on.   ∎

19.1 Scope and Binding

In order to model phenomena, i.e., to express concepts, and their properties and/or computations involving these, it is often wise to introduce identifiers that then designate these phenomena cum concepts. These identifiers are thus associated with values (over which properties and/or computations are expressed). These identifiers have a certain text over which they are supposed to be used, i.e., over which they are valid. We call this the *scope of the identifier*. Some such identifiers designate constants, i.e., values which are expressed and do not change. These are the identifiers we think of in application specification (programming). Other such identifiers designate possibly changing values, i.e., the identifiers name declared (storable) variables whose value may be reassigned (reexpressed). We shall deal with this kind of variable in Chap. 20. The constant (even though they are also called "variable") identifiers are given value once. We say they are *bound*. This section is about such identifiers, their scope and binding. As for a number of technicalities of binding we refer to Sect. 19.6, on the topics of bindings, typings, patterns and matching.

We find that there are basically five kinds of situations in which identifiers are being defined, and thus for which the notions of scope and binding become relevant. They are:

1. **let** definitions
2. function definitions
3. **case** constructs
4. comprehended expressions
5. quantified expressions

In Sects. 19.1.2–19.1.6 we refer, in brackets, to the above numerals.

We now treat the binding and scope issues as they arise in the above forms. Our treatment will be 'esoteric'. That is: It assumes that you are already familiar with our earlier coverage of these forms. Thus we summarise.

19.1.1 Binding Patterns — An Informal Exposition

Characterisation. By a *binding pattern* we mean a structure of usually free and always distinct identifiers or "wildcards" (_), that are bound to, i.e., equated with, a similarly structured value such that one can establish a one-to-one relationship between the identifiers and components of the value.   ■

In earlier chapters on sets, Cartesians, lists and maps we presented binding patterns like:

let {a} ∪ s = set **in** ... **end**
let (a,b,...,c) = cart **in** ... **end**
let ⟨a⟩ˆℓ = list **in** ... **end**   and   **let** ℓˆ⟨a⟩ = list **in** ... **end**
let [a↦b] ∪ m = map **in** ... **end**

Here the patterns are:

{a} ∪ s, (a,b,...,c), ⟨a⟩ˆℓ, ℓˆ⟨a⟩, [a↦b] ∪ m

We assume that set, cart, list and map are of the right size: That is, that set, list, and map are nonempty, and cart has the right number of immediate components, commensurate with the Cartesian binding pattern (a,b,...,c).

We now extend the above forms with wildcards _:

let {a,_} ∪ s = set **in** ... **end**
let (a,_,...,c) = cart **in** ... **end**
let ⟨a,_,b⟩ˆℓ = list **in** ... **end**
let [a↦b,_] ∪ m = map **in** ... **end**

These forms only make sense if set has at least two elements, list has at least three elements, and map at least two "pairings". If such is the case then the idea is that s is any set, derived from the set set by removing any two elements; that ℓ is the list derived from the list list by removing the first three elements, and that m is any map derived from the map map by removing arbitrary pairings.

In the following we shall assume that a wildcard is treated as if it was a free identifier! That is, our expositions will not take wildcards into specific consideration, but just assume that they may be used, i.e., that they may occur in the generic presentations of bindings given.

To summarise, and to generalise: to patterns, which are structures of usually free identifiers we now add the possibility of also having wildcards, bound identifiers and constants appearing in patterns. The bound identifiers are, naturally, bound to something, namely a value, i.e., a(nother) constant.[1] A binding, as treated in this chapter, is now the pairing of a pattern and a value. The value presents itself in a number of ways: (i) through the evaluation of an expression with which the pattern is paired (with the pairing operator being an equality symbol, =) — as in the **let** constructs; (ii) through an argument

---

[1]That latter binding is provided by the context of the text in which the pattern occurs — with such a context usually being provided for by the evaluation configuration's context, i.e., environment component.

value provided in a function invocation and then paired with the formal parameter list of the function definition; (iii) through the typed quantification as in comprehensions and predicate expressions; (iv) or through the **case e of** construct where, alternatively, one after the other, of the case selection clauses, the pattern left-hand side of these are paired to the value of expression **e** of the **case e of** header. All this will now be treated in some detail.

19.1.2 "let" Construct Scope and Binding [1]

The **let** construct is also treated in Sect. 19.2. So we only present a simplest, albeit schematic example:

>   **let** pattern = $\mathcal{E}(...)$ **in** $\mathcal{B}$(id_1,id_2,...,id_n) **end**

Let Δ be a metalinguistic "observer" function which extracts all identifiers from a *pattern*. Then, for the above **pattern**, we have:

> Δ(pattern) = {id_1,id_2,...,id_n}

The free identifiers {id_1,id_2,...,id_n} of binding_pattern are introduced by the left-hand (of =) construct, binding_pattern. They are *bound* to the values that satisfy the *defining equation* binding_pattern = $\mathcal{D}$(id_1,id_2,...,id_n). And their *scope* is the *body expression*, $\mathcal{B}$(id_1,id_2,...,id_n), of the clause above. The defining equation may give rise to a finite (including zero) or an infinite number of models in which these free identifiers are bound to values that satisfy the equation.

Example 19.1 *Simple "let" Bindings:* We present a simple — rather construed — example, to be studied by the reader:

type
>   A = **Bool** × (**Int** × **Real** × (**Text** × **Char**))

value
>   f: A → (**Int** | **Text**)
>   f(a) ≡ **let** (b,(i,r,(t,c))) = a **in if** b **then** i + **int** r **else** t^⟨c⟩ **end end**

(Here $\Delta(b, (i, r, (t, c))) = \{b, i, r, t, c\}$.)   ∎

For further examples of let definition bindings we refer to Sects. 7.7.2, 13.2.3, 14.2.3–14.2.4, 15.2.3, and 16.2.3.

19.1.3 Function Definition Scope and Binding [2]

We refer to Chap. 11 for an earlier presentation of this material. The form of function definitions for which it is meaningful to talk about introduction, binding and scope of identifiers are:

value
    f: A $\overset{\sim}{\to}$ B
    f(pattern) $\equiv$ $\mathcal{E}$(a_1,...,a_m)
    pre: $\mathcal{P}$(a_1,...,a_m)

    f(arg_pattern) **as** res_pattern
    pre: $\mathcal{P}$(a_1,...,a_m)
    post: $\mathcal{P}$(a_1,...,a_m,r_1,...,r_n)

where:
    {a_1,...,a_m} = Δ(arg_pattern)
    {r_1,...,r_n} = Δ(res_pattern)

By argument_pattern we mean a pattern with one or more free identifiers. These are the identifiers we shall be referring to. result_pattern is a pattern with free identifiers only. The form argument_pattern in the function definition header f(argument_pattern) introduces the identifiers. The signature f: A $\to$ B generally binds these free identifiers to types. The specific binding of the free identifiers of the argument_patterns occurs whenever the function f is invoked: f(argument). The scope of f and the free identifiers is the rest of the function definition, the body and the pre condition: $\mathcal{E}$(id_1,id_2,...,id_n) **pre:** $\mathcal{P}$(id_1,id_2,...,id_n).

Example 19.2 *Simple Function Definition Bindings:* Again a somewhat construed example, to be studied by the reader:

type
    A = **Bool** $\times$ **Real**
    B = **Int** $\times$ **Nat**
    C = **Real** $\times$ **Real**
value
    f: A $\to$ (B | C)
    f(b,r) $\equiv$ **if** b **then** (int r,abs(r$-$int r)) **else** ($-$abs r,abs r) **end**

    f(b,r) **as** (ir,nr)
        post ir = **if** b **then** int r **else** $-$abs r **end** $\wedge$
                nr = **if** b **then** abs(r$-$int r) **else** abs r **end**

■

For further examples of function definition bindings we refer to Chap. 11.

19.1.4 "case" Construct Scope and Binding [3]

We only treat the scope and binding of the **case** construct now. For other facets of the **case** construct see Sect. 19.5. The **case** construct schematically appears as:

    case expr **of**
        choice_pattern_1 $\to$ expr_1,

        choice_pattern_2 → expr_2,

        ...

        choice_pattern_n_or_wild_card → expr_n
    end

where choice_pattern_i and choice_pattern_n_or_wild_card are patterns usually with one or more free identifiers. The free identifiers (not shown, but implied, above) are introduced in the choice_pattern_i clauses immediately to the left of the → s. They are bound to values as per the *matching* afforded between the **cases expr of** expression value part and the pattern. And their scope is the expr_i immediately to the right of the corresponding →.

Example 19.3 *Case Bindings:* Next in the line of our construed examples we bring the following, to be studied by the reader:

type
    A == mkB(s_i:**Int**) | mkC(s_i:**Int**,s_j:**Int**) | mkD(s_i:**Int**,s_j:**Int**,s_k:**Int**)
value
    f: A → (**Int** | **Nat** | **Real**)
    f(a) ≡
        case a **of**
            mkB(iv) → iv,
            mkC(iv,jv) → **if** iv≥0 **then** −iv **else** jv **end**
            mkD(iv,jv,kv) → **if** kv≠0 **then** iv/kv **else** iv/(kv+0.000001) **end**
        end

                                                          ■

For further examples of case construct bindings we refer to Sect. 14.4.1.

19.1.5 Comprehensions: Scope and Binding [4]

There are three forms of comprehended expressions:

    { E(a) | a:A • P(a) },
    ⟨ E(i) | i **in** index_list • P(i) ⟩,
    [D(a) ↦ R(a) | a:A • P(a)].

The identifiers a, i and a (lines 1, 2 and 3, respectively, above) are named and typed (i.e., generally bound) in respective clause parts: a:A, i **in** index_list and a:A. They are being specifically bound to specific values by the optional part P(a). And their scope is E(a), E(i), respectively D(a)↦ R(a). We leave it to the reader to "retell the story" above, but based on appropriate patterns and their free identifiers. For specific examples of comprehension bindings we refer to Sects. 13.2.2, 15.2.2 and 16.2.2.

19.1.6 Quantifications: Scope and Binding [5]

There are three forms of quantified expressions:

$$\forall\ a{:}A \bullet P(a), \quad \exists\ a{:}A \bullet P(a), \quad \exists\ !\ a{:}A \bullet P(a)$$

We refer to Chap. 9, Sect. 9.5.4.

The identifier a is introduced and typed in the a:A part of the quantified expressions. And the scope of the defined identifier a is the remaining text: P(a). We leave it to the reader to "retell the story" above, but based on appropriate patterns and their free identifiers.

For specific examples of quantified expressions we refer to Sects. 9.5.4–9.5.7.

19.2 Intuition

First, it is important to note that we have already given quite a lot of examples of uses of the **let ... in ... end** clause. Second, it is important to state that in this entire section we are not going to present any further examples of applicative specifications.

We have already seen that operator/operand expressions can express quite complex values. And, as we shall see, expressions can indeed express all the values we ever wish to express, through the use of fix points. The last three sentences were brought in in order that we may justify, from an untraditional angle, our focus on expressions, that is, functions, as a full-blown specification cum programming language.

19.2.1 Simple "let a $= \mathcal{E}_d$ in $\mathcal{E}_b(a)$ end"

We continue this attempt at justification. To decompose the expression of values we introduce the:

let a $= \mathcal{E}_d$ **in** $\mathcal{E}_b(a)$ **end**

clause. It is an expanded form of:

$$(\lambda a.\mathcal{E}_b(a))(\mathcal{E}_d)$$

that is, of defining a function, $\lambda a.\mathcal{E}_b(a)$, and of applying that function to an argument, $\mathcal{E}_d$. The scope of a is $\mathcal{E}_b(a)$.

An intuition about the expression: **let** a $= \mathcal{E}_d$ **in** $\mathcal{E}_b(a)$ **end** is that it defines the variable a, to not really be a variable in the sense of attaining a varying value, but that it defines a to attain a constant value throughout the scope $\mathcal{E}_b(a)$. That intuition makes the clause **let** a $= \mathcal{E}_d$ **in** into a so-called single assignment. This two step approach of first binding a constant value to a, and then using this value, i.e., a, in a context — in which other such bindings and uses take place — allows for a "divide and conquer" principle of expressing values.

19.2.2 Recursive "let f(a) = $\mathcal{E}_d$(f) in $\mathcal{E}_b$(f,a) end"

We saw, in Sect. 7.8, how a recursive definition, as of f in:

> **let** f(a) = E(f) **in** B(f,a) **end**
> /* which is the same as */
> **let** f = λa:A • E(f) **in** B(f,a) **end**

amounts to:

> **let** f = **YF** **in** B(f,a) **end**
> F ≡ λg•λa•(E(g))
> *The Fix Point Identity Law:* **YF** = F(**YF**)

This explains and thus allows the use of recursive definitions.

19.2.3 Predicative "let a:A • $\mathcal{P}$(a) in $\mathcal{E}$(a) end"

The typing construct:

> **let** a:A • $\mathcal{P}$(a) **in** $\mathcal{B}$(a) **end**

expresses, in colloquial terms, the selection of an a value of type A which satisfies a predicate $\mathcal{P}$(a) for evaluation in the body $\mathcal{B}$(a).

19.2.4 Multiple "let a_i = $\mathcal{E}_{d_i}$ in $\mathcal{E}_b$(a_i) end"

In general, we allow for multiple, mixed and compound binding pattern definitions:

> **let** a:A • P_1(a), b:B • P_2(a,b), ..., c:C • P_n(a,b,...,c),
>   p_a = E_1(a,b,...,c),
>   p_b = E_2(a,b,...,c,p_a),
>   ...,
>   p_c = E_n(a,b,...,c,p_a,p_b,...,) **in**
> B(a,b,...,c,p_a,p_b,...,p_c) **end**

where p_a, p_b, ... p_c are binding patterns of free identifiers (and possible wildcards), and where the order of the defining clauses above is important.

The above is shorthand for:

> **let** a:A • P_1(a) **in let** b:B • P_2(a,b) **in** ..., **let** c:C • P_n(a,b,...,c) **in**
>   **let** p_a = E_1(a,b,...,c) **in**
>   **let** p_b = E_2(a,b,...,c,p_a) **in**
>   ...,
>   **let** p_c = E_n(a,b,...,c,p_a,p_b,...) **in**
>   B(a,b,...,c,p_a,p_b,...,p_c)
> **end end** ... **end end end** ... **end**

This rewriting explains the scope of the defined names.

Now, what is the meaning of all this? We have not imposed, so far, any restrictions on the forms of the defining expressions. (That is, those on the right-hand side of the equations and in the typing predicates.) The answer, without going into renewed detail, is simple: The meaning of a compound set of multiple and mixed **let** bindings, i.e., excluding the body B(a,b,...,c,p_a,p_b,...,p_c), is the set of all models that contain bindings of all free identifiers a,b,...,c, and all free identifiers in the binding patterns p_a,p_b,...,p_c, to such values that make the equations and predicates hold.

Please do not bother about how these equations (etc.) are 'solved'. Just focus on the properties they define. We are specifying, not algorithmically programming! Please note that we can thus not use the above multiple **let** clauses to define two or more functions that are mutually recursive. That is,

value
    f: A → B
    f(a) ≡
        let f1 = λ x:X • $\mathcal{E}$(f2,a,x),
            f2 = λ y:Y • $\mathcal{E}$(f1,a,y) **in**
        let x = ..., y = ... **in**
        ... f1(x) ... f2(y) ... **end end**

is not an acceptable definition.

But we can define any set of mutually recursive functions as proper **value** definitions of a **class** definition. Such function definitions — momentarily disregarding any possible name clashes (i.e., two or more in different **class** definitions having the same name) — can be considered defined at the "outermost" level of of definitions, declarations, etc., of a full specification.

19.2.5 Literals and Identifiers

Literals

The simplest kind of expression is the literals, that is, names of constants: numerals, Booleans, characters, etc.

    0, 1, 2, ..., −1, −2, ...
    0.0, 1.41, 2.71, 3.15, ...
    true, false
    "a", "b", ..., "z", ..., "abc", ...

Identifiers

An almost equally simple kind of expressions are the identifiers which, for example through their occurrence in function argument/value bindings, in **let** clause bindings and in **case** choice bindings, are bound to values:

a, b, ..., id, name, ...

Some identifiers may designate enumerated type values.

19.3 Operator/Operand Expressions

The operator or connective/operand expressions of RSL are the prefix, infix and suffix expressions:

⟨Expr⟩ ::=
        ⟨Prefix_Op⟩ ⟨Expr⟩
      | ⟨Expr⟩ ⟨Infix_Op⟩ ⟨Expr⟩
      | ⟨Expr⟩ ⟨Suffix_Op⟩
      | ...
⟨Prefix_Op⟩ ::=
      $-$ | $\sim$ | $\cup$ | $\cap$ | **card** | **len** | **inds** | **elems** | **hd** | **tl** | **dom** | **rng**
⟨Infix_Op⟩ ::=
      $=$ | $\neq$ | $\equiv$ | $+$ | $-$ | $*$ | $\uparrow$ | $/$ | $<$ | $\leq$ | $\geq$ | $>$ | $\wedge$ | $\vee$ | $\Rightarrow$
      | $\in$ | $\notin$ | $\cup$ | $\cap$ | $\setminus$ | $\subset$ | $\subseteq$ | $\supseteq$ | $\supset$ | $\widehat{}$ | $\dagger$ | $\circ$
⟨Suffix_Op⟩ ::= !

Expression values are expected to be of types commensurate with the operators.

    The prefix unary operators or connectives are: arithmetic (negation), Boolean (negation), set (distributed union and intersection, cardinality), list (length, indices, elements, head, tail), map (definition set, map range set). The infix binary operators or connectives are: general equality, inequality and equivalence; arithmetic (addition, subtraction, multiplication, division, exponentiation), Boolean (conjunction, disjunction, implication), set (element membership or non-membership, union, intersection, complement, proper subset, subset, superset, proper superset), list (concatenation), map (union, override, restriction) and function (composition). The (only) suffix unary operator is: arithmetic (factorial). Infix expressions are evaluated left to right.

19.4 Enumerated and Comprehended Expressions

We continue our RSL "Reference Manual-like" survey of RSL's applicative language features. For expressing sets, Cartesians, lists and maps explicitly there are the enumerated and comprehended forms:

{a_1,a_2,...,a_n}, {E(a)|a:A•P(a)}
(a_1,a_2,...,a_n), ⟨E(ids)|b_p **in** lst_ex•P(ids)⟩   **where:** ids = Δ(b_p)
[a_1↦b_1, ..., a_n↦b_n], [D(a)↦R(a)|a:A: P(a)]

That is, the identifiers, ids, occurring in E(ids), are the free identifiers of the binding pattern b_p, and lst_ex is a list expression.

19.5 Conditional Expressions

The conditional expressions are:

> **if** b_expr **then** c_expr **else** a_expr **end**

> **if** b_expr **then** c_expr **end** ≡ /∗ same as: ∗/
>   **if** b_expr **then** c_expr **else skip end**

> **case** expr **of**
>   choice_pattern_1 → expr_1,
>   choice_pattern_2 → expr_2,
>   ...
>   choice_pattern_n_or_wild_card → expr_n
> **end**

where choice_patter_n_or_wild_card is either a choice_pattern or a wild_card (_).
 For the situation where the choice_patterns do not or at least not significantly-contain free identifiers we could say that the construct:

> **case** expr **of**
>   choice_pattern_1 → expr_1,
>   choice_pattern_2 → expr_2,
>   ...
>   choice_pattern_n_or_wild_card → expr_n
> **end**

is not a conditional, but a selection expression. Thus there are basically two different situations in which we make use of the **case** construct: For selection purposes, or for "multi-way", i.e., more than two, conditional decisions.

Example 19.4 *Conditional versus Selection "case"s:* We leave it to the reader to study, i.e., to "decipher" the below example — it serves no practical purpose, but illustrates the idea of a conditional use of the **case** construct:

type
  A = **Int** | (**Int** × **Int**) | (**Int** × **Int** × **Int**)
value
  f: A → **Bool**
  f(a) ≡
    case a **of**
      7 → **true**, (7,_) → **true**, (7,_,_) → **true**, _ → **false**
    end

The next example shall then, likewise, illustrate the idea of selection:

$$A = \mathbf{Int} \mid (\mathbf{Int} \times \mathbf{Int}) \mid (\mathbf{Int} \times \mathbf{Int} \times \mathbf{Int})$$

value

   f: A → **Real**

   f(a) ≡

     case a **of**

       (7,j) → j/3, (7,j,k) → j∗k/5, _ → a/7

     end

∎

Repeated **if ... then ... else ... end**s can be written:

   if b

     then c

     else

       if b′

         then c′

         else

           if b″

             then c″

   end end end

But can be abbreviated:

   if b **then** c

   elsif b′ **then** c′

   elsif b″ **then** c″

   end

using the **elsif** construct.

19.6 Bindings, Typings, Patterns and Matching

> Pattern: ...; matrix, a mould; a figure in wood or metal
> from which a mould is made for casting; ...
>
> *(1598) The Shorter Oxford English Dictionary*
> *On Historial Principles [350]*

This section can be skipped, but is written so as to be readable in and by itself. Hence it repeats some of the material in earlier sections of this chapter, albeit in a more general form.

19.6.1 The Issues

Earlier we dealt with the concepts of *bindings, typings, patterns* and *matching* (Sect. 13.2.3 (sets), Sects. 14.4.1–14.4.2 (Cartesians), Sect. 15.2.3 (lists), and Sect. 16.2.3 (maps)). We shall here summarise these and additionally consider the construct of *record patterns*.

The two main issues are: first, that we need to express the choice of named values of desired types, and for that we use the concepts of binding and typing; Second, we need to express the decomposition of composite values into named subcomponents, and for that we use the concepts of patterns and matching.

Syntactic Issues of Convenience

The concepts of binding, typing, pattern and matching, are not abstraction concepts, they are merely technicality concepts of linguistic convenience of expressibility.

Also, we shall not strictly follow RSL's formal syntax. Instead, we shall generalise the syntax for expressing bindings and patterns, thereby coercing the two to more or less coincide! First, however, we treat a notion of binding forms, then the matchings necessary for these bindings to work as intended, and finally the notion of typing.

19.6.2 An Essence of Bindings and Patterns

The three concepts, bindings, typings and patterns, are closely related.

Bindings

In a typical binding, for example,

> **let** (a,(b,c)) = v **in** $\mathcal{E}$(a,b,c,v) **end**

the clause **let** (a,(b,c)) = v is the binding. It defines the free variables a, b and c of the pattern to value components of v which had better match the left-hand side pattern (a,(b,c)).

Patterns

In a typical use of patterns:

> **case** v **of**
> $\qquad$ (a,(b,**true**)) → $\mathcal{E}_i$(a,b),
> $\qquad$ (a,(b,c)) → $\mathcal{E}_j$(a,b,c),
> $\qquad$ (a,b) → $\mathcal{E}_k$(a,b),
> $\qquad$ ...
> $\qquad$ _ → $\mathcal{E}_v$(v)
> **end**

each of the clauses (a,(b,**true**)), (a,(b,c)), (a,b) and _, are choice patterns. The full forms, for example, (a,(b,**true**)) → $\mathcal{E}_i$(a,b), are bindings as now outlined.

If the value expression v designates a pair whose second element is a pair — whose second element is the truth value **true** — then a and b are defined to be bound to the respective first element values in the evaluation of $\mathcal{E}_i$(a,b).

If the value expression v designates a pair whose second element is a pair — whose second element is any value other than the truth value **true** — then a, b and c are defined to be bound to the respective first and second element values in the evaluation of $\mathcal{E}_j$(a,b,c).

If the value expression v designates a pair whose second element is a not a pair, then a and b are defined to be bound to the respective first and second element values in the evaluation of $\mathcal{E}_k$(a,b).

Otherwise $\mathcal{E}_v$(v) is evaluated.

The previous four paragraphs explained aspects of a matching between patterns and values. Note that sequential evaluation of the **case** clause: "From top to bottom, left to right" permits proper selection of patterns and bindings.

Bindings and Patterns: Apparent Differences

Binding patterns, as explained in terms of the **let** clause, thus contain a restricted form of pattern: We do not allow value literals (i.e., names of constants), but we do allow "*wildcards*": _. All free binding pattern identifiers are distinct.

Choice patterns, as explained in terms of the **case** clause, allow their patterns to contain value literals, both free and bound identifiers, and wildcards, _. Distinct usages of binding and choice patterns are: Binding patterns are also used, besides in **let** clauses, in quantified typings, see below. Choice patterns are also used, besides in **case** clauses, in function parameter clauses, see below. An example of the use of patterns in function parameter clauses is given in Example 11.2.

Binding and Typing

We first introduced the concept of binding and typing in Sect. 9.3: ∀ b,b′:**Bool**, where b and b′ were bound to some value in **Bool**, and where ∀ b,b′:**Bool** represented a typing. Further examples were given in Sect. 9.5.2: [3] ∀ x:X•E(x), [4] ∃ x:X•E(x), [5] ∃ ! x:X•E(x). They represent three schematic typings. We briefly and informally introduced the concepts of typing and binding on Sect. 9.5.2.

● ● ●

In the following we shall treat the subject of bindings, typings, patterns and matching more systematically.

19.6.3 Binding Patterns

By a binding we shall understand an association of identifiers with values. Binding is thus a semantic concept. It is denoted by such syntactic concepts as patterns, **let** and **case ... of** clauses.

Review of Earlier Material

Sections 13.2.3 (sets), 14.2.4 (Cartesians), 15.2.3 (lists), and 16.2.3 (maps) have introduced the following schematic bindings:

[1] **let** $\{a\_1,a\_2,...,a\_n\} \cup s = \mathcal{V}set$ **in** ... **end**
    pre: card $\mathcal{V}set \geq n$
    assert: card $\mathcal{V}set = n \Rightarrow s=\{\}$

[2] **let** $(a\_1,a\_2,...,a\_n) = product$ **in** ... **end**
    pre: product $-$ a Cartesian having exactly n components

[3] **let** $\langle a\_1,a\_2,...,a\_m \rangle \hat{} \ell = \mathcal{V}list$ **in** ... **end**
    pre: len list $\geq m$
    assert: len $\mathcal{V}list = m \Rightarrow \ell=\langle \rangle$

[4] **let** $[a\_1 \mapsto b\_1, a\_2 \mapsto b\_2,...,a\_n \mapsto b\_n] \cup m = \mathcal{V}map$ **in** ... **end**
    pre: card dom $\mathcal{V}map \geq n$
    assert: card dom $\mathcal{V}map = n \Rightarrow m=[\,]$

In all of the above, the left-hand side identifiers indeed do designate free, distinct identifiers, not arbitrary expressions. The "mystical" $\mathcal{V}e$ refers, rather informally, to the value of the expression e.

These identifiers are being bound to values by the definitions which the four clauses prescribe. In the set decomposition, [1], the nondeterministic naming of n arbitrary components and the remaining set is defined. In the Cartesian decomposition, [2], the deterministic naming of the n specific components is defined. In the list decomposition, [3], the deterministic naming of the n first list elements and the remaining list is defined. In the map decomposition, [4], the nondeterministic naming of n arbitrary definition set elements and their map associated range elements and the remaining map is defined.

Only the Cartesian and the list bindings are part of the "official" RSL syntax. The others are useful and expressive, but will not be accepted by the RAISE tool set.

The schematic examples above can be pseudo formalised. First, we repeat the above schematic bindings:

[1] **let** $\{a\_1,a\_2,...,a\_n\} \cup s = set$ **in** ... **end**
[2] **let** $(a\_1,a\_2,...,a\_n) = pro$ **in** ... **end**
[3] **let** $\langle a\_1,a\_2,...,a\_m \rangle \hat{} n\ell= list$ **in** ... **end**
[4] **let** $[a\_1 \mapsto b\_1, a\_2 \mapsto b\_2,...,a\_n \mapsto b\_n] \cup m = map$ **in** ... **end**

If the set, product, list and map (expression) values are as shown below:

[1] set $\equiv$ {v_1,v_2,...,v_n} $\cup$ sv
[2] pro $\equiv$ (v_1,v_2,...,v_n)
[3] list $\equiv$ ⟨v_1,v_2,...,v_m⟩^vℓ
[4] map $\equiv$ [v_1↦w_1,v_2↦w_2,...,v_n↦w_n] $\cup$ mv

then the bindings, the associations of the free left-hand side identifiers to element values, are as further shown:

[1] $set\rho \equiv [a\_1{\mapsto}v\_1,a\_2{\mapsto}v\_2,...,a\_n{\mapsto}v\_n,s{\mapsto}sv]$
[2] $pro\rho \equiv [a\_1{\mapsto}v\_1,a\_2{\mapsto}v\_2,...,a\_n{\mapsto}v\_n]$
[3] $list\rho \equiv [a\_1{\mapsto}v\_1,a\_2{\mapsto}v\_2,...,a\_m{\mapsto}v\_m,n\ell{\mapsto}v\ell]$
[4] $map\rho \equiv [a\_1{\mapsto}v\_1,a\_2{\mapsto}v\_2...,,b\_n{\mapsto}w\_n]$
      $\cup [b\_1{\mapsto}w\_1,b\_2{\mapsto}w\_2,...,b\_n{\mapsto}w\_n,m{\mapsto}mv]$

The above thus motivates the use of the term 'binding': The ρ suffix-named maps represent bindings of identifiers to values.

We have, for reason of pedagogics, used three type fonts above: The roman formulas represent ordinary, albeit schematised (...), RSL text. The sans serif formulas represent schematic value definitions, using RSL to explain RSL. The *italic formulas* represent semantic values implied by the ordinary RSL text, again using RSL to explain RSL.

Record Binding Patterns

One form of binding remains to be introduced, one that uses the record binding pattern:

[5] **let** mk_A(b,c,...,d) = v **in** $\mathcal{E}$(b,c,...,d) **end**

Here we assume that the value designated by the expression v is of the type designated by mk_A. Assume, for example:

type
    A == mk_A(β:B,γ:C,...,δ:D)

The binding **let** mk_A(b,c,...,d) = v is only syntactically correct if v:A. The effect of the binding is the association:

[5] $rec\rho = [b{\mapsto}\beta(v),c{\mapsto}\gamma(v),...,d{\mapsto}\delta(v)]$

General Forms of Binding Patterns

In all of the above schematic RSL examples we have only illustrated rather simple patterns. Usually composite syntactic structures whose immediate elements were free identifiers.

In a series of examples we will now go through a number of micro-steps. Together they illustrate a version of a specification language type, value, binding and pattern system — one very close to, but not exactly that of the predominant specification language of these volumes. Each micro-step "settles" one item of a development and its documentation.

Example 19.5 *Informal Description of Binding Patterns:* We now generalise patterns, whether binding patterns or choice patterns, to have immediate elements themselves be respective forms of patterns.

In narrative, i.e., in informal, but concise text we describe binding patterns as follows: An identifier is a binding pattern. A set enumeration of a finite set of one or more distinct binding patterns preceded, or usually followed, by an optional simple identifier is a binding pattern. A Cartesian grouping of a finite, non-empty list of distinct binding patterns is a binding pattern. A non-empty, finite list of alternatively either finite, non-empty lists of one or more distinct binding patterns and simple identifiers is a binding pattern. A map enumeration of a finite set of one or more distinct pairs of binding patterns preceded, or usually followed, by an optional simple identifier is a binding pattern. A record expression consisting of an already defined constructor name and a list of one or more binding patterns, is a binding pattern. A "wildcard" (_) is a binding pattern. All free identifiers of a binding pattern must be distinct. ∎

Example 19.6 *Formal Description of Binding Patterns:* The above narrative can be formalised. We intersperse some schematic examples.

type
   Id
   B$'$ = Bid | Bse | BCa | Bli | Bma | Bre | Wil
   B = {| b:B$'$ • wf_B(b) |}
   Bid == mk_nm(id:Id)
        Ex.: a
   Bse == mk_se(se:B-**set**,on:Onm)
         Ex.: {b_1,b_2,b_3}
         Ex.: {b_i,b_j,b_k} ∪ s
   Onm = nil | Bid

   BCa == mk_Ca(ca:B*)
         Ex.: (b_1,(b_21,b_22),(b_31,b_32,b_33,b_34))
   Bli == mk_li(tu:B*,on:Onm)

Ex.: $\langle b\_1,b\_2 \rangle \hat{\ } \ell$

Bma == mk_ma(ma:(B $\underset{m}{\rightarrow}$ B),on:Onm)

Ex.: $[b\_11 \mapsto b\_12,b\_21 \mapsto b22,b\_31 \mapsto b\_32]$

Ex.: $[b\_i1 \mapsto b\_i2,b\_j1 \mapsto bj2,b\_k1 \mapsto b\_k2] \cup m$

Bre == mk_re(sn:Sn,ca:B*)

Ex.: mk_X(b_1,b_2,b_3)

Ex.: mk_Y(b_1)

Wil == wildcard

∎

Example 19.7 *Formalisation of Well-formedness Constraints:* Just looking at binding patterns, the only constraint to be formalised is the distinctness of identifiers. Since patterns may be recursively nested, and since the identifier distinctness criterion applies across all levels of recursive embedding, we need, after some reflection (i.e., analysis), to define a function which both checks embedded patterns for identifier distinctness, and which also yields, besides the truth or falsity of identifier distinctness, the set of embedded identifiers.

There are three comments to make with respect to the specification given next: (1) It exemplifies the use of choice patterns in two forms: as function parameters (see the many definitions of the wfB function) and in the **case** clause (see the definition of the wfBS function). (2) The definition does not work! Well, of course it works, but one cannot define the semantics of a language in itself, and this is what we seemingly try to do! So, if you believe it works, it works. And, if you think it does not work, then it does not work! It is as simple as that![2] (3) Just to define distinctness of all possibly and arbitrarily embedded identifiers takes 37 lines of specification. Please consider the triviality of expressing: *All occurrence of identifiers in a binding pattern must be distinct*, and yet it takes more than 30 lines to define this. Hardly convincing — till you consider programming it in Java! Many seemingly innocent requirements turn out to become rather cumbersome to formalise, and sometimes, in fact, usually — but not always — harder to program. On the other hand, once formally specified, as here, "coding up" the Standard ML, Java, C++, C# or other programming language code becomes rather straightforward.

value

wf_B: B′ → **Bool**

wf_B(b) ≡ **let** (ids,tf) = wfB(b) **in** tf **end**

---

[2]Try the following definition: *An x is a y, and: A y is an x.* If you thought 1 is a choice for y, then it is also a choice (solution) for x. But so would any entity (mathematical or otherwise) be! Defining a language by using the same language leads to the above forms of circularities.

wfB: B$'$ → Id-set × **Bool**

wfB(mk_nm(id)) ≡ ({id},**true**)

wfB(mk_se(se,mk_nm(id))) ≡

   let (ids,tf) = wfS(se) **in** (ids ∪ {id},tf ∧ id∉ ids) **end**

wfB(mk_se(se,nil)) ≡ **let** (ids,tf) = wfS(se) **in** (ids,tf) **end**

wfS: B-set → Id-set × **Bool**

wfS(se) ≡ wfL(⟨b | b:B$'$ • b ∈ se⟩)

wfL: B$'^*$ → Id-set × **Bool**

wfL(bl) ≡

   let ts = ⟨wfB(bl(i))|i **in inds** bl⟩,

      tr = ∀ i:**Nat** • {i,i+1} ∈ **inds** ts

        ⇒ **let** (idsi,tf)=ts(i), (idsj,_)=ts(i+1) **in**

             idsi ∩ idsj={} ∧ tf **end**,

      ns = ∪{**let** (ids,_)=ts(i) **in** ids **end**|i:**Nat**•i ∈ **inds** ts} **in**

   (ns,tr) **end**

wfB(mk_Ca(bl)) ≡ wfL(bl)

wfB(mk_li(bl)) ≡ wfL(bl)

wfB(mk_ma(bm,ni)) ≡

   let wfm = (**card dom** bm = **card rng** bm),

      (ids,tr) = wfL(⟨bm(d)|d:B$'$•d ∈ **dom** bm⟩),

      (ids$'$,tr$'$) = wfL(⟨bm(d)|d:B$'$•d ∈ **dom** bm⟩),

      (ids$''$,tr$''$) =

         case ni **of**

            mk_nm(id) → ({id},id∉ ids ∪ ids$'$)

            nil → ({},**true**) **end in**

   (ids ∪ ids$'$ ∪ ids$''$,

     wf ∧ tr ∧ tr$'$ ∧ ids ∩ ids$'$ = {} ∧ tr$''$) **end**

wfB(mk_re(,bl)) ≡ wfL(bl)

                                                   ■

Comment

Since one cannot define the semantics of a language in itself, that is, by writing down some formulas that one thinks works, we have to resort to first understanding an informal explanation, or one expressed in another, already properly defined specification language (usually discrete mathematics). Once we have understood that other description, we can then use that understanding, to exemplify — as do the definitions of the above functions — uses of bindings and binding and choice patterns.

More to Come

We have yet to define the syntactic correctness of the binding clause: the left-hand side binding pattern and the right-hand side expression. And we have also to define the creation of a binding as exemplified in the schematics examples given earlier. We will leave that to Sect. 19.6.5.

19.6.4 Typings

The "formal" story on typings will here be given rather briefly. There are basically two forms of typings: In **let** clauses, and in quantified (predicate) expressions. Specifically:

> **let** $(a,(b,c)):(A \times (B \times C)) \bullet \mathcal{P}(a,b,c)$ **in** $\mathcal{E}(a,b,c)$ **end**
> $\forall (a,(b,c)):(A \times (B \times C)) \bullet \mathcal{P}_1(a,b,c) \Rightarrow \mathcal{P}_2(a,b,c)$

Generally:

> **let** Car_bin_pat : Car_typ_exp $\bullet$ Pre_exp **in** ... **end**
> $\forall$ Car_bin_pat : Car_typ_exp $\bullet$ Pre_exp $\Rightarrow$ Pre_exp

Thus we allow only simple binding patterns involving at most Cartesian types, or, as shown next, just simple typings:

> **let** a:A $\bullet$ $\mathcal{P}_1(a) \Rightarrow \mathcal{P}_2(a)$ **in** $\mathcal{E}(a)$ **end**
> $\forall$ a:A $\bullet$ $\mathcal{P}_1(a) \Rightarrow \mathcal{P}_2(a)$

In all the typings the implication may be omitted:

> **let** a:A $\bullet$ $\mathcal{P}(a)$ **in** $\mathcal{E}(a)$ **end**
> $\forall$ a:A $\bullet$ $\mathcal{P}(a)$

19.6.5 Choice Patterns and Bindings

In this section we will present a simplified version of RSL's type/value matching concept: We will not take into account any notion of subtypes.

Example 19.8 *Choice Patterns and Bindings: Binding and Value Syntaxes:* To arrive at choice patterns we generalise binding patterns as follows: Wherever an identifier may occur (as in binding patterns) we allow values to occur. A binding is now a pair: Either a binding pattern or a choice pattern, and a value. A formal syntax for choice patterns and bindings is given next.

type
  Id, Wild
  Bind′ = C × VAL
  Bind = {| (c,v):Bind′ • wf_Bind(c,v) |}

  C′ = Cid | Cse | CCa | Cli | Cma | Cre | VAL | Wil
  C = {| c:C′ • wf_C(c) |}
  Cid == mk_ccn(id:Id)
  Cse == mk_ccs(se:C-**set**,oc:OC)
  OC = nil | Cid
  CCa == mk_ccc(ca:C*)
  Cli == mk_ccl(li:C*,oc:OC)
  Cma == mk_ccm(ma:(C $\overrightarrow{m}$ C),oc:OC)
  Cre == mk_ccr(sn:Sn,ca:C*)
  Wil == wildcard

  VAL = AtV | SeV | CaV | LiV | MaV | ReV
  AtoV = Intg | Boolean | Character | String
  Intg :: **Int**, Boolean :: **Bool**
  Character :: **Char**, String :: **Text**
  SeV :: VAL-**set**
  CaV :: VAL*
  LiV :: VAL*
  MaV :: VAL $\overrightarrow{m}$ VAL
  ReV :: sn:Sn cl:VAL*

Comments

Well-formedness of choice patterns is as for binding patterns: Distinctness of
all identifiers, and, in addition, well-formedness of values. Well-formedness
of bindings amounts to well-formedness of patterns, well-formedness of values
and structural compatibility between the left-hand side pattern and the right-
hand side value.   ∎

Example 19.9 *Choice Patterns and Bindings: Type Syntax:* To define well-
formedness of values we define first a notion of value type. Based on that we
then define well-formedness of values. But first, atomic values are well-formed.
All values of a set value must be of the same value type. All values of a list
value must be of the same value type. All values of the definition set of a map
value set must be of the same value type. All values of the range set of a map
value set must be of the same value type. All value components of a record
value must be well-formed.

type

Typ = Aty | Sty | Cty | Lty | Mty | Rty
Aty == integer | boolean | character | string
Sty :: Typ
Cty :: Typ*
Lty :: Typ
Mty :: d:Typ r:Typ
Rty :: s:Sn lt:Typ*

∎

Example 19.10 *Choice Patterns and Bindings: Value Type Extraction:*
xty extracts the **type** of a non-void value:

value
    xty: VAL $\overset{\sim}{\to}$ Typ
    xty(v) ≡
        case v **of**
            mk_Intg(_) → integer,
            mk_Boolean(_) → boolean,
            mk_Character(_) → character,
            mk_String(_) → string
            mk_SeV(vs) →
                case vs **of** {}→**chaos** v ∪ vs'→mk_Sty(xty(v)) **end**
            mk_CaV(vl) → mk_Cty(⟨xty(vl(i))|i **in inds** vl⟩)
            mk_LiV(vl) →
                case vl **of** ⟨⟩→**chaos**,v ⌢ vl'→mk_Lty(xty(v)) **end**
            mk_MaV(vm) →
                case vm **of**
                    []→**chaos**,[d↦r] ∪ vm'→mk_Mty(xty(d),xty(r))
                end
        end

∎

Example 19.11 *Choice Patterns and Bindings: Formalisation of Well-Formedness:*

value
    wf_Bind: Bind' → **Bool**
    wf_Bind(c,v) ≡ wf_C(c) ∧ wf_VAL(v) ∧ wfBind(c,v)
    wf_C: C → **Bool** /* similar to wf_B */

    wf_VAL: VAL → **Bool**
    wf_VAL(v) ≡
        case v **of**

$$\text{mk\_SeV(vs)} \rightarrow \forall \text{ v}',\text{v}'':\text{VAL} \bullet \{\text{v}',\text{v}''\} \subseteq \text{vs}$$
$$\Rightarrow \text{wf\_VAL(v}') \wedge \text{wf\_VAL(v}'') \wedge \text{xty(v}') = \text{xty(v}'')$$
$$\text{mk\_Ca(vl)} \rightarrow \forall \text{ i:\textbf{Nat}} \bullet \text{i} \in \text{indx vl} \Rightarrow \text{wf\_VAL(vl(i))}$$
$$\text{mk\_LiV(vl)} \rightarrow \forall \text{ i,i}':\textbf{Nat} \bullet \{\text{i,i}'\}\subseteq\text{inds vl}$$
$$\Rightarrow \text{wf\_VAL(vl(i))} \wedge \text{xty(vl(i))} = \text{xty(vl(i}'))$$
$$\text{mk\_MaV(vm)} \rightarrow \forall \text{ v,v}':\text{VAL}\bullet \{\text{v,v}'\} \subseteq \text{vs}$$
$$\Rightarrow \text{wf\_VAL(v}') \wedge \text{wf\_VAL(vm(v}'))$$
$$\wedge \text{xty(d)=xty(d}') \wedge \text{xty(vm(d))=xty(vm(d}'))$$
$$\_ \rightarrow \textbf{true}$$
   end

wfBind: Bind$'$ × VAL → **Bool**

wfBind(mk_ccn(id),v) ≡ **true**,
wfBind(wildcard,v) ≡ **true**

wfBind(mk_ccs(cs,_),mk_SeV(vs)) ≡
   card cs ≤ **card** vs ∧
   let cl = mklist(cs), vl = mklist(vs) **in**
   ∃ im:IM •**dom** im = **inds** cl ∧ **rng** im ⊆ **inds** vl
      ⇒ ∀ i:**Nat** • i ∈ **inds** cl ⇒ wfBind(cl(i),bl(bi(i))) **end**

mklist: (VAL|C)-**set** → (VAL|C)*
mklist(vs) ≡
   if vs={} **then** ⟨⟩ **else let** {v} ∪ vs$'$ **in** vs **in** ⟨v⟩^mklist(vs$'$) **end end**

Since we are allowed to have different binding patterns for distinctly (to be nondeterministically) selected set value elements we introduce a technicality: Make the sets into lists and postulate a bijective index map. The idea is that if the binding is well-formed, then there exist such choice pattern and set element value lists and a bijection between choice/values that are well-formed.

type
   IM$'$ = **Nat** −m− **Nat**
   IM = {|im:IM$'$ • wf_IM(im) |}
value
   wf_IM: IM$'$ → **Bool**
   wf_IM(im) ≡
      dom im={1..**card dom** im} ∧
      card rng im = **card dom** im

   wfBind(mk_ccc(cl),mk_CaV(vl)) ≡
      len cl = **len** vl ∧
      ∀ i:**Nat** • i ∈ **inds** cl
         ⇒ wfBind(cl(i),vl(i))

wfBind(mk_ccl(cl,_),mk_LiV(vl)) ≡
   len cl = **len** vl ∧
   ∀ i:**Nat** • i ∈ **inds** cl
     ⇒ wfBind(cl(i),vl(i))

wfBind(mk_ccm(cm,_),mk_MaV(vm)) ≡
   card dom cm ≤ **card dom** vm ∧
   ∃ vm′,vm″:MaV •
     vm = vm′ ∪ vm″ ∧
     card dom cm = **card dom** vm′ ⇒
       wf_recursive_descent(cm,vm′)

wf_recursive_descent: (C $\overrightarrow{m}$ C) × MaV → **Bool**
wf_recursive_descent(cm,vm)
   ∃ c:C,v:VAL • c ∈ **dom** cm ∧ v ∈ **dom** vm
     ⇒ wfBind(c,v) ∧ wfBind(cm(c),vm(v)) ∧
       wf_recursive_descent(cm \ {c},vm \ {v})
   pre card dom cm = **card dom** vm

wfBind(mk_ccr(sn,cl),mk_ReV(sn′,vl)) ≡
   sn = sn′ ∧ **len** cl = **len** vl ∧
   ∀ i:**Nat** • i ∈ indx cl ⇒
     wfBind(cl(i),vl(i))

Example 19.12 *Choice Patterns and Binding: Formalisation of Binding:*
   Any value can be bound to a choice pattern identifier. A wildcard binds
nothing. All bindings depend on their a priori well-formedness. This is especially relevant for set and map bindings. Their nondeterministic nature is
reflected in the definition, below, of their binding, in much the same way
as for their well-formedness. A binding syntactically is a pair of a syntactic
pattern and a semantic value, while semantically it is a semantic denotation,
here modelled, obviously, as a map from syntactic identifiers to values. Note
how the Bind function "worms" its way into embedded identifiers, finding
their associated value, bringing out the resulting binding, while summing up
(union-ing) all contributions ("at outer levels").

type
   BIN = Id $\overrightarrow{m}$ VAL
value
   Bind: C × VAL → BIN
   Bind(mk_ccn(id),v) ≡ [id↦v]
   Bind(wildcard,v) ≡ []

Bind(mk_ccs(cs,on),mk_SeV(vs)) ≡
  let cl = mklist(cs), vl = mklist(vs),
      im:IM • **dom** im=**inds** cl ∧ **rng** im⊆**inds** vl
        ⇒ ∀ i:**Nat** • i ∈ **inds** cl
          ⇒ wfBind(cl(i),bl(bi(i))) **in**
  ∪ { Bind(cl(i),vl(i)) | i **in inds** cl }
  ∪ **case** on **of**
      nil → [],
      mk_nm(id)→[id↦{vl(i)|i:**Nat**•i ∈ **inds** vl**rng** im}] **end end**

Bind(mk_ccc(cl),mk_CaV(vl)) ≡ ∪ { Bind(cl(i),vl(i)) | i **in inds** cl }

Bind(mk_ccl(cl,on),mk_LiV(vl)) ≡
  ∪ { Bind(cl(i),vl(i)) | i:**Nat** • i ∈ **inds** cl }
  ∪ **case** on **of**
      nil → [], mk_nm(id) → [id↦⟨vl(i)|**len** cl<i≤**len** vl⟩] **end**

Bind(mk_ccm(cm,on),mk_MaV(vm)) ≡
  let (ρ,vm′) = recursive_bind(cm,vm) **in**
  case on **of** nil → [], mk_nm(id) → [id↦vm′] **end**
  ∪ ρ **end**

recursive_bind: (C ⇸ C) × MaV → BIN × MaV
recursive_bind(cm,vm) ≡
  if cm = [] **then** ([],vm) **else**
  let c:C,v:VAL • c ∈ **dom** cm ∧ v ∈ **dom** vm
                  ⇒ wfBind(c,v) ∧ wfBind(cm(c),vm(v)) **in**
  let cvρ = Bind(c,v),
      (restρ,vm′) = recursive_bind(cm \\ {c},vm \\ {v}) **in**
  (cvρ ∪ restρ,vm′)
  end end end

Bind(mk_ccr(_,cl),mk_ReV(_,vl)) ≡ ∪ { Bind(cl(i),vl(i)) | i **in inds** cl }

∎

Some Observations

In the examples above, you may have observed that we defined **Bind** in terms
of a set of equations:

Bind(mk_ccn(id),v) ≡ [id↦v]
Bind(wildcard,v) ≡ []
Bind(mk_ccs(cs,on),mk_SeV(vs)) ≡ ...

Bind(mk_ccc(cl),mk_CaV(vl)) ≡ ...
Bind(mk_ccl(cl,on),mk_LiV(vl)) ≡ ...
Bind(mk_ccm(cm,on),mk_MaV(vm)) ≡ ...
Bind(mk_ccr(_,cl),mk_ReV(_,vl)) ≡ ...

You may then have observed that we have not specified, in the definition of Bind, what happens if a pair of arguments to that function does not "fit" the patterns actually dealt with. What about the others? Well, first of all, the pre-condition for invocation of Bind(c,v) is that wfBind(c,v) holds. That takes care of all the others. Second, we could define Bind by the **case** construct — obviously also using choice patterns:

Bind(c,v) ≡
   case (c,v) **of**
      (mk_ccn(id),v) → [id↦v],
      (wildcard,v) → [],
      (mk_ccs(cs,on),mk_SeV(vs)) → ...,
      (mk_ccc(cl),mk_CaV(vl)) → ...,
      (mk_ccl(cl,on),mk_LiV(vl)) → ...,
      (mk_ccm(cm,on),mk_MaV(vm)) → ...,
      (mk_ccr(_,cl),mk_ReV(_,vl)) → ...,
      _ → **chaos end**

making it clear what happens! The latest definition also shows that the two styles are interchangeable.

19.6.6 Summary

This section, especially the formalisations of pattern, value and binding well-formedness, the formal concepts of values, their types and type extraction (observation) functions, and the final definition of the binding function, amounted to a rather large section. On one hand, we introduced the RSL concepts of patterns and bindings so that we could make free and good use of them in our abstractions, while, on the other hand, we described the structure (syntax) and meaning (semantics) of these specification linguistic notions. That gave rise to a lengthy section, but then it gave us a chance to illustrate how we describe and formalise a classic language problem.

We remind the reader that our "story", in this section, on types is a simplified version of RSL's type concept: We did not include the concept of subtypes in our model.

19.7 Review and Discussion

19.7.1 General

We have briefly reviewed what we could consider the expression sublanguage of RSL. We use the term 'expression sublanguage' to signal that, in RSL, there is really no difference between what we normally consider to be purely value-returning expressions and purely state-changing (simply side-effect-causing) statements. In fact, we illustrated a clause, **skip**, which designates the (void) **Unit** value of no side-effect.

19.7.2 Principles and Techniques

This section presents principles that spring from Sect. 19.6.

Modelling of types and values and their relations were illustrated in Example 16.8 and discussed in Sect. 19.6.5. We developed a concrete syntax for values, which are expected to be of the defined types, functions for extracting, from a value, "its" type, functions for expressing whether a value is well-formed ("in and by itself") and functions for expressing whether a value is well-formed wrt. a given type.

As a modelling principle related to maps, we mentioned the concepts of configurations as consisting of contexts and states. In the present section contexts arose again as the concept "constructed" to maintain bindings: associations of identifiers to values. Hence we can enunciate two principles:

Principles. *Typed Values:* When modelling values consider their type. If values are typed (we say *strongly typed*), then make sure that there is a homomorphism between values and types, that a function can be defined which determines the type of any value, and that a well-formedness predicate can be expressed which examines whether a value is of a given type.   ∎

Principles. *Binding Contexts:* When a phenomenon is analysed into having a — contextually speaking — constant identity in the form of a name and value, in fact, when several such phenomena are so analysed, then — for each suitable class of such phenomena — model these facts by establishing a context, modelled as a map from phenomena and attribute names to values.

A phenomenon is said to be contextually a constant, when, within a certain — temporally "long" — period of observation, or, say, within a spatially "long" description (or prescription) — the phenomenon stands in the same, fixed relation between name and value.   ∎

19.8 Bibliographical Notes

Applicative specification programming is a form of functional programming. Current functional programming languages are constrained to have their programs be subject to interpretation or compilation and execution by machines. The RSL applicative programming subset is not so constrained.

Leading functional programming languages are Standard ML [389] and Haskell [498]. Exciting textbooks on functional programming are [50,51,261, 474].

19.9 Exercises

The function definitions of the exercises of this section are all to be expressed in the functional, i.e., applicative style.

Exercises 19.1, 19.2 and 19.3 are followed-up by Exercises 20.1, 20.2 and 20.3 and 21.5, 21.6 and 21.7, respectively.

Exercises 19.4, 19.5 and 19.6 continue our line of exercises anchored in Appendix Chap. A.

• • •

Exercise 19.1. *The Grocery Store, I.* You are to complete the answers to the referenced exercises by providing a formal model of entities and functions. Thus you must formalise a notion of grocery store.

Hints: Follow, in your initial modelling the following narrative, slavishly:

1. A grocery store consists of a store, a warehouse, a catalogue and a checkout.
2. The store consists of a set of one or more uniquely named shelf racks (i.e., set of shelves).
3. Each shelf rack (i.e., each set of shelves) consists of a set of one or more uniquely named (shelf) segments.
4. A shelf contains zero, one or more items of merchandise of the same type.
5. From segment identifiers one can observe the type of merchandise (to be) displayed on the identified segment.
6. From an item of merchandise one can observe its sales price.
7. A warehouse consists of one or more uniquely merchandise-typed bins.
8. Each bin consists of one or more items of merchandise of the type of the bin.
9. A catalogue records for every merchandise type the following information: Sale price, purchase price, gross (number of items when ordering), recommended minimum amount of items on shelf that triggers replenishment, set of names of wholesalers from which this type of item can be ordered and on which shelf racks and segments items of this type shall be displayed.
10. A checkout (register) can be modelled just by the cash (i.e., monies) it contains.
11. A client can be modelled by a shopping cart (which may be empty), a purse (of monies) and a bag (which may be empty).

12. Carts and bags can be modelled by the number of items that they contain of respective types.
13. A wholesaler can be modelled by the number of items the wholesaler stores in the inventory, per type, and a cash register.

You are then to model the visit of a client to the grocery store as a sequence of one or more selects, followed by a checkout. Please define the syntactic type of visits, that is, a script which for every type of merchandise lists the quantity to be selected. (That script is either prepared beforehand, by noting it on a scrap of paper or in the mind, or "entries" in the script occur as the result of seeing merchandise on the shelf.) Define the semantics of a fixed visit script. For a client to select merchandise from a store shelf segment is only meaningful if that shelf segment contains at least one item of merchandise. An out-of-stock item is treated as "skipping" that script entry.

Hints: We suggest you try to structure the visit function as follows: The client with the visit script goes around, i.e., *visits*, the entire grocery store: First (i) *selecting* one or more items of merchandise, as per the script, from shelf segments, and then (ii) *checking out*. The result is a changed grocery store (less merchandise on the shelves, more money in the cash register), and a client (with en empty cart, a full bag and some less money!). For the client to select (i.e., transfer from shelf segments to the shopping cart) items of merchandise, listed in the script by item and quantity, that client must first *identify* a shelf rack and segment carrying that type of merchandise. The selection is nondeterministic since there may be more than one shelf segment carrying a certain type of merchandise. Selections proceed one by one: The client selects a next type of item from the script to identify in the store, selects the amount stated, or less if there is not enough, and decreases the segment quantity listed in the script by the amount selected. If all have been selected, then the item is stricken from the script. If none can be selected the item is also stricken.

Next you are to model the replenishment of store shelf segments from the warehouse, and warehouse shelf segments from wholesalers. Guess yourself how such replenishments could take place, and hence be modelled! See, however, the hint below.

A grocery store can then be modelled by a sequence of one or more visits, henceforth referred to as shopping, alternating with replenishment actions. You can model shopping as a strict sequence with the assumption that there is only one checkout counter, and that clients are thus served sequentially. The obvious possibility that clients may concurrently be selecting from shelves is abstracted, and the possibility that more than one client simultaneously attempts to and/or could possibly succeed in selecting merchandise from the same shelf segment is ruled out. Specify the syntactic type of client shopping and define the semantics of such a sequence of visits. Make sure that the grocery store staff keeps shelf segments replenished.

If you believe that the above description is incomplete, please state so, and provide the completing text.

Hint: To model the nondeterminism of either doing something, a little bit, or doing something more of the same, cf. replenishment, we suggest the following schema:

value
    transition: X → X
    transition(x) ≡
      if stop_condition_met(x)
        then x
        else let x′ = one_step_transform(x) **in** x′ ⌈⌉ transition(x′) **end**
      end

The value of expression a⌈⌉b is either a or b — the choice is left internally nondeterministic (i.e, left open).

The present exercise is to be solved in the imperative style in Exercise 20.1, and in the concurrent style in Exercise 21.9.

Exercise 19.2. *The Anarchic Factory, I.* Please read the problem formulation texts of the above referenced exercises carefully. You are to model the anarchic factory. A suggestion that might be worth following is to define a state which consists of four components: (i) a set of uniquely identified production cells, (ii) a set of uniquely identified fork trucks, (iii) a parts inventory and (iv) a product warehouse.

Also define plan scripts, i.e., the truck logistics (one per truck) and the production cell schedules (one per cell). Collect all scripts into the production plan.

Follow, in your initial modelling, the following narrative, slavishly:

Hints on Modelling Factory Configurations

1. A factory consists of an inventory, a set of uniquely identified trucks, a set of uniquely identified production cells and a warehouse.
2. An inventory consists of parts.
3. A production cell consists of an in-tray, an "agent capable of performing an operation" and an out-tray.
4. In-trays and out-trays contain parts. The out-trays contain only parts of one kind, i.e., with all having the same part number.
5. An "agent capable of performing an operation" exhibits two things: the signature of the operation, and the operation itself.
6. The signature of an operation lists, for each incoming part number, how many of that part it takes to perform the operation, and the part number of the resulting part.
7. The operation is a function over parts, and into a part, of its signature.
8. By parts we may understand the following model, something that for an actual part lists its quantity, i.e., number of occurrences in parts.

9. We may model a truck as the parts it is carrying to either a named cell or to the warehouse, that is: It maps (some) cell identifiers into parts, and/or a warehouse enumerated token likewise into parts.

10. The in-tray of a cell should only contain parts commensurate with the signature of its operation.

11. Similarly for the out-tray.

Hints on Modelling the Production Plans

1. A production plan consists of a cell production schedule and a truck schedule.

2. A cell schedule lists, for some cells, the quantity of parts to be produced by that cell.

3. A truck schedule has two things: which parts to convey to which production cells, and which parts to convey between which cells, or between cells and the warehouse.

Hints on Modelling Factory Behaviours

1. A factory transition, from one to a next, possibly changed, state can be expressed as follows:

2. A factory has either fulfilled its plan or not.

3. If not fulfilled, then
   (a) Either (i) there are some trucks and cells which, according to the plan, yet have work to do, or (ii) there are just some trucks, or (iii) just some cells, which, according to the plan, yet have work to do;
   (b) or (iv) there are some trucks, or (v) just some cells, which, according to the plan, yet have work to do, or (vi) there are no "live" trucks or cells.

4. Due to "programming" notation limitations, one could formulate the factory behaviour as just done above: Either/or (i), or (ii), or ... or (vi)!

5. For each of the three kinds (i, ii=iv, iii=v) of "liveness" we then define separate transition functions.

6. Each of the possibly alternatively expressed transitions (i–v) continues into another factory behaviour.

7. Thus the factory evolves, either toward dead-lock or to fulfilling its plan!

Hints on Modelling Truck Behaviours

1. Either a truck is loading, from the inventory or from cells,

2. or it is unloading, onto cells or the warehouse.

3. The truck behaviour expresses this choice internal nondeterministically.

We warn you: there are many subsidiary functions to deal with. Define at least the major ones and one of the "minor" ones.

Hints on Modelling Cell Behaviours

1. For every valid operation of a production cell its production schedule is reduced by one, its in-tray has that many fewer parts which are needed to perform the operation and its out-tray has one more resulting part.
2. An operation is valid if its production schedule is not exhausted and if there are the necessary input parts for its operation. The production cell of a valid operation is said to be 'live'.
3. In any step, i.e., transition, of the factory, zero, one or more live production cells may be selected for (valid) operations.

The present exercise is to be solved in the imperative style in Exercise 20.2 and in the concurrent style in Exercise 21.10.

Exercise 19.3. *The Document System, I.*
This exercise is formulated in several iterations. Narrative descriptions of the universe of discourse alternate with problem statements.

1. Iteration I:
   (a) The document handling system consists of:
       i. A finite set of one or more uniquely identified places (cum institutions, public administration offices, enterprises, businesses, etc.),
       ii. and a finite set of uniquely identified citizens.
   (b) From places one can observe the following three kinds of entities:
       i. Either a non-activated, or an activated directory,
       ii. a set of one or more uniquely identified staff members
       iii. and a set of uniquely identified locations.
   (c) There are the two notions of
       i. documents, and
       ii. dossiers;
       iii. the latter are (i.e., contain) sets of zero, one or more documents.
   (d) A directory can be thought of as a hierarchy that maps directory names onto sets of documents and/or dossiers and subdirectories.
   (e) Documents as well as dossiers are uniquely identified.
   (f) Given a location, one can observe whether it contains documents and or dossiers.
   (g) From a document one can observe its unique identification.
   (h) From a dossier one can observe its unique identification.
2. Please formalise the concepts of system, places, directories, etc.
   (a) A document is either a master document, or a copy of a document, or it is a version of a copy.
   (b) From a document one can observe whether its most recent status is that of a master, a copy or a version.
   (c) From a copy or a version one can observe the document from which it was copied, respectively on the basis of which it was edited.
   (d) By a document event we mean the location and time of its creation, copying, or editing.

(e) From a document one can observe the ("historic", most recent) identity of the location of its creation, copying or editing, whichever is the most recent event.

(f) From a document one can observe the ("historic", most recent) identity of the person who created, copied, or edited the document, whichever is the most recent event.

(g) From a document one can observe the ("historic") time its creation, copying or editing, whichever is the most recent event.

3. Please formalise documents as sorts with observers.

(a) Thus one can trace the ("historic") sequence of documents, and their location and time of document event, from a present document, back through all previous documents to its ancestor master document.

4. Please formalise the document history function.

5. Iteration II:

We observe, in the descriptions given so far, a few loose ends. So we continue.

To the above narratives join:

(a) A document or a dossier, i.e., also any document in a dossier, is
   i. either residing in a directory, and then in at most one,
   ii. or it is "on loan" to, or with some, i.e., possessed by a, person (possibly via other persons),
   iii. or it is residing in a location, in (or at) which a person has put it. The above description is applicable also to documents and dossiers which have so far not been associated with a directory.

(b) From a document or a dossier, i.e., also from any document in a dossier, one can observe whether it belongs to, and if so then where in, a directory by place identification and directory path name.

(c) Documents or dossiers absent from a directory may be so indicated, and the indication may either say that its whereabouts are unknown, or that it is with some person or at some location in some place, or with a citizen.

6. Please formalise the revised directories and person, location and document and dossier observers.

7. Iteration III:

We need to define some notions:

- Descendant:
  ⋆ A version, d', of a document, d, is a descendant of d.
  ⋆ A copy, d', of a document, d, is a descendant of d.
  ⋆ If a document d' is a descendant of a document d, and document d'' is a descendant of d', then d'' is a descendant of d.

- Ancestor:
  ⋆ A version, d', of a document, d, has d as its ancestor.
  ⋆ A copy, d', of a document, d, has d as its ancestor.

⋆ If a document d is an ancestor of a document d', and document d' is an ancestor of d'', then d is an ancestor of d''.

- "Belong" to: If one from a document can observe a place identification, p_i, and a directory path, π_{p_i}, then that document is said to belong to the directory at p_i and in the position designated by the directory path π_{p_i}.

Now to some more narrative:

(a) a document and all its descendants, if any of these belong to a directory, at some directory position (by place identifier and path name), then all such documents "belong" to that same directory position — whether actually present or absent.

(b) How that is handled, in the domain, is sketched now:

   i. If a master (including any of its versions) is made to "belong" to a directory position, before any copies have been made, then all such copies (and versions) will inherit knowledge about that directory position.

   ii. If a copy (including any of its versions) is made to "belong" to a directory position, before any copies have been made, then all such copies (and versions) will inherit knowledge about that directory position.

   iii. Thus it is entirely possible for a copy to "belong" to a directory position, without its ancestors doing so.

   iv. And it is entirely possible for two different copies — deriving from some common, i.e. "shared" ancestor document — to "belong" to different directory positions — provided their common, i.e. "shared" ancestor document did not "belong" to a directory position.

(c) One might think of other rules governing the relationship between, on one hand, documents and dossiers, and, on the other hand, directories:

   i. Either no rules whatsoever: Documents and dossiers can "belong" anywhere without restrictions, or:

   ii. Ancestors to some copy may belong to some position in a directory in one place, while the copy of its descendants may belong to another position the same directory or some other directory in another place.

8. Please formalise well-formedness constraints.

9. Document, dossier and directory operations:

(a) Staff and clients create documents, which they then possess.

(b) Staff create dossiers, initially empty, which they then possess.

(c) Staff may copy and edit documents they possess (and that they then continue to possess).

(d) Clients may pass own, created, i.e., possessed documents onto place staff, as master documents. The client no longer possesses the passed document, but the place staff person does.

(e) Whether clients have "copied" such or other documents is of no concern to the present document system.

(f) Staff may insert documents in dossiers. They must possess both the document and the dossier.

(g) Staff may insert documents and dossiers in directories. They must initially possess the document or the dossier. After the insert they no longer possess the document or the dossier.

(h) Staff may "borrow" (i.e., "remove", albeit thought of to be "temporarily") documents or dossiers from directories. After the borrow the staff person possesses the borrowed document or dossier.

(i) Staff may put documents or dossiers (they possess) "away" in locations, after which they no longer possess the document or dossier.

(j) Same or other staff may take possession of documents and dossiers from locations.

(k) Staff may send (possessed) documents and dossiers from "their" place to staff at other places. Possession changes from one person to another person.

(l) Staff may send such (possessed) documents and dossiers (i.e., "on loan" from other places) to yet other staff at yet other places.

(m) Staff may return (possessed) documents and dossiers sent from other places back to staff persons at places of origin or from where they were received (i.e., "last sent/last received").

(n) Documents and dossiers may be shredded.

(o) Staff may send (possessed) documents (not dossiers) to clients, at which point these documents cease to exist within the system of places. (And they can never be returned from clients!)

10. Please formalise the command syntax and the command interpretation functions.

Exercise 19.4. *An Applicative Domain Model of Transportation Nets.* We refer to Appendix A, Sect. A.1, *Transportation Net*.

We summarise a narrative of *Transportation Nets*: Transportation nets consists of a set of uniquely identified segments, a set of uniquely identified connections (or connectors). For each segment (represented by its unique identifier) there are one or two (direction) triplets which describe, besides the segment identifier, the identifiers of the two connections the identified segment is connected to: One if a one-way segment, two if a two-way segment. (We may call this part the structure part of a transportation net.) Segments have two kinds of attributes: static and dynamic. The static attributes include segment names, segment length, and other. The dynamic attributes include whether the segment is open or closed in one or the other direction, or both. Connections have two kinds of attributes: static and dynamic. The static attributes include connection name. The dynamic attributes include what we could call the state of the semaphore: for each identifier of a segment incident upon the connection there is associated a possibly empty set of identifiers of segments emanating from that connection.

1. Formalise a concrete type system and indicate well-formedness constraints for the transportation nets described above.

Over the lifetime of a transportation net it gets built up: from an "empty net" (no segments and no connections, and hence no structure), segments and connections are added and removed, and the states of segments and connections change. We will treat these changes as the result of performing certain operations on a net. Each of these operations will be represented by a command. The interpretation of the command then brings about the change.

2. Define the syntax and semantics of the command which initialises a transportation net.
3. Define the syntax and semantics of the command which adds a segment to a transportation net. State appropriate conditions that must be satisfied before successful interpretaion of this command.
   To add a segment three possibilities exist: One adds a segment whose connector identifiers are connector identifiers of the net, so one has to state the segment and two connector identifiers. Or one adds a segment one of whose connector identifiers is a connector identifier of the net, so one has to state the segment, a connector identifier and a connector. Or one adds a segment whose connector identifiers are not connector identifiers of the net, so one has to state the segment and two connectors.
4. Define the syntax and semantics of the command which removes a segment to a transportation net. State appropriate conditions that must be satisfied before successful interpretaion of this command.
5. The lifetime of a net can thus be represented by a sequence of commands as described above. Formalise such a sequence and express appropriate well-formedness conditions on such sequences.

Exercise 19.5. *An Applicative Domain Model of Container Logistics.* We refer to Appendix A, Sect. A.2, *Container Logistics.*

We summarise a narrative of *Container Logistics*: There is given five sets of phenomena: A set of uniquely named container terminals, a set of uniquely named container ships, a set of uniquely identified containers, a set of uniquely named shipping routes, and a set of uniquely named trucks. A container terminal consists of a quay where zero, one or more container ships may be docked, and of a container pool (a storage area) where zero, one or more containers may be temporarily stored. Container ships and container terminal pools consist of one or more uniquely named bays, each bay consists of one or more uniquely named rows, and a row consists of one or more uniquely named (container) stacks. A container stack consists of zero, one or more containers. A container consists of a container box, with or without freight, and, if with freight, then the container box also carries a waybill. A waybill consists of the unique container identifier, its own unique waybill identifier, and a list of sailings. Each sailing is a triple: The name of a container ship and the pair of names of container terminals served by the named ship and from, respectively to which the container identified by the waybill is to be transported. The list of sailings must be well-formed: If two or more sailings, then the "to" terminal named in a "non-last" entry of the list must be the same as the "from" terminal named in the next entry of that list. A shipping route is a pair: The name of a container ship and a route. The route is a list of two or more trips. A trip is just the name of a container terminal. A route is subject to well-formedness: If ti are names of container terminals, then ⟨t1,t2,...,tn−1,tn,tn−1,...,t2,t1⟩ is a well-formed route of n container terminal visits, on an outward journey, and n−1 container terminal visits, on a return journey. Trucks carry at most one container: either from an outside to a container terminal pool area, or to a container ship, or from a container ship or a container terminal pool area to an outside.

1. Define a concrete type system for the above container logistics system components.
2. Indicate appropriate well-formedness predicates.

At some stage, i.e, in some state of the container logistics system, a number of container ships are plying the waters between container terminals according to their shipping route, and a "remaining" number of container ships are docked in container terminals — also according to their shipping route. While in container terminals containers — so designated by their waybills — are being moved between container ships and container terminal pools: either unloaded or loaded.

Define the syntax and semantics of the following six movement commands:

3. Move a container from a ship to the pool. The locations on the ship and in the pool are identified by bay/row/stack/cell identifiers.
4. Move a container from a container terminal pool to a ship. The locations on the ship and in the pool are identified by bay/row/stack/cell identifiers.
5. Move a container from a truck to a ship. The location on the ship is identified by bay/row/stack/cell identifiers.
6. Move a container from a truck to a container terminal pool. The location of the pool area is identified by bay/row/stack/cell identifiers.
7. Move a container from a ship to a truck. The location on the ship is identified by bay/row/stack/cell identifiers.
8. Move a container from a container terminal pool to a truck. The location in the container terminal pool is identified by bay/row/stack/cell identifiers.

and of the following three ship movement commands:

9. A ship at sea requests permission to enter and dock at a container terminal. The request can either be fulfilled in which case the ship is informed

of its quay location, or the request can not be fulfilled in which case the ship is so informed.

10. A ship which has been granted a request for permission to enter and dock at a container terminal enters and docks at the informed location.
11. A ship leaves its quay location and the container terminal.

Quay locations are sequences of adjacent quay positions. (The quay consists of a non-zero number of quay positions. Each container ship, when docking, takes up a fixed number of quay positions.

Exercise 19.6. *An Applicative Domain Model of Financial Service Industries.* We refer to Appendix A, Sect. A.3, *Financial Service Industry*.

We assume a bank to be represented by the following three applicatively expressed components: (i) a *client catalogue* which to every client of the bank lists two things: (i.1) some administrative information about the client (name, address, etc.) and (i.2) the one or more account numbers that this client has with the bank; (ii) an *account catalogue* which for every account of the bank lists two things: (ii.1) some computational information about the account: (ii.1.a) whether it is a demand/depost account or a mortgage, or some other form of account, (ii.1.b) what the present interest[3] and yield[4] rates are for this account, etc. and (ii.2) which one or more clients (share) this account; and (iii) the *accounts* which for every account number associate an account balance, that is, a number which if it is positive indicates how much money the client(s) has in this account and which if it is negative indicates how much money the clients owe the bank.

1. Define the command syntax for the following ten transactions:
   (a) *open* and
   (b) *close* an account,
   (c) *deposit* into,
   (d) *withdraw* from,
   (e) *accrue yield*, and
   (f) *pay interests* on a deposit/demand account, partially or fully
   (g) *repay* (including paying interests and fees) on, and
   (h) *increase* a mortgage (i.e., a loan) account;
   (i) *transferring* funds between two accounts; and
   (j) *obtain statement* of transactions since last obtaining such a statement.
2. Define the meaning of some of these commands, for example commands numbered a, c, g, i and j.

---

[3]The interest rate is for the interest charged if the account balance is negative, as it would normally be for a mortgage or a loan account.

[4]The yield rate is for the yield paid to the customer when the account balance is positive.

20

Imperative Specification Programming

- The **prerequisites** for studying this chapter are that you have understood most, if not all, of what has been covered in previous chapters and that you are interested in bridging previously given applicatively specified models to today's programming languages such as `Java` or `C#`.
- The **aims** are to introduce the imperative constructs of RSL: assignable variables, assignments, statements (as opposed to expressions) such as while loops, etc., to illustrate definitions of the semantics of imperative programming languages in a spectrum from applicative, to mixed applicative/imperative, to imperative models, and to otherwise show how one can convert applicative models into imperative models.
- The **objective** is to enable the reader to become fluent in imperative modelling.
- The **treatment** is reasonably formal.

Classically, *machine languages* and the early so-called higher-level *programming languages* were all imperative programming languages. We refer to the languages known through assembler and autocoder programming, and to such programming languages as `FORTRAN` [14], `COBOL` [12], `Algol` 60 [22, 24], `Pascal` [314, 523, 524] or `C` [321]. In this section we shall briefly review the imperative constructs of the RSL specification language, and we shall exemplify how one can define their semantics.

Characterisation. By *imperative programing* we shall understand programming in which a central notion is that of assignable variables. These are variables for which there is an associated notion of storage and of storage locations. The contents of these locations, that is, the values of the variable, may, and usually do change as a result of interpretation of imperative programs. ∎

Characterisation. By *imperative specification programming* we shall understand an abstract, preferably property-oriented form of *imperative programming*, one in which we deploy abstract types — and so on. ∎

20.1 Intuition

Imperative, colloquially speaking, means: *"Do this, then do that"*, as an imperial command! In order to *"first do something, then something else,"* some remembrance of *"where were we, where are we?"* need be recorded. The "recording device" is called a state. The state of a computation is a summary of all of the past computation. To "carry" or "contain" the state we use assignable variables. Variables are state components, also called locations, whose contents, the value, is remembered.

20.2 Imperative Combinators: A λ-Calculus

As in ordinary imperative programming languages, the RAISE Specification Language allows: 0, typed, possibly initialised variable *declarations*, *"statements"* (all statements are expressions in RSL; 1, *assignment*; 2, **skip**; 3, *sequences*; 4–7, *conditionals*; 5, 6, 8, *iterations*; and 9, *expressions* containing state variable references.

> 0. **variable** v:Type := expression
> 1. v := expr
> 2. **skip**
> 3. stm_1;stm_2;...;stm_n
> 4. **if** expr **then** stm_c **else** stm_a **end**
> 5. **while** expr **do** stm **end**
> 6. **do** stmt **until** expr **end**
> 7. **case** e **of**: p_1→S_1(p_1),...,p_n→S_n(p_n) **end**
> 8. **for** b **in** list_expr • P(b) **do** S(b) **end**
> 9. v

where p_i is a choice pattern, typically of the forms id, or (b1,...,bn), where id are identifiers and bj are choice patterns. These numbered expressions are covered in the sections that follow.

The λ-formulas shown below are not to be read as RSL specifications, but as explanatory notes in a small subset of a mathematical notation basically borrowed from Chap. 7 and from the map notation taken from Chap. 16. The semantics of RSL is a bit more complicated than these simple λ-formulas. They are therefore presented more to familiarise you with the λ-calculus as a tool for sketching meanings than to give a fully satisfactory semantics of RSL.

20.2.1 [0] "variable" Declarations

Among new expressions we have variables: 9. v. They look like, but are not the same as, the applicative variables, which designate values. The imperative variables designate locations — with these latter designating values.

The state of the meaning of an imperative RSL specification is built from the variables declared in that specification. Every declaration:

- 0. **variable** v:Type := expression;

which is allocated, that is, which is interpreted designates a state component. Here that state component is of **type** Type and is initialised to the value of the expression.

To simplify, we can explain declaration and initialisation, as designated above, by the sequence of pseudo-RSL and of λ-notation expressions now being unfolded:

First, we have the variable declaration and initialisation:

ppt
    variable v := e;
ppt$'$

which occurs in some text. That text is being interpreted by an interpreter.[1] The interpreter proceeds from program (text) point ppt to program point ppt$'$ [2]. At each program point the interpreter maintains a state $(\sigma : \Sigma)$.[3] It maps locations to values.

type $\Sigma = \text{LOC} \overrightarrow{m} \text{VAL}$

Thus, at program point ppt the interpreter interprets the variable declaration and initialisation in a state:

let $\sigma:\Sigma \cdot P(\sigma)$ **in**

...

end

The interpreter now "obeys" the prescription of the declaration and initialisation clause by (1) finding a "fresh", hitherto unused location, loc, by (2) obtaining the value val of e, and (3) by updating the state accordingly:

(1)   **let** loc:LOC $\cdot$ loc $\notin$ **dom** σ,
(2)   val $= \mathcal{V}(e)(\sigma)$ **in**
(3)   **let** $\sigma' = \sigma \cup [\text{loc} \mapsto \text{val}]$ **in**

    ...

    end end

---

[1] For statements the interpreter function is named $\mathcal{I}$ while for expressions it is named $\mathcal{V}$.

[2] When now telling the story through the mind of an interpreter our explanation becomes operational. From the operational behaviour of the interpreter we shall "lift" to the meaning of program texts as functions.

[3] We presently use the term 'state'. We could, as well, in this example, have used the term 'storage'.

where val is the value of the initialisation expression e eValuated[4] in the input state σ; and where σ' : Σ is now the state at program point ppt'. Declaration and initialisation, "lifting" the explanation, can thus be considered to be the function:

$$\lambda\sigma{:}\Sigma \bullet \sigma \cup [\ loc \mapsto \mathcal{V}(e)(\sigma)\ ]$$

What happened to v? The answer is: It became part of an *environment*, a semantic component maintained by the interpreter:

type
  LOC, VAL
  $\rho{:}\text{ENV} = V \xrightarrow{\ \widetilde{m}\ } \text{LOC}$
  $\sigma{:}\text{STG} = \text{LOC} \xrightarrow{\ \widetilde{m}\ } \text{VAL}$
value
  $\mathcal{I}$: RSL_Text $\xrightarrow{\sim}$ ENV $\xrightarrow{\sim}$ STATE $\xrightarrow{\sim}$ STATE

  $\mathcal{I}[\textbf{variable } v := e; \text{txt}](\rho)(\sigma) \equiv$
    let loc:LOC $\bullet$ loc $\notin$ **dom** σ,
      val $= \mathcal{V}(e)(\rho)(\sigma)$ **in**
    let $\sigma' = \sigma \cup [\ loc \mapsto val\ ]$ **in**
    $\mathcal{I}[\text{txt}](\rho \dagger [v \mapsto loc])(\sigma')$
    end end

Hence we can conclude that variable declaration (and initialisation) denotes functions from state to state, actually from configurations of environments and storages to such configurations, since also the environment got "updated". In the following we shall, however, maintain the simplistic view of state-to-state transforming functions as being the denotation of the imperative statements of RSL.

On the background of the above detailed explication, we can now speed up our story on the "sketch" λ-notation semantics of RSL's imperative features. In that story we will omit references to environments.

20.2.2 [1] Assignments: "var := expression"

The RSL state (value) can be changed only through an assignment action:

- 1. v := expr

where the variable v is given the value of the expression.

---

[4]We show a rather free-wheeling use type fonts: $\mathcal{V}$ refer to the name, $\mathcal{V}$, of the semantics valuation function presented later [9]. Similar for the use of the $\mathcal{I}$ name elow and b[3].

$\lambda\sigma:\Sigma \cdot \sigma \dagger [\ loc \mapsto val\ ]$
where:
  $loc \in \mathbf{dom}\ \sigma \land loc \equiv \text{location of v} \land val \equiv \mathcal{V}(e)(\sigma)$

20.2.3 [9] State Expressions

There is a new type of clause, the impure variable expression:

- 9. v

On the left-hand side of an assignment statement it designates a *storage location*. As an expression, and as proper part of expressions, it designates the *content* at (or of) a storage location.[5]

  $\mathcal{V}: \text{RSL\_Text} \overset{\sim}{\to} \text{ENV} \overset{\sim}{\to} \text{STATE} \overset{\sim}{\to} \text{VAL}$
  $\mathcal{V}(v)(\sigma) \equiv \sigma(l)\ \mathbf{where:}\ l \equiv \mathcal{L}ocation(v)$

20.2.4 [2] "skip": No-Action

There is a *no state change* action:

- 2. **skip**.

It denotes the state-to-state changing identity function:

  $\mathcal{I}(\mathbf{skip}) \equiv \lambda\sigma:\Sigma \cdot \sigma$

20.2.5 [3] Statement Sequencing (;)

If stm_i (for i=1,...,n) is a statement, then:

- 3. stm_1;stm_2;...;stm_n

designates a conventional statement list.

  $\mathcal{I}(s\_1;s\_2) \equiv \lambda\sigma:\Sigma \cdot \mathcal{I}(s\_2)(\mathcal{I}(s\_1)(\sigma))$

---

[5]Elsewhere in these volumes we sometimes prefix expression occurrences of imperative variable names by the contents-taking operator: $\underline{\mathbf{c}}$. Thus imperative v's always designate locations, and $\underline{\mathbf{c}}$ v the value stored at those locations — making the above explanation a bit less convolute!

20.2.6 [4] "if ... then ... else ... end"

The classical:

- 4. **if** expr **then** stm_c **else** stm_a **end**

is evaluated as you would expect. Reflexively:

$\mathcal{I}$(**if** e **then** c_s **else** a_s **end**) $\equiv$
  $\lambda\sigma:\Sigma \bullet$
    let b $= \mathcal{V}$(e)(σ) **in**
    if b **then** $\mathcal{I}$(c_s)σ' **else** $\mathcal{I}$(a_s)σ'
    end end

20.2.7 [5–6] "while ... do ... end", and "do ... until ... end"

There are two more conditional statements, also referred to as iteration statements:

- 5. **while** expr **do** stm **end**

and

- 6. **do** stmt **until** expr **end**.

The last two statements can be explained as the fix points of

  while e **do** s **end** $\equiv$
    if e **then** (s;**while** e **do** s **end**) **else skip end**

  do s **until** e **end** $\equiv$
    (s;**while** e **do** s **end**)

20.2.8 [7] "case ... of ... end"

Let e be an expression which evaluates to some value, v, and let p_i be choice patterns which introduce some structures of identifiers. Statements S_i(p_i) contains (some, but not necessarily all of) the (free) identifiers of p_i. Evaluation of:

- 7. **case** e **of**: p_1$\rightarrow$s_1(p_1),...,p_n$\rightarrow$s_n(p_n) **end**

then proceeds by matching the structure of the value v against the elements of the binding-list $\langle$p_1,...,p_n$\rangle$ until a first is found which matches the structure of v. If such a first, i, in order 1 to n, is found, then s_i(p_i) is interpreted in the context of the new bindings provided by the matching of p_i to v. If none is found and p_n is not the *wildcard* (_) then **chaos** ensues, otherwise s_n(p_n) is interpreted.

20.2.9 [8] "for... in ... do... end"

Let b be a pattern which introduces some structure of identifiers, and let list_expr be a list-valued expression whose evaluation yields a list, say ⟨e1,...,en⟩. The statement s(b) contains (some, but not necessarily all of) the (free) identifiers of b. Evaluation of:

- 8. **for** b **in** list_expr • p(b) **do** s(b) **end**

then proceeds by processing each element ei of the list ⟨e1,...,en⟩ in order from e1 to en. If evaluation of the predicate p(b) in the context of the definitions obtained by matching ei against the binding b deterministically yields **true**, then s(b) is evaluated in this same context, otherwise it is skipped.

20.3 Variable References: Pointers

In Sect. 20.2 we covered the imperative language constructs of the specification language RSL such as we shall be using them. The RSL constructs are quite familiar, and at the core of all imperative programming languages. The difference is that in RSL we allow for any value of any of the definable abstract or concrete types to be stored — except references to variable locations. In this section we shall be discussing and exemplifying other imperative language constructs — such as you will find in some programming languages. Please observe that the constructs that we shall now be discussing are not part of RSL.

20.3.1 A Discourse on Simple References

We have modelled assignable variables in terms of a storage, above referred to by a Greek letter sigma (σ). The storage maps locations into values. Among values, in many programming languages, but not in the RSL specification language, one can have locations as "storable" values. Locations are thus considered "first class citizens", thus reflecting a view that there may be entities which are not storable values. In those same programming languages that were implied above, procedures may not be treated as storable values. We shall look at models for such programming languages.

Let a programming language allow variables that store values of type "**ref**erence to variables of type A":

dcl v : **ref** A

Now, for this to make sense we must either allow dynamic, "on-the-fly" **al**location of locations (whose contents are of type A):

dcl v : **ref** A := **alloc** e

where the expression e is of type A. Or we must allow assignment of the location of declared variables of type A to such reference variables:

dcl a : A;
dcl v : **ref** A := **ref** a;

or both. Usually both situations hold in order to make "things" hang together.[6]

Instead of using the syntactic form **ref** a to designate, not the contents of the variable a, but its location, one could turn things around: Let a designate the location, and c̲ a the contents.

20.3.2 Dynamic Allocation and Referencing

We now present a model of typed references: integer, Boolean and record locations designate integer, Boolean, respectively record values. Record values consist of two or more uniquely identified values. Locations are values.

Example 20.1 *A Simple Model of Dynamic Records:*
We model a "toy" imperative programming language in which one may declare variables of type integer, Boolean, record or reference, and in which one may dynamically allocate (and possibly also free, i.e., deallocate) unnamed variables of type record. Storage is thus a collection of uniquely located values. Any two distinctly located values, that is, any two storage cells, are "disjoint", they do not overlap — in whatever sense this term: 'overlap' may have in your mind![7]. Integer, Boolean and record type variables contain, when properly initialised, values of respective types: Integer values (i.e., integers), Boolean values and record values. A variable of type reference is to contain a reference (only) to a dynamically allocated record or the nil (void, null) reference. A value of type reference is either a reference to a dynamically allocated record or is nil. Record values are sets (fields) of uniquely, and statically identified simple values. Thus we do not allow record values embedded in record values. A simple value is either an integer, a Boolean or a possibly nil reference value.

---

[6]If we can designate one kind of value assignment, as of dynamically allocated locations, then why not from statically, i.e., textually, implied allocations as for variable declarations? Symmetry seems to be a good language design principle as it enables consistency of expression and adheres to a principle of *every denotable value being storable*.

[7]In our mind overlap refers to the possibility that one may think of storage as a list of consecutively indexed storage cells where one might think of Boolean valued storage cells occupying one bit, of integer valued storage cells occupying 32 bits, of location valued storage cells occupying 16 bits, and of record values occupying several such storage cells. Overlap now means that an index to a separately declared, say integer variable "shares" bits with another, now, say a location valued variable. Such overlaps are possible due to the way in which most computers address storage cells to begin at a byte (i.e., an eight bit) boundary.

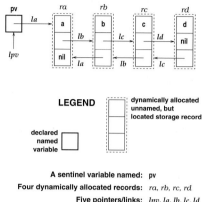

A sentinel variable named: pv

Four dynamically allocated records: *ra, rb, rc, rd*

Five pointers/links: *lpv, la, lb, lc, ld*

Fig. 20.1. An example dynamically allocated data structure

Intuition

Figure 20.1 illustrates a fragment of a storage in which one reference variable, named **pv**, has been declared, and there have been four (dynamic) allocations of records **ra**, **rb**, **rc** and **rd**. Each of the records has three fields, i.e., all records seem to be of the same type, and otherwise they each contain two fields of type reference to records of the record type shown.

ra, rb, rc and *rd* are not identifiers declared in a program text. They are just names we introduced in order to speak about the problem. There are no program text names for dynamically allocated variables. They are "reachable" only through chains of references, where such a chain (of one or more indirect references) is anchored in a program text declared and thus identified reference variable.

Formalisation — Storage, Locations and Values

Locations may only designate, i.e., refer, point or link, to "whole" variables, whether explicitly declared or dynamically allocated. For reasons of abstraction we mark locations as either being integer locations, Boolean locations, reference locations or record locations. Similar, obviously, for values, where a reference value can be either a whole location or **nil**. Record locations are atomic and do not further identify the structure of the possibly referenced record values. This is a gross simplification, which makes our example shorter, but it does not make it less relevant.

type
    Nm, Tn, 1LOC

$$\text{STG}' = \text{LOC} \underset{m}{\rightarrow} \text{VAL}$$

$$\text{LOC} = \text{SLOC} \mid \text{RLOC}$$
$$\text{SLOC} == \text{mkintl(i:1LOC)} \mid \text{mkbooll(b:1LOC)}$$
$$\text{RLOC} == \text{mkrecl(1loc:1LOC)}$$

$$\text{VAL} = \text{SVAL} \mid \text{RVAL}$$
$$\text{SVAL} == \text{mkintv(i:\textbf{Int})} \mid \text{mkboolv(b:\textbf{Bool})} \mid \text{LOCV}$$
$$\text{LVAL} == \text{nil} \mid \text{RLOC}$$
$$\text{RVAL} == \text{mkrecv(rval:(Nm} \underset{m}{\rightarrow} \text{SVAL))}$$

Location and Value Types

With locations and with values we can thus associate their type. And we will do so systematically, while also defining a function that observes the type of locations and values.

type
$$\text{1Typ} = \text{STyp} \mid \text{record}$$
$$\text{STyp} == \text{integer} \mid \text{boolean}$$

$$\text{Typ} = \text{1Typ} \mid \text{RTyp}$$
$$\text{RTyp} == \text{mkrect(rt:(Rn} \underset{m}{\rightarrow} \text{1Typ))}$$

value
$$\text{1typ: (VAL|LOC)} \rightarrow \text{1Typ}$$
$$\text{1typ(mkintv(\_))} \equiv \text{integer}$$
$$\text{1typ(mkintl(\_))} \equiv \text{integer}$$
$$\text{1typ(mkboolv(\_))} \equiv \text{boolean}$$
$$\text{1typ(mkbooll(\_))} \equiv \text{boolean}$$
$$\text{1typ(nil)} \equiv \text{record}$$
$$\text{1typ(mkrecv(\_))} \equiv \text{record}$$
$$\text{1typ(mkrecl(\_))} \equiv \text{record}$$

$$\text{typ: VAL} \rightarrow \text{Typ}$$
$$\text{typ(v)} \equiv$$
    case v **of**
        mkrecv(rv)
            $\rightarrow$ mkrect([r$\mapsto$1typ(rv(r))|r:Rn•r $\in$ **dom** rv]),
           _ $\rightarrow$ 1typ(v) **end**

Storage Invariant

Now we are ready to define an invariant on storages: Location and value types must match, and all values that contain or are references are references to allocated records.

type
   STG = {| stg:STG′ • wfSTG(stg) |}
value
   wfSTG: STG′ → STG
   wfSTG(stg) ≡
     ∀ loc:LOC • loc ∈ **dom** stg ⇒ ltyp(loc) = ltyp(stg(loc)) ∧
     ∀ val:VAL • val ∈ **rng** stg ⇒
       case val **of**
         mkrecv(rval) →
           ∀ v:VAL • v ∈ **rng** rval ⇒
             case v **of** mkrecl(_) → v ∈ **dom** stg, _ → **true end**,
         mkrecl(_) → val ∈ **dom** stg, _ → **true**
       end

Semantic Operations

The following primitive, i.e., basic operations on storages can now be defined: allocation of suitably typed storage location, extension of storage, reading storage values, and overriding (overwriting) of such.

value
   get_LOC: Typ → STG → LOC
   get_LOC(t)(σ) ≡
     let ℓ:LOC • ℓ∉ **dom** σ ∧ ltyp(ℓ)=t **in** ℓ **end**

   extend_STG: LOC × VAL → STG → STG
   extend_STG(ℓ,v)(σ) ≡ σ ∪ [ℓ↦v]

   get_VAL: LOC → STG → VAL
   get_VAL(ℓ)(σ) ≡ σ(ℓ)

   override_STG: LOC × VAL → STG → STG
   override_STG(ℓ,v)(σ) ≡ σ † [ℓ↦v]

The Syntactic Forms

Seven syntactic forms are necessary to suitably exploit the semantic machinery, now that the storage model is partly established: (i) declaration of named scalar and record variables of any type, (ii) allocation of unnamed record storage cells of simple type, (iii) reading whole, included record values, from storage, (iv) obtaining reference values, (v) selecting field values of a record value and (vi) assigning values to declared simple variables, including assigning to fields of record variables.

> Dcl :: v:Vn val:VAL
> Alo :: v:Vn rv:RVAL
> Rea :: Vn
> Sel :: v:Vn rn:Rn
> Asg :: v:Vn f:Fld ex:Exp
> Fld == null | mkRn(rn:Rn)
> Exp == Rea | Sel | Loc
> Loc :: v:Vn

Semantics

The rest should now be trivial. Environments, ENV, keep track of locations of declared, named variables.

type
> ENV = Vn $\overrightarrow{m}$ LOC

value
> elab_Dcl: Dcl → STG → STG × ENV × LOC
> elab_Dcl(mkDcl(v,val))(ρ)(σ) ≡
>   **let** loc = get_LOC(1typ(val)) **in**
>   (extend_STG(loc,val)(σ),[v↦loc],loc) **end**
>
> int_Alo: Alo → STG → STG
> int_Alo(mkAlo(v,mkRVAL(rval)))(ρ)(σ) ≡
>   **let** loc = get_LOC(record) **in**
>   override_STG(ρ(v),loc)(extend_STG(loc,val)(σ)) **end**
>   **pre** v ∈ **dom** ρ ∧ 1typ(σ(ρ(v)))=record
>
> eval_Rea: Rea → ENV → STG → VAL
> eval_Rea(mkRea(v))(ρ)(σ) ≡ get_VAL(ρ(v))(σ)
>   **pre:** v ∈ **dom** ρ(v) ∧ ρ(v) ∈ **dom** σ
>
> eval_Sel: Sel → ENV → STG → VAL
> eval_Sel(mkSel(v,r))(ρ)(σ) ≡ (get_VAL(ρ(v))(σ))(r)
>   **pre:** r ∈ **dom** σ(ρ(v))

int_Asg: Asg → ENV → STG → STG
int_Asg(v,f,e)(ρ)(σ) ≡
   let loc=ρ(v),
        old=σ(ρ(v)),
        new = eval_Exp(e)(ρ)(σ) **in**
   case f **of**
      mkRn(rn) → extend_STG(loc,old†[rn↦new])(σ),
      null → extend_STG(loc,new)(σ) **end**
   end
   pre: v ∈ **dom** ρ(v) ∧ ρ(v) ∈ **dom** σ ∧ f≠null ⇒ rn ∈ **dom** old

eval_Exp: Exp → ENV → STG → VAL
eval_Exp(e)(ρ)(σ) ≡
   case e **of**:
      mkRea(v) → eval_Rea(mkRea(v))(ρ)(σ),
      mkSel(v,r) → eval_Sel(mkSel(v,r))(ρ)(σ),
      mkLoc(v) → ρ(v), ...
   end
   pre v ∈ **dom** ρ ...

Discussion I — The Example

We have illustrated a rather simple language. It illustrates basic notions of dynamically allocated storage, references to such storage, assignments to record fields and pointer "chasing": pointers being assigned to declared variables, selected as expression values, and assigned to fields of declared or dynamically allocated records.

    We have assumed a rather loose typing discipline, much too loose for our liking. But then we chose this looseness only in order to avoid having to show even more text, informal as well as formal: static and/or dynamic type checking. We shall have an opportunity later to also illustrate such facets. ∎

20.3.3 Discussion: Semantics First, Then Syntax

Example 20.1 significantly illustrated the following important development principle:

Principles. *First Semantics Then Syntax:* When investigating a phenomenon in a domain, when prescribing requirements, or when designing a software device, analyse and construct first the semantic algebras (entities, and operations), then design the syntax "to go with" the semantics. ∎

20.3.4 Discussion: Type Homomorphisms

Example 20.1 significantly illustrated another important development principle:

Principles. *Type, Value and Location Homomorphisms:* When modelling types, values and locations (of some storage) it is prudent to ensure that there exists one or more appropriate homomorphisms between the three sets of entities: types, values and locations.   ∎

The above principle may appear a bit cryptic. Especially since we have not at all been sufficiently precise about what we mean by the type, the value and the location algebras. Please refer to the definitions of the LOC, the VAL and the Type types in Example 20.1. They define the entities of respective algebras. Please refer to the definition of the 1typ function. It represents a homomorphism between the entities of the LOC and VAL, on one hand, and Typ on the other hand.

The type and value part of the homomorphism principle was already illustrated in Example 19.10 and Example 19.11.

20.3.5 The Notion of State

We speak of the storage model of assignable variables as a state model. The use of the term state is one of pragmatics. Its use shall signal to the reader that the 'state' component value changes value "quite often, rapidly". That is, 'state' is a temporal notion. The thing that makes it change value, i.e., that makes the state change, is, of course, the assignments prescribed by statements. So, storage, as a notion connected to prescriptions of programs of an imperative programming language, is a state notion.

20.4 Function Definitions and Expressions

We continue the line of explaining the RSL imperative constructs, which we left at the end of Sect. 20.2. A number of issues need be resolved: Is there really a difference between RSL statements and RSL expressions? The answer is: No there is no fundamental difference (but see below). What is the 'value', then, of a statement? The answer is: It is designated by (), and is of type **Unit** (again, see below). But there is a slight difference between RSL statements and RSL expressions. We may distinguish between pure and impure expressions, including read-only expressions. Finally, what is the signature (i.e., the type) of functions which access variables? The answer is: It involves specifying to which variables we need (have) **read** access, and to which we need have **write** access. We now deal with these issues, in a slightly different order.

20.4.1 The Unit Type Expression, I

In our signatures, in Example 20.1 (Sect. 20.3.2), for functions that applied to or yielded values of type storage (**STG**) we explicitly listed the type **STG**. Now what are we to do when the state, with the use of declared RSL variables, in a sense becomes "hidden"? We refer to that state by using **Unit.**

The literal **Unit** is a type literal. It designates that there is a value of type **Unit.** We (arbitrarily) designate this value by (). The type literal **Unit** is used in function signatures. So, let us see how and why.

20.4.2 Imperative Functions

We define three functions which all access a globally declared variable:

variable k:**Nat** := 0;
value
    step: **Unit** → **write** k **Unit**
    step() ≡ k := 7

    incr: **Unit** → **read** k **write** k **Nat**
    incr() ≡ step();k

    get: **Unit** → **read** k **Nat**
    get() ≡ k

The signature of step defines that step applies to a value of type **Unit** (the first occurrence of **Unit**) and that it **writes** onto the variable k. The signature also defines that step only prescribes a *side effect* on the state (the second occurrence of **Unit**). By default, the **write** access descriptor allows for reading (but not yielding to "an outside") the value of the variable. The signature of incr defines that incr applies to a value of type **Unit** and that it writes onto and reads from and yields a value that depends on the value of the variable k. The signature of incr defines that incr applies to a value of type **Unit** and that it reads from the variable k, and yields a value that depends on the value of the variable k.

20.4.3 Read/Write Access Descriptions

The clauses:

    write u_1, u_2, ..., u_m
    read v_1, v_2, ..., v_n

are called *access descriptions*. They are part of potentially side effect prescribing total and partial function signatures:

value
    tf: typ_ex_a → acc_des_1,...,acc_des_n typ_ex_r
    pf: typ_ex_a $\overset{\sim}{\to}$ acc_des_1,...,acc_des_n typ_ex_r

20.4.4 Local Variables

Variables are either declared globally or they are declared *local* to an expression:

    local variable_declaration **in** expression **end**

For example,

value
    fact: **Nat** → **Nat**
    fact(n) ≡
        local variable k:**Nat** := n, **variable** r:**Nat** := 1 **in**
        while k≠0 **do** r := r ∗ k ; k := k − 1 **end**
        r **end**

Observe that the signature of the factorial function does not refer to the local state.

20.4.5 The Unit Type Expression, II

When we say informally that a clause of the specification language RSL is a statement, we mean that it is of type **Unit.** That is, it "delivers" the value () of type **Unit.** We review the RSL clauses that may be of type **Unit:**[8]

    0. **variable** v:Type := expr
    1. v := expr
    2. **skip**
    3. stm_1;stm_2;...;stm_n
    4. **if** expr **then** stm_c **else** stm_a **end**
    5. **while** expr **do** stm_w **end**
    6. **do** stmt_u **until** expr **end**
    7. **case** e **of:** p_1→s_1(p_1),...,p_n→s_n(p_n) **end**
    8. **for** b **in** list_expr • P(b) **do** s(b) **end**

---

[8]They will be of type **Unit** only if in formulas 0–8 we can assume that clauses stm_1,..., stm_n, stm_c, stm_a, stm_w, stmt_u, s_1(p_1), ..., s_n(p_n), and s(b) are all statements, i.e., of type **Unit,** and that the clause expr is an expression yielding a proper (i.e., a non-**Unit**) value.

Clauses 0–2 are of type **Unit.** Clauses stm_w, stm_u, and s(b) must be of type **Unit** for clauses 5, 6, and 8 to be well-formed. They are then of type **Unit.** For all i in the range 1..n−1, stm_i, of clause 3, must be of type **Unit** for that clause to be well-formed. If stm_n of clause 3 is of type A then clause 4 is of type A. (That includes type **Unit.**) If clauses stm_c and stm_a (of clause 4) are of a type different from **Unit,** then they must both be of the same type B.[9] If clauses stm_n, stm_c, stm_a and s_i(p_i) (above) are of type **Unit,** then clauses 3 and 4 are of type **Unit.** If clauses s_i(p_i) (of clause 4) are of a type different from **Unit,** then they must all have the same maximal[10] type, say A, which is then the type of clause 7.

20.4.6 Pure Expressions

An expression which does not prescribe access to assignable variables[11] is called a pure expression. For specifications expressed in RSL to "hang to-gether", a number of RSL expression forms permit only pure expressions. These are P(a) in the let clause forms shown below, and expr, in variable initialisa-tions, see below. Further, all identifiers of argument_pattern and result_patterns must be free in the forms also shown below:

> **let** a:A • P(a) **in** ... **end**
> **variable** v:A := expr
> binding_pattern /∗ any such ∗/
> f(argument_pattern) **as** result_pattern

To the above add some forms we have yet to meet: actual array parame-ters, comprehended access and those in which there must also only be pure expressions.

20.4.7 Read-Only Expressions

An expression which prescribes access to assignable variables[12] but which does not imply side effects[13] is called a read-only expression. For specifications expressed in RSL to "hang together", a number of RSL expression forms permit only pure or read-only expressions. The cases for pure expressions (only) was

---

[9]We omit in this part of the book treatment of the possibility that the types of stm_c and stm_a are different, say, both being different subtypes of type B, or one being of type B and another being a subtype of B. In those cases the type of clause 4 is B, known as the maximal type of the two types of stm_c and stm_a.

[10]The concept of maximal type is mentioned in Footnote 9.

[11]— and which does not prescribe reading from (or writing to) channels, as we shall see in Chap. 21.

[12]— or which is allowed to prescribe reading from channels, as we shall see in Chap. 21.

[13]Thus the expression is not allowed to prescribe writing to channels.

mentioned above. So we mention (below) the cases where both pure and (or) read-only expressions may be used, but not side effect prescribing expressions. These are P(a), e_1, e_2, ..., e_n, ll(a), d_i, r_i, d(a) and r(a) in:

choice_pattern
∀ a:A • P(a), ∃ a:A • P(a), ∃! a:A • P(a),
{e_1..e_n}, {e_1,e_2,...,e_n}, {e(a)|a:A • P(a)}
⟨e(a)|b **in** ll(a)⟩
[d_1↦r_1,d_2↦r_2,...,d_n↦r_n],[d(a)↦r(a)|a:A•P(a)]
□ P(a)

where identifiers in the choice_pattern may be bound to assignable variables. In addition, expressions occurring in **axiom**s, and **pre-, post-**conditions are to be pure or read-only expressions.

Note that side effects are allowed in list element formations e(a), since their construction is ordered. (They are allowed since we have not explicitly mentioned them!) Such an ordering is not expressible for sets and maps. Similarly, Cartesian expressions also are not restricted to read-only, but can contain side effect prescribing expressions, although we do not advise this for abstract specifications.

Quantification over States (□)

So far, axioms have been illustrated only in connection with applicative specifications, i.e., pure expressions. What happens when we wish to access assignable variables in an axiom? The answer is: Then we must express that when the axiom is true it is true for all states. This can be achieved by quantifying over all states as expressed by the □ quantifier. The state quantification expression □ P(a) allows P(a) to be read-only. The entire expression □ P(a) is pure since it quantifies over all possible states. The truth value of □ P(a) is **true** if P(a) holds for all possible values of all declared variables, otherwise it is **false**. Previous uses of axioms:

axiom P(a)

now amount to:

axiom □ P(a).

20.4.8 Equivalence (≡) and Equality (=)

Two operators that look alike need be clearly understood: ≡, equivalence, and =, equality.

Equivalence ($\equiv$)

The equivalence expression consisting of two read-only expressions:

  expr_1 $\equiv$ expr_2

is evaluated in all states. If it holds in all states, then the value of expr_1$\equiv$expr_2 is **true,** otherwise it is **false.**

 If the expressions expr_1 and expr_2 prescribe side effects, then they must have the same side effect on variables and return the same value in order to hold. If one of the expressions yields **chaos**, then they must both yield **chaos** for the equivalence to hold. The equivalence expression itself, as a whole, never yields **chaos.**

 If, as we shall see later, one expression prescribes nondeterminism, then they must both prescribe exactly the same nondeterminism for the equivalence to hold.

Conditional Equivalence

We can constrain axioms:

  axiom expr_1 $\equiv$ expr_2 **pre** P(a)

for example as used in:

variable ctr:**Nat** := 0
value
  decr: **Unit** $\overset{\sim}{\rightarrow}$ **write** ctr **Nat**
  decr() $\equiv$ ctr := ctr $-$ 1 ; ctr   **pre** ctr > 0

have expr_1$\equiv$expr_2 **pre** P(a) being equivalent to

  (P(a) $\equiv$ **true**) $\Rightarrow$ (expr_1 $\equiv$ expr_2)

Equality ($=$)

If two expressions, expr_1, expr_2, do not access assignable variables, i.e., have no side effects, do not evaluate to **chaos** and are both deterministic, then $=$ and $\equiv$ mean the same. If not, then $=$ and $\equiv$ do not mean the same.

 The equality expr_1 $=$ expr_2 is an expression of type Boolean. If one or both expressions evaluate to **chaos, chaos** is yielded. Otherwise the values yielded by evaluation of the above, left to right, are compared and either **true** or **false** is yielded. Side effects may occur, and they will then result, i.e., be effected, but they are not part of the comparison.

20.5 Translations: Applicative to Imperative

In this section we treat three simple topics: (i) the translation of some forms of simple applicative function definitions into likewise simple imperative function definitions together with the simple declaration of variables; (ii) the translation of some forms of simple applicative recursive function definitions into likewise simple imperative function definitions together with the simple declaration of a variable; and (iii) specialising the two former translation schemes — the translation of not-quite-so-simple forms of applicative recursive function definitions into slightly less simple imperative function definitions together with the declaration of suitable variables.

20.5.1 Applicative to Imperative Translations

Consider the following kind of function definition, i.e., function schema:

type
    A, B, Σ
value
    f_α: A $\rightarrow$ Σ $\rightarrow$ Σ $\times$ B
    $f_\alpha(a)(\sigma) \equiv$ **let** b $= g_\alpha(a)(\sigma)$, $\sigma' = h_\alpha(a)(\sigma)$ **in** (σ',b) **end**

    g_α: A $\rightarrow$ Σ $\rightarrow$ B, ...

    h_α: A $\rightarrow$ Σ $\rightarrow$ Σ
    $h_\alpha(a)(\sigma) \equiv ... \sigma'$

Let us, by fiat, claim that Σ represents "our" state space, i.e., a type of states. Then we say that f is a state-changing function that yields a result, while h is just a state-changing function.
    Let us instead consider:

type
    A, B
variable
    s:Σ := ...
value
    f_ι: A $\rightarrow$ **read, write** s B
    $f_\iota(a) \equiv$ **let** b $= g_\iota(a)$ **in** s := $h_\iota(a)$; b **end**

    g_ι: A $\rightarrow$ **read** s B

    h_ι: A $\rightarrow$ **write** s Unit
    $h_\iota(a) \equiv ...$ s := σ'

We ask the reader to accept the claim that the two functions, f_α and f_ι, compute the same type B results[14] for corresponding pairs of f_α state arguments, σ, and initialisations of the global variable s.

Now, what can we learn from this example? We claim that we can conclude that given a suitable form of function definitions f_α, one may be able to find an imperative function f_ι that computes the "same results' for corresponding pairs of state arguments and variable initialisations.

20.5.2 Recursive to Iterative Translations

Let us consider the following simple example of an applicative, recursive function definition:

type
    A, B
value
    f_α: A $\overset{\sim}{\to}$ B
    $f_\alpha(a) \equiv$ **if** $p_\alpha(a)$ **then** $g_\alpha(a)$ **else** $f_\alpha(h_\alpha(a))$ **end**

    p_α: A $\to$ **Bool**
    g_α: A $\to$ B
    h_α: A $\to$ A

f_α is partial since the predicate p_α may yield **false** for all relevant a's.

One may think of first invoking f_α with the value initial_a. Function f_α could be "imperialised" into likewise partial f_ι:

variable
    v:A := initial_a ;
value
    f_ι: **Unit** $\overset{\sim}{\to}$ **read, write** v B
    $f_\iota() \equiv$ **if** $p_\iota(v)$ **then** $g_\iota(v)$ **else** $(v := h_\iota(v); f_\iota())$ **end**

    p_ι: A $\to$ **read** v **Bool**
    g_ι: A $\to$ **read** v B
    h_ι: A $\to$ **read** v A

or even:

value
    f_ι: **Unit** $\overset{\sim}{\to}$ **read, write** v B
    $f_\iota() \equiv$ **while** $\sim p_\iota(v)$ **do** $v := h_\iota(v)$ **end**; $g_\iota(v)$

---

[14]By the "same result" we loosely mean that the values observed from any invocation of the two functions with corresponding arguments, respectively initialisations, are the same. What is not compared, and what, in a sense, is not comparable, is the "side effect" left on the global state by the imperative function invocation vis-a-vis the fact that there is not such a side effect when invoking the applicative functions.

We again ask the reader to accept the claim that the two functions, f_α and f_ι, computes the same results for corresponding pairs of f_α arguments and initialisations of the global variable v.

What can we learn from this example?

We can conclude that, given a suitable form of recursive function definitions f_α, one may be able to find an imperative function f_ι that computes the same results for corresponding pairs of arguments and variable initialisations.

20.5.3 Applicative to Imperative Schemas

This section is based on the work of Burstall and Darlington: [174]. Later work appears in [34]. The gist of this section is that a number of recursive, applicative (i.e., functional) programs (cum specifications), can be transformed into nonrecursive, imperative (and iterative) programs (cum specifications).

We follow [174] closely. For each of a number of applicative, recursive schemas is given one, two or three nonrecursive, imperative schemas, together with some conditions, one for each imperative schema, that must be fulfilled of the abstract, functional operators of the applicative, recursive schema for it to be transformable into the given imperative schema.

We start, as does [174], with an example.

---- Example ----

```
type                          reverse: A* → Unit
  A                           reverse(alv) ≡
value                           if alv = ⟨⟩
  reverse: A* → A*                then
  reverse(al) ≡                     result:=⟨⟩
    if al=⟨⟩                      else
      then ⟨⟩                       result:=⟨hd alv⟩^⟨⟩;
      else reverse(tl al)^⟨hd al⟩   alv:=tl alv ;
    end                           while alv ≠ ⟨⟩ do
                                    result:=⟨hd alv⟩^result;
variable                          alv:=tl alv
  alv:A* := al;                  end
  result:A*                      result:=⟨⟩^result
                              end
value
```

The applicative version of **reverse** (list) is easy to understand, whereas the imperative version is contorted, i.e., difficult to understand. Hence it is difficult to see that the two do essentially the same job.

Schemas

We now show a number of schemas: Triples of (i) an abstract, schematic applicative and recursive program, (ii) an abstract, schematic imperative (nonrecursive) program, and (iii) a set of one or more equations that the abstract functional operators of (i) must satisfy, when one tries to apply it to a concrete applicative and recursive program in order to transform it to a concrete, imperative (and nonrecursive, but usually iterative) program.

————————————————— Schema 1 —————————————————

- Recursion Schema:

  $f(x) \equiv$ **if** a **then** b **else** h(d,f(e)) **end**

————————————————— Transformation 1.I —————————————————

- Iterative Schema 1.I:

  if a
      then
          result := b
      else
          result := d ; x := e ;
          while $\sim$a **do**
              result := h(result,d) ; x := e
          end
          result := h(result,b)
      end

- Equation and Condition:

  $h(h(\alpha,\beta),\gamma) \equiv h(\alpha,h(\beta,\gamma))$
  x does not occur free in h

————————————————— Example: Factorial Function —————————————————

The factorial function:

$\text{fact}(n) \equiv$ **if** n=0 **then** 1 **else** n $*$ fact(n$-$1) **end**

is an instance of Schema 1.I. With

$a \equiv (n=0)$, b=1, d =n, e=n$-$1, h=$*$

we get:

$\text{fact}(n) \equiv$
    if n=0

```
      then
          result := 1
      else
          result := n ; n := n−1 ;
          while n≠0 do
              result := result * n ;
              n := n−1
          end ;
          result := result * 1
end
```

_____ Transformation 1.II _____

- Iterative Schema:

    ```
    result := b ;
    while ~a do
        result := h(d,result) ; x := e
    end
    ```

- Equation and Conditions:

    $h(\alpha,h(\beta,\gamma)) \equiv h(\beta,h(\alpha,\gamma))$
    x does not occur free in h or b

_____ Example: Factorial Function _____

The factorial function:

$fact(n) \equiv$ **if** $n=0$ **then** 1 **else** $n * fact(n−1)$ **end**

is an instance of Schema 1.II. We get:

```
result := 1
while n≠0 do
    result := n * result ; n := n − 1
end
```

_____ Transformation 1.III _____

- Iterative Schema:

    ```
    result := b ; xsave := x ;
    x := "unique x such that a" ;
    ```

```
while ~x do
    x := "inverse of e"(x) ; result := h(d,result)
end
```

- Conditions:

    There is a unique x such that a is true exists and the inverse of
    e exists. x does not occur free in b or h.

───────────────────── Schema 2 ─────────────────────

- Recursion Schema:

    $f(x1,x2) \equiv$ **if** a **then** b **else** h(d,f(e1,e2)) **end**

───────────────────── Transformation ─────────────────────

- Iterative Schema:

    ```
    result := b ;
    while ~a do
        result := h(d,result) ; xsave := e1 ; x2 := e2 ; x1 := xsave
    end
    ```

- Equation and Conditions:

    $h(\alpha,h(\beta,\gamma)) \equiv h(\beta,h(\alpha,\gamma))$
    x1 does not occur free in h or b
    x2 does not occur free in h or b

───────────────────── Example: Set Union ─────────────────────

The concrete set union function:

type
    E
value
    set_union: **E-set** × **E-set** → **E-set**
    set_union(s1,s2) ≡
        if s1={}
            then s2
            else
                result := choose(s1) ∪. set_union(s1 \. choose(s1),s2)
        end

    choose: **E-set** → E

given two identical sets, s and s', selects
the same e:E in s and s': choose(s) $\equiv$ choose(s')

∪. : E × E-set → E-set

\. : E-set × E → E-set

is an instance of Schema 2. We get:

```
result := s2 ;
while s1≠{} do
    result := choose(s1) ∪. result ;
    s1 := s1 \. choose(s1)
end
```

_____ Schema 3 _____

- **Recursion Schema:**

    f(x) $\equiv$ **if** a **then** b **else** h(f(d1),f(d2)) **end**

_____ Transformation 3.I _____

- **Iterative Schema:**

    ```
    result := b ; xsave := x ; x := "unique x such that a" ;
    while ~a do
        x := "inverse of d1"(x) ; result := h(result,result)
    end
    ```

- **Equation and Conditions:**

    d1 = d2

    x does not occur free in h or b. There is a unique x such that a
    exists and such that the inverse of d1 exists.

_____ Transformation 3.II _____

- **Iterative Schema:**

    ```
    y1 := b ; y2 := b ; result := b ;
    while ~a do
        result := h(y1,y2) ; y1 := y2 ; y2 := result ; x := d
    ```

end

- Equations:

    $h(\alpha,h(\beta,\gamma)) \equiv h(\beta,h(\alpha,\gamma))$
    d1 $\equiv$ d2 **with** every occurrence **of** x replaced by d2

_____ Example: Fibonacci Function _____

The Fibonacci function:

   $fib(n) \equiv$ **if** n=0∨n=1 **then** 1 **else** fib(n−1) + fib(n−2) **end**

is an example of Schema 3.II. We get:

   y1 := 1 ; y2 := 1 ; result := 1 ;
   while ∼(n=0∨n=1) **do**
       result := y1 + y2 ; y1 := y2 ; y2 := result ; x := n − 1
   end

_____ Transformation 3.III _____

- Iterative Schema:

       result := b ;
       while ∼a **do**
           result := h(result,result) ; x := d1
       end

- Equation and Condition:

       d1 $\equiv$ d2
       x does not occur free **in** h or b

_____ Schema 4 _____

- Recursion Schema:

       $f(x) \equiv$ **if** a **then** b **else** h(f(d)) **end**

_____ Transformation 4.I _____

- Iterative Schema:

while ~a **do** x := d **end** ; result b

- Equations:

  h ≡ λ x•x

_____ Transformation 4.II _____

- Iterative Schema:

  result := b ; xsave := x ; x := "unique x such that a" ;
  while x ≠ xsave **do**
      x := "inverse of d"(x) ; result := h(result)
  end

- Conditions:

  x does not occur free in h or b. There is a unique x such that a
  exists and such that the inverse of d exists.

_____ Schema 5 _____

- Recursion Schema:

  f(x,y) ≡ **if** a **then** b **else** h(f(d1,d2)) **end**

_____ Transformation _____

- Iterative Schema:

  while ~a **do**
      xsave := d1 ; y := d2 ; x := xsave
  end
  result := b

- Equations:

  h ≡ λ x•x

We do not illustrate examples of uses of all schemas, but refer the reader to
works by Cooper [160], Strong [488], and Burstall and Darlington [142, 173,
174].

20.5.4 Correctness, Principles, Techniques and Tools

Characterisation. By *correctness of transformation* we mean that the imperative function's result value is identical to the applicative function application value. ∎

This is not proved for the individual schema above. We refer to [142, 160, 173, 174, 488] for examples of such proofs.

Principles. *Translations from Applicative Function Definitions into Imperative Function Definitions:* Usually we start with sorts, observer and selector function signatures and axioms over these. That is, we begin purely axiomatically. Then we "transform" into applicative, typically recursive function definitions. After that we transform to imperative definitions, including iterative ones. ∎

20.6 Styles of Configuration Modelling

In the model-oriented style of abstraction there are a number of styles of specifying contexts and states using the sequential style in up to four variations, of which we illustrate three:

- both *applicative* contexts and states, Example 20.2
- combinations of *applicative* contexts and *imperative* states, Example 20.3
- and both *imperative* contexts and states, Example 20.4

We shall now examine these modelling styles. The examination will be wrt. a fragment, basically imperative programming language, very much in the style of the imperative parts of RSL.

20.6.1 Applicative Contexts and States

We now formalise the context and state concepts of the RSL-like language introduced above. We start with a model that is expressed in the applicative (i.e., functional) style.

Example 20.2 *An Applicative Context and State Style Model:*

Syntactic and Semantic Types

As usual, we start by defining the syntactic and semantic types. In this example we start with the syntactic types — since the readers and the designers are normally expected to be rather familiar with conventional programming languages we bring the semantic types second. Normally it is advisable to first design the semantic types.

Syntactic Types

type
0. VarDef = V × Expr
1. Stmt == Asg(v:V,e:Expr)
2. | donothing
3. | Lst(sl:Stmt*)
4. | Cnd(e:Expr,ts:Stmt,fs:Stmt)
5. | Whi(e:Expr,s:Stmt)
6. | Rep(s:Stmt,e:Expr)
7. | Cas(e:Expr,cl:(Bind × Stmt)*)
8. | For(b:Bind,le:Expr,pe:Expr,s:Stmt)

Semantic Types:

ρ:ENV = (Id $\overrightarrow{m}$ VAL) ∪ (V $\overrightarrow{m}$ LOC)
σ:Σ = LOC $\overrightarrow{m}$ Val
Val = VAL | Val*
VAL = **Int** | **Bool** | ... | Ω

The Identifiers (mentioned in the environment) are those of formal function parameters and let and case expression and statement bindings. The Variables (mentioned in the environment) are those of declared variable names. ENV is the context; Σ is the state.

We separate out as *auxiliary* function definitions those of gL: obtain (get) a free location, i.e., a location of storage not yet in use; AEnv: extend (override) the environment — seen as a form of "allocate"; AStg: allocate storage (space and initialize); and gV: obtain (get) value from storage location. These auxiliary functions will be redefined as we move from applicative to imperative style specifications. And one new auxiliary function will be added later. Comparing these auxiliary function definitions reveals a lot about the essence of the individual styles.

Auxiliary Functions

value
    gL: Σ → LOC
    gL(σ) ≡ **let** l:LOC • l $\notin$ **dom** σ **in** l **end**

    AEnv: ENV → ENV → ENV
    AEnv(env)ρ ≡ ρ † env

    AStg: Σ → Σ $\overset{\sim}{\rightarrow}$ Σ
    AStg(stg)σ ≡ σ ∪ stg

$gV: V \rightarrow ENV \overset{\sim}{\rightarrow} \Sigma \overset{\sim}{\rightarrow} VAL$
$gV(v)\rho\sigma \equiv \sigma(\rho(v))$

Simple Interpretation Functions

$V: VarDef \rightarrow ENV \overset{\sim}{\rightarrow} \Sigma \overset{\sim}{\rightarrow} \Sigma \times ENV$
$E: Expr \rightarrow ENV \overset{\sim}{\rightarrow} \Sigma \overset{\sim}{\rightarrow} Val$
$I: Stmt \rightarrow ENV \overset{\sim}{\rightarrow} \Sigma \overset{\sim}{\rightarrow} \Sigma$

$V(v,e)\rho\sigma \equiv$
   let $l = gL(\sigma)$, $val = E(e)\rho\sigma$ **in**
   $(AStg([l\mapsto val])\sigma, AEnv([v\mapsto l])\rho)$ **end**

E: almost as defined above, but without dynamic tests!
$E(v)\rho\sigma \equiv gV(v)\rho\sigma, ..., $ etc.

$I(Asg(v,e))\rho\sigma \equiv \sigma \dagger [\rho(v) \mapsto E(e)\rho\sigma]$

$I(donothing)\rho\sigma \equiv \sigma$

Composite Interpretation Functions

$I(Lst(sl))\rho\sigma \equiv$ **if** $sl=\langle\rangle$ **then** σ **else** $(I(tl\ sl)\rho)(I(hd\ sl)\sigma)$ **end**

$I(Cnd(e,c,a))\rho\sigma \equiv$ **if** $E(e)\rho\sigma$ **then** $I(s)\rho\sigma$ **else** $I(a)\rho\sigma$ **end**

$I(Whi(e,s))\rho\sigma \equiv$ **if** $E(e)\rho\sigma$ **then** $(I(Whi(e,s))\rho)(I(c)\rho\sigma)$ **else skip end**

$I(Rep(s,e))\rho\sigma \equiv (I(Whi(e,s))\rho)(I(s)\rho\sigma)$

Context-Creating Interpretation Functions

$I(Cas(e,cl))\rho\sigma \equiv$ **let** $v = E(e)\rho\sigma$ **in** $M(v,cl)\rho\sigma$ **end**

$M: Val \times Case^* \overset{\sim}{\rightarrow} ENV \overset{\sim}{\rightarrow} \Sigma \overset{\sim}{\rightarrow} \Sigma$
$M(v,cl)\rho\sigma \equiv$
   if $cl=\langle\rangle$ **then chaos else**
   let $(b,s) =$ **hd** cl **in let** $(t,env) = B(b,v)$ **in**
   if t **then** $I(s)(AEnv(env)\rho)\sigma$ **else** $M(v,tl\ cl)\rho\sigma$ **end**

end end end

$I(For(b,le,pe,s))\rho\sigma \equiv \textbf{let } vl = E(le)\rho\sigma \textbf{ in } S(b,vl,pe,s)\rho\sigma \textbf{ end}$

$S: Bind \times VAL^* \times Expr \times Stmt \overset{\sim}{\to} ENV \overset{\sim}{\to} \Sigma \overset{\sim}{\to} \Sigma$
$S(b,vl,pe,s)\rho\sigma \equiv$
    if $vl=\langle\rangle$ **then** σ **else**
    let $(\_,env) = B(b,\textbf{hd } vl)$ **in**
    if $E(pe)(AEnv(env)\rho)\sigma$
        then $S(b,\textbf{tl } vl,pe,s)(\rho)(I(s)(AEnv(env)\rho)\sigma)$
        else $S(b,\textbf{tl } vl,pe,s)\rho\sigma$ **end**
    end end

We comment on the applicative context and state model. ρ : ENV models the context. σ : Σ models the state. The computation intervalS of variables are "indefinite": from the point at which a variable is allocated till "the end of time" or when and if a *free variable* action could or would occur, whichever comes first. At any textual point there is a pair (ρ,σ) "at work": It is the configuration at that point. The fact that there may be a number of invocations of the interpretation functions E, I, M and S extant, i.e., "alive" — as seen from the point of view of the machine which performs the interpretation according to the interpretation function definitions — relates to a notion of meta-metastate of the interpreter machine, not to the notion of context and state of the "thing" (here a language fragment) being modelled. ∎

Summary, Applicative Contexts and States

We have shown that the concepts of context and state can be suitably separated and treated as separable parts of a specification, but that they relate. That is, when a variable location has been obtained and is being state allocated, then its binding to a variable name in a context (i.e., an environment) is expressed "at the same time"! We have also shown that obtaining a variable value is expressed as the "double application" of a state to the result of applying a context to a name.

    We have further illustrated that the context concept is syntactic: For any point of a specification in some (formal) language, and for any system, there is a statically knowable number of names (identifiers) being defined by (or therein). Furthermore, the state concept is temporal: For any point of a specification in some (formal) language, and for any system, the state value is only knowable at run time, i.e., when exercising the system (prescribed by the specification).

Characterisation. By an *applicative context* we understand a concept of context which has been modelled in the functional style. ∎

Characterisation. By an *applicative state* we understand a concept of state which has been modelled in the functional style.   ∎

Techniques. *Applicative Contexts:* Usually we model an applicative context as a simple Cartesian product (i.e., grouping) of a fixed number of context components, when their number is a priori fixed and known, or as a simple set or list of context components or a map of context component names to (context or possibly state) component associations — when the number of components is definite and knowable, but where contexts and components may change, thereby bringing change in the "size" of context.   ∎

The Cartesian context components may themselves be lists, sets or maps.

Techniques. *Applicative States:* Usually we model an applicative state either as a simple Cartesian product (i.e., grouping) of a fixed number of state components — when their number is a priori fixed and known — or as a simple set or list of state components or a map of state components to (state) component associations — when the number of components is indefinite and otherwise depends on the designated (the prescribed) behaviours (of specification interpretations or of systems).   ∎

The Cartesian state components may themselves be lists, sets or maps.

Techniques. *Applicative Contexts vs. State Function Arguments:* When defining functions that apply to contexts and states — besides other arguments — these latter are listed as first the formal parameters, then the context and finally the state.   ∎

20.6.2 Applicative Contexts and Imperative States

We continue now with a combined applicative and imperative model of the state concept of the RSL-like language.

Example 20.3 *An Applicative Context and Imperative State Style Model:*
We continue with the same syntactic types as were defined earlier (cf. Example 20.2). While the binding of variable names and binding identifiers remain "stable" over the interpretation of syntactically well-defined specification texts, the storage will (usually) change for every statement being interpreted within that text. We therefore introduce a storage **variable stg**, of **type** Σ, our first metastate component, and change the gL, AStg, gV, V, E, I, M and S function definitions accordingly. Note that the metastate is the aggregation of specification declared **variables** and their values. In this case the metastate reflects (colloquially: "is the same as") the state of the modelled language fragment.

Metastate and Auxiliary Functions

variable
  stg:Σ := [];
value
  gL: **Unit** → **read** stg LOC
  gL() ≡ **let** l:LOC • l ∉ **dom** stg **in** l **end**

  AEnv: ENV → ENV → ENV
  AEnv(env)ρ ≡ ρ † env /* Unchanged ! */

  AStg: Σ → **read** stg **write** stg **Unit**
  AStg(σ) ≡ stg := stg ∪ σ

  gV: V → ENV $\xrightarrow{\sim}$ **read** stg VAL
  gV(v)ρ ≡ stg(ρ(v))

Simple Interpretation Functions

  V: VarDef → ENV $\xrightarrow{\sim}$ **read** stg **write** stg ENV
  E: Expr → ENV $\xrightarrow{\sim}$ **read** stg **write** stg Val
  I: Stmt → ENV $\xrightarrow{\sim}$ **read** stg **write** stg **Unit**

  V(v,e)ρ ≡
      let l = gL(), val = E(e)ρ **in**
      AStg([l↦val]); AEnv([v↦l])ρ **end**

  E(v)ρ() ≡ gV(v)ρ

  I(Asg(v,e))ρ ≡ stg := stg † [ρ(v) ↦ E(e)ρ]
  I(donothing)ρ ≡ **skip**

Composite Interpretation Functions

  I(Lst(sl))ρ ≡ **if** sl=⟨⟩ **then** **skip** **else** I(hd sl)ρ;I(tl sl)ρ **end**

  I(Cnd(e,c,a))ρ ≡ **if** E(e)ρ **then** I(c)ρ **else** I(a)ρ **end**

  I(Whi(e,s))ρ ≡ **while** E(e)ρ **do** I(s)ρ **end**

  I(Rep(s,e))ρ ≡ I(s)ρ;I(Whi(e,s))ρ

Context-Creating Interpretation Functions

$I(Cas(e,cl))\rho \equiv$ **let** $v = E(e)\rho$ **in** $M(v,cl)\rho$ **end**

$M: Val \times Case^* \overset{\sim}{\to} ENV \overset{\sim}{\to}$ **read** stg **write** stg **Unit**
$M(v,cl)\rho \equiv$
    if $cl=\langle\rangle$ **then chaos else**
    let $(b,s) =$ **hd** cl **in let** $(t,env) = B(b,v)$ **in**
    if t **then** $I(s)(AEnv(env)\rho)$ **else** $M(v,$**tl** $cl)\rho$ **end**
    end end end

$I(For(b,le,pe,s))\rho \equiv$ **let** $vl = E(le)\rho$ **in** $S(b,vl,pe,s)\rho$ **end**

$S: Bind \times VAL^* \times Expr \times Stmt \overset{\sim}{\to} ENV \overset{\sim}{\to}$ **read** stg **write** stg **Unit**
$S(b,vl,pe,s)\rho \equiv$
    if $vl=\langle\rangle$ **then skip else**
    let $(,env) = B(b,$**hd** $vl)$ **in**
    if $E(pe)(AEnv(env)\rho)$
        then $(I(s)(AEnv(env)\rho);S(b,$**tl** $vl,pe,s)\rho)$
        else $S(b,$**tl** $vl,pe,s)\rho$ **end**
    end end

We comment on the applicative context and imperative state model. As before, $\rho : ENV$ models the context. Now stg $: \Sigma$ models the state, and is itself a state component of the model, i.e., is the metastate. And, as before, $(\rho:ENV,stg:\Sigma)$ models configurations.

Notice, by inspecting, line by line, and pairwise, the interpretation functions (V, E, I, M, S), the way in which arguments "disappear" (being replaced by reference to a global metastate) and the way in which the interpretation functions (typically the composite) are structured wrt. their composite syntactical arguments. The above remarks apply equally well to the next — the imperative context and state style — model. ∎

Summary, Applicative Contexts and Imperative States

We have continued our demonstration of applicative contexts, but have modelled states imperatively. The model state component is now being represented by a specification metastate component. Now the explicit state parameter of applicative state models has disappeared, being replaced by references to a global metastate component. In an imperative state model it is less obvious, where in a specification state, changes are prescribed, but the number of interpretation and auxiliary function arguments is usually smaller, and often significantly so! It is still obvious where, in a specification context, changes are prescribed and where no changes are prescribed.

Characterisation. By an *imperative state* we mean a concept of state which has been modelled in the imperative style.   ∎

Techniques. *Imperative States:* In abstract specifications, it really is a matter of style as to when to model a state imperatively: you must weigh the number of arguments (more for applicative, fewer for imperative), and the number and style of interpretation and auxiliary function definitions. Usually, however, the choice of state modelling moves from applicative to imperative as we reify (develop) our specification into more concrete, more executable designs.   ∎

20.6.3 Imperative Contexts and States

We finish our sequence of three context/state model styles with an imperative model of the RSL-like language.

Example 20.4 *An Imperative Context and State Style Model:*
We continue with the same syntactic types as were defined earlier (cf. Example 20.2). Environments obey a stack-property: Whenever a binding is processed, a "new" environment is created. Its computation interval is that piece of text to which it is applied (by the interpreter). "Surrounding" text interpretation takes place in an "old" environment. We therefore decide to also introduce a **variable** env_stk, of **type** ENV*, to change the gV, AEnv, V, E, I, M and S functions accordingly, and to introduce a new auxiliary function: FEnv: Free Environment. As AEnv now "stacks" (pushes onto the environment stack) a new environment, FEnv "un-stacks" (pops) that environment.

The metastate now models the configuration concept of the language fragment whose semantics is being (operationally) specified.

Metastate

variable
    env_stk:ENV* := ⟨[ ]⟩;
    stg:Σ := [ ];

Auxiliary Functions

value
    gL: **Unit** → **read** stg LOC
    gL() ≡ **let** l:LOC • l ∉ **dom** stg **in** l **end** /∗ Unchanged ∗/

    AEnv: ENV → **read** env_stk **write** env_stk **Unit**
    AEnv(env) ≡ env_stk := ⟨**hd** env_stk † env⟩⌢env_stk

FEnv: **Unit** → **read** env_stk **write** env_stk **Unit**
FEnv() ≡ env_stk := **tl** env_stk /* New! */

AStg: Σ → **read** stg **write** stg **Unit**
AStg(σ) ≡ stg := stg ∪ σ /* Unchanged */

gV: V $\overset{\sim}{\to}$ **read** stg,env_stk VAL
gV(v) ≡ stg((**hd** env_stk)(v))

Simple Interpretation Functions

V: VarDef → **read,write** env_stk,stg **Unit**
E: Expr → **read,write** env_stk,stg Val
I: Stmt → **read,write** env_stk,stg **Unit**

V(v,e) ≡ **let** l = gL(), val = E(e) **in** AStg([l↦val]); AEnv([v↦l]) **end**

E(v) ≡ gV(v)

I(Asg(v,e)) ≡ stg := stg † [(**hd** env_stk)(v) ↦ E(e)]

I(donothing) ≡ **skip**

Composite Interpretation Functions

I(Lst(sl)) ≡ **if** sl=⟨⟩ **then skip else** I(hd sl);I(tl sl) **end**

I(Cnd(e,c,a)) ≡ **if** E(e) **then** I(c) **else** I(a) **end**

I(Whi(e,s)) ≡ **while** E(e) **do** I(s) **end**

I(Rep(s,e)) ≡ I(s);I(Whi(e,s))

Context-Creating Interpretation Functions

I(Cas(e,cl)) ≡ **let** v = E(e) **in** M(v,cl) **end**

M: Val × Case* $\overset{\sim}{\to}$ **read,write** env_stk,stg **Unit**
M(v,cl) ≡

> **if** cl=⟨⟩ **then chaos else**
> **let** (b,s) = **hd** cl **in let** (t,env) = B(b,v) **in**
> **if** t
>   **then** (AEnv(env);I(s);FEnv())
>   **else** M(v,**tl** cl) **end**
> **end end end**

$I(For(b,le,pe,s)) \equiv$ **let** vl = E(le) **in** S(b,vl,pe,s) **end**

> S: Bind × VAL* × Expr × Stmt $\overset{\sim}{\to}$ **read,write** env_stk,stg **Unit**
> S(b,vl,pe,s) $\equiv$
>   **if** vl=⟨⟩ **then skip else**
>   **let** (,env) = B(b,**hd** vl) **in**
>   AEnv(env);
>   **if** E(pe)
>   **then** (I(s);FEnv();S(b,**tl** vl,pe,s))
>   **else** (FEnv();S(b,**tl** vl,pe,s))
>   **end end end**

We comment on the imperative context and state model. Now the top of the environment stack, **hd** env_stk:ENV, models the context. stg : Σ still models the state, and thus remains a state component of the model. And, as before, (**hd** env_stk:ENV,stg:Σ) models configurations. The metastate, env_stk:ENV*,stg:Σ, is just that. Notice the explicit stacking and un-stacking of environments. The specification text between a "closest" such pair of allocate and free environment actions (AEnv, respectively FEnv) models the scope of a binding, that is, its context.   ∎

Summary, Imperative Contexts and States

We have seen how the block-structured concepts of specification of text names to their designations (incl. denotations) is modelled imperatively, and as stacks, that is, reflecting the block structure, i.e., the nested or embedded or scope-limited redefinitional nature of such concepts. And we have seen how the beginning and ending of a context, i.e., of a scope of the defined names, lead to matching pairs of stacking and un-stacking of contexts. Now it may be less obvious as to where, in a specification, a context is defined, used and "ends" — unless one is careful in finding suitable "expressional" ways of designating the pairs of stackings and un-stackings.

Characterisation. By an *imperative context* we understand a concept of context modelled in the imperative style.   ∎

Techniques. *Imperative Contexts (I):* We usually model contexts imperatively as we develop our abstract specifications (where the contexts usually were applicatively modelled) into more concrete specifications, that is, as we move closer to, or develop actual software designs.   ∎

Techniques. *Imperative Block-Structured Contexts (II):* Contexts may be recursively defined, as are the bindings of names to their designations in specification (hence also programming) languages. In such cases imperative contexts are usually modelled as stacks of context models.   ∎

Techniques. *Imperative Block-Structured Contexts (III):* To help the reader to more easily observe that a block-structured context concept "is at play" in an imperative definition, we advise that suitable auxiliary stack (allocate) and un-stack (free) functions be defined and deployed.   ∎

20.6.4 Summary of Sequential Models

The three models shown so far have all had 'sequentiality' in common: The applicative style 'sequentiality' is illustrated by **let** $a = b$ **in** c **end** and more generally, by the 'call-by-value', 'inside-out' and 'left-to-right' evaluation of expressions The imperative style 'sequentiality' is illustrated by 'left-to-right' interpretation of RSL: statement lists, structured statements and assignment statements.

20.7 Review and Discussion

20.7.1 Review

We introduced the imperative language constructs of RSL. We sketched their mathematical meaning — in terms of state-to-state changing functions — in some form of λ-notation. We then discussed notions of location values: Values that are references to storage cells keeping other values; and we showed, in an extensive example, how to model a "toy" programming language having reference values. We then showed how to relate certain simple forms of applicative function definitions to similarly simple imperative function definitions. Finally, we modelled another simple "toy" programming language, which exhibits scope of identifiers, in three different styles: applicatively, imperatively and a "mix" of both. These last three models, in a slightly different order, also exemplified the notion, and thus reinforced our understanding, of contexts (environments) and states (storages).

20.7.2 Discussion

Which is a "better" style of programming: functional, as in `Standard ML` (`SML`), or imperative, as in `Fortran`? We believe that it does not make sense to try to answer this question by nominating either of the two styles as a "winner". It may seem, on first study, that functional programming is so much more "clean", elegant, expressive, and as versatile as imperative programming. But then the laws of imperative programming are as beautiful as are those of functional programming, to wit: [290, 449].

What separates the two styles of programming wrt. actual languages is not that one is functional, and the other is imperative, but that one offers data types that are more suitable for one kind of problem, and that the other offers other data types that are more suitable for other kinds of problems. Thus — as an example — `Standard ML` (`SML`) offers language constructs to go with its special offering of data types that have proven to be very useful in specifying computations over structured values: trees, records, etc. On the other hand `Fortran` is still considered, by some, to be most appropriate for scientific computations involving arrays (vectors, matrices, etc.) of floating-point data. The moral: We need many different kinds of programming, as well as specification languages.

20.8 Bibliographical Notes

There are four main sets of references to be made at this point.

20.8.1 Theory of Computation

First there are the references to the work of John McCarthy, [365–368]:

- Recursive Functions of Symbolic Expressions and Their Computation by Machines. *Communications of the ACM* 3(4):184–195, 1960 [365].
- Towards a Mathematical Science of Computation. In C.M. Popplewell, editor, *IFIP World Congress Proceedings*, pp. 21–28, 1962 [366].
- A Basis for a Mathematical Theory of Computation. In *Computer Programming and Formal Systems*. North-Holland, Amsterdam, 1963 [367].
- A Formal Description of a Subset of ALGOL. in *Formal Language Description Languages,* IFIP TC-2 Work. Conf., Baden. Ed. T.B. Steel. North-Holland, Amsterdam, 1966 [368].

20.8.2 A Type Theory for the λ-Calculus

Then there are the references to the works of Christopher Strachey and Dana Scott [463, 469]. We only mention two:

- D.S. Scott and C. Strachey. Towards a Mathematical Semantics for Computer Languages. In *Computers and Automata*, Vol. 21 of *Microwave Research Inst. Symposia*, pp. 19–46, 1971.
- D.S. Scott. Outline of a Mathematical Theory of Computation. In *Proc. 4th Ann. Princeton Conf. on Inf. Sci. and Sys.*, p. 169, 1970.

20.8.3 Source Program Transformation Works

There are basically two schools of thought to refer to here, the Burstall–Darlington school, which we have followed [142, 173, 174]:

- J. Darlington and R. M. Burstall. A System Which Automatically Improves Programs. *Acta Informatica*, 6:41–60, 1976 [174].
- R. M. Burstall and J. Darlington. A Transformation System for Developing Recursive Programs. *Journal of ACM*, 24(1):44–67, 1977 [142].
- J. Darlington. A Synthesis of Several Sorting Algorithms. *Acta Informatica*, 11:1–30, 1978 [173].

and the Munich CIP project as covered in [35]:

- F.L. Bauer: Program Development by Stepwise Transformations — The Project CIP. Appendix: Programming Languages Under Educational and Under Professional Aspects, pp. 237–272.
- F.L. Bauer, M. Broy, H. Partsch, P. Pepper, H. Wössner: Systematics of Transformation Rules, pp. 273–289.
- H. Wössner, P. Pepper, H. Partsch, F.L. Bauer: Special Transformation Techniques, pp. 290–321.
- P. Pepper: A Study on Transformational Semantics, pp. 322–405.
- F.L. Bauer: Detailization and Lazy Evaluation, Infinite Objects and Pointer Representation, pp. 406–420.
- H. Partsch, M. Broy: Examples for Change of Types and Object Structures, pp. 421–463.

20.8.4 Laws of Imperative Programming

Finally there is a reference to work by Hoare et al. on laws of imperative programming [290]:

- C.A.R. Hoare, I.J. Hayes, J.F. He, C.C. Morgan, A.W. Roscoe, J.W. Sanders, I.H. Sørensen, J.M. Spivey, and B. Sufrin. Laws of Programming. *Communications of the ACM* 30(8):672–686, 770, 1987.

We find these references to have formed an important basis for and a summary of many of the facets covered in the present chapter.

20.9 Exercises

We give only a few exercises, but they are a bit on the large side. We trust that lecturers using this text can make up simple exercises requiring imperative solutions. The function definitions of the exercises of this chapter are basically to be expressed in the imperative style.

Exercises 20.1, 20.2 and 20.3 are preceded by Exercises 19.1, 19.2 and 19.3, respectively. They are continued in Exercises 21.5, 21.6 and 21.7, respectively.

• • •

Exercise 20.1. *The Grocery Store, II.* You are basically asked to repeat Exercise 19.1, but now on the basis of an imperative state. We suggest that any configuration component that is either changed (as a state component), or is often referred to (as a context component), be made into a variable component. Thus, a suggestion is to maintain the following variables: (i) The warehouse, (ii) the store, (iii) a set, clients, of uniquely identified clients — embodying, in principle, only their purse, i.e., some monies — (iv) with their shopping carts and (v) their bags, and (vi) the check-out counter, which essentially contains the cash register, the wholesaler inventories and their wholesaler cash registers. Now, redefine the functions that were given as solutions to Exercise 19.1, but now in the imperative style.

In the applicative definition style all state component values were arguments to many, and results of many defined functions. In the present, imperative style definition these state component values need to be given an initial value to be assigned to respective variables.

If you believe that the above description is incomplete, please state why, and provide the completing text.

The present exercise is to be solved in the concurrent style in Exercise 21.9.

Exercise 20.2. *The Anarchic Factory, II.* We refer to Exercise 19.2; please read the problem formulation texts of those exercises carefully.

Now, in this version of a formalisation of the factory model you are to convert the configuration (context and state) components into state variables. A suggestion is to maintain the following state components in terms of variables: (i) the inventory, (iii) the trucks, which is a set of uniquely identified trucks, (ii) the cells, which is also a set of uniquely identified production cells, and (iv) the product warehouse. The rest is as in Exercise 19.2, formalise the non-deterministic single state transition function and the function that iterates over a(n entire) production plan, etc.

The present exercise is to be solved in the concurrent style in Exercise 21.10.

Exercise 20.3. *The Document System, II.* Please read the problem formulation texts of Exercise 19.3 carefully.

1. In this exercise make the system components:

(a) the set of all place directories a single global variable,

(b) the set of all place persons a single global variable,

(c) the set of all citizens a single global variable,

(d) the set of all document identifiers in use a single global variable, and

(e) the set of all dossier identifiers in use a single global variable.

2. Define all variable types clearly.

3. Now redefine the syntax of commands, replacing explicit mentioning of persons, documents, dossiers and locations by their identifiers.

4. And redefine, in the imperative style, all semantic interpretation functions.

The present exercise is to be solved in the concurrent style in Exercise 21.11.

Exercise 20.4. ♣ *An Imperative Domain Model of Transportation Nets.* We refer to Appendix A, Sect. A.1, *Transportation Net.*

We refer to Exercise 19.4. Please read the problem formulation of that exercise carefully.

You are basically asked to repeat Exercise 19.4, but now on the basis of an imperative state. We suggest that any configuration component that is either changed (as a state component), or is often referred to (as a context component), be made into a variable component. Thus, a suggestion is to maintain the following variables: (i) the static segments, (ii) the dynamic segments, (iii) the static connectors, (iv) the dynamic connectors, and (v) the graph of the network (i.e., the structure part of the net). Based on these five variables redefine the operations mentioned in items 3–5 of Exercise 19.4.

Exercise 20.5. ♣ *An Imperative Domain Model of Container Logistics.* We refer to Appendix A, Sect. A.2, *Container Logistics.*

We refer to Exercise 19.5. Please read the problem formulation of that exercise carefully.

You are basically asked to repeat Exercise 19.5, but now on the basis of an imperative state. We suggest that any configuration component that is either changed (as a state component), or is often referred to (as a context component), be made into a variable component. Thus, a suggestion is to maintain the following gloabal state variables: ships, the container storage area of a specific container terminal, and the quay of that terminal. Based on these three variables redefine the operations mentioned in items 3–11 of Exercise 19.5.

Exercise 20.6. ♣ *An Imperative Domain Model of Financial Service Industries.* We refer to Appendix A, Sect. A.3, *Financial Service Industry.*

We refer to Exercise 19.6. Please read the problem formulation of that exercises carefully.

You are basically asked to repeat Exercise 19.6, but now on the basis of an imperative state. We suggest that any configuration component that is either changed (as a state component), or is often referred to (as a context component), be made into a variable component. Thus, a suggestion is to maintain the following variables: client catalogue, account catalogue and accounts. Based on these three global state variables redefine the operations mentioned in items 1–2 of Exercise 19.6.

Concurrent Specification Programming

- The **prerequisites** for studying this chapter are that you have understood most, if not all, of what has been covered in previous chapters *and* you are interested in modelling concurrent behaviours.
- The **aims** are to motivate and introduce both simple CSP and the RAISE version of CSP, RSL/CSP, and to show a number of principles and techniques for modelling concurrent behaviours using RSL.
- The **objective** is to set the reader firmly on the road to modelling concurrent systems such as distributed systems, client/server systems, etc.
- The **treatment** is semiformal.

In this chapter we introduce a notation for expressing parallelism (also called concurrency): First we present a pure notation, a formal language, CSP: *Communicating Sequential Processes* [288, 289, 448, 456]. Then we present this notation's embedding in RSL.

Characterisation. By *concurrent programming* we shall understand programming with processes as a central notion: where processes are combined (in parallel) to form concurrent processes, where synchronous or asynchronous interaction between processes can be specified, and so on. ∎

Characterisation. By *parallel programming* we mean the same as *concurrent programming*. ∎

Characterisation. By *concurrent specification programming* we shall understand an abstract, property-oriented form of *concurrent programming*, one in which (relative or absolute) progress of processes is left unspecified, where choice between actions of proceses can be left unspecified (i.e., nondeterministic), and in which we deploy abstract types, and so on. ∎

In Vol. 2, Chaps. 12–14 we shall introduce three sets of predominantly graphical notations: *Petri Nets* [313, 421, 435–437], *Message Sequence Charts*

[302–304] and *Live Sequence Charts* [171, 270, 325], and *Statecharts* [265, 266, 268, 269, 271].

In this chapter we bring in a number of principles and techniques for modelling concurrent behaviours and the interaction between behaviours. We do so in a number of steps: First, in Sect. 21.1, we informally examine some basic notions of behaviours. Then, in Sect. 21.2, on a per intuition basis, we present some behaviour scenarios and show their possible formalisation using RSL's CSP sublanguage. But this sublanguage is not formally introduced. Following that, in Sect. 21.3, we present the "bare bones" of CSP. After all these preliminaries we introduce, more systematically, the RSL/CSP sublanguage in Sect. 21.4, and, in Sect. 21.5, we suggest a calculus for transforming applicative, respectively imperative, RSL specifications into RSL/CSP specifications. In Vol. 2, Chap. 15 we cover extensions to the RSL/CSP sublanguage. These allow us to deal with "real time" and with time durations. Throughout we present many examples.

21.1 Behaviour and Process Abstractions

Characterisation. *Behaviour* is defined in Merriam–Webster's Collegiate Dictionary [373]: *(i) the manner of conducting oneself, (ii) anything that an organism does involving action and response to stimulation, (iii) the response of an individual, group, or species to its environment, (iv) the way in which someone behaves, an instance of such behavior, (v) the way in which something functions or operates.*   ∎

By behaviour we shall understand the organism to be anything spanning from a human, via any phenomena in "Mother Nature", to an interpreter or a machine or a computer.

Characterisation. Merriam–Webster [373] defines *process as (i) a natural phenomenon marked by gradual changes that lead toward a particular result, (ii) a natural continuing activity or function, (iii) a series of actions or operations conducing to an end, or more particularly (iv) a continuous operation or treatment especially in manufacture.*   ∎

We shall, more or less, take the two terms, 'behaviour' and 'process', as being synonymous. The only difference is a pragmatic one: When we use the term 'behaviour' we refer to an as yet unanalysed, hence not yet formalised, but otherwise precisely described understanding of some actual-world phenomenon. And when we refer to the term 'process' we refer to an analysed, precisely narrated and/or formalised specification of a behaviour, typically as we expect it to be more or less implemented by computer.

21.1.1 Introduction

Entities are the "things" we can point to: *bank accounts, trains, timetables, people, rail nets, etc.*. Entities can be subject to actions: queries concerning (i.e., observations of) their state, i.e., predicates and functions (viz.: *account balance, train speed, journey duration, etc.*); and also operations that possibly alter their states, i.e., generator functions (viz.: *deposit, accelerate, reschedule, etc.*).

Any particular entity can be seen from the point of view of the sequences of actions that apply to it (viz.: *open account, alternation of one or more deposits into or one or more withdrawals from the account, ended by a close account*). Such a sequence of actions may, for certain actions in the sequence, involve two or more entities for which other action sequences are defined (viz.: *transfer between accounts, running train according to timetable schedule, etc.*). We therefore see that action sequences may interact. In this section we shall investigate means for describing interaction sequences, or as they are also called, behaviours or processes. That is, we shall otherwise — with the above caveat in mind — in general, treat the two terms behaviour and process synonymously.

There are many examples in this chapter. You may wish to "scan" the section to get an immediate, informal grasp of the ideas discussed in it. The various forms of text between the examples — *section, paragraph and other headers, definitions, comments, principles, techniques* and other text — should reasonably directly inform you!

21.1.2 On Process and Other Abstractions

In *abstraction* and in *modelling* we have at our disposal a number of abstraction styles. These are either property-oriented (cf. Sect. 12.2) or model-oriented (cf. Sect. 12.4). Within the former we usually speak of *algebraic* or *axiomatic* (cf. Sects. 8.5, respectively 9.6) abstractions. Axiomatically and algebraically expressed models differ less materially than do denotationally and computationally expressed models. Within the latter we can distinguish between *denotation* abstraction (cf. Vol. 2, Sect. 3.2) and *computation* abstraction (cf. Vol. 2, Sect. 3.3).

In this section we shall introduce yet another form of abstraction and modelling: it is *operational* (as are computation models). Do not confuse operation abstraction with operational abstraction. In *operation abstraction* we abstract *individual* (usually basic, i.e., primitive) *operations* (i.e., functions and predicates) over abstracted entities. In *operational abstraction* we focus upon, but do not necessarily detail, specific *sequences of operations* of a system.

Denotation abstraction (Vol. 2, Chap. 3, Sect. 3.3.3) was first introduced around 1970 in order to model the meaning of computer programs, typically of imperative languages. The *denotation* of a computer program is then seen as some mathematical function. *Denotation abstraction* can, however, also be applied to other than computing concepts. We shall elsewhere in these volumes illustrate the denotation abstraction of facets of banks, aspects of railways, etc.

Computation abstraction (Vol. 2, Chap. 3, Sect. 3.3.3) was likewise first introduced around 1964 in order to model abstract executions of computer programs. The term *computation abstraction* emphasises the concept computation. In the actual world we may not think of some phenomena as computations, but rather as sequences of actions. In this case we prefer to use the term *operational abstraction* when modelling the sequence aspect of these sequences of actions.

When seemingly independent, concurrently operating phenomena (i.e., processes) occasionally interact, and when we wish to model both the concurrency and the interaction, then we apply *process abstraction*. So *process abstraction* is a more general form of *operational abstraction*. Several tools and techniques are offered for the modelling of processes:

- The CSP-oriented techniques and tools where a system of processes is defined in terms of abstract, textual programs (Sects. 21.2–21.4). Seminal references to CSP are [288, 289, 448, 456].
- The Petri net-oriented techniques and tools, where a system of processes is defined in terms of a diagrammatic net of places, transitions and tokens (Vol. 2, Chap. 12 and [313, 421, 435–437]).
- The statechart-oriented techniques and tools, where a system of processes is defined in terms of a diagrammatic net of iteratively embedded groupings of boxes of state machines with transitions between states and or boxes (Vol. 2, Chap. 14 and [265, 266, 268, 269, 271]).
- The live sequence chart-oriented techniques and tools by means of which statecharts are "glued" together and external protocols are imposed on otherwise "freely" occurring ("external") events (Vol. 2, Chap. 13 and [171, 270, 325]).

In this chapter we shall exclusively illustrate some process concepts using the CSP-approach — couched, however, in the RSL/CSP subset.

21.2 Intuition

We shall discuss the behaviour (i.e., the process) concepts of this chapter.

21.2.1 Illustrative Rendezvous Scenarios

In this section we shall attempt to motivate and illustrate the notion of processes as partially independent, but interacting phenomena. In doing so we shall be introducing both informal, graphic and formal, textual notation. The formal (in this case some variant of CSP) notation will not (yet) be formally introduced — only by way of annotated examples. There will be many examples. We start by relating some scenarios.

Example 21.1 *Four Rendezvous Scenarios:* We present a number of scenarios. Their purpose is to let us introduce a number of process concepts and, informally, notation to go with these.

(1) ***One sender, one receiver.*** Two persons, P and Q, walk in opposite directions down a street, towards each other. One person, say P, carries a letter for the other person, Q. Some previous agreement, i.e., a protocol, has been established between the two persons that an exchange of a letter is to take place.[1] They walk, most likely, at different and, in any case, unpredictable speeds. The speeds may vary, and they may be zero. The letter deliverer and the letter receiver are willing to hand over, resp. to receive, i.e., to 'relay', the letter at any point. As they are walking, the two persons are not performing any activities other than walking and being willing to 'relay'. And as they meet — i.e., as they rendezvous — the delivering person "hands over" the letter which is simultaneously received by the receiving person. After they have relayed the letter they both walk on in their respective directions.

If either P or Q refuses to walk, then the combined process fails, i.e., *deadlocks.*

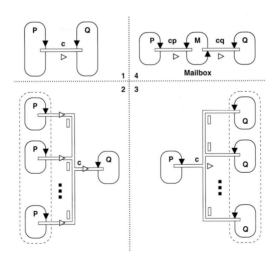

Fig. 21.1. Four schematic "rendezvous" classes

---

[1]The compositional aspects of each of the four kinds of "rendezvous" classes of the diagrams of Fig. 21.1 and of the four corresponding formal specifications "embody" this "agreement".

Variants on the scenario above could be:

(2) **Any sender, one receiver.** The letter sender may be any one of a number of willing persons, P_1, P_2, ..., P_m, but the letter, and then at most one, is receivable only by a specific person Q, say standing still on the street. We consider P_1, P_2, ..., P_m and Q as being processes. The various P_i are walking, each at their own speed, as was P in the previous scenario, but now in any direction, up or down, the street, and hence meeting Q sooner or later — with the first one so meeting delivering the letter.

If either Q refuses, or all P_i refuse to walk, then the combined process fails, i.e., *deadlocks*.

(3) **One sender, any receiver.** The letter sender, P, is thought of as a fixed person, say standing still on the street, but the letter may be received by the "first" of a number of willing recipients, Q_1, Q_2, ..., Q_n. We consider, i.e., we abstract P, Q_1, Q_2, ..., and Q_n as being processes. The various Q_i are walking, each at their own speed, as was Q in the previous scenario, but now in any direction, up or down, the street, and hence meeting P sooner or later — with the first one so meeting receiving the letter.

If either P refuses, or all Q_i refuse to walk, then the combined process fails, i.e., the combined process fails, or *deadlocks*.

(4) **Send/receive via a mailbox.** Letters are posted in an at most one letter capacity mailbox, M, by a sender, or any number of senders, and retrieved from that mailbox by a receiver, or any number of receivers. We consider P_1, P_2, ..., P_m Q_1, Q_2, ..., Q_n and M as being processes.

If no P_i puts a letter in the mailbox, then any Q_j attempting to fetch the letter *deadlocks*.

$$\bullet \quad \bullet \quad \bullet$$

Cyclic versions of the initial scenario and the three subsequent variations described above are illustrated in Fig. 21.1's respective four cases: 1–4. By a cyclic version we mean one in which we model the repeated behaviour: Scenarios (1–4) are repeated indefinitely. Thus scenario (1) could be rephrased: The same person P, after having delivered the letter to person Q, starts all over again, possibly after some other activities which we do not detail, i.e., from which we abstract, walking down the same street with a new letter for person Q, where that person again is ready, possibly after some other activities which we do not detail, i.e., from which we abstract, to receive a letter and indicates this willingness by again walking down that street! Similar rewordings can be made for scenarios 2–4.

We will explain the graphics of Fig. 21.1. For simplicity and generality we have shown all processes as rounded-edge boxes with arrows.

The thick line of the rounded-edge boxes is intended to designate a cyclic sequence of actions including the event-causing actions. The arrows are intended to show direction of execution (black) or communication (white). (We either place the arrows on or next to the action list or channel; and we either show these arrows for all instances or summarise them meaningfully, the latter as in case 3.) The horizontal bars "touching" ("overlapping") two or more boxes are intended to show synchronisation and communication rendezvous. The tiny rectangles ([]) along the rendezvous of parts **2** and **3** are intended to show nondeterministic choice as to from which of the (2) **P**'s (3, **Q**'s) **Q** (resp. **P**) will accept input. In part **4** the **mailbox** process **M** alternates between being ready to receive a letter from **P** and delivering that letter to **Q**. The four "box and arrow" diagrams of Fig. 21.1 correspond to the four sets of abstract process (i.e., function) definitions of the below Schematic "Rendezvous" Specifications 1–2–3 and Schematic "Rendezvous" Specification 4.

Schematic "Rendezvous" Specifications 1–2–3

type Info
channel c,cp,cq:Info
value
    P: **Unit** → **out** c **Unit**
    P() ≡ **let** i = write_letter() **in** c ! i **end** ; P()

    Q: **Unit** → **in** c **Unit**
    Q() ≡ **let** i = c ? **in** read_letter(i) **end** ; Q()

    write_letter: **Unit** → Info, read_letter: Info → **Unit**

    S1: **Unit** → **Unit**, S1() ≡ P() ‖ Q()
    S2: **Nat Unit** → **Unit**, S2(m) ≡ ‖ { P() | x:{1..m} } ‖ Q()
    S3: **Nat Unit** → **Unit**, S3(n) ≡ P() ‖ (‖ { Q() | x:{1..n} })

Process S1 is the parallel composition (‖) of processes P and Q. Process S2 is the parallel composition of process Q with the parallel, distributed composition of processes P, one for each index set 1..m. Process S3 is the parallel composition of process P with the parallel, distributed composition of processes Q, one for each index set 1..n.

Info is the type of the information contained in the letter. c is what is known as a channel between P and Q in parts 1–3. Channels allow pairs of processes to share events; cp and cq are the channels between P and M, respectively between M and Q. P writes a letter, hands it over on channel c to Q — as prescribed by the output [!] / input [?] pair (c ! i,c ?).

This is true in all parts 1–3. In part 1 it is simply so: Two processes (P and Q) share channel c, and thus share events. In part 2 many (m) processes P share the same channel c with one process Q. Q will not know which of the m P processes sent the letter to Q. In part 3 many (n) processes Q share same channel c with one process P. P will not know which of the n Q processes received the letter. All P and Q processes are cyclic: P produces letters, and Q consumes letters. They both cycle for each production, resp. consumption.

Schematic "Rendezvous" Specification 4

S4: **Unit** → **Unit**, S4() ≡ P'() ‖ M() ‖ Q'()

P': **Unit** → **out** cp **Unit**
P'() ≡ **let** i = write_letter() **in** cp ! i **end** ; P'()

M: **Unit** → **in** cp **out** cq **Unit**
M() ≡ **let** i = cp ? **in** cq ! i **end** ; M()

Q': **Unit** → **in** cq **Unit**
Q'() ≡ **let** i = cq ? **in** read_letter(i) **end** ; Q'()

Process P' now sends (i.e., drops) the letter to (i.e., in) mailbox M. The relation between P' and M is as between P and Q in part 1. Process q now receives (i.e., fetches) the letter from mailbox M. The relation between M and Q' is as between P and Q in part 1. Process M is a one-item buffer, it alternates between receiving and sending. It recycles for each pair of receive–sends. ∎

21.2.2 Diagram and Notation Summary

Example 21.1 thus served as more than just an example: It also, in a serious yet informal, manner introduced core concepts of CSP and hence RSL/CSP. As such, the reader is very strongly advised to study that example carefully.

So we have introduced the concepts of processes and their "rendezvous" output (!) and input (?) synchronisation and communication. We have sketched informal ways of picturing process structures (cf. Fig. 21.1); and we have informally shown formal notations (Figs. 21.1 and 21.1). Before going on to a more systematic, formal introduction of a (so-called "pure") notation for [T]CSP [288, 448, 456] and the corresponding CSP-like notation for the process concepts of RSL [236, 238], in Sects. 21.3 and 21.4, we will further review, illustrate and thus motivate the CSP process concepts.

21.2.3 On a Trace Semantics

In this section we provide a very rough sketch of a possible *semantics* of a CSP-like language. For authoritative, and certainly more proper, accounts of such semantics we refer to [288, 448, 456].

Actions change the data as well as the control state[2] and are thought of as taking place instantaneously, i.e., with no observable time duration.

---

[2]By a data state we understand "something" that records and remembers the values of various usually named data items, like a storage. By a control state we understand the interpreter's awareness of the point in a program cum specification text which is being interpreted by the interpreter.

Processes, from one viewpoint, can be said to be sequences of actions. *Events* are phenomena that also take place instantaneously, but which, in and by themselves, do not change the data state, but (usually) cause actions to take place, i.e., be "triggered", thereby changing the control state. *Processes*, from another viewpoint, can be said to be sequences of events and — if causing actions — then possibly also sequences of actions. A process can exchange information with another process through what we shall call synchronised events (Fig. 21.2). *Systems* may consist of many processes synchronising on events and exchanging (communicating) information during such synchronised 'rendezvous'.

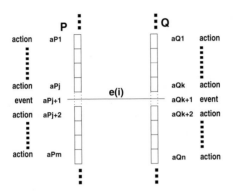

**Processes P and Q Rendezvous
to cause Event e(i) after respective
execution of Actions aPj, resp. aQk**

Fig. 21.2. Stylised "rendezvous" situation

The *behaviour* of systems can, for example, be the set of sequences (traces) of externally observable events, or can, more generally, be the set of traces of both externally and internally observable events.

For the conceptual example of Fig. 21.2 the system is that of the parallel ($\|$) combination of processes P and Q: P$\|$Q. The external behaviour is: $\{\langle e(i)\rangle\}$. The internal behaviour — expressed, as above, in some metalinguistic notation — is:

$$\{\{\langle\ aP1, \ldots, aPj\ \rangle \bowtie \langle\ aQ1, \ldots, aQk\ \rangle\}$$
$$\widehat{}\ \langle\{\ aPj+1, e(i), aQk+1\ \}\rangle\widehat{}$$
$$\{\langle\ aPj+2, \ldots, aPm\ \rangle \bowtie \langle\ aQk+2, \ldots, aQn\ \rangle\}\}.$$

The expression means: any interleaved and/or concurrent string ($\bowtie$) of P and Q actions from 1 up to j, respectively k, then the composite action/event, $\{aPj+1,e(i),aQk+1\}$, and then any interleaved and/or concurrent string ($\bowtie$) of P and Q actions from j+2 up to m, respectively k+2 up to n. The external behaviour is the internal behaviour "minus" all the actions (being projected "away").

Example 21.2 *Some Trace Semantics:* Let there be given the following three processes composed into one overall process:

type
    M
channel
    pq: M, qr: M
value
    S: **Unit** → **Unit**
    P: **Unit** → **out** pq **Unit**
    Q: **Unit** → **in** pq, **out** qr **Unit**
    R: **Unit** → **in** qr **Unit**

    S() ≡ P() ‖ Q() ‖ R()

    P() ≡ a1 ; pq!m ; a2 ; P()
    Q() ≡ b1 ; **let** m = pq? **in** qr!m **end** ; b2; Q()
    R() ≡ c1 ; qr ? ; c2 ; R()

Traces observed of P, Q and R are:

$\mathcal{P}$: ⟨a1;pq!m;a2;a1;pq!m;a2;a1;pq!m;a2;a1;...⟩
$\mathcal{Q}$: ⟨b1;pq?;qr!m;b2;b1;pq?;qr!m;b2;b1;pq?;qr!m;b2;b1;...⟩
$\mathcal{R}$: ⟨c1;qr?;c2;c1;qr?;c2;c1;qr?;c2;c1;...⟩

Traces potentially observable of S are:

$\mathcal{S}$: {⟨a1;b1;c1;{pq!m‖pq?};a2;{qr!m‖qr?};b2;{pq!m‖pq?};c2;...⟩,
    ⟨a1;b1;c1;{pq!m‖pq?};{qr!m‖qr?};a2;b2;{pq!m‖pq?};c2;...⟩,
    ⟨a1;b1;{pq!m‖pq?};c1;{qr!m‖qr?};a2;c2;b2;{pq!m‖pq?};...⟩,
    ... }

■

21.2.4 Some Characterisations: Processes, Etcetera

One way of expressing the meaning of a process expression, that is, an expression which contains communication primitives such as output (c!e) and input (c?), is to express it as a set of traces of observable (output/input) events.

Characterisation. By a *process* we (semantically) mean a trace.   ■

Characterisation. By a *process definition* we syntactically mean a function definition, and semantically a set of traces.   ■

Characterisation. By *concurrent processes* we mean a set of two or more processes. ∎

It makes little sense to speak of one concurrent process. But we can talk of one process, namely a sequential occurrence of some actions.

Characterisation. By the *global process environment* we mean the surroundings with which the process may interact, i.e., share in events, but excluding other defined and channel-connected processes. ∎

Characterisation. By a *process environment* we mean the set of other processes and the global surroundings from which the process may receive input and (or) to which it may deliver output, that is, with which the process may interact, i.e., share in events. ∎

Characterisation. By an *event* we mean a process event, the occurrence of an input (from the environment, including another process) or an output (to the environment, including another process) or both. The latter designates an internal event. ∎

We shall later distinguish between internal (or local) and external (global) events, and hence between observable and nonobservable events.

Characterisation. By an *externally observable process trace*, or just an *external trace*, we mean a sequence of process events. ∎

In addition to events one could, as was mentioned earlier, include as part of traces the occurrence of certain non-input/non-output actions. We shall refrain from doing so.

21.2.5 Principle of Process Modelling

So when do we choose to introduce processes into our models? The answer is not that straightforward. We can indeed model processes without introducing the explicit process (channel, output, input) notation so far informally illustrated, for example, by nondeterministically defined transition functions over configurations that contain set- or map-oriented values whose elements model the control state of individual processes.

Principles. *Process Modelling:* We choose to model, in terms of processes and events, phenomena in the real world, i.e., "in some application domain", or in computing, when we wish to emphasise concurrently interacting components, that is, how they synchronise and communicate. ∎

Components ≡ Processes

The concept of *component*[3] is perhaps the one that we will rather assume for granted. However:

Characterisation. By a *component* we shall loosely understand a structured set of [variable or constant] (i) values [modelling certain nouns], (ii) predicates, [observer] functions and [generator] operations over these [modelling certain verbs], (iii) and events that stand for willingness to "communicate", i.e., to accept and/or present values to other components, including that of an "outside" [external] world.   ∎

In this sense a component becomes synonymous with what we shall now call a process. The concept of 'object', as in object-oriented programming [1] and [376–378], is sometimes used where we here use the term component — or "our" notion of 'component' is (then) a set of such objects (object modules). We shall, in Vol. 2, Chap. 10, elaborate more on object-oriented specification and the relationship between our concept of component (i.e., process or process definition) and that of the more commonly accepted use of objects and object-orientedness. Meanwhile, let us consider some component examples.

21.2.6 Informal Examples

Example 21.3 *Atomic Component — A Bank Account:* When we informally speak of the phenomena that can be observed in connection with a bank account, we may first bring up such things as: (i) The balance (or cash, a noun), the credit limit (noun), the interest rate (noun), the yield (noun); and (ii) the opening (verb) of, the deposit (verb) into, the withdrawal (verb) from and the closing (verb) of an account. Then we may identify (iii) the events that trigger the opening, deposit, withdrawal and closing actions. We may thus consider a bank account — with this structure of (i) values, (ii) actions (predicates, functions, operations), and (iii) ability to respond to external events (to open, to deposit, etc.) — to be a component, i.e., a process.   ∎

Components are either atomic or composite. In the latter case we can — often more or less arbitrarily — show a decomposition of a component into two or more subcomponents.

Example 21.4 *Composite Component — A Bank:* Likewise, continuing the above example, we can speak of a bank as consisting of any number of bank accounts, i.e., as a composite component of proper constituent bank account components. Other proper constituent components are: the customers (who own the accounts), the bank tellers (whether humans or machines) who services the accounts as instructed by customers, etc.   ∎

---

[3]We shall later, in Vol. 3, Chaps. 26–27, present a more general concept of component.

In the above we have stressed the "internals" of the atomic components. When considering the composite components we may wish to emphasise the interaction between components.

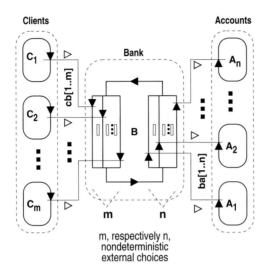

Fig. 21.3. A fifth schematic "rendezvous" class

Example 21.5 *One-Way Composite Component Interaction:* We illustrate a simple one-way client-to-account deposit. A customer may instruct a bank teller to deposit monies handed over from the customer to the bank teller into an appropriate account, and we see an interaction between three "atomic" components: the client(s), the bank teller(s) and the account(s).

This scenario is very much like part 4 in Fig. 21.1, see also Fig. 21.3. Figure 21.3 shows a set of distinct client processes. A client may have one or more accounts and clients may share accounts. For each distinct account there is an account process. The bank (i.e., the bank teller) is a process. It is at any one time willing to input a cash-to-account (a,d) request from any client (c). There are as many channels into (out from) the bank process as there are distinct clients (resp. accounts).

Using formal notation we can expand on the informal picture of Fig. 21.3.

type
    Cash, Cash, Cidx, Aidx
channel
    { cb[c]:(Aidx×Cash) | c:Cidx }
    { ba[a]:Cash | a:Aidx }
value

S5: **Unit** → **Unit**
S5() ≡ Clients() || B() || Accounts()

Clients: **Unit** → **out** { cb[c] | c:Cidx } **Unit**
Clients() ≡ || { C(c) | c:Cidx }

C: c:Cidx → **out** cp[c] **Unit**
C(c) ≡ **let** (a,d):(Aidx×Cash) = ... **in** cb[c] ! (a,d) **end** ; C(c)

type
   A_Bals = Aindex $\overrightarrow{m}$ Cash
value
   abals: A_Bals

Accounts: **Unit** → **in** { ba[a] | a:AIndex } **Unit**
Accounts() ≡ || { A(a,abals(a)) | a:AIndex }

A: a:Aindex × Balance → **in** ba[a] **Unit**
A(a,d) ≡ **let** d′ = ba[a] ? **in** A(a,d+d′) **end**

B: **Unit** → **in** { cb[c] | c:Cidx } **out** { ba[a] | a:Aidx } **Unit**
B() ≡ [] {**let** (a,d) = cb[c] ? **in** ba[a] ! d **end** | c:Cidx} ; B()

We comment on the deposit example. With respect to the use of notation above, there are Cindex client-to-bank channels, and Aindex bank-to-account channels. The banking system (S5) consists of a number of concurrent processes: Cindex clients, Aindex accounts and one bank. From each client process there is one output channel, and into each account process there is one input channel. Each client and each account process cycles around depositing, respectively cashing monies. The bank process is nondeterministically willing ([]) to engage in a rendezvous with any client process, and passes any such input onto the appropriate account.

Generally speaking, we illustrated a banking system of many clients and many accounts. We only modelled the deposit behaviour from the client via the bank teller to the account. We did not model any reverse behaviour, for example, informing the client as to the new balance of the account. So the two bundles of channels were both one-way channels. We shall later show an example with two-way channels. ∎

Example 21.6 *Multiple, Diverse Component Interaction:* We illustrate composite component interaction. At regular intervals, as instructed by some service scripts associated with several distinct kinds of accounts, transfers of monies may take place between these. For example, a regular repayment of a loan may involve the following components, operations and interactions: An

appropriate repayment amount, p, is communicated from client k to the bank's
script servicing component se (3).[4] Based on the loan debt and its interest
rate (d,ir) (4), and this repayment (p), a distribution of annuity (a), fee (f)
and interest (i) is calculated.[5] The loan repayment sum total, p, is subtracted
from the balance, b, of the demand/deposit account, dd_a, of the client (5).
A loan service fee, f, is added to the (loan service) fee account, f_a, of the
bank (7). The interest on the balance of the loan since the last repayment is
added to the interest account, i_a, of the bank (8), and the difference, a, (the
effective repayment), between the repayment, p, and the sum of the fee and
the interest is subtracted from the principal, p, of the mortgage account, m_a,
of the client (6).

In process modelling the above we are stressing the communications. As
we shall see, the above can be formally modelled as below.

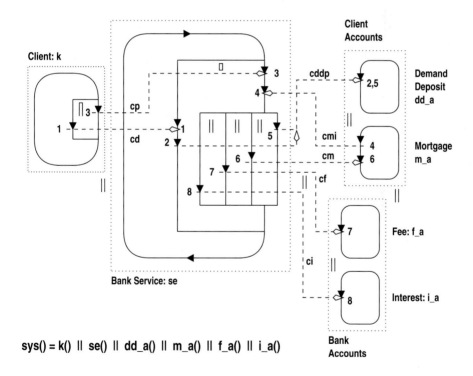

Fig. 21.4. A loan repayment scenario

---

[4]For references (3–8) we refer to Fig. 21.4.
[5]See line four of the body of the definition of the se process below.

type

    Monies,Deposit,Loan,

    Interest_Income,Fee_Income = **Int**,

    Interest = Rat

channel

    cp,cd,cddp,cm,cf,ci:Monies, cmi:Interest

value

    sys: **Unit** → **Unit**,

    sys() ≡ se() ‖ k() ‖ dd_a(b) ‖ m_a(p) ‖ f_a(f) ‖ i_a(i)

    k: **Unit** → **out** cp,cd **Unit**

    k() ≡

        (**let** p:Nat • /* p is some repayment, 1 */ **in** cp ! p **end**

      ⊓

        let d:**Nat** • /* d is some deposit, 2 */ **in** cd ! d **end**)

     ; k()

    se: **Unit** → **in** cd,cp,cmi **out** cddp,cm,cf,ci **Unit**

    se() ≡

        ((**let** d = cd ? **in** cddp ! d **end**) /* 1,2 */

      []

        (**let** (p,(ir,ℓ)) = (cp ?,cmi ?) **in** /* 3,4 */

        let (a,f,iv) = o(p,ℓ,ir) **in**

        (cddp ! (−p) ‖ cm ! a ‖ cf ! f ‖ ci ! iv) **end end**)) /* 5,6,7,8 */

     ; se()

    dd_a: Deposit → **in** cddp **Unit**

    dd_a(b) ≡ dd_a(b + cddp ?) /* 2,5 */

    m_a: Interest × Loan → **out** cmi **in** cm **Unit**

    m_a(ir,ℓ) ≡ cmi ! (ir,ℓ) ; m_a(ir,ℓ− cm ?) /* 4;6 */

    f_a: Fee_Income → **in** cf **Unit**

    f_a(f) ≡ f_a(f + cf ?) /* 7 */

    i_a: Interest Income → **in** ci **Unit**

    i_a(i) ≡ i_a(i + ci ?) /* 8 */

The formulas above express:

- The composite component, a bank, consists of:
  - ⋆ a customer, k, connected to the bank (service), se, via channels cd, cp
  - ⋆ that customer's demand/deposit account, dd_a, connected to the bank (service) via channels cdb, cddp

- ⋆ that customer's mortgage account, m_a, connected to the bank (service) via channel cm
- ⋆ a bank fees income account, f_a, connected to the bank (service) via channel cf
- ⋆ a bank interest income account, i_a, connected to the bank (service) via channel ci
- The customer demand/deposit account is willing, at any time, to nonde-terministically engage in communication with the service: either accepting (?) a deposit or loan repayment (2 or 5), or delivering (!) information about the loan balance and interest rate (4).
- We model this "externally inflicted" behaviour by (what is called) the *external nondeterministic choice*, $\lceil\rceil$[6], operation.
- The service component, in a nondeterministic external choice, $\lceil\rceil$, either accepts a customer deposit (cd?) or a mortgage payment (cp?).
- The deposit is communicated (cddp!d) to the demand/deposit account component.
- The fee, interest and annuity payments are communicated in parallel (∥) to each of the respective accounts: bank fees income (cf!f), bank interest income (ci!i) and client mortgage (cm!a) account components.
- The customer is unpredictable, may issue either a deposit or a repayment interaction with the bank.
- We model this "self-inflicted" behaviour by (what is called) the *internal nondeterministic choice*, $\lceil\rceil$[7], operation.

■

Characterisation. By a *nondeterministic external choice* we mean a non-deterministic decision which is effected, not by actions prescribed by the text in which the $\lceil\rceil$ operator occurs, but by actions in other processes. That is, speaking operationally, the process honouring the $\lceil\rceil$ operation does so by "listening" to the environment.   ■

Characterisation. By *nondeterministic internal choice* we mean a nondeter-ministic decision that is implied by the text in which the $\lceil\rceil$ operator occurs. Speaking operationally, the decision is taken locally by the process itself, not as the result of any event in its surroundings.   ■

21.2.7 Some Modelling Comments — An Aside

Examples 21.5 and 21.6 illustrated one-way communication, from clients via the bank to accounts. Example 21.5 illustrated bank "multiplexing" between

---

[6]See the definition of what is meant by nondeterministic external choice right after this example.

[7]See the definition of what is meant by nondeterministic internal choice right after this example.

several (m) clients and several (n) accounts. Example 21.6 illustrated a bank
with just one client and one pair of client demand/deposit and mortgage
accounts. Needless to say, a more realistic banking system would combine the
above. Also, we have here chosen to model each account as a process. It is
reasonable to model each client as a separate process, in that the collection
of all clients can be seen as a set of independently and concurrently operating
components. To model the large set of all accounts as a similarly large set of
seemingly independent and concurrent processes can perhaps be considered a
"trick": It makes, we believe, the banking system operation more transparent.
In the next — and final — example of this introductory section we augment
the first example with an account balance response being sent back from the
account via the bank to the client.

21.2.8 Examples Continued

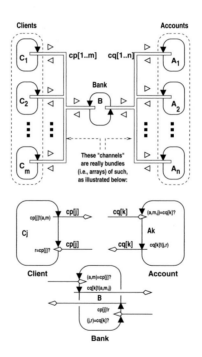

Fig. 21.5. Two-way component interaction

Example 21.7 *Two-Way Component Interaction:* The present example
"contains" that of the one-way component interaction of Example 21.5. Each
of the client, bank and account process definitions are to be augmented as
shown in Fig. 21.5 and in the formulas that follow (cf. Fig. 21.3 and the
formulas in Example 21.5).

type
    Cash, Balance, CIndex, AIndex
    CtoB = AIndex × Cash,
    BtoC = Balance,
    BtoA = Cindex × Cash,
    AtoB = Cindex × Balance
channel
    cb[1..m] CtoB|BtoC, ba[1..n] BtoA|AtoB
value
    S6: **Unit** → **Unit**
    S6() ≡
        ‖ { C(c) | c:CIndex } ‖ B() ‖
        ‖ { A(a,b,r) | a:AIndex, b:Balance, r:Response • ... }

    C: c:CIndex → **out** cp[c] **Unit**
    C(c) ≡
        let (a,d):(AIndex×Cash) = ... **in**
        cb[c] ! (d,a) **end let** r = cb[c] ? **in** C(c) **end**

    B: **Unit** → **in,out** {cb[c]|c:CIndex} **in,out** {ba[a]|a:AIndex} **Unit**
    B() ≡ [] {**let** (d,a) = cb[c] ? **in** ba[a] ! (c,d) **end** | c:Cindex} []
        [] {**let** (c,b) = ba[a] ? **in** bc[c] ! b **end** | a:Aindex} ; B()

    A: a:Aindex × Balance → **in,out** ba[a] **Unit**
    A(a,b) ≡ **let** (c,m) = ba[a] ? **in** ba[a] ! (m+b) ; A(a,m+b) **end**

We explain the formulas above. Both the C and the A definitions specify pairs of communications: deposit output followed by a response input, respectively a deposit input followed by a balance response output. Since many client deposits may occur while account deposit registrations take place, client identity is passed on to the account, which "returns" this identity to the bank — thus removing a need for the bank to keep track of client-to-account associations. The bank is thus willing, at any moment, to engage in any deposit and in any response communication from clients, respectively accounts. This is expressed using the nondeterministic external choice combinator [].   ■

21.2.9 Some System Channel Configurations

We have seen, so far, a number of configurations of channels and processes. Figure 21.6 attempts to diagram a few generic configurations of processes and channels. There may be channels between P, Q, P_j and Q_i processes and other (non-P, etc., and non-Q, etc.) processes, but they are not shown. We shall comment on each of these configurations:

[A] An event (a synchronisation and communication) between P and some Q_i prevents any other such event for the duration of the $P - Q_i$ event. Any other Q_j process (for $j \neq i$) may engage in other events with other processes, or own actions during the $P - Q_i$ event.

[B] An event (a synchronisation and communication) between P and Q_i prevents any other Q_j from engaging in an event with P for the duration of the $P - Q_i$ event. Any other Q_j process (for $j \neq i$) may engage in other events with other non-P processes, or own actions during the $P-Q_i$ event.

[C] An event (a synchronisation and communication) between some P_j and some Q_i prevents any other such $P_k - Q_\ell$ event for the duration of the $Pj - Qi$ event. Any other P_k and Q_ℓ processes (for $k \neq j$ and $j \neq i$) may engage in other events with other non-P and non-Q processes, or own actions during the $P_j - Q_i$ event.

[D] An event (a synchronisation and communication) between some P_j and some Q_i prevents any other $P_j - Q_k$ event for the duration of the Pj_Qi event, but does not prevent a $P_\ell - Q_k$ event for $\ell \neq i$ and $k \neq j$. Etcetera. Please analyse other possible process engagements yourself!

[E] Etcetera. Please analyse the diagram yourself!

We leave it as an exercise to provide schemas for each of the five cases ([A–E]) above (see Exercise 21.1).

21.2.10 Concurrency Concepts — A Summary

Characterisation. *Events* are atomic and instantaneous; they "occur". Events are basic (primitive) elements of processes. Processes are, from a certain level of abstraction, composed from events. Events are used to mark important points in the (temporal or partially ordered) history of a system (i.e., a process). Typically events may stand for a process having reached a certain control (and data) state (a summary of past actions), or for some undefined (or undefinable) environment spontaneously wishing to interact, that is, synchronise and communicate with some process.   ∎

Characterisation. A *sequential process* is an ordered (i.e., sequential) set of operations (i.e., actions) on a data state. (Many processes will be cyclic.) Some actions may simply change a data state. Others may cause the synchronisation between two processes and the communication, i.e., transfer of values from one process to the other. In any case, the control state changes.   ∎

Characterisation. *Blocked Process:* When a process is unable to progress, i.e., to commence a next action, then it is said to be *blocked*. A process description prescribes the conditions under which events may occur, and thus the conditions under which they may be blocked.   ∎

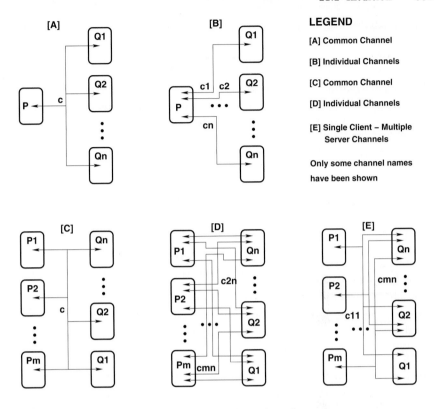

Fig. 21.6. Some system channel configurations

Characterisation. A *parallel process* is a usually unordered (i.e., not predictable) set of sequential process operations (i.e., actions) on own or shared data states. ▪

Characterisation. *Action:* Events usually "trigger" *actions*, that is, operations upon the data state of a process. As we shall later see, events may stand for output from one process and the corresponding input to another process, that is, for synchronisation and exchange of information between processes. ▪

Characterisation. *Channel:* Synchronisation of (e.g., two) and communication between processes "takes place" over (i.e., on) *channels. Channels* allow processes connected to the channels to share events. ▪

Characterisation. *Behaviour:* Sets of observable sequences of events and/or actions of a process or a set of processes. Observations are usually made on "what goes on" on a channel (between processes). The sets may be finite or infinite. ▪

Characterisation. A *trace* is a single sequence of events and/or actions of a postulated or actual process. A *trace* is either of finite or infinite length. A *behaviour* is a set of traces. A *process* usually denotes a behaviour.   ∎

Characterisation. *Environment:* Channels may be connected, at one end, to a process, but at the other end may be left "dangling". Such channels help define aspects of an *environment:* something "external" to or "outside" the collection of processes of main concern. Thus defined processes can share events with an environment: they can react to events from or "deliver" events to the environment.
                                                                                ∎

21.3 Communicating Sequential Processes, CSP

In the previous section we have provided intuitive examples of concurrent specifications expressed in RSL/CSP. In those examples (of that notation) can be found a lot of syntactic details, that may clutter the presentation. In the present section we shall therefore show the CSP notation, a "purest" form of *Communicating Sequential Processes,* in order to show the utter elegance of the underlying concepts and their accompanying notation.

  This section thus goes back to the origins of CSP by presenting a "cleanest", simplest view of an essence of CSP. The "language" of CSP to be presented here is to processes what the λ-calculus is to functions.[8] We shall only cover its language constructs and explain their meaning informally. We shall not delve into issues of mathematical models for the semantics of the CSP variant covered here. Instead we refer to [288, 448, 456].

  First we bring some preliminaries on processes and events. Then, in eleven "easy pieces", we cover the major process combinators ($\rightarrow$, [], $\sqcap$, ? [input], ! [output] and $\parallel$) as well as some basic and compound process expressions, and a few laws.

21.3.1 Preliminaries: Processes and Events

By $\mathcal{P}, \mathcal{P}', \ldots, \mathcal{P}'', \mathcal{Q}, \ldots$ we mean processes. Not process descriptions, but processes "themselves". By Pn, Pn', ..., Pn'', Qn, ... we mean process names (process names are process expressions). By Pe, Pe', ..., Pe'', Qe, ... we mean process expressions, in general.

  Thus:

Pn ≡ Pe

---

[8]An even more "frugal" and foundational language for experimenting with process notions is that of ccs [388, 453].

gives the name Pn to the process expression (or description) Pe. Pn may occur (hence recursively) in Pe. However, we shall deliberately "confuse" processes with their names or prescribing expressions whenever the examples are simple. By a, a', ..., a", b, ... we mean events.

Events are presently considered atomic. Later we shall structure events over (sets of) sets of values (and channels).

21.3.2 Process Combinators, Etcetera

stop: A Basic Process

- **stop:**

The process **stop** is unable to perform (issue, generate, participate in) any events.

Prefix

- $a \rightarrow P$

is a process which is **ready** to engage in the event a. If the event a occurs the process will then behave as P.[9]

Definitions

- $Pn \equiv Pe$

Pn is an identifier (a name), and the expression, Pe, defines the process of that name to **behave** as the process expression Pe prescribes. That expression may contain the name Pn (as well as much else).

- *Example:*

  $Q \equiv e \rightarrow Q$

  Q is the process whose behaviour is the singleton set of the infinite trace of the same event e.

⫿: External Nondeterministic Choice

- $P \;\sqcap\; Q$

Operationally you may think of any one trace of $P \;\sqcap\; Q$ being either P or Q. Which one is "selected" is nondeterministically determined by the environment of $P \;\sqcap\; Q$. The process $P \;\sqcap\; Q$ is available to engage in the events of either P or Q.

---

[9]In RSL semicolon, ";", is used where CSP uses $\rightarrow$.

- *Example:*

  P ≡ requestA → performX ▯ requestB → performY

  P is the process which is willing to engage in either event *requestA* or *requestB*. If event *requestA* is chosen then *P* behaves like *performX*.

The environment offers the events *requestA* and *requestB*.

⊓: Internal Nondeterministic Choice

We write:

- *P* ⊓ *Q*

to denote the internal nondeterministic choice between processes *P* and *Q*. The *environment* has no influence over which of the two alternatives is chosen; but one is chosen "at random".

- *Example:*

  P ≡ reqA → (actA1 ⊓ actA2) ▯ reqB → (actB1 ⊓ actB2)

  Process *P* engages either in the behaviours *actA1* ⊓ *actA2* or *actB1* ⊓ *actB2* depending on the external nondeterministic (▯) choices *reqA* and *reqB*. The process *actA1* ⊓ *actA2* behaves either like *actA1* or *actA2* — chosen nondeterministically by an internal choice. The situation is similar for process *actB1* ⊓ *actB2*.

CSP Law (I)

  a → (P ⊓ Q) ≡ (a → P) ⊓ (a → Q)

Compound Events

Sets of related events can be compounded. In CSP we can write:

  ▯ e:{a.1,a.2,a.3} • e → P ≡ a.1 → P ▯ a.2 → P ▯ a.3 → P7
  ▯ i:{1,2,3} • a.i → P ≡ (a.1 → P) ▯ (a.2 → P) ▯ (a.3 → P)

In RSL [236] we "move" the typing (e : {a.1, a.2, a.3}) out of the expression part and into a **channel** declaration clause:

type
    C == a.1 | a.2 | a.3
channel
    c:C
value
    ... c!e ; P ... /∗ or ∗/ **let** v = c? **in** P(v) **end**

Input and Output

External choice, in CSP, corresponds to **input**, internal choice to **output**:

$$c \ ? \ k{:}K \to P(k) \ \equiv \ [] \ k{:}K \bullet c.k \to P(k)$$
$$d \ ! \ k{:}K \to Q(k) \ \equiv \ [] \ k{:}K \bullet d.k \to P(k)$$

The order of listing is immaterial. For the above example we have chosen non-deterministic external choice [] as the connective. It means: whichever other process or processes that are willing to engage in communication on channels c, c1, c2, ..., cn, will nondeterministically determine which of the alternatives is chosen. If none are willing, at a certain moment, then the above-described process is (temporarily) blocked. If exactly one is willing, say a process Q on channel ci, then the corresponding alternative is (deterministically) chosen. If two or more other processes on channels c, cj, ..., ck are willing to communicate then one of them is nondeterministically chosen and together with the corresponding alternative performs the interaction.

Had we instead chosen nondeterministic internal choice, $\lceil \rceil$, then one of the alternatives would have been chosen (at random) and communication would occur only when and if another, external process is, or becomes willing to synchronise and communicate.

In RSL **input** and **output** can be "mixed":

channel
    c:C, c':C', c1:C1, c2:C2, ..., cn:Cn
value
    /* either nondeterministic input */
       let u = c1? **in** P(u) **end** [] **let** v = c2? **in** Q(v) **end** [] ...
    /* or nondeterministic output */
       c1!e1 ; P' [] c2!e2 ; P'' [] ...
    /* or both (mixed) */
       c1!e1 ; P' [] **let** u = c? **in** P(u) **end** [] c2!e2 ; P'' [] ...

||: Parallel Composition

- $P \parallel Q$

denotes the parallel composition of processes P and Q. Colloquially, i.e., speaking 'operationally', process $P \parallel Q$ describes a process as consisting of two other processes that "run in parallel" while cooperating on shared events.

Shared Events

Process expressions P and Q will often contain expressions listing the same, that is, "shared" events. Shared events are events of the same alphabetic name:

- $\alpha\,P$: alphabet of P, etc.

If:

$$\alpha\,P \cap \alpha\,Q = \{a,b,c\}$$

then processes P and Q share events a, b, c and are thus willing to engage in these simultaneously.

$$x \rightarrow P \parallel x \rightarrow Q \;\equiv\; x \rightarrow (P\parallel Q)$$

If αP does not contain event z and if αQ does not contain event y then:

$$y \rightarrow P \parallel z \rightarrow Q \;\equiv\; (y \rightarrow (P\parallel(z{\rightarrow}Q))) \; [] \; (z \rightarrow ((y{\rightarrow}P)\parallel Q))$$

CSP Law (II)

if
$$P \equiv [] \; e{:}A \bullet e \rightarrow P(e)$$
$$Q \equiv [] \; e{:}B \bullet e \rightarrow Q(e)$$
then
$$P \parallel Q \equiv$$
$$[] \; e{:}A \setminus \alpha\,Q \bullet e \rightarrow (P(e)\parallel Q)$$
$$[]$$
$$[] \; e{:}B \setminus \alpha\,P \bullet e \rightarrow (P\parallel Q(e))$$
$$[]$$
$$[] \; e{:}A \cap B \bullet e \rightarrow (P(e)\parallel Q(e))$$
end

• • •

We bring a summary of this section in Fig. 21.7.

21.3.3 Discussion

We encourage the study of concurrency as a whole subject, say in the form of a full semester course. The topic was covered only partially in the present chapter. For concurrency seen from the perspective of CSP, we refer to three eminent texts: [288, 448, 456].

Simple event	Events occur, have no time-duration, cause actions, change the control state	e
Input/-output	As events, but include actions: output, respectively input, latter changes the data state	c!expr, c?var
Process	P, Q are process expressions that designate sequences of one or more actions and events	P, Q, ...
stop	The no-effect action	**stop**
Prefix	e→P is a process expression: event e followed by process P, where e may be c!expr or c?var. P is a process expression	e→P
External choice	P[]Q is a process expression: P, Q are process expressions	P[]Q
Internal choice	P⊓Q is a process expression: P, Q are process expressions	P⊓Q
Parallel composition	P, Q are process expressions. The designated processes proceed in parallel	P‖Q
Process definition	Pn is a process identifier, P a process expression; (a) an argument (a may be free in P), and where a process identifier in P is a process expression	Pn(a)≡P
Shared event	Upon event e the above process makes the transition to P‖Q, e is shared between P and Q.	(e→P) ‖(e→Q)

Fig. 21.7. Summary of CSP concepts and notation

21.4 The RSL/CSP Process Combinators

In Sect. 21.3 we formally introduced the concept of CSP-like processes. In Sect. 21.2 we intuitively motivated and informally used a notation which is derived from CSP and has been adopted for RSL. In this section we will briefly, but systematically review this notation, the RSL/CSP "sublanguage", which is RSL-like. That is, this language is not exactly a subset of RSL. We have taken some liberties wrt. arrays of channels and how we name channels in function (i.e., process) type clauses. We shall elsewhere show that our deviation can be explained in terms of RSL. In the following we shall cover this RSL-like notation, syntactical construct by construct.

21.4.1 RSL-like Channels

Channels are the means for synchronising processes and communicating values (i.e., messages). Channels lead from a "surrounding" outside (the environment) to defined processes, or lead to such a surrounding from defined processes, or channels are placed between, i.e., "infixed" defined processes, or combinations of the above. We may speak of single channels or of an indexed set of channels. The latter are intended wherever our system of processes involves similarly indexed sets of like processes. Channels must, in RSL, be declared:

type
    C /* C can designate any type */
    Cindex /* Cindex designates a finite set */
channel
    c1,c2,...,cn:C /* n≥1 */
    { c[i]:C | I:CIndex }

Channels ci can communicate values of type C. c is like an array of channels. c[i] for i ranging over the finite set of enumerations Cindex is otherwise like any channel ci.

21.4.2 RSL **Communication Clauses**

Systems are either composed from a fixed set of processes or from a combination of one or more fixed and one or more sets of indexed processes. Correspondingly, we speak of fixed, constant named output/input communications, respectively of varying, indexed output/input communications. We presently treat the former kind of communications.

Simple Input/Output Clauses

We assume that c designates a declared channel. There are basically two communication clauses. First, input expressions:

    c ?
    let v = c ? **in** E(v) **end**

The first clause above designates a value expression and expresses willingness to input a value from channel c. The second clause above also designates a value expression, with the embedded value expression c? value being bound to variable v.
    The output clause:

    c ! expr

designates an output statement, that is, an expression, and expresses an offer of the value of expression expr for communication on channel c. As an expression it has the **Unit** type value ().
    Sometimes an input (c?) is from an undefined process of a (globally) surrounding environment, and sometimes an output (c!expr) is to an undefined process of a (globally) surrounding environment. And sometimes — in a set of processes — there are groups of (two or more) processes which define "matching" output/inputs — one or more of c!e and one or more of c?.
    We refer to examples already given in Figs. 21.5 and 21.7.

21.4.3 RSL Processes

Simple Process Definitions

We assume that both the two clauses $S(a)$ and $S(...)$ are statement clauses, i.e., of type **Unit**. We likewise assume that all channels c_{i_j} and c_{o_k} are being properly declared (elsewhere).

value
    P: A → **in** c_i1,c_i2,...,c_im /* m ≥ 0 */
           out c_o1,c_o2,...,c_on /* n ≥ 0 */
           Unit
    P(a) ≡ $S(a)$

    Q: **Unit** → **in** c_i1,c_i2,...,c_im /* m ≥ 0 */
             out c_o1,c_o2,...,c_on /* n ≥ 0 */
             Unit
    Q() ≡ $S(...)$

Process P takes [optional] input arguments in A, is willing to, i.e., may, receive input over channels c_i1, ..., c_im, and is willing to, i.e., may, output over channels c_o1, ..., c_om. Process P's signature ends with **Unit** to designate that no explicit value is returned, i.e., that the P process either recurses (i.e., "loops") indefinitely or "ends" with the interpretation of a clause of type **Unit**. Process Q takes no input and delivers no output, but is otherwise as is P.

    Instead of **input channels** c_i1, c_i2,...,c_im and **output** c_o1, c_o2,...,c_om, one could write **any** in either or both places. This expresses that process P is willing to engage in communication on any channel.

    The function, i.e., the process definition

value
    R: **Unit** → **any** B
    R() ≡ ... ? ... ! ... b

designates a process which may engage in input/output over any channel, and which yields a value of type B.

Processes and Their Definitions

Please note the distinction between a process definition or a process expression, on one hand, and a process, on the other hand. The former are pieces of text, syntactic "things". The latter is a semantic phenomenon, invisible to the human eye! Processes communicate, not process expressions or process definitions. They prescribe communications.

Process Invocations

Processes get started whenever a process invocation takes place. Invocations of processes are prescribed as follows:

P(a), Q()

The argument a can be thought of as a state. The process, as described by the named process definition, is started whenever a process invocation expression is elaborated. A recursive invocation, P(a'), then means that a state has been updated.

Example 21.8 *A Buffer Process Definition:*

type
    V
channel
    in_ch,out_ch:V
value
    Buffer: V* → **in** in_ch **out** out_ch **Unit**
    Buffer(q) ≡
        let v = in_ch? **in** Buffer(q^⟨v⟩) **end**
        ⫿
        out_ch!hd q; Buffer(**tl** q)

The Buffer process is willing, at any time, to receive input values — which it then appends to its queue buffer before resuming being a Buffer process with that new queue state — or to output the head, i.e., the oldest member of the queue before resuming being a Buffer process with a new, "shorter" queue. ∎

Array Channel Process Definitions

Let the intention be that CI_index and CJ_index designate finite, enumerable token sets.

type
    A_idx, B_idx
channel
    { c_in[c] | c:A_idx }, { c_out[c] | c:B_idx }
value
    P: a:A_idx × b:B_idx →
            in c_in[a] **out** c_out[b] **Unit**
    P(i,j) ≡
        ... **let** v = c_in[i] ? **in**
            ... c_out[j] ! e ... **end** ...

The above process signature is nonstandard RSL. Note the binding of the channel array indices from the left of the $\rightarrow$ to the right.

In Vol. 2, Chap. 10 we will show that the above is a shorthand for a more elaborate set of RSL **scheme** (and hence **class**) and **object** definitions and declarations.

value

> Q: **Unit** $\rightarrow$ **in** $\{c\_in[c]|c:CA\_index\}$ **out** $\{c\_out[c]|c:CB\_index\}$ **Unit**
> Q() $\equiv$
> $\quad$ ⌷ { **let** v = c_in[c'] ? **in**
> $\quad\quad$ ⊓ { c_out[c''] ! v | c'':CB_index } **end** | c':CA_index }

Q prescribes the external nondeterministic input of a value v from any of a number of channels c_in[c'], followed by the internal nondeterministic output of that value to one of a number of channels c_out[c''].

21.4.4 Parallel Process Combinator

Typically a system of concurrently operating components can be expressed as the parallel composition of component processes.

Let P_i designate expressions.

> P_1 || P_2 || ... || P_n

The above expresses the parallel composition of n processes. Evaluation of each individual P_i in P_1||P_2||...||P_n proceeds in parallel. Figures 21.1, 21.1, 21.5, 21.6, and 21.7 illustrated systems (S1, S2, S3, S5, S5, sys and S6) of processes.

21.4.5 Nondeterministic External Choice

Let P_i designate expressions. Then:

> P_1 ⌷ P_2 ⌷ ... ⌷ P_n

expresses the parallel nondeterministic external choice between n processes. Let, for example (omitting type clauses),

> P1() $\equiv$ **let** v = c ? **in** E1(v) **end**
> P2() $\equiv$ **let** v = c ? **in** E2(v) **end**
> Q() $\equiv$ (c ! e)
> R() $\equiv$ (P1() ⌷ P2()) || Q()

The value of expression e is communicated to either the first or the second of the ⌷ argument processes and hence is evaluated either under E1 or under E2. Which one is chosen (left, P1, or right P2), is not shown explicitly, but one is chosen. Wrt. (P1() ⌷ P2()) we say that Q() is a surrounding process, and vice versa. (P1() ⌷ P2()) is willing to engage in communication with its surrounding, and Q() likewise.

21.4.6 Nondeterministic Internal Choice

Let P_i designate expressions all of which are of the same type. Then

P_1 ⌈⌉ P_2 ⌈⌉ ... ⌈⌉ P_n

expresses the parallel nondeterministic internal choice between n processes. Either P_1, or P_2, or, ..., or P_n is chosen — only the choice is internal nondeterministic, i.e., not dependent on any possibly surrounding processes.

Example 21.9 A "Rolling a Dice" Process Definition: To express the arbitrary selection among a finite set of enumerated possibilities we make use of nondeterministic internal choice

type
    Dice = one | two | three | four | five | six
value
    P: **Unit** → Dice
    P() ≡ one ⌈⌉ two ⌈⌉ three ⌈⌉ four ⌈⌉ five ⌈⌉ six

Invocation of P() "randomly" yields a face of a dice.   ∎

21.4.7 Interlock Combinator

Sometimes it is necessary to force two concurrent processes to prioritise their mutual communication — over other such. For that RSL offers the *interlock combinator*:

    pe_1 ‖ pe_2.

The above interlock composition is evaluated as follows: The two expressions are evaluated concurrently. If one of them comes to an end before the other, evaluation continues with that other. However, during the concurrent evaluation, any communication external to pe_1‖pe_2 is prevented. Thus pe_1‖pe_2 expresses that the two processes are forced to communicate only with one another, until one of them terminates.

21.4.8 Summary

We provide a check list summary of RSL/CSP clauses:

• *Channel:*	**channel** c:C
• *Input:*	c? and **let** v = c? **in** Pe **end**
• *Output:*	c!r
• *Process expressions:*	Pe_1 ; Pe_2 ; ... ; Pe_n
• *Parallelism:*	Pe_1 ‖ Pe_2 ‖ ... ‖ Pe_n

- *External nondeterminism:* $Pe\_1 \; [] \; Pe\_2 \; [] \; ... \; [] \; Pe\_n$
- *Internal nondeterminism:* $Pe\_1 \; \sqcap \; Pe\_2 \; \sqcap \; ... \; \sqcap \; Pe\_n$
- *Interlocking:* $Pe\_1 \; \# \; Pe\_2$
- *Process definition:* $Pn: A \rightarrow \textbf{in } c\_i \textbf{ out } c\_j \textbf{ Unit}$
  $Pn(a) \equiv Pe$

21.4.9 A Note of Caution

We remind the reader that the present book's function signatures, when it comes to such functions which define processes using channels (etc.), go beyond "standard" (i.e., tool-supported) RSL, in allowing a kind of "dependent" types:

type
    X_Idx, Y_Idx, M, A, ...
channel
    { c[x,y]:M | x:X_Idx,y:Y_Idx }
value
    f: x:X_Idx × A → **in** { c[x,y] | y:Y_Idx } ...

In the function f signature x is being bound "to the left" of → and is being "used" "to the right" of →, in delimiting the channels from which to input.

21.5 Translation Schemas

In Sect. 20.5 we gave a brief treatment of translations from applicative (i.e., functional) to imperative specifications. In the present section we shall do likewise for translations from applicative and, or via, imperative specifications to parallel process-oriented specifications.

In a few "stages" we shall be "massaging" some formulas into other formulas. Then we shall examine the validity of this "massaging".

21.5.1 Stage I: An Applicative Schema

Let us consider the following schema:

type
    A, B
value
    f: A → **Unit**
    g: A → A
    h: A → **Unit**

    f(a) ≡ (**let** a′ = g(a) **in** f(a′) **end** $\sqcap$ h(a) ; f(a))

Annotation. We explain, as far as we can, the above abstract program specification schema: f can be considered a "main" function. f is initially invoked with some argument, say a. f nondeterministically, internal choice, selects between either expressing the clause to the left of the ⌈⌉ operator, or to the right. In the former case f is ("tail" recursively) invoked with an "updated" version of a, now named a′. Or f chooses the "simpler" right clause, first expressing the **Unit** value clause h(a), and then proceeding by (also in this case), a tail recursive invocation of f with the "original" argument a. And so on.

21.5.2 Stage II: A Simple Reformulation

The above schema defines the behaviour of f as a nondeterministic internal choice behaviour between two processes: **let** $a' = g(a)$ **in** f(a′) **end** and h(a) ; f(a). Let us call them g′ and h′:

type
    A, B
value
    f: A → **Unit**
    g: A → A
    g′,h,h′: A → **Unit**

    f(a) ≡ g′(a) ⌈⌉ h′(a)
    g′(a) ≡ **let** $a' = g(a)$ **in** f(a′) **end**
    h′(a) ≡ h(a) ; f(a)

Let us examine the above: It seems that f is a main process. It seems that a is like a state variable, being used and updated (by g′), or just used and "passed on", by h′. In other words, the two processes G and H both require access to the shared state, but the two processes' g, respectively h, "actions" cannot proceed in parallel. Observe that f is not recursive, but g′ and h′ are.

21.5.3 Stage III: Introducing Parallelism

What about the following idea: "Split out", i.e., decompose, f into two three parallel processes F, G and H. In this case F "maintains" the global state a, and G and H reread, respectively rewrite that global state:

type
    A, B
channel
    fg:A, fh:A
value
    S: A → **Unit**
    F: A → **out** fg,fh **Unit**

G: **Unit** → **in** fg **Unit**
H: **Unit** → **in** fh **Unit**
g: A → A
h: A → **Unit**

S(a) ≡ F(a) || G() || H()
F(a) ≡ fg!a ⊓ fh!a
G() ≡ **let** a = fg ? **in let** a′ = g(a) **in** F(a′) **end end**
H() ≡ **let** a = fh ? **in** h(a) ; F(a) **end**

Annotation. Let us explain the above abstract program specification schema: A system process, S, has been introduced. S expresses the parallel composition of three processes: F, G and H. F communicates with both G and H. That is, they both communicate with F. They do so over separate channels: fg, respectively fh. F nondeterministically (internal choice) expresses either G() or H(). G "mimics" the left clause of the body of definition f of stage I, i.e., g′ of stage II. H "mimics" the right clause of the body of definition f of stage I, h′ of stage II. Observe that F is not recursive, but G and H are.

21.5.4 Stage IV: A Simple Reformulation

Instead of using the "tail" recursive invocations of F from both G and H, "passing" on appropriate arguments to the F process, we communicate, over a (new) channel, a possibly updated value of the argument (a′). Since H need not communicate any new A value, we let it, for sake of "symmetry", communicate a "tick", indicating, for whatever it is worth, completion.

A variant of F, G and H could thus be:

type
    Tick == tick
channel
    fg:A, fh:A, gf:A, hf:Tick
value
    F: A → **out** fg,fh **in** gf,hf **Unit**
    G: **Unit** → **in** fg **out** gf **Unit**
    H: **Unit** → **in** fh **out** hf **Unit**

F(a) ≡
    (fg!a ; **let** a′ = gf ? **in** F(a′) **end**)
    ⊓
    (fh!a ; **let** t = hf ? **in** F(a) **end**)

G() ≡ **let** a = fg ? **in let** a′ = g(a) **in** gf!a′ **end end** ; G()
H() ≡ **let** a = fh ? **in** gh!tick ; h(a) **end** ; H()

Annotation. First, there really was no need for separate, directed channels between F and G, and G and F, etcetera. One channel would have sufficed. We then explain, as far as we can, the above abstract program specification schema. All we have done, in and at this stage, is to augment the definition with two new channels and let F take care of its own continuation — in the form of its explicit "tail" recursion. At the same time we had to keep both G and H going, so they continue to have their "tail" recursions. Now we see some stylistic differences between the two models of stage III and stage IV: In stage III neither F, G nor H were recursive. But, as F invoked either G or H, these in return invoked F. In stage IV all processes are recursive.

21.5.5 Stage Relations

Now we have to stop and consider! Is the above "development", from stage I via stage II and stage III to stage IV, correct? And, what, after all, do we mean by correctness?

It is clear that the four stages of formulas do not exhibit the same functions, and, where they do "share" some function names, that the function signatures are not the same. So, from that point of view, the four stages do not "compute the same thing". But they are comparable. We claim that the sequence of state updates of the four models are the same — and ask the reader's acceptance of that!

To "prove" that claim will take us too far off our software engineering specification and design "track", and into the specifics of *programming methodology*. But we can hint at one approach of obtaining some assurance that the stages do relate. That is by rewriting later stages into forms akin to earlier stages. We leave that, however, to another time and place. Thus we ask the reader to carefully check what's going on, within and between the above four stages. RSL, as it stands today, does have a powerful proof system, but not powerful enough to handle these kinds of development stages.

In general, since we are, in this case, "transgressing" from applicative to imperative RSL, and from either of these to concurrent, i.e., parallel RSL, we are in fact trying to integrate various formal notations. The subject of integrating such formal notations is as of summer 2005 a subject that is being very much studied and researched. Many integrations are being proposed. We have shown those with which applicative RSL, i.e., the core of RSL, has been integrated from the inception of RSL, in the late 1980s.

In Vol. 2 we shall illustrate further, more recent integrations. They include integration of (i) RSL with ER[10] (cum UML Class) Diagrams, Chap. 10; of (ii) RSL with Petri Nets, Chap. 12 [313, 421, 435–437]; of (iii) RSL with Live Sequence Charts, Chap. 13 [171, 270, 325]; of (iv) RSL with Statecharts, Chap. 14 [265, 266, 268, 269, 271]; and of (v) RSL with Duration Calculus, Chap. 15 [537, 538]. Then we shall revert to the problem of assuring "sameness".

---

[10]ER: entity relationship [148, 149].

21.5.6 Stage V: An Imperative Reformulation

In Sect. 20.5.2 we saw that an applicative function could be "imperialised". So we now do with F:

variable
  σ:A
value
  F: **Unit** → **read,write** σ **out** fg,fh **in** gf,hf **Unit**
  F() ≡
    (fg!σ ; σ := gf ? ; F())
    ⌈⌉
    (fh!σ ; **let** t = hf ? **in** F() **end**)

We can even turn tail recursion into an imperative loop:

variable
  σ:A
value
  F: **Unit** → **read,write** σ **out** fg,fh **in** gf,hf **Unit**
  F() ≡
    while true do
      (fg!σ ; σ := gf ?)
      ⌈⌉
      (fh!σ ; **let** t = hf ? **in skip end**)
    end

21.5.7 Some Remarks

This ends our informal, yet systematic, sequence of stages of "comparable" and "believably correct" developments. The idea of this section has been to give you some hints as how to turn applicative and recursive function definitions into imperative process definitions.

21.6 Parallelism and Concurrency: A Discussion

21.6.1 CSP and RSL/CSP

This chapter, on parallel specification programming, has focused on CSP, and for good reasons. CSP provides an elegant way of expressing concurrency. Furthermore, CSP blends well with RSL.

Learning RSL/CSP will enable the reader to quickly adapt to, i.e., learn and use, "pure" CSP. "Pure" CSP — with its tool support for model checking [447], a means of proving that certain CSP satisfy expected properties — is very useful as a separate tool for investigating specific specifications of (specific) concurrent system proposals.

21.6.2 Modelling Techniques

In Sects. 21.2 and 21.5 we gave many examples of modelling techniques. In the next volumes of this book, i.e., in Vols. 2 and 3, we shall have ample opportunity to bring more examples — and from the current and the future ones there will be enough examples to draw from when you are confronted with a concurrent systems modelling problem.

21.7 Bibliographical Notes

We have repeatedly given the following references: [288, 448] and [456].The originator of CSP is C.A.R. Hoare. His first published paper on CSP was [287]. His book, [288], has been carefully edited by Jim Davies [179]. It is now available electronically [289] and is the definitive reference on CSP. Bill Roscoe's book [448] covers the same ground, and more: It has twice as many pages and provides more industry-oriented examples. It also introduces the reader to technology support for CSP. Steve Schneider's book [456] is perhaps a bit more of a textbook where Hoare's was a monograph and Roscoe's is somewhat in between. Schneider's book additionally extends CSP into Timed CSP (TCSP). A final reference is [229]. It is to the Internet Web (home) page of **Formal Systems (Europe)** whose toolset FDR2 provides a model-checker and other CSP tools. Through subpages access is provided to documents on the CSP syntax of 'programs' (cum specifications) that can be accepted by the FDR2 tool.

21.8 Exercises

The function definitions of the exercises of this chapter are basically to be expressed in the parallel programming style.

Exercises 21.9, 21.10 and 21.11 are preceded by Exercises 19.1, 19.2 and 19.3, and Exercises 20.1, 20.2 and 20.3, respectively.

• • •

Exercise 21.1. *System Channel Configurations.* Please review Sect. 21.2.9, and suggest formal specifications of P, P_i, Q, and Q_j function definition schema and channel structures to cater to each of the five ([A–E]) system channel configurations.

Hint: You are to assume that the functions P, P_i, Q and Q_j do not interact, i.e., engage in events, with other processes.

Exercise 21.2. *Single Producer-/Consumer-Bounded Repository.* There are given three behaviours: a **producer**, a **repository**, and a **consumer**. The producer (occasionally) produces entities and delivers them to the repository. The repository accepts producer-manufactured entities and, upon request, hands them on to the consumer. The consumer consumes entities by (occasionally) requesting these from the repository. The repository delivers entities in the order in which they were received. The repository can keep at most b entities.

Define types of entities and of entity requests (from consumers), two (or three) channels and the four behaviours: producer, repository, consumer and their aggregation into a **system** behaviour.

Exercise 21.3. *Multiple Producer-/Consumer-Bounded Repository.* We refer to Exercise 21.2. All you need, for this exercise, is to read the formulation of that exercise.

There are given $m + n + 1$ behaviours: m **producers**, p_i, a **repository**, and n **consumers**, c_j. Any producer may deposit an entity with the repository, and any consumer may request an entity from the repository. The repository marks every received entity with a unique identity of its producer. The entities delivered to consumers are marked with this identity. The repository otherwise delivers the marked entities in the order of their receipt.

Define types of entities and of entity requests (from consumers), the m channels between producers and the repository, the either n or $2n$ channels between the repository and the consumers, and the four behaviours: producer, repository, consumer and their combined system.

Exercise 21.4. *Shared Storage.* A number of **computation** processes share a common **storage**. We see this common **storage** to record, for distinct **locations**, a **value**. We see the computation processes performing the following operations on the shared storage: (i) requesting **allocation** of new storage locations, (ii) storing (**initial**) values in these, (iii) **updating** with, i.e., changing existing values to, new given values at identified, i.e., given, locations; (iv) requesting the **value** at a given (i.e., identified) location, (v) and requesting the **deallocation**, i.e., the freeing or removal, of an identified location. We finally allow processes to (vi) **pass on** locations to one another — according to some further unspecified protocol.

Define the type of storages, i.e., of locations and values and their combination into storages. Define the type of channels between computation processes and between these and the storage process — the latter is thus thought of as the only process which "keeps", i.e., maintains, the storage. Finally, define the two kinds of behaviours: computation processes which occasionally perform one of the actions (i–vi), and the storage behaviour.

Exercise 21.5. *Synchronous Multiple-Client/Single-Server System.* A **client** is a behaviour which, at its own volition, generates **requests** to a **server** to **perform** some — amongst a finite number of — identified actions (on a server state). The client, in addition to providing a name, i.e., an identifier, of the action to be performed, may, or may not — depending on the (arity of the) identified action — also provide some input arguments, i.e., a (finite) sequence of (zero, one or more) values to the identified action. That is, actions are possibly state-changing and definitely value-returning functions. The **server** is then, after successful or failed action, to return a result (of having performed, or failed to perform such an action) to the client. Failure occurs whenever a client provides an unknown action name, or a wrong number of argument values. The result, "good" or "bad", shall be accepted by the client. That client, after having issued the request, has (patiently) waited for a result.

A server, on the other hand, is a behaviour which, prompted by the client, performs identified actions with possible arguments and on its, i.e., the server state. Thus the server is to maintain a catalogue of functions. The catalogue records the unique names of the functions, their finite arities (0 or more) and "the function itself", that is, the denotation of the function identifier. Typically such a function denotation is of type: total function from arguments and state to possibly changed states and results. We leave argument and result values further unspecified.

Define the types of server function catalogues and states, and of client-to-server and server-to-client messages. Also define the (generic) client and the server behaviours as well as that of the combined system: m clients and one server.

Exercise 21.6. *Asynchronous Multiple-Client/Single-Server System.* We refer to Exercise 21.5. You need not have solved that exercise, but you need to have read its problem formulation before you now read on.

The only difference between the problem of the present exercise and that of the referenced exercise is that the client does not "patiently" await completion of server actions, but may proceed to other behaviours. Sooner or later it is, however, expected that the client requests the result from a previously requested action. To enable this — and the interleaving of other requesting clients, and even that any client may, at different times, request actions the return of whose results is pending — we assume that the clients provide unique identification of their action requests. These unique action request identifications are then presented by the client when finally requesting the results.

Define the types of server function catalogues and states, and of client-to-server and server-to-client messages. Also define the system, the (generic) client and the server behaviours.

Exercise 21.7. *Synchronous Multiple-Client/Multiple-Server System:* We refer to Exercise 21.5. You need not have solved that exercise, but you need to have read its problem formulation before you now read on.

The only difference between the problem of the present exercise and that of the referenced exercise is that there are now many servers, i.e., more than one. Any server is ready to accept any action request, and all servers serve the same actions.

Define the types of server function catalogues and states, and of client-to-server and server-to-client messages. Also define the system, the client and the server behaviours.

Exercise 21.8. *A UNIX Pipe.* A UNIX pipeline is a sequence of processes, π_i, one for each command, cmd_i, of a sequence of UNIX commands:

cmd_1(argl_1) | cmd_2(argl_2) | ... | cmd_n(argl_n)

Each command cmd_i (is a name which) denotes a function, f_i, and each argument list argl_i is a list of values, vl_i. Each argument argl_i[j] for j in {1..**len** argl_i} is a list of characters. (Here **len** argl_i may be 0.) Each function f_i process π_i, for all i, produces, little by little, a result, r_i, which is a sequence of characters. Functions f_i, for $i \geq 2$, however, all accept one more input argument, namely the one produced by $f_{i-1}(\langle r_{i-1}\rangle \hat{\ } vl_i)$. Correspondingly each "next" (in the pipe line) function f_{i+1} process π_{i+1}, for $i < $ **len** argl_i, may consume that output, provided it is ready to do so. Thus, as soon as the function process π_i has produced some such partial result it "outputs" it to a pipe-buffer (i.e., a process) $\wp_i^{i+1}$ for $1 \leq i <$**len** argl_i (Fig. 21.8). It is from this buffer that function process π_{i+1} may or will (eventually) request it.

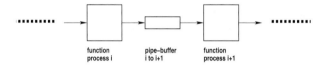

function   pipe-buffer   function
process i   i to i+1   process i+1

Fig. 21.8. A fragment system: some pipe processes

Define the three kinds of processes: the **system**, the **function_process** and the **pipe_buffer**, their channels, and the type of commands, arguments, states and function catalogues (cf. Exercise 21.5). The system process accepts a pipe specification and for each command-argument list item the system process starts} function process, and for each pair of adjacent such a pipe-buffer process. Let an external input channel receive the piped command lists, and an output channel deliver the result, little by little, of the "last" function process.

Figure 21.9 illustrates which processes receive which inputs.

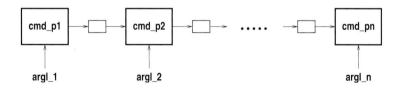

cmd_p1   cmd_p2   .....   cmd_pn

argl_1   argl_2   argl_n

Fig. 21.9. Some pipe processes and their arguments

Exercise 21.9. *The Grocery Store, III.* We continue Exercises 19.1 and 20.1. Whereas these exercises suggested serial (in effect, "single-process") behaviour of a grocery store, we shall now suggest a behaviour in which several clients may simultaneously select merchandise. We suggest, however, that no two or more clients can access a shelf segment simultaneously; at most one can access a shelf segment. Similarly for checkout: There is just one staff and one cash register. Once you have a parallel process solution to the current problem you can easily lift these (and other) restrictions.

Thus the nine state components suggested in Exercise 20.1 are now to be thought of as a set of $3 \times k + m + n + 1 + 1 + 2 \times w$ processes: (1) k client, (2) k shopping cart, (3) k bag, (4) m store shelf segments, (5) n inventory shelf segments (one for each type of merchandise, where $m \geq n$), (6) one cash register, (7) one catalog, (8) w wholesaler inventory and (9) w wholesaler cash register processes.

The initialisation prescribed for the nine global state components are now *distributed* over respective processes (Fig 21.10).

We consider, finally, as a new kind of process, (10) the staff as a single process: This is a small, friendly country store. The staff process did not find its way into a state component in the imperative model. It was, however, the actor which performed the checkout and the replenishments actions. That checkout/replenishment actor had no "state", i.e., no "memory".

Now a shopping script is a prescription for the behaviour of a client — whose state components, thus, are basically those of the script and the purse.

The somewhat elaborate nondeterminism expected from solutions to Exercises 19.1 and 20.1 is now to be expressed by the parallel process combinators ||, [], and ⊓, as well as by the output/input combinators ! and ?.

Please define all relevant types, all relevant channels (and their types) and all relevant behaviours, that is, in addition to those mentioned above, also the "overall" system process. Assume an appropriate initialisation of store and inventory shelves.

If you believe that the above description is incomplete, please state so, and provide the completing text.

Exercise 21.10. *The Anarchic Factory, III.* We continue Exercises 19.2 and 20.2. Please read the problem formulation texts of the above referenced exercises carefully.

The six state components suggested in Exercise 20.2 are now to be thought of as a set of four kinds of processes: m fork trucks, each with their own schedule, n production cells, each with their own schedule, one parts inventory, and one products warehouse. That is, the schedules are folded into the state of the fork truck and production cell agents. The remarks concerning initialising the individual processes appropriately as outlined in Fig. 21.10 also apply to this exercise.

Please define all relevant types, all relevant channels (and their types) and all relevant behaviours, that is, in addition to those mentioned above,

To give you an idea what is meant by *"the global state components being distributed over respective processes"* consider the following: A composite state component, for a system of n "actors", maps a finite set of n unique actor identifiers to actor states:

value
    n:**Nat**
type
    Uid **axiom** |Uid|=n /∗ cardinality of Uid is n ∗/
    AΣ
    Actors = Uid $\overrightarrow{m}$ AΣ
value
    actors:Actors
variable
    agents:Actors := actors

The agents variable is not really needed to understand the concept of distributing a composite state over n process states. It is only brought in here to show the transition from applicative *via* imperative to parallel specification programming.
For each "actor" we now establish a process and "distribute" the actor states over these n processes:

value
    system() ≡ || { actor(uid)(actors(uid)) | uid:Uid }

The actors(uid) argument to the actor function, i.e., process, definition represents one, the uid, component of the state. The actor function will usually "locally update" this state:

value
    actor: Uid → AΣ → **Unit**
    actor(uid)(aσ) ≡ ... **let** aσ' = ... **in** actor(uid)(aσ') **end**

Fig. 21.10. Single global state to multiple process state distribution

also the "overall" **system** process. Assume an appropriate initialisation of the inventory.

If you believe that the above description is incomplete, please state why, and provide the completing text.

Exercise 21.11. *The Document System, III.* We continue Exercises 19.3 and 20.3. Please read the problem formulation texts of those exercises carefully.

1. In this exercise make the system components:
    (a) the set of all d place directories into d parallel processes
    (b) the set of all m persons into m parallel processes, where m is the sum of all persons in all places

(c) the set of all c citizens into c parallel processes
(d) the set of all document identifiers in use into a process
(e) the set of all dossier identifiers in use into a process
(f) time into a process.

2. Define all appropriate channels.
3. Define all process types clearly.
4. Now redefine the syntax of commands, replacing explicit mentioning of persons, documents, dossiers and locations by their process identifiers.
5. Redefine all semantic interpretation functions as auxiliary functions within the generic person process.

Exercise 21.12. ♣ *A Concurrent Domain Model of Transportation Nets.* We refer to Appendix A, Sect. A.1, *Transportation Net*.

We refer to Exercises 19.4 and 20.4. Please read the problem formulation of those exercises carefully.

In Exercise 20.4 we suggested five state variables: (i) the static segments, (ii) the dynamic segments, (iii) the static connectors, (iv) the dynamic connectors, and (v) the graph of the network (i.e., the structure part of the net). In the present exercise we suggest to represent each of these as a process. And we ask you to reformulate solutions to question 4 of Exercise 19.4.

Exercise 21.13. ♣ *A Concurrent Domain Model of Container Logistics.* We refer to Appendix A, Sect. A.2, *Container Logistics*.

We refer to Exercises 19.5 and 20.5. Please read the problem formulation of those exercises carefully.

In Exercises we suggested the declaration of three global state variables: (i) ships, (ii) the container storage area of a specific container terminal, and (iii) the quay of that terminal. In the present exercise we suggest to represent each of these as a process. Based on these three processes redefine the operations mentioned in items 3–11 of Exercise 19.5.

Exercise 21.14. ♣ *A Concurrent Domain Model of Financial Service Industries.* We refer to Appendix A, Sect. A.3, *Financial Service Industry*.

We refer to Exercises 19.6 and 20.6. Please read the problem formulation of those exercises carefully.

In Exercise 20.6 we suggested the declaration of three global state variables: client catalogue, account catalogue and accounts. In the present exercise we suggest to represent each of these as a process. Based on these three processes redefine the operations mentioned in items 1–2 of Exercise 19.6.

Part VI

AND SO ON!

Etcetera!

22.1 What Have We Covered?

We claim that we have, in the present volume, covered the following core aspects of software engineering:

- Chaps. 2–9: a minimum necessary background in **discrete mathematics**: numbers, sets, Cartesians, types, functions, λ-calculus, algebras and logics
- Chaps. 10–18: basic principles and techniques of **abstraction and modelling** as expressible in RSL: atomic types and values, function definitions, property- and model-oriented abstractions, sets, Cartesians, lists, maps, higher-order functions and types
- Chaps. 19–21 **specification programming**: applicative, imperative and concurrent specification programming

The main objective of Vol. 1 has been to give the reader a firm foundation in abstraction and modelling.

22.2 What Is Next?

In the next volume of this three-volume book we shall cover further essential aspects of software engineering:

- **Specification facets:** Volume 2, Chaps. 2–5 — hierarchies and compositions, denotations and computations, configurations: contexts and states, and time, space and time/space
- **Semiotics:** Volume 2, Chaps. 6–9 — pragmatics, semantics, syntax, and semiotics
- **Advanced specification techniques:** Volume 2, Chaps. 10–15 — modularisation, automata and machines, Petri nets, message sequence charts and live sequence charts, statecharts, and the quantitative models of time (duration calculus). Chaps. 12–14 represent a major contribution by Christian Krog Madsen.

- **Language definitions:** Volume 2, Chaps. 16–19 — a simple applicative language, SAL, a simple imperative language, SIL, a simple modular imperative language, SMIL, and a simple parallel language, SPIL

The main objective of Vol. 2 is to make the reader a professional in the area of formal specification, as concerns both classical software devices as well as devices that possess temporal and concurrent properties.

22.3 What Is Next-Next?

In the third volume of this three-volume book we shall then "wind up" the specification and programming methodological aspects of software engineering by covering the essential spectrum of development phases from:

- **domain engineering** via
- **requirements engineering** to
- **software Design.**

More specifically we cover the following stages of these phases:

- **Domain engineering:** Volume 3, Chaps. 8–16 — an overview of domain engineering, domain stakeholders, domain attributes, domain facets, domain acquisition, domain analysis and concept formation, domain verification and validation, towards domain theories, and the domain engineering process model
- **Requirements engineering:** Volume 3, Chaps. 17–24 — overview of requirements engineering, requirements stakeholders, requirements facets, requirements acquisition, requirements analysis and concept formation, requirements verification and validation, requirements satisfiability and feasibility, and the requirements engineering process model
- **Software design:** Volume 3, Chaps. 25–30 — hardware/software codesign, software architecture design, a case study in component design, domain-specific architectures, coding (etc.), and the triptych computing systems design process model

To properly set the stage for study of the above major phases of software development we first bring in some preliminary material:

- **The paperwork:** Volume 3, Chap. 2 — documents
- **The conceptual framework:** Volume 3, Chaps. 3–4 — methods and methodology, and models and modelling
- **Descriptions: theory and practice:** Volume 3, Chaps. 5–7 — phenomena and concepts, on defining and on definitions, and Jackson's description principles

A final technical chapter closes the specification and programming methodological aspects of software engineering by covering:

- **The triptych development process model** — Volume 3, Chap. 31

The main objective of Vol. 3 is to make the reader a professional in the complete and full range of software development: from domains via requirements to software.

22.4 A Caveat

As pointed out, the reader must not forget that these volumes provide only one, albeit a major, facet of what is needed in "real" development:

- **Problem frame specialties.** These first three volumes do cover many facets of such software applications as is usually classified by the terms: (i) administrative data processing; (ii) enterprise resource planning (ERP); (iii) compilers and interpreters; (iv) distributed (client/server, etc.) systems, (v) production planning, monitoring and control systems; (vi) database management systems; (vii) embedded real-time safety-critical systems, and the like. But to become a real professional in any one of these areas requires more than these volumes can give you. So you are well advised to study special texts on such things as (a) formal semantics and compiler techniques, (b) data communication, cryptography and distributed systems, (c) database systems, (d) real-time embedded software, etc.
- **Management:** Issues not covered by these volumees are: engineering management, configuration management (version monitoring and control), people management (capability maturity model, risk management, quality management), project planning (monitoring and control, project graphs, resource allocation and scheduling etc.), development cost management, contracts and contract management, market analysis, product cost estimates, consultancy and instantiation costs, marketing and sales, maintenance and service, business plans, financial matters, ISO 9000, ISO 9001 and ISO 9000-3, IEEE and ACM standards, software tool standards, etc. We entertain some hope that a volume could be produced, one whose objective would be to show that formal techniques fit "hand-in-glove" with many current management concepts, while, in cases, warranting some new looks!

22.5 Formal Methods *"Lite"*

In Vol. 3, Chap. 32, Sect. 32.2 we bring an analysis of the issues of "myths and commandments" of formal methods.

Suffice it for this volume to state that we do not believe in formal methods, but we use formal methods whenever the development of a piece of software is done by more than one person, or whenever that software eventually will be used by any person other than the one who developed it, i.e., "always". But let us also state that we use formal methods "lite": We, ourselves, emphasise formal specification, in all phases, in reasonably "connected" stages and steps. But we seldom prove any properties: We assert that the developments we record do satisfy correctness criteria; but we "leave the details" to others. We do so on the experienced background that formal specification in carefully monitored and controlled phases, stages and steps — recording suitable abstraction (retrieve) functions, all appropriate invariants, etc. — seems to capture the proverbial "99.99%" of "believed" bugs. For those customers who need more formal assurance we know which kinds of developments we can provably relate, which kinds of properties we can formally verify — but in these volumes we cover only the proverbial "99.99%".

22.6 Bibliographical Notes

These volumes are the fruits of many years of my own work also. That work is recorded in the following documents: [37, 55–114, 116–121, 123–130, 228, 257, 352, 431, 490]

Part VII

APPENDIXES

A

Common Exercise Topics

In this appendix we bring some initial formulations of some problem domains for which a number of exercises, marked ♣, will then be posed in subsequent chapters of this volume. References are given below.

A.1 Transportation Nets

By a transportation net we understand a composition of road nets (of various kinds: public roads, toll roads [viz.: toll booth or electronically road priced], free ways, etc.), rail nets, nets of air traffic corridors, and nets of shipping lanes. Common, we claim, to all these nets are their composition from segments (street or road segments, rail lines between stations, air corridors, etc.), and connections (street intersections, railway stations, airports and harbours).

So nets, segments and connections (or intersections) are important concepts. They abstract phenomena such as mentioned above (roads, lines, and lanes, respectively street corners, train stations, airports and harbours).

Segments may be decomposed into blocks, i.e., a segment being a sequence of blocks. And blocks (hence segments), as well as connections, may contain zero, one or more conveyors (cars, trains [usually at most one], air crafts or ships). Conveyors may move — so that traffic can be abstracted as a function from time to positions of conveyors (in, or within, blocks and connections).

Issues of allocation, scheduling and control of traffic can then be approached.

Exercises related to this topic are: 2.6, 3.3, 4.4, 5.1, 5.2, 5.3, 8.1, 9.1, 10.2, 11.1, 12.4, 13.5, 14.6, 15.15, 16.12, 18.1, 19.4, 20.4 and 21.12.

Examples 9.8 and 9.12 also relate to this exercise topic.

A.2 Container Logistics

A container terminal is a special kind of harbour — at the "borderline" between ocean and land. Roughly a container terminal consists of a harbour basin, shielded from the ocean, on one side, by jetties, and otherwise bordering to one or more (land located) quays. Finally, also on land, each container terminal has a container storage area.

A container terminal is so organised as to serve in the loading and unloading of containers onto, respectively from container ships. Before loading, and after unloading containers, these are usually kept, on shore, i.e., on land, in the container storage area. Containers on container ships and in container storage areas are kept in stacks — and we can talk about container ships and container storage areas being organised into 'bays' of 'rows' of stacks of containers.

Quays are where container ships are positioned when being loaded and unloaded. Ship/shore cranes parked at locations (with up to several such per ship position) perform this loading and unloading, from, respectively onto terminal trucks or container trucks. The former move containers between container ships and container storage areas and deposit and fetch their containers in, respectively from container storage area stacks by means of container storage area cranes. In other words: A Quay consists of a sequence of quay locations, with any subsequence of locations designating a quay position.

Container ships may contain more containers than destined for the container terminal they may currently be visiting. And container storage area stacks may contain containers destined for further container ship transport to usually several, "next", container terminals.

Container ships as well as containers have sailing routes, respectively waybills, where both the former and the latter imply a sequence of container terminals, to be visited, respectively at which to be transferred (unloaded from one container ship and loaded onto another container ship via temporary storage in the container storage area of the transfer container terminal).

Exercises related to this topic are: 2.7, 3.4, 4.5 5.1, 5.2, 5.3, 8.2, 9.2, 10.3, 11.2, 12.5, 13.6, 14.7, 15.16, 16.13, 18.2, 19.5, 20.5, and 21.13.

Examples 9.9 and 9.13 also relate to this exercise topic.

A.3 Financial Service Industry

A, or the, financial service industry (of a country, of a region, or of the world) consists of banks, insurance companies, securities instrument brokers and (stock) exchanges, as well as of portfolio management and other financial market operators.

In banks customers can open and close accounts, deposit and withdraw funds, establish and terminate loans, borrow ("against") and pay back loans, etc. A customer may have several deposit and/or loan (and/or other) accounts.

Several customers may share accounts. Funds may be transferred between accounts in same or different banks.

Customers may request (order) the buying or selling of securities instruments through a broker (to be transacted at a securities instrument (eg., stock) exchange. A 'buy' ['sell'] request names a securities instrument, states time interval of request being valid (i.e., during which it should, if possible, be effected), states price interval ("lo, hi") within which transaction should, if possible, be effected (with "hi" ["lo"], for 'buy' ['sell'] orders, designating an absolute limit, while the "lo" ['hi'] being an "OK, you may effect transaction" limit). The lacing of a buy or sell order results in the exercise of a unique order code (to be retained by the customer and broker). At a securities instrument (eg.. stock) exchange several buy and sell orders may have associated (overlapping) time and price intervals such that transaction can be concluded (by traders). If an order cannot be effected it is withdrawn. Customers may direct funds from or to bank accounts (and is so stated in placed orders). A set of buy and sell orders naming the same securities instrument may constitute the basis for a transaction. The sum of the sell quantities must "be close" or equal to the sum of buy quantities; the time of the transaction must be within the time intervals stated in all these orders; and the transacted price must within the price intervals stated in all these orders. Which transactions are eventually concluded is not a computable decision. It is ("highly") nondeterministic — to some even chaotic.

In the set of exercises related to this topic we forgo any consideration of other than banks, brokers and exchanges (incl. traders).

Exercises related to this topic are: 2.8, 3.5, 4.6, 5.1, 5.2, 5.3, 8.3, 9.3, 10.4, 11.3, 12.6, 13.7, 14.8, 15.17, 16.14, 18.3, 19.6, 20.6, and 21.14.

Examples 9.10 and 9.14 also relate to this exercise topic.

A.4 Summary References to Exercises

Topic	Transportation Nets	Container Logistics	Finance Industry
Numbers	2.6	2.7	2.8
Sets (I)	3.3	3.4	3.5
Cartesians (I)	4.4	4.5	4.6
Types (I)	5.1, 5.2 and 5.3 for all three topics		
Algebras	8.1	8.2	8.3
Logic	9.1	9.2	9.3
Atomicity	10.2	10.3	10.4
Functions	11.1	11.2	11.3
Abstraction	12.4	12.5	12.6
Sets (II)	13.5	13.6	13.7
Cartesians (II)	14.6	14.7	14.8
Lists	15.15	15.16	15.17
Maps	16.12	16.13	16.14
Types	18.1	18.2	18.3
Applicativeness	19.4	19.5	19.6
Imperativeness	20.4	20.5	20.6
Concurrency	21.12	21.13	21.14

B

Glossary

- There is no **prerequisite** for studying this chapter.
- The **aims** are to put the concept of a glossary in the context of like notions of dictionaries, ontologies, taxonomies, terminologies and thesauri and to explain important computer science, computing science and software engineering terms.
- The **objective** is to make the reader professional in the use of terms.
- The **treatment** is systematic.

For parts of 17 of the 788 entries we have quoted from [373]. There are 19 such uses of [350] and four of [227] in this appendix.

In any *software development project* it is important:

- to define the terms before their first use,
- to maintain, including adjust, update and extend, such a glossary of term definitions, and
- to adhere to the definitions.

A list of terms specific to the overlapping areas of informatics, the computer and computing sciences and to software engineering is presented. Each term is described: delineated, characterised, in cases defined, and examples are sometimes illustrated. The list is simply alphabetically sorted. No attempt has been made to construct a thesaurus, a taxonomy or an ontology.

The terms, and especially their descriptions, may not coincide or subsume, or be subsumed by descriptions given in standard glossaries or textbooks of the field. Thus this terminology represents a personal, yet sufficiently honed newest glossary.

> This appendix is very personal, yet, we believe, both scientifically and technically, "correct". The gloss, the selection of entries (which terms to include, which to exclude), and their characterisation, in some cases definition, is our choice. The gloss thus reflects our view of the field of software engineering. One may rightfully claim, we believe, that from this gloss there emerges the contours of an ontology for, or of, software engineering.

B.1 Categories of Reference Lists
On Glossaries, Dictionaries, Encyclopædia, Ontologies, Taxonomies, Terminologies and Thesauri

An important function of glossaries, dictionaries, etc., is to make sure that terms that may seem esoteric do not remain so.

> **Esoteric:** designed for or understood by the specially initiated alone, of or relating to knowledge that is restricted to a small group, limited to a small circle
>
> *Merriam–Webster's Collegiate Dictionary [373]*

B.1.1 Glossary

According to [350] a *gloss* is "a word inserted between the lines or in the margin as an explanatory rendering of a word in the text; hence a similar rendering in a glossary or dictionary. Also, a comment, explanation, interpretation." Furthermore according to [350] a *glossary* is therefore "a collection of glosses, a list with explanations of abstruse, antiquated, dialictical, or technical terms; a partial dictionary." [137] provides a *Glossary of Z Notation*.

B.1.2 Dictionary

According to [350] a *dictionary* is "a book dealing with the words of a language, so as to set forth their orthography, pronunciation, signification, and use, their synonyms, derivation, history, or at least some of these; the words are arranged in some stated order, now, usually, alphabetical; a word book, vocabulary, lexicon. And, by extension: A book on information or reference, on any subject or branch of knowledge, the items of which are arranged alphabetically." Standard dictionaries are [350, 373, 412].

B.1.3 Encyclopædia

According to [350], an *encyclopædia* is "a circle of learning, a general course of instruction. A work containing information on all branches of knowledge, usually arranged alphabetically (1644). A work containing exhaustive information on some one art or branch of knowledge, arranged systematically." [207] is, perhaps, the most "famous" encyclopædia.

B.1.4 Ontology

By *ontology* is meant [350]: "the science or study of being; that department of metaphysics which relates to the being or essence of things, or to being in the abstract." By *an ontology* we shall mean a document which, in a systematic arrangement explains, in a logical manner, a number of abstract concepts.

B.1.5 Taxonomy

By *taxonomy* is meant [350]: "classification, especially in relation to its general laws or principles; that department of science, or of a particular science or subject, which consists in or relates to classification."

B.1.6 Terminology

By a *term* is here meant [350]: "a word or phrase used in a definite or precise sense in some particular subject, as a science or art; a technical expression." More widely: "*Any word or group of words expressing a notion or conception, or denoting an object of thought.*" By *terminology* is meant [350]: "the doctrine or scientific study of terms; the system of terms belonging to a science or subject; technical terms collectively; nomenclature." [341] provides a terminology of *Dependable Computing and Fault Tolerance: Concepts and Terminology*.

B.1.7 Thesaurus

By *thesaurus* is, in general, meant [350]: "a 'treasury' or 'storehouse' of knowledge, as a dictionary, encyclopædia or the like. (1736)" The thesaurus [445] has set a unique standard for and "the" meaning, now, of the term 'thesaurus'.

B.2 Typography and Spelling

Some comments are in order:

- A term *definition* consists of two or three parts.

- ⋆ The first part consists of a natural (the index) number, the term being defined and a colon (:). The term subpart is the *definiendum*.
  - ⋆ The second part is the term definition body, the *definiens*.
  - ⋆ Optional third parts — in parentheses — expand on the definiens, contrast it to other terms, or other.
- The definiendum is a one, two or three word **boldfaced term**.
- The definiens consists of free text which may contain uses of (other, or the same) defined terms.
- *Terms* written in *sans serif italicized font* stand for defined terms.
- Definiens (second part) text ending with [373] (or [350]) represents quotes.
- For reasons of cross-referencing we have spelled the terms α, β and λ as Alpha (alpha), Beta (beta) and Lambda (lambda).
- And we have rewritten the technical terms α-renaming, β-reduction and λ-calculus, conversion and expression (etc.) into Alpha-renaming, Beta-reduction and Lambda-expression, etc., while keeping the hyphens.

B.3 The Glosses

$$\boxed{\ \mathcal{A}}$$

1. **Abstract:** Something which focuses on essential properties. Abstract is a relation: something is abstract with respect to something else (which possesses — what is considered — inessential properties).
2. **Abstract algebra:** An *abstract algebra* is an algebra whose carrier elements and whose functions are defined by *postulates* (*axioms*, *laws*) which specify general properties, rather than values, of functions. (Abstract algebras are also referred to as *postulational*, or *axiomatic algebras*. The axiomatic approach to the study of algebras forms the cornerstone of so-called modern algebra [349].)
3. **Abstract data type:** An *abstract data type* is a set of values for which no external world or computer (i.e., data) representation is being defined, together with a set of abstractly defined functions over these data values.
4. **Abstraction:** 'The art of abstracting. The act of separating in thought; a mere idea; something visionary.'
5. **Abstraction function:** An *abstraction function* is a function which applies to *values* of a *concrete type* and yields values of — what is said to be a corresponding — *abstract type*. (Same as *retrieve function*.)
6. **Abstract syntax:** An *abstract syntax* is a set of rules, often in the form of an *axiom system*, or in the form of a set of *sort definitions*, which defines a set of structures without prescribing a precise external world, or a computer (i.e., data) representation of those structures.
7. **Abstract type:** An *abstract type* is the same as an *abstract data type*, except that no functions over the data values have been specified.

8. **Accessibility:** We say that a *resource* is accessible by another resource, if that other resource can make use of the former resource. (Accessibility is a *dependability requirement*. Usually accessibility is considered a *machine* property. As such, accessibility is (to be) expressed in a *machine requirements* document.)

9. **Acceptor:** An acceptor is a device, like a *finite state automaton* of a *pushdown automaton*, which, when given (i.e., presented with) character strings (or, in general, finite structures), purported to belong to a language, can recognise, i.e., can decide, whether these character strings belong to that language.

10. **Acquirer:** The legal entity, a person, an institution or a firm which orders some *development* to take place. (Synonymous terms are *client* and *customer*.)

11. **Acquisition:** The common term means purchase. Here we mean the collection of *knowledge* (about a *domain*, about some *requirements*, or about some *software*). This collection takes place in an interaction between the *developers* and representatives of the *client* (*users*, etc.). (A synonym term is *elicitation*.)

12. **Action:** By an action we shall understand something who potentially changes a *state*.

13. **Activation stack:** See the *Comment* field of the *function activation* entry.

14. **Active:** By active is understood a *phenomenon* which, over *time*, changes *value*, and does so either by itself, *autonomously*, or also because it is "instructed" (i.e., is "bid" (see *biddable*), or "programmed" (see *programmable*) to do so). (Contrast to *inert* and *reactive*.)

15. **Actor:** By an actor we shall understand someone which carries out an *action*. (A synonymous term for actor is *agent*.)

16. **Actual argument:** When a function is invoked it is usually applied to a list of values, the actual *arguments*. (See also *formal parameter*.)

17. **Actuator:** By an actuator we shall understand an electronic, a mechanical, or an electromechanical device which carries out an *action* that influences some physical *value*. (Usually actuators, together with *sensors*, are placed in *reactive* systems, and are linked to *controllers*. Cf. *sensor*.)

18. **Acyclic:** Acyclicity is normally thought of as a property of graphs. (Hence see next entry: *acyclic graph*.)

19. **Acyclic graph:** An acyclic graph is usually thought of as a *directed graph* in which there is no nonempty *path*, in the direction of the *arrows*, from any *node* to itself. (Often acyclic graphs are called directed acyclic graphs, *DAGs*. An undirected graph which is acyclic is a *tree*.)

20. **Adaptive:** By adaptive we mean some thing that can adapt or arrange itself to a changing *context*, a changing *environment*.

21. **Adaptive maintenance:** By adaptive maintenance we mean an update, as here, of software, to fit (to adapt) to a changing environment. (Adaptive maintenance is required when new input/output media are attached to the existing software, or when a new, underlying database management system

is to be used (instead of an older such), etc. We also refer to *corrective maintenance, perfective maintenance*, and *preventive maintenance*.)

22. **Address:** An address is the same as a *link*, a *pointer* or a *reference*: Something which refers to, i.e., designates something (typically something else). (By an address we shall here, in a narrow sense, understand the *location*, the place, or position in some *storage* at which some *data* is *store*d or kept.)

23. **Ad hoc polymorphism:** See Comment field of *polymorphic*.

24. **Agent:** By an agent we mean the same as an *actor* — a human or a machine (i.e., robot). (The two terms *actor* and *agent* are here considered to be synonymous.)

25. **AI:** Abbreviation for artificial intelligence. (We shall refrain from positing (including risking) a definition of the term AI. Instead we refer to John McCarthy's home page [369].)

26. **Algebra:** An algebra is here taken to just mean: A set of *values*, A, the *carrier* of the algebra, and a set of *functions*, Φ, on these values such that the result values are within the set of values: $\Phi = A^* \to A$. (We make the distinction between *universal algebras*, *abstract algebras* and *concrete algebras*. See also *heterogeneous algebras*, *partial algebras* and *total algebras*.)

27. **Algebraic semantics:** By an algebraic semantics we understand a *semantics* which denotes one, or a (finite or infinite) set of zero, one or more *algebras*. (Usually an algebraic semantics is expressed in terms of (i) *sort* definitions, (ii) *function signatures* and (iii) *axioms*.)

28. **Algebraic systems:** An algebraic system is an *algebra*. (We use the term *system* as an entity with two clearly separable parts: the *carrier* of the algebra and the *functions* of the algebra. We distinguish between *concrete algebras*, *abstract algebras* and *universal algebras* — here listed in order of increasing *abstraction*.)

29. **Algebraic type:** An algebraic type is here considered the same as a *sort*. (That is, algebraic types are specified as are *algebraic systems*.)

30. **Algol:** Algol stands for Algorithmic Language. (`Algol 60` designed in the period 1958–1960 [24]. It became a reference standard for future language designs (Algol W [531], Algol 68 [510], Pascal [292, 314, 522] and others.)

31. **Algorithm:** The notion of an algorithm is so important that we will give a number of not necessarily complementary definitions, and will then discuss these.

   • By an algorithm we shall understand a precise prescription for carrying out an orderly, finite set of *operations* on a set of *data* in order to calculate (*compute*) a result. (This is a version of the classical definition. It is compatible with computability in the sense of *Turing machines* and *Lambda-calculus*. Other terms for algorithm are: effective procedure, and abstract program.)

   • Let there be given a possibly infinite set of *states*, S, let there be given a possibly infinite set of initial states, I, where $I \subseteq S$, and let there be given a next state function $f : S \to S$. (C, where $C =$

(Q, I, f) is an initialised, *deterministic transition* system.) A sequence $s_0, s_1, \ldots, s_{i-1}, s_i, \ldots, s_m$ such that $f(s_{i-1}) = s_i$ is a *computation*. An algorithm, A, is a C with final states O, i.e.: $A = (Q, I, f, O)$, where $O \subseteq S$, such that each computation ends with a state s_m in O. (This is basically Don Knuth's definition [326]. In that definition a state is a collection of identified data, i.e., a formalised representation of information, i.e., of computable data. Thus Knuth's definition is still Turing and Lambda-calculus "compatible".)

- There is given the same definition as just above with the generalisation that a state is any association of variables to phenomena, whether the latter are representable "inside" the computer or not. (This is basically Yuri Gurevitch's definition of an algorithm [253, 438, 439]. As such this definition goes beyond Turing machine and Lambda-calculus "compatibility". That is, captures more!)

32. **Algorithmic:** Adjective form of *algorithm*.

33. **Allocate:** To apportion for a specific purpose or to particular persons or things, to distribute tasks among human and automated components. (We shall here use the term generally for the allocation of *resources* (see also *resource allocation*), specifically for *storage* to *assignable variables*. In the general sense, allocation, as the name implies, has some spatial qualities about it: allocation to spatial positions. In the special sense we can indeed talk of storage space.)

34. **Alphabet:** A finite collection of script symbols called the letters of the alphabet.

35. **Alpha-renaming:** By alpha-renaming (α-renaming) we mean the substitution of a *binding identifier*, with another, the "new", identifier, in some *Lambda-expression* (statement or clause), such that all free occurrences of that binding identifier in that expression (statement or clause) are replaced by the new identifier, and such that that new identifier is not already bound in that expression (statement or clause). (Alpha-renaming is a concept of the *Lambda-calculus*.)

36. **Ambiguous:** A *sentence* is ambiguous if it is open to more than one *interpretation*, i.e., has more than one *model* and these models are not *isomorphic*.

37. **Analogic:** Equivalence or likeness of relations. Resemblance of relations or attributes as a ground of reasoning. Also: Presumptive reasoning based on the assumption that if things have some similar attributes, their other attributes will be similar [350].

38. **Analogue:** A representative in another class or group [350]. (Used in these volumes in the sense above, not in the sense of electrical engineering or control theory.)

39. **Analysis:** The resolution of anything complex into simple elements. A determination of proper components. The tracing of things to their sources; the discovery of general principles underlying concrete phenomena [350]. (In conventional mathematics analysis pertains to continuous phenomena,

e.g. differential and integral calculi. Our analysis is more related to hybrid systems of both discrete and continuous phenomena, or often to just discrete ones.)

40. **Analytic:** Of, or pertaining to, or in accordance with *analysis*.

41. **Analytic grammar:** A *grammar*, i.e., a *syntax* whose designated sentences (in general: Structures) can be subject to *analysis*, i.e., where the syntactic composition can be revealed through *analysis*.

42. **Anomaly:** Deviation from the normal.

43. **Anthropomorphic:** Attributing a human personality to anything impersonal or irrational [350]. (See *anthropomorphism*. It seems to be a "disease" of programmers to attribute their programs with human properties: "The program does so-and-so; and after that, it then goes on to do such-and-such," etcetera. Programs, to recall, are, as are any description is, a mere syntactic, i.e., static text. As such they certainly can "do nothing". But they may prescribe that certain actions are effected by machine — when a machine interprets ("executes") the program text!)

44. **Anthropomorphism:** Ascription of a human form and attributes to the Deity, or of a human attribute or personality to anything impersonal or irrational [350]. (See *anthropomorphic*.)

45. **Application:** By an application we shall understand either of two rather different things: (i) the application of a function to an *argument*, and (ii) the use of software for some specific purpose (i.e., the application). (See next entry for variant (ii).)

46. **Application domain:** An area of activity which some *software* is to support (or supports) or partially or fully automate (resp. automates). (We normally omit the prefix 'application' and just use the term *domain*.)

47. **Applicative:** The term applicative is used in connection with applicative programming. It is hence understood as programming where applying functions to *argument*s is a main form of expression, and hence designates function application as a main form of operation. (Thus the terms applicative and *functional* are here used synonymously.)

48. **Applicative programming:** See the term *applicative* just above. (Thus the terms applicative programming and *functional programming* are here used synonymously.)

49. **Applicative programming language:** Same as *functional programming language*.

50. **Arc:** Same as an *edge*. (Used normally in connection with *graph*s.)

51. **Architecture:** The structure and content of *software* as perceived by their *user*s and in the context of the *application domain*. (The term architecture is here used in a rather narrow sense when compared with the more common use in civil engineering.)

52. **Argument:** A *value* provided (possibly as part of an argument list) when invoking a function.

53. **Arity:** By the arity of a *function* (i.e., an *operation*) we understand the number (0, 1, or more) of *argument*s that the function applies to. (Usually

a function applies to an argument list, and the arity is therefore the length of this list.)

54. **Arrow:** A directed *edge*. (*Branches* are arrows.)
55. **Artefact:** An artificial product [350]. (Anything designed or constructed by humans or machines, which is made by humans.)
56. **Artifact:** Same term as *artefact*.
57. **Artificial intelligence:** See *AI*.
58. **Assertion:** By an assertion we mean the act of stating positively usually in anticipation of denial or objection. (In the context of *specifications* and *programs* an assertion is usually in the form of a pair of *predicates* "attached" to the specification text, to the program text, and expressing properties that are believed to hold before any interpretation of the text; that is, "a before" and "an after", or, as we shall also call it: a **pre-** and a **post-**condition.)
59. **Assignable variable:** By an assignable variable we understand an entity of a program text which *denotes* a *storage location* whose associated *value* can be changed by an *assignment*. (Usually, in the context of specifications and programs, assignable variables are declared.)
60. **Assignment:** By an assignment we mean an update to, a change of a *storage location*. (Usually, in the context of specifications and programs, assignments are prescribed by assignment statements.)
61. **Associative:** Property of a binary operator o: If for all values a, b and c, $(a\ o\ b)\ o\ c\ =\ a\ o\ (b\ o\ c)$, then o is said to be an associative operator. (Addition ($+$) and multiplication ($*$) of natural numbers are associative operators.)
62. **Asynchronous:** Not *synchronous*. (In the context of computing we say that two or more *processes* — some of which may represent the world external to the computing device — are asynchronous if occurrences of the *events* of these processes are not (a priori) coordinated.)
63. **Atomic:** In the context of software engineering atomic means: A *phenomenon* (a *concept*, an *entity*, a *value*) which consists of no proper subparts, i.e., no proper subphenomena, subconcepts, subentities or subvalues other than itself. (When we consider a phenomenon, a concept, an entity, a value, to be atomic, then it is often a matter of choice, with the choice reflecting a level of abstraction.)
64. **Attribute:** We use the term attribute only in connection with values of composite type. An attribute is now whether a composite value possesses a certain property, or what value it has for a certain component part. (An example is that of database (e.g., SQL) relations (i.e., tabular data structures): Columns of a table (i.e., a relation) are usually labelled with a name designating the attribute (type) for values of that column. Another example is that, say, of a Cartesian: $A = B \times C \times D$. A can be said to have the attributes B, C, and D. Yet other examples are $M = A \xrightarrow{\text{\tiny{m}}} B$, S = A-**set** and $L = A^*$. M is said to have attributes A and B. S is said to have attribute A. L is said to have attribute A. In general we make the distinction between

an entity consisting of subentities (being decomposable into proper parts, cf. *subentity*), and the entities having attributes. A person, like me, has a height attribute, but my height cannot be "composed away from me"!)

65. **Attribute grammar:** A grammar, usually expressed as a *BNF grammar*, where, to each *rule*, and to each nonterminal, of the left-hand side or of the right-hand side of the rule, there is associated one or more (attribute) *assignable variables* together with a set of single assignments to some of these variables — such that the assignment expression variables are those of the attribute variables of the rule.

66. **Automaton:** An automaton is a device with *states*, *inputs*, some states designated as final states, and with a next state *transition* function which to every state and input designates a next state. (There may be a finite, or there may be an infinite number of states. The next state transition function may be *deterministic* or *nondeterministic*.)

67. **Automorphism:** An *isomorphism* that maps an algebra into itself is an automorphism. (We refer to Sect. 8.4.4. See also *endomorphism*, *epimorphism*, *homomorphism*, *monomorphism*.)

68. **Autonomous:** A *phenomenon* (a *concept*, an *entity*) is said to be autonomous if it changes *value* at its own discretion or without influence from an *environment*. (Rephrasing the above we get: (i) A phenomenon is said to be of, or possess, the autonomous active dynamic attribute if it changes value only on its own volition — that is, it cannot also change value as a result of external stimuli; (ii) or when its actions cannot be controlled in any way: That is, they are a "law onto themselves and their surroundings". We speak of such *phenomena* as being *dynamic*. Other dynamic *active* phenomena may be *active* or *reactive*.)

69. **Availability:** We say that a *resource* is available for use by other resources, if within a reasonable time interval these other resources can make use of the former resource. (Availability is a *dependability requirement*. Usually availability is considered a *machine* property. As such availability is (to be) expressed in a *machine requirements* document.)

70. **Axiom:** An established rule or principle or a self-evident truth.

71. **Axiomatic specification:** A *specification* presented, i.e., given, in terms of a set of *axioms*. (Usually an axiomatic specification also includes definitions of *sorts* and *function signatures*.)

72. **Axiom system:** Same as *axiomatic specification*.

$\mathcal{B}$

---

73. **B:** B stands for Bourbaki, pseudonym for a group of mostly French mathematicians which began meeting in the 1930s, aiming to write a thorough unified set-theoretic account of all mathematics. They had tremendous influence on the way mathematics has been done since. (The founding of the Bourbaki group is described in André Weil's autobiography, titled something like "memoir of an apprenticeship" (orig. Souvenirs

D'apprentissage). There is a usable book on Bourbaki by J. Fang. Liliane Beaulieu has a book forthcoming, which you can sample in "A Parisian Cafe and Ten Proto-Bourbaki Meetings 1934–1935" in the Mathematical Intelligencer 15 no. 1 (1993) 27–35. From `http://www.faqs.org/faqs/-sci-math-faq/bourbaki/` (2004). Founding members were: Henri Cartan, Claude Chevalley, Jean Coulomb, Jean Delsarte, Jean Dieudonné, Charles Ehresmann, René de Possel, Szolem Mandelbrojt, André Weil. From: `http://www.bourbaki.ens.fr/` (2004). B also stands for a model-oriented specification language [3].)

74. **Behaviour:** By behaviour we shall understand the way in which something functions or operates. (In the context of *domain engineering* behaviour is a concept associated with *phenomena*, in particular manifest *entities*. And then behaviour is that which can be observed about the *value* of the *entity* and its *interaction* with an *environment*.)

75. **Beta-reduction:** By Beta-reduction we understand the substitution whereby all *free* occurrences of a designated *variable* in a *Lambda-expression* are replaced by *Lambda-expression* (in which some *Alpha-renamings* may have to be made first).

76. **Biddable:** A *phenomenon* is biddable if it can be advised (through a "contractual arrangement") on which *action*s are expected of it in various *states*. (A biddable phenomenon does not have to take these actions, but then the "contractual arrangement" need no longer be honoured by other phenomena (other [sub]domains) with which it *interacts* (i.e., shares phenomena).)

77. **Bijection:** See *bijective function*.

78. **Bijective function:** A total *surjective function* which maps all *values* of its postulated *definition set* into all distinct values of its postulated *range*set is called bijective. (See also *injective function* and *surjective function*.)

79. **Binding:** By binding we mean a pairing of, usually, an *identifier*, a *name*, with some *resource*. (In the context of software engineering we find such bindings as: (i) of an *assignable variable* to a *storage location*, (ii) of a *procedure name* to a procedure *denotation*, etc.)

80. **Block:** By a block we shall here understand a textual entity, one that is suitably delineated. (In the context of software engineering a block is normally some partial *specification* which locally introduces some (*applicative*, i.e., expression) constant definitions (i.e., **let .. in .. end**), or some (*imperative*, i.e., statement) local variable declarations (i.e., **begin dcl .. ; .. end**).)

81. **Block-structured programming language:** A *programming language* is said to be block-structured if it permits such program constructs (incl. *procedures*) whose *semantics* amount to the creation of a local identifier *scope*, and where such can be nested, zero, one or more within another.

82. **BNF:** Abbreviation for Backus–Naur Form (Grammar). (See *BNF Grammar*.)

83. **BNF grammar:** By BNF Grammar we mean a concrete, linear textual representation of a *grammar*, i.e., a *syntax*, one that *designate*s a set of strings. (A BNF Grammar usually is represented in the form of a set of *rule*s. Each rule has a *nonterminal* left-hand-side *symbol* and a finite set of zero, one or more alternative right-hand-side strings of *terminal* and nonterminal symbols.)

84. **Boolean:** By Boolean we mean a data type of logical values (**true** and **false**), and a set of connectives: $\sim$, $\wedge$, $\vee$, and $\Rightarrow$. (Boolean derives from the name of the mathematician George Boole.)

85. **Boolean connective:** By a *Boolean connective* we mean either of the Boolean operators: $\wedge$, $\vee$, $\Rightarrow$ (or $\supset$), $\sim$ (or $\neg$).

86. **Bound:** The concept of being bound is associated with (i) *identifier*s (i.e., *name*s) and *expression*s, and (ii) with *name*s (i.e., *identifier*s) and *resource*s. An identifier is said to be either *free* or bound in an expression based on certain rules being satisfied or not. If an identifier is bound in an expression then bound occurrences of that identifier are bound to the same resource. If a name is bound to some resource then all bound occurrences of that name *denote* that resource. (Cf. *free*.)

87. **BPR:** See *business process reengineering*

88. **Branch:** Almost the same as an *edge*, except that branches are directed, i.e., are (like) *arrow*s. (Used usually in connection with *tree*s.)

89. **Brief:** By a brief is understood a *document*, or a part of a document which informs about a *phase* , or a *stage* , or a *step* of *development*. (A brief thus contains *information*.)

90. **Business process:** By a business process we shall understand a *behaviour* of an enterprise, a business, an institution, a factory. (Thus a business process reflects the ways in which a business conducts its affairs, and is a *facet* of the *domain*. Other facets of an enterprise are those of its *intrinsics, management and organisation* (a facet closely related, of course, to business processes), *support technology*, *rules and regulations*, and *human behaviour*.)

91. **Business process engineering:** By *business process engineering* we shall understand the *design*, the determination, of *business process*es. (In doing business process engineering one is basically designing, i.e., prescribing entirely new business processes.)

92. **Business process reengineering:** By *business process reengineering* we shall understand the re*design*, the change, of *business process*es. (In doing business process reengineering one is basically carrying out *change management*.)

	C

93. **Calculate:** Given an expression and an applicable *rule* of a *calculus*, to change the former expression into a resulting expression. (Same as *compute*.)

94. **Calculation:** A sequence of steps which, from an initial expression, following rules of a *calculus*, *calculate*s another, perhaps the same, expression. (Same as *computation*.)

95. **Calculus:** A method of *computation* or *calculation* in a special notation. (From mathematics we know the differential and the integral calculi, and also the Laplace calculus. From metamathematics we have learned of the λ-calculus. From logic we know of the Boolean (propositional) calculus.)

96. **Capture:** The term capture is used in connection with *domain knowledge* (i.e., *domain capture*) and with *requirements acquisition*. It shall indicate the act of acquiring, of obtaining, of writing down, domain knowledge, respectively requirements.

97. **Carrier:** By a carrier is understood a, or the set of *entities* of an *algebra* — the former in the case of a *heterogeneous algebra*.

98. **Cartesian:** By a Cartesian is understood an ordered product, a fixed grouping, a fixed composition, of *entities*. (Cartesian derives from the name of the French mathematician René Descartes.)

99. **C.C.I.T.T:** Abbreviation for Comité Consultative Internationale de Telegraphie et Telephonie. (CCITT is an alternative form of reference.)

100. **Change management:** Same as *business process reengineering*.

101. **Channel:** By a channel is understood a means of *interaction*, i.e., of *communication* and possibly of *synchronisation* between *behaviour*s. (In the context of computing we can think of channels as being either input, or output, or both input and output channels.)

102. **Chaos:** By **chaos** we understand the totally undefined *behaviour*: Anything may happen! (In the context of computing **chaos** may, for example, be the *designation* for the never-ending, the never-terminating *process*.)

103. **CHI:** Abbreviation for Computer Human Interface. (Same as *HCI*.)

104. **CHILL:** Abbreviation for CCITT's High Level Language. (See [145,254].)

105. **Class:** By a class we mean either of two things: a **class** *clause*, as in RSL, or a set of *entities* defined by some *specification*, typically a *predicate*.

106. **Clause:** By a clause is meant an *expression*, designating a *value*, or a *statement*, designating a *state* change, or a sentential form, which designates both a value and a state change. (When we use the term clause we mean it mostly in the latter sense of both designating a value and a side effect.)

107. **Client:** By a client we mean any of three things: (i) The legal body (a person or a company) which orders the development of some software, or (ii) a *process* or a *behaviour* which *interact*s with another process or behaviour (i.e., the *server*), in order to have that server perform some *action*s on behalf of the client, or (iii) a user of some software (i.e., computing system). (We shall normally use the term customer in the first or in the second sense (i, ii).)

108. **Closure:** By a closure is usually meant some transitive closure of a relation $\Re$: If $a\Re b$ and $b\Re c$ then $a\Re c$, and so forth. To this we shall add another meaning, used in connection with implementation of (for example) procedures: Denotationally a procedure, when invoked, in some calling environ-

ment, is to be interpreted in the defining environment. Hence a procedure closure is a pair: The procedure text and the defining environment.

109. **Code:** By code we mean a *program* which is expressed in the machine language of a computer.

110. **Coding:** By coding we shall here, simply, mean the act of programming in a machine, i.e., in a computer-close language. (Thus we do not, except where explicitly so mentioned, mean the encoding of one string of characters into another, say for *communication* over a possibly faulty communication *channel* (usually with the decoding of the encoded string "back" into the original, or a similar string).)

111. **Cohesion:** Cohesion expresses a measure of "closeness", of "dependency", of "sticking together" among a set of entities. (In the context of software engineering cohesion is, as it is here, a term used to express a dependency relation between *module*s of a *specification* or a *program*. Two modules have a higher cohesion the larger the number of cross-references (to types and values, including, in particular functions) there are among them.)

112. **Collision:** Collision, as used here, means that two (or more) occurrences of the same identifier, of which at least one is free, and which at some stage occurred in different text parts, are brought together, say by function application (i.e., macro-expansion) and thereby become bound. (Collision is a concept introduced in the Lambda-calculus, see Vol. 1, Chap. 7, Sect. 7.7.4.3. Collision is an undesirable effect. See also *confusion*.)

113. **Communication:** A *process* by which *information* is exchanged between individuals (*behaviour*s, *process*es) through a common *system* of *symbol*s, *sign*s, or *protocol*s.

114. **Commutative:** Property of a binary operator o: If for all values a and b, $a \; o \; b = b \; o \; a$, then o is said to be a commutative operator. (Addition (+) and multiplication (*) of natural numbers are commutative operators.)

115. **Compilation:** By a compilation we shall mean the conversion, the *translation*, of one formal text to another, usually a high-level program text to a low-level machine code text.

116. **Compiler:** By a compiler we understand a device (usually a software package) which given *sentence*s (i.e., *source program*s) in one language, generates sentences (i.e., *target program*s) in another language. (Usually the source and the target languages are related as follows: The source language is normally a so-called "higher-order" language, like Java, and the target language is normally a "lower (abstraction) level" language, like Java Byte Code (or a computer machine language) for which an interpreter is readily available.)

117. **Compiler dictionary:** By a compiler dictionary we shall understand a composite data structure (with a varying number of entries) and a fixed number of operations. The data structure values reflect properties of a program text being compiled. These properties could be: types of some program text variable, type structure of some program text type name, program point of definition of some (goto) label, etc. The possibly hierar-

chical, i.e., recursively nested, structure of the compiler dictionary further reflects a similarly hierarchical structure of the program text being compiled. The operations include those that insert, update, and search for entries in the compiler dictionary.

118. **Compile time:** By compile time we understand that time interval during which a *source program* is being compiled and during which certain analyses, and hence decisions, can be made about, and actions taken with respect to the source program (to be, i.e., being, compiled) — such as *type checking*, name *scope checking*, etc. (Contrast to *run time*.)

119. **Compiling algorithm:** By a compiling algorithm we shall understand a specification which, for every rule in a syntax (of a *source programming* language), prescribes which *target programming* language data structure to generate. (We refer to Vol. 2, Chap. 16 (Sects. 16.8–16.10) for "our story" on compiling algorithms.)

120. **Complete:** We say that a *proof system* is complete if all true sentences are provable.

121. **Completeness:** Noun form of the *complete* adjective.

122. **Component:** By a component we shall here understand a set of type definitions and component local variable declarations, i.e., a component local state, this together with a (usually complete) set of modules, such that these modules together implement a set of concepts and facilities, i.e., functions, that are judged to relate to one another.

123. **Component design:** By a component design we shall understand the *design* of (one or more) *components*. (We shall refer to Vol. 3, Chaps. 28–29 for "our story" on component design.)

124. **Composite:** We say that a *phenomenon*, a *concept*, is composite when it is possible, and meaningful, to consider that phenomenon or concept as analysable into two or more subphenomena or subconcepts.

125. **Composition:** By composition we mean the way in which a *phenomenon*, a *concept*, is "put together" (i.e., composed) into a *composite phenomenon*, resp. *concept*.

126. **Compositional:** We say that two or more *phenomena* or *concepts* are compositional if it is meaningful to *compose* these phenomena and/or concepts. (Typically a *denotational semantics* is expressed compositionally: By composing the semantics of sentence parts into the semantics of the composition of the sentence parts.)

127. **Compositional documentation:** By compositional documentation we mean a development, or a presentation (of that development), of, as here, some *description* (*prescription* or *specification*), in which some notion of "smallest", i.e., atomic phenomena and concepts are developed (resp. presented) first, then their compositions, etc., until some notion of full, complete development (etc.) has been achieved. (See also *composition, compositional* and *hierarchical documentation*.)

128. **Comprehension:** By comprehension we shall here mean *set, list* or *map* comprehension, that is, the expression, of a set, a list, respectively a map,

by a predicate over the elements of the set, list or pairings of the map, that belong to the set, list, respectively the map.

129. **Computation:** See *calculation*.

130. **Computational linguistics:** The study and knowledge of the *syntax* and *semantics* of *language* based on notions of *computer science* and *computing science*. (Thus computational linguistics emphasises those aspects of language whose analysis (*recognition*), or synthesis (*generation*), can be mechanised.)

131. **Computational data+control requirements:** By a computational data + control requirements we mean a requirements which express how the dynamics of computations or data (may) warrant interaction between the machine and its environment, hence is an *interface requirements facet*. (See also *shared data initialisation requirements*, *shared data refreshment requirements*, *man-machine dialogue requirements*, *man-machine physiological requirements*, and *machine-machine dialogue requirements*.)

132. **Computational semantics:** By a computational semantics we mean a specification of the semantics of a language which emphasises run-time computations, i.e., state-to-next-state transitions, as effected when following the prescriptions of programs. (Terms similar in meaning to computational semantics are *operational semantics* and *structural operational semantics*.)

133. **Compute:** Given an expression and an applicable *rule* of a *calculus*, to change the former expression into a resulting expression. (Same as *calculate*.)

134. **Computer Science:** The study and knowledge of the phenomena that can exist inside computers.

135. **Computing Science:** The study and knowledge of how to construct those phenomena that can exist inside computers.

136. **Computing system:** A combination of *hardware* and *software* that together make meaningful *computation*s possible.

137. **Concept:** An abstract or generic idea generalised from phenomena or concepts. (A working definition of a concept has it comprising two components: The *extension* and the *intension*. A word of warning: Whenever we describe something claimed to be a "real instance", i.e., a physical *phenomenon*, then even the description becomes that of a concept, not of "that real thing"!)

138. **Concept formation:** The forming, the enunciation, the *analysis*, and definition of *concepts* (on the basis, as here, of *analysis* of the *universe of discourse* (be it a *domain* or some *requirements*)). (Domain and requirements concept formation(s) is treated in Vol. 3, Chaps. 13 (Domain Analysis and Concept Formation) and 21 (Requirements Analysis and Concept Formation).)

139. **Concrete:** By concrete we understand a *phenomenon* or, even, a *concept*, whose explication, as far as is possible, considers all that can be observed about the phenomenon, respectively the concept. (We shall, however, use

the term concrete more loosely: To characterise that something, being specified, is "more concrete" (possessing more properties) than something else, which has been specified, and which is thus considered "more abstract" (possessing fewer properties [considered more relevant]).)

140. **Concrete algebra:** A *concrete algebra* is an algebra whose carrier is some known set of mathematical elements and whose functions are known, i.e., well-defined. That is, the *model*s of both the carrier and all the functions are pre-established. (Concrete algebras are the level of the empirical (actual) world of mathematics and its applications, where one deals with specific sets of elements (integers, Booleans, reals, etc.), and where operations on these sets that are defined by rules or algorithms or combinations. In general one "knows" a concrete algebra when one knows what the elements of the carrier A are and how to *evaluate* the functions $\phi_i : \Phi$ over A [349].)

141. **Concrete syntax:** A *concrete syntax* is a syntax which prescribes actual, computer representable *data structure*s. (Typically a *BNF Grammar* is a concrete syntax.)

142. **Concrete type:** A *concrete type* is a type which prescribes actual, computer representable *data structure*s. (Typically the type definitions of programming languages designate concrete types.)

143. **Concurrency:** By concurrency we mean the simultaneous existence of two or more *behaviour*s, i.e., two or more *process*es. (That is, a *phenomenon* is said to exhibit concurrency when one can analyse the phenomenon into two or more *concurrent* phenomena.)

144. **Concurrent:** Two (or more) *event*s can be said to occur concurrently, i.e., be concurrent, when one cannot meaningfully describe any one of these events to ("always") "occur" before any other of these events. (Thus concurrent systems are systems of two or more processes (behaviours) where the simultaneous happening of "things" (i.e., events) is deemed beneficial, or useful, or, at least, to take place!)

145. **Configuration:** By a configuration we shall here understand the *composition* of two or more *semantic value*s. (Usually we shall decompose a configuration into parts such that each part enjoys a *temporal* relationship with respect to the other parts: being "more *dynamic*", being "more *static*", etc. More specifically, we shall typically model the semantics of *imperative* programming languages in terms of *semantic function*s over configurations composed from *environment*s and *storage*s.)

146. **Conformance:** Conformance is a relation between two *document*s (A and B). B is said to conform to A, if everything A specifies is satisfied by B. (Conformance is thus, here, taken to be the same as *correct*ness, i.e., *congruence*. Usually conformance is used in standardisation documents: *Any system claiming to follow this standard must show conformance to it.*)

147. **Confusion:** Confusion, as used here, means that two (or more) occurrences of the same identifier, bound to possibly different values, may be

confused in that it is difficult from a smaller context of the text in which they occur to discern, to decide, which meanings, which values, the various occurrences are bound to. (Confusion is a concept introduced in the Lambda-calculus, see Vol. 1, Chap. 7, Sect. 7.7.4.3. Confusion is an OK, albeit annoying, effect! See also *collision*.)

148. **Congruence:** An *algebra*, A, is said to be congruent with another algebra, B, if, for every operation, o_B, and suitable set of arguments, $b_1, b_2, \ldots, b_n$, to that operation, in B, there corresponds an operation, o_A, and a suitable set of arguments, $a_1, a_2, \ldots, a_n$, in A such that $o_A(a_1, a_2, \ldots, a_n) = o_B(b_1, b_2, \ldots, b_n)$. (Compare this definition to that of *conformance*. The difference is one between a precise, mathematical meaning of congruence, as contrasted to an informal meaning of conformance.)

149. **Conjunction:** Being combined, being conjoined, composed. (We shall mostly think of conjunction as the (meaning of the) logical connective "and": $\wedge$.)

150. **Connection:** Connection is a topological notion, and, as such, is also an ontological concept related to "parts and wholes", where parts may be, or may not be connected, i.e., "so close" to one another, that there can be no other parts "inserted in between".

151. **Connector:** We shall here, by a connector, mean a hardware, or some software device that "connects" two like devices, hardware+hardware, or software+software. (Typically, in software engineering, when "connecting" two independently developed *components*, one deploys a connector in order to connect them.)

152. **Connective:** By a connective is here meant one of the Boolean "operators": "and" $\wedge$, "or" $\vee$, "imply" $\Rightarrow$, and "negation" $\sim$.

153. **Consistent:** A set of *axioms* is said to be consistent if, by means of these, and some *deduction rules*, one cannot *prove* a property and its negation.

154. **Consistency:** Being *consistent* (throughout).

155. **Constraint:** By a constraint we shall here, in a somewhat narrow sense, understand a property that must be satisfied by certain values of a given type. (That is: The type may define more values than are to be satisfied by the constraint. We also use the terms *data invariant*, or *well-formedness*. The term constraint has taken on a larger meaning than propagated in this book. We refer to *constraint programming, constraint satisfaction problems*, etc. For a seminal text book we refer to [18]. In constraint programming a constraint, as expressed in a problem model, and hence in a constraint program, is a relation on a sequence of values of (a sequence of) variables of that program. As you see, the difference, in the two meanings of 'constraint', really, is minor.)

156. **Constructor:** By a constructor we mean either of two, albeit related, things, a type constructor, or a value constructor. By a type constructor we mean an operator on types which when applied to types, say A, constructs another type, say B. By a value constructor we mean a some-

times distributed fix operator which when applied to one or more values constructs a value of a different type. (Examples of type constructors are -set, $\times$, *, $^\omega$, $\overset{\sim}{\twoheadrightarrow}$, $\rightarrow$, $\overset{\sim}{\rightarrow}$ (sets, Cartesians, finite lists, finite and infinite lists, maps, total functions, partial functions), and mk_B. Examples of value constructors are: $\{\bullet,\bullet,...,\bullet\}$, $(\bullet,\bullet,...,\bullet)$, $\langle\bullet,\bullet,...,\bullet\rangle$, $[\bullet\mapsto\bullet,\bullet\mapsto\bullet,...,\bullet\mapsto\bullet]$ and mk_B($\bullet,\bullet,...,\bullet$), etc., (sets, Cartesians, lists, maps, and variant records).)

157. **Context:** There are two related meanings: (i) the parts of a discourse that surround some text and (ii) the interrelated conditions in which something is understood. (The former meaning emphasises *syntactical* properties, i.e., speaks of a syntactic context; the latter, we claim, *semantical* properties (i.e., semantic context). We shall often, by a syntactic context speak of the *scope* of an *identifier*: the text (parts) over which the identifier is defined, i.e., is *bound*. And by a semantic context we then speak of the *environment* in which an *identifier* is *bound* to its semantic meaning. As such semantic contexts go, hand-in-hand, in *configurations*, with *states*.)

158. **Context-Free:** By context-free we mean that something is defined free of any considerations of the *context* in which that "something" (otherwise) occurs. (We shall use the context-free concept extensively: *context-free grammar* and *context-free syntax*, etc. The *type definition rules* of RSL have a context-free interpretation.)

159. **Context-Free language:** By a context-free language we mean a *language* which can be generated by a *context-free syntax*. (See *generator*.)

160. **Context-Free Grammar:** See *context-free syntax*.

161. **Context-Free Syntax:** By a context-free syntax we shall understand a type system consisting of type definitions in which right-hand-side occurrences of defined *type names* can be freely substituted for any of a variety of their definitions. (Typically a *BNF grammar* specifies a context-free syntax.)

162. **Context-Sensitive Grammar:** See *context-sensitive syntax*.

163. **Context-Sensitive Syntax:** By a context-sensitive syntax we may understand a type system consisting of ordinary type definitions in which right-hand-side occurrences of defined *type names* cannot be freely substituted for any of a variety of their definitions, but may only be substituted provided these right-hand-side type names (i.e., *nonterminals*) occur in specified contexts (of other type names or *literals*). (Usually a context-sensitive syntax can be specified by a set of rules where both left-hand and right-hand sides are composite type expressions. The left-hand-side composite expression then specifies the contexts in which the right-hand side may be substituted.)

164. **Continuation:** By a continuation we shall, rather technically, understand a state-to-state transformation function, specifically one that is the denotation of a *program point*, that is, of any computation as from that program point (i.e., *label*) onwards — until program *termination*.

165. **Continuous:** Of a mathematical curve, i.e., function: 'Having the property that the absolute value of the numerical difference between the value

at a given point and the value at any point in a neighborhood of the given point can be made as close to zero as desired by choosing the neighborhood small enough' [373].

166. **Contract:** A legally binding agreement between two or more parties — hence a document describing the conditions of the contract. (To us, in software development, a contract specifies what is to be developed (a *domain description*, a *requirements prescription*, or a *software design*), how it might, or must be developed, criteria for acceptance of what has been developed, delivery dates for the developed items, who the "parties" to the contract are: the *client* and the *developer*, etc.)

167. **Control:** To control has two meanings: to check, test or verify by evidence or experiments, and to exercise restraining or directing influence over, to regulate. (We shall mostly mean the second form. And we shall often use the term 'control' in conjunction with the term '*monitor*ing'.)

168. **Controller:** By a controller we here mean a *computing system*, which interfaces with some physical environment, a *reactive* system, i.e., a plant, and which, by temporally sensing (i.e., sampling) characteristic values of that plant, and by similarly regularly activating *actuator*s in the plant, can make the plant behave according to desired prescriptions. (We stress the reactive system nature of the plant to be controlled. See also *sensor*.)

169. **Conversion:** By conversion we shall here, in a rather limiting sense, with a base in the *Lambda-calculus*, understand either an *Alpha-renaming* or a *Beta-reduction* of some *Lambda-expression*. (We refer to Chap. 7.)

170. **Correct:** See next entry: *correctness*.

171. **Correctness:** Correctness is a relation between two specifications A and B: B is correct with respect to A if every property of what is specified in A is a property of B. (Compare to *conformance* and *congruence*.)

172. **Corrective maintenance:** By corrective maintenance we understand a change, predicated by a specification A, to a specification, B', resulting in a specification, B'', such that B'' satisfies more properties of A than does B'. (That is: Specification B' is in error in that it is not *correct* with respect to A. But B'' is an improvement over B'. Hopefully B'' is then correct wrt. A. We also refer to *adaptive maintenance*, *perfective maintenance*, and *preventive maintenance*.)

173. **CSP:** Abbreviation for Communicating Sequential Processes. (See [288, 448] and Chap. 21. Also, but not in this book, a term that covers constraint satisfaction problem (or programming).)

174. **Curry:** Name of American mathematician: Haskell B. Curry. Also a verb: to Curry — see *Currying*.

175. **Curried:** A *function invocation*, commonly written $f(a_1, a_2, ..., a_n)$, is said to be Curried when instead written: $f(a_1)(a_2)...(a_n)$. (The act of rewriting a function invocation into Curried form is called *Currying*.)

176. **Currying:** A *function signature*, normally written, f: $A \times B \times ... \times C \rightarrow D$ can be Curried into being written f: $A \rightarrow B \rightarrow ... \rightarrow C \rightarrow D$. The act of doing so is called Currying.

177. **Customer:** By a customer we mean either of three things: (i) the *client*, a person, or a company, which orders the development of some software, or (ii) a *client process* or a *behaviour* which *interacts* with another process or behaviour (i.e., the *server*), in order to have that server perform some *action*s on behalf of the client, or (iii) a user of some software (i.e., computing system). (We shall normally use the term customer in the third sense (iii).)

	$\mathcal{D}$

178. **DAG:** Abbreviation for directed (i.e., oriented) *acyclic graph*.
179. **Dangling reference:** A reference is usually a "pointer", a "link" to some resource. A dangling reference is a reference where that resource has been lost, i.e., has been removed. (Usually the reference is a location and the location has been "freed", i.e., deallocated.)
180. **Data:** Data is formalised representation of information. (In our context information is what we may know, informally, and even express, in words, or informal text or diagrams, etc. Data is correspondingly the internal computer, including database representation of such information.)
181. **Database:** By a database we shall generally understand a large collection of data. More specifically we shall, by a database, imply that the data are organised according to certain data structuring and data *query* and *update* principles. (Classically, three forms of (data structured) databases can be identified: The *hierarchical*, the *network*, and the *relational* database forms. We refer to [176, 177] for seminal coverage, and to [62, 65, 124, 125] for formalisation, of these database forms.)
182. **Database schema:** By a database schema we understand a *type definition* of the structure of the data kept in a database.
183. **Data abstraction:** Data abstraction takes place when we abstract from the particular formal representation of data.
184. **Data invariant:** By a *data* invariant is understood some property that is expected to hold for all instances of the data. (We use the term 'data' colloquially, and really should say type invariance, or variable content invariance. Then 'instances' can be equated with values. See also *constraint*.)
185. **Data refinement:** Data refinement is a relation. It holds between a pair of data if one can be said to be a "more concrete" implementation of the other. (The whole point of *data abstraction*, in earlier *phase*s, *stage*s and *step*s of *development*, is that we can later concretise, i.e., data refine.)
186. **Data reification:** Same as *data refinement*. (To reify is to render something abstract as a material or concrete thing.)
187. **Data structure:** By a data structure we shall normally understand a composition of *data value*s, for example, in the "believed" form of a linked *list*, a *tree*, a *graph* or the like. (As in contrast to an *information structure*, a data structure (by our using the term *data*) is bound to some computer representation.)

188. **Data transformation:** Same as *data refinement* and, hence, *data reification*.

189. **Data type:** By a *data type* is understood a set of *value*s and a set of *function*s over these values — whether *abstract* or *concrete*.

190. **DC:** DC stands for Duration Calculus. (The duration calculi are specific temporal logics over continuous time intervals [537,538])

191. **Decidable:** A formal logic system is decidable if there is an *algorithm* which prescribes *computation*s that can determine whether any given sentence in the system is a theorem.

192. **Declaration:** A declaration prescribes the allocation of a resource of the kind declared: (i) A variable, i.e., a location in some storage; (ii) a channel between active processes; (iii) an object, i.e., a process possessing a local state; etc.

193. **Decomposition:** By a decomposition is meant the presentation of the parts of a *composite* "thing".

194. **Deduce:** To perform a *deduction*, see next. (Cf. *infer*.)

195. **Deduction:** A form of reasoning where a conclusion about particulars follows from general premises. (Thus deduction goes from the general (case) to the specific (case). See contrast to *induction*: inferring from specific cases to general cases.)

196. **Deduction rule:** A *rule* for performing *deduction*s.

197. **Definiendum:** The left-hand side of a *definition*, that which is to be defined.

198. **Definiens:** The right-hand side of a *definition*, that which is defining "something".

199. **Definite:** Something which has specified limits. (Watch out for the four terms: *finite, infinite, definite* and *indefinite*.)

200. **Definition:** A definition defines something, makes it conceptually "manifest". A definition consists of two parts: a *definiendum*, normally considered the left-hand part of a definition, and a *definiens*, normally considered the right-hand part (the body) of a definition.

201. **Definition set:** By a definition set we mean, given a *function*, the set of *value*s for which the function is defined, i.e., for which, when it is *applied* to a member of the definition set yields a proper value. (Cf., *range set*.)

202. **Delimiter:** A delimiter delimits something: marks the start, and/or end of that thing. (A delimiter thus is a syntactic notion.)

203. **Denotation:** A direct specific meaning as distinct from an implied or associated idea [373]. (By a denotation we shall, in our context, associate the idea of mathematical functions: That is, of the *denotational semantics* standing for functions.)

204. **Denotational:** Being a *denotation*.

205. **Denotational semantics:** By a denotational semantics we mean a *semantics* which to *atomic* syntactical notions associate simple mathematical structures (usually *function*s, or *set*s of *trace*s, or *algebra*s), and which to

composite syntactical notions prescribe a semantics which is the *functional composition* of the denotational semantics of the *composition* parts.

206. **Denote:** Designates a mathematical meaning according to the principles of *denotational semantics*. (Sometimes we use the looser term designate.)

207. **Dependability:** Dependability is defined as the property of a *machine* such that reliance can justifiably be placed on the service it delivers [432]. (See definition of the related terms: *error*, *failure*, *fault* and *machine service*.)

208. **Dependability requirements:** By *requirements* concerning dependability we mean any such requirements which deal with either *accessibility* requirements, or *availability* requirements, or *integrity* requirements, or *reliability* requirements, or *robustness* requirements, or *safety* requirements, or *security* requirements, or *robustness* requirements.

209. **Describe:** To describe something is to create, in the mind of the reader, a *model* of that something. The thing, to be describable, must be either a physically manifest *phenomenon*, or a concept derived from such phenomena. Furthermore, to be describable it must be possible to create, to formulate a mathematical, i.e., a formal description of that something. (This delineation of description is narrow. It is too narrow for, for example, philosophical or literary, or historical, or psychological discourse. But it is probably too wide for a *software engineering*, or a *computing science* discourse. See also *description*.)

210. **Description:** By a description is, in our context, meant some text which designates something, i.e., for which, eventually, a mathematical *model* can be established. (We readily accept that our characterisation of the term 'description' is narrow. That is: We take as a guiding principle, as a dogma, that an informal text, a *rough sketch*, a *narrative*, is not a description unless one can eventually demonstrate a mathematical model that somehow relates to, i.e., "models" that informal text. To further paraphrase our concern about "describability", we now state that a description is a description of the *entities*, *functions*, *events* and *behaviours* of a further designated universe of discourse: That is, a description of a *domain*, a *prescription* of *requirements*, or a *specification* of a *software design*.)

211. **Design:** By a design we mean the *specification* of a *concrete artefact*, something that can either be physically manifested, like a chair, or conceptually demonstrated, like a software program.

212. **Designate:** To designate is to present a reference to, to point out, something. (See also *denote* and *designation*.)

213. **Designation:** The relation between a *syntactic* marker and the semantic thing signified. (See also *denote* and *designate*.)

214. **Destructor:** By a destructor we shall here understand a *function* which applies to a *composite value* and yields a further specified part (i.e., a subpart) of that value. (Examples of destructors in RSL are the list index-

ing function, and the selector functions of a variant record. They do not destroy anything, however.)

215. **Deterministic:** In a narrow sense we shall say that a behaviour, a process, a set of actions, is deterministic if the outcome of the behaviour, etc., can be predicted: Is always the same given the same "starting conditions", i.e., the same initial *configuration* (from which the behaviour, etc., proceeds). (See also *nondeterministic*.)

216. **Developer:** The person, or the company, which constructs an *artefact*, as here, a *domain description*, or a *requirements prescription*, or a *software design*.

217. **Development:** The set of actions that are carried out in order to construct an *artefact*.

218. **Diagram:** A usually two-dimensional drawing, a figure. (Sometimes a diagram is annotated with informal and *formal* text.)

219. **Dialogue:** A "conversation" between two *agent*s (men or machines). (We thus speak of man-machine dialogues as carried out over *CHI*s (*HCI*s).)

220. **Didactics:** Systematic instruction based on a clear conceptualisation of the bases, of the foundations, upon which what is being instructed rests. (One may speak of the didactics of a field of knowledge, such as, for example, software engineering. We believe that the present three volume book represents such a clearly conceptualised didactics, i.e., a foundationally consistent and complete basis.)

221. **Directed graph:** A directed graph is a *graph* all of whose *edge*s are directed, i.e., are *arrow*s.

222. **Directory:** A collection of directions. (We shall here take the more limited view of a directory as being a list of names of, i.e., references to *resource*s.)

223. **Discharge:** We use the term discharge in a very narrow sense, namely that of discharging a proof obligation, i.e., by carrying out a proof.

224. **Discrete:** As opposed to *continuous*: consisting of distinct or unconnected elements [373].

225. **Disjunction:** Being separated, being disjoined, decomposed. (We shall mostly think of disjunction as the (meaning of the) logical connective "or": ∨.)

226. **Document:** By a document is meant any text, whether informal or *formal*, whether *informative*, *descriptive* (or *prescriptive*) or *analytic*. (Descriptive documents may be *rough sketch*es, *terminologies*, *narrative*s, or *formal*. Informative documents are not *descriptive*. Analytic documents "describe" relations between documents, *verification* and *validation*, or describe properties of a document.)

227. **Documentation requirements:** By documentation requirements we mean requirements which state which kinds of documents shall make up the deliverable, what these documents shall contain and how they express what they contain.

228. **Domain:** Same as *application domain*; hence see that term for a characterisation. (The term domain is the preferred term.)

229. **Domain acquisition:** The act of acquiring, of gathering, *domain knowledge*, and of analysing and recording this knowledge.

230. **Domain analysis:** The act of analysing recorded *domain knowledge* in search of (common) properties of phenomena, or relating what may be considered separate phenomena.

231. **Domain capture:** The act of gathering *domain knowledge*, of collecting it — usually from domain *stakeholders*.

232. **Domain description:** A textual, informal or formal document which describes the domain. (Usually a domain description is a set of documents with many parts recording many facets of the domain: The *intrinsics, business processes, support technology, management and organisation, rules and regulations*, and the *human behaviours*.)

233. **Domain description unit:** By a domain description unit we understand a short, "one- or two-liner", possibly *rough-sketch description* of some property of a *domain phenomenon*, i.e., some property of an *entity*, some property of a *function*, of an *event*, or some property of a *behaviour*. (Usually domain description units are the smallest textual, sentential fragments elicited from domain *stakeholders*.)

234. **Domain determination:** Domain determination is a *domain requirements facet*. It is an operation performed on a *domain description* cum *requirements prescription*. Any *nondeterminism* expressed by either of these specifications which is not desirable for some required software design must be made deterministic (by this *requirements engineer* performed operation). (Other domain requirements facets are: *domain projection, domain instantiation, domain extension* and *domain fitting.*)

235. **Domain development:** By domain development we shall understand the *development* of a *domain description*. (All aspects are included in development: *domain acquisition*, domain *analysis*, domain *model*ling, domain *validation* and domain *verification*.)

236. **Domain engineer:** A domain engineer is a *software engineer* who performs *domain engineering*. (Other forms of *software engineers* are: *requirements engineers* and *software designers* (cum *programmers*).)

237. **Domain engineering:** The engineering of the development of a *domain description*, from identification of *domain stakeholders*, via *domain acquisition, domain analysis* and *domain description* to *domain validation* and *domain verification*.

238. **Domain extension:** Domain extension is a *domain requirements facet*. It is an operation performed on a *domain description* cum *requirements prescription*. It effectively extends a *domain description* by entities, functions, events and/or behaviours conceptually possible, but not necessarily humanly feasible in the domain. (Other domain requirements facets are: *domain projection, domain determination, domain instantiation* and *domain fitting*.)

239. **Domain facet:** By a domain facet we understand one amongst a finite set of generic ways of analysing a domain: A view of the domain, such

that the different facets cover conceptually different views, and such that these views together cover the domain. (We consider here the following domain facets: *business process, intrinsics, support technology, management and organisation, rules and regulations,* and *human behaviour*.)

240. **Domain fitting:** Domain fitting is a *domain requirements facet*. It is an operation performed on a *domain description* cum *requirements prescription*. It effectively combines one *domain description* (cum *domain requirements*) with another [*domain description*, respectively *domain requirements*]. (Other domain requirements facets are: *domain projection, domain determination, domain instantiation* and *domain extension*.)

241. **Domain initialisation:** Domain initialisation is an *interface requirements facet*. It is an operation performed on a *requirements prescription*. For an explanation see *shared data initialisation* (its 'equivalent'). (Other *interface requirements facets* are: *shared data refreshment, computational data+control, man-machine dialogue, man-machine physiological* and *machine-machine dialogue requirements*.)

242. **Domain instantiation:** Domain instantiation is a *domain requirements facet*. It is an operation performed on a *domain description* (cum *requirements prescription*). Where, in a domain description certain *entities* and *functions* are left undefined, domain instantiation means that these entities or functions are now instantiated into constant *values*. (Other requirements facets are: *domain projection, domain determination, domain extension* and *domain fitting*.)

243. **Domain knowledge:** By domain knowledge we mean that which a particular group of people, all basically engaged in the "same kind of activities", know about that domain of activity", and what they believe that other people know and believe about the same domain. (We shall, in our context, strictly limit ourselves to "knowledge", staying short of "beliefs", and we shall similarly strictly limit ourselves to assume just one "actual" world, not any number of "possible" worlds. More specifically, we shall strictly limit our treatment of domain knowledge to stay clear of the (albeit very exciting) area of reasoning about knowledge and belief between people (and agents) [223, 285].)

244. **Domain projection:** Domain projection is a *domain requirements facet*. It is an operation performed on a *domain description* cum *requirements prescription*. The operation basically "removes" from a description definitions of those *entities* (including their *type definitions*), *functions, events* and *behaviours* that are not to be considered in the *requirements*. (The removed phenomena and concepts are thus projected "away". Other domain requirements facets are: *domain determination, domain instantiation, domain extension* and *domain fitting*.)

245. **Domain validation:** By domain validation we rather mean: '*validation of a domain description*', and by that we mean the informal assurance that a description purported to cover the *entities, functions, events* and *behaviours* of a further designated domain indeed does cover that domain

in a reasonably representative manner. (Domain validation is, necessarily, an informal activity: It basically involves a guided reading of a domain description (being validated) by *stakeholder*s of the domain, and ends in an evaluation report written by these domain *stakeholder* readers.)

246. **Domain verification:** By domain verification we mean *verification* of claimed properties of a domain description, and by that we mean the formal assurance that a description indeed does possess those claimed properties. (The usual principles, techniques and tools of verification apply here.)

247. **Domain requirements:** By domain *requirements* we understand such requirements — save those of *business process reengineering* — which can be expressed solely by using professional terms of the *domain*. (Domain requirements constitute one requirements *facet*. Others requirements facets are: *business process reengineering*, *interface requirements* and *machine requirements*.)

248. **Domain requirements facet:** By *domain requirements* facets we understand such domain requirements that basically arise from either of the following operations on *domain description*s (cum *requirements prescription*s): *domain projection*, *domain determination*, *domain extension*, *domain instantiation* and *domain fitting*.

249. **Dynamic:** An *entity* is said to be dynamic if its value changes over time, i.e., it is subjected, somehow, to actions. (We distinguish three kinds of dynamic entities: *inert*, *active* and *reactive*. This is in contrast to *static*.)

250. **Dynamic typing:** Enforcement of *type checking* at *run time*. (A language is said to be dynamically typed if it is not *statically typed*.)

$$\mathcal{E}$$

251. **Edge:** A line, a connection, between two *node*s of a *graph* or a *tree*. (Other terms for the same idea are: *arc* and *branch*.)

252. **Elaborate:** See next: *elaboration*.

253. **Elaboration:** The three terms *elaboration*, *evaluation* and *interpretation* essentially cover the same idea: that of obtaining the meaning of a syntactical item in some *configuration*, or as a function from configurations to *value*s. Given that configuration typically consists of *static environment*s and *dynamic state*s (or *storage*s), we use the term elaboration in the more narrow sense of designating, or yielding functions from syntactical items to functions from configurations to pairs of states and values.

254. **Elicitation:** To elicit, to extract. (See also: *acquisition*. We consider elicitation to be part of acquisition. Acquisition is more than elicitation. Elicitation, to us, is primarily the act of extracting information, i.e., knowledge. Acquisition is that plus more: Namely the preparation of what and how to elicit and the postprocessing of that which has been elicited — in preparation of proper analysis. Elicitation applies both to domain and to requirements elicitation.)

255. **Embedded:** Being an integral part of something else. (When something is embedded in something else, then that something else is said to surround the embedded thing.)

256. **Embedded system:** A *system* which is an integral part of a larger system. (We shall use the term embedded system primarily in the context of the larger, 'surrounding' system being *reactive* and/or *hard real time*.)

257. **Endomorphism:** A *homomorphism* that maps an algebra into itself is an endomorphism. (We refer to Sect. 8.4.4 on page 132. See also *automorphism*, *epimorphism*, *isomorphism*, *monomorphism*.)

258. **Engineer:** An engineer is a person who "walks the bridge" between science and technology: (i) Constructing, i.e., designing, *technology* based on scientific insight, and (ii) analysing technology for its possible scientific content.

259. **Engineering:** Engineering is the design of *technology* based on scientific insight, and the analysis of technology for its possible scientific content. (In the context of this glossary we single out three forms of engineering: *domain engineering*, *requirements engineering* and *software design*; together we call them *software engineering*. The technology constructed by the *domain engineer* is a *domain description*. The technology constructed by the *requirements engineer* is a *requirements prescription*. The technology constructed by the *software design*er is *software*.)

260. **Enrichment:** The addition of a property to something already existing. (We shall use the term enrich in connection with a collection (i.e., a RSL **scheme** or a RSL **class**) — of definitions, declaration and axioms — being '**extended with**' further such definitions, declaration and axioms.)

261. **Entity:** By an entity we shall loosely understand something fixed, immobile, static — although that thing may move, but after it has moved it is essentially the same thing, an entity. (We shall take the narrow view of an entity, being in contrast to a *function*, and an *event*, and a *behaviour*; that entities "roughly correspond" to what we shall think of as *value*s, i.e., as *information* or *data*. We shall further allow entities to be either *atomic* or *composite*, i.e., in the latter case having decomposable subentities (cf. *subentity*). Finally entities may have nondecomposable *attribute*s.)

262. **Enumerable:** By enumerable we mean that a set of elements satisfies a *proposition*, i.e., can be logically characterised.

263. **Enumeration:** To list, one after another. (We shall use the term enumeration in connection with the syntactic expression of a "small", i.e., definite, number of elements of a(n enumerated) *set*, *list* or *map*.)

264. **Environment:** A context, that is, in our case (i.e., usage), the ("more static") part of a *configuration* in which some syntactic entity is *elaborated*, *evaluated*, or *interpreted*. (In our "metacontext", i.e., that of software engineering, environments, when deployed in the elaboration (etc.) of, typically, specifications or programs, record, i.e., list, associate, identifiers of the specification or program text with their meaning.)

265. **Epimorphism:** If a *homomorphism* ϕ is a *surjective function* then ϕ is an epimorphism. (We refer to Sect. 8.4.4 on page 132. See also *automorphism, endomorphism, isomorphism, monomorphism.*)

266. **Epistemology:** The study of knowledge. (Contrast, please, to *ontology.*)

267. **Error:** An error is an action that produces an incorrect result. An error is that part of a *machine state* which is "liable to lead to subsequent failure". An error affecting the *machine service* is an indication that a *failure* occurs or has occurred [432]. (An error is caused by a *fault.*)

268. **Evaluate:** See next: *evaluation.*

269. **Evaluation:** The three terms *elaboration, evaluation* and *interpretation* essentially cover the same idea: that of obtaining the meaning of a syntactical item in some *configuration*, or as a function from configurations to *values*. Given that configuration typically consists of *static environments* and *dynamic states* (or *storages*), we use the term evaluation in the more narrow sense of designating, or yielding functions from syntactical items to functions from configurations to values.

270. **Event:** Something that occurs instantaneously. (We shall, in our context, take events as being manifested by certain *state* changes, and by certain *interactions* between *behaviours* or *processes*. The occurrence of events may "trigger" actions. How the triggering, i.e., the *invocation* of *functions* are brought about is usually left implied, or unspecified.)

271. **Expression:** An expression, in our context (i.e., that of software engineering), is a syntactical entity which, through *evaluation*, designates a *value*.

272. **Extension:** We shall here take extension to be the same as *enrichment*. (The extension of a *concept* is all the individuals falling under the concept [405].)

273. **Extensional:** Concerned with objective reality [373]. (Please observe a shift here: We do not understand the term extensional as 'relating to, or marked by extension in the above sense, but in contrast to *intensional*.)

$\mathcal{F}$

---

274. **Facet:** By a facet we understand one amongst a finite set of generic ways of analysing and presenting a *domain*, a *requirements* or a *software design*: a view of the universe of discourse, such that the different facets cover conceptually different views, and such that these views together cover that universe of discourse. (Examples of domain facets are *intrinsics, business processes, support technology, management and organisation, rules and regulations* and *human behaviour*. Examples of requirements facets are *business process reengineering, domain requirements, interface requirements* and *machine requirements*. Examples of software design facets are *software architecture, component design, module design,* etc.)

275. **Failure:** A *fault* may result in a failure. A *machine* failure occurs when the delivered *machine service* deviates from fulfilling the machine function,

the latter being what the machine is aimed at [432]. (A failure is thus something relative to a *specification*, and is due to a *fault*. Failures are concerned with such things as *accessibility*, *availability*, *reliability*, *safety* and *security*.)

276. **Fault:** The adjudged (i.e., the 'so judged') or hypothesised cause of an *error* [432]. (An *error* is caused by a fault, i.e., faults cause errors. A software fault is the consequence of a human *error* in the development of that software.)

277. **Finite:** Of a fixed number less than infinity, or of a fixed structure that does not "flow" into perpetuity as would any *information structure* that just goes on and on. (Watch out for the four terms: *finite*, *infinite*, *definite* and *indefinite*.)

278. **Finite state automaton:** By a finite state automaton we understand an *automaton* whose state set is finite. (We shall usually consider only what is known as Moore automata: that is, automata which have some final states.)

279. **Finite state machine:** By a finite state machine we understand an extended *finite state automaton*. The extension amounts simply to the following: Every transition (caused by an input, in a state, to another state) also yields an output. (We shall thus consider only what is known as Mealy machines. The output is intended to designate some action, or some signal, to be considered by an environment of the machine.)

280. **Finite state transducer:** By a finite state transducer we simply mean the same as a finite state machine. (The machine in question is said to transduce, to "translate" any sequence of inputs to some corresponding sequence of outputs.)

281. **First-order:** We say that a *predicate logic* is first order when quantified variables are not allowed to range over functions. (If they range over functions we call the logic a *higher-order* logic [406, 419]. Similar remarks can be made for general first-order functions, respectively higher-order functions.)

282. **Fix point:** The fix point of a function, F, is any value, f, for which $Ff = f$. A function may have any number of fixed points from none (e.g., $Fx = x + 1$) to infinitely many (e.g., $Fx = x$). The fixed point combinator, written as either "**fix**" or "**Y**" will return the fixed point of a function. (The fix point identity is $\mathbf{Y}F = F(\mathbf{Y}F)$.)

283. **Flowchart:** A diagram (a chart), for example of circles (input, output), annotated (square) boxes, annotated diamonds and infixed arrows, that shows step by step flow through an algorithm.

284. **Formal:** By formal we shall, in our context (i.e., that of software engineering), mean a language, a system, an argument (a way of reasoning), a program or a specification whose syntax and semantics is based on (rules of) mathematics (including mathematical logic).

285. **Formal definition:** Same as *formal description*, *formal prescription* or *formal specification*.

286. **Formal development:** Same as the standard meaning of the composition of *formal* and *development*. (We usually speak of a spectrum of development modes: *systematic development*, *rigorous development*, and formal development. Formal software development, to us, is at the "formalistic" extreme of the three modes of development: Complete *formal specifications* are always constructed, for all (phases and) stages of development; all *proof obligations* are expressed; and all are discharged (i.e., proved to hold).)

287. **Formal description:** A *formal description* of something. (Usually we use the term formal description only in connection with *formalisation* of *domains*.)

288. **Formalisation:** The act of making a formal specification of something elsewhere informally specified; or the document which results therefrom.

289. **Formal method:** By a formal method we mean a *method* whose techniques and tools[1] are *formally* based. (It is common to hear that some notation is claimed to be that of a formal method — where it then turns out that few, if any, of the building blocks of that notation have any formal foundation. This is especially true of many diagrammatic notations. UML is a case in point — much is presently being done to formalise subsets of UML [408].)

290. **Formal parameter:** By a formal parameter we mean an identification (say a naming and a typing), in a *function definition*'s *function signature*, of an argument of the function, a place-holder for *actual arguments*.

291. **Formal prescription:** Same as *formal definition* or *formal specification*. (Usually we use the term formal prescription only in connection with *formalisation* of *requirements*.)

292. **Formal specification:** A *formalisation* of something. (Same as *formal definition*, *formal description* or *formal prescription*. Usually we use the term formal specification only in connection with *formalisation* of *software designs*.)

293. **Free:** The concept of being free is associated with (i) *identifiers* (i.e., *names*) and *expressions*, and (ii) with *names* (i.e., *identifiers*) and *resources*. An identifier is said to be either *bound* or free in an expression based on certain rules being satisfied or not. If an identifier is free in an expression then nothing is said about what free occurrences of that identifier are bound to. (Cf. *bound*.)

294. **Freeing:** The removal of *storage locations*, or of *stack activations*.

295. **Frontier:** The concept of frontier is here associated with *trees*. Visualise that tree as represented as a flat diagram with no crosses (i.e., intersecting) *branches*. A frontier of a tree is a reading of the leaves (cf. *leaf*) of the tree

---

[1]Tools include specification and programming languages as such, as well as all the software tools relating to these languages (editors, syntax checkers, theorem provers, proof assistants, model checkers, specification and program (flow) analysers, interpreters, compilers, etc.).

in one of the two possible directions, say left to right or right to left. (See *tree traversal*.)

296. **FUNARG:** A specification or a programming language is said to enjoy, i.e. possess, the FUNARG property if *values* of *function invocations* may be *functions* defined locally to the invoked function. (LISP has the FUNARG property. So does SAL, a simple applicative language defined in Vol. 2, Chap. 15.)

297. **Full algebra:** A full *algebra* is a *total algebra*.

298. **Function:** By a function we understand something which when *applied* to a *value*, called an *argument*, yields a value called a *result*. (Functions can be modelled as sets of (argument, result) pair — in which case applying a function to an argument amounts to "searching" for an appropriate pair. If several such pairs have the same argument (value), the function is said to be *nondeterministic*. If a function is applied to an argument for which there is no appropriate pair, then the function is said to be partial; otherwise it is a total function.)

299. **Function activation:** When, in an operational, i.e., computational ("mechanical") sense, a function is being applied, then some resources have to be set aside in order to carry out, to handle, the application. This is what we shall call a function activation. (Typically a function activation, for conventional *block-structured* languages (like C#, Java, Standard ML [261, 277, 470]), is implemented by means (also) of a stack-like data structure: Function invocation then implies the stacking (pushing) of a stack activation on that stack, i.e., the *activation stack* (a circular reference!). Elaboration of the function definition body means that intermediate values are pushed and popped from the topmost activation element, etc., and that completion of the function application means that the top stack activation is popped.)

300. **Functional:** A function whose arguments are allowed themselves to be functions is called a functional. (The *fix point* (finding) function is a functional.)

301. **Functional programming:** By functional programming we mean the same as *applicative programming*: In its barest rendition functional programming involves just three things: definition of functions, functions as ordinary *values*, and *function application* (i.e., *function invocation*). (Most current functional programming languages (Haskell, Miranda, Standard ML) go well beyond just providing the three basic building blocks of functional programming [389, 498, 502].)

302. **Functional programming language:** By a functional programming language we mean a *programming language* whose principal values are functions and whose principal operations on these values are their creation (i.e., definition), their application (i.e., invocation) and their composition. (Functional programming languages of interest today, 2005, are (alphabetically listed): CAML [146, 147, 162, 346, 518], Haskell [498], Miranda [502],

Scheme [2, 206, 247] and SML (Standard ML) [261, 389]. LISP 1.5 was a first functional programming language [370].)

303. **Function application:** The act of applying a function to an argument is called a function application. (See 'comment' field of *function activation* just above.)

304. **Function definition:** A *function definition*, as does any definition, consists of a *definiens* and a *definiendum*. The definiens is a *function signature*, and the definiendum is a clause, typically an expression. (Cf. *Lambda-functions*.)

305. **Function invocation:** Same as *function application*. (See parenthesized remark of entry 299 (*function activation*).)

306. **Function signature:** By a function signature we mean a text which presents the name of the function, the types of its argument values and the type(s) of its result value(s).

$\mathcal{G}$

---

307. **Garbage:** By garbage we shall here understand those (computing) *resources* which can no longer be referenced. (Usually we restrict our 'garbage' concern to that of *storage location*s that can no longer be accessed because there are no references to them.)

308. **Garbage collector:** To speak of garbage collection we must first introduce the notions of allocatable *storage*, i.e., storage — what shall be known as free, i.e., unallocated — *locations* (including those that can be considered *garbage*). By a garbage collector we shall here understand a device, a software program or a hardware mechanism which "returns" to a set of free locations that can subsequently be made available for *allocation*.

309. **Generate:** By generate we shall understand that which can be associated both with a *grammar* and with an *automaton*: namely a *language*, i.e., a set of strings. Either accepted as *input* to a *finite state automaton*, or *denote*d by a *grammar*. (Acceptance by an automaton means that the automaton is started in an initial state and upon completion of reading the input is in a final state. Generation by a grammar means the recursive (i.e., repeated) *substitution* of *nonterminals* of a grammar *rule* left-hand side with the left-hand sides of the rules whose right-hand side is the substituted nonterminal.)

310. **Generator:** A generator is a concept: It can be thought of as a device, i.e., a software program or a machine mechanism, which outputs typically sequences of structures — typically symbols. (A *BNF Grammar* can thus be said to generate the (usually infinite) set of strings, i.e., of sentence of the designated language. A *finite state machine* can likewise be said to be a generator: Upon being presented with any input string it generates an output string (a *transduction*).)

311. **Generator function:** To speak of a generator function we need first introduce the concept of a *sort* "of interest". A generator function is a

function which when applied to arguments of some kind, i.e., types, yields a value of the type of the sort "of interest". (Typically the sort "of interest" can be thought of as the state (a stack, a queue, etc.).)

312. **Generic programming:** See entry 514 (*polymorphic*).

313. **Glossary:** See Sect. B.1.1.

314. **Grammar:** See *syntax*, in general, or *regular syntax*, *context-free syntax*, *context-sensitive syntax* and *BNF* in specific.

315. **Grand state:** "Grand state" is a colloquial term. It is meant to have the same meaning as *configuration*. (The colloquialism is used in the context of, for example, praising a software engineer as "being one who really knows how to design the grand state for some universe of discourse" being specified.)

316. **Graph:** By a graph we shall here mean the term as usually used in the discrete mathematics discipline of graph theory: as a (usually, but not necessarily finite) set of *nodes* (*vertexes*), some of which may be connected by (one or more) *arcs* (*edges*, lines). (A graph edge defines a *path* of length one. If there is a path from one node to another, and from that other node to yet a third node, then the graph, by transitivity, defines a path from the first to the third node, etc. A graph can be either an *acyclic graph* (no path "cycles back") or a *cyclic graph*, a *directed graph* (edges are one-directional arrows) or an *undirected graph* [41, 42, 272, 409].)

317. **Ground term:** A ground term is either an *identifier* or a *value literal*. (The identifier is then assumed to be bound to a value. The value literal typically is an alphanumeric string designating, for example, an integer, a real, a truth value, a character, etc.)

318. **Grouping:** By grouping we mean the ordered, finite collection, into a *Cartesian*, of mathematical structures (i.e., *values*).

$\mathcal{H}$

---

319. **Hard real time:** By hard real time we mean a *real time* property where the exact, i.e., absolute timing, or time interval, is of essence. (Thus, if a system is said to enjoy, or must possess, a certain real time property, for example, (i) the system must emit a certain signal on the 11th of December 2005 at 17:20:30 hours[2], or (ii) that a response signal must be issued after an interval of exactly 1234 days, 5 hours, 6 minutes, and 7 seconds plus/minus 8 microseconds (from when an initiating signal was received), then it is hard real time. Cf. *soft real time*.)

320. **Hardware:** By hardware is meant the physical embodiment of a computer: its electronics, its boards, the racks, cables, button, lamps, etc.

321. **HCI:** Abbreviation for human computer interface. (Same as *CHI*, and same as *man-machine* interface.)

---

[2]That time is when the current author hopes to celebrate the exact hour of his anniversary of 40 years of marriage to Kari Skallerud!

322. **Heap:** By a heap is here meant an unordered, finite collection, i.e., a set, of *storage location*s, such that each of these locations can be said to be allocated (for some purpose), and such that a freeing, i.e., deallocation, of these locations usually does not follow the inverse order of their allocation. (Thus a heap works in contrast to an *activation stack* — complementary, so to speak! Typically a *garbage collector* is involved in helping to secure locations on the heap available for allocation.)

323. **Heterogeneous algebra:** A heterogeneous *algebra* is an algebra whose carrier A is an indexed set of carriers: A_1, $A_2,\ldots, A_m$, and whose functions, $\phi_{i_n} : \Phi$, or *arity* n, are of *type*: $A_{i_1} \times A_{i_2} \times \cdots \times A_{i_n} \to A_j$ where i_k, for all $k \in \{1,\ldots,n\}$, are in the set $\{1, 2,\ldots, m\}$.

324. **Hiding:** Hiding is a concept related to *module*s. In fact, it is a main purpose of syntactically providing the module mechanism. You have, somewhat mechanistically, to imagine a group of (developers of) modules. One module mentions (i.e., uses), say, functions defined in other modules. But those other modules, besides, in order to define those "exported" functions, define auxiliary functions (types, etc.) that "reveal" details of implementation which it is not necessary to divulge. (One may wish, later, in "the life of that module", to change those implementation decisions.) Hence, by syntactic means, such as, for example, *export, import* and *hide* clauses, the developer requests the module compiling system to statically (or otherwise) secure that other modules cannot "inspect" those auxiliary functions, types, etc. (We refer to [413–417]. Parnas must be credited, among others, for having skillfully propagated the hiding concept.)

325. **Hierarchy:** By a hierarchy we understand a conceptual decomposition of resources into what can be "pictured" as a *tree*-like structure (and where the emphasis is on the root of the structure).

326. **Hierarchical:** By something being hierarchical we mean that that something forms a *hierarchy*. (See also *compositional*.)

327. **Hierarchical documentation:** By hierarchical documentation we mean a development, or a presentation (of that development), of, as here, some *description* (*prescription* or *specification*), in which a notion of "largest", overall, phenomena and concepts are developed (resp. presented) first, then their decompositions into component phenomena and concepts, etc., until some notion of atomic, i.e., "smallest" development (etc.) has been achieved. (See also *hierarchy* (just above) and *compositional documentation*.)

328. **Higher-order:** A *functional* or a *value* whose *definition set* or *range set* values are *function*s. (See, in contrast, *first-order*.)

329. **Homeomorphism:** A function that is a one-to-one mapping between sets such that both the function and its inverse are continuous. (Not to be confused with *homomorphism*.)

330. **Homomorphism:** A *function*, $\phi : A \to A'$, from values of the carrier A of one *algebra* (A, Ω) to values of the carrier A' of another algebra (A', Ω') is said to be a homomorphism (same as a morphism) from (A, Ω)

to (A', Ω'), if for any $\omega : \Omega$ and for any $a_i : A$, there is a corresponding $\omega' : \Omega'$ such that: $\phi(\omega(a_1, a_2, ..., a_n)) = \omega'(\phi(a_1), \phi(a_2), ..., \phi(a_n))$. (We refer to Sect. 8.4.4. See also *automorphism, endomorphism, epimorphism, isomorphism* and *monomorphism*.)

331. **Homomorphic principle:** The homomorphic principle advises the software engineer to formulate *function definition*s such that they express a *homomorphism*. (It is a basic tenet of a *denotational semantics definition* that it is expressed as a *homomorphism*.)

332. **Human behaviour:** By human behaviour we shall here understand the way a human follows the enterprise *rules and regulations* as well as interacts with a *machine*: dutifully honouring specified (machine *dialogue*) *protocol*s, or negligently so, or sloppily not quite so, or even criminally not so! (Human behaviour is a *facet* of the *domain* (of the enterprise). We shall thus model human behaviour also in terms of it failing to react properly, i.e., humans as *nondeterministic agent*s! Other facets of an enterprise are those of its *intrinsics, business process*es, *support technology, management and organisation*, and *rules and regulations*.)

333. **Hybrid:** Something heterogeneous, something (as a computing device) that has two different types of components (*software*, respectively hardware, the latter including, besides the digital computer, also *controller*s (*sensor*s, *actuator*s)) performing essentially the same function by cooperating on computing "*that same*" function. (Typically we speak of, i.e., deploy hybridicity when *monitor*ing and *control*ling *reactive system*s — but then hybridicity additionally, to us, means a combination in which the *controller* handles analog matters of continuity, and the *software* plus computer handles discrete matters. Finally, for a conventional analogue *controller* there is usually but one "decision mode". With the software-directed computing system there is now the possibility of multiple discrete + continuous *controller* "regimes".)

334. **Hypothesis:** An assumption made for the sake of argument.

$\mathcal{I}$

335. **Icon:** A pictorial representation, an image, a sign whose form (shape, etc.) suggests its meaning. (A graphic symbol on a computer display screen which suggests the purpose of an available *function* or *value* which *designate*s that *entity*.)

336. **Iconic:** Adjective form of *icon*.

337. **Identification:** The pointing out of a relation, an association, between an *identifier* and that "thing", that *phenomenon*, it *designate*s, i.e., it stands for or identifies.

338. **Identifier:** A name. (Usually represented by a string of alphanumeric characters, sometimes with properly infixed "-"s or "_"s.)

339. **Imperative:** Expressive of a command [373]. (We take imperative to more specifically be a reflection of *do this, then do that*. That is, of the

use of a *state*-based programming approach, i.e., of the use of an *imperative programming language*. See also *indicative*, *optative*, and *putative*.)

340. **Imperative programming:** Programming, *imperatively*, "with" references to *storage locations* and the updates of those, i.e., of *states*. (Imperative programming seems to be the classical, first way of programming digital computers.)

341. **Imperative programming language:** A programming language which, significantly, offers language constructs for the creation and manipulation of variables, i.e., *storages* and their *locations*. (Typical imperative programming languages were, in "ye olde days", `Fortran, Cobol, Algol 60, PL/I, Pascal, C,` etc. [12–14, 24, 24, 321]. Today programming languages like `C++, Java, C#,` etc. [277, 470, 489] additionally offer *module* cum *object* "features".)

342. **Implementation:** By an implementation we understand a computer program that is made suitable for *compilation* or *interpretation* by a *machine*. (See next entry: *implementation relation*.)

343. **Implementation relation:** By an *implementation* relation we understand a logical relation of *correctness* between a *software design specification* and an *implementation* (i.e., a computer program made suitable for *compilation* or *interpretation* by a *machine*).

344. **Incarnation:** A particular instance of a value, usually a state. (We shall here use the term incarnation to designate any one activation on an *activation stack* — where such an incarnation, i.e., activation, represents a program *block* or *function* (or procedure, or *subroutine*) *invocation*.)

345. **Incomplete:** We say that a *proof system* is incomplete if not all true sentences are provable.

346. **Incompleteness:** Noun form of the *incomplete* adjective.

347. **Inconsistent:** A set of *axioms* is said to be inconsistent if, by means of these, and some *deduction rules*, one can *prove* a property and its negation.

348. **Indefinite:** Not definite, i.e., of a fixed number or a specific property, but it is not known, at the point of uttering the term 'indefinite', what that number or property is. (Watch out for the four terms: *finite, infinite, definite* and *indefinite*.)

349. **Indicative:** Stating an objective fact. (See also *imperative, optative* and *putative*.)

350. **Induce:** The use of *induction*. (To conclude a general property from special cases.)

351. **Induction:** Inference of a general property from particular instances. (On the basis of several, "similar" cases one may infer a general, say, principle or property. In contrast to *deduction*: from general (e.g., from laws) to specific instances.)

352. **Inductive:** The use of *induction*.

353. **In extension:** A concept of logic. In extension is a correlative word that indicates the reference of a term or concept. (When we speak of functions

in extension, we shall therefore mean it in the sense of presenting "all details", the "inner workings" of that function. Contrast to *in intension*.)

354. **Inert:** A *dynamic phenomenon* is said to be inert if it cannot change *value* of its own volition, i.e., by itself, but only through the *interaction* between that *phenomenon* and a change-instigating *environment*. An inert phenomenon only changes value as the result of external stimuli. These stimuli prescribe exactly which new value they are to change to. (Contrast to *active* and *reactive*.)

355. **Infer:** Common term for *deduce* or *induce*.

356. **Inference rule:** Same as *deduction rule*.

357. **Infinite:** As you would think of it: not finite! (Watch out for the four terms: *finite, infinite, definite* and *indefinite*.)

358. **Informal:** Not formal! (We normally, by an informal specification mean one which may be precise (i.e., unambiguous, and even concise), but which, for example is expressed in natural, yet (domain specific) professional language — i.e., a language which does not have a precise semantics let alone a formal *proof system*. The UML notation is an example of an informal language [408].)

359. **Informatics:** The confluence of (i) *applications*, (ii) *computer science*, (iii) *computing science* [i.e., the art [326–328] (1968–1973), craft [441] (1981), discipline [194] (1976), logic [275] (1984), practice [276] (1993–2004), and science [245] (1981) of programming], (iv) *software engineering* and (v) *mathematics*.

360. **Information:** The communication or reception of knowledge. (By information we thus mean something which, in contrast to *data*, informs us. No computer representation is, let alone any efficiency criteria are, assumed. Data as such does, i.e., bit patterns do, not 'inform' us.)

361. **Information structure:** By an information structure we shall normally understand a composition of more "formally" represented (i.e., structured) *information*, for example, in the "believed" form of *table*, a *tree*, a *graph*, etc. (In contrast to *data structure*, an information structure does not necessarily have a computer representation, let alone an "efficient" such.)

362. **Informative documentation:** By informative documentation we understand texts which *inform*, but which do not (essentially) describe that which a *development* is to develop. (Informative documentation is balanced by *descriptive* and *analytic documentation* to make up the full documentation of a *development*.)

363. **Infrastructure:** According to the World Bank: *'Infrastructure' is an umbrella term for many activities referred to as 'social overhead capital' by some development economists, and encompasses activities that share technical and economic features (such as economies of scale and spillovers from users to nonusers).* We shall use the term as follows: Infrastructures are concerned with supporting other systems or activities. Computing systems for infrastructures are thus likely to be distributed and concerned in particular with supporting communication of information, control, people

and materials. Issues of (for example) openness, timeliness, security, lack of corruption, and resilience are often important. (Winston Churchill is quoted to have said, during a debate in the House of Commons, in 1946: ... *The young Labourite speaker that we have just listened to, clearly wishes to impress upon his constituency the fact that he has gone to Eton and Oxford since he now uses such fashionable terms as 'infra-structures'.*)

364. **Inheritance:** The act of inheriting' a 'property. (The term inheritance, in software engineering, is deployed in connection with a relationship between two pieces (i.e., *modules*) of specification and/or program texts A and B. B may be said to *inherit* some *type*, or *variable*, or *value* definitions from A.)

365. **In intension:** A concept of logic: In intension is a correlative word that indicates the internal content of a term or concept that constitutes its formal definition. (When we speak of functions in intension, we shall therefore mean it in the sense of presenting only the "input/output" relation of the function. Contrast to *in extension*.)

366. **Injection:** A mathematical function, f, that is a one-to-one mapping from *definition set* A to *range set* B. (That is, if for some a in A, $f(a)$ yields a b, then for all $a : A$ all $b : B$ are yielded and there is a unique a for each b, or, which is the same, there is an *inverse function*, f^{-1}, such that $f^{-1}(f(a)) = a$ for all $a : A$. See also *bijection* and *surjection*.)

367. **Injective function:** A *function* which maps *values* of its postulated *definition set* into some, but not all, of its postulated *range set* is called injective. (See also *bijective function* and *surjective function* .)

368. **In-order:** A special order of *tree traversal* in which visits are made to nodes of trees and subtrees as follows: First the tree root is visited and "marked" as having been in-order visited. Then for each subtree a subtree in-order traversal is made, in the order left to right (or right to left). When a tree, whose number of subtrees is zero, is in-order traversed, then just that tree's root is visited (and that tree has then been in-order traversed) and (the leaf) is "marked" as having been visited. After each subtree visit the root (of the tree of which the subtree is a subtree) is revisited, i.e., again "marked" as having been in-order visited. (Cf. Fig. B.4: a left to right in-order traversal of that tree yields the following sequence of "markings": AQCQALXLFLAKUKJKZMZKA. Cf. also Fig. B.1 on the following page).

369. **Input:** By input we mean the *communication* of *information* (*data*) from an outside, an *environment*, to a *phenomenon* "within" our universe of discourse. (More colloquially, and more generally: Input can be thought of as *value*(s) transferred over *channel*(s) to, or between *process*es. Cf. *output*. In a narrow sense we talk of input to an *automaton* (i.e., a *finite state automaton* or a *pushdown automaton*) and a *machine* (here in the sense of, for example, a *finite state machine* (or a *pushdown machine*)).)

370. **Input alphabet:** The set of *symbols input* to an *automaton* or a *machine* in the sense of, for example, a *finite state machine* or a *pushdown machine*.

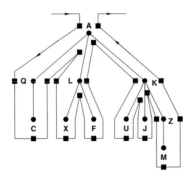

Fig. B.1. A left-to-right in-order tree traversal

371. **Instance:** An individual, a thing, an *entity*. (We shall usually think of an 'instance' as a *value*.)

372. **Instantiation:** 'To represent (an abstraction) by a concrete *instance*' [373]. (We shall sometimes be using the term 'instantiation' in lieu of a *function invocation* on an *activation stack*.)

373. **Installation manual:** A *document* which describes how a *computing system* is to be installed. (A special case of 'installation' is the downloading of *software* onto a *computing system*. See also *training manual* and *user manual*.)

374. **Intangible:** Not *tangible*.

375. **Integrity:** By a *machine* having integrity we mean that that machine remains unimpaired, i.e., has no faults, errors and failures, and remains so even in the situations where the environment of the machine has faults, errors and failures. (Integrity is a *dependability requirement*.)

376. **Intension:** Intension indicates the internal content of a term. (See also *in intension*. The intension of a *concept* is the collection of the properties possessed jointly by all conceivable individuals falling under the concept [405]. The intension determines the *extension* [405].)

377. **Intensional:** Adjective form of *intension*.

378. **Interact:** The term interact here addresses the phenomenon of one *behaviour* acting in unison, simultaneously, *concurrent*ly, with another behaviour, including one behaviour influencing another behaviour. (See also *interaction*.)

379. **Interaction:** Two-way reciprocal action.

380. **Interface:** Boundary between two disjoint sets of communicating phenomena or concepts. (We shall think of the systems as *behaviour*s or *processes*, the boundary as being *channel*s, and the communications as *input*s and *output*s.)

381. **Interface requirements:** By interface requirements we understand the expression of expectations as to which software-software, or software-hardware *interface* places (i.e., *channel*s), *input*s and *output*s (including

the *semiotics* of these input/outputs) there shall be in some contemplated *computing system*. (Interface requirements can often, usefully, be classified in terms of *shared data initialisation requirements, shared data refreshment requirements, computational data+control requirements, man-machine dialogue requirements, man-machine physiological requirements* and *machine-machine dialogue requirements*. Interface requirements constitute one requirements *facet*. Other requirements facets are: *business process reengineering, domain requirements* and *machine requirements*.)

382. **Interface requirements facet:** See *interface requirements* for a list of facets: *shared data initialisation, shared data refreshment, computational data+control, man-machine dialogue, man-machine physiological* and *machine-machine dialogue requirements*.

383. **Interpret:** See next: *interpretation*.

384. **Interpretation:** The three terms *elaboration, evaluation* and *interpretation* essentially cover the same idea: that of obtaining the meaning of a syntactical item in some *configuration*, or as a function from configurations to *values*. Given that configuration typically consists of *static environments* and *dynamic states* (or *storages*), we use the term interpretation in the more narrow sense of designating, or yielding functions from syntactical items to functions from configurations to states.

385. **Interpreter:** An interpreter is an *agent*, a *machine*, which performs *interpretations*.

386. **Intrinsics:** By the intrinsics of a *domain* we shall understand those phenomena and concepts of a domain which are basic to any of the other facets, with such a domain intrinsics initially covering at least one specific, hence named, *stakeholder* view. (Intrinsics is thus one of several *domain* facets. Others include: *business processes, support technology, management and organisation, rules and regulations,* and *human behaviour*.)

387. **Invariant:** By an invariant we mean a property that holds of a *phenomenon* or a *concept*, both before and after any *action* involving that phenomenon or a concept. (A case in point is usually an *information* or a *data structure*: Assume an action, say a repeated one (e.g., a while loop). We say that the action (i.e., the while loop) preserves an invariant, i.e., usually a *proposition*, if the proposition holds true of the *state* before and the state after any *interpretation* of the while loop. Invariance is here seen separate from the *well-formedness* of an *information* or a *data structure*. We refer to the explication of *well-formedness*!)

388. **Inverse function:** See *injection*.

389. **Invocation:** See *function invocation*.

390. **Isomorphic:** One to one. (See *isomorphism*.)

391. **Isomorphism:** If a *homomorphism* ϕ is a *bijective function* then ϕ is an isomorphism. (See also *automorphism, endomorphism, epimorphism* and *monomorphism*.)

	$\mathcal{J}$

392. **J:** The **J** operator (**J** for **J**ump) was introduced (before 1965) by Peter Landin as a *functional* used to explain the creation and use of program *closure*s, and these again are used to model the *denotation* of *label*s. (We refer to [172, 334–336, 340]. Cf. www.dcs.qmw.ac.uk/~peterl/danvy/.)

	$\mathcal{K}$

393. **Keyword:** A significant word from a title or document. (See *KWIC*.)
394. **Knowledge:** What is, or what can be known. The body of truth, information, and principles acquired by mankind [373]. (See *epistemology* and *ontology*. *A priori knowledge:* Knowledge that is independent of all particular experiences. *A posteriori knowledge:* Knowledge, which derives from experience alone.)
395. **Knowledge engineering:** The representation and modelling of knowledge. (The construction of ontological and epistemological knowledge and its manipulation. Involves such subdisciplines as *modal logic*s (promise and commitment, knowledge and belief), *speech act* theories, *agent* theories, etc. Knowledge engineering usually is concerned with the knowledge that one agent may have about another agent.)
396. **KWIC:** Abbreviation for keyword-in-context (A classical software application. Cf. Example 15.10.)

	$\mathcal{L}$

397. **Label:** Same as named *program point*.
398. **Lambda-application:** Within the confines of the *Lambda-calculus*, *Lambda-application* is the same as *function application*. (Subject, however, to simple *term-rewriting* using (say just) *Alpha-renaming* and *Beta-reduction*.)
399. **Lambda-calculus:** A *calculus* for expressing and "manipulating" functions. The Lambda-calculus (λ-calculus) is a de facto "standard" for "what is computable". See *Lambda-expression*s. As a *calculus* it prescribes a language, the language of *Lambda-expression*s, a set of *conversion* rules — these apply to *Lambda-expression*s and result in *Lambda-expression*s. They "mimic" *function definition* and *function application*. The seminal texts on the Lambda-calculi are [26, 27, 29, 153].
400. **Lambda-combination:** See *Lambda-application*.
401. **Lambda-expression:** The language of the "pure" (i.e., simple, but fully powerful) *Lambda-calculus* has three kinds of Lambda-expressions: *Lambda-variable*s, *Lambda-function*s and *Lambda-application*s.
402. **Lambda-function:** By a Lambda-function we understand a *Lambda-expression* of the form $\lambda x \cdot e$, where x is a binding variable and e is a

Lambda-expression. (It is usually the case that e contains *free* occurrences of x — these being bound by the binding variable in $\lambda x \cdot e$.)

403. **Lambda-variable:** The x in the *Lambda-function* expression $\lambda x \cdot e$: both the formal parameter, the first x you see in $\lambda x \cdot e$, and all the *free* occurrences of x in the *block* (i.e., body) expression e.

404. **Language:** By a language we shall understand a possibly infinite set of *sentences* which follow some *syntax*, express some *semantics* and are uttered, or written down, due to some *pragmatics*.

405. **Law:** A law is a rule of conduct prescribed as binding or enforced by a controlling authority. (We shall take the term law in the specific sense of law of Nature (cf., Ampére's Law, Boyle's Law, the conservation laws (of mass-energy, electric charge, linear and angular momentum), Newton's Laws, Ohm's Law, etc.), and laws of Mathematics (cf. "law of the excluded middle" (as in logic: a proposition must either be true, or false, not both, and not none)).)

406. **Leaf:** A leaf is a *node* in a *tree* for which there are no sub*trees* of that node. (Thus a leaf is a concept of *trees*. Cf. Fig. B.4 on page 644.)

407. **Lemma:** An auxiliary *proposition* used in the demonstration of another proposition. (Instead of proposition we could use the term *theorem*.)

408. **Lexical analysis:** The analysis of a *sentence* into its constituent *words*. (Sentences also are usually "decorated" with such signs as for example punctuation marks (, . : ;), delimiters (( ) [ ], etc.), and other symbols (? !, etc.). Lexical analysis therefore is a process which serves to recognise which character sequences are words and which are not (i.e., which are delimiters, etc.).)

409. **Lexicographic:** The principles and practices of establishing, maintaining and using a dictionary. (We shall, in software engineering, mostly be using the term 'lexicographic' in connection with compilers and, more rarely, database schemas — although, as the definition implies, it is of relevance in any context where a computing system builds, maintains and uses a dictionary.)

410. **Lexicographical order:** The order, i.e., sequence, in which entries of a dictionary appear. (More specifically, the lexicographical ordering of entries in a *compiler dictionary* is, for a *block-structured programming language*, determined by the nesting structure of *blocks*. The dictionary itself, generally "mimics" the nesting structure of the language.)

411. **Link:** A link is the same as a *pointer*, an *address* or a *reference*: something which refers to, i.e., designates something (typically something else).

412. **Lifted function:** A lifted function, say of type $A \rightarrow B \rightarrow C$, has been created from a function of type $B \rightarrow C$ by 'lifting' it, i.e., by abstracting it in a variable, say a of type A. (Assume $\lambda b : B \cdot \mathcal{E}(b)$ to be a function of type $B \rightarrow C$. Now $\lambda a : A \cdot \lambda b : B \cdot \mathcal{E}(b)$ is a lifted version of $\lambda b : B \cdot \mathcal{E}(b)$. An example is **and:** $\lambda b_1, b_2 : \textbf{Bool} \cdot b_1 \wedge b_2$, Boolean conjunction. We lift **and** to be a function, $\wedge_T$, over time: $\lambda t : T \cdot b_1(t) \wedge b_2(t)$, where the variables

b_1, b_2 typically could be (e.g., assignable) variables whose values change over time.)

413. **Linguistics:** The study and knowledge of the *syntax*, *semantics* and *pragmatics* of *language*(s).

414. **List:** A list is an ordered sequence of zero, one or more not necessarily distinct entities.

415. **Literal:** A term whose use in software engineering, i.e., programming, shall mean: an identifier which denotes a constant, or is a keyword. (Usually that identifier is emphasised. Examples of RSL literals are: **Bool, true, false, chaos, if, then, else, end, let, in,** and the numerals $0, 1, 2., ..., 1234.5678$, etc.)

416. **Live Sequence Chart:** The Live Sequence Chart language is a special graphic notation for expressing communication between and coordination and timing of processes. (See [171, 270, 325].)

417. **Location:** By a location is meant an area of *storage*.

418. **Logic:** The principles and criteria of validity of inference and deduction, that is, the mathematics of the formal principles of reasoning. (We refer to Vol. 1, Chap. 9 for our survey treatment of mathematical logic.)

419. **Logic programming:** Logic programming is programming based on an interpreter which either performs deductions or inductions, or both. (In logic programming the chief values are those of the Booleans, and the chief forms of expressions are those of propositions and predicates.)

420. **Logic programming language:** By a *logic programming* language is meant a language which allows one to express, to prescribe, *logic programming*. (The classical logic programming language is Prolog [295, 351].)

421. **Loose specification:** By a loose specification is understood a specification which either *underspecifies* a problem, or specifies this problem *nondeterministically*.

$\mathcal{M}$

---

422. **Machine:** By the machine we understand the *hardware* plus *software* that implements some *requirements*, i.e., a *computing system*. (This definition follows that of M.A. Jackson [308].)

423. **Machine-Machine dialogue requirements:** By machine-machine dialogue requirements we understand the *syntax* (incl. sequential structure), and *semantics* (i.e., meaning) of the communications (i.e., messages) transferred in either direction over the automated interface between *machines* (including supporting technologies). (See also *computational data+control requirements*, *shared data initialisation requirements*, *shared data refreshment requirements*, *man-machine dialogue requirements*, and *man-machine physiological requirements*.)

424. **Machine requirements:** By *machine requirements* we understand *requirements* put specifically to, i.e., expected specifically from, the *machine*. (We normally analyse machine requirements into *performance re-*

quirements, dependability requirements, maintenance requirements, platform requirements and *documentation requirements.)*

425. **Machine service:** The service delivered by a machine is its *behaviour* as it is perceptible by its user(s), where a user is a human, another machine, or a(nother) system which *interacts* with it [432].

426. **Macro:** Macros have the same syntax as procedures, that is, a pair of a *signature* (i.e., a macro name followed by a formal argument list of distinct identifiers (i.e., the *formal parameters*)) and a macro body, a text. Syntactically we can distinguish between macro definitions and macro *invocations*. Semantically, invocations, in some text, of the macro name and an *actual argument* list are then to be thought of as an expansion of that part of the text with the macro (definition) body and such that formal parameters are replaced (*macro substitution*) by actual arguments. Semantically a macro is different from a *procedure* in that a macro expansion takes place in a *context*, i.e., an *environment*, where *free* identifiers of the macro body are replaced by their value as defined at the place of the occurrence of the macro invocation. Whereas, for a procedure, the free identifiers of a procedure body are bound to their value at the point where the procedure was defined. (Thus the difference between a macro and a procedure is the difference between *evaluation* in a calling, versus in a defining environment.)

427. **Macro substitution:** See under *macros*.

428. **Maintenance:** By maintenance we shall here, for software, mean change to *software*, i.e., its various *documents*, due to needs for (i) adapting that software to new *platforms*, (ii) correcting that software due to observed software errors, (iii) improving certain performance properties of the *machine* of which the software is part, or (iv) avoiding potential problems with that machine. (We refer to subcategories of maintenance: *adaptive maintenance, corrective maintenance, perfective maintenance* and *preventive maintenance.*)

429. **Maintenance requirements:** By *maintenance requirements* we understand requirements which express expectations on how the *machine* being desired (i.e., required) is expected to be maintained. (We also refer to *adaptive maintenance, corrective maintenance, perfective maintenance* and *preventive maintenance.*)

430. **Management and organisation:** By management and organisation we mean those *facets* of a *domain* which are representative of relations between the various management levels of an enterprise, and between these and non-management staff, i.e., "blue-collar" workers. (As such, management and organisation is about formulating strategical, tactical and operational goals for the enterprise, of communicating and "translating" these goals into action to be done by management and staff, in general, and to "backstop" when "things do not 'work out'", i.e., handling complaints from "above" and "below". Other facets of an enterprise are those of its

intrinsics, business processes, support technology, rules and regulations and *human behaviour*.)

431. **Man-machine dialogue:** By man-machinedialogues we understand actual instantiations of *user* interactions with *machines*, and machine interactions with users: what input the users provide, what output the machine initiates, the interdependencies of these inputs/outputs, their temporal and spatial constraints, including response times, input/output media (locations), etc. (

432. **Man-machine dialogue requirements:** By man-machine dialogue requirements we understand those *interface requirements* which express expectations on, i.e., mandates the *protocol* according to which *users* are to interact with the *machine*, and the machine with the users. (See *man-machine dialogue*. For other *interface requirements* see *computational data+control requirements, shared data initialisation requirements, shared data refreshment requirements, man-machine physiological requirements* and *machine-machine dialogue requirements*.))

433. **Man-machine physiological requirements:** By man-machine physiological requirements we understand those *interface requirements* which express expectations on, i.e., mandates, the form and appearance of ways in which the *man-machine dialogue* utilises such physiological devices as visual display screens, keyboards, "mouses" (and other tactile instruments), audio microphones and loudspeakers, television cameras, etc. (See also *computational data+control requirements, shared data initialisation requirements, shared data refreshment requirements, man-machine dialogue requirements* and *machine-machine dialogue requirements*.)

434. **Map:** A map is like a *function*, but is here thought of as an *enumerable* set of pairs of argument/result values. (Thus the *definition set* of a map is usually decidable, i.e., whether an entity is a member of a definition set of a map or not can usually be decided.)

435. **Mechanical semantics:** By a mechanical semantics we understand the same as an *operational semantics* (which is again basically the same as a *computational semantics*), i.e., a semantics of a language specified using concrete constructs (like stacks, program pointers, etc.), and otherwise as defined in *operational semantics* and *computational semantics*.

436. **Mereology:** The theory of parthood relations: of the relations of part to whole and the relations of part to part within a whole. (Mereology is often considered a branch of *ontology*. Leading investigators of mereology were Franz Brentano, Edmund Husserl, Stanislaw Lesniewski [355,383,473,479, 480,493] and Leonard and Goodman [345].)

437. **Meta-IV:** Meta-IV stands for the fourth metalanguage (for programing language definition conceived at the IBM Vienna Laboratory in the 1960s and 1970s). (Meta-IV is pronounced meta-four.)

438. **Metalanguage:** By a metalanguage is understood a *language* which is used to explain another language, either its *syntax*, or its *semantics*, or its *pragmatics*, or two or all of these! (One cannot explain any language using

itself. That would lead to any interpretation of what is explained being a valid solution, in other words: Nonsense. RSL thus cannot be used to explain RSL. Typically formal specification languages are metalanguages: being used to explain, for example, the semantics of ordinary programming languages.)

439. **Metalinguistic:** We say that a language is used in a metalinguistic manner when it is being deployed to explain some other language. (And we also say that when we examine a language, like we could, for example, examine RSL, and when we use a subset of RSL to make that analysis, then that subset of RSL is used metalinguistically (wrt. all of RSL).)

440. **Metaphysics:** We quote from: http://mally.stanford.edu/: "Whereas physics is the attempt to discover the laws that govern fundamental concrete objects, metaphysics is the attempt to discover the laws that systematize the fundamental abstract objects presupposed by physical science, such as natural numbers, real numbers, functions, sets and properties, physically possible objects and events, to name just a few. The goal of metaphysics, therefore, is to develop a formal ontology, i.e., a formally precise systematization of these abstract objects. Such a theory will be compatible with the world view of natural science if the abstract objects postulated by the theory are conceived as patterns of the natural world." (Metaphysics may, to other scientists and philosophers, mean more or other, but for software engineering the characterisation just given suffices.)

441. **Method:** By a method we shall here understand a set of *principles* for selecting and using a number of *techniques* and *tools* in order to construct some *artefact*. (This is our leading definition — one that sets out our methodological quest: to identify, enumerate and explain the principles, the techniques and, in cases, the tools — notably where the latter are specification and programming languages. (Yes, languages are tools.))

442. **Methodology:** By methodology we understand the study and knowledge of *methods*, one, but usually two or more. (In some dialects of English, methodology is confused with method.)

443. **Mixed computation:** By a mixed computation we understand the same as by a *partial evaluation*. (The term mixed computation was used notably by Andrei Petrovich Ershov [214–221], in my mind the "father" of Russian computing science.)

444. **Modal logic:** A modal is an expression (like "necessarily" or "possibly") that is used to qualify the truth of a judgment. Modal logic is, strictly speaking, the study of the deductive behavior of the expressions "it is necessary that" and "it is possible that". (The term "modal logic" may be used more broadly for a family of related systems. These include logics for belief, for tense and other temporal expressions, for the deontic (moral) expressions such as "it is obligatory that", "it is permitted that" and many others. An understanding of modal logic is particularly valuable in the formal analysis of philosophical argument, where expressions from

the modal family are both common and confusing. Modal logic also has important applications in computer science [536].)

445. **Model:** A model is the mathematical meaning of a description (of a domain), or a prescription (of requirements), or a specification (of software), i.e., is the meaning of a specification of some universe of discourse. (The meaning can be understood either as a mathematical function, as for a *denotational semantics* meaning, or an *algebra* as for an *algebraic semantics* or a *denotational semantics* meaning, etc. The essence is that the model is some mathematical structure.)

446. **Model-oriented:** A specification (description, prescription) is said to be model-oriented if the specification (etc.) *denotes* a *model*. (Contrast to *property-oriented*.)

447. **Model-oriented type:** A type is said to be model-oriented if its specification *designates* a *model*. (Contrast to *property-oriented type*.)

448. **Modularisation:** The act of structuring a text using *modules*.

449. **Module:** By a module we shall understand a clearly delineated text which denotes either a single complex quantity, as does, usually, an *object*, or a possibly empty, possibly infinite set of *models* of objects. (The RSL module concept is manifested in the use of one or more of the RSL *class* (**class ... end**), *object* (**object** identifier **class ... end**, etc.), and *scheme* (**scheme** identifier **class ... end**), etc., constructs. We refer to [54, 169, 170] and to [413, 414] for original, early papers on modules.)

450. **Module design:** By module design we shall understand the *design* of (one or more) *modules*.

451. **Monitor:** Syntactically a monitor is "a programming language construct which encapsulates variables, access procedures and initialisation code within an abstract data type. The monitor's variable may only be accessed via its access procedures and only one process may be actively accessing the monitor at any one time. The access procedures are critical sections." Semantically "a monitor may have a queue of processes which are waiting to access it" [227].

452. **Monomorphism:** If a *homomorphism* ϕ is an *injective function* then ϕ is an isomorphism. (See also *automorphism*, *endomorphism*, *epimorphism*, and *monomorphism*.)

453. **Monotonic:** A function, $f : A \to B$, is monotonic, if for all a, a' in the definition set A of f, and some ordering relations, $\sqsubseteq$, on a and B, we have that if $a \sqsubseteq a'$ then $f(a) \sqsubseteq f(a')$.

454. **Mood:** A conscious state of mind, as here, of a specification. (We can thus express an *indicative* mood, an *optative* mood, a *putative* mood or an *imperative* mood. Our use of these various forms of moods is due to Michael Jackson [308].)

455. **Morphism:** Same as *homomorphism*.

456. **Morphology:** (i) A study and description of word formation (as inflection, derivation, and compounding) in language; (ii) the system of word-

forming elements and processes in a language; (iii) a study of structure or form [373].

457. **Multi-dimensional:** A composite (i.e., a non*atomic*) *entity* is a multi-dimensional *entity* if some relations between properly contained (i.e., constituent) subentities (cf. *subentity*) can only be described by both forward and backward references, and/or with recursive references. (This is in contrast to *one-dimensional* entities.)

458. **Multimedia:** The use of various forms of input/output media in the man-machine interface: Text, two-dimensional graphics, voice (audio), video, and tactile instruments (like "mouse").

$\mathcal{N}$

---

459. **Name:** A name is syntactically (generally an expression, but usually it is) a simple alphanumeric identifier. Semantically a name denotes (i.e., designates) "something". Pragmatically a name is used to uniquely identify that "something". (Shakespeare: Romeo: "What's in a name?" Juliet to Romeo: "That which we call a rose by any other name would smell as sweet.")

460. **Naming:** The action of allocating a unique name to a value.

461. **Narrative:** By a narrative we shall understand a document text which, in precise, unambiguous language, introduces and describes (prescribes, specifies) all relevant properties of entities, functions, events and behaviours, of a set of phenomena and concepts, in such a way that two or more readers will basically obtain the same idea as to what is being described (prescribed, specified). (More commonly: Something that is narrated, a story.)

462. **Natural language:** By a natural language we shall understand a language like Arabic, Chinese, English, French, Russian, Spanish, etc. — one that is spoken today, 2005, by people, has a body of literature, etc. (In contrast to natural languages we have (i) professional languages, like the languages of medical doctors, or lawyers, or skilled craftsmen like carpenters, etc.; and we have (ii) formal languages like software specification languages, programming languages, and the languages of first-order predicate logics, etc.)

463. **Network:** By a network we shall understand the same as a directed, but not necessarily *acyclic graph*. (Our only use of it here is in connection with network *databases*.)

464. **Node:** A point in some *graph* or *tree*.

465. **Nondeterminate:** Same as *nondeterministic*.

466. **Nondeterministic:** A property of a specification: May, on purpose, i.e., deliberately have more than one meaning. (A specification which is ambiguous also has more than one meaning, but its ambiguity is of overriding concern: It is not 'nondeterministic' (and certainly not 'deterministic'!).)

467. **Nondeterminism:** A *nondeterministic* specification models nondeterminism.

468. **Nonstrict:** Nonstrictness is a property associated with functions. A function is nonstrict, in certain or all arguments, if, for undefined values of these it may still yield a defined value. (See also *strict functions*.)

469. **Nonterminal:** The concept of a nonterminal (together with the concept of a *terminal*) is a concept associated with the *rule of grammars*. (See that term: *rule of grammar* for a full explanation.)

470. **Notation:** By a notation we shall usually understand a reasonably precisely delineated language. (Some notations are textual, as are programming notations or specification languages; some are diagrammatic, as are, for example, *Petri nets*, *statecharts*, *live sequence charts*, etc.)

471. **Noun:** Something, a name, that refers to an *entity*, a quality, a *state*, an *action*, or a *concept*. Something that may serve as the subject of a *verb*. (But beware: In English many nouns can be "verbed", and many verbs can be "nouned"!)

	O

472. **Object:** An instance of the *data structure* and *behaviour* defined by the object's *class*. Each object has its own *values* for the instance *variables* of its class and can respond to the *functions* defined by its class. (Various *specification languages*, object Z [144, 199, 200], RSL, etc., each have their own, further refined, meaning for the term 'object', and so do *object-oriented programming language* (viz., C++ [489], Java [10, 20, 243, 348, 470, 511], C# [277, 381, 382, 422] and so on).)

473. **Object-oriented:** We say that a program is *object-oriented* if its main structure is determined by a *modularisation* into a *class*, that is, a cluster of *types*, *variables* and *procedures*, each such set acting as a separate *abstract data type*. Similarly we say that a *programming language* is object-oriented if it specifically offers language constructs to express the appropriate *modularisation*. (Object-orientedness became a mantra of the 1990s: Everything had to be object-oriented. And many programming problems are indeed well served by being structured around some object-oriented notion. The first *object-oriented programming language* was Simula 67 [54].)

474. **Observer:** By an observer we mean basically the same as an *observer function*.

475. **Observer function:** An observer function is a *function* which when "applied" to an *entity* (a *phenomenon* or a *concept*) yields subentities or attributes of that entity (without "destroying" that entity). (Thus we do not make a distinction between functions that observe subentities (cf. *subentity*) and functions that observe *attributes*. You may wish to make distinctions between the two kinds of observer function. You can do so by some simple *naming* convention: assign names the prefix obs_ when

you mean to observe subentities, and **attr_** when you mean to observe attributes. Vol. 3 Chap. 5 introduces these concepts.)

476. **One-dimensional:** A composite *entity* is a one-dimensional *entity* if all relations between properly contained (i.e., constituent) subentities can be described by either no references to other subentities, or only by backward or only by forward references. (This is in contrast to *multi-dimensional* entities. Thus arrays of arbitrary order (vectors, matrices, tensors) are usually one-dimensional.)

477. **Ontology:** In philosophy: A systematic account of Existence. To us: An explicit formal specification of how to represent the phenomena, concepts and other entities that are assumed to exist in some area of interest (some universe of discourse) and the relationships that hold among them. (Further clarification: An ontology is a catalogue of *concepts* and their relationships — including properties as relationships to other concepts. See Sect. B.1.4.)

478. **Operation:** By an operation we shall mean a *function*, or an *action* (i.e., the effect of function *invocation*). (The context determines which of these two strongly related meanings are being referred to.)

479. **Operational:** We say that a *specification* (a *description*, a *prescription*), say of a *function*, is operational if what it explains is explained in terms of how that thing, **how** that phenomenon, or concept, operates (rather than by **what** it achieves). (Usually operational definitions are *model oriented* (in contrast to *property oriented*).)

480. **Operational abstraction:** Although a definition (a *specification*, a *description*, or a *prescription*) may be said, or claimed, to be *operational*, it may still provide *abstraction* in that the *model-oriented* concepts of the definition are not themselves directly representable or performable by humans or computers. (This is in contrast to *denotational abstraction*s or *algebra*ic (or *axioma*tic) *abstraction*s.)

481. **Operational semantics:** A *definition* of a *language semantics* that is *operational*. (See also *structural operational semantics*.)

482. **Operation reification:** To speak of *operation reification* one must first be able to refer to an abstract, usually *property-oriented*, specification of the operation. Then, by operation *reification* we mean a *specification* which indicates how the operation might be (possibly efficiently) implemented. (Cf. *data reification* and *operation transformation*.)

483. **Operation transformation:** To speak of *operation reification* one must first be able to refer to an abstract, usually *property-oriented*, specification of the operation. Then, by operation *transformation* we mean a *specification* which is, somehow, *calculate*d from the abstract specification. (Three nice books on such calculi are: [21, 50, 390].)

484. **Optative:** Expressive of wish or desire. (See also *imperative*, *indicative*, and *putative*.)

485. **Organisation:** By organisation we shall here, in a narrow sense, only mean the administrative or functional structure of an enterprise, a pub-

lic or private administration, or of a set of services, as for example in a consumer/retailer/wholesaler/producer/distributor market, or in a financial services industry, etc.

486. **Organisation and management:** The composite term organisation and management applies in connection with *organisation*s as outlined just above. The term then emphasises the relations between the organisation and its management. (For more, see *management and organisation*.)

487. **Output:** By output we mean the *communication* of *information* (*data*) to an outside, an *environment*, from a *phenomenon* "within" our universe of discourse. (More colloquially, and more generally: output can be thought of as *value*(s) transferred over *channel*(s) from, or between, *processes*. Cf. *input*. In a narrow sense we talk of output from a *machine* (e.g., a *finite state machine* or a *pushdown machine*).)

488. **Output alphabet:** The set of *symbols* *output* from a *machine* in the sense of, for example, a *finite state machine* or a *pushdown machine*.

489. **Overloaded:** The concept of 'overloaded' is a concept related to *function symbol*s, i.e., *function name*s. A function name is said to be overloaded if there exists two or more distinct *signature*s for that function name. (Typically overloaded function symbols are '+', which applies, possibly, in some notation, to addition of integers, addition of reals, etc., and '=', which applies, possibly, in some notation, to comparison of any pair of *value*s of the same *type*.)

$$P$$

490. **Paradigm:** A philosophical and theoretical framework of a scientific school or discipline within which theories, laws and generalizations and the experiments performed in support of them are formulated; a philosophical or theoretical framework of any kind. (Software engineering is full of paradigms: Object-orientedness is one.)

491. **Paradox:** A statement that is seemingly contradictory or opposed to common sense and yet is perhaps true. An apparently sound argument leading to a contradiction. (Some famous examples are Russell's Paradox[3] and the Liar Paradox.[4] Most paradoxes stem from some kind of self-reference.)

492. **Parallel programming language:** A *programming language* whose major kinds of concepts are *process*es, process *composition* [putting processes in parallel and *nondeterministic* {internal or external} choice of process *elaboration*], and synchronisation and communication between processes. (A main example of a practical parallel programming language is occam [301], and of a specificational 'programming' language is CSP [288,448,456].

---

[3]If R is the set of all sets which do not contain themselves, does R contain itself? If it does then it doesn't and vice versa.

[4]"This sentence is false" or "I am lying".

Most recent *imperative programming language*s (Java, C#, etc.) provide for programming constructs (e.g., threads) that somehow mimic parallel programming.)

493. **Parameter:** Same as *formal parameter*.

494. **Parametric polymorphism:** See the parenthesised part of the *polymorphic* entry.

495. **Parameterised:** We say that a *definition*, of a *class* (or of a *function*) is parameterised if an *instantiation* of an *object* of the class (respectively an *invocation* of the function) allows an *actual argument* to be substituted (cf. *substitution*) into the class definition (function body) for every occurrence of the [formal] *parameter*.

496. **Parser:** A parser is an *algorithm*, say embodied as a *software program*, which accepts text strings, and, if the text string is generated by a suitable *grammar*, then it will yield a *parse tree* of that string. (See *generator*.)

497. **Parse tree:** To speak of a parse tree we assume the presence of a string of *terminal*s and *nonterminal*s, and of a *grammar*. A parse tree is a *tree* such that each subtree (of a *root* and its immediate descendants, whether *terminal*s or *nonterminal*s) corresponds to a *rule* of the grammar, and hence such that the *frontier* of the tree is the given string.

498. **Parsing:** The act of attempting to construct a *parse tree* from a *grammar* and a text string.

499. **Part:** To speak of parts we must be able to speak of "parts and wholes". That is: We assume some *mereology*, i.e., a theory of parthood relations: of the relations of part to whole and the relations of part to part within a whole.

500. **Partial algebra:** A partial *algebra* is an algebra whose functions are not defined for all combinations of arguments over the carrier.

501. **Partial evaluation:** To speak of partial evaluation we must first speak of *evaluation*. Normally evaluation is a *process*, as well as the result of that process, whereby an *expression* in some language is evaluated in some *context* which binds every *free identifier* of the expression to some *value*. A partial evaluation is an evaluation in whose context not all free identifiers are bound to (hence, defined) values. The result of a partial evaluation is therefore a symbolic evaluation, one in which the resulting value is expressed in terms of actual values and the undefined free identifiers. (We refer to [115, 320].)

502. **Path:** The concept of paths is usually associated with *graph*s and *tree*s (i.e., networks). A path is then a sequence of one or more graph edges or tree branches such that two consecutive edges (branches) share a node of the graph (or [root] of a tree). (We shall also use the term *route* synonymously with paths.)

503. **Pattern:** We shall take a pattern, p, (as in RSL) to mean an expression with identifiers, a, and constants, k, as follows. Basis clauses: Any identifier a is a pattern, and any constant, k, is a pattern. Inductive clause: If $p_1, p_2, \ldots, p_m$ are patterns, then so are $(p_1, p_2, \ldots, p_m)$,

$< p_1, p_2, \ldots, p_m >, \{p_1, p_2, \ldots, p_m\}, [p_{d_1} \mapsto p_{r_1}, p_{d_2} \mapsto p_{r_2}, \ldots, p_{d_m} \mapsto p_{r_m}]$, and so are: $\langle p \rangle \hat{\ } a, a \hat{\ } \langle p \rangle, \{p\} \cup a$, and $[p_{d_1} \mapsto p_{r_1}] \cup a$. (The idea is that a pattern, p, is "held up against" a value, v, "of the same kind" and then we attempt to "match" the pattern, p, with the value, v, and if a matching can be made, then the free identifiers of p are bound to respective component values of v.)

504. **Perfective maintenance:** By perfective maintenance we mean an update, as here, of software, to achieve a more desirable use of resources: time, storage space, equipment. (We also refer to *adaptive maintenance*, *corrective maintenance* and *preventive maintenance*.)

505. **Performance:** By performance we, here, in the context of computing, mean quantitative figures for the use of computing resources: time, storage space, equipment.

506. **Performance requirements:** By performance requirements we mean *requirements* which express *performance* properties (desiderata).

507. **Petri net:** The Petri net language is a special graphic notation for expressing concurrency of actions, and simultaneity of events, of processes. (See [313, 421, 435–437].)

508. **Phase:** By a phase we shall here, in the context of software development, understand either the *domain development* phase, the *requirements development* phase, or the *software design* phase.

509. **Phenomenon:** By a phenomenon we shall mean a physically manifest "thing". (Something that can be sensed by humans (seen, heard, touched, smelled or tasted), or can be measured by physical apparatus: Electricity (voltage, current, etc.), mechanics (length, time and hence velocity, acceleration, etc.), chemistry, etc.)

510. **Phenomenology:** Phenomenology is the study of structures of consciousness as experienced from the first-person point of view [536].

511. **Platform:** By a platform, we shall, in the context of computing, understand a *machine*: Some computer (i.e., hardware) equipment and some software systems. (Typical examples of platforms are: `Microsoft Windows` running on an `IBM ThinkPad Series T` model, or `Trusted Solaris` operating system with an `Oracle Database` 10*g* running on a `Sun Fire E25K Server`.)

512. **Platform requirements:** By platform requirements we mean *requirements* which express *platform* properties (desiderata). (There can be several platform requirements: One set for the platform on which software shall be developed. Another set for the platform(s) on which software shall be utilised. A third set for the platform on which software shall be demonstrated. And a fourth set for the platform on which software shall be maintained. These platforms need not always be the same.)

513. **Pointer:** A pointer is the same as an *address*, a *link*, or a *reference*: something which refers to, i.e., designates something (typically something else).

514. **Polymorphic:** Polymorphy is a concept associated with functions and the type of the values to which the function applies. If, as for the length

of a list function, **len**, that function applies to lists of elements of any type, then we say the **len**gth function is polymorphic. So, in general, the ability to appear in many forms; the quality or state of being able to assume different forms. From Wikipedia, the Free Enclycopedia [519]:

> In computer science, polymorphism is the idea of allowing the same code to be used with different types, resulting in more general and abstract implementations. The concept of polymorphism applies to functions as well as types: A function that can evaluate to and be applied to values of different types is known as a polymorphic function. A data type that contains elements of an unspecified type is known as a polymorphic data type. There are two fundamentally different kinds of polymorphism: If the range of actual types that can be used is finite and the combinations must be specified individually prior to use, it is called *ad hoc polymorphism*. If all code is written without mention of any specific type and thus can be used transparently with any number of new types, it is called *parametric polymorphism*. Programming using the latter kind is called *generic programming*, particularly in the object-oriented community. However, in many statically typed functional programming languages the notion of parametric polymorphism is so deeply ingrained that most *programmers* simply take it for granted.

515. **Portability:** Portability is a concept associated with *software*, more specifically with the *programs* (or *data*). Software is (or files, including *data base* records, are) said to be portable if it (they), with ease, can be "ported" to, i.e., made to "run" on, a new *platform* and/or compile with a different compiler, respectively different database management system.

516. **Post-condition:** The concept of post-condition is associated with function application. The post-condition of a function f is a predicate p_{o_f} which expresses the relation between argument a and result r values that the function f defines. If a represent argument values, r corresponding result values and f the function, then $f(a) = r$ can be expressed by the post-condition predicate p_{o_f}, namely, for all applicable a and r the predicate p_{o_f} expresses the truth of $p_{o_f}(a, r)$. (See also *pre-condition*.)

517. **Postfix:** The concept of postfix is basically a syntactic one, and is associated with operator/operand expressions. It is one about the displayed position of a unary (i.e., a monadic) operator with respect to its operand (expression). An expression is said to be in postfix form if a monadic operator is shown, is displayed, after the expression to which it applies. (Typically the factorial operator, say !, is shown after its operand expression, viz. 7!.)

518. **Post-order:** A special order of *tree traversal* in which visits are made to nodes of trees and subtrees as follows: First, for each subtree, a subtree post-order traversal is made, in the order left to right (or right to left). When a tree, whose number of subtrees is zero, is post-order traversed,

then just that tree's root is visited (and that tree has then been post-order traversed) and (the leaf) is "marked" as having been post-order visited. After each subtree visit the root of the tree of which the subtree is a subtree is revisited and now it is "marked" as having been visited. (Cf. Fig. B.4 on page 644: A left to right post-order traversal of that tree yields

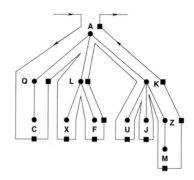

Fig. B.2. A left to right post-order tree traversal

the following sequence of "markings": CQXFLUJMZKA; cf. also Fig. B.2).

519. **Pragmatics:** Pragmatics is the (i) study and (ii) practice of the factors that govern our choice of language in social interaction and the effects of our choice on others. (We use the term pragmatics in connection with the use of language, as complemented by the *semantics* and *syntax* of language.)

520. **Pre-condition:** The concept of pre-condition is associated with function application where the function being applied is a partial function. That is: for some arguments of its definition set the function yields **chaos**, that is, does not terminate. The pre-consition of the function is then a predicate which expresses those values of the arguments for which the function application terminates, that is, yields a result value. (See *weakest pre-condition*.)

521. **Predicate:** A predicate is a truth-valued expression involving terms over arbitrary values, well-formed formula relating terms and with *Boolean connectives* and *quantifiers*.

522. **Predicate logic:** A predicate logic is a language of *predicates* (given by some *formal syntax*) and a *proof system*.

523. **Pre-order:** A special order of *tree traversal* in which visits are made to nodes of trees and subtrees as follows: First to the root of the tree with that root now being "marked" as having been pre-order visited. Then for each subtree a subtree pre-order traversal is made, in the order left to right (or right to left). When a tree, whose number of subtrees is zero, is pre-order traversed, then just that tree's root is visited (and that tree has then been pre-order traversed) and the leaf is then "marked" as having

been pre-order visited. (Cf. Fig. B.4 on page 644: A right-to-left pre-

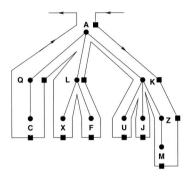

Fig. B.3. A right-to-left pre-order tree traversal

order traversal of that tree yields the following sequence of "markings":
AKZMJULFXQC. Cf. also Fig. B.3).

524. **Presentation:** By presentation we mean the syntactic *documen*tation of the results of some *development*.

525. **Prescription:** A prescription is a specification which prescribes some-thing designatable, i.e., which states what shall be achieved. (Usually the term 'prescription' is used only in connection with *requirements* prescrip-tions.)

526. **Preventive maintenance:** By preventive maintenance — of a *machine* — we mean that a set of special tests are performed on that *machine* in order to ascertain whether the *machine* needs *adaptive maintenance*, and/or *corrective maintenance*, and/or *perfective maintenance*. (If so, then an update, as here, of software, has to be made in order to achieve suitable *integrity* or *robustness* of the *machine*.)

527. **Principle:** An accepted or professed rule of action or conduct, ..., a fundamental doctrine, right rules of conduct, ... [484]. (The concept of principle, as we bring it forth, relates strongly to that of *method*. The concept of principle is "fluid". Usually, by a method, some people under-stand an orderliness. Our definition puts the orderliness as part of overall principles. Also, one usually expects analysis and construction to be effi-cient and to result in efficient artifacts. Also this we relegate to be implied by some principles, techniques and tools.)

528. **Procedure:** By a procedure we mean the same as a *function*. (Same as *routine* or *subroutine*.)

529. **Process:** By a process we understand a sequence of actions and events. The events designate interaction with some environment of the process.

530. **Program:** A program, in some *programming language*, is a formal text which can be subject to *interpretation* by a computer. (Sometimes we use

the term *code* instead of program, namely when the program is expressed in the machine language of a computer.)

531. **Programmable:** An *active dynamic phenomenon* has the programmable (active dynamic) attribute if its *action*s (hence *state* changes) over a future time interval can be accurately prescribed. (Cf. *autonomous* and *biddable*.)

532. **Programmer:** A person who does *software design*.

533. **Program point:** By a program point we shall here understand any point in a program text (whether of an *applicative programming language* (i.e., *functional programming language*), an *imperative programming language*, or a *logic programming language*) between any two textually neighbouring *token*s. (The idea of a program point is the following: Assume an *interpreter* of programs of the designated kind. Such an interpreter, at any step of its *interpretation process*, can be thought of as interpreting a special token, or a sequence of neighbouring tokens, in both cases: "between two program points".)

534. **Program organisation:** By program organisation we loosely mean how a *program* (i.e., its text) is structured into, for example, *module*s (eg., *class*es), *procedure*s, etc.

535. **Programming:** The act of constructing *program*s. From [227]:
    1: The art of debugging a blank sheet of paper (or, in these days of on-line editing, the art of debugging an empty file). 2: A pastime similar to banging one's head against a wall, but with fewer opportunities for reward. 3: The most fun you can have with your clothes on (although clothes are not mandatory).

536. **Programming language:** A language for expressing *program*s, i.e., a language with a precise *syntax*, a *semantics* and some textbooks which provides remnants of the *pragmatics* that was originally intended for that programming language. (See next entry: *programming language type*.)

537. **Programming language type:** With a *programming language* one can associate a *type*. Typically the name of that type intends to reveal the type of a main paradigm, or a main data type of the language. (Examples are: *functional programming language* (major data type is functions, major operations are definition of functions, application of functions and composition of functions), *logic programming language* (major kinds of expressions are ground terms in a Boolean algebra, propositions and predicates), *imperative programming language* (major kinds of language constructs are declaration of assignable variables, and assignment to variables, and a more or less indispensable kind of data type is references [locations, addresses, pointers]), and *parallel programming language*.)

538. **Projection:** By projection we shall here, in a somewhat narrow sense, mean a technique that applies to *domain description*s and yields *requirements prescription*s. Basically projection "reduces" a domain description by "removing" (or, but rarely, *hiding*) *entities*, *function*s, *event*s and *behaviour*s from the domain description. (If the domain description is an informal one, say in English, it may have expressed that certain enti-

ties, functions, events and behaviours *might* be in (some instantiations of) the domain. If not "projected away" the similar, i.e., informal requirements prescription will express that these entities, functions, events and behaviours *shall* be in the domain and hence *will* be in the environment of the *machine* being requirements prescribed.)

539. **Proof:** A *proof* of a theorem, ϕ, from a set, Γ, of sentences of some *formal propositional* or *predicate* language, $\mathcal{L}$, is a finite sequence of sentences, ϕ_1, ϕ_2, ..., ϕ_n, where $\phi = \phi_1$, where $\phi_n = $ **true**, and in which each ϕ_i is either an *axiom* of $\mathcal{L}$, or a member of Γ, or follows from earlier ϕ_j's by an *inference rule* of $\mathcal{L}$.

540. **Proof obligation:** A clause of a program may only be (dynamically) well-defined if the values of clause parts lie in certain ranges (viz. no division by zero). We say that such clauses raise proof obligations, i.e., an obligation to prove a property. (Classically it may not be statically (i.e., compile time) checkable that certain expression values lie within certain *subtypes*. Discharging a proof may help ensure such constraints.)

541. **Proof rule:** Same as *inference rule* or *axiom*.

542. **Proof system:** A *consistent* and (relative) *complete* set of *proof rules*.

543. **Property:** A quality belonging and especially peculiar to an individual or thing; an *attribute* common to all members of a class. (Hence: "Not a property owned by someone, but a property possessed by something".)

544. **Property-oriented:** A specification (description, prescription) is said to be property-oriented if the specification (etc.) expresses *attributes*. (Contrast to *model oriented*.)

545. **Proposition:** An expression in language which has a truth value.

546. **Protocol:** A set of formal rules describing how to exchange messages, between a human user and a *machine*, or, more classically, across a network. (Low-level protocols define the electrical and physical standards to be observed, bit and byte ordering, and the transmission and error detection and correction of the bit stream. High-level protocols deal with the data formatting, including the syntax of messages, the terminal-to-computer dialogue, character sets, sequencing of messages, etc.)

547. **Pure functional programming language:** A *functional programming language* is said to be pure if none of its constructs designates *side-effects*.

548. **Pushdown stack:** A pushdown stack is a simple *stack*. (Usually a simple stack has just the following operations: *push* an element onto the stack, *pop* the top element from the stack, and observe the *top* element of the stack.)

549. **Pushdown automaton:** A pushdown automaton is an *automaton* with the addition of a *pushdown stack* such that (i) the pushdown automaton *input* is provided both from an environment external to the pushdown automaton and from the *top* of the pushdown stack, (ii) the pushdown automaton *output* is provided to the pushdown stack by being *pushed* onto the top of that stack, and (iii) such that the pushdown automaton may

direct an element to be *popped* from the pushdown stack. (The pushdown automaton still has the notion of the final states of the *automaton*.)

550. **Pushdown machine:** A pushdown (stack) machine is like a *pushdown automaton* with the addition that now the pushdown machine also provides *output* to the environment of the pushdown machine.

551. **Putative:** Commonly accepted or supposed, that is, assumed to exist or to have existed. (See also *imperative*, *indicative* and *optative*.)

$\mathcal{Q}$

---

552. **Quality:** Specific and essential character. (Quality is an *attribute*, a *property*, a characteristic (something has character).)

553. **Quantification:** The operation of quantifying. (See *quantifier*. The x (the y) is quantifying expression $\forall x : X \cdot P(x)$ (respectively $\exists y : Y \cdot Q(y)$).)

554. **Quantifier:** A marker that quantifies. It is a prefixed operator that binds the variables in a logical formula by specifying their possible range of *value*s. (Colloquially we speak of the **universal** and the **existential** quantifiers, $\forall$, respectively $\exists$. Typically a quantified expression is then of either of the forms $\forall x : X \cdot P(x)$ and $\exists y : Y \cdot Q(y)$. They 'read': For all quantities x of type X it is the case that the predicate $P(x)$ holds; respectively: There exists a quantity y of type Y such that the predicate $Q(y)$ holds.)

555. **Quantity:** An indefinite *value*. (See the *quantifier* entry: The quantities in $P(x)$ (respectively $Q(y)$) are of type X (respectively Y). y is indefinite in that it is one of the quantities of Y, but which one is not said.)

556. **Query:** A request for information, generally as a formal request to a *database*.

557. **Query language:** A *formal language* for expressing queries (cf. *query*). (The most well-known query language, today, 2005, is SQL [178].)

558. **Queue:** A queue is an *abstract data type* with a queue data structure and, typically, the following operations: enqueue (insert into one end of the queue), dequeue (remove from the other end of the queue). Axioms then determine specific queue properties. (See Example 8.6.)

$\mathcal{R}$

---

559. **Radix:** In a positional representation of numbers, that integer by which the significance of one digit place must be multiplied to give the significance of the next higher digit place. (Conventional decimal numbers are radix ten, binary numbers are radix two.)

560. **RAISE:** RAISE stands for Rigorous Approach to Industrial Software Engineering. (RAISE refers to a method, The RAISE Method [238], a specification language, RSL [236], and "comes" with a set of tools. For more on RSL we refer to Part III of this volume.)

561. **Range:** The concept of range is here used in connection with functions. Same as *range set*. See next entry.

562. **Range set:** Given a *function*, its range set is that set of *values* which is yielded when the function is *applied* to each member of its *definition set*.

563. **Reactive:** A *phenomenon* is said to be reactive if the phenomenon performs *actions* in response to external stimuli. Thus three properties must be satisfied for a system to be of reactive dynamic attribute: (i) An interface must be definable in terms of (ii) provision of input stimuli and (iii) observation of (state) reaction. (Contrast to *inert* and *active*.)

564. **Reactive system:** A *system* whose main phenomena are chiefly *reactive*. (See the *reactive* entry just above.)

565. **Real time:** We say that a *phenomenon* is real time if its behaviour somehow must guarantee a response to an external event within a given time. (Cf. *hard real time* and *soft real time*.)

566. **Reasoning:** Reasoning is the ability to *infer*, i.e., to make *deductions* or *inductions*. (Automated reasoning is concerned with the building and use of computing systems that automate this process. The overall goal is to mechanise different forms of reasoning.)

567. **Recogniser:** A recogniser is an *algorithm* which can decide whether a string can be *generated* by a given *grammar* of a *language*. (Typically a recogniser can be abstractly formulated as a *finite state automaton* for a *regular language*, and as a *pushdown automaton* for a *context-free language*.)

568. **Recognition rule:** A recognition rule is a text which describes some *phenomenon*, that is, a possibly singleton *class* of such (i.e., their embodied *concept*, i.e., *type*), such that it is uniquely decidable, by a human, whether a phenomenon satisfies the rule or not, i.e., is a member of the class, or not. (The recognition rule concept used here is due to Michael A. Jackson [308].)

569. **Recursion:** Recursion is a concept associated both with the *function definitions* and with *data type definitions*. A function definition [a data type] is said to possess recursion if it is defined in terms of itself. (Cf. with the slightly different concept of *recursive*.)

570. **Recursive:** Recursive is a concept associated with *functions*. A function is said to be recursive if, in the course of the evaluation of an invocation of the function, that function is repeatedly invoked. (Cf. with the slightly different concept of *recursion*.)

571. **Reengineering:** By reengineering we shall, in a narrow sense, only consider the reengineering of business processes. Thus, to us, reengineering is the same as *business process reengineering*. (Reengineering is also used in the wider sense of a major change to some already existing engineering *artefact*.)

572. **Reference:** A reference is the same as an *address*, a *link*, or a *pointer*: something which refers to, i.e., designates something (typically something else).

573. **Referential transparency:** A concept which is associated with certain kinds of *programming* or *specification language* constructs, namely those

whose *interpretation* does not entail *side effects*. (A *pure functional programming language* is said to be referentially transparent.)

574. **Refinement:** Refinement is a *relation* between two *specifications*: One specification, D, is said to be a refinement of another specification, S, if all the properties that can be observed of S can be observed in D. Usually this is expressed as $D \sqsubseteq S$. (Set-theoretically it works the other way around: in $D \supseteq S$, D allows behaviours not accounted for in S.)

575. **Refutable assertion:** A refutable assertion is an assertion that might be refuted (i.e., convincingly shown to be false). (Einstein's theory of relativity, in a sense, refuted Newton's laws of mechanics. Both theories amount to assertions.)

576. **Refutation:** A refutation is a statement that (convincingly) refutes an assertion. (Lakatos [330] drew a distinction between refutation (evidence that counts against a theory) and rejection (deciding that the original theory has to be replaced by another theory). We can still use Newton's theory provided we stay within certain boundaries, within which that theory is much easier to handle than Einstein's theory.)

577. **Regular expression:** To introduce the notion of regular expression we assume an *alphabet*, A, say finite. Basis clause: For any a in the alphabet, a is a regular expression. Inductive clause: If r and r' are regular expressions, then so are rr', (r), $r \mid r'$, and $r^\star$. (The denotation, $\mathcal{L}(r)$, of a regular expression r is defined as follows: (i) If r is of the form a, for a in the alphabet A, then $\mathcal{L}(a) = \{a\}$; (ii) if r is of the form rr' then $\mathcal{L}(rr') = \{s \mid s : \mathcal{L}(r), s'\mathcal{L}(r') : s = s'^\frown s''\}$; (iii) or if r is of the form (r') then $\mathcal{L}((r')) = \{s \mid s : \mathcal{L}(r')\}$; (iv) or if r is of the form $r \mid r'$ then $\mathcal{L}(r \mid r') = \{s \mid s \in \mathcal{L}(r) \vee s' \in \mathcal{L}(r')\}$; (v) or if r is of the form $r^\star$ then $\mathcal{L}(r^\star) = \{s \mid s = <> \vee s \in \mathcal{L}(r) \vee s' \in \mathcal{L}(rr) \vee s' \in \mathcal{L}(rrr) \vee \ldots\}$ where $<>$ is the empty string, idempotent under concatenation.)

578. **Regular grammar:** See *regular syntax*.

579. **Regular language:** By a regular language we understand a *language* which is the denotation of a *regular expression*. (Some simple forms of *grammars*, that is, *regular syntax*es, also generate regular languages.)

580. **Regular syntax:** A regular syntax is a *syntax* which denotes (i.e., which *generates*) a *regular language*.

581. **Reification:** The result of a *reify* action. (See also *data reification*, *operation reification* and *refinement*.)

582. **Reify:** To regard (something *abstract*) as a material or *concrete* thing. (Our use of the term is more *operational*: To take an *abstract* thing and turn it into a less abstract, more *concrete* thing.)

583. **Relation:** By a relation we usually understand either a mathematical *entity* or an *information structure* consisting of a set of (relation) tuples (like rows in a *table*). The mathematical entity, a relation, can be thought of, also, as a possibly infinite set of n-groupings (i.e., *Cartesians* of the same *arity*), such that if $(a, b, \cdots, c, d, \cdots, e, f)$ is such an n-tuple, then we may say that $(a, b, \cdots, c)$ (a relation argument) relates to $(d, \cdots, e, f)$ (a

relation result). Thus *functions* are special kinds of relations, namely where every argument relates to exactly one result. (Relations, as information structures, are well-known in *relational databases*.)

584. **Relational database:** A *database* whose *data types* are (i) *atomic values*, (ii) *tuples* of these, and *relations* seen as sets of *tuples*. (The relational database model is due to E.F. Codd [156].)

585. **Reliability:** A system being *reliable* — in the context of a machine being dependable — means some measure of continuous correct service, that is: Measure of time to *failure*. (Cf. *dependability* [being dependable].) (Reliability is a *dependability requirement*. Usually reliability is considered a *machine* property. As such, accessibility is (to be) expressed in a *machine requirements* document.)

586. **Renaming:** By renaming we mean *Alpha-renaming*. (Renaming, in this sense, is a concept of the *Lambda-calculus*.)

587. **Rendezvous:** Rendezvous is a concept related to parallel processes. It stands for a way of synchronising a number, usually two, of processes. (In CSP the pairing of output (!) / input (?) clauses designating the same channel provides a language construct for rendezvous.)

588. **Representation abstraction:** By *representation abstraction* of [typed] values we mean a specification which does not hint at a particular data (structure) model, that is, which is not implementation biased. (Usually a representation abstraction (of data) is either *property oriented* or is *model oriented*. In the latter case it is then expressed, typically, in terms of mathematical entities such as sets, Cartesians, lists, maps and functions.)

589. **Requirements:** A condition or capability needed by a user to solve a problem or achieve an objective [299].

590. **Requirements acquisition:** The gathering and enunciation of *requirements*. (Requirements acquisition comprises the activities of preparation, requirements *elicitation* (i.e. *requirements capture*) and preliminary requirements evaluation (i.e., requirements vetting).)

591. **Requirements analysis:** By *requirements analysis* we understand a reading of requirements acquisition (rough) prescription units, (i) with the aim of forming concepts from these requirements prescription units, (ii) as well as with the aim of discovering inconsistencies, conflicts and incompletenesses within these requirements prescription units, and (iii) with the aim of evaluating whether a requirements can be objectively shown to hold, and if so what kinds of tests (etc.) ought be devised.

592. **Requirements capture:** By requirements capture we mean the act of eliciting, of obtaining, of extracting, requirements from *stakeholders*. (For practical purposes requirements capture is synonymous with *requirements elicitation*.)

593. **Requirements definition:** Proper *definitional* part of a *requirements prescription*.

594. **Requirements development:** By requirements development we shall understand the *development* of a *requirements prescription*. (All aspects are

included in development: *requirements acquisition*, requirements *analysis*, requirements *model*ling, requirements *validation* and requirements *verification*.)

595. **Requirements elicitation:** By requirements elicitation we mean the actual extraction of *requirements* from *stakeholders*.

596. **Requirements engineer:** A requirements engineer is a *software engineer* who performs *requirements engineering*. (Other forms of *software engineers* are *domain engineers* and *software design*ers (cum *programmer*).)

597. **Requirements engineering:** The engineering of the development of a *requirements prescription*, from identification of *requirements stakeholders*, via *requirements acquisition*, *requirements analysis*, and *requirements prescription* to requirements *validation* and requirements *verification*.

598. **Requirements facet:** A requirements facet is a view of the requirements — "seen from a *domain description*" — such as *domain projection*, *domain determination*, *domain instantiation*, *domain extension*, *domain fitting* or *domain initialisation*.

599. **Requirements prescription:** By a *requirements prescription* we mean just that: the prescription of some requirements. (Sometimes, by requirements prescription, we mean a relatively complete and consistent specification of all requirements, and sometimes just a *requirements prescription unit*.)

600. **Requirements prescription unit:** By a *requirements prescription* unit we understand a short, "one or two liner", possibly *rough sketch*, *prescription* of some property of a *domain requirements*, an *interface requirements*, or a *machine requirements*. (Usually prescription prescription units are the smallest textual, sentential fragments elicited from requirements *stakeholders*.)

601. **Requirements specification:** Same as *requirements prescription* — the preferred term.

602. **Requirements validation:** By requirements validation we rather mean the *validation* of a *requirements prescription*.

603. **Resource:** From Old French *ressourse relief, resource, from resourdre to relieve, literally, to rise again, from Latin resurgere ... an ability to meet and handle a situation* [373] (being resourceful). (In computing we deal with computing resources such as *storage*, *time* and further computing equipment. Many computing applications handle enterprise resources such as enterprise staff, production equipment, building or land space, production time, etc.)

604. **Resource allocation:** The *allocation* of *resources*.

605. **Resource scheduling:** The *scheduling* of *resources*.

606. **Retrieval:** Used here in two senses: The general (typically *database*-oriented) sense of 'the retrieval [the fetching] of data (of obtaining information) from a repository of such'. And the special sense of 'the retrieval of an abstraction from a concretisation', i.e., abstracting a concept from a

phenomenon (or another, more operational concept). (See the next entry for the latter meaning.)

607. **Retrieve function:** By a *retrieve function* we shall understand a function that applies to *values* of some *type*, the "more concrete, operational" type, and yields *values* of some *type* claimed to be more *abstract*. (Same as *abstraction function*.)

608. **Rewrite:** The replacement of some text or structure by some other text, respectively structure. (See *rewrite rule*.)

609. **Rewrite rule:** A rewrite rule is a directed equation: *lhs* = *rhs*. The left- and right-hand sides are *patterns*. If some *text* can be decomposed into three parts, i.e., $text_0 = text_1 \,\widehat{}\, text_2 \,\widehat{}\, text_3$, where $text_1$ and/or $text_3$ may be empty texts, and where $text_2 = lhs$, then an application of the rewrite rule *lhs* = *rhs* to $text_0$ yields $text_1 \,\widehat{}\, rhs \,\widehat{}\, text_3$. (The equation *lhs* = *rhs* is said to be directed in that this rule does not prescribe that a subtext equal to *rhs* is to be rewritten into *lhs*.)

610. **Rewrite system:** Rewrite systems are sets of *rewrite rule*s used to compute, by repeatedly replacing subterms of a given formula with equal terms, until the simplest form possible is obtained [184]. (Rewrite systems form a both theoretically and practically interesting subject. They abound in instrumenting *theorem proving*, and the *interpretation* of notably *algebraic semantics specification language*s, cf. CafeOBJ [191,193] and Maude [140,154,374].)

611. **Rigorous:** Favoring rigor, i.e., being precise.

612. **Rigorous development:** Same as the composed meaning of the two terms *rigorous* and *development*. (We usually speak of a spectrum of development modes: *systematic development*, rigorous development and *formal development*. Rigorous software development, to us, "falls" somewhere between the two other modes of development: (Always) complete *formal specification*s are constructed, for all (phases and) stages of development; some, but usually not all *proof obligation*s are expressed; and usually only a few are discharged (i.e., proved to hold).)

613. **Robustness:** A *system* is robust — in the context of a *machine* being *dependable* — if it retains all its *dependability* attributes (i.e., properties) after *failure* and after *maintenance*. (Robustness is (thus) a *dependability requirement*.)

614. **Root:** A root is a *node* of a *tree* which is not a sub*tree* of a larger, *embedding* (*embedded*) tree.

615. **Rough sketch:** By a rough sketch — in the context of *descriptive software development documentation* — we shall understand a *document* text which describes something which is not yet consistent and complete, and/or which may still be too concrete, and/or overlapping, and/or repetitive in its descriptions, and/or with which the describer has yet to be fully satisfied.

616. **Route:** Same as *path*.

617. **Routine:** Same as *procedure*.

618. **RSL:** RSL stands for the RAISE [238] Specification Language [236]. (For more on RSL we refer to Part III.)
619. **Rule:** A regulating principle. (We use the concept of rules in several different contexts: *rewrite rule*, *rule of grammar* and *rules and regulations*.)
620. **Rule of grammar:** A grammar is made up of one or more rules. A rule has a (left-hand-side) *definiendum* and a (right-hand-side) *definiens*. The definiendum is usually a single *identifier*. The definiens is usually a possibly empty string of *identifiers*. These identifiers are either *terminals* or *nonterminals*. A definiendum identifier is a nonterminal. In a grammar all nonterminals have a defining rule. Those identifiers which do not appear as a definiendum of a rule are thence considered terminals.
621. **Rules and regulations:** By rules and regulations we mean guidelines that are intended to be adhered to by the enterprise staff and enterprise customers (i.e., users, clients) in conducting their "business", i.e., their actions within, and with, the enterprise. (Other facets of an enterprise are those of its *intrinsics*, *business processes*, *support technology*, *management and organisation* and *human behaviour*.)
622. **Run time:** The time (or time interval) during which a software *program* is subject to *interpretation* by a computer. (The term run time is usually deployed in order to distinguish between that concept and the concept of *compile time*.)

$$S$$

623. **Safety:** By safety — in the context of a *machine* being *dependable* — we mean some measure of continuous delivery of service of either correct service, or incorrect service after benign *failure*, that is, measure of time to catastrophic failure. (Safety is a *dependability requirement*. Usually safety is considered a *machine* property. As such safety is (to be) expressed in a *machine requirements document*.)
624. **Safety critical:** A *system* whose *failure* may cause injury or death to human beings, or serious loss of property, or serious disruption of services or production, is said to be safety critical.
625. **Satisfiable:** A *predicate* is said to be *satisfied* if it is true for at least one *interpretation*. (In this context think of an interpretation as a *binding* of all *free variables* of the predicate expression to *values*. Cf. *valid*.)
626. **Schedule:** A schedule is a *syntactic composite concept*. A schedule is a *prescription* for (usually where and) when some *resources* are to be present, i.e., *information* about being spatially and temporally available. (As such a schedule usually also includes some *allocation information*.)
627. **Scheduling:** The act of providing, of constructing, a *schedule*.
628. **Schema:** A structured framework or plan. (We shall also use the term 'schema' in connection with, i.e., as a *rewrite rule* and some *axioms* that apply to, for example, applicative program texts and rewrite into imperative program texts, cf. Sect. 20.5.3.)

629. **Scheme:** See *schema*.
630. **Scope:** We shall use the term scope in two sufficiently different senses: (1) In *programming* the scope of an *identifier* is the region of a *program* text within which it represents a certain thing. This usually extends from the place where it is declared to the end of the smallest enclosing *block* (begin/end or procedure/function body). An inner block may contain a redeclaration of the same identifier, in which case the scope of the outer declaration does not include (is shadowed, occluded, blocked off or obstructed by) the scope of the inner. (2) We also use the term scope in the context of the degree to which a project *scope* and *span* extends: Scope being the "larger, wider" delineation of what a project "is all about", *span* being the "narrower", more precise extent.
631. **Scope check:** Usually a function performed by a *compiler* concerning the definition (declaration) and places of use of identifiers of *program* texts. (Thus the use of *scope* is that of the first (1) sense of item 630.)
632. **Script:** By a domain script we shall understand the structured, almost, if not outright, formally expressed, wording of a rule or a regulation (cf. *rules and regulations*) that has legally binding power, that is, which may be contested in a court of law.
633. **Secure:** To properly define the concept of secure, we first assume the concept of an authorised user. Now, a *system* is said to be secure if an un-authorised user, when supposedly making use of that system, (i) is not able to find out what the system does, (ii) is not able to find out how it does 'whatever' it does do, and (iii), after some such "use", does not know whether he/she knows! (The above characterisation represents an unattainable proposition. As a characterisation it is acceptable. But it does not hint at ways and means of implementing secure systems. Once such a system is believed implemented the characterisation can, however be used as a guide in devising tests that may reveal to which extent the system indeed is secure. Secure systems usually deploy some forms of authorisation and encryption mechanisms in guarding access to system functions.)
634. **Security:** When we say that a *system* exhibits security we mean that it is *secure*. (Security is a *dependability requirement*. Usually security is considered a *machine* property. As such security is (to be) expressed in a *machine requirements* document.)
635. **Selector:** By a selector (a selector function) we understand a function which is applicable to *values* of a certain, defined, composed *type*, and which yields a proper component of that value. The function itself is defined by the *type definition*.
636. **Semantics:** Semantics is the study and knowledge [incl. specification] of meaning in language [165]. (We make the distinction between the *pragmatics*, the semantics and the *syntax* of languages. Leading textbooks on semantics of programming languages are [183, 252, 443, 454, 497, 521].)

637. **Semantic function:** A semantics function is a function which when applied to *syntactic values* yields their *semantic values*.

638. **Semantic type:** By a semantic type we mean a *type* that defines *semantic values*.

639. **Semiotics:** Semiotics, as used by us, is the study and knowledge of *pragmatics*, *semantics* and *syntax* of language(s).

640. **Sensor:** A sensor can be thought of as a piece of *technology* (an electronic, a mechanical or an electromechanical device) that senses, i.e., measures, a physical *value*. (A sensor is in contrast to an *actuator*.)

641. **Sentence:** (i) A word, clause, or phrase or a group of clauses or phrases forming a syntactic unit which expresses an assertion, a question, a command, a wish, an exclamation, or the performance of an action, that in writing usually begins with a capital letter and concludes with appropriate end punctuation, and that in speaking is distinguished by characteristic patterns of stress, pitch and pauses; (ii) a mathematical or logical statement (as an equation or a proposition) in words or symbols [373].

642. **Sequential:** Arranged in a sequence, following a linear order, one after another.

643. **Sequential process:** A process is sequential if all its observable actions can be, or are, ordered in sequence.

644. **Server:** By a server we mean a *process* or a *behaviour* which *interacts* with another process or behaviour (i.e., a *client*) in order for the server to perform some *action*s on behalf of the client.

645. **Set:** We understand a set as a mathematical entity, something that is not mathematically defined, but is a concept that is taken for granted. (Thus by a set we understand the same as a collection, an aggregation, of distinct entities. Membership (of an entity) of a set is also a mathematical concept which is likewise taken for granted, i.e., undefined.)

646. **Set theoretic:** We say that something is set theoretically understood or explained if its understanding or explanation is based on *sets*.

647. **Shared data:** See *shared phenomenon*.

648. **Shared data initialisation:** By shared data initialisation we understand an *operation* that (initially) creates a *data structure* that reflects, i.e., models, some *shared phenomenon* in the *machine*. (See also *shared data refreshment*.)

649. **Shared data initialisation requirements:** *Requirements* for *shared data initialisation*. (See also *computational data+control requirements*, *shared data refreshment requirements*, *man-machine dialogue requirements*, *man-machine physiological requirements*, and *machine-machine dialogue requirements*.)

650. **Shared data refreshment:** By shared data refreshment we understand a *machine operation* which, at prescribed intervals, or in response to prescribed events updates an (originally initialised) *shared data* structure. (See also *shared data initialisation*.)

651. **Shared data refreshment requirements:** *Requirements* for *shared data refreshment*. (See also *computational data+control requirements*, *shared data initialisation requirements*, *man-machine dialogue requirements*, *man-machine physiological requirements*, and *machine-machine dialogue requirements*.)

652. **Shared information:** See *shared phenomenon*.

653. **Shared phenomenon:** A shared phenomenon is a phenomenon which is present in some *domain* (say in the form of facts, *knowledge* or *information*) and which is also represented in the *machine* (say in the form of *data*). (See also *shared data* and *shared information*.)

654. **Side effect:** A language construct that designates the modification of the state of a system is said to be a side-effect-producing construct. (Typical side effect constructs are assignment, input and output. A *programming language* "without side effects" is said to be a *pure functional programming language*.)

655. **Sign:** Same as *symbol*.

656. **Signature:** See *function signature*.

657. **Simulation:** The imitation of the functioning of one system or process by means of the functioning of another. (Attempting to predict aspects of the behaviour of some system by creating an approximate (mathematical) model of it. This can be done by physical modelling, by writing a special-purpose computer program or using a more general simulation package, probably still aimed at a particular kind of simulation [227].)

658. **Soft real time:** By soft real time we mean a *real time* property where the exact, i.e., absolute timing, or time interval, is only of loose, approximate essence. (Cf., *hard real time*.)

659. **Software:** By software we understand not only the code that when "submitted" to a computer enables desired computations to take place, but also all the documentation that went into its development (i.e., its *domain description*, *requirements specification*, its complete *software design* (all stages and steps of *refinement* and *transformation*), the *installation manual*, *training manual*, and the *user manual*).

660. **Software component:** Same as *component*.

661. **Software architecture:** By a software architecture we mean a first kind of specification of software — after requirements — one which indicates **how** the software is to handle the given requirements in terms of *software components* and their interconnection — though without detailing (i.e., designing) these software components.

662. **Software design:** By software design we shall understand the determination of which *components*, which *modules* and which *algorithms* shall implement the *requirements* — together with all the *documents* that usually make up properly documented *software*. (Software design entails *programming*, but programming is a "narrower" field of activity than software design in that programming usually excludes many documentation aspects.)

663. **Software design specification:** The *specification* of a *software design*.

664. **Software development:** To us, software development includes all three phases of *software development*: *domain development*, *requirements development* and *software design*.

665. **Software development project:** A *software* development project is a planning, research and development project whose aim is to construct *software*.

666. **Software engineer:** A software engineer is an *engineer* who performs one or more of the functions of *software engineering*. (These functions include *domain engineering*, *requirements engineering* and *software design* (incl. *programming*).)

667. **Software engineering:** The confluence of the science, logic, discipline, craft and art of *domain engineering*, *requirements engineering* and *software design*.

668. **Sort:** A sort is a collection, a structure, of, at present, further unspecified entities. (That is, same as an *algebraic type*. When we say "at present, further unspecified", we mean that the (values of the) sort may be subject to constraining axioms. When we say "a structure", we mean that "this set" is not necessarily a *set* in the simple sense of mathematics, but may be a collection whose members satisfy certain interrelations, for example, some *partially ordered set*, some *neighbourhood set* or other.)

669. **Sort definition:** The *definition* of a *sort*. (Usually a sort definition consists of the (introduction of) a type name, some (typically *observer function* and *generator function*) *signatures*, and some *axioms* relating sort *values* and *functions*.)

670. **Source program:** By a source program we mean a *program* (text) in some *programming language*. (The term source is used in contrast to target: the result of compiling a source text for some target *machine*.)

671. **Span:** Span is here used, in contrast to *scope*, more specifically in the context of the degree to which a project *scope* and *span* extend: Scope being the "larger, wider" delineation of what a project "is all about", *span* being the "narrower", more precise extent.

672. **Specification:** We use the term 'specification" to cover the concepts of *domain descriptions*, *requirements prescriptions* and *software designs*. More specifically a specification is a *definition*, usually consisting of many definitions.

673. **Specification language:** By a specification language we understand a *formal language* capable of expressing *formal specifications*. (We refer to such formal specification languages as: ASM [439], B & eventB [3,4,143], CASL [49,395,399], CafeOBJ [191,193], RSL [236,237], VDM-SL [120,226] and Z [281,476,477,533].)

674. **Stack:** A stack is an *abstract data type* with a stack data structure and, typically, the following operations: push (onto the top of the stack), pop (remove from the top of the stack). Axioms then determine specific stack properties. (See Example 8.5.)

675. **Stack activation:** Generally: The topmost element of a stack. Specifically, when a stack is used to record the local states of blocks of a block-structured programming language's blocks or procedure bodies (they are also blocks), then each stack element, i.e., each stack activation, records such a local state and — what is known as static and dynamic — pointers chain such activations together which correspond to the lexicographic scope of the program, respectively the calling invocation of the blocks. (We refer to Vol. 2, Chap. 16, Sect. 16.6.1 for a thorough treatment of stack activations.)

676. **Stage:** (i) By a development stage we shall understand a set of development activities which either starts from nothing and results in a complete phase documentation, or which starts from a complete phase documentation of kind stage, and results in a complete phase documentation of another stage kind. (ii) By a development stage we shall understand a set of development activities such that some (one or more) activities have created new, externally conceivable (i.e., observable) properties of what is being described, whereas some (zero, one or more) other activities have refined previous properties. (Typical development stages are: *domain intrinsics*, *domain support technologies*, *domain management and organisation*, *domain rules and regulations*, etc., and *domain requirements*, *interface requirements*, and *machine requirements*, etc.)

677. **Stakeholder:** By a *domain (requirements, software design)*[5] stakeholder we shall understand a person, or a group of persons, "united" somehow in their common interest in, or dependency on the domain (requirements, software design); or an institution, an enterprise, or a group of such, (again) characterised (and, again, loosely) by their common interest in, or dependency on the domain (requirements, software design). (The three stakeholder groups usually overlap.)

678. **Stakeholder perspective:** By a *stakeholder* perspective we shall understand the, or an, understanding of the *universe of discourse* shared by the specifically identified stakeholder group — a view that may differ from one stakeholder group to another stakeholder group of the same universe of discourse.

679. **State:** By a state we shall, in the context of computer *programs*, understand a summary of past *computations*, and, in the context of *domains*, a suitably selected set of *dynamic entities*.

680. **Statechart:** The Statechart language is a special graphic notation for expressing communication between and coordination and timing of processes. (See [265, 266, 268, 269, 271].)

681. **Statement:** We shall take the rather narrow view that a statement is a *programming language* construct which *denotes* a *state*-to-state function. (Pure expressions are then programming language constructs which de-

---

[5]These three areas of concern form three *universes of discourse*.

note state-to-value functions (i.e., with no *side effect*), whereas "impure" expressions, also called clauses, denote state-to-state-and-value functions.)

682. **Static:** An *entity* is static if it is not subject to *actions* that change its *value*. (In contrast to *dynamic*.)

683. **Static semantics:** The concept of static semantics is one that applies to *syntactic entities*, typically *programs* or *specifications* of *programming languages*, respectively *specification languages*. The static semantics of such a language is now a *predicate* that applies to *programs* (respectively *specifications*) and yields true if the *program* (*specification*) is syntactically well formed according to the static semantics criteria, typically that certain relations are satisfied between dispersed parts of the *program* (*specification*) texts.

684. **Static typing:** Enforcement of *type checking* at *compile time*. (A *programming language* (or a *specification language*) is said to be statically typed if its *programs* (resp. *specifications*) can be statically *type checked*.)

685. **Step:** By a development step we shall understand a refinement of a domain description (or a requirements prescription, or a software design specification) module, from a more abstract to a more concrete description.

686. **Stepwise development:** By a stepwise development we shall understand a *development* that undergoes *phases*, *stages* or *steps* of development, i.e., can be characterised by pairs of two adjoining *phase steps*, a last *phase step* and a (first) next *phase step*, or two adjoining *stage steps*.

687. **Stepwise refinement:** By a stepwise refinement we understand a pair of adjoining *development steps* where the transition from one *step* to the next *step* is characterised by a *refinement*. (Refinement is thus always stepwise refinement.)

688. **Store:** Same as *store*; see next.

689. **Storage:** By storage we shall understand a *function* from *locations* to *values*. (Thus we emphasise the mathematical character of storage rather than any technological character (such as disk storage, etc.).)

690. **Strict function:** A strict function is a function which yields **chaos** (i.e., is undefined) if any of the function arguments are undefined (i.e., **chaos**). (In RSL the logical connectives are not strict. All other functions, built-in or defined, are strict.)

691. **Strongest post-condition:** See *weakest pre-condition*.

692. **Structure:** The term 'structure' is understood rather loosely. Normally we shall understand a structure as a mathematical structure, such as an *algebra*, or a *predicate logic*, or a *Lambda-calculus*, or some defined abstraction (a *scheme* or a *class*). (Set theory is a (mathematical) structure. So are RSL's Cartesian, list and map data types.)

693. **Structural operational semantics:** By a structural operational semantics we understand an *operational semantics* which is expressed in terms of a number of *transition rules*. (See [428].)

694. **Subentity:** A subentity is a proper part of a (thus) non-*atomic entity*. (Do not confuse a subentity of an entity with an *attribute* of that entity (or of that subentity).)

695. **Substitution:** By substitution we mean the replacement of a token (viz.: an identifier) by a structure, usually a text. (The most common form of substitution is that of *Beta-reduction* (in the *Lambda-Calculus*). Substitution is a "simpler" form of *rewriting*.)

696. **Subroutine:** Same as *routine*.

697. **Subtype:** To speak of a subtype we must first be able to speak of a *type*, i.e., colloquially, a (suitably structured) set of *values*. A subtype of a type is then a (suitably structured) and proper subset of the values of the type. (Usually we shall, in RSL, think of a predicate, p, that applies to all members of the type, T, and singles out a proper subset whose elements satisfy the predicate: $\{a \mid a : T \cdot p(a)\}$.)

698. **Support technology:** By a support technology we understand a *facet* of a *domain*, one which reflects its (current) dependency on mechanical, electro-mechanical, electronic and other technologies (i.e., tools) in order to carry out its *business processes*. (Other facets of an enterprise are those of its *intrinsics, business processes, management and organisation, rules and regulations* and *human behaviour*.)

699. **Surjection:** A *surjective function* represents surjection. (See also *bijection* and *injection*.)

700. **Surjective function:** A *function* which maps *values* of its postulated *definition set* into all of its postulated *range set* is called surjective. (See also *bijective function* and *injective function*.)

701. **Symbol:** Something that stands for or suggests something else, that is, an arbitrary or conventional sign used in writing.

702. **Synchronisation:** By synchronisation we understand the act of ensuring *synchronism* between occurrence of designated *events* in two or more *processes*. (Usually synchronisation between occurrence of designated events in two or more processes entails the exchange of *information*, i.e., *data*, between these processes, i.e., *communication*.)

703. **Synchronism:** A chronological arrangement of *events*.

704. **Synchronous:** Happening, existing, or arising at precisely the same *time* indicating *synchronism*.

705. **Synopsis:** By a synopsis we shall understand a composition of *informative documentation* and *rough-sketch description* of some project.

706. **Syntax:** By syntax we mean (i) the ways in which words are arranged to show meaning (cf. *semantics*) within and between sentences, and (ii) rules for forming textuseisyntactically correct sentences. (See also *regular syntax, context-free syntax, context-sensitive syntax* and *BNF* for specifics.)

707. **Synthesis:** The construction of an *artefact*.

708. **Synthetic:** Result of *synthesis*: not *analytic*.

709. **System:** A regularly interacting or interdependent group of phenomena or concepts forming a whole, that is, a group of devices or artificial objects

or an organization forming a network especially for producing something or serving a common purpose. (This book will have its own characterisation of the concept of a system (commensurate, however, with the above encircling characterisation); cf. Vol. 2, Sect. 9.5's treatment of system.)

710. **Systematic development:** Systematic development of software is *formal development "lite"*! (We usually speak of a spectrum of development modes: systematic development, *rigorous development*, and *formal development*. Systems software development, to us, is at the "informal" extreme of the three modes of development: *formal specifications* are constructed, but maybe not for all stages of development; and usually no proof obligations are expressed, let alone proved. The three volumes of this series of textbooks in software engineering can thus be said to expound primarily the systematic approach.)

711. **Systems engineering:** By systems engineering we shall here understand computing systems engineering: The confluence of developing *hardware* and *software* solutions to *requirements*.

T

712. **Table:** By a table we understand an *information structure* which can be thought of as an ordered *list* of rows, each row consisting of an ordered *list* of entries, each consisting of some *information*. (When thought of as a *data structure*, a table is normally thought of as either a matrix or a *relation*.)

713. **Tangibility:** Noun of *tangible*.

714. **Tangible:** Physically manifest. That is, can be humanly sensed: heard, seen, smelled, tasted, or touched, or physically measured by a physical apparatus: length (meter, m), mass (kilogram, kg), time (second, s), electric current (Ampere, A), thermodynamic temperature (Kelvin, K), amount of substance (mole, mol), luminous intensity (candela, cd).

715. **Target program:** The concept of target program stems from the fact that *programs* of ordinary *programming languages* need to be translated into some intermediary language or final machine, i.e., computer hardware, language, before their designated computations (i.e., interpretations) can take place. By a target program we understand such an intermediary or final program. (Besides the final target languages made up from the repertoire of computer hardware instructions and computer (bit, byte, half-word, word, double-word and variable field) data formats, special intermediary languages have been devised: P-code [198] (into which Pascal programs can be translated) [11,138,292,314,522–524], A-code [197] (into which Ada programs can be translated) [128,516], etc.)

716. **Taxonomy:** See Sect. B.1.5.

717. **Technique:** A procedure, an approach, to accomplish something.

718. **Technology:** We shall in these volumes be using the term technology to stand for the results of applying scientific and engineering insight. This,

we think, is more in line with current usage of the term IT, information technology.

719. **Temporal:** Of or relating to time, including sequence of time, or to time intervals (i.e., durations).

720. **Temporal logic:** A(ny) *logic* over *temporal phenomena*. (We refer to Vol. 2, Chap. 15 for our survey treatment of some temporal logics.)

721. **Term:** From [350]: A word or phrase used in a definite or precise sense in some particular subject, as a science or art; a technical expression. More widely: any word or group of words expressing a notion or conception, or denoting an object of thought. (Thus, in RSL, a term is a *clause*, an *expression*, a *statement*, which has a *value* (statements have the **Unit** value).)

722. **Terminal:** By a terminal we shall mean a terminal *symbol* which (in contrast to a *nonterminal* symbol) designates something specific.

723. **Termination:** The concept of termination is associated with that of an *algorithm*. We say that an algorithm, when subject to *interpretation* (colloquially: 'execution'), may, or may not terminate. That is, may halt, or may "go on forever, forever looping". (Whether an algorithm terminates is *undecidable*.)

724. **Terminology:** By terminology is meant ([350]): The doctrine or scientific study of terms; the system of terms belonging to a science or subject; technical terms collectively; nomenclature.

725. **Term rewriting:** Same as *rewriting*.

726. **Test:** A test is a means to conduct *testing*. (Typically such a test is a set of data values provided to a program (or a specification) as values for its *free variables*. *Testing* then evaluates the program (resp., interprets (symbolically) the specification) to obtain a result (value) which is then compared with what is (believed to be) the, or a, correct result. See Vol. 3, Sects. 14.3.2, 22.3.2 and 29.5.3 for treatments of the concept of test.)

727. **Testing:** Testing is a systematic effort to refute a claim of correctness of one (e.g., a concrete) specification (for example a program) with respect to another (the abstract) specification. (See Vol. 3, Sects. 14.3.2, 22.3.2, and 29.5.3 for treatments of the concept of testing.)

728. **Theorem:** A theorem is a *sentence* that is *provable* without assumptions, that is "purely" from *axioms* and *inference rules*.

729. **Theorem prover:** A mechanical, i.e., a computerised means for *theorem proving*. (Well-known theorem provers are: PVS [410, 411] and HOL/Isabelle [406].)

730. **Theorem proving:** The act of *proving theorems*.

731. **Theory:** A formal theory is a *formal language*, a set of *axioms* and *inference rules* for *sentences* in this language, and is a set of *theorems* proved about sentences of this language using the axioms and inference rules. A mathematical theory leaves out the strict formality (i.e., the *proof* system) requirements and relies on mathematical proofs that have stood the social test of having been scrutinised by mathematicians.

732. **Thesaurus:** See Sect. B.1.7.

733. **Three-valued logic:** Standard logics are two value: **true** and **false**. A three-valued logic is a logic for which the Boolean connectives accept a third value, usually referred to as the *undefined*, or *chaotic* (*nontermination* of operand *expression evaluation*). (There can be, and are, many three-valued logics. RSL has one set of definitions of the outcome of Boolean ground term evaluation with **chaos** operands. LPF is a logic for partial functions sugggested as a logic for VDM [32, 150]. John McCarthy [367] first broached the topic of three-valued logics in computing.)

734. **Time:** Time is often a notion that is taken for granted. But one may do well, or better, in trying to understand time as some point set that satisfies certain axioms. Time and space are also often related (via [other] physically manifest "things"). Again their interrelationship needs to be made precise. (In comparative concurrency semantics one usually distinguishes between linear time and branching time semantic equivalences [504]. We refer to our treatment of time and space in Vol. 2 Chap. 5, to Johan van Benthem's book *The Logic of Time* [503], and to Wayne D. Blizard's paper *A Formal Theory of Objects, Space and Time* [134].)

735. **Token:** Something given or shown as an identity. (When, in RSL, we define a *sort* with no "constraining" axioms, we basically mean to define a set of tokens; cf. Sect. 10.5.)

736. **Tool:** An instrument or apparatus used in performing an operation. (The tools most relevant to us, in software engineering, are the *specification* and *programming languages* as well as the *software* packages that aid us in the development of (other) software.)

737. **Topology:** (i) A branch of mathematics concerned with those properties of geometric configurations (as point sets) which are unaltered by elastic deformations (as a stretching or a twisting) that are *homeomorphisms*; (ii) the set of all open subsets of a *topological space* (i.e., being or involving properties unaltered under a homeomorphism [continuity and connectedness are topological properties]) [373].

738. **Total algebra:** A total *algebra* is an algebra all of whose functions are total over the carrier.

739. **Trace:** The concept of trace is linked to the concept of a *behaviour*. Trace is then defined as a sequence of *actions* and *events*. ()

740. **Training manual:** A *document* which can serve as a basis for a (possibly self-study) course in how to use a *computing system*. (See also *installation manual* and *user manual*.)

741. **Transaction:** General: A communicative action or activity involving two *agents* that reciprocally influence each other. (Special: The term transaction has come to be used, in computing, notably in connection with the use of database management systems (DBMS, or similar multiuser systems): A transaction is then a unit of interaction with a DBMS (etc.). To further qualify as being a transaction, it must be handled, by the DBMS (etc.), in a coherent and reliable way independent of other transactions.)

742. **Transduce:** To convert (a physical signal, or a message) into another form.

743. **Transducer:** A device that is actuated by power from one system and supplies power usually in another form to a second system. (*Finite state machines* and *pushdown stack machines* are considered transducers.)

744. **Transformation:** The operation of changing one configuration or expression into another in accordance with a precise rule. (We consider the results of *substitution*, of *translation* and of *rewriting* to be transformations of what the *substitution*, the *translation* and the *rewriting* was applied to.)

745. **Transition:** Passage from one state, stage, subject or place to another; a movement, development, or evolution from one form, stage or style to another [373].

746. **Transition rule:** A *rule*, of such a form that it can specify how any of a well-defined class of *states* of a *machine* may make *transitions* to another state, possibly *nondeterministically* to any one of a well-defined number of other states. (The seminal 1981 report *A Structural Approach to Operational Semantics*, by Gordon D. Plotkin [427], set a de facto standard for formulating transition rules (exploring their theoretical properties and uses).)

747. **Translate:** See *translation*.

748. **Translation:** An act, process or instance of translating, i.e., of rendering from one language into another.

749. **Translator:** Same as a *compiler*.

750. **Tree:** An *acyclic* un-*directed graph*. Thus a tree (i) has a *root*, which is a *node*, and (ii) zero, one or more, possibly (*branch* or *edge*) *label*led subtrees. Trees or subtrees with no further subtrees have their roots being equated with leaves. Nodes may be labelled. (This characterisation allows for trees with no labels, with only labelled nodes, with only labelled branches, with labelled nodes and branches, or with only some nodes and some branches being labelled. The characterisation usually is interpreted as only allowing finite trees, but one could dispense of the "finite applicability" of the above (i–ii) clauses, to allow infinite trees. The branch concept, akin to the *edge* concept, amounts, however, to a directed edge, i.e., an *arrow*. We refer specifically to *parse trees*. See also a "redefinition" of trees as found just below, under *tree traversal*, including Fig. B.4.)

751. **Tree traversal:** A way of visiting (all) the *nodes* of a *tree*. Redefine the notion of a *tree* as just given above: Now a tree is a root node and an ordered set (i.e., like a list) of zero, one or more subtrees; each subtree is a tree. Roots are labelled. Hence subtrees are labelled. A tree with an empty set of subtrees is called a leaf. Their roots are the leaves. A tree traversal is now a way of visiting, in some order, as indicated by the order of subtrees, (all) the nodes: the root, the branch nodes and leaves, of a tree. (See the tree of Fig. B.4 on the next page. It will be referred to in entries *in-order*, *post-order* and *pre-order*.)

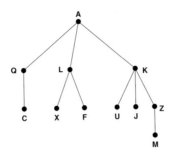

Fig. B.4. A labelled, ordered tree

752. **Triptych:** An ancient Roman writing tablet with three waxed leaves hinged together; a picture (as an altarpiece) or carving in three panels side by side [373]. (The trilogy of the *phases* of *software development*, *domain engineering*, *requirements engineering* and *software design* as promulgated by this trilogy of volumes!)

753. **Tuple:** A grouping of values. (Like 2-tuplets, quintuplets, etc. Used extensively, at least in the early days, in the field of relational databases — where a tuple was like a row in a relation (i.e., table).)

754. **Turing machine:** A hypothetical machine defined in 1935–1936 by Alan Turing and used for computability theory proofs. It can be understood as consisting of a *finite state machine* and an infinitely long "tape" with symbols (chosen from some finite set) written at regular intervals. A pointer marks the current position and the machine is in one of states. At each step the machine reads the symbol at the current position on the tape. For each combination of current state and symbol read, the finite state machine specifies the new state and either a symbol to write to the tape or a direction to move the pointer (left or right) or to halt [227]. (Turing machines are equivalent, in computational power, to the *Lambda-calculus*.)

755. **Type:** Generally a certain kind of set of *values*. (See *algebraic type*, *model-oriented type*, *programming language type* and *sort*.)

756. **Type check:** The concept of type check arises from the concepts of *function signatures* and function *arguments*. If arguments are not of the appropriate type then a type check yields an *error* result. (By appropriate *static typing* of *declarations* of *variables* of a *programming language* or a *specification language* one can perform static type checking (i.e., at *compile time*).)

757. **Type constructor:** A type constructor is an operation that applies to *types* and yields a *type*. (The type constructors of RSL include the power set constructors: **-set** and **-infset**, the Cartesian constructor: ×, the list constructors: * and $^\omega$, the map constructor: $\overrightarrow{m}$, the total and partial function space constructors: → and $\xrightarrow{\sim}$, the union type constructor: |, and others.)

758. **Type definition:** A type definition semantically associates a *type name* with a *type*. Syntactically, as, for example, in RSL, a type definition is either a *sort* definition or is a *definition* whose right-hand side is a *type expression*.

759. **Type expression:** A type expression semantically denotes a *type*. Syntactically, as, for example, in RSL, a type expression is an expression involving *type names* and *type constructors*, and, rarely, *terminals*.

760. **Type name:** A type name is usually just a simple *identifier*.

761. **Typing:** By typing we mean the association of *types* with *variables*. (Usually such an association is afforded by pairing a *variable identifier* with a *type name* in the variable *declaration*. See also *dynamic typing* and *static typing*.)

$$\mathcal{U}$$

762. **UML:** Universal Modelling Language. A hodgepodge of notations for expressing requirements and designs of computing systems. (Vol. 2, Chaps. 10, and 12–14 outlines our attempt to "UML"-ize formal techniques.)

763. **Universal algebra:** A universal *algebra* is an *abstract algebra* where we leave the postulates (axioms, laws) unspecified. (The universal level of abstract, the viewpoint of universal algebras, represents for us [349], the high water mark of abstraction in the treatment of *algebraic systems*.)

764. **Underspecify:** By an underspecified expression, typically an identifier, we mean one which for repeated occurrences in a specification text always yields the same value, but what the specific value is, is not knowable. (Cf. *nondeterministic* or *loose specification*.)

765. **Undecidable:** A formal logic system is undecidable if there is no *algorithm* which prescribes *computations* that can determine whether any given sentence in the system is a theorem.

766. **Universe of discourse:** That which is being talked about; that which is being discussed; that which is the subject of our concern. (The four most prevalent universes of discourse of this book, this series of volumes on software engineering, are: *software development methodology*, *domains*, *requirements* and *software design*.)

767. **Update:** By an update we shall understand a change of value of a variable, including also the parts, or all, of a *database*.

768. **Update problem:** By the update problem we shall understand that data stored in a *database* usually reflect some state of a domain, but that changes in the external state of that domain are not always properly, including timely, reflected in the database.

769. **User:** By a user we shall understand a person who uses a *computing system*, or a *machine* (i.e., another computing system) which *interfaces* with the former. (Not to be confused with *client* or *stakeholder*.)

770. **User-friendly:** A "lofty" term that is often used in the following context: "*A computing system, a machine, a software package, is required to be*

user-friendly" — without the requestor further prescribing the meaning of that term. Our definition of the term user-friendly is as follows: A *machine* (software + hardware) is said to be user-friendly (i–ii) if the *shared phenomena* of the application *domain* (and *machine*) are each implemented in a transparent, one-to-one manner, and such that no IT jargon, but common application *domain terminology* is used in their (i.1) accessing, (i.2) *invocation* (by a human *user*), and (i.3) display (by the machine); i.e., (ii) if the *interface requirements* have all been carefully expressed (commensurate, in further detailed ways: ..., with the user psyche) and correctly implemented; and (iii) if the machine otherwise satisfies a number of *performance* and *dependability requirements* that are commensurate, in further detailed ways: ..., with the user psyche.

771. **User manual:** A *document* which a regular user of a *computing system* refers to when in doubt concerning the use of some features of that system. (See also *installation manual* and *training manual*.)

V

---

772. **Valid:** A *predicate* is said to be *valid* if it is true for all *interpretations*. (In this context think of an interpretation as a *binding* of all *free variables* of the predicate expression to *values*; cf. *satisfiable*.)

773. **Validation:** (Let, in the following *universe of discourse* stand consistently for either *domain, requirements* or *software design*.) By universe of discourse validation we understand the assurance, with universe of discourse *stakeholders*, that the specifications produced as a result of universe of discourse acquisition, universe of discourse analysis and *concept formation*, and universe of discourse domain *modelling* are commensurate with how the stakeholder views the universe of discourse. (*Domain* and *requirements validation* is treated in Vol. 3, Chaps. 14 and 22.)

774. **Valuation:** Same as *evaluation*.

775. **Value:** From (assumed) Vulgar Latin *valuta*, from feminine of *valutus*, past participle of Latin *valere* to be worth, be strong [373]. (Commensurate with that definition, value, to us, in the context of programming (i.e., of software engineering), is whatever mathematically founded *abstraction* can be captured by our *type* and *axiom systems*. (Hence numbers, truth values, *tokens*, sets, Cartesians, lists, maps, functions, etc., of, or over, these.))

776. **Variable:** (i) From Latin *variabilis*, from *variare* to vary; (ii) able or apt to vary; (iii) subject to variation or changes [373]. (Commensurate with that definition, a variable, to us, in the context of programming (i.e., of software engineering), is a *placeholder*, for example, a *storage location* whose *contents* may change. A variable, further, to us, has a name, the variable's identifier, by which it can be referred.)

777. **VDM:** VDM stands for the Vienna Development Method [120, 121]. (VDM-SL (SL for Specification Language) was the first formal specification language

to have an international standard: VDM-SL, ISO/IEC 13817-1: 1996. The author of this book coined the name VDM in 1974 while working with Hans Bekič, Cliff B. Jones, Wolfgang Henhapl and Peter Lucas, on what became the VDM description of PL/I. The IBM Vienna Laboratory, in Austria, had, in the 1960s, researched and developed semantics descriptions [38–40, 354] of PL/I, a programming language of that time. "JAN" (John A.N.) Lee [342] is believed to have coined the name VDL [343, 353] for the notation (the Vienna Definition Language) used in those semantics definitions. So the letter M follows, lexicographically, the letter L, hence VDM.)

778. **VDM–SL:** VDM-SL stands for the VDM Specification Language. (See entry VDM above. Between 1974 and the late 1980s VDM-SL was referred to by the acronym Meta-IV: the fourth metalanguage (for language definition) conceived at the IBM Vienna Laboratory during the 1960s and 1970s.)

779. **Verb:** A *word* that characteristically is the grammatical centre of a sentence and expresses an act, occurrence or mode of being that in various languages is inflected for agreement with the subject, for tense, for voice, for mood, or for aspect, and that typically has rather full descriptive meaning and characterizing quality but is sometimes nearly devoid of these especially when used as an auxiliary or linking verb [373]. (We shall often find, in modelling, that we model verbs as *functions* (incl. *predicates*).)

780. **Verification:** By verification we mean the process of determining whether or not a specification (a description, a prescription) fulfills a stated property. (That stated property could (i) either be a property of the specification itself, or (ii) that the specification relates, somehow, i.e., is correct with respect to some other specification.)

781. **Verify:** Same, for all practical purposes, as *verification*.

782. **Vertex:** Same as an *edge*.

W

---

783. **Waterfall diagram:** By a waterfall diagram is understood a two-dimensional diagram with a number of boxes placed, say, on a diagonal, from a top left corner of the diagram to a lower right corner, such that the individual boxes are sufficiently spaced apart, i.e., do not overlap, and such that arrows (i.e., "the water") infix adjacent boxes along a perceived diagonal line. (The idea is then that a preceding box, from which an arrow emanates, designates a software development activity that must, somehow, be concluded before activity can start on the software development activity designated by the box upon which the infix arrow is incident.)

784. **Weakest pre-condition:** The condition that characterizes the set of all initial states, such that activation will certainly result in a properly terminating happening leaving the system in a final state satisfying a given post-condition, is called "the weakest pre-condition corresponding to that post-condition". (We call it "weakest", because the weaker a condition,

the more states satisfy it and we aim here at characterising all possible starting states that are certain to lead to a desired final state.)

785. **Well-formedness:** By well-formedness we mean a concept related to the way in which *information* or *data structure* definitions may be given. Usually these are given in terms of *type definitions*. And sometimes it is not possible, due to the *context-free* nature of type definitions. (Well-formedness is here seen separate from the *invariant* over an *information* or a *data structure*. We refer to the explication of *invariant*!)

786. **Wildcard:** A special symbol that stands for one or more characters. (Many operating systems and applications support wildcards for identifying files and directories. This enables you to select multiple files with a single specification. Typical wildcard designators are * (asterisk) and _ (underscore).)

787. **Word:** A speech sound or series of speech sounds or a character or series of juxtaposed characters that symbolizes and communicates a meaning without being divisible into smaller units capable of independent use [373].

Z

---

788. **Z:** Z stands for Zermelo (Frankel), a set theoretician. (Z also stands for a model-oriented specification language [281, 476, 478, 533].)

C

Indexes

- The **prerequisite** for studying this chapter is that you need to look up where a term has been defined or is used.
- The **aim** is to illustrate the breadth and depth, the variety and multitude of terms used in these volumes.
- The **objective** is to satisfy your needs.
- The **treatment** is systematic.

Appendix B contains an extensive glossary.

C.1 Symbols Index

Symbol, Greek: Mark, token, ticket, watchword, outward sign, covenant.

Symbol, Meaning: Something that stands for, represents, or denotes something else; a material object representing, or taken to represent, something immaterial or abstract (1590); a written character or mark used to represent something; a letter, figure, or sign conventionally standing for some object, process, etc. (1620)

The SHORTER OXFORD ENGLISH DICTIONARY
On Historical Principles [350]

An attempt has been made to structure the symbols index. You may have to look in more than one place to find a cross-reference to the first appearances of the symbol, literal or abbreviation that you are looking for.

C.1.1 Operators

Literal Operators

abs absolute number (positive), 207

card set cardinality, 55, 56, 192, 264, 269

dom map definition set (domain), 349, 352, 353

elems list elements, 68, 70, 193, 322, 324, 325

hd list head, 68, 193, 322, 324, 325

inds list indices, 68, 70, 193, 322, 324, 325

int make integer from real, 50, 207

len list length, 68, 69, 193, 322, 324, 325

real make real from integer, 50, 207

rng map range, 349, 352, 353

tl list tail, 68, 193, 322, 324, 325

Y fix point operator, 119–121

α alpha renaming, 113, 115

αP process alphabet, 536

β beta reduction, 113, 115

B^A function space, 93

Relational Operators

$<$ less than, numbers, 207

≤ less than or equal, numbers, 207
= equality, 485
    Boolean connective, 143
    Cartesians, 300
    enumerated tokens, 208, 209
    general tokens, 214
    lists, 322, 324, 325
    maps, 352, 349, 353
    numbers, 207
    sets, 55, 56, 192, 264, 268, 269
≡ equivalence, 484
    enumerated tokens, 208, 209
    general tokens, 214
    numbers, 207
={} is_ empty_ set operator, 192
≠, in-equality, non-equivalence
    Boolean connective, 143
    Cartesians, 300
    enumerated tokens, 208, 209
    general tokens, 214
    lists, 322, 324, 325
    maps, 349, 352, 353
    numbers, 207
    sets, 55, 56, 264, 268, 269
≥ greater than or equal to
    numbers, 207
> greater than
    numbers, 207
⊂ proper subset, 55, 56, 192, 264, 268
⊆ subset, 55, 56, 192, 264, 268

Arithmetic Operators

* multiplication, numbers, 207
+ addition, numbers, 207
- subtraction, numbers, 207
/ division, numbers, 207

Boolean Connectives

~ Boolean connective (not, negation),
    57, 143, 157
∨ Boolean connective (disjunction, in-
    clusive or logical or), 57, 143,
    157

∧ Boolean connective (conjunction,
    logical and), 57, 143, 157
⇒ Boolean connective (implication),
    143, 158
= Boolean connective (equality), 143,
    485
≡ Boolean connective (identical), 143

Set Operators &c.

card set cardinality, 55, 56, 192, 264,
    269

∈ set membership, 55, 56, 264, 268,
    269
∉ not member of, 57
∩ set intersection, 55, 56, 192, 264,
    268
∪ set union, 55, 56, 192, 264, 268 (map
    union, 349, 352, 353)
/ set difference, 55, 56, 264, 268
\ set complement (restriction by), 55,
    56, 192, 264, 268 (also see
    map)
⊂ proper subset, 55, 56, 192, 264, 268
⊆ subset, 55, 56, 192, 264, 268

{} empty set, 56, (overloaded function
    symbol) 191
{ open set brace, 56, 266
} close set brace, 56, 266
{•} singleton set function, 192
{∘, ∘, . . . , ∘} set enumeration, 58, 265,
    266
{∘ | ∘ : ∘ • ∘} set comprehension, 57,
    58, 270
| in: set comprehension, 58, 270
.. set range, 267

Cartesian Composition

(∘, ∘, . . . , ∘) Cartesian composition,
    63, 64, 295, 297, 298

List Operators &c.

elems list elements, 68, 70, 193, 322, 324, 325
hd list head, 68, 193, 322, 324, 325
inds list indices, 68, 70, 193, 322, 324, 325
len list length, 68, 69, 193, 322, 324, 325
tl list tail, 68, 193, 322, 324, 325

⌢ list concatenation, 67, 193, 322, 324, 325
$\ell(i)$ list element selection, 68, 70, 193, 322, 324

⟨⟩ empty list (overloaded function symbol, singleton list function), 193
⟨o, ... , o⟩ list enumeration, 323, 324
⟨o|o **in** o•o⟩ list comprehension, 327

Map Operators &c.

dom map definition set (domain), 349, 352, 353
rng map range, 349, 352, 353

∪ map union, 349, 352, 353 (set union, 55, 56, 192, 264, 268)
† map override, 349, 352, 353
° map composition, 349, 352, 353
·(·) map application, 349, 353
\ map restriction by, 349, 352, 353 (also see set)
o(o) map application, 352
/ map restriction to, 349, 352, 353 (also see set)

] map value constructor, 351
[map value constructor, 351
↦ map value constructor, 351

[o↦o, ..., o↦o] map enumeration, 352
[o ↦ o | o • o] map comprehension, 354
[o↦o] map value constructor, 351

Process Combinators

; process sequencing, 468, 471, 533
→ process combinator (sequencing), 533
! output to channel, 517, 535, 538
? input from channel, 517, 535, 538
[] nondeterministic external choice, 527, 533
⊓ nondeterministic internal choice, 527, 534
|| parallel combinator (composition), 517, 535

Comprehension

| part of comprehension expression
list: ⟨ o | o **in** o • o ⟩, 327
map: [o ↦ o | o • o], 354
set: {o | o : o • o}, 270

C.1.2 Constructors

Atomic Types

Bool Boolean type, 81, 143
Char Chracter type, 81, 212
Int integer type, 48, 81, 206
Nat natural number type, 46, 206, 207
Real real number type, 49, 206, 207
Text text type, 212

Composite Types

-infset infinite power set type constructor, 105, 265
-set finite power set type constructor, 105, 265
× Cartesian type constructor, 64, 82, 296
* finite list type constructor, 322
$^\omega$ infinite and finite list type constructor, 322

Function Constructs

Deconstructors

C.1.3 Constant Value Literals

C.1.4 Combinators

Statement Combinators

Clause Combinators

Specification Combinators

C.1.5 Calculi

λ The λ Calculus, 109–125

The Predicate Calculi

C.1.6 Abbreviations

Roman lettered abbreviations designate concepts, teletype lettered abbreviations designate languages.

C.2 Concepts Index

Conceive: To grasp with the mind.

Conception: The act of conceiving, apprehension, imagination.

Concept: The product of the faculty of conception, an idea of a class of objects, a general notion.

The SHORTER OXFORD ENGLISH DICTIONARY
On Historical Principles [350]

The terms: a concept, an idea, a notion, an apprehension and an imagination are treated as similar terms. The concept index also lists common abbreviations.

C.3 Characterisations and Definitions Index

Definition: The setting of bounds, limitation.
The action of determining a question at issue, of defining.
A precise statement of the essential nature of a thing.
A declaration of the signification of a word or phrase.

The SHORTER OXFORD ENGLISH DICTIONARY
On Historical Principles [350]

We shall list both characterisations and definitions. The latter are usually more formally expressed than the former.

C.4 Authors Index

Author: The person who originates or gives existence to anything;
an inventor, constructor, or founder.

He who gives rise to an action, event, circumstance, or state of things.

One who sets forth written statements;
the writer or composer of a treatise or book.

The SHORTER OXFORD ENGLISH DICTIONARY
On Historical Principles [350]

The authors listed here (many with [references] to (usually) their main books)
are (co)authors of publications cited on the referenced page(s). Not all referenced publications have their authors listed here — but a very high proportion
have been listed here!

References

1. M. Abadi, L. Cardelli: *A Theory of Objects* (Springer, New York, USA 1996)
2. H. Abelson, G.J. Sussman, J. Sussman: *Structure and Interpretation of Computer Programs* (MIT Press, USA 1996)
3. J.-R. Abrial: *The B Book: Assigning Programs to Meanings* (Cambridge University Press, UK 1996)
4. J.-R. Abrial, L. Mussat. *Event B Reference Manual (Editor: Thierry Lecomte)*, June 2001. Report of EU IST Project Matisse IST-1999-11435.
5. J.-R. Abrial, S.A. Schuman, B. Meyer: Specification Language. In: *On the Construction of Programs: An Advanced Course*, ed by R.M. McKeag, A.M. Macnaghten (Cambridge University Press, 1980) pp 343–410
6. J.-R. Abrial, I.H. Sørensen: KWIC-index generation. In: *Program Specification: Proceedings of a Workshop*, vol 134 of *Lecture Notes in Computer Science*, ed by J. Staunstrup (Springer, 1981) pp 88–95
7. A. Aho, J. Hopcroft, J. Ullman: *The Design of Computer Algorithms* (Addison-Wesley, USA 1974)
8. A.V. Aho, R. Sethi, J.D. Ullman: *Compilers: Principles, Techniques, and Tools* (Addison-Wesley, USA 1977, 1986)
9. R. Alur, D.L. Dill: *A Theory of Timed Automata.* Theoretical Computer Science **126**, 2 (1994) pp 183–235
10. Edited by J. Alves-Foss: *Formal Syntax and Semantics of Java* (Springer, 1998)
11. D. Andrews, W. Henhapl: Pascal. In: *[121]* (Prentice Hall, 1982) pp 175–252
12. ANSI X3.23-1974: The COBOL Programming Language. Technical Report, American National Standards Institute, Standards on Computers and Information Processing (1974)
13. ANSI X3.53-1976: The PL/I Programming Language. Technical Report, American National Standards Institute, Standards on Computers and Information Processing (1976)
14. ANSI X3.9-1966: The FORTRAN Programming Language. Technical Report, American National Standards Institute, Standards on Computers and Information Processing (1966)
15. K. Apt: *Ten Years of Hoare's Logic: A Survey — Part I.* ACM Trans. on Prog. Lang. and Systems **3** (1981) pp 431–483
16. K. Apt: *Ten Years of Hoare's Logic: A Survey — Part II: Nondeterminism.* Theoretical Computer Science **28** (1984) pp 83–110

688   References

17. K.R. Apt: *From Logic Programming to Prolog* (Prentice Hall, 1997)
18. K.R. Apt: *Principles of Constraint Programming* (Cambridge University Press, August 2003)
19. K.R. Apt, E.-R. Olderog: *Verification of Sequential and Concurrent Programs* (Springer, 1997)
20. K. Arnold, J. Gosling, D. Holmes: *The Java Programming Language* (Addison-Wesley, US 1996)
21. R.-J. Back, J. von Wright: *Refinement Calculus: A Systematic Introduction* (Springer, Heidelberg, 1998)
22. J.W. Backus: The Syntax and Semantics of the proposed International Algebraic Language of the Zürich ACM-GAMM Conference. In: *ICIP Proceedings, Paris 1959* (Butterworth's, London, 1960) pp 125–132
23. J.W. Backus: *Can Programming Be Liberated from the von Neumann Style? A Functional Style and Its Algebra of Programs.* Communications of the ACM **21**, 8 (1978) pp 613–641
24. J.W. Backus, P. Naur: *Revised Report on the Algorithmic Language ALGOL 60.* Communications of the ACM **6**, 1 (1963) pp 1–1
25. H.P. Barendregt: The Type Free Lambda Calculus. In: *[33]* (North-Holland, Amsterdam, 1977) pp 1091–1132
26. H.P. Barendregt: *The Lambda Caculus — Its Syntax and Semantics* (North-Holland, Amsterdam, 1981)
27. H.P. Barendregt: *Introduction to Lambda Calculus.* Niew Archief Voor Wiskunde **4** (1984) pp 337–372
28. H.P. Barendregt: Functional Programming and Lambda Calculus. In: *[344]* — vol.B., ed by J. Leeuwen (North-Holland, Amsterdam, 1990) pp 321–363
29. H.P. Barendregt: *The Lambda Calculus*, no 103 of *Studies in Logic and the Foundations of Mathematics*, revised edn (North-Holland, Amsterdam 1991)
30. Edited by J. Barnes: *The Complete Works of Aristotle; I and II* (Princeton University Press, NJ, USA 1984)
31. W. Barnstone: *Border of a Dream: Selected Poems of Antonio Machado* (Copper Canyon Press, WA, USA 2003)
32. H. Barringer, J. Cheng, C.B. Jones: *A logic covering undefinedness in program proofs.* Acta Informatica **21** (1984) pp 251–269
33. Edited by J. Barwise: *Handbook of Mathematical Logic* (North-Holland, Amsterdam, 1977)
34. F. Bauer, H. Wössner: *Algorithmic Language and Program Development* (Springer, 1982)
35. F.L. Bauer, M. Broy, editors. *Program Construction, International Summer School, July 26–August 6, 1978, Marktoberdorf, Germany*, volume 69 of *Lecture Notes in Computer Science*. Springer, 1979.
36. H. Bekič: Programming Languages and Their Definition. In: *Lecture Notes in Computer Science, Vol. 177*, ed by C.B. Jones (Springer, 1984)
37. H. Bekič, D. Bjørner, W. Henhapl, C.B. Jones, P. Lucas: A Formal Definition of a PL/I Subset. Technical Report 25.139, Vienna, Austria (1974)
38. H. Bekič, P. Lucas, K. Walk, et al.: Formal Definition of PL/I, ULD Version I. Technical Report, IBM Laboratory, Vienna (1966)
39. H. Bekič, P. Lucas, K. Walk, et al.: Formal Definition of PL/I, ULD Version II. Technical Report, IBM Laboratory, Vienna (1968)
40. H. Bekič, P. Lucas, K. Walk, et al.: Formal Definition of PL/I, ULD Version III. IBM Laboratory, Vienna, 1969.

41. C. Berge: *Théorie des Graphes et ses Applications* (Dunod, Paris, 1958)
42. C. Berge: *Graphs*, vol 6 of *Mathematical Library*, second revised edition of part 1 of the 1973 english version edn (North-Holland, 1985)
43. J. Bergstra, J. Heering, P. Klint: *Algebraic Specification* (Addison-Wesley, ACM Press, 1989)
44. E. Berlekamp, J. Conway, R. Guy: *Winning Ways for Your Mathematical Plays, vol. 1* (Academic Press, 1982)
45. E. Berlekamp, J. Conway, R. Guy: *Winning Ways for Your Mathematical Plays, vol. 2* (Academic Press, 1982)
46. P. Bernays: *Axiomatic Set Theory* (Dover, NY, USA 1991)
47. G. Berry. *Proof, Language and Interaction: Essays in Honour of Robin Milner*, chapter The Foundations of Esterel. MIT Press, 1998.
48. G. Berry, G. Gonthier: *The Esterel Synchronous Programming Language: Design, Semantics, Implementation.* Science of Computer Programming **19**, 2 (1992) pp 87–152
49. M. Bidoit, P.D. Mosses: CASL *User Manual* (Springer, 2004)
50. R. Bird, O. de Moor: *Algebra of Programming* (Prentice Hall, September 1996)
51. R.S. Bird, P. Wadler: *Introduction to Functional Programming* (Prentice Hall, 1988)
52. G. Birkhoff: *Lattice Theory,* 3 edn (American Mathematical Society, Providence, RI 1967)
53. G. Birkhoff, S. MacLane: *A Survey of Modern Algebra* (Macmillan, 1956)
54. G. Birtwistle, O.-J.Dahl, B. Myhrhaug, K. Nygaard: *SIMULA* begin (Studentlitteratur, Sweden, 1974)
55. D. Bjørner: Programming Languages: Formal Development of Interpreters and Compilers. In: *International Computing Symposium 77* (North-Holland, Amsterdam, 1977) pp 1–21
56. D. Bjørner: Programming Languages: Linguistics and Semantics. In: *International Computing Symposium 77* (North-Holland, Amsterdam, 1977) pp 511–536
57. D. Bjørner: Programming in the Meta-Language: A Tutorial. In: *The Vienna Development Method: The Meta-Language, [120]*, ed by D. Bjørner, C.B. Jones (Springer, 1978) pp 24–217
58. D. Bjørner: Software Abstraction Principles: Tutorial Examples of an Operating System Command Language Specification and a PL/I-like On-Condition Language Definition. In: *The Vienna Development Method: The Meta-Language, [120]*, ed by D. Bjørner, C.B. Jones (Springer, 1978) pp 337–374
59. D. Bjørner: The Systematic Development of a Compiling Algorithm. In: *Le Point sur la Compilation*, ed by Amirchahy, Neel (INRIA, Paris, 1979) pp 45–88
60. D. Bjørner: The Vienna Development Method: Software Abstraction and Program Synthesis. In: *Mathematical Studies of Information Processing*, vol 75 of *LNCS* (Springer, 1979)
61. Edited by D. Bjørner: *Abstract Software Specifications*, vol 86 of *LNCS* (Springer, 1980)
62. D. Bjørner: Application of Formal Models. In: *Data Bases* (INFOTECH Proceedings, 1980)

63. D. Bjørner: Experiments in Block-Structured GOTO-Modelling: Exits vs. Continuations. In: *Abstract Software Specification, [61]*, vol 86 of *LNCS*, ed by D. Bjørner (Springer, 1980) pp 216–247

64. D. Bjørner: Formal Description of Programming Concepts: a Software Engineering Viewpoint. In: *MFCS'80, Lecture Notes Vol. 88* (Springer, 1980) pp 1–21

65. D. Bjørner: Formalization of Data Base Models. In: *Abstract Software Specification, [61]*, vol 86 of *LNCS*, ed by D. Bjørner (Springer, 1980) pp 144–215

66. D. Bjørner: The VDM Principles of Software Specification and Program Design. In: *TC2 Work. Conf. on Formalisation of Programming Concepts, Peniscola, Spain* (Springer, LNCS Vol. 107 1981) pp 44–74

67. D. Bjørner: Realization of Database Management Systems. In: *See [121]* (Prentice Hall, 1982) pp 443–456

68. D. Bjørner: Rigorous Development of Interpreters and Compilers. In: *See [121]* (Prentice Hall, 1982) pp 271–320

69. D. Bjørner: Stepwise Transformation of Software Architectures. In: *See [121]* (Prentice Hall, 1982) pp 353–378

70. D. Bjørner: Software Architectures and Programming Systems Design. Vols. I–VI. Techn. Univ. of Denmark (1983–1987)

71. D. Bjørner: Project Graphs and Meta-Programs: Towards a Theory of Software Development. In: *Proc. Capri '86 Conf. on Innovative Software Factories and Ada, Lecture Notes on Computer Science*, ed by N. Habermann, U. Montanari (Springer, 1986)

72. D. Bjørner: Software Development Graphs — A Unifying Concept for Software Development? In: *Vol. 241 of Lecture Notes in Computer Science: Foundations of Software Technology and Theoretical Computer Science*, ed by K. Nori (Springer, 1986) pp 1–9

73. D. Bjørner: *Software Engineering and Programming: Past-Present-Future*. IPSJ: Inform. Proc. Soc. of Japan **8**, 4 (1986) pp 265–270

74. D. Bjørner: On the Use of Formal Methods in Software Development. In: *Proc. of 9th International Conf. on Software Engineering, Monterey, California* (1987) pp 17–29

75. D. Bjørner: The Stepwise Development of Software Development Graphs: Meta-Programming VDM Developments. In: *See [122]*, vol 252 of *LNCS* (Springer, Heidelberg, 1987) pp 77–96

76. D. Bjørner: *Facets of Software Development: Computer Science & Programming, Engineering & Management*. J. of Comput. Sci. & Techn. **4**, 3 (1989) pp 193–203

77. D. Bjørner: Specification and Transformation: Methodology Aspects of the Vienna Development Method. In: *TAPSOFT'89*, vol 352 of *Lecture Notes in Computer Science* (Springer, Heidelberg, 1989) pp 1–35

78. D. Bjørner: Formal Software Development: Requirements for a CASE. In: *European Symposium on Software Development Environment and CASE Technology, Königswinter, FRG, June 17–21* (Springer, Heidelberg, 1991)

79. D. Bjørner: Formal Specification Is an Experimental Science (in English). In: *Intl. Conf. on Perspectives of System Informatics* (1991)

80. D. Bjørner: *Formal Specification Is an Experimental Science (in Russian)*. Programmirovanie **6** (1991) pp 24–43

81. D. Bjørner: Towards a Meaning of 'M' in VDM. In: *Formal Description of Programming Concepts*, ed by E. Neuhold, M. Paul (Springer, Heidelberg, 1991) pp 137–258

82. D. Bjørner: From Research to Practice: Self-reliance of the Developing World Through Software Technology: Usage, Education & Training, Development & Research, pp 65–71. In: *Information Processing '92, IFIP World Congress '92, Madrid*, ed by J. van Leeuwen (IFIP Transaction A-12: Algorithms, Software, Architecture, North-Holland 1992)

83. D. Bjørner: Trustworthy Computing Systems: The ProCoS Experience. In: *14'th ICSE: Intl. Conf. on Software Eng., Melbourne, Australia* (ACM Press, 1992) pp 15–34

84. D. Bjørner. *Formal Models of Robots: Geometry & Kinematics*, chapter 3, pages 37–58. Eds.: W. Roscoe and J. Woodcock, *A Classical Mind*, Festschrift for C.A.R. Hoare. Prentice Hall, January 1994.

85. D. Bjørner: Prospects for a Viable Software Industry — Enterprise Models, Design Calculi, and Reusable Modules. In: *First ACM Japan Chapter Conference* (World Scientific, Singapore 1994)

86. D. Bjørner: Software Systems Engineering — From Domain Analysis to Requirements Capture: An Air Traffic Control Example. In: *2nd Asia-Pacific Software Engineering Conference (APSEC '95)* (IEEE Computer Society, 1995)

87. D. Bjørner: From Domain Engineering via Requirements to Software. Formal Specification and Design Calculi. In: *SOFSEM'97*, vol 1338 of *Lecture Notes in Computer Science* (Springer, 1997) pp 219–248

88. D. Bjørner: Challenges in Domain Modelling — Algebraic or Otherwise. Research, Department of Information Technology, Technical University of Denmark, Denmark (1998)

89. D. Bjørner: Domains as Prerequisites for Requirements and Software &c. In: *RTSE'97: Requirements Targeted Software and Systems Engineering*, vol 1526 of *Lecture Notes in Computer Science*, ed by M. Broy, B. Rumpe (Springer, Heidelberg 1998) pp 1–41

90. D. Bjørner: Formal Methods in the 21st Century — An Assessment of Today, Predictions for The Future — Panel position presented at the ICSE'98, Kyoto, Japan. Technical Report, Department of Information Technology, Technical University of Denmark (1998)

91. D. Bjørner: Issues in International Cooperative Research — Why Not Asian, African or Latin American 'Esprits'? Research, Department of Information Technology, Technical University of Denmark, DK–2800 Lyngby, Denmark (1998)

92. D. Bjørner: A Triptych Software Development Paradigm: Domain, Requirements and Software. Towards a Model Development of a Decision Support System for Sustainable Development. In: *Festschrift to Hans Langmaack: Correct Systems Design: Recent Insight and Advances*, vol 1710 of *Lecture Notes in Computer Science*, ed by E.-R. Olderog, B. Steffen (Springer, 1999) pp 29–60

93. D. Bjørner: Challenge 2000: some aspects of: "How to Create a Software Industry". In: *Proceedings of CSIC'99, Ed.: R. Jalili* (1999)

94. D. Bjørner: *Where Do Software Architectures Come from? Systematic Development from Domains and Requirements. A Re-assessment of Software Engineering?* South African Journal of Computer Science **22** (1999) pp 3–13

95. D. Bjørner: Domain Engineering, A Software Engineering Discipline in Need of Research. In: *SOFSEM'2000: Theory and Practice of Informatics*, vol 1963 of *Lecture Notes in Computer Science* (Springer) pp 1–17

96. D. Bjørner: Domain Modelling: Resource Management Strategics, Tactics & Operations, Decision Support and Algorithmic Software. In: *Millennial Perspectives in Computer Science*, ed by J. Davies, B. Roscoe, J. Woodcock (Palgrave, UK 2000) pp 23–40

97. D. Bjørner: Formal Software Techniques in Railway Systems. In: *9th IFAC Symposium on Control in Transportation Systems*, ed by E. Schnieder (DVI 2000) pp 1–12

98. D. Bjørner: Informatics: A Truly Interdisciplinary Science — Computing Science and Mathematics. In: *9th Intl. Colloquium on Numerical Analysis and Computer Science with Applications*, ed by D. Bainov (Academic Publications, Bulgaria 2000)

99. D. Bjørner: Informatics: A Truly Interdisciplinary Science — Prospects for an Emerging World. In: *Information Technology and Communication — at the Dawn of the New Millennium*, ed by S. Balasubramanian (AIT Press, 2000) pp 71–84

100. D. Bjørner: *Pinnacles of Software Engineering: 25 Years of Formal Methods*. Annals of Software Engineering **10** (2000) pp 11–66

101. D. Bjørner: Informatics Models of Infrastructure Domains. In: *Computer Science and Information Technologies* (Institute for Informatics and Automation Problems, Yerevan, Armenia 2001) pp 13–73

102. D. Bjørner: On Formal Techniques in Protocol Engineering: Example Challenges. In: *Formal Techniques for Networks and Distributed Systems* (Eds.: Myungchul Kim, Byoungmoon Chin, Sungwon Kang and Danhyung Lee) (Kluwer, 2001) pp 395–420

103. D. Bjørner: Some Thoughts on Teaching Software Engineering – Central Rôles of Semantics. In: *Liber Amicorum: Professor Jaco de Bakker* (Stichting Centrum voor Wiskunde en Informatica, Amsterdam, The Netherlands 2002) pp 27–45

104. D. Bjørner: Domain Engineering: A "Radical Innovation" for Systems and Software Engineering? In: *Verification: Theory and Practice*, vol 2772 of *Lecture Notes in Computer Science* (Springer, Heidelberg 2003)

105. D. Bjørner: Dynamics of Railway Nets: On an Interface Between Automatic Control and Software Engineering. In: *CTS2003: 10th IFAC Symposium on Control in Transportation Systems* (Elsevier Science, Oxford, UK 2003)

106. D. Bjørner: Logics of Formal Software Specification Languages — The Possible Worlds cum Domain Problem. In: *Fourth Pan-Hellenic Symposium on Logic*, ed by L. Kirousis (Univ. of Thessaloniki, 2003)

107. D. Bjørner: New Results and Trends in Formal Techniques for the Development of Software for Transportation Systems. In: *FORMS 2003: Symposium on Formal Methods for Railway Operation and Control Systems* (Institut für Verkehrssicherheit und Automatisierungstechnik, Techn. Univ. of Braunschweig, Germany, 2003)

108. D. Bjørner. *"What Is a Method?" — An Essay on Some Aspects of Software Engineering*, chapter 9, pages 175–203. Monographs in Computer Science. IFIP: International Federation for Information Processing. Springer, NY, USA, 2003. Programming Methodology: Recent Work by Members of IFIP Working Group 2.3. Eds.: Annabelle McIver and Carroll Morgan.

109. D. Bjørner: What Is an Infrastructure? In: *Formal Methods at the Crossroads. From Panacea to Foundational Support* (Springer, Heidelberg, Germany 2003)

110. D. Bjørner: Towards "Posit & Prove" Design Calculi for Requirements Engineering and Software Design. In: *From Object-Orientation to Formal Methods – Essays in Memory of Ole-Johan Dahl*, Lecture Notes in Computer Science, Vol. 2635 (Springer, 2004)

111. D. Bjørner: *Domain Engineering: "Upstream" from Requirements Engineering and Software Design.* US ONR + Univ. of Genoa Workshop, Santa Margherita Ligure (June 2000)

112. D. Bjørner, J.R. Cuéllar: *Software Engineering Education: Rôles of Formal Specification and Design Calculi.* Annals of Software Engineering **6** (1998) pp 365–410

113. D. Bjørner, Y.L. Dong, S. Prehn: Domain Analyses: A Case Study of Station Management. In: KICS'94: *Kunming International CASE Symposium, Yunnan Province, China* (1994)

114. D. Bjørner, L. Druffel: Industrial Experience in Using Formal Methods. In: *Intl. Conf. on Software Engineering* (IEEE Computer Society Press, 1990) pp 264–266

115. Edited by D. Bjørner, A. Ershov, N. Jones: *Partial Evaluation and Mixed Computation. Proceedings of the IFIP TC2 Workshop, Gammel Avernæs, Denmark, October 1987* (North-Holland, 1988)

116. D. Bjørner, C. George, S. Prehn. *Scheduling and Rescheduling of Trains*, chapter 8, pages 157–184. *Industrial Strength Formal Methods in Practice*, Eds.: Michael G. Hinchey and Jonathan P. Bowen. FACIT, Springer, London, England, 1999.

117. D. Bjørner, C.W. George, A.E. Haxthausen et al.: "UML"-ising Formal Techniques. In: *INT 2004: Third International Workshop on Integration of Specification Techniques for Applications in Engineering*, vol 3147 of *Lecture Notes in Computer Science* (Springer, 2004, ETAPS, Barcelona, Spain) pp 423–450

118. D. Bjørner, C.W. George, S. Prehn: Computing Systems for Railways — A Rôle for Domain Engineering. Relations to Requirements Engineering and Software for Control Applications. In: *Integrated Design and Process Technology. Editors: Bernd Kraemer and John C. Petterson* (Society for Design and Process Science, Texas, USA 2002)

119. D. Bjørner, A.E. Haxthausen, K. Havelund: *Formal, Model-Oriented Software Development Methods: From VDM to ProCoS, and from RAISE to LaCoS.* Future Generation Computer Systems (North-Holland, 1992)

120. Edited by D. Bjørner, C. Jones: *The Vienna Development Method: The Meta-Language*, vol 61 of *LNCS* (Springer, 1978)

121. Edited by D. Bjørner, C. Jones: *Formal Specification and Software Development* (Prentice Hall, 1982)

122. D. Bjørner, C. Jones, M.M. an Airchinnigh, E. Neuhold, editors. *VDM – A Formal Method at Work.* Proc. VDM-Europe Symposium 1987, Brussels, Belgium, Springer, Lecture Notes in Computer Science, Vol. 252, 1987.

123. D. Bjørner, S. Koussobe, R. Noussi, G. Satchok: Michael Jackson's Problem Frames: Towards Methodological Principles of Selecting and Applying Formal Software Development Techniques and Tools. In: *ICFEM'97: Intl. Conf. on "Formal Engineering Methods", Hiroshima, Japan*, ed by L. ShaoQi, M. Hinchley (IEEE Computer Society Press, CA, USA 1997) pp 263–271

124. D. Bjørner, H.H. Løvengreen: Formal Semantics of Data Bases. In: *8th Int'l. Very Large Data Base Conf.* (VLDB Found. 1982)

125. D. Bjørner, H.H. Løvengreen: Formalization of Data Models. In: *Formal Specification and Software Development, [121]* (Prentice Hall, 1982) pp 379–442

126. D. Bjørner, M. Nielsen: Meta Programs and Project Graphs. In: *ETW: Esprit Technical Week* (Elsevier, 1985) pp 479–491

127. D. Bjørner, J. Nilsson: Algorithmic & Knowledge Based Methods — Do They "Unify"? — with Some Programme Remarks for UNU/IIST. In: *International Conference on Fifth Generation Computer Systems: FGCS'92* (ICOT, 1992) pp (Separate folder, "191–198")

128. Edited by D. Bjørner, O. Oest: *Towards a Formal Description of Ada*, vol 98 of *LNCS* (Springer, 1980)

129. D. Bjørner, O.N. Oest: The DDC Ada Compiler Development Project. In: *Towards a Formal Description of Ada, [128]*, vol 98 of *LNCS*, ed by D. Bjørner, O.N. Oest (Springer, 1980) pp 1–19

130. D. Bjørner, S. Prehn: Software Engineering Aspects of VDM. In: *Theory and Practice of Software Technology*, ed by D. Ferrari (North-Holland, Amsterdam, 1983)

131. A. Blikle: *MetaSoft Primer; Towards a Metalanguage for Applied Denotational Semantics*, vol 288 of *Lecture Notes in Computer Science* (Springer, 1987)

132. A. Blikle: *A Guided Tour of the Mathematics of MetaSoft.* Information Processing Letters **29** (1988) pp 81–86

133. A. Blikle: Three-valued predicates for software specification and validation. In: *[135]* (1988) pp 243–266

134. W.D. Blizard: *A Formal Theory of Objects, Space and Time.* The Journal of Symbolic Logic **55**, 1 (1990) pp 74–89

135. R. Bloomfield, L. Marshall, R. Jones, editors. *VDM – The Way Ahead.* Proc. 2nd VDM-Europe Symposium 1988, Dublin, Ireland, Springer, Lecture Notes in Computer Science, Vol. 328, September 1988.

136. G.S. Boolos, R.C. Jeffrey: *Computability and Logic* (Cambridge University Press, September 29, 1989)

137. J.P. Bowen: *Glossary of Z Notation.* Information and Software Technology **37**, 5–6 (1995) pp 333–334

138. British Standards Institution: Specification for Computer Programming Language Pascal. Technical Report BS6192, BSI (1982)

139. M. Broy, K. Stølen: *Specification and Development of Interactive Systems — Focus on Streams, Interfaces and Refinement* (Springer, NY, USA and Heidelberg, Germany 2001)

140. R. Bruni, J. Meseguer: Generalized Rewrite Theories. In: *Automata, Languages and Programming. 30th International Colloquium, ICALP 2003, Eindhoven, The Netherlands, June 30–July 4, 2003. Proceedings*, vol 2719 of *Lecture Notes in Computer Science*, ed by J.C.M. Baeten, J.K.Lenstra, J.Parrow, G.J. Woeginger (Springer, 2003) pp 252–266

141. E. Burke: *Reflections on the Revolution in France, Ed. Conor Cruise O'Brien* (Hammondsworth, 1790 (1968))

142. R.M. Burstall, J. Darlington: *A Transformation System for Developing Recursive Programs.* Journal of ACM **24**, 1 (1977) pp 44–67

143. D. Cansell, D. Méry: *Logical Foundations of the B Method.* Computing and Informatics **22**, 1–2 (2003)

144. D. Carrington, D.J. Duke, R. Duke et al.: Object-Z: An Object-Oriented Extension to Z. In: *Formal Description Techniques, II (FORTE'89)*, ed by S. Vuong (Elsevier — (North-Holland), 1990) pp 281–296

145. C.C.I.T.T.: The Specification of CHILL. Technical Report Recommendation Z200, International Telegraph and Telephone Consultative Committee, Geneva, Switzerland (1980)

146. E. Chailloux, P. Manoury, B. Pagano: *Developing Applications With Objective Caml* (Project Cristal, INRIA, France 2004)

147. E. Chailloux, P. Manoury, B. Pagano: *Développement d'applications avec Objective Caml* (Éditions O'Reilly, Paris, France 2000)

148. P.P. Chen: *The Entity-Relationship Model — Toward a Unified View of Data.* ACM Trans. Database Syst **1**, 1 (1976) pp 9–36

149. P.P. Chen, editor. *Entity–Relationship Approach to Systems Analysis and Design. Proc. 1st International Conference on the Entity–Relationship Approach.* North-Holland, 1980.

150. J. Cheng: A Logic for Partial Functions. PhD Thesis, Department of Computer Science, University of Manchester (1986)

151. J. Cheng, C. Jones: On the usability of logics which handle partial functions. In: *Proceedings of the Third Refinement Workshop*, ed by C. Morgan, J. Woodcock (Springer, 1990)

152. A. Church: *The Calculi of Lambda-Conversion*, vol 6 of *Annals of Mathematical Studies* (Princeton University Press, USA 1941)

153. A. Church: *Introduction to Mathematical Logic* (Princeton University Press, USA 1956)

154. M. Clavel, F. Durán, S. Eker et al: The Maude 2.0 System. In: *Rewriting Techniques and Applications (RTA 2003)*, no 2706 of *Lecture Notes in Computer Science*, ed by Robert Nieuwenhuis (Springer, 2003) pp 76–87

155. G. Clemmensen, O. Oest: Formal Specification and Development of an Ada Compiler – A VDM Case Study. In: *Proc. 7th International Conf. on Software Engineering, 26.–29. March 1984, Orlando, Florida* (IEEE Press, 1984) pp 430–440

156. E.F. Codd: *A Relational Model For Large Shared Databank.* Communications of the ACM **13**, 6 (1970) pp 377–387

157. P. Cohn: *Universal Algebra*, rev. edn ((Harper and Row) D. Reidel, Boston (1965) 1981)

158. P. Cohn: *Classical Algebra* (Wiley, 2001)

159. J. Conway: *On Numbers and Games* (Academic Press, 1976)

160. D. Cooper: *The Equivalence of Certain Computations.* Computer Journal **9** (1966) pp 45–52

161. T.H. Cormen, C.E. Leiserson, R.L. Rivest, C. Stein: *Introduction to Algorithms*, 2nd edn (McGraw-Hill and MIT Press, 2001)

162. G. Cousineau, M. Mauny: *The Functional Approach to Programming* (Cambridge University Press, UK 1998)

163. P. Cousot: *Abstract Interpretation.* ACM Computing Surveys **28**, 2 (1996) pp 324–328

164. P. Cousot, R. Cousot: Abstract Interpretation: A Unified Lattice Model for Static Analysis of Programs by Construction or Approximation of Fixpoints. In: *4th POPL: Principles of Programming and Languages* (ACM Press, 1977) pp 238–252

165. D. Crystal: *The Cambridge Encyclopedia of Language* (Cambridge University Press, 1987, 1988)

166. H.B. Curry, R. Feys: *Combinatory Logic I* (North-Holland, Amsterdam, 1968)

167. H.B. Curry, J.R. Hindley, J.P. Seldin: *Combinatory Logic II* (North-Holland, Amsterdam, 1972)

168. O.-J. Dahl, E.W. Dijkstra, C.A.R. Hoare: *Structured Programming* (Academic Press, 1972)

169. O.-J. Dahl, C.A.R. Hoare: Hierarchical Program Structures. In: *[168]* (Academic Press, 1972) pp 197–220

170. O.-J. Dahl, K. Nygaard: *SIMULA – An ALGOL-based Simulation Language*. Communications of the ACM **9**, 9 (1966) pp 671–678

171. W. Damm, D. Harel: *LSCs: Breathing Life into Message Sequence Charts*. Formal Methods in System Design **19** (2001) pp 45–80

172. O. Danvy: A Rational Deconstruction of Landin's SECD Machine. Research RS 03–33, BRICS: Basic Research in Computer Science, University of Århus, Denmark (2003)

173. J. Darlington: *A Synthesis of Several Sorting Algorithms*. Acta Informatica **11** (1978) pp 1–30

174. J. Darlington, R.M. Burstall: *A System Which Automatically Improves Programs*. Acta Informatica **6** (1976) pp 41–60

175. J. Darlington, P. Henderson, D. Turner: *Functional Programming and Its Applications* (Cambridge Univ. Press, 1982)

176. C. Date: *An Introduction to Database Systems, I* (Addison-Wesley, 1981)

177. C. Date: *An Introduction to Database Systems, II* (Addison-Wesley, 1983)

178. C. Date, H. Darwen: *A Guide to the SQL Standard* (Addison-Wesley Professional, November 8, 1996)

179. J. Davies. Announcement: Electronic version of Communicating Sequential Processes (CSP). Published electronically: http://www.usingcsp.com/, 2004. Announcing revised edition of [288].

180. M. Davis: *Computability and Undecidability* (McGraw-Hill, 1958)

181. R.E. Davis: *Truth, Deduction, and Computation* (Computer Science Press, New York, USA 1989)

182. J. de Bakker: *Mathematical Theory of Programming Correctness* (Prentice Hall, 1980)

183. J. de Bakker: *Control Flow Semantics* (MIT Press, USA, 1995)

184. N. Dershowitz, J.-P. Jouannaud: Rewrite Systems. In: *Handbook of Theoretical Computer Science, Volume B: Formal Models and Semantics*, ed by J. van Leeuwen (Elsevier, 1990) pp 243–320

185. R. Descartes: *Discours de la méthode pour bien conduire sa raison et chercher la vérité dans les sciences, with three appendices: La Dioptrique, Les Météores, and La Géométrie* (Leyden, The Netherlands 1637)

186. R. Descartes: *La Géométrie* (France, 1637)

187. R. Descartes: *Discourse on Method and Related Writings (from: Discourse on the Method of Rightly Conducting the Reason, and Seeking Truth in the Sciences)* (France and Penguin Classics, 1637, respectively February 28, 2000)

188. R. Descartes: *Discourse on Method and Related Writings* (Penguin Classics, 2000)

189. R. Descartes: *Discourse on Method, Optics, Geometry, and Meteorology* (Hackett Publishing Co, Cambridge, USA 2001)

190. R. Diaconescu, K. Futatsugi: Logical Semantics of CafeOBJ. Research Report IS-RR-96-0024S, JAIST, Japan (1996)

191. R. Diaconescu, K. Futatsugi: *CafeOBJ Report: The Language, Proof Techniques, and Methodologies for Object-Oriented Algebraic Specification* (World Scientific, Singapore, 1998)

192. R. Diaconescu, K. Futatsugi, S. Iida: CafeOBJ Jewels. In: *CAFE: An Industrial-Strength Algebraic Formal Method* (Elsevier, 2000) pp 33–60

193. R. Diaconescu, K. Futatsugi, K. Ogata: *CafeOBJ: Logical Foundations and Methodology*. Computing and Informatics **22**, 1–2 (2003)

194. E. Dijkstra: *A Discipline of Programming* (Prentice Hall, 1976)

195. E. Dijkstra, W. Feijen: *A Method of Programming* (Addison-Wesley, 1988)

196. E. Dijkstra, C. Scholten: *Predicate Calculus and Program Semantics* (Springer, 1990)

197. O. Dommergaard: The Design of a Virtual Machine for Ada. In: *[61]* (Springer, 1980) pp 463–605

198. O. Dommergaard, S. Bodilsen: A Formal Definition of P-Code. Technical Report, Dept. of Comp. Sci., Techn. Univ. of Denmark (1980)

199. D.J. Duke, R. Duke: Towards a Semantics for Object-Z. In: *VDM and Z – Formal Methods in Software Development*, vol 428 of *Lecture Notes in Computer Science*, ed by D. Bjørner, C.A.R. Hoare, H. Langmaack (Springer, 1990) pp 244–261

200. R. Duke, P. King, G.A. Rose, G. Smith: The Object-Z Specification Language. In: *Technology of Object-Oriented Languages and Systems: TOOLS 5*, ed by T. Korson et al. (Prentice Hall, 1991) pp 465–483

201. E.H. Dürr, L. Dusink: Role of VDM(++) in the Development of a Real-Time Tracking and Tracing System. In: *FME'93: Industrial-Strength Formal Methods*, ed by J. Woodcock, P. Larsen (Springer, 1993) pp 64–72

202. E.H. Dürr, S. Goldsack. *Formal Methods and Object Technology*, chapter 6 Concurrency and Real-Time in VDM++, pages 86–112. Springer (Eds. S.J. Goldsack and S.J.H. Kent), London, 1996.

203. E.H. Dürr, J. van Katwijk: VDM^{++} – A Formal Specification Language for Object-Oriented Designs. In: *Technology of Object-oriented Languages and Systems*, ed by B.M. Heeg, B. Magnusson (Prentice Hall, 1992) pp 63–78

204. E.H. Dürr, W. Lourens, J. van Katwijk: The Use of the Formal Specification Language VDM^{++} for Data Acquisition Systems. In: *New Computing Techniques in Physics Research II*, ed by D. Perret-Gallix (World Scientific, Singapore 1992) pp 47–52

205. B. Dutertre: Complete Proof System for First-Order Interval Temporal Logic. In: *Proceedings of the 10th Annual IEEE Symposium on Logic in Computer Science* (IEEE CS, 1995) pp 36–43

206. R.K. Dybvig: *The Scheme Programming Language* (MIT Press, Cambridge, USA 2003)

207. Encyclopædia Brittanica.   Encyclopædia Brittanica.   Merriam-Webster/Brittanica: Access over the Web: http://www.eb.com:180/, 1999.

208. H. Ehrig, B. Mahr: *Fundamentals of Algebraic Specification 1, Equations and Initial Semantics* (EATCS Monographs on Theoretical Computer Science, vol. 6, Springer, 1985)

209. H. Ehrig, B. Mahr: *Fundamentals of Algebraic Specification 2, Module Specifications and Constraints* (EATCS Monographs on Theoretical Computer Science, vol. 21, Springer, 1990)

210. H.B. Enderton: *A Mathematical Introduction to Logic* (Academic Press, New York, 1974)

211. H.B. Enderton: *Elements of Set Theory* (Elsevier, Amsterdam, The Netherlands 23 May 1977)

212. E. Engeler: *Symposium on Semantics of Algorithmic Languages*, vol 188 of *Lecture Notes in Mathematics* (Springer, 1971)

213. S.S. Epp: *Discrete Matematics with Applications*, third edn (Thomson, Brooks/Cole, California, USA 2004)

214. A. Ershov: *On the Essence of Translation.* Computer Software and System Programming **3**, 5 (1977) pp 332–346

215. A. Ershov: *On the Partial Computation Principle.* Information Processing Letters **6**, 2 (1977) pp 38–41

216. A. Ershov: *Mixed Computation: Potential Applications and Problems for Study.* Theoretical Computer Science **18** (1982) pp 41–67

217. A. Ershov: *On Futamura Projections.* BIT (Japan) **12**, 14 (1982) pp 4–5

218. A. Ershov: On Mixed Computation: Informal Account of the Strict and Polyvariant Computational Schemes. In: *Control Flow and Data Flow: Concepts of Distributed Programming. NATO ASI Series F: Computer and System Sciences, vol. 14*, ed by M. Broy (Springer, 1985) pp 107–120

219. A. Ershov, D. Bjørner, Y. Futamura et al., editors. *Special Issue: Selected Papers from the Workshop on Partial Evaluation and Mixed Computation, 1987 (New Generation Computing, vol. 6, nos. 2,3).* Ohmsha and Springer, 1988.

220. A. Ershov, V. Grushetsky: An Implementation-Oriented Method for Describing Algorithmic Languages. In: *Information Processing 77, Toronto, Canada*, ed by B. Gilchrist (North-Holland, 1977) pp 117–122

221. A. Ershov, V. Itkin: Correctness of Mixed Computation in Algol-like Programs. In: *Mathematical Foundations of Computer Science, Tatranská Lomnica, Czechoslovakia. (Lecture Notes in Computer Science, vol. 53)*, ed by J. Gruska (Springer, 1977) pp 59–77

222. A. Evans Jr.: The Lambda-Calculus and Its Relation to Programming Languages. Unpubl. Notes, MIT (1972)

223. R. Fagin, J.Y. Halpern, Y. Moses, M.Y. Vardi: *Reasoning About Knowledge* (MIT Press 1996)

224. W. Feijen, A. van Gasteren, D. Gries, J. Misra, editors. *Beauty Is Our Business*, Texts and Monographs in Computer Science, New York, NY, USA, 1990. Springer. A Birthday Salute to Edsger W. Dijkstra.

225. A. Field, P. Harrison: *Functional Programming* (Addison-Wesley, 1988)

226. J.S. Fitzgerald, P.G. Larsen: *Developing Software Using VDM-SL* (Cambridge University Press, UK 1997)

227. FOLDOC: The free online dictionary of computing. Electronically, on the Web: `http://wombat.doc.ic.ac.uk/foldoc/foldoc.cgi?ISWIM`, 2004.

228. P. Folkjær, D. Bjørner: A Formal Model of a Generalised CSP-like Language. In: *Proc. IFIP'80*, ed by S. Lavington (North-Holland, Amsterdam, 1980) pp 95–99

229. Formal Systems Europe. Home of the FDR2. Published on the Internet: `http://www.fsel.com/`, 2003.

230. A. Fraenkel, Y. Bar-Hillel, A. Levy: *Foundations of Set Theory*, 2nd revised edn (Elsevier Science, Amsterdam, The Netherlands 1973)

231. Y. Futamura: *Partial Evaluation of Computation Process – An Approach to a Compiler-Compiler.* Systems, Computers, Controls **2**, 5 (1971) pp 45–50

232. K. Futatsugi, R. Diaconescu: *CafeOBJ Report — The Language, Proof Techniques, and Methodologies for Object-Oriented Algebraic Specification* (World Scientific, Singapore 1998)

233. K. Futatsugi, J. Goguen, J.-P. Jouannaud, J. Meseguer: Principles of OBJ-2. In: *12th Ann. Symp. on Principles of Programming* (ACM, 1985) pp 52–66

234. K. Futatsugi, A. Nakagawa, T. Tamai, editors. *CAFE: An Industrial-Strength Algebraic Formal Method,* Proceedings from an April 1998 Symposium, Numazu, Japan, Elsevier 2000

235. J. Gallier: *Logic for Computer Science: Foundations of Automatic Theorem Proving* (Harper and Row, NY, USA, 1986)

236. C.W. George, P. Haff, K. Havelund et al: *The RAISE Specification Language* (Prentice Hall, UK 1992)

237. C.W. George, A.E. Haxthausen: *The Logic of the RAISE Specification Language.* Computing and Informatics **22**, 1–2 (2003)

238. C.W. George, A.E. Haxthausen, S. Hughes et al: *The RAISE Method* (Prentice Hall, UK 1995)

239. C.W. George, H.D. Van, T. Janowski, R. Moore: *Case Studies Using the RAISE Method* (Springer, London 2002)

240. C. Ghezzi, M. Jazayeri, D. Mandrioli: *Fundamentals of Software Engineering* (Prentice Hall, 2002)

241. J.-Y. Girard, Y. Lafont, P. Taylor: *Proofs and Types,* vol 7, Cambridge Tracts in Theoretical Computer Science edn (Cambridge Univ. Press, UK 1989)

242. Edited by M.J.C. Gordon, T.F. Melham: *Introduction to HOL: A Theorem Proving Environment for Higher-Order Logic* (Cambridge University Press, UK 1993)

243. J. Gosling, F. Yellin: *The Java Language Specification* (ACM Press, 1996)

244. D. Gries: *Compiler Construction for Digital Computers* (Wiley, NY, 1971)

245. D. Gries: *The Science of Programming* (Springer, 1981)

246. D. Gries, F.B. Schneider: *A Logical Approach to Discrete Math* (Springer, 1993)

247. O. Grillmeyer: *Exploring Computer Science with Scheme* (Springer, New York, USA 1998)

248. P.L. Guernic, M.L. Borgne, T. Gauthier, C.L. Maire: Programming Real Time Applications with Signal. In: *Another Look at Real Time Programming,* vol Special Issue of *Proceedings of the IEEE* (1991)

249. I. Guessarian: *Algebraic Semantics* (Springer, 1981)

250. C. Gunter, J. Mitchell: *Theoretical Aspects of Object-Oriented Programming* (MIT Press, USA, 1994)

251. C. Gunter, D. Scott: Semantic Domains. In: *[344] — vol. B.,* ed by J. Leeuwen (North-Holland, Amsterdam, 1990) pp 633–674

252. C. Gunther: *Semantics of Programming Languages* (MIT Press, USA, 1992)

253. Y. Gurevich: *Sequential Abstract State Machines Capture Sequential Algorithms.* ACM Transactions on Computational Logic **1**, 1 (2000) pp 77–111

254. Edited by P. Haff: *The Formal Definition of CHILL* (ITU (Intl. Telecom. Union), Geneva, Switzerland 1981)

255. P. Haff, A. Olsen: Use of VDM Within CCITT. In: *[122]* (Springer, 1987) pp 324–330

256. N. Halbwachs, P. Caspi, Pilaud: The Synchronous Dataflow Programming Language Lustre. In: *Another Look at Real Time Programming*, vol Special Issue of *Proceedings of the IEEE* (1991)

257. P. Hall, D. Bjørner, Z. Mikolajuk: Decision Support Systems for Sustainable Development: Experience and Potential — a Position Paper. Administrative Report 80, UNU/IIST, Macau (1996)

258. P.R. Halmos: *Naive Set Theory* (Springer, Heidelberg, 1998)

259. A. Hamilton: *Logic for Mathematicians* (Cambridge University Press, 1978, revised ed.: 1988)

260. A. Hamilton: *Numbers, Sets and Axioms: the Apparatus of Mathematics* (Cambridge University Press, 1982)

261. M.R. Hansen, H. Rischel: *Functional Programming in Standard ML* (Addison-Wesley, 1997)

262. S. Harbinson: *Modula 3* (Prentice Hall, USA 1992)

263. G. Hardy: *A Course of Pure Mathematics* (Cambridge University Press, England, 1908, 1943–4, 1949)

264. D. Harel: *Algorithmics —The Spirit of Computing* (Addison-Wesley, 1987)

265. D. Harel: *Statecharts: A Visual Formalism for Complex Systems*. Science of Computer Programming **8**, 3 (1987) pp 231–274

266. D. Harel: *On Visual Formalisms*. Communications of the ACM **33**, 5 (1988)

267. D. Harel: *The Science of Computing — Exploring the Nature and Power of Algorithms* (Addison-Wesley, April 1989)

268. D. Harel, E. Gery: *Executable Object Modeling with Statecharts*. IEEE Computer **30**, 7 (1997) pp 31–42

269. D. Harel, H. Lachover, A. Naamad et al: *STATEMATE: A Working Environment for the Development of Complex Reactive Systems*. Software Engineering **16**, 4 (1990) pp 403–414

270. D. Harel, R. Marelly: *Come, Let's Play – Scenario-Based Programming Using LSCs and the Play-Engine* (Springer, 2003)

271. D. Harel, A. Naamad: *The STATEMATE Semantics of Statecharts*. ACM Transactions on Software Engineering and Methodology (TOSEM) **5**, 4 (1996) pp 293–333

272. F. Harrary: *Graph Theory* (Addison-Wesley, 1972)

273. F. Hausdorff: *Set Theory* (Oxford University Press, UK 1991)

274. A.E. Haxthausen, X. Yong: Linking DC together with TRSL. In: *Proceedings of 2nd International Conference on Integrated Formal Methods (IFM 2000), Schloss Dagstuhl, Germany, November 2000*, no 1945 of *Lecture Notes in Computer Science* (Springer, 2000) pp 25–44

275. E. Hehner: *The Logic of Programming* (Prentice Hall, 1984)

276. E. Hehner: *A Practical Theory of Programming*, 2nd edn (Springer, 1993)

277. A. Hejlsberg, S. Wiltamuth, P. Golde: *The C# Programming Language* (Addison-Wesley, USA 2003)

278. P. Henderson: *Functional Programming: Application and Implementation* (Prentice Hall, 1980)

279. J.L. Hennessy, D.A. Patterson: *Computer Architecture: a Quantitative Approach* (Morgan Kaufmann, 1995)

280. M. Hennessy: *Algebraic Theory of Processes* (MIT Press, Cambridge, USA, 1988)

281. M.C. Henson, S. Reeves, J.P. Bowen: *Z Logic and Its Consequences*. Computing and Informatics **22**, 1–2 (2003)

282. J.R. Hindley: *Basic Simple Type Theory* (Cambridge University Press, October 2002)

283. J.R. Hindley, B. Lercher, J.P. Seldin: *Introduction to Combinatory Logic* (Cambridge University Press, 1972)

284. J.R. Hindley, J.P. Seldin: *Introduction to Combinators and λ-Calculus*, vol 1 of *London Mathematical Society, Student Texts* (Cambridge University Press, 1986)

285. J. Hintikka: *Knowledge and Belief: An Introduction to the Logic of the Two Notions* (Cornell University Press, NY, USA 1962)

286. C.A.R. Hoare: Notes on Data Structuring. In: *[168]* (1972) pp 83–174

287. C.A.R. Hoare: *Communicating Sequential Processes*. Communications of the ACM **21**, 8 (1978)

288. C.A.R. Hoare: *Communicating Sequential Processes* (Prentice Hall, 1985)

289. C.A.R. Hoare. Communicating Sequential Processes. Published electronically: http://www.usingcsp.com/cspbook.pdf, 2004. Second edition of [288]. See also http://www.usingcsp.com/.

290. C.A.R. Hoare, et al.: *Laws of Programming*. Communications of the ACM **30**, 8 (1987) pp 672–686, 770

291. C.A.R. Hoare, J.F. He: *Unifying Theories of Programming* (Prentice Hall, 1997)

292. C.A.R. Hoare, N. Wirth: *An Axiomatic Definition of the Programming Language PASCAL*. Acta Informatica **2** (1973) pp 335–355

293. A. Hodges: *Alan Turing: the Enigma* (Random House, London, UK 1992)

294. W. Hodges: *Logic* (Penguin Books, 1977)

295. C.J. Hogger: *Essentials of Logic Programming* (Clarendon Press, 1990)

296. J. Hopcroft, J. Ullman: *Introduction to Automata Theory, Languages and Computation* (Addison-Wesley, 1979)

297. I. Horebeek, J. Lewi: *Algebraic Specifications in Software Engineering. An Introduction* (Springer, New York, NY, 1989)

298. W. Humphrey: *Managing the Software Process* (Addison-Wesley, 1989)

299. IEEE CS. IEEE Standard Glossary of Software Engineering Terminology, 1990. IEEE Std.610.12.

300. D.C. Ince: *The Collected Works of A.M. Turing: Mechanical Intelligence* (North-Holland, Amsterdam, The Netherlands 1992)

301. Inmos Ltd.: specification of instruction set & Specification of floating point unit instructions. In: *Transputer Instruction Set – A Compiler writer's guide* (Prentice Hall, UK 1988) pp 127–161

302. ITU-T. CCITT Recommendation Z.120: Message Sequence Chart (MSC), 1992.

303. ITU-T. ITU-T Recommendation Z.120: Message Sequence Chart (MSC), 1996.

304. ITU-T. ITU-T Recommendation Z.120: Message Sequence Chart (MSC), 1999.

305. M.A. Jackson: *Principles of Program Design* (Academic Press, 1969)

306. M.A. Jackson: *System Design* (Prentice Hall, 1985)

307. M.A. Jackson: *Problems, methods and specialisation*. Software Engineering Journal **9**, 6 (1994) pp 249–255

308. M.A. Jackson: *Software Requirements & Specifications: a lexicon of practice, principles and prejudices* (Addison-Wesley, UK 1995)

309. M.A. Jackson: *Software Hakubutsushi: sekai to kikai no kijutsu (Software Requirements & Specifications: a lexicon of practice, principles and prejudices)* (Toppan Company, Japan 1997)

310. M.A. Jackson: *Problem Frames — Analyzing and Structuring Software Development Problems* (Addison-Wesley, UK 2001)

311. M.A. Jackson, G. Twaddle: *Business Process Implementation — Building Workflow Systems* (Addison-Wesley, 1997)

312. J. Jaffar, S. Michaylov: Methodology and Implementation of a CLP System. Technical Report, IBM Research, Yorktown (1987)

313. K. Jensen: *Coloured Petri Nets*, vol 1: Basic Concepts (234 pages + xii), Vol. 2: Analysis Methods (174 pages + x), Vol. 3: Practical Use (265 pages + xi) of *EATCS Monographs in Theoretical Computer Science* (Springer, Heidelberg 1985, revised and corrected second version: 1997)

314. K. Jensen, N. Wirth: *Pascal User Manual and Report*, vol 18 of *LNCS* (Springer, 1976)

315. C.B. Jones: Denotational Semantics of GOTO: an Exit Formulation and Its Relation to Continuations. In: *[120]* (Springer, 1978) pp 278–304

316. C.B. Jones: *Systematic Software Development Using VDM* (Prentice Hall, 1986)

317. C.B. Jones: *Systematic Software Development Using VDM*, 2nd edn (Prentice Hall, 1990)

318. C.B. Jones, K. Middelburg: *A Typed Logic of Partial Functions Reconstructed Classically.* Acta Informatica **31**, 5 (1994) pp 399–430

319. N.D. Jones: *Computability and Complexity — From a Programming Point of View* (MIT Press, USA, 1996)

320. N.D. Jones, C. Gomard, P. Sestoft: *Partial Evaluation and Automatic Program Generation* (Prentice Hall, 1993)

321. B. Kernighan, D. Ritchie: *C Programming Language*, 2nd edn (Prentice Hall, 1989)

322. S.C. Kleene: *Lambda-definability and recursiveness.* Duke Math. J. **2** (1936) pp 340–53

323. S.C. Kleene: *Introduction to Meta-mathematics* (Van Nostrand, New York and Toronto, 1952)

324. S.C. Kleene: *Mathematical Logic* (Dover Publications, 2002)

325. J. Klose, H. Wittke: An Automata Based Interpretation of Live Sequence Charts. In: *TACAS 2001*, ed by T. Margaria, W. Yi (Springer, 2001) pp 512–527

326. D. Knuth: *The Art of Computer Programming, Vol. 1: Fundamental Algorithms* (Addison-Wesley, USA, 1968)

327. D. Knuth: *The Art of Computer Programming, Vol. 2.: Seminumerical Algorithms* (Addison-Wesley, USA, 1969)

328. D. Knuth: *The Art of Computer Programming, Vol. 3: Searching & Sorting* (Addison-Wesley, USA, 1973)

329. B. Konikowska, A. Tarlecki, A. Blikle: A Three-alued Logic for Software Specification and Validation. In: *[135]* (1988) pp 218–242

330. I. Lakatos: *Proofs and Refutations: The Logic of Mathematical Discovery (Eds.: J. Worrall and E.G. Zahar)* (Cambridge University Press, UK 1976)

331. L. Lamport: *The Temporal Logic of Actions.* ACM Transactions on Programming Languages and Systems **16**, 3 (1994) pp 872–923

332. L. Lamport: *Specifying Systems* (Addison-Wesley, USA 2002)

333. P. Landin: *The Mechanical Evaluation of Expressions.* Computer Journal **6**, 4 (1964) pp 308–320

334. P. Landin: *A Correspondence Between ALGOL 60 and Church's Lambda-Notation (in 2 parts)*. Communications of the ACM **8**, 2-3 (1965) pp 89–101 and 158–165

335. P. Landin: A Generalization of Jumps and Labels. Technical Report, Univac Sys. Prgr. Res. Grp., NY (1965)

336. P. Landin: Getting Rid of Labels. Technical Report, Univac Sys. Prgr. Res. Grp., NY (1965)

337. P. Landin: A Formal Description of ALGOL 60. In: *[483]* (1966) pp 266–294

338. P. Landin: A Lambda Calculus Approach. In: *Advances in Programming and Non-numeric Computations*, ed by L. Fox (Pergamon Press, 1966) pp 97–141

339. P. Landin: *The Next 700 Programming Languages*. Communications of the ACM **9**, 3 (1966) pp 157–166

340. P. Landin. Histories of discoveries of continuations: belles-lettres with equivocal tenses, 1997. In O. Danvy, editor, ACM SIGPLAN Workshop on Continuations, Number NS-96-13 in BRICS Notes Series, 1997.

341. J. Laprie: Dependable computing and fault-tolerance: concepts and terminology. In: *15th. Int. Symp. on Fault-Tolerant Computing* (IEEE, 1985)

342. J. Lee: *Computer Semantics* (Van Nostrand Reinhold, 1972)

343. J. Lee, W. Delmore: The Vienna Definition Language, A Generalization of Instruction Definitions. In: *ACM SIGPLAN Symp. on Programming Language Definitions, San Francisco* (1969)

344. Edited by J. van Leeuwen: *Handbook of Theoretical Computer Science, Volumes A and B* (Elsevier, 1990)

345. H. Leonard, N. Goodman: *The Calculus of Individuals and Its Uses*. Journal of Symbolic Logic **5** (1940) pp 45–55

346. X. Leroy, P. Weis: *Manuel de Référence du langage Caml* (InterEditions, Paris, France 1993)

347. S. Levi, A. Agrawala: *Real-Time System Design* (McGraw-Hill, NY, USA 1990)

348. T. Lindholm, F. Yellin: *The Java Virtual Machine Specification* (ACM Press Books, 1996)

349. J. Lipson: *Elements of Algebra and Algebraic Computing* (Addison-Wesley, USA 1981)

350. W. Little, H. Fowler, J. Coulson, C. Onions: *The Shorter Oxford English Dictionary on Historical Principles* (Clarendon Press, UK, 1987)

351. J. Lloyd: *Foundation of Logic Programming* (Springer, 1984)

352. H.H. Løvengreen, D. Bjørner: On a Formal Model of the Tasking Concepts in Ada. In: *ACM SIGPLAN Ada Symp.* (1980)

353. P. Lucas: *Formal Semantics of Programming Languages: VDL*. IBM Journal of Devt. and Res. **25**, 5 (1981) pp 549–561

354. P. Lucas, K. Walk: *On the Formal Description of PL/I*. Annual Review Automatic Programming Part 3 **6**, 3 (1969)

355. E. Luschei: *The Logical Systems of Lesniewski* (North-Holland, Amsterdam, The Netherlands 1962)

356. J. Lützen: *Joseph Liouville 1809-1882: Master of Pure and Applied Mathematics*, vol 15 of *Studies in the History of Mathematics and Physical Sciences* (Springer, New York – Berlin 1990)

357. N. Lynch: *Distributed Algorithms* (Morgan Kaufmann Publishers, 1996)

358. C. MacPherson: *Burke* (Oxford University Press, 1980)

359. Z. Manna: *Mathematical Theory of Computation* (McGraw-Hill, 1974)

360. Z. Manna, A. Pnueli: *The Temporal Logic of Reactive Systems: Specifications* (Addison-Wesley, 1991)

361. Z. Manna, A. Pnueli: *The Temporal Logic of Reactive Systems: Safety* (Addison-Wesley, 1995)

362. Z. Manna, R. Waldinger: *The Logical Basis for Computer Programming, Vols.1–2* (Addison-Wesley, 1985–90)

363. W. Mao: *Modern Cryptography: Theory and Practice* (Pearson Professional Education, Prentice Hall, 2003)

364. D. May: *occam* (Prentice Hall, UK 1982)

365. J. McCarthy: *Recursive Functions of Symbolic Expressions and Their Computation by Machines, Part I.* Communications of the ACM **3**, 4 (1960) pp 184–195

366. J. McCarthy: Towards a Mathematical Science of Computation. In: *IFIP World Congress Proceedings*, ed by C. Popplewell (1962) pp 21–28

367. J. McCarthy: A Basis for a Mathematical Theory of Computation. In: *Computer Programming and Formal Systems* (North-Holland, Amsterdam, 1963)

368. J. McCarthy: A Formal Description of a Subset of ALGOL. In: *[483]* (1966)

369. J. McCarthy. Artificial Intellingence. Electronically, on the Web: http://-www-formal.stanford.edu/jmc/, 2004.

370. J. McCarthy, et al.: *LISP 1.5, Programmer's Manual* (The MIT Press, USA 1962)

371. K. Mehlhorn: *Data Structures and Algorithms: 3 vols.: 1: Multi-dimensional Searching and Computational Geometry, 2: Graph Algorithms and NP-Completeness, 3: Sorting and Searching* (Springer, 1984)

372. E. Mendelsohn: *Introduction to Mathematical Logic*, 4th edn (Lewis Publishers, International Thomson Publishing, June 1, 1997)

373. Merriam-Webster. Online Dictionary: http://www.m-w.com/home.htm, 2004. Merriam-Webster, USA.

374. J. Meseguer: Software Specification and Verification in Rewriting Logic. NATO Advanced Study Institute (2003)

375. B. Meyer: *On Formalism in Specifications.* IEEE Software **2**, 1 (1985) pp 6–26

376. B. Meyer: *Object-oriented Software Construction* (Prentice Hall, 1988)

377. B. Meyer: *Eiffel: The Language*, second revised edn (Prentice Hall, USA 1992)

378. B. Meyer: *Object–oriented Software Construction*, second revised edn (Prentice Hall, USA 1997)

379. J. Meyer, T. Downing, A. Shulmann: *Java Virtual Machine* (O'Reilly & Associates, 1997)

380. G. Michaelson: *Introduction to Functional Programming Through Lambda-Calculus* (Addison-Wesley, 1989)

381. Microsoft Corporation: *MCAD/MCSD Self-Paced Training Kit: Developing Web Applications with Microsoft Visual Basic .NET and Microsoft Visual C# .NET* (Microsoft Corporation, Redmond, WA, USA 2002)

382. Microsoft Corporation: *MCAD/MCSD Self-Paced Training Kit: Developing Windows-Based Applications with Microsoft Visual Basic .NET and Microsoft Visual C# .NET* (Microsoft Corporation, Redmond, WA, USA 2002)

383. D. Miéville, D. Vernant: *Stanislaw Lesniewski aujourd'hui* Grenoble, October 8-10, 1992 (Neuchâtel, 1996)

384. P. Millican, A. Clark: *The Legacy of Alan Turing: Machines and Thought* (Oxford University Press, UK 1999)

385. R. Milne, C. Strachey: *A Theory of Programming Language Semantics* (Chapman and Hall, London, Halsted Press/Wiley, NY 1976)

386. R. Milner: *Calculus of Communication Systems*, vol 94 of *Lecture Notes in Computer Science* (Springer, 1980)

387. R. Milner: *Communication and Concurrency* (Prentice Hall, 1989)

388. R. Milner: *Communicating and Mobile Systems: The π–Calculus* (Cambridge University Press, 1999)

389. R. Milner, M. Tofte, R. Harper: *The Definition of Standard ML* (MIT Press, USA and UK, 1990)

390. C.C. Morgan: *Programming from Specifications* (Prentice Hall, UK 1990)

391. J. Morris: Lambda-Calculus Models of Programming Languages. PhD Thesis, Lab. for Computer Science, Mass. Inst. of Techn., Cambridge, USA, TR-57 (1968)

392. L. Morris: The Next 700 Programming Language Descriptions. Unpubl. ms., Univ. of Essex, Comp. Ctr. (1970)

393. L. Morris: Advice on Structuring Compilers and Proving Them Correct. In: *Principles of Programming Languages, SIGPLAN/SIGACT Symposium, ACM Conference Record/Proceedings* (1973) pp 144–152

394. Y.N. Moschovakis: *Notes on Set Theory* (Springer, Heidelberg, 1994)

395. T. Mossakowski, A.E. Haxthausen, D. Sanella, A. Tarlecki: *CASL — The Common Algebraic Specification Language: Semantics and Proof Theory*. Computing and Informatics **22**, 1–2 (2003)

396. P.D. Mosses: *Action Semantics* (Cambridge University Press, 1992)

397. P.D. Mosses: *CoFI: The Common Framework Initiative for Algebraic Specification*. Bull. EATCS **59** (1996) pp 127–132

398. P.D. Mosses: CASL for CafeOBJ users. In: *CAFE: An Industrial-Strength Algebraic Formal Method* (Elsevier, 2000) pp 121–144

399. Edited by P.D. Mosses: CASL *Reference Manual*, vol 2960 of *LNCS* (Springer, Heidelberg 2004)

400. B.C. Moszkowski: *Executing Temporal Logic Programs* (Cambridge University Press, UK 1986)

401. Edited by G. Nelson: *Systems Programming in Modula 3* (Prentice Hall, USA 1991)

402. A. Nerode, R. Shore: *Logic for Applications* (Springer, 1997)

403. D.E. Newton: *Alan Turing* (Xlibris Corporation, 2003)

404. J.F. Nilsson: Formal Vienna Development Method Models of PROLOG. In: *Implementations of PROLOG*, ed by J. Campbell (Ellis Horwood Series: Artificial Intelligence, 1984) pp 281–308

405. J.F. Nilsson. Some Foundational Issues in Ontological Engineering, October 30 – Novewmber 1 2002. Lecture slides for a PhD Course in *Representation Formalisms for Ontologies*, Techn. Univ. of Denmark.

406. T. Nipkow, L.C. Paulson, M. Wenzel: *Isabelle/HOL, A Proof Assistant for Higher-Order Logic*, vol 2283 of *LNCS* (Springer, Heidelberg, Germany, 2002)

407. B. Nordström, K. Petersson, J.M. Smith: *Programming in Martin-Löf's Type Theory An Introduction*, vol 7 of *International Series of Monographs on Computer Science* (Clarendon Press, Oxford University Press, UK 1990) p 232

408. Object Management Group: *OMG Unified Modelling Language Specification*, version 1.5 edn (OMG/UML, http://www.omg.org/uml/ 2003)

409. O. Ore: *Graphs and Their Uses* (The Mathematical Association of America, 1963)

410. S. Owre, N. Shankar, J.M. Rushby, D.W.J. Stringer-Calvert. *PVS Language Reference*. Computer Science Laboratory, SRI International, CA, 1999.

411. S. Owre, N. Shankar, J.M. Rushby, D.W.J. Stringer-Calvert. *PVS System Guide*. Computer Science Laboratory, SRI International, Menlo Park, CA, Sept. 1999.

412. Oxford University Press: *The Oxford Dictionary of Quotations* (Oxford University Press, UK 1974)

413. D.L. Parnas: *On the criteria to be used in Decomposing Systems into Modules.* Communications of the ACM **15**, 12 (1972) pp 1053–1058

414. D.L. Parnas: *A technique for Software Module Specification with Examples.* Communications of the ACM **14**, 5 (1972)

415. D.L. Parnas: *Software Fundamentals: Collected Papers, Eds.: David M. Weiss and Daniel M. Hoffmann* (Addison-Wesley, 2001)

416. D.L. Parnas, P.C. Clements: *A Rational Design Process: How and Why to Fake it.* IEEE Trans. Software Engineering **12**, 2 (1986) pp 251–257

417. D.L. Parnas, P.C. Clements, D.M. Weiss: Enhancing reusability with information hiding. In: *Tutorial: Software Reusability (Ed.: Peter Freeman)* (IEEE Press, 1986) pp 83–90

418. D.A. Patterson, J.L. Hennessy: *Computer Organization and Design* (Morgan Kaufmann, 1998)

419. L. Paulson: Isabelle: The Next 700 Theorem Provers. In: *Logic in Computer Science*, ed by P. Oddifreddi (Academic Press, 1990) pp 361–386

420. R. Penner: *Discrete Mathematics, Proof Techniques and Mathematical Structures* (World Scientific, Singapore 1999)

421. C.A. Petri: *Kommunikation mit Automaten* (Bonn: Institut für Instrumentelle Mathematik, Schriften des IIM Nr. 2, 1962)

422. C. Petzold: *Programming Windows with C# (Core Reference)* (Microsoft Corporation, Redmond, WA, USA 2001)

423. S.L. Pfleeger: *Software Engineering, Theory and Practice*, 2nd edn (Prentice Hall, 2001)

424. B. Pierce: *Types and Programming Languages* (MIT Press, 2002)

425. M. Piff: *Discrete Mathematics, An Introduction for Software Engineers* (Cambridge University Press, UK 1991)

426. G.D. Plotkin: *Call-by-Name, Call-by-Value and the Lambda Calculus.* Theoretical Computer Science **1** (1975) pp 125–159

427. G.D. Plotkin: A Structural Approach to Operational Semantics. Technical Report, Comp. Sci. Dept., Aarhus Univ., Denmark; DAIMI-FN-19 (1981)

428. G.D. Plotkin: *A Structural Approach Operational Semantics.* Journal of Logic and Algebraic Programming **60–61** (2004) pp 17–139

429. A. Pnueli: The Temporal Logic of Programs. In: *Proceedings of the 18th IEEE Symposium on Foundations of Computer Science* (IEEE CS, 1977) pp 46–57

430. R.S. Pressman: *Software Engineering, A Practitioner's Approach*, 5th edn (McGraw-Hill, 1981–2001)

431. M. Pěnička, A.K. Strupchanska, D. Bjørner: Train Maintenance Routing. In: *FORMS 2003: Symposium on Formal Methods for Railway Operation and Control Systems* (L'Harmattan Hongrie, 2003)

432. B. Randell: On Failures and Faults. In: *FME 2003: Formal Methods*, vol 2805 of *Lecture Notes in Computer Science* (Springer, 2003) pp 18–39

433. C. Read: *Elements of Functional Programming* (Addison-Wesley, 1989)

434. M. Reiser: *The* OBERON *System, User Guide and Programmer's Manual* (Addison-Wesley, 1991)

435. W. Reisig: *Petri Nets: An Introduction*, vol 4 of *EATCS Monographs in Theoretical Computer Science* (Springer, 1985)

436. W. Reisig: *A Primer in Petri Net Design* (Springer, 1992)

437. W. Reisig: *Elements of Distributed Algorithms: Modelling and Analysis with Petri Nets* (Springer, 1998)

438. W. Reisig: *On Gurevich's Theorem for Sequential Algorithms*. Acta Informatica (2003)

439. W. Reisig: *The Expressive Power of Abstract-State Machines*. Computing and Informatics **22**, 1–2 (2003)

440. J.C. Reynolds: On the Relation Between Direct and Continuation Semantics. In: *International Colloquium on Automata, Languages and Programming, European Association for Theoretical Computer Science* (Springer, 1974) pp 157–168

441. J.C. Reynolds: *The Craft of Programming* (Prentice Hall, 1981)

442. J.C. Reynolds: *Theories of Programming Languages* (Cambridge University Press, UK 1998)

443. J.C. Reynolds: *The Semantics of Programming Languages* (Cambridge University Press, UK 1999)

444. H.R. Rogers: *Theory of Recursive Functions and Effective Computability* (McGraw-Hill, 1967)

445. P. Roget: *Roget's Thesaurus* (Collins, London and Glasgow, 1974)

446. Edited by A.W. Roscoe: *A Classical Mind: Essays in Honour of C.A.R. Hoare* (Prentice Hall, 1994)

447. A.W. Roscoe. *Model Checking CSP*, pages 353–378. Prentice Hall, 1994

448. A.W. Roscoe: *Theory and Practice of Concurrency* (Prentice Hall, 1997)

449. A.W. Roscoe, C.A.R. Hoare: *Laws of occam Programming*. Theoretical Computer Science **60** (1988) pp 177–229

450. Edited by A.W. Roscoe, J.C.P. Woodcock: *A Millennium Perspective on Informatics* (Palgrave, 2001)

451. J. Rushby: Formal Methods and the Certification of Critical Systems. Technical Report SRI-CSL-93-7, Computer Science Laboratory, SRI International, Menlo Park, CA., USA (1993)

452. J. Rushby: Formal Methods and Their Role in the Certification of Critical Systems. Technical Report SRI-CSL-95-1, Computer Science Laboratory, SRI International, Menlo Park, CA (1995)

453. D. Sangiorgio, D. Walker: *The π-Calculus* (Cambridge University Press, 2001)

454. D.A. Schmidt: *Denotational Semantics: a Methodology for Language Development* (Allyn & Bacon, 1986)

455. D.A. Schmidt: *The Structure of Typed Programming Languages* (MIT Press, 1994)

456. S. Schneider: *Concurrent and Real-Time Systems — The CSP Approach* (Wiley, UK 2000)

457. J.R. Schoenfeld: *Mathematical Logic* (A.K. Peters, 2001)

458. D. Scott: The Lattice of Flow Diagrams. In: *[212]* (1970) pp 311–366

459. D. Scott: Outline of a Mathematical Theory of Computation. In: *Proc. 4th Ann. Princeton Conf. on Inf. Sci. and Sys.* (1970) p 169

460. D. Scott: Continuous Lattices. In: *Toposes, Algebraic Geometry and Logic*, ed by F. Lawvere (Springer, Lecture Notes in Mathematics, Vol. 274 1972) pp 97–136

461. D. Scott: Data Types as Lattices. Unpublished Lecture Notes, Amsterdam (1972)

462. D. Scott: Lattice Theory, Data Types and Semantics. In: *Symp. Formal Semantics*, pp 67–106, ed by R. Rustin (Prentice Hall, 1972)

463. D. Scott: Mathematical Concepts in Programming Language Semantics. In: *Proc. AFIPS, Spring Joint Computer Conference, 40* (1972) pp 225–234

464. D. Scott: Lattice-Theoretic Models for Various Type Free Calculi. In: *Proc. 4th Int'l. Congr. for Logic Methodology and the Philosophy of Science*, Bucharest (North-Holland, Amsterdam, 1973) pp 157–187

465. D. Scott: λ-Calculus and Computer Science Theory. In: *Lecture Notes in Computer Science, Vol. 37*, ed by C. Böhm (Springer, 1975)

466. D. Scott: *Data Types as Lattices*. SIAM Journal on Computer Science **5**, 3 (1976) pp 522–587

467. D. Scott: Domains for Denotational Semantics. In: *International Colloquium on Automata, Languages and Programming, European Association for Theoretical Computer Science* (Springer, 1982) pp 577–613

468. D. Scott: Some Ordered Sets in Computer Science. In: *Ordered Sets*, ed by I. Rival (Reidel Publ., 1982) pp 677–718

469. D. Scott, C. Strachey: Towards a Mathematical Semantics for Computer Languages. In: *Computers and Automata*, vol 21 of *Microwave Research Inst. Symposia* (1971) pp 19–46

470. P. Sestoft: *Java Precisely* (MIT Press, 2002)

471. R. Sethi, A. Tang: *Constructing Call-by-Value Continuation Semantics*. Journal of the ACM **27** (1980) pp 580–597

472. N. Shankar: *Metamathematics, Machines and Gödel's Proof* (Cambridge University Press, UK 1994)

473. P.M. Simons. *Leśniewski's Logic and Its Relation to Classical and Free Logics*. In: Foundations of Logic and Linguistics: Problems and Their Solutions, Georg Dorn and P. Weingartner (Eds.). Plenum Press, NY, 1985.

474. S. Sokołowski: *Applicative Higher-Order Programming: the Standard ML Perspective* (Chapman and Hall, 1991)

475. I. Sommerville: *Software Engineering*, 6th edn (Addison-Wesley, 1982–2001)

476. J.M. Spivey: *Understanding Z: A Specification Language and Its Formal Semantics*, vol 3 of *Cambridge Tracts in Theoretical Computer Science* (Cambridge University Press, 1988)

477. J.M. Spivey: *The Z Notation: A Reference Manual* (Prentice Hall, UK 1989)

478. J.M. Spivey: *The Z Notation: A Reference Manual*, 2nd edn (Prentice Hall, 1992)

479. Edited by J.T.J. Srzednicki, Z. Stachniak: *Lesniewski's lecture notes in logic* (Dordrecht, 1988)

480. J.T.J. Srzednicki, Z. Stachniak: *Lesniewski's systems protothetic* (Dordrecht, 1998)

481. D.F. Stanat, D.F. McAllister: *Discrete Mathematics for Computer Science* (Prentice Hall, 1977)

482. Edited by J. Staunstrup, W. Wolff: *Hardware/Software Co-design: Principles and Practice* (Kluwer Academic Press, The Netherlands 1997)

483. Edited by T.B. Steel: *Formal Language Description Languages,* IFIP TC-2 Work. Conf., Baden (North-Holland, Amsterdam, 1966)

484. Edited by J. Stein: *The Random House American Everyday Dictionary* (Random House, NY, USA 1949, 1961)

485. C. Strachey: Fundamental Concepts in Programming Languages. Unpubl. Lecture Notes, NATO Summer School, Copenhagen, 1967, and Programming Research Group, Oxford Univ. (1968)

486. C. Strachey: The Varieties of Programming Languages. Techn. Monograph 10, Programming Research Group, Oxford Univ. (1973)

487. C. Strachey: Continuations: A Mathematical Semantics which can deal with Full Jumps. Techn. Monograph, Programming Research Group, Oxford Univ. (1974)

488. H. Strong: Translating Recursion Equations into Flow Charts. In: *Proceedings 2nd Annual ACM Symposium on Theory of Computig (SToC)* (1970) pp 184–197

489. B. Stroustrup: *C++ Programming Language* (Addison-Wesley, 1986)

490. A.K. Strupchanska, M. Pěnička, D. Bjørner: Railway Staff Rostering. In: *FORMS 2003: Symposium on Formal Methods for Railway Operation and Control Systems* (L'Harmattan Hongrie, 2003)

491. P.R. Suppes: *Axiomatic Set Theory* (Dover, NY, USA 7 May 1973)

492. P.R. Suppes, S. Hill: *A First Course in Mathematical Logic* (Dover, July 1, 2002)

493. Edited by S.J. Surma, J.T. Srzednicki, D.I. Barnett, V.F. Rickey: *Stanislaw Lesniewski: Collected Works (2 Vols.)* (Dordrecht, Boston – New York 1988)

494. V.G. Szebehely: *Adventures in Celestial Mechanics. A First Course in the Theory of Orbits* (University of Texas Press, USA 1993)

495. R. Tarjan: *Data Structures and Network Algorithms* (SIAM: Soc. for Ind. & Appl. Math., 1983)

496. R. Tennent: *Principles of Programming Languages* (Prentice Hall, 1981)

497. R. Tennent: *The Semantics of Programming Languages* (Prentice Hall, 1997)

498. S. Thompson: *Haskell: The Craft of Functional Programming,* 2nd edn (Addison-Wesley, 1999)

499. F.X. Tong: *From the Soil — The Foundations of Chinese Society: XiangTu ZhongGuo* (University of California Press, USA (1947) 1992)

500. G. Tourlakis: *Lectures in Logic and Set Theory: Volume 2, Set Theory* (Cambridge University Press, UK 2003)

501. W.A. Triebel: *The 80386, 80486, and Pentium Microprocessors* (Prentice Hall, 1998)

502. D. Turner: Miranda: A Non-strict Functional Language with Polymorphic Types. In: *Functional Programming Languages and Computer Architectures,* no 201 of *Lecture Notes in Computer Science,* ed by J. Jouannaud (Springer, Heidelberg, Germany, 1985)

503. J. van Benthem: *The Logic of Time,* vol 156 of *Synthese Library: Studies in Epistemology, Logic, Methhodology, and Philosophy of Science (Editor: Jaakko Hintika),* 2nd edn (Kluwer Academic, The Netherlands 1991)

504. R. van Glabbeek, P. Weijland. Branching Time and Abstraction in Bisimulation Semantics. Electronically, on the Web: `http://theory.stanford.-edu/~rvg/abstraction/abstraction.html`, Centrum voor Wiskunde en Informatica, Postbus 94079, 1090 GB Amsterdam, The Netherlands, January 1996.

505. W. van Orman Quine: *Set Theory and Its Logic* (Harvard University Press, USA 1969)

506. W. van Orman Quine: *From a Logical Point of View* (Harvard Univ. Press, USA 1980)

507. W. van Orman Quine: *Word and Object* (MIT Press, USA 1960)

508. W. van Orman Quine: *Pursuit of Truth*, paperback edn (Harvard Univ. Press, USA 1992)

509. W. van Orman Quine: *Mathematical Logic* (Harvard University Press, 1979)

510. A. van Wijngaarden: *Report on the Algorithmic Language ALGOL 68.* Acta Informatica **5** (1975) pp 1–236

511. B. Venners: *Inside the Java 2.0 Virtual Machine (Enterprise Computing)* (McGraw-Hill, 1999)

512. H. van Vliet: *Software Engineering: Principles and Practice* (Wiley, UK 2000)

513. C. Wadsworth: Semantics and Pragmatics of the Lambda-Calculus. PhD Thesis, Programming Research Group, Oxford Univ., (1971)

514. M. Wand: *Continuation-Based Program Transformation Strategies.* Journal of the ACM **27** (1980) pp 164–180

515. M. Wand: *Induction, Recursion and Programming* (North-Holland, Amsterdam, 1980)

516. D. Watt, B. Wichmann, W. Findlay: *Ada: Language and Methodology* (Prentice Hall, 1986)

517. P. Wegner: *Programming Languages, Information Structures, and Machine Organization* (McGraw-Hill, 1968)

518. P. Weis, X. Leroy: *Le langage Caml* (Dunod, Paris, France 1999)

519. Wikipedia: Polymorphism. In: *Internet* (Published: http://en.wikipedia.org/-wiki/Polymorphism_(computer_science), 2005)

520. Å. Wikström: *Functional Programming Using Standard ML* (Prentice Hall, 1984)

521. G. Winskel: *The Formal Semantics of Programming Languages* (The MIT Press, USA, 1993)

522. N. Wirth: *The Programming Language PASCAL.* Acta Informatica **1**, 1 (1971) pp 35–63

523. N. Wirth: *Systematic Programming* (Prentice Hall, 1973)

524. N. Wirth: *Algorithms + Data Structures = Programs* (Prentice Hall, 1976)

525. N. Wirth: *Programming in Modula-2* (Springer, Heidelberg, 1982)

526. N. Wirth: *From Modula to Oberon.* Software — Practice and Experience **18** (1988) pp 661–670

527. N. Wirth: *The Programming Language Oberon.* Software — Practice and Experience **18** (1988) pp 671–690

528. N. Wirth: *The Programming Language Oberon.* Software — Practice and Experience **18** (1988) pp 671–690

529. N. Wirth, J. Gutknecht: *The Oberon System.* Software — Practice and Experience **19**, 9 (1989) pp 857–893

530. N. Wirth, J. Gutknecht: *The Oberon Project* (Addison-Wesley, 1992)

531. N. Wirth, C.A.R. Hoare: *A Contribution to the Development of ALGOL.* Communications of the ACM **9**, 6 (1966) pp 413–432

532. D.A. Wolfram: *The Clausal Theory of Types* (Cambridge University Press, March 1993)

533. J.C.P. Woodcock, J. Davies: *Using Z: Specification, Proof and Refinement* (Prentice Hall, 1996)

534. J.C.P. Woodcock, M. Loomes: *Software Engineering Mathematics* (Pitman, London, 1988)

535. Y. Xia, C.W. George: An Operational Semantics for Timed RAISE. In: *FM'99 — Formal Methods*, ed by J.M. Wing, J. Woodcock, J. Davies (Springer, 1999) pp 1008–1027

536. E.N. Zalta: Logic. In: *The Stanford Encyclopedia of Philosophy* (Published: http://plato.stanford.edu/, Winter 2003)

537. C.C. Zhou, M.R. Hansen: *Duration Calculus: A Formal Approach to Real-Time Systems* (Springer, 2004)

538. C.C. Zhou, C.A.R. Hoare, A.P. Ravn: *A Calculus of Durations*. Information Proc. Letters **40**, 5 (1992)

Texts in Theoretical Computer Science · An EATCS Series